# THE LETTERS OF BASIL LANNEAU GILDERSLEEVE

# The Letters of
# BASIL LANNEAU GILDERSLEEVE

Edited by
WARD W. BRIGGS, JR.

THE JOHNS HOPKINS UNIVERSITY PRESS
Baltimore and London

The Johns Hopkins University Press
701 West 40th Street, Baltimore, Maryland 21211

The Johns Hopkins Press Ltd., London

The paper used in this publication meets the
minimum requirements of American National Standard for
Information Sciences—Permanence of Paper for
Printed Library Materials, ANSI Z39.48-1984.

LIBRARY OF CONGRESS CATALOGING-IN-PUBLICATION DATA

Gildersleeve, Basil L. (Basil Lanneau), 1831–1924.
The letters of Basil Lanneau Gildersleeve.

Includes index.
1. Gildersleeve, Basil L. (Basil Lanneau),
1831–1924—Correspondence.   2. Classicists—United
States—Correspondence.   3. Scholars—United States—
Correspondence.   I. Briggs, Ward W.   II. Title.
PA85.G48A4   1987          880′.092′4          87-4133
ISBN 0-8018-2876-7 (alk. paper)

To
WILLIAM M. CALDER III

# ❧ CONTENTS ❧

# ❦ ILLUSTRATIONS ❧

ix

# ❦ ACKNOWLEDGMENTS ❧

A project such as the present one is necessarily dependent on the cooperation of many people, both in this country and in Europe. I am of course grateful to those institutions and individuals who have provided me with copies of both the letters reproduced here and others that I have not been able to publish. A very special debt is owed to Katharine Lane Weems of Boston and Manchester, Basil Lanneau Gildersleeve's beloved granddaughter, who has welcomed my interest with her far-famed kindness and generosity, in which virtues she provides a living contact with the spirit of her grandfather. Edward Weeks, editor emeritus of the *Atlantic,* is also to be thanked for his support.

Charles Norwood and Susie R. Mowbray have answered many questions about the Lanneau family, as Benjamin Gildersleeve IV has filled in gaps in the records of the Gildersleeves. My teacher T. R. S. Broughton and his wife Annie Leigh, grand-niece of Gildersleeve, have provided a wealth of genealogical material on the "cousinwealth" of the Colston family.

For information about his University of Virginia period, I am indebted to Richard H. F. Lindemann of the Manuscripts Department, Alderman Library, University of Virginia, and to Arthur F. Stocker. Thomas Connelly and Richard J. Hellinger, Archivist of the United States Military Academy, have both provided and checked information on the Civil War and Reconstruction politics. For the Hopkins years, I am of course indebted to the staff of the Ferdinand Hamburger, Jr., Archives at Johns Hopkins. I also wish to express special thanks to my friend Robert L. Fowler for sharing the results of his very careful catalogue of the Hopkins Archive, not only with me but with many others whose research touches on Gildersleeve. His work has been at my side throughout this project. Another friend who has very generously shared a great deal of his own carefully collected information, including letter No. 79, is P. G. Naiditch. For unstinting assistance at the Johns Hopkins Special Collections, I must thank Ann Gwyn, assistant library director for Special Collections, and especially Lisa A. Minklei and Mary H. Lis. A similar debt is owed to James Stimpert of the Johns Hopkins Archives. My debt to Hugh Hawkins' work is expressed elsewhere. For providing me with a great deal of information about Sewanee, Trudy Mignery and Anne Armour deserve my thanks. A special debt is owed to Hugo Schmidt for sharing his knowledge of German literature and folksongs and to Georg Krotkoff for his help with Oriental matters.

I am additionally indebted to Leo Sirota, Dr. Richard S. Conte, Professors J. K. Newman, Roger M. Savory, G. M. Wickens, Marshall Fishwick, Friedrich Solmsen, Jay Bolter, John Francis Latimer, G. Ross Roy, Mr. William M. Calder IV, Shayne Mitchell of the Warburg Institute, and Elizabeth C. Hadas. My thanks also to Brenda Britton, Jane Zha, and Rich Galloway, who helped with checking and typing; and to David Chesnutt, Joel Myerson, and Buford Norman for technical assistance. The Reference Department of the Thomas Cooper Library and the South Caroliniana Collection at the University of South Carolina have given of unstinting aid, and I am particularly grateful to Alexander Gilchrist, Michael Freeman, and Henry G. Fulmer. To Peter Dreyer, who has read the final typescript twice with the most meticulous care, I owe a singular debt of gratitude for salvation from a multitude of howlers and inconsistencies.

Two of my colleagues deserve special thanks. James N. Hardin has come to my aid often with his broad and deep knowledge of German language, literature, and history. Patrick G. Scott has sharpened my vision, corrected errors of all kinds, and provided the necessary information on more occasions than I can enumerate. My obligations to the wisdom and patience of both these fine colleagues and friends are perhaps unrepayable. I am also grateful to the Office of Sponsored Programs and Research of the University of South Carolina for grants that supported part of the research for this book and to the Carolina Venture Fund for publication assistance. Finally, I must thank Catherine J. Castner for her unlimited help and support throughout this project.

# ❦ INTRODUCTION ❧

This collection presents its subject as classicist, Southerner, and man of letters and is edited with classical, historical, and educational scholars, both American and foreign, in mind. Basil Lanneau Gildersleeve was born the second of ten children to the Reverend Benjamin Gildersleeve (1791–1875) and his third wife, Emma Louisa Lanneau (1805–59), daughter of the prominent Charlestonian Bazile Lanneau (1746–1833), on 23 October 1831, ten years after Napoleon died and six years before Victoria assumed the British throne. He saw America grow from a provincial republic governed by a rude, but heroic, general from Tennessee to a world power managed by a laconic politician from Vermont. While Gildersleeve watched his region restore itself after the horrors of the Civil War, and his country rise to compete with Europe and the rest of the world economically and militarily, he was instrumental in raising American classical scholarship to a level of excellence fully equal in many areas to that of the Europeans who trained him. The sense of isolation that compelled Thomas Jefferson to stock his new university in Virginia with Englishmen yielded in time to a growing sense of pride in the works and men of American classical scholarship and a decided (and perhaps unjust) hostility to German manners and methods both before and after World War I.

Gildersleeve's ties to Charleston identified him forever in his own mind as a Charlestonian, as one who took part in the history and character of a particular place and time in American life. He defended it with his pen and sword in the Civil War and extolled it in aftertimes to an international audience with all the fervor he employed to extol the value of the classics and the good work of his countrymen.

Since my wish is to present Gildersleeve here in the full range of his interests and accomplishments, and since there is no full-scale (or even half-scale) biography, I have selected many of these letters to account for the main events of his life, and a few simply to reflect the charm and grace of his personality; most do both. For the present, this collection will stand in lieu of a much-needed biography and may perhaps provide someone with a basis for further investigation of this remarkable American life. I have given full notes where possible, sometimes giving information that every classicist knows from the philological cradle, sometimes names and dates that are central to American history, but may not be known to the average European.

Some readers will already know Gildersleeve as a revered American icon: as a classicist of the greatest literary breadth and scholarly depth, as a Southerner who took notions of honor and hard work to be of the highest importance, as one who stood for the noble ideals of his German training and helped transplant them permanently to this country. I hope all readers will also find Gildersleeve's very human qualities on display here as well: his deep affection for his friends, his flashes of temper against plagiarists or fools, the passions for Germany and Italy that animated his youth, the "patient deep despair" that characterized his last years. The reader will find throughout the letters a touching and even engaging *Selbstironie* that moderates the despair of his adult years over the loss of the Old South that he knew and loved so intimately, and over his own sense of failure in living up to the promise and ideals of his German years. One will also find the contradictions Whitman promises us are in every man. Like anyone, Gildersleeve could change his mind about men over the years, as he did in the cases of Seymour and Howells, but the fidelity he showed Hübner, possibly at cost to his career, the constant loyalty and affection he gave his friends in Charlottesville, and his sincere attachment to Wiggins and Sewanee further ennoble the author of these letters.

Clearly his deepest professional relationship was with the most frequent recipient of letters in this collection (forty-six), Daniel Coit Gilman (1831–1908), the founding president of the Johns Hopkins University, whom Gildersleeve met at around the time of his father's death (1875) and who seems, in that period when "the whole aspect of life is strangely altered when the headship is changed" (No. 62), to have filled a position Gildersleeve later compared to that of "the head of the house" (No. 112). Gildersleeve had always professed a desire to be a journalist, as his father had been, and he never wholly retired from writing for the popular press, but Gilman gave him a new figure to emulate, as well as serve, and towards the end, Gildersleeve credits him in his characteristically generous and self-effacing way with nearly every positive aspect of his career (No. 131).

The Greek of the section titles comes from Gildersleeve's interpretation of the four virtues of a man's life in Pindar *Nem.* 3 (No. 109).

## THE LETTERS

Gildersleeve speaks of "the hundreds of letters I write each year" (No. 154), and he may have written more than ten thousand letters during his life. The majority were on the trivial business of *AJP* and have vanished with their day's sun. Later in life, he was obliged to write letters of thanks to the many who sent him birthday greetings every year (Nos. 119, 154, 159, 163–64, 168, 180, 189). By his eightieth birthday the number of well-wishers had grown so large that he was forced to have printed cards of thanks sent out. He answered most of his correspondence immediately and is apologetic for delays of more than a few days. His most personal letters were put in his pocketbook and saved for the following Sunday, the day of the week he consecrated to his "favourite correspondence" (BLG to Shorey, 5 April 1914 [Chicago]) with close friends such as Hübner (Nos. 2–3, 5–7, 57, 61, 68, 117), Minor (No. 35), Gilman (Nos. 50, 90), Wiggins (Nos. 78, 107), Wheeler (Nos. 95, 108), Seymour (Nos. 130, 135), K. F. Smith (No. 147), Goodell (No. 148), C. F. Smith (Nos. 160, 164, 168 ), Thornton (No. 181), or to special occasions (Nos. 106, 109, 114, 127), perhaps a habit inculcated by his religious father. Many of the letters in the present selection that concern more practical matters were written on Mondays (Nos. 13, 29, 30, 36, 40, 53, 58, 73, 77, 79–81, 83, 85–86, 89, 91–94, 97, 103–4, 113, 122–23, 134, 143, 149, 151–52, 156, 171, 174, 179, 181–82, 186, 188).

At Gildersleeve's death, his children burned all the letters that were in his house, presumably including his cherished correspondence with Ritschl, Schneidewin, Usener, James Russell Lowell, Ralph Waldo Emerson, and, with the exception of one letter, Wilamowitz. Presumably all of his family correspondence was destroyed at the same time, since no letters of any kind to his immediate family have survived.

What has survived in Baltimore are the letters that were in the office space accorded him in Gilman Hall when the Homewood campus was opened in 1916 (No. 173), an office space he never used. These letters and papers make up the bulk of the Gildersleeve Archive, which is housed in the Special Collections of the Milton S. Eisenhower Library at Johns Hopkins.

I have located some 1,600 letters in various repositories in Europe and America, and some of these must represent the best of his correspondence. Amazingly for a man who wrote so many letters and was so constantly pressed for time, he wrote drafts (e.g., No. 155) of nearly all but his most perfunctory letters, and these drafts (along with typed copies of other letters) comprise the greater part of the surviving correspondence. Most of the letters from Johns Hopkins in the present collection (excepting those to Gilman and Miller) are drafts (Nos. 110, 113, 121–23, 125–26, 147, 149–50). Only with the failure of his eyes and the employment of a secretary did he send typewritten letters and keep carbon copies (Nos. 157, 162, 165, 166), but even then he insisted on writing important and/or personal letters by hand, again with drafts (Nos. 158, 161).

The letters of the Hopkins period are generally written in black ink with a fine nib on 5¹/₂" × 8¹/₂" ecru *AJP* stationery. His personal letters are usually on plain paper or, beginning with No. 78, have the 1002 Belvidere Terrace letterhead. Printed letterheads are given within braces ({ }; e.g., No. 15). The signature is regularly underscored and I have kept it so here.

For this selection I have chosen 191 letters, an arbitrary number to be sure. I might easily have chosen 291 letters or more without including any that showed traces of the ordinary or failed to show another facet of their author's life and character. The present collection covers a period of seventy years, from 1853, shortly after he completed his doctorate, to 1923, barely two months before his death at the age of ninety-two.

## EDITORIAL METHOD

Because Gildersleeve was often obliged to write letters or copy drafts at finger speed, his handwriting, which is crisp and elegant when the product of repose, becomes very difficult to decipher, his punctuation becomes more anarchic than usual, and his text is occasionally mottled with other blemishes of haste, including errors of year (Nos. 19, 20, 21) or month (No. 41). I have consequently made silent corrections of punctuation, commas, unclosed quotations, dittographs, and the like. If Gildersleeve misdates a letter, I have so noted it in order that those who might want to find the original will have the catalogued date. On the other hand, I have transcribed his punctuation, even when it is irregular by modern standards (see No. 64), I have retained his spellings of "sate" (for "sat"), "staid" (for "stayed"), "inclosed," "can not," every body," "any thing," "type writer," and the like, and respected the comparative absence of hyphens, as in "twenty seven." Strike-throughs are of intrinsic interest and have been noted in the text thus: "~~save only~~"; I have noted his insertions with slashes thus: "on /one of/ the benches," and noted my own insertions with brackets thus: "while we [in marg.: 'Sechsen'] were resting." Two letters employ their own signs: in No. 150 I have indicated various stages of the text, and in No. 167 I have noted omissions in the printed form of the letter.

Citations of letters in this selection are by their number, e.g., "see No. 133." Citations of letters not included in this selection are by correspondent, with the location in brackets, e.g., "BLG to Hübner, 21 May 1853 [Berlin]." Letters that are cited without location are at Johns Hopkins.

Quotations of one or two words in a foreign language are translated within brackets in the text; longer passages are translated in the notes. Some single words of common knowledge, such as *gravitas*, are left untranslated. One letter (No. 116), written by Gildersleeve in German, is translated entire.

In one place Gildersleeve describes the style of his published writings as "kaleidoscopic,"[1] and elsewhere he laments the result: "True, the points of my shafts have often failed to reach their mark because so few German critics are possessed of a knowledge of idiomatic English, or if that is too bold a word for an American, the kind of English in which I indulge."[2] The reader will find the same style in many of the letters: regionalisms, archaisms, slang, literary locutions, and word-play, all heavily admixed with literary, political, historical, and biblical allusions. Writing to classicists, he often felt obliged to quote the ancients; writing to literary men, he cites more modern poets, and the language of the Bible is never far from his thoughts with all his correspondents. Full annotation of these heavily allusive letters is beyond my powers and would probably unnecessarily encumber the text. I have not tried to note every allusion or unfamiliar word. Citations in the notes will give only a hint, not a catalogue, of the vast variety of his background to any non-English-speaking, non-Christian, non-Southern, non-literary readers.

I have also tried to give biographical sketches of all the classicists Gildersleeve mentions, largely because there is no convenient source at present for the information and because, if members of my own profession are largely ignorant of their recent predecessors, there is no reason to imagine that non-classicists will know these figures or be able readily to locate the scattered sources in which the information is available.

There is no separate bibliography, but I would like to give special notice to the works that have been of greatest service to me. For the genealogy of the Gildersleeve family, Willard H. Gildersleeve's *Gildersleeve Pioneers* (Rutland, Vt: Tuttle Publishing Co., 1941) and Susie R. Mowbray and Charles S. Norwood's *Bazile Lanneau of Charleston, 1746–1833: A Family History* (Goldsboro, N.C.: Hilburn Printing Corp., 1985) are indispensible, but the latter must be used with caution. For the University of Virginia years, D. M. R. Culbreth gives a remarkable portrait in his *The University of Virginia: Memories of Her Student-Life and Professors* (New York: Neale Publishing Co., 1908). Hugh Hawkins' *Pioneer: A History of the Johns Hopkins University, 1874–1889* is simply one of the best college histories written. And, finally, Robert L. Fowler's "The Gildersleeve Archive," *Briggs-Benario*, 62–105, to which I have referred in the Acknowledgments, must be noted again here as an exemplary piece of work.

1. *AJP* 31 (1910): 109 ( = *SBM*, 196). See E. Christian Kopff, "Gildersleeve in American Literature: The 'Kaleidoscopic Style,' " *Briggs-Benario*, 56–61.
2. *AJP* 36 (1915): 242 ( = *SBM*, 332).

# ❦ ABBREVIATIONS ❧

| | |
|---|---|
| *ADB* | *Allgemeine Deutsche Biographie.* 56 vols. Leipzig: Duncker & Humblot, 1875–1912. |
| *AJP* | *American Journal of Philology.* Founded by B. L. Gildersleeve in 1880. Baltimore: Johns Hopkins University Press. |
| APA | American Philological Association |
| *Barringer* | Paul Brandon Barringer et al., *University of Virginia: Its History, Influence, Equipment and Characteristics.* 2 vols. New York: Lewis Publishing Co., 1904. |
| *BLG* | Basil Lanneau Gildersleeve. |
| *Briggs-Benario* | Ward W. Briggs, Jr., and Herbert W. Benario, *Basil Lanneau Gildersleeve: An American Classicist.* Baltimore: Johns Hopkins University Press, 1986. |
| *Bruce* | Philip Alexander Bruce, *History of the University of Virginia, 1819–1919: The Lengthened Shadow of One Man.* 5 vols. New York: Macmillan Co., 1921. |
| *CAMWS* | Classical Association of the Middle West and South. |
| *Creed* | B. L. Gildersleeve, "The Creed of the Old South." *Atlantic* 69 (January 1892): 75–87. Reprinted in *The Creed of the Old South,* 7–52. Baltimore: Johns Hopkins Press, 1915. |
| *Culbreth* | David M. R. Culbreth M.D., *The University of Virginia: Memories of Her Student-Life and Professors.* New York: Neale Publishing Co., 1908. |
| *DAB* | *Dictionary of American Biography.* 20 vols. New York: Scribner, 1928–36. Supplements 1 & 2, 1944. Supplement 3 (1941–45), 1973. |
| *DNB* | *Dictionary of National Biography.* Founded by George Smith. Edited by Sir Leslie Stephen and Sir Sidney Lee. 22 vols. (Vol. 22 is Supplement 1.) Lon- |

|           | don: Oxford University Press, 1949–50. Supplement 2 (1901–11), 1920. Supplement 3 (1912–21), 1927. Supplement 4 (1922–30), 1937. Supplement 5 (1931–40), 1949. Supplement 6 (1941–50), 1959. |
|-----------|-----|
| *E&S* | B. L. Gildersleeve, *Essays and Studies.* Baltimore: N. Murray, 1890. Reprint, New York: Alfred Hafner, 1924; Johnson Reprint Co., 1968. |
| *Formative Influences* | B. L. Gildersleeve, "Formative Influences." *The Forum* 10 (February 1891): 607–17. |
| *Franklin* | Fabian Franklin, *The Life of Daniel Coit Gilman.* New York: Dodd, Mead, 1910. Chapters 1–3 written respectively by William C. Gilman, Emily H. Whitney, and William Carey Jones. |
| *French* | John C. French, *A History of the University Founded by Johns Hopkins.* Baltimore: Johns Hopkins Press, 1946. |
| *Hawkins* | Hugh Hawkins, *Pioneer: A History of the Johns Hopkins University, 1874–1889.* Ithaca, N.Y.: Cornell University Press, 1960. |
| *H&H* | B. L. Gildersleeve, *Hellas and Hesperia; or, The Vitality of Greek Studies in America.* New York: Holt, 1909. |
| JHU | The Johns Hopkins University. |
| *NatCAB* | *National Cyclopedia of American Biography.* 63 vols. New York: James T. White, 1893–1984. |
| *NDB* | *Neue Deutsche Biographie.* 14 vols. Berlin: Duncker & Humblot, 1953–. |
| *NYTimes* | *New York Times* |
| *Pindar* | B. L. Gildersleeve, *Pindar: The Olympian and Pythian Odes.* New York: Harper and Bros., 1885; revised 1890. Reprint, Amsterdam: Hakkert, 1965; St. Clair Shores, Mich.: Scholarly Press, 1970. |
| *Professorial Types* | B. L. Gildersleeve, "Professorial Types." *The Hopkinsian* 1 (1893): 11–18. |
| *Sandys* | John Edwin Sandys, *A History of Classical Scholarship,* vol. 3, *The Eighteenth Century in Germany, and the Nineteenth Century in Europe and the United States of America.* Cambridge: Cambridge University Press, 1908. |

| | |
|---|---|
| *SBM* | *Selections from the Brief Mention of Basil Lanneau Gildersleeve.* Edited by Charles William Emil Miller. Baltimore: The Johns Hopkins Press, 1930. |
| *Selected Correspondence* | *Ulrich von Wilamowitz-Moellendorff: Selected Correspondence,* 1869–1931. Edited by William M. Calder III. *Antiqua* 23. Naples: Jovene, 1983. |
| *60 Days* | B. L. Gildersleeve, "My Sixty Days in Greece: I. The Olympic Games, Old and New; II. A Spartan School; III. My Travelling Companions." *Atlantic* 79 (February, March, May 1897): 199–212, 301–12, 630–41. |
| *Southerner* | B. L. Gildersleeve, "A Southerner in the Peloponnesian War." *Atlantic* 80 (September 1897): 330–42; reprinted in *Creed,* 55–103. |
| *Studies* | *Studies in Honor of Basil L. Gildersleeve.* Baltimore: Johns Hopkins Press, 1902. |
| *Syntax* | *Syntax of Classical Greek from Homer to Demosthenes, Part I,* with C. W. E. Miller. New York: American Book Co., 1900. Reprint, Gröningen: Peter Stork, 1980. |
| *University Work* | B. L. Gildersleeve, "University Work in America and Classical Philology." *Princeton Review* 55 (May 1879): 511–36. Reprinted in *E&S,* 87–123. |
| UVa | University of Virginia |
| *WhAm* | *Who Was Who in America: Historical Volume, 1607–1896.* Revised ed., Chicago: Marquis Who's Who, 1967. |
| *WhAm 1* | *Who Was Who in America.* Vol. 1, *1897–1942.* Chicago: A. N. Marquis Co., 1943. |
| *WhAm 5* | *Who Was Who in America.* Vol. 5, *1969–1973.* Chicago: Marquis Who's Who, 1973. |

All periodical abbreviations are those of *L'Année philologique.* References to ancient authors and their works follow the abbreviations of Liddell and Scott's *Greek-English Lexicon* (Oxford: Clarendon Press, 1978) and the *Oxford Latin Dictionary,* edited by P. G. W. Glare (Oxford: Clarendon Press, 1982).

# CHRONOLOGY OF
# BASIL LANNEAU GILDERSLEEVE

1831      Born in grandparents' home at 3 Pitt St., Charleston, S.C., on 23 October.

1836      Reads Gospel of John in Greek.

1840      Family moves to 5 Pitt St.

1844–45      Enrolled at College of Charleston.

1845      Family finances oblige a move to Richmond, Va., where his father, Benjamin Gildersleeve, buys *Watchman of the South*. The family arrives in Richmond on 13 August, Benjamin and Emma's wedding anniversary.

1845–46      Enrolled at Jefferson College, Washington, Pa.

1846–49      Enrolled at Princeton; graduates fourth of seventy-nine in class of '49.

1848      Accidentally shoots himself in face with his "frogging piece." He grows a full beard in Germany to hide the resulting scar.

1850–51      Enrolled at Berlin for the winter semester.

1851–52      Enrolled at Göttingen for spring and winter semesters.

1852      Enrolled at Bonn for spring and winter semesters 1852–53; meets Emil Hübner, with whom he celebrates his twenty-first birthday. Father builds house at 117 West Grace St., Richmond.

1853      Receives Ph.D. from Göttingen on 14 March; tours Europe with the Dingles before leaving for America on 13 July; during the winter serves as private tutor to Blake family of "Board House," near Wiggins, S.C.

1854      Visits Charleston in the spring, sees Hayne and other members of the Simms circle. Gildersleeve's "maiden article," "The Necessity of the Classics," *Southern Quarterly Review* 26, n.s., 10 (July 1854): 145–67, published.

1856      Elected professor of Greek at the University of Virginia in October; moves into Pavilion I.

| | |
|---|---|
| 1858 | Trip to Cuba; Gildersleeve's brother Ben enrolls at the University of Virginia and lives with him. |
| 1859 | Gildersleeve's mother, Emma Lanneau Gildersleeve, dies on 21 September. |
| 1860 | Trip to Europe; visits Ritschl. |
| 1861 | On staff of Col. William Gilham, 21st Virginia Infantry, in the summer. |
| 1863 | Private, Co. D., 1st Regt., First Virginia Cavalry (under Fitzhugh Lee) in the summer. |
| 1863–64 | Writes editorials for the *Richmond Examiner*. |
| 1864 | On staff of Gen. John B. Gordon. Wounded in skirmish at Weyer's Cave, Va., on 25 September while carrying orders for Gordon. Recuperates for five months at Hillandale, the Colston estate in Albemarle Co., Va. |
| 1866 | Marries Elizabeth Fisher Colston at Hillandale on 15 September. |
| 1867 | *Latin Grammar* published (New York: Richardson). |
| 1869 | Receives LL.D. from College of William and Mary. Son Raleigh Colston born on 6 June (died 12 September 1944). |
| 1871 | Son Basil Seymour born on 10 March (died 2 October 1871). |
| 1872 | Daughter Emma Louisa born on 15 June (died 13 September 1954). |
| 1874 | Son Benjamin F. born on 12 January (died 20 July 1874). |
| 1875 | *The Satires of A. Persius Flaccus* published (New York: Harper and Bros.). Gilman, looking for faculty for Johns Hopkins, visits Charlottesville. Father Benjamin dies on 20 June in Tazewell, Va. Gildersleeve accepts appointment as first faculty member at Johns Hopkins on 11 December. |
| 1877 | *The Apologies of Justin Martyr* published (New York: Harper and Bros.). |
| 1877–78 | First presidency of APA. |
| 1878 | Gardiner Martin Lane visits Gildersleeve. |
| 1880 | First issue of *AJP* appears in January. Gildersleeve in Europe seeking faculty and promoting *AJP* from 7 May to 22 September. |
| 1883 | Lectures and holds examinations at the University of the South, Sewanee, Tenn. |
| 1884 | Gives summer course at Sewanee from 29 July to 19 September; receives D.C.L. from Sewanee. |

1885     *Pindar: The Olympian and Pythian Odes* published in April (New York: Harper and Bros.).

1886     Lectures at Sewanee from 14 July to 18 September on "Aristophanes and His Times"; Receives LL.D. from Harvard.

1887     Lectures at Sewanee from 6 August to 10 September on "Outlines of Hermeneutics."

1888     Takes family to Europe; Raleigh enrolls at Technische Hochschule, Charlottenberg; Betty and Emma stay in Berlin for two years.

1889     Visits family in Europe in summer.

1890     *Essays and Studies* published (Baltimore: N. Murray). Visits family in Europe in summer; Betty and Emma return on 1 December.

1891     Family moves to 1002 Belvidere Terrace (N. Calvert St.) in September.

1892     "The Creed of the Old South," *Atlantic* 69 (January 1892): 75–87, published.

1893     Visits Charleston for last time on 22 December.

1894     Moves seminar to 14 McCoy Hall.

1896     Trip to Greece, 21 March–8 September.

1897     "A Southerner in the Peloponnesian War," *Atlantic* 80 (September 1897): 330–42, published.

1898     Emma marries Gardiner Martin Lane in Christ Church, Baltimore, on 8 June.

1899     Granddaughter Katharine Ward Lane born on 22 February. Gildersleeve receives L.H.D. from Princeton on his Jubilee.

1900     *Syntax of Classical Greek, Part I*, with C. W. E. Miller, published (New York: American Book Co.).

1901     Hübner dies on 21 February. Gilman retires from Johns Hopkins on 1 September. Gildersleeve receives LL.D. from Yale on 23 October.

1902     *Studies in Honor of Basil L. Gildersleeve* published on 20 February (Baltimore: Johns Hopkins Press, 1902) and presented to Gildersleeve by his students.

1903     Elected to American Philosophical Society on 7 April.

1905     Receives D.Litt. from Cambridge on 14 June; receives D.Litt. from Oxford on 28 June; elected to National Institute of Arts and Letters.

1907     Visits Wilamowitz in Berlin in spring.

1908    Elected to American Academy of Arts and Letters. Gilman
        dies on 13 October. Gives inaugural Barbour-Page Lectures,
        "Hellas and Hesperia," at the University of Virginia on 19–21
        November.

1911    *Syntax of Classical Greek, Part II*, with C. W. E. Miller,
        published (New York: American Book Co.).

1914    Gardiner Lane dies on 3 October.

1915    Gildersleeve retires from Johns Hopkins on 22 May. Betty's
        "attack" forces Gildersleeve to decline (11 December) Wheel-
        er's offer of a Sather Lectureship.

1916    Gildersleeve suffers heart attack on 29 February.

1924    Dies of pneumonia caused by bronchial infection on 9 Janu-
        ary; buried in University Cemetery, Charlottesville, Va., on 14
        January.

# ❦ LOCATIONS OF LETTERS ❧

Abbreviations used in the text are in italics.

American Academy and Institute of Arts and Letters, New York.
*Berlin* = Deutsche Staatsbibliothek, Berlin, DDR.
Bodleian Library, Oxford.
*Bonn* = S2103, Universitätsbibliothek, Bonn, FRD.
Bryn Mawr College, Bryn Mawr, Pa.
*California* = Benjamin Ide Wheeler Papers (C-B1044), Bancroft Library, University of California, Berkeley.
Cambridge University Library.
*Chicago* = Paul Shorey Papers, Box 2, Folder 2, University of Chicago Archives, Chicago.
"Collegiana," *Virginia University Magazine* 15, no. 1 (October 1876): 98–99.
*Columbia* = Edmund C. Stedman Papers, Rare Book and Manuscript Library, Columbia University, New York.
*Cornell* = John M. Olin Library, Cornell University, Ithaca, N.Y.
*Culbreth* = David M. R. Culbreth, M.D., *The University of Virginia: Memories of Her Student-Life and Professors* (New York: Neale Publishing Co., 1908), 402.
*Dickinson* = Dickinson College Library, Carlisle, Pa.
"Dr. Gildersleeve at Ninety-Two," *Alumni Bulletin University of Virginia,* 3d ser., 17, no. 1 (January 1924): 132–33.
"Dr. Gildersleeve's Birthday," ibid., 200.
*Duke* = William R. Perkins Library, Duke University, Durham, N.C.
Glasgow University.
*Göttingen* = Signatur: Cod. MS. Wilamowitz 442, Niedersächsiche Staats- und Universitätsbibliothek, Göttingen, FRD.
Hamilton College Library, Clinton, N.Y.
*Harvard* = Harvard University Archives, Cambridge, Mass.
*Houghton* = Houghton Library, Harvard University, Cambridge, Mass.
*JHU-BLG* = Basil Lanneau Gildersleeve Collection, MS. 5, Special

Collections, Milton S. Eisenhower Library, Johns Hopkins University, Baltimore.

*-Gilman* = Daniel Coit Gilman Collection, MS. 1, Special Collections, Milton S. Eisenhower Library, Johns Hopkins University, Baltimore.

*Maryland Historical Society* = McIlvain Collection, MS. 1081, Manuscripts Division, Maryland Historical Society Library, Baltimore.

*New York Public Library-BLG* = Basil L. Gildersleeve, Miscellaneous Papers, Rare Books and Manuscripts Division, New York Public Library, Astor, Lenox, and Tilden Foundations.

*-Century* = Century Company Records, Rare Books and Manuscripts Division, New York Public Library, Astor, Lenox, and Tilden Foundations.

Charles S. Norwood, Goldsboro, N.C.

Mary E. Phillips, *Edgar Allan Poe the Man* (Chicago: John C. Winston Co., 1926), 1442–43.

Edgar Allan Poe Museum, Richmond, Va.

*St. Andrews* = University of St. Andrews, Fife, Scotland.

*Sewanee* = Archives, University of the South, Sewanee, Tenn.

*Smith* = Charles Forster Smith, "Basil Lanneau Gildersleeve: An Intimate View," *Sewanee Review* 32 (April 1924): 162–75.

Staatsbibliothek Preussischer Kulturbesitz, Berlin, FRD.

*Stanford* = Henry Rushton Fairclough Papers, SC 21, Stanford University Archives, Stanford, Calif.

State Historical Society of Wisconsin, Madison, Wis.

*Testimonials in Favour of Alfred Edward Housman, Late Scholar of St. John's College, Oxford, A Candidate for the Professorship of Latin in University College, London* (Cambridge: University Press, 1892).

*UNC-Bain* = Charles W. Bain Papers (2739-B), Southern Historical Collection, Library of the University of North Carolina at Chapel Hill.

*UNC-Tucker* = Tucker Family Papers (2605), Southern Historical Collection, Library of the University of North Carolina at Chapel Hill.

*UVa-Alderman* = Edwin A. Alderman Papers (1001)

*-Barbour* = Barbour Family Papers (1486)

*-"Enchanted Years"* = "The Enchanted Years" Collection (38–429)

*-Gordon* = Correspondence of Armistead Gordon (38–145)

*-Maupin* = Papers of the Maupin family (4105)

*-Minor* = Papers of the Minor Family (38–602)

*-Robinson* = Papers of Leigh Robinson (438)

*-Savage* = Papers of A. D. Savage (10079)

*-Thornton* = Papers of William Mynn Thornton (2077-b)

Manuscripts Department, University of Virginia Library, Charlottesville, Va.

*Vanderbilt* = Edwin Mims Papers, Special Collections, Jean and Alex-
  ander Heard Library, Vanderbilt University, Nashville, Tenn.
Virginia Historical Society, Richmond, Va.
*Yale-Gilman* = Daniel Coit Gilman Papers
  *-Goodell* = Thomas D. Goodell Papers
  *-Seymour* = Seymour Family Papers
  *-Whitney* = William D. Whitney Family Papers
  Yale University Library, Yale University, New Haven, Conn.

# THE LETTERS OF BASIL LANNEAU GILDERSLEEVE

# ❦ 1 ❧

## *SOPHROSYNE*: BEGINNINGS, 1851–1856

"I was a Charlestonian first, Carolinian next, and then a southerner—on my mother's side a southerner beyond dispute."[1] Basil Lanneau Gildersleeve was born at the home of the grandfather after whom he was named,[2] Bazile Lanneau (1746–1833), a Charleston single-house at 3 Pitt Street, where his mother had gone for her lying-in. His father, the Reverend Benjamin Gildersleeve (1791–1875), never had his own parish and had come to Charleston in 1826 to found the *Charleston Observer,* a Presbyterian newspaper. On 13 August 1828 he married his third wife, Emma Louisa Lanneau (1805–59). The Gildersleeves lived at 40 St. Philips Street, and around 1840, presumably with money inherited from Emma's father, built a house at 5 Pitt Street, where the family, of which Basil was the first son, would grow up. Three sisters and two brothers were born in Charleston (one brother, Gilbert Snowden, was born following the move to Richmond), and three children died in infancy.[3]

Benjamin Gildersleeve had educated himself prior to attending Middlebury College (A.B. 1814), Hopewell Seminary in Athens, Ga., and Princeton Theological Seminary, from which he graduated in 1817.[4] He likewise provided his precocious son's early education up to the age of thirteen, and Basil subsequently expressed his sense of the overlap of the paternal and the academic: "The father is lost in the teacher or the teacher in the father":[5]

After I left the nursery, until I was between twelve and thirteen, my father was my only teacher. My lessons were heard at odd hours, often when my father was tired from work; and hard was the work that would tire that heroic soul. It was, as I remember it, a very tumultuous affair, that earliest education of mine. I could read when I was between three and four years of age, and I signalized the completion of my fifth year by reading the Bible from cover to cover. Needless to say, the reading was without the understanding.[6]

I knew Greek as early as I knew anything. When I was five years old I read the Gospel of John in Greek and I have virtually thought in Greek ever since.[7]

1

A lad of less than twelve, I translated the so-called Anacreon into English rhyme, untroubled by questions of higher criticism and pagan morality.[8]

Latin I learned at a tender age, and I "got through" Caesar, Sallust, Cicero, Virgil, and Horace before the time when boys of to-day have fairly mastered the rudiments. . . . French I picked up after a fashion. I had read sundry plays of Corneille, Racine, and Molière before I was fourteen. . . . Of German I knew only a few words . . . of Spanish I had learned something in a private class at Richmond.[9]

His English reading included his father's favorite, Milton, but not Shakespeare, whom his father considered "immoral," and whom he could only read on Saturdays at the home of "an ungodly great-uncle," who would declaim his favorite passages and recall memorable performances for his rapt nephew. Novels were similarly prohibited, but the boy read Poe (see No. 167) and obtained the Waverly novels of Sir Walter Scott by subterfuge from "the 'dour' old custodian of the Apprentices' Library—a Scotchman."[10]

At around the age of twelve, his father delivered him to William E. Bailey, a Charleston teacher of the classics, who prepared the boy to enter the College of Charleston in 1845 at the age of thirteen, in the class of Sam Lord, David Ramsay, and Richardson Miles.[11]

At this time his lifelong compulsion to write began to manifest itself, and Basil soon realized, with a frustration that would be equally lifelong, that although he had the "poetic temperament," he was nevertheless "unblessed by poetic power."[12] His first publications were poems for a children's newspaper in Charleston and hymns to be sung at the Juvenile Missionary Society;[13] his last published work was a sonnet to South Carolina.

Whatever the successes of Basil Gildersleeve's later life, he maintained that "the roots go back to the first fourteen years,"[14] when his father taught him the piety of duty and Charleston taught him about the nobility and code of the Southern way of life at its apogee.

In 1845 the state of the family's finances forced Benjamin Gildersleeve to buy another Presbyterian newspaper, the *Watchman of the South,* merge it with the *Observer,* and move the family to Richmond, where they arrived on 13 August, the anniversary of Benjamin and Emma's wedding. Here he edited the *Watchman and Observer* until 1856, when, with associates, he bought and published his third newspaper, the *Central Presbyterian,* which lasted until 1860.

Basil "pleaded" with his father to let him attend the University of Virginia, but his father had other ideas about the "godless university" in Charlottesville, and Basil was packed off to Jefferson College (now Washington and Jefferson College) in Canonsburg, Pa.,[15] where he "scamped his lessons" and wrote in his diary of his disgust at the immaturity of the students and the unprofessionalism of the faculty in much the same terms he would use sixty years later: "In my boyhood there was nothing but a text-book with a few pictures, and a posing demonstrator, who, when he succeeded, had the air of an adroit conjurer, when he failed, the attitude of a baffled rat-catcher."[16] Easily overtopping his classmates, he finished first in his class, but when one of the few admirable people Basil found in Canonsburg, Jefferson's President Robert J. Breckinridge (1800–71), resigned, Basil begged to transfer, this time to Yale, where an uncle had gone and his father had once intended to go.[17] But his father's choice was his own alma mater, Princeton, whose vice-president and professor of Greek was Benjamin Gildersleeve's former classmate John Maclean, and which was a favorite school for Southerners of the day. (Indeed, Basil's two roommates at 30 East College were Virginians.)

He entered Princeton at the age of fifteen in 1847 and graduated fourth in his class of seventy-nine in 1849 at seventeen. At Princeton he continued his extensive reading: "I gave a couple of hours to my classes each day, and then ho! for the wide field of literature—English, French, German, Italian, Spanish."[18] Some Princetonians impressed him, particularly the physicist Joseph Henry, the chemist John Torrey, and the mathematician Stephen Alexander. But again he found the instruction in his chosen field "hit-or-miss." The Reverend John Maclean, vice-president of the college and professor of Greek, although a friend, was an indifferent teacher at best.[19]

Basil's disillusion extended beyond the American educational system. Something deeper had altered the once-religious youth, as revealed in his account of the time his "frogging-piece" exploded in his face during a "frog hunt near Dr. Scudder's" in Princeton. In the face of death, the minister's son recurred not to the Good Book, but to Carlyle:

> I recalled a bright summer day in 1848, sixty-four years ago, when I sate beneath a tree awaiting the arrival of a surgeon to dress a gun-shot wound that I had just received, and how with the affected stoicism of a boy, I sent up to my room for a copy of Sartor Resartus that I might finish the chapter of the Everlasting Yea, if the worst came to the worst. I did not know the pretty anecdote of Solon, who wished to learn the last sweet thing of Sappho's before he died.[20]

"Good old Johnny" Maclean "watched over me when I lay grievously hurt at the house where that angel, Miss Mary [Maclean's sister], prepared delicacies for me,"[21] but this was the only effect his Greek teacher Maclean seems to have had.

"The most important of all the teachers I ever had"[22] was Goethe, whom he encountered via Carlyle. Goethe took the place in his heart and mind that had once been occupied by his religion, and Gildersleeve describes his solitary walks with Goethe in his head as if he were on his own road to Damascus:

> My acquaintance with Goethe goes back to the beginning of my Teutonomaniac period in 1847, and I doubt whether any boy of my age ever devoured so much of Goethe in so short a time. There was not much that I left unread from Goetz von Berlichingen to the Second Part of Faust. His lyrics were my delight and I learned many of his "Sprüche" by heart. But while I enjoyed the light and warmth of my luminary, I did not inquire too curiously in what sign of the zodiac my sun was standing, or whose star, not to say petticoat was in the ascendant, Frederike's, Frau von Stein's or Ulrike von Levetsow's. Since that far-off time every recess of Goethe's life has been explored and every sinuosity of his long career has been lighted up.[23]

> Goethe's aphorisms were my daily food. I committed my favorite passages to memory. I repeated them over and over to myself in my long solitary rambles, and Goethe was my mainstay at a time when my faith had suffered an eclipse. This was the epoch of my Teutonomania, the time when I read German, wrote German, listened to German, and even talked German—to myself if I could not find any long-suffering German to submit to my experiments.[24]

He had begun reading William Howitt's *Student-Life of Germany*[25] at Jefferson and had recorded in his diary his calculation that he could live at Heidelberg on 500–600 gilders a year, 300–400 less than Howitt's estimate. But he had another year to wait following his graduation from Princeton.

He returned to Richmond in the summer of 1849 and was given a job as classical master at the school of Dr. Socrates Maupin (see "Correspondents"), where he taught for a year, chiefly to earn the money to finance his German education, and began work on a long, semi-autobiographical novel. "I undertook to teach what I had never properly learned myself, and I practised myself in Greek and Latin composition with the help of such manuals as were available,"[26] drilling the boys out of Kühner's Greek grammar.

Finally, in the summer of 1850, he boarded the tobacco boat *Hermine* and sailed from Richmond to Bremen. "I had no plan, I had no mentor."[27] His arrival in Berlin for the winter semester of 1850–51 must have been a cultural, linguistic, and educational shock to the nineteen-year-old Southerner.[28] He spent his time trying to accommodate himself to a large city, getting used to the language, and imposing discipline upon himself after his easy semesters in America. "An imaginative, impulsive, *prime-sautier* boy, proud, shy, self-conscious,"[29] he was once again called to "the duty of work" that his father had so thoroughly ingrained in him by both precept and example. At matriculation he met one of the great influences of his life, the Pindarist August Boeckh (No. 50, n. 3), whose "teaching made a passionate classicist out of an amateurish student of literature."[30] Boeckh felt that "Grammar is the highest problem of science"[31] and, like Gildersleeve in later life, was able to inspire great devotion in his pupils, while remaining aloof from them.[32] Gildersleeve's other professors were Johannes Franz (1804-51), "the first real teacher of Greek I ever had," who influenced his "whole life and whole teaching,"[33] and Friedrich August Maercker (1804-89). But there were only five Americans at the Friedrich-Wilhelms-Universität that year, among them W. D. Whitney (No. 8), and Gildersleeve met few locals: "Of my German fellow-students during my one semester in Berlin (1850-51) I saw little and remember less."[34] It is no wonder he stayed only a semester and left "profoundly discouraged."[35]

He made his way quickly to the George-August-Universität, Göttingen, long a popular German university for Charlestonians,[36] where he spent the spring semester of 1851 and winter semester of 1851-52. Now he was with his Charleston friends Sam Lord, David Ramsay, and G. W. Dingle, with whom he roomed at Weenderstrasse 59; his "Charlestownian" friend, George M. Lane (No. 22, n. 1), who had been at Göttingen since 1847; and Francis J. Child (No. 21, n. 1). He became friends with his German classmates August Baumeister (1830-1922) and Eduard von Wölfflin (1831-1908). His professors were Karl Friedrich Hermann (No. 5, n. 5), Heinrich Ritter (1791-1869), and Friedrich Wilhelm Schneidewin (see No. 157), who warmly received him in his home, and whom he recalled as "one of my favorite teachers."[37]

At Rheinische Friedrich-Wilhelms-Universität, Bonn, he encountered the "sons of Belial flown with lust and wine," and among the "sundry young Palatines" of his boardinghouse[38] during the spring semester of 1852 was Lane. By the winter semester of 1852-53, he had found among his fellows Johannes Vahlen (No. 164, n. 7) and the man with whom he would form a great friendship that would last for nearly sixty years, Emil Hübner. For an even longer period, Gildersleeve kept before him in his study a bust of the Bonn Latinist Friedrich Wilhelm Ritschl (No. 23, n. 2), who welcomed him into his home and later corresponded with him.[39] His other professors were Joseph von Aschbach (1801-82), Friedrich Gottlieb Welcker (1784-1868), Franz Ritter (1803-75), Moriz Schmidt (1823-93), Johannes Adolf Overbeck (1826-95), Ludwig Schopen (1799-1867), and the young Jacob Bernays (No. 7, n. 9), who "led me into the study that resulted in my doctoral dissertation."[40]

He returned to Göttingen to defend his dissertation, *De Porphyrii studiis capitum Homericis trias* (Göttingen: E. A. Huthius, 1853), and swear his oath on the Ides of March.[41] He saw the Hübners in Berlin before beginning his European tour in April (No. 2). On July 13 he sailed for home, arriving on the 25th with a paucity of prospects equal to his superb education and a multitude of memories of his German friends and teachers.

1. *Formative Influences*: 608.

2. He is also supposed to have been named after the Reverend Basil Manly, a prominent Charlestonian, as was a cousin, Basil Manly Lanneau (1841–1915).

3. For the family tree, see Susie R. Mowbray and Charles S. Norwood, *Bazile Lanneau of Charleston, 1746–1833* (Goldsboro, N.C.: Hilburn Printing Corp., 1985), 59.

4. The second son of Finch Gildersleeve (see genealogy, No. 122), Benjamin Gildersleeve was given 100 acres of the family farm on his twenty-first birthday by his father, but he had found his religion the year before and went off to Middlebury College. Since he had been teaching in local schools from the age of thirteen, he at first determined to be a teacher. He became master at a new classical school at Mt. Zion, Ga. (1814–17), was licensed by the Hopewell Presbytery in 1815, and was ordained in August 1820. He spent 1817 at Princeton Theological Seminary and in 1819 became founding editor of the *Missionary*. Following his own illness and the death of his first wife (Sarah Elliott) in 1820, the paper began to fail, and after his recovery, he was obliged to preach itinerantly in Georgia and South Carolina for two years to pay the bills. His second wife (Frances Langston) died in 1825 on their first wedding anniversary, and their young daughter died in 1828. On 1 January 1827, he published the first issue of the *Charleston Observer* (see, further, introduction to this chapter). When his third wife, Emma, died after a long illness, he gave up editing and returned to preaching. Late in his life his eyesight failed (as did Basil's), but having memorized large amounts of scripture and many hymns, he was able to continue preaching. See W. Gildersleeve, *Gildersleeve Pioneers* (Rutland, Vt.: Tuttle Publishing, 1941), 242–49, S. R. Mowbray and C. S. Norwood (cited n. 3 above), 25–28 (with portrait).

5. *Formative Influences*: 616.

6. *AJP* 5 (1884): 341.

7. *Columbia* (S.C.) *State*, 30 November 1919: 9.

8. *H&H*, 19–20. See also *Formative Influences:* 611: "I still own a prize copy of Plato given to me in 1843 by our scholarly family physician, Dr. Samuel H. Dickson. The version of the 'Crito' which I undertook in order to show myself worthy of the gift is still among my papers."

9. *Formative Influences*: 611. On his Latin reading, see "A Novice of 1850," *Johns Hopkins Alumni Magazine* 1, no. 1 (November 1912): 4: "I do not think that I was exceptional, I read before I was fifteen all Caesar's Gallic War, all Vergil, all Horace, a number of Cicero's Orations, the Laelius and the Cato, Sallust, Juvenal, parts of Tacitus. These I recall distinctly, as also Cicero's De Oratore, of which my father, my principal teacher, happened to own a fine old edition."

10. *Formative Influences*: 612.

11. See No. 12, nn. 15 and 16, and No. 65.

12. See No. 12, n. 3; No. 138, n. 14.

13. No. 12, n. 3.

14. *Formative Influences*: 116.

15. See No. 153.

16. *H&H*, 29

17. "The College in the Forties," *Princeton Alumni Weekly* 16, no. 16 (26 January 1916): 376, *Gildersleeve Pioneers* (cited n. 4 above), 244.

18. "College in the Forties" (cited n. 17 above), 379.

19. John Maclean (1800–86) was ordained by the Presbyterian Church in 1828 and in the next year was named instructor of Greek and vice-president of the college. In 1847 he was made professor of Greek, and in 1854, president of the university. *DAB*, 12: 128–29.

20. "Third lecture on Greek poetry." Reprinted with permission of the University of Mississippi Library. "As to his beard, he told us that his "frogging piece" accidentally went off and scarred his face, and his beard was meant to hide the scar." Letter of Thomas W. Dickson in *Johns Hopkins Magazine* (July 1974): 23.

21. "College in the Forties": 377.

22. *Formative Influences*: 614.

23. *AJP* 23 (1902): 110–11 ( = *SBM*, 79).

24. *Formative Influences*: 613–14.

25. William Howitt, *The Student-Life of Germany* (Philadelphia: Carey and Hart, 1842).

26. "Novice of 1850" (cited n. 9 above): 5.

27. Ibid.: 5–6.

28. "Of my special preparation for philological work the less said the better. . . . But I had enough German to understand the lectures and that was something" (*Professorial Types*: 14). See also "Novice of 1850": 3–6, esp. 5.

29. *Formative Influences*: 612.

30. *H&H*, 42.

31. *University Work*: 108.

32. Gildersleeve recorded his first meeting with Boeckh, shortly after arriving on campus. After keeping Gildersleeve and a colleague waiting, he invited them into his study: "The distinguished philologist was exceedingly monosyllabic—asked me my name—told me to hold my matriculation—gave me leave to depart and bowed me out" (diary, 1850–53, in Hopkins Archives, quoted by R. L. Fowler, "The Gildersleeve Archive," *Briggs-Benario*, 73). On Gildersleeve's own aloofness from students, see Nos. 160 and 164.

33. *H&H*, 33. See also "Novice of 1850": 7.

34. *AJP* 22 (1901): 229 ( = *SBM*, 66). In addition to his diaries, Gildersleeve saved most of his student notebooks from the period; see Fowler (cited n. 32 above), 64–6.

35. "Novice of 1850": 8.

36. See Daniel B. Shumway, "The American Students of the University of Göttingen," *German American Annals* 12, nos. 5–6 (n.s. 8, 5–6) (September–December 1910): 171–207. For a description of Göttingen in contrast to Berlin, see *Professorial Types*: 6–7.

37. *AJP* 37 (1916): 501 ( = *SBM*, 356).

38. "Modest Critique of 'A Sketch after Landseer,' " *Southern Literary Messenger* 20 (1854): 119–20.

39. *AJP* 5 (1884): 340.

40. *AJP* 32 (1911): 360 ( = *SBM*, 232).

41. His committee included Christoph Wilhelm Mitscherlich, C. Fr. Gauss, Georg Heinrich August Ewald, J. Fr. L. Hausmann, Karl Heinrich Hoeck, Georg W. Waitz, and Georg Weber. For the diploma and other aspects of his German education, see John T. Krumpelmann, *Southern Scholars in Goethe's Germany* (Chapel Hill, N.C.: University of North Carolina Press, n.d.), 105–6.

## 1 To: "Homefolks"
### *JHU-BLG*[1]

Saturday–Oct. 22, 1853

I have before me a huge pile of letters written by me to the homefolks during my three year absence—I have resolved upon going through the drudgery of looking over them if perchance a jewel may be found on the dunghill.—

Jan^y 1, 1851 The American college is in my opinion a palpable absurdity—in which the attempt to unite freedom + submission produces daily the most ridiculous incongruities. A good school like a German Gymnasium—where boys <u>must</u> learn—or a good university like that of Berlin—where men <u>may</u>—but no such amphibious affair—where boys <u>may</u> learn—and men <u>cannot</u>[2]—

===

May 9, 1851 I have rejected the black lines—I beseech you to congratulate me upon my progress in this department of penmanship—I who once could not write without black lines save only on ruled paper ~~save only~~ without feeling the glow of ingenuous shame at the towardness and frowardness of my files can now write under the above-mentioned trying circumstances without the least chagrin— — —

===

I was quite diverted with a flower-boy who came up to a friend and myself while we [in marg.: "Sechsen"] were resting on /one of/ the benches in the park and besought us to buy his violets. I gave him (c.) a cent for a Lilliputian bunch—moved by his incessant "my dear—dear Sir" which sounds much more plaintive in German than in English. He then besieged my friend who commenced to haggle with him. He finally offered him 4 bunches for 3 c. and as my friend was about to pull out the tin I attempted to trick him. "Give him, my boy," I said, " 3 bunches + then we should have together 4. I have paid you one c. already + he will pay you 2 so that you will have 3 c. for your 4 bunches." "Paid for already" he replied quick as lightning. A carriage rolled by—as he finished his business transactions with us and the last I saw of him was his outstretched arms and trotting legs— —Moral: We threw the violets away— —

===

During the last days of my stay in Berlin I discussed with considerable zeal the subject of games + sports—It would have diverted you highly to have seen my landlady and myself making with all the glow of artistic fervor cocked-hats—boat-biddies + salt-cellars—Thus far we kept pace with each other but she could not make a fly-trap—and therein I bore off the prize but not without trouble for I had almost forgotten how. Neither of us was able to bring a pocket handkerchief rabbit into existence and I mourned over my inability to represent the whole series of combinations of the fingers in my 'Here's my lady's cradle—here's my lady's knife + fork—and here's my ladie's [sic] table' or however the formula runs[3]—

===

Book-auction. The business was transacted in the 3^d story of three—more than 2000 volumes to be sold and three hours a day allotted—The

clerk sat at one end of the table—the ~~bid~~ auctioneers on one side and as
many of the bidders as could be accommodated sate round about the
same—The rest stood—Every one was provided with a catalogue— +
there was no bepraising of the books—The articles in question were thrown
on the table as the number was called—and the curious inspected it. N⁰
1553—8-8¹/₂-9-9¹/₂ +c—20 for the first time—for the 2ᵈ time—for the—
bam or rather bim went the little hammer—Grebeustein—The catalogue
numbering 48 pp. was sold for about a cent—the profits to be given to the
poor—a questionable sort of charity—

===

The Nightingale—A nightingale is bearing [sic] her throat with melody
just opposite my window. It ~~seems~~ is almost painfully delicious to hear
these birds when they sing from the depths of their throats. It seems as if
the little things would vibrate to death—

===

I am unfortunately more like that Simon of Cyrene who helped bear the
cross[4] than like Simon the sorcerer who would fain buy the spirit of prophesy[5]—

===

Do you remember the chiding question of the nursery? 'Will you have it
now or wait until you can get it?' I have found the same question of wide
application in life beyond the confines of the nursery.

===

When I have come /out/ of a company where I have talked a great deal I
feel like running my head against a wall for having made such a fool of
myself and when I have said nothing I feel like knocking the aforemen-
tioned excrescence off for having played dummy in decent society—

===

I cherish the most solemn awe of holy things and it has been the case
with me that this very feeling has brought me to the use of light expressions
as we read of the pangs of the dying extorting laughter—

===

I am now my own master but not master of myself—a considerable difference—

===

I hope to grow in grease if not in grace.

===

A German girl goes to church with true piety and a gilt edged hymnbook
on Sunday morning—takes a walk and admires the beauties of nature ~~after
coffee~~ in the afternoon—or rather in the after-coffee—and receives the
friends of the family at night. Sometimes she goes to church twice on a
Sunday—but then she regards herself as a little saint. Wednesday night
prayer-meetings are unheard-of. Feasts + festivals as prescribed by the

calendar and the Most High (meaning the sublunary potentate of Pumpernickel) she religiously observes. She never speaks lightly of religion nor likes to hear it lightly spoken of and is according to her own benighted view of the subject a good Christian—

==

One of the Professors here has reached the 50$^{\text{th}}$ year of his Doctorate—and this <u>Jubilee</u> was necessarily celebrated. The students formed a torch-light procession arrayed according to their different clubs and societies and marched to the dwelling of the old man—The committee went up—congratulated—and took wine—The old man put his snowy head out of the window—and amid a very creditable silence thanked the students in a very brief speech—it was a wet night and the professor was learned in the practice of medicine and fearful of catarrh—Whereupon they gave a hearty "vivat" and withdrew to fortify themselves for their Jubilee with beer— —A shrewd old Aulic counsellor[6] with a rubicund face + a cigar in his mouth leans over the sill of his colleague's house and looks whimsically at the assembled multitude.

==

Moses broke both tables of the law in his anger—I am afraid of breaking one in self-mistrust.

==

I must renew my request for the Psyche of the Eros you sent me lately—the Alter Ego—in short the other half of the hundred.

==

Unaided by the bigoted unity of a sect or the Briarean[7] multiplicity of a party.

==

In America one sees on the doors more frequently "push" than "pull"[8] and a man's best trumpeter is himself—

==

I would fain linger around these fountains /of learning/ year after year but if I can borrow the divining rod I shall content myself with searching for the hidden springs at home—

==

I sometimes choke with merriment at the idea that a set of young persons should come together and dance from 8 at night until 3 in the morning with the speed of dromedaries and the energy of bears—

==

Little did I expect this abruptly conical end of my study in Germany. I had pictured to myself a cylinder or a cube or a sphere as the emblem of my well-finished course—

==

Among students beer is the standard as water is in hydrostatics

==

Ich habe den ganzen Misthaufen durchsucht—durchwühlt—u. finde am Ende leider nur Mistkäfer[9]—

1. These fragments were copied into the last pages of his 1850–53 diary.
2. Cf. "Classics and Colleges," *Princeton Review* 54 (July 1878): 81 ( = *E&S*, 64): "The *curriculum* must be simplified for the college side; the elective principle must be the norm for the university side. There must be no such incongruous blending of the two as is seen all over the country, so that it would not be hard to point out institutions in which college work is done on university principles and university work is done on college principles. There are things that must be learned by the dead pull, and no amount of scientific presentation will be of any practical avail; and, on the other hand, there are high ranges that cannot be traversed without the discursive faculty."
3. Gildersleeve describes a series of creations made by folding paper or manipulating strings. See E. Landells, *The Boy's Own Toy-Maker* (London: Griffith and Farran, 1866) for many of the figures.
4. Matt. 27:32; Mark 15:21; Luke 23:26.
5. Also called Simon Magus: Acts 8:5-24.
6. The Aulic Council was the privy council of the Holy Roman Emperors from 1501 to 1806.
7. I.e., like Briareus, with a hundred hands, often used connotatively; *OED* s.v. "Briareus."
8. See "Our Southern Colleges," *New Eclectic Magazine* 5 (August 1869): 214.
9. "I have searched the entire dung-heap—rummaged through it—and find at the end only dung-beetles."

2 To: EMIL HÜBNER
*Berlin*

Richmond, Vª Aug. 28, 1853

My dear Hübner—
Your persevering silence would discourage any other than myself from the attempt to keep up communication with one apparently so averse to correspondence, did I not feel the necessity of holding spiritual communion with my transatlantic home of which you must consent to be the representative. My last bull was issued from Dresden + as far as I recollect towards the end of May.[1]—From that time then to this I will relate the brief history of my wanderings although I should perhaps ignorance/e/ your ignorance on the subject and pass over to something equally uninteresting. After parting from your kind family + receiving from your father a copy of his "Germania"[2] that I always admired so much I turned my face

toward Saxon Switzerland[3] where I passed two of the most delightful days of my life clambering over the mountains with a young lady from Greves [sic] her mother being only the obligato [sic] accompaniment. Thence I journeyed on to Prague + Vienna where I suffered considerably from the bad arrangements of Austrian railroads—for we broke down between Badenbach + Prague—and from the impertinence of Austrian custom house officers—and from risés [sic] of the Austrian police. I was not over delighted with Vienna. My expectations had been raised to a very high pitch and came down parachute-like from my eminence. But I suppose that the charm of Viennese life consists in or rather is only to be appreciated by means of permanent residence + I was there but a few days. My original plan was to have ascended the Danube + then to have crossed the country to Stuttgart + Strasburg but I did not have the patience requisite for the slow conveyance + turning round shook off the dust from my feet + went by express to Cologne. Here I remained a morning to rest from the fatiguing journey that I had taken + felt sorely tempted to run over to Bonn for a day. An undefinable feeling of apprehension for which I can + could in no wise account kept me back from the trip and so I proceeded to Brussels. From Brussels with which I was much pleased I went to Paris where friends received me[4] + where a life of sight seeing commenced which lasted during the month of my sojourn. How a Londoner can exist in his smoky grim dismal looking wilderness of houses after having seen Paris + how he can have the face to praise English fare after having dined at a Continental table I with my cosmopolitan notions can in no wise understand. I betrayed my French original[5] in Paris by moving about with mercurial lightness + the English side[6] of my character by every shade of dulness from brown study up to violent spleen during the week of my abode in London. The quicker London is used up the better in my opinion + I have not the slightest desire to see old England's shore again. You will find the Englishman however a much better fellow at home than abroad—and he is certainly the best guide + the kindest animal to strangers that I have ever met with in all my travels. Respectable men will set you right very often without your asking them + then bolt as if they had picked your pockets. The only fun that I had in London was to ride on the top of the 'bus. I have traversed the metropolis in all directions in this way + know the great arteries of London's brick + mortar sytem pretty well. The difficulties are very much exaggerated—London + Paris—and especially the latter—are with regard to their main streets nothing like such complexities as Vienna.—If you had been with me in London I might have prolonged my stay because your lively temper renders even disagreeabilities agreeable but I had nothing except my 'penseroso' disposition for company—+ feeling accordingly blue jumped on the [sic] board the Carnatic[7] at Liverpool on the 13th ult.—

ten days thereafter touched my native shore + on the 25<sup>th</sup> was restored to the unexpecting arms of my loving family.[8]—Thus I have been more than a month at home[9]—having nothing to do—my books still under way—a prey to fearful ennui. Great changes have been + are about to be operated in my family. My brother has declared himself definitely for merchandize [sic][10] + is in Charleston where he will probably reside. My two elder sisters are both to be married[11]—the one in October coming—the other next spring according to the brief tenor of American engagements—and so one of the liveliest noisiest houses in the town is to be rendered mute.—My plans are not very definite—I think however that I shall remain in Richmond for a year at least—as no great inducements have yet been held out to leave it. I shall keep bachelor's hall + act as the "guide philosopher + friend" to a limited number of youth at $100 a head which will bring me /in/ a little pocket money—from 1500 to 1800 Thalers a year—with which I can buy gloves—cigar + light reading. Richmond is beautifully situated + looks from the third story window at which I am sitting as if she it had put on its Sunday best for the occasion. It is built on 7 hills and is washed by a beautiful river—a mile wide—which is dammed up by a huge bed of rocks over which it foams and tumbles quite picturesquely.[12] The winter promises to be a gay one—rich + pretty girls are said to abound + could I forget the higher advantages of your more intellectual life I might be contented. But the word Germany is enough to bring up a sigh + I try to bridge over the future which lies before my return. By the by they are trying to make the German element pervade our community.[13] I was in a <u>Kneipe</u> [bar] the other evening with a beer garden attached—a flaming hand bill announced a Drittes Garten Concert[14]—and really I might have thought that some good genius had translated me were it /not/ for the Entrée which cost 12$\frac{1}{2}$ cts a decidedly un-german denomination. The beer is really not so bad.—They have a society of 'Turners' likewise[15]—whether a "turning" will become as popular as "logger-beer" (lager-bier) drinking remains to be seen. We are certainly a great nation.—I have a little spite against a professor in this good state who has published a work on Latin Grammar[16]—with more exalted pretensions than we usually find— + I think of blowing him up in an elaborate article. Could I use Ritschl's lectures on L.G.[17] it would help me along wonderfully. Could you lend me your <u>Heft</u> [notebook] for transcription or would that be too daring a request? I suppose you will think of the Horatian "nequicquam deus abscidit"[18]—but I can't help it. I can get it in 15 days copy it in 15 + you can receive it in 15—so that if you can do without your Vade Mecum for 6 weeks I may hope you will incur no expense whatever as postage is payable on this side—and there is no risk whatever in the transmission—Give my best respects to your family in Dresden[19] + to Mr. + Mrs. Bendemann[20] in Berlin. Do you see anything of D[r] Sommer[21] nowadays—Greet him in my name if you do, likewise Krantz.[22] Write soon

Yours sincerely
B. L. Gildersleeve

Richmond ~~V~~[a]
Virginia   U.S. of America

1. 21 May 1853 [Berlin].
2. For a description of this representation of Germany immediately after the turmoil of 1848, see "Classics and Colleges," *Princeton Review* 54 (July 1878): 75 ( = *E&S*, 55).
3. I.e., Sächsischer Schweiz, a resort area near Dresden, part of the Elbessandstein Mountains that flank the Elbe, near modern Czechoslovakia.
4. He stayed with G. W. Dingle (see No. 12) at 390, rue St. Honoré.
5. For the Lanneaus, see No. 144.
6. On Richard Gildersleeve, see No. 122, n. 5.
7. The *Carnatic*, a 650-ton barque of the Stitt and Co. line running between Liverpool and Charleston. It sailed on the 14th for New Orleans.
8. See genealogy, No. 122. Gildersleeve's youngest sister, Johannah Frances Gildersleeve (Mrs. Henry Barrington) Pratt (1836-1904), remembered his homecoming in a letter to her children of 28 October 1901: "Father did not recognize him. It did take us days to realize that the slim youth, not out of his teens, could have become during his absence from home a broad-shouldered and fully bearded man."
9. In 1852 Rev. Gildersleeve had built a three-story house at 117 West Grace Street in the center of the city. See Mary Wingfield Scott, *Old Richmond Neighborhoods* (Richmond: William Byrd Press, 1950), fig. 146, facing p. 167.
10. Benjamin, who was eighteen, had moved to Charleston to begin a career in business, but he was not successful and in 1858-59 he attended the University of Virginia. He never returned to business, but spent his life after the war as a farmer.
11. The household was not actually reduced. Emma Lanneau Gildersleeve (1830-84) married Robert Howard on 12 October 1853, and lived in the Grace Street house, as did Mary Hannah Gildersleeve (1833-70), who married Samuel W. Jeter and stayed on to take care of her father following her mother's death in 1859.
12. The Falls of the James River, seven miles above Richmond, a site settled by Huguenots in 1699.
13. Regular German immigration to Virginia began in 1837 as a source of laborers for the James River and Kanawha Canal, which began in Richmond and ran 196 miles to Buchanan, Va. After strikes and general disenchantment in 1839, many Germans moved to Richmond and by 1853, "provided with his own churches, social, fraternal, and relief organizations, militia company, theatrical club, and newspaper, the German immigrant began to feel at home" (Klaus Wust, *The Virginia Germans* [Charlottesville: University Press of Virginia, 1969], 208). In the last years before the Civil War, Germans made up nearly a quarter of Richmond's white population. See, further, Wust, 203-17.
14. Probably in a series of concerts sponsored by the recently formed *Gesang-Verein Virginia*, which was organized at the hall of August Schad on Broad Street.
15. The *Sociale Turnverein* held lectures and exercise classes at Simon Steinlein's Monticello Hall (on Broad Street across from Schad's Hall), promoting the prescriptions of the *Turnvater* Friedrich Ludwig Jahn (1778-1852), who felt that German morale could be shored up in the years following the Napoleonic Wars by the moral and physical benefits of gymnas-

tic exercises. For a summary of his programme, see "Treatise on Gymnastics," *Am. Quart. Rev.* 3 (March 1828): 126–50.

16. Probably the work of his future colleague at the University of Virginia, Gessner Harrison (1807–62), *An Exposition of Some of the Laws of Latin Grammar* (New York: Harper and Bros., 1852). Gildersleeve wrote Hübner on 13 November 1853 [Berlin] that he had decided against the project. On Harrison and Gildersleeve, see No. 5, n. 9. For Gildersleeve on Harrison, see *AJP* 35 (1914): 497.

17. Gildersleeve did not take Friedrich Ritschl's (see No. 23, n. 2) course on Latin grammar at Bonn.

18. Hor. *Carm.* 1.3.21: nequiquam deus abscidit / prudens Oceano dissociabili / terras. ("In vain did the wise god divide the land by the incompatible Ocean.")

19. Hübner's father, Julius Hübner (1806–82), was a well-known portraitist of the Düsseldorf school, who lived in Dresden. *ADB* 50: 774–77.

20. Eduard Julius Friedrich Bendemann (1811–89) was E. Hübner's uncle and a well-known Berlin artist. He collaborated with J. Hübner on the illustrations for *Das Nibelungenlied*, ed. G. O. Marbach (Leipzig: O. & G. Wigand, 1840), and was also known for *Frescoes in the Royal Palace in Dresden* with explanations by J. G. Droysen (E. Hübner's father-in-law) (New York: Stroefer and Kirchner, 1859). *NDB*, 2: 36–37. Gildersleeve made "assiduous visits" to the Bendemanns, with whom Hübner's sister was staying, several times in May 1853 (BLG to Hübner, 21 May 1853 [Berlin]).

21. Dr. Wilhelm Sommer (1828–1904), school inspector and author of *Praktische Aufsatzschule für Elementarschüler*) and *Deutsche Sprachlehre*, 20th ed., ed. R. Zimmerman (both Paderborn: Schüningh, 1883–94 and 1929 respectively).

22. Probably Joseph Krantz of Düsseldorf, who had been a student at Bonn and published "Über die iambischen Tetrameter bei Terentius," *RhM* 8 (1853): 531–60.


3 To: Emil Hübner
*Berlin*

Richmond Vᵃ Sept. 10. 1854

Greatly do I rejoice—beloved Aemilius—to see your familiar handwriting once more. I had deemed myself forgotten and with apparent reason for the postmark of your letter before the last was Nov. 10. 1853. Now let me assure /you/ that (barring the heavy postage which Elihu Burritt[1] has not yet succeeded in reducing) there is no manner of difficulty in conducting a correspondence with us ~~Trans~~ Cisatlantic Barbarians. On the 18th. of August you sit down near a window of your beautiful residence and divide a half hour between your paper and the blooming garden below and on the 5ᵗʰ of Sept. I shall be reading that paper and longing to see your face again. To be sure accidents will happen in the carriage—and pamphlets and newspapers are often thrown out as bitter experience hath taught me for the same mail brought me your letter but failed to bring me your dissertation.[2] Let me congratulate you. You have passed through your academic career pleasantly and profitably and have crowned yourself at its close with glory and honour. Would that I could have held such an even tenor in my way and that my flight had /not/ been like that of the swallow in the first scrap of German I ever read—"Nicht hoch u. nur rückweise"[3] So you are about to address yourself to the stern duties of a teacher's life. I tried that profession some years ago and shall try it again. It is as we Americans say "a hard row to hoe" but you will have the consolation of being in Berlin while I vegetate in this miserable "nest". By the way if you meet with a certain William A. Ingham[4]—Attaché of the American legation at Berlin cultivate him for my sake. He is an old college-mate of mine and a man of very good sense.

When such an interval of time elapses between letters from friend to friend, the communications must consist in a great measure of personal narrative: and so, even at the risk of being tedious, I will set forth all my history. A few weeks after my last letter I was seized with an intestinal disorder resembling wind-colic and inflammation of the bowels combined—the which cost me intense agony and came very near putting a period to my existence. Drastic purging and heroic bleeding saved my life but left me to crawl about a shadow of my former self. After recovering I went to work somewhat languidly + wrote a review article in which I demonstrated that the great Yankee nation needed the classics as much if not more than any other[5]—The article was wretchedly misprinted—very feebly commended—and the author remains to this day unpaid. Besides this I have written a few critiques[6]—all of which have excited some attention and called down fiery indignation on my head. My lighter articles in one of which I make mention of our achievements in Frankfort[7] /either/ fell dead from the periodical press—or were not considered suitable for the public so that I augur very little good from /this/ very beginning.—Last spring I revisited Charleston the place of my birth which I had not seen for 9 years—renewed old associations which were not altogether pleasant and met several friends who had studied with me in Germany.[8] No sooner had I returned from this excursion and set myself to work than I was attacked by another complication of disorders. When I became convalescent I was ordered by my physician to the mountains of Virginia—the Blue Ridge of which you have haply heard[9]—and I have returned thence after an absence of six weeks—determined to turn over a new leaf and start afresh. I need not rehearse my disappointments which are neither few nor small. A situation as Redacteur was offered me conditionally and after long haggling the whole affair went fell through.[10] Another situation as Professor at a college in the north was presented for my acceptance. I accepted and by accepting lost the a lucrative and pleasant position at the South.[11] The Professorship did not become vacant and thus "inter duas sellas dissidium"[12]—I have an offer before me now but it /is/ from the far South-west down in Mississippi[13]—and I cannot make up my mind to such a move.—This winter I shall give a few private lessons—write a few magazine and review articles and make preparations for a school edition of one of Plautus' plays.[14] Perhaps I shall deliver a few lectures here and in the neighboring towns. This latter is, if successful, the easiest method of making money. In most American cities there are associations called Lycaea Athenaea—library societies etc. which engage lectures for the winter season at so much a lecture. Here they pay very little—25 dol's for each lecture; but I could easily trump up 3 lectures on almost any subject—and I could repeat them in Fredericksburg and Petersburg and perhaps Norfolk so that I could earn 300 dol's in ~~season~~ 3 or 4 weeks.—If this miscellaneous employment succeeds I shall make a desparate effort to revisit Europe next Autumn and of course I shall steer directly for Italy.—By the way I have been reading Platen's correspondence. I have been threatening to write an article on the author of the "romantische Oedipus" but the difficulty of translating specimen passages has kept me back.[15] I have written a few Ghazels in imitation of him—but the "profanum vulgus" would not or could not see the beauty of the verse.—[16]

I have treated you to a long chapter of disappointments. Success is not so easy in our country and /although/ my foreign education may give me a local reputation the reputation is not worth the fees for the Doctor's hat. Richmond can show two doctors of philosophy besides myself and one of these a Prizeman! In a few years German diplomas will be a drug on the market but in a few years I hope to be beyond the necessity of employing such extrinsic recommendation.

But I have been far too egotistical. Pardon me. The most minute details about yourself would interest me and I have voluntarily attributed ~~the~~ a like interest to you. Present me kindly to your family in Dresden and to your grandparents in Berlin.—I direct to Dresden as winter has not yet come.—

Yours affectionately
B. L. Gildersleeve

1. Elihu Burritt (1810–79), autodidact and pacifist. When the Crimean War halted his campaign for European peace, he began to press for reduced international postage rates. *DAB*, 3: 328–30.

2. *Quaestiones onomatologicae Latinae* (Bonn: Carl George, 1854).

3. Lessing, *Fables*, book 3.1, no. 19: "[Der Sperling zum Strausz:] du kannst nicht fliegen; ich aber fliege, obgleich nicht hoch, obgleich nur rückweise" ([The sparrow to the ostrich:] You do not know how to fly; I however fly, though not high, and only in fits and starts).

4. William A. Ingham (1827–1913), a native of Bucks County, Pa., was in Gildersleeve's class (1849) at Princeton. See "College in the Forties," *Princeton Alumni Weekly* 16, no. 16 (26 January 1916): 377. He returned from Germany and was admitted to the Philadelphia bar in 1855. He was president of the Union Improvement Co., the Highland Coal Co., and several other corporations. *WhAm* 1: 618.

5. "The Necessity of the Classics," review of *Grundriss der Griechischen Litteratur* by G. Bernhardy, *Southern Quarterly Review* (Columbia, S.C.), 26 (n.s. 10) (July 1854): 145–67.

6. He may have wished "Modest Critique of 'A Sketch after Landseer,' " *Southern Literary Messenger* 20 (December 1854): 118 -20, to be anonymous, for he signed the piece "Chrysobrachion" ("Golden Sleeves"), the Greek name given him by Johannes Franz for his Schola Graeca at Berlin, 1850-51.

7. Possibly the Frankfurt adventures included in *Schlafhausen* (see following letter, n. 8).

8. He was the guest of his cousin Fleetwood Lanneau II (No. 161) and would have renewed his associations with the "Hayne Set" and the Simms Circle (see No. 12, n. 4). Among his Charlestonian friends from Germany were David Ramsay, the Dingle brothers, and Samuel Lord, Jr. (No. 12, nn. 15-17). The Charlestonians W. K. Bachmann, who took a law degree from Göttingen at this time, and Joseph E. Carr, who studied at Berlin, may have been acquaintances.

9. His fictionalized account of this sabbatical is in "The Black Mountain Jaunt" and "Hickory Nut Gap," both in the 1853 diary in the Gildersleeve Archive.

10. "Shortly after my return from Europe in 1853, it was proposed that I should enter the service of the College [Princeton], but the position offered me turned out to be so far inferior to what I, a conceited youngster, deemed my due as a Ph.D. with high honours from a German university, that the negotiations were broken off with some show of anger on both sides" ("College in the Forties" [cited n. 4 above]: 375).

11. The universities in question are not known.

12. "Falling between two chairs."

13. John Newton Waddel (1812-95) had held the chair of ancient languages from the founding of the University of Mississippi in 1848 and wanted the chair divided. But a suitable candidate was not found until 1854 when Wilson G. Richardson became professor of Latin. Waddel retired the next year and was replaced as professor of Greek by Henry Whitehorne. See *Historical Catalogue of the University of Mississippi, 1849–1909* (Nashville: Marshall and Bruce Co., 1910), 26-34 and John N. Waddell, *Memorials of Academic Life* (Richmond: Presbyterian Committee of Publication, 1891), 305.

14. Heavily under the influence of the Bonn Plautus scholar Friedrich Ritschl (see No. 23, n. 2), from whom he took a course in the *Miles Gloriosus* in the winter semester 1852-53, Gildersleeve had written Hübner on 13 November 1853 [Berlin] that he was "going through Ritschl's Prolegomena . . . preparatory to the critical study of Plautus," but he never published on Plautus.

15. He eventually wrote "Platen's Poems," *Southern Review* 4 (October 1868): 434-65 ( = *E&S*, 401-50), ostensibly in review of five works dealing with Platen from the years 1836-55 and employing extensive translations. See also *AJP* 40 (1919): 450-51 ( = *SBM*, 395-96). Of the article, John T. Krumpelmann, *Southern Scholars in Goethe's Germany* (Chapel Hill: University of North Carolina Press, n.d.), 119, says: "It was then, and probably remains today, the most authentic evaluation of that poet ever to appear in an English periodical." One of the works was the "correspondence" mentioned here, *Briefwechsel zwischen August Graf von Platen und Johannes Minckwite* (Leipzig, 1836).

16. "Occidental Ghazels," *Southern Literary Messenger* 18 (March 1852): 173.


## 4 To: EMIL HÜBNER
### Berlin

Richmond Vᵃ Oct. 10. 1855

Both of us are afflicted with a sad disease of diffidence—my dearly beloved Aemilianus. Each of us has been fancying that he has been forgotten by the other—a grievous error, if you testify aright. Let us for the future take our mutual regard for granted and proceed on that pleasant supposition. A frequent interchange of letters is impossible under the circumstances but we must not suffer the correspondence to drop wholly. I am sure you would not if you could have seen the joy with which I received your letter. It thrilled me with the pleasure of former days so different from the pleasure of the present. I thought of our first meeting—of our growing intimacy—of our common studies—of our walks and of our excursions—and of those minutes, when the joyous soul of conviviality threw off the yoke of conventional laws—and my lethargic spirit quickened its pace to keep step with your's [sic]. Indeed I fear to look back to my residence in Germany. "That way lies madness"[1] or if not madness—discontent, repining, uneasy yearning. So you /see/ there is a portion of bitter even in your letter—"Surgit amari aliquid"[2]—Were I disposed to envy I might envy you the noble activity with which you are blessed.[3] It is a great thing to feel that you are living to some end—that you are actually contributing something to the sum of human knowledge—that your labors will not perish—even if your name disappears.—There is no such prospect for me—I can aspire to nothing more than a "Ragout von Andrew Johannesen[?]" a <u>rifacimento</u> [recasting] of foreign material. Hash-maker in general to the United States.

You need expect—after such a preamble—no brilliant recital of successes and triumphs.—Three or four professorships have been offered to me but I have declined them all.[4] The salaries varied from 700 to 1000 dollars. The dollar being about 1 g. 10 sqr. of your money. But you must consider in the first /place/ that a professor in this country has harder work to perform than any teacher in your gym/n/asia—and especially if the college is a small one—and all those to which I was invited were newly founded institutions. Then the price of living is much higher than in Germany and the reputation to be gained in such positions is too small to satisfy my foolish cravings.—I have tried literature—To be sure my experiments have not been made on a larger scale but the small essays I have made give me no reason to expect great success— — Last autumn, when m̶ I was completely <u>á sec</u> [broke] I received an advantageous offer from a very wealthy Englishman, who resides in South Carolina.[5] $100 per month—and everything found what you call—freie Station. My employment was to consist in teaching his four children. I held the situation for ten months and then threw it up. Result: a thorough disgust for teaching—freedom from debt and $600 in the bank.—I thought at one time that I would persevere in this employment until I could amass enough to defray the expense of another visit to Europe—But I had no aim and object on the other side of the waters—nothing to steady me as formerly and an idle residence in Europe requires a fortune.—While I was indulging these day-dreams my thought turned instinctively to E̶u̶r̶o̶p̶e̶ /Italy/ and last winter I took up my

Italian again—by way of preparation.—But I quietly buried this dream with so many others and now your letter has awakened my longing in full force—and perhaps—I dare not hope it—perhaps a way may /still/ be found and we may still meet in Rome—I have written this very day to one of the New York journals—offering my services as foreign correspondent.[6] If the man will give me anything—$600-$500-$400— I will start as soon as possible.

Please write to me from Italy more frequently than you would under ordinary circumstances and let me know something in relation to the expenses of living and travel. If I were in Germany now I would join you— even with my little pittance. But it costs too much to cross the herring-pond.[7] I have another plan with the same tendency—to write I have a work partly descriptive partly nonsensical on hand.[8] It is nearly half-finished and if I can sell the copy-right for a decent amount I will cross the water next summer and hunt you up in Naples.—Or again: You remember our very small party of two on occasion of my 21$^{st}$ birthday—the [year] at which we attain our majority in this country and in England. Well three years have passed since then. In a few days I shall be 24 years old and my friends insinuate that I ought to take to myself a wife.[9]—We marry early in America you know. Now, if I do marry, I must marry a fortune—as my patrimony is almost nothing and my profession of vagrant is not very lucrative. And in that case too, I shall go to Europe. When I left the continent two years ago I resolved to return once in five years and 1858 is still afar off.[10] So I will live in hope— —I am pleasantly situated at home for the present—The climate of Richmond is very fine at this season of the year and your Italian skies cannot be more brilliant. I have at my disposal a fine mare—which adds greatly to my enjoyment of life—passionately devoted as I am to that kind of exercise—Indeed I am surrounded by every temporal comfort—but alas! my mind is ill at ease. There is no greater curse than to be a man of half intent. Much better to be perfectly stolid.

But I have been indulging too much in the doleful strain—provoked thereto—I suppose—by your happy letter.—Present my best regards to our common acquaintances. I remember them all better than you imagine.—Degenkolb[11]—Kock[12]—Ravené[13]—all of them are present to my mind—and I am once more standing at your window and looking down upon the broad Rhine.

Please present my best regards to your Father and his family and write to me from the "seven hill'd city."

Yours affectionately,
B. L. Gildersleeve

1. King Lear 3.4.21
2. Lucr. 4.1134: *Surgit amari aliquid quod in ipsis floribus angat* (Something bitter rises which chokes men even in the midst of flowers).

3. Hübner was setting off to Italy to gather inscriptions and prepare *De senatus populique Romanis actis* (Leipzig: B. G. Teubner, 1859).

4. See preceding letter.

5. In the fall of 1854, Gildersleeve was hired to tutor the six children of Daniel Blake (1803–73) and his wife Emma Middleton Rutledge (d. 1853) at "Board House," so named because it was the first house built of clapboards in the region where the Cuchold Creek and Combahee come together. It was unusual that even a man of Blake's education (St. John's College, Cambridge) would hire someone of Gildersleeve's training as a mere tutor; luckily for Blake, he was desperate to take the job. Gildersleeve later described it as having "tasted the salt bread of a tutorship in a private family" (*Formative Influences*: 615–16). See John H. Rice, Jr., "Basil Lanneau Gildersleeve: Paladin of South Carolina," *Columbia State*, 27 January 1924, pt. 1: 15, and for the Blake family, see *SC Hist. and Gen. Mag.* 1 (1900): 165–66.

6. The journal is unknown, but Gildersleeve continued to pursue the possibility of a career in journalism, telling the *Baltimore Sun* on 12 October 1911: "About this time [1856] I had an invitation to become editor of a Democratic newspaper in Springfield, Mass. While I was considering this offer I had the opportunity of becoming a member of the faculty of the University of Virginia, and so my life's work was decided." See also BLG to W. H. Page, 12 June 1883 [Houghton], No. 141, and *AJP* 35 (1914): 498.

7. A humorous term for the Atlantic Ocean both in English (*OED*, s.v. "herring-pond") and German (Heinz Küpper, *Illustriertes Lexikon der Deutschen Umgangs Sprache* [Stuttgart: Klett, 1983], s.v. "Heringsteich").

8. He may mean his semi-autobiographical novel set partly in America, partly in Germany, in two volumes, *Schlafhausen; or, One Year of Mr. Alfred Thistledown's Life*, dated October 1855, and *Schlafhausen; or, Confessions of a Very Young Man*, dated February 1856. The MS exists in the Hopkins Archive. See, further, No. 8.

9. For a glimpse of his "courtship" in this season, see No. 163. For his marriage, see No. 12, n. 9.

10. See No. 7.

11. Heinrich Degenkolb (1832–1909) devoted himself to the study of Roman law and finished his dissertation at Berlin in 1855.

12. Theodor Kock (1820–91), another Berlin student, who would direct a *gymnasium* in Berlin (1860–82) and edit *Comicorum Atticorum fragmenta*, 3 vols. (Leipzig: B. G. Teubner, 1880–88). *NDB*, 12: 286, *JhrB* 29 (1902): 44–49, *Sandys*, 155–56.

13. Probably Louis Ravené (1823–79), a German businessman and patron of the arts, *Geheimrat* for commerce (as had been his father, the art collector Peter Louis Ravené [1793–1861]), and from 1874 to his death consul-general in Berlin for the Austro-Hungarian Empire.

## 5 To: EMIL HÜBNER
### *Berlin*

Richmond April 27, 1856

Again I have followed you through the wonders of Rome; again I have drawn near to my friend and listened to his enthusiastic descriptions. Alas! it was not Rome but Becker's Plan[1]: it was /not/ Hübner but only a thin sheet of paper. Again the phlegmatic, the impassive Gildersleeve has forgotten his petrified nature, has suffered his heart to swell his pulse to beat higher. At the first reading of your letter—my dear Hübner—this ill-fated young man became extravagant: he indulged in sighs and wishes and long, aimless rambles: every thought was Italy; every other word was Italy: and his friends and relations became alarmed at his unreasonable conduct. At length the tumult subsided and he became comparatively /quiet/ but now that he attempts to respond to your kind summons, the pen trembles in his hand. My whole heart's desire goes forth to[wards] Italy as it once did towards Germany and yet I must call the vain longing back. I fear me, I shall never pledge you in Falernian.[2] My destiny is now hanging in the balance.[3] A few weeks will decide it. If I am successful in my attempt, I shall have a competence for life and with the competence a tether, which will not allow me much liberty of motion. Once every three or four years I shall be able to run over to Europe for four or five months and that will be all. If I do not succeed I shall go to work mechanically and in a couple of years from the present time "ho for Italy." My next letter will probably contain the result.

However, if we cannot see each other in person, we can sympathize in spirit for with our great diversity of ~~spirit~~ disposition, there is combined in strange union a great similarity of intellectual tendencies.

Nescis quod certe est quod me tibi temperat astrum![4] Your letters have been the complement of our friendship. They have brought me that confidence, which I had unlearned in a treacherous world. They have proven to me that our intercourse was not merely the result of accident, that it was the natural and indestructible growth of spiritual affinities. Do not relax the grasp, which keeps us together across the wide interval of waters. You will soon be the only living link, which binds me to the farther shores for death has robbed me of dear friends, kind and revered teachers. Hermann[5] is gone and Schneidewin[6], for whom I felt a real and deep affection, has followed. The other day I had to write to Göttingen for testimonials and there was but one person in the whole town to whom I could address myself. Do not forget your humble brother-philologian from the height of your epigraphic and topographic achievements. He needs all your encouragement and consolation.

But I must not and will not be lachrymose. If we cannot transplant German philology to our uncongenial soil, there are other German institutions, which promise to establish themselves in permanence and among these is the venerable institution of "lagerbier." It is only a few years since lager-bier gained a footing in the northern cities and now it has /spread to/ the South, ~~and~~ opens its saloons on every street and if you could dine with me to-day you might drink cerevisian out of Roisdorfer jugs![7] Think of that and admire the progress of civilization. I myself have made an attempt to introduce divinities into Latium[8]—or to speak more plainly "Dichterspre-chen" [poetic language] into the schools of Virginia.[9] Indeed I am sanguine of success and I hope that my name will go down to posterity with the Cadmuses and the Cecropses. Other German elements assert themselves from time to time. Have I not heard negroes whistling the tune of "wenn ich ein Vöglein wär?"[10] Have I not heard a "loafer" (g.d. gamin) singing the English words of "wenn die Schwalben heimwärts ziehn"[11] and did not my memory lead me gently back to the hotel at Rolandseck[12] where our dessert was enlivened by the appearance of three musical urchins, who attempted the performance of that very tune in the shrillest of falsettos. Is your memory as faithful as mine?

But I dare not trust myself in the past. My present is joyless. My future uncertain. When I can see my way clearly and arrive at some definite conclusion, I will write to you at greater length.

Accept this scrawl as the /an/ instalment of my debt and believe me to be in America as well as in Germany, any where, every where and at all times

Yours affectionately<br>
B. L. Gildersleeve

May 4, 1856.

I had laid this letter aside. I could not resolve to send off so miserable, so brief an answer to your long letter. But I am in such a strait at present that I must make up my mind to this or nothing—and anything rather than nothing—anything rather than suffer you to suppose that I have forgotten you. Recent developments encourage me to hope that I shall be able after all to devote my life to my favorite science and in that case I should feel the necessity of your friendship more than ever. It would not be difficult for me to enter with enthusiasm into your "geliebten ephigraphica" but I am unfortunately with[out] resources. I only wish that the results of the investigations were collected in an accessible form. Namque parabilem amo.[13] I have examined all the book catalogues which I get—I have seen nothing "epochemachendes" [epoch-making] at least as far as I could conjecture. If you spend next winter in Italy I shall probably torment you with commissions and I warn you now to prepare for heavy impositions on your good nature.—You have the goodness to praise my style—my style!! There is no such thing as style now a days in the English language. It is all mannerism or chaos.—I have a great horror of both these extremes and consequently fall into one or the other as often as I undertake to write anything for the press—You consider us lucky because we can use the Germans as heavers of wood and drawers of water in our intellectual labours. Ah me! there is a pleasure in original investigation, which no adornment of foreign productions can equal. Ours is far the less noble office. E.g. some laborious individual writes a life of Frischlin in 575 octavo pages—I know nothing about Frischlin—but I buy the book. Of the 575 octavo pages I make 36—adding a few moral and philological observations—it is printed in one of our numerous reviews[14]—I receive after long waiting about as many dollars as there are pages in the article—and that is learned authorship—that is the heavy artillery of literature in this country.—As for our school-editions of the classics they are all plagiarisms and very bad ones from the German.[15]—I mentioned Frischlin just now because he was foremost in my mind—and he was foremost in my mind because I have before me the irksome task of copying the brouillon [rough draft] of the article, which I have manufactured in the manner above indicated.—If you should come across ~~the book of~~ Strauss's book[16] and you have abundance of time glance through it—some parts of it are quite amusing + interesting. I take a great interest in the history of philology and the lives of philologians—and I am only waiting for D<sup>r</sup> Bernays's book on Scaliger[17]—to perpetuate another essay of the same sort. But enough of my feeble essays—'Επιφυλλί-δες ταῦτ' ἐστὶ καὶ στωμύλματα[18]—when I next write —it may be from the beauties of the Hudson or the majesty of Niagara—I can tell you whether I am to be a philologian or not—and I dread the announcement in either case.[19] If I am successful, I shall be the recipient of a salary such as few German philologians dream of—if I am not, I shall be grieved to announce the departure of my most cherished hopes. In the one case I shall blush—in the other I shall turn pale. How unreservedly I write to you—how I open my whole heart to you as I did in those other days.—Go out into ~~your~~ /the/ hoar antiquity /which surrounds you/ and forget the agitations and vacillations of your friend in the eternal sorrow and eternal joy of your mistress and my mistress—of the mistress of the world.—

Adieu.—

1. Wilhelm Adolf Becker (1796–1846) wrote *Handbuch der römischen Alterthümer*, *Die römische Topographie in Rom*, and *Zür römischen Topographie* (Leipzig: Weidmann, respectively 1843–67, 1844, 1845). *NDB*, 2: 229–31.

2. A very good, but not the best, Roman wine from a district in the north of Campania. It required ten years to mature and is the wine most mentioned by Horace.

3. See following letter.

4. Persius 5.51: "There is certainly some star that 'blends my being with thine.' " Gildersleeve so translates *me tibi temperat* in his *Persius* (No. 14, n. 5), 163.

5. Karl Friedrich Hermann (1804–55), editor of Plato, was, in Gildersleeve's words, "the most eminent of the classical philologists at Göttingen" (*Professorial Types*: 7), but he was not a good lecturer (ibid. and *AJP* 5 [1884]: 340). Nonetheless, ". . . no one, however prejudiced, could fail to recognize Hermann's wide learning and broad vision, no one could fail to be borne on by the turbulent flow of his discourse" (*Professorial Types*, ibid.). Gildersleeve took Hermann's courses in the history of Greek literature (summer semester 1851) and in the history of Latin literature (winter semester 1851–52).

6. Friedrich Wilhelm Schneidewin (1810-1856), from whom Gildersleeve took Latin syntax (summer semester 1851) and Greek syntax and elegiac poetry in the winter semester 1851–52. See, further, No. 157, nn. 1, 3.

7. Cerevisarian = beer. Roisdorf is a village four miles from Bonn containing a mineral spring.

8. As Aeneas brought the gods of Troy to Italy; see Virg. *Aen.* 1.6: *inferretque deos Latio.*

9. It was considered a source of friction between Gildersleeve and his Latin colleague at the University of Virginia, Gessner Harrison (1807-62), that the former tried to impose the pronunciation then in European vogue. See W. Briggs, "Basil L. Gildersleeve at the University of Virginia," *Briggs-Benario*, 13-14. On his early (i.e., pre-Schmidtean) enthusiasms for Greek metrics, see *AJP* 33 (1912): 233 ( = *SBM*, 250) and Milton Humphreys' obituary in *UVa Alumni News* 12 (January 1924): 132.

10. Gildersleeve may have learned both of these songs from *Deutsche Lieder nebst ihren Melodien* (Leipzig: R. Freise, 1843), later revised as *Allgemeines Deutsches Kommersbuch*, ed. F. Silcher and F. Erk (Lahr: M. Schauenburg, 1858); this song is no. 546, entitled "Flug der Liebe."

11. The words were written by K. Herloßsohn (1804-49) in 1830; the music was composed by Franz Abt (1819-95) in 1842. The English version is called "When the Swallows Homeward Fly"; see *Love Songs the Whole World Sings*, ed. Albert E. Wier (New York: D. Appleton-Century Co., 1916), 206-7.

12. The Rolandseck Hotel in the village on the Rhine, nine miles SE of Bonn, featured a garden restaurant.

13. Hor. *Sat*. 1.2.119: *Namque parabilem amo venerem facilemque* (For I love a ready and easy pleasure).

14. "Nicodemus Frischlin," *Quarterly Review of the Methodist Episcopal Church, South*, 10 (July 1856): 348-82. The biography in question is David Friderich Strauss (see following letter, n. 3), *Leben und Schriften des Dichters und Philologen Nicodemus Frischlin* (Frankfurt: Literarische anstalt [J. Rütten], 1856). See also *AJP* 8 (1887): 253; 33 (1912): 230-32 ( = *SBM*, 249-50).

15. E.g., Raphael Kühner's (1802-78) *Elementargrammatik der lateinischen Sprache und Ausführliche Grammatik* (Hannover: Hahn, 1845) was "translated and remodelled" as *Elementary Grammar of the Latin Language* by James Tift Champlin (1811-82) (Boston: J. Monroe, 1853), as well as *Kühner's Latin Exercise-Book* and *Kühner's Latin Grammar* (both Boston: Phillips, Sampson, 1851 and 1850) respectively); Johan Nicolai Madvig's (No. 17, n. 2) *Lateinische Sprachlehre für Schulen* (Braunschweig: F. Vieweg & Sohn, 1844) was translated as *A Latin Grammar for the Use of Schools* by Rev. George Woods (Boston: Ginn, 1870); and Gildersleeve's *Latin Grammar* relied heavily on Karl August Julius Lattmann (1818-1898) and Heinrich Dietrich Müller's (1819-1893) *Kleine lateinische Grammatik* (Göttingen: Vandenhoeck & Ruprecht, 1864). In 1830 a review of Charles Anthon's *Horace* said, "A critical edition of a classical author, elaborated in America, by an American, and for American consumption, is a new thing under the sun." Quoted by Meyer Reinhold, *Classica Americana* (Detroit: Wayne State University Press, 1984), 186.

16. See n. 14 above.

17. Jacob Bernays, *Joseph Justus Scaliger* (Berlin: W. Hertz, 1855). Gildersleeve never wrote the essay.

18. Ar. *Frogs* 92: "All that is grapes left for gleaners [i.e. poetasters], chattering."

19. See following letter.

# ❦ 2 ❧

## *ANDREIA:* VIRGINIA AND THE WAR, 1857–1875

Gildersleeve continued "to endure the hardest discipline of all—the discipline of waiting for what I considered a suitable sphere,"[1] writing, reviewing, and working again on a novel. But he pushed his candidacy for the leading classics chair in the South (No. 141), and "in the Autumn of 1856 I was elected professor of Greek in the University of Virginia. My only regret was that I was in port so early. I was not yet twenty-five."[2]

Young, proud to the point of arrogance, bored with provincialism to the point of contempt, he was not a popular teacher in the four years before the Civil War.[3] His conduct towards both the students and the residents of Charlottesville was at one point chastised by the faculty.[4] Moreover, his German training forced him into a professional conflict with the erstwhile classicist Gessner Harrison (No. 2, n. 16; No. 5, n. 9), who had been trained thirty years earlier by the Englishman George Long (1800–1879). The conflict arose over the correct pronunciation of the ancient languages, and even when Gildersleeve left the university twenty years later, generally revered if not beloved, a Richmond editorial declared, "Now we shall have the Greek of the Greeks, not the Greek of Gildersleeve."[5] But Harrison, terribly overworked for decades, had no heart for the conflict and left the university within three years of Gildersleeve's arrival.

Gildersleeve continued to look overseas for his inspiration, maintaining his correspondence with Hübner and even visiting Ritschl (No. 23, n. 2) in 1860[6] during what would be his last trip for twenty years, his last delight before the conflagration of 1861.

All four Gildersleeve brothers enlisted in the first year of the war (No. 9, n. 3), and their father enlisted in the Richmond Home Guard at seventy. All five survived the war. Gildersleeve fought perhaps more powerfully with the pen than with the sword. He served as aide-de-camp in Gen. Fitzhugh Lee's command in 1861, as a private in the First Virginia Cavalry in 1863 (No. 9), and as aide (captain) on the staff of Gen. John B. Gordon in 1864. He therefore earned "the right to teach Southern youths for nine months . . . by sharing the fortunes of their fathers and brothers at the front for three."[7] He fought the war on another front as well, writing sixty-three editorials between October 1863 and August 1864 for the *Richmond Examiner* that "showed up the selfishness of the farming class and [prophesied] the improvement of the currency."[8] Finally wounded carrying orders at the skirmish at Weyer's Cave, Va., in September 1864 (No. 12, n. 8), he was carried off the field and brought to the Colston estate in Albemarle Co., Va., where he recuperated and fell in love with the eldest of Raleigh Colston's three beautiful daughters, Elizabeth Fisher ("Betty"). After the war, he returned to "Hillandale" to marry her (No. 12, n. 9).

Gildersleeve's personality changed greatly after the war. With the sober responsibilities of marriage, the special introspection afforded the champions of a losing cause, the destitution of friends like Hayne and Chamberlayne (see "Correspondents"), the poverty of his once flourishing region, and, in time, the death of two of his sons in infancy, he seemed to his students preoccupied and much older than his years.[9] Cut off from Europe and with his crippled leg a constant reminder of the war, he began to identify more and more with the "lame Spartan schoolmaster Tyrtaeus." He became a more industrious and demanding teacher than he had been before.[10] He prepared nearly seventy lectures a semester with only meagre library holdings, teaching Greek history, literature, and three levels of Greek language each term. For six years he also did the same for Latin.

In the ten years after the war, he produced the first and revised editions of his *Latin Grammar, Latin Exercise-Book, Latin Reader,* and *Latin Primer,* his edition of Persius, and nine major articles (No. 12, nn. 5 and 6), most reprinted in *E&S*.

His family life was one of great happiness, marred only by the loss of infant sons (No. 12, n. 10; No. 13, n. 1). His surviving son Raleigh was born in 1869, and Emma, whom he would call "the light of our house" (No. 107), in 1872. The homes they kept both off campus and on the university's incomparable colonnade were sites of frequent receptions for students and Charlottesville society.

His two decades at the University of Virginia would have made an illustrious career for anyone else: he was the leading classicist of his region, he had a generation of devoted pupils throughout the South, he was a spokesman for the best in Southern education and an exemplar of the noble and ruined ways of the Old South. In many ways he was already a legend, if not an institution. But it was really an apprenticeship. As Gildersleeve put it, "If a man has a conscience he cannot be an indolent teacher [at the University of Virginia]; 'the genius of the place is hard work,' as the sons of the university love to repeat. There was nothing there to lure one away from hard work, and I stuck to my business of preparing lectures and correcting exercises. My motto was 'Grow, not climb,' and I was content to wait."[11]

1. *Formative Influences*: 615.
2. Ibid.: 616.
3. For a portrait of one in his position, see *University Work*: 515-17 ( = *E&S*, 94-95).
4. See the letter of W. J. N. Robinson to S. Schooler, quoted in W. Briggs, "Basil L. Gildersleeve at the University of Virginia," *Briggs-Benario*, 13.
5. Thomas W. Dickson, "Letter," *Johns Hopkins Magazine* 25, no. 5 (September 1974): 2.
6. *Southerner*: 334.
7. *Creed*: 75.
8. *Southerner*: 341.
9. *Culbreth*, 397.
10. C. F. Smith, "Basil Lanneau Gildersleeve: An Intimate View," *Sewanee Review* 32 (April 1924): 165.
11. *Formative Influences*: 616.

### 6 To: EMIL HÜBNER
#### *Berlin*

University of Vᵃ Janʸ 18. 1857

My dear Hübner—there is a forcible saying in our forcible language that "Hell is paved with good intentions"—If then this really be the case a good portion of that pavement must be formed by my resolutions to write a long answer to your second Italian letter. But as I was prevented in former days by paucity of material so I must now urge the want of time—for I have at last been caught and tethered. And then I can return you no just equivalent for /your/ sketches of Italy and the course of your studies and achievements—all my discourse must be of myself and of my personal history.— So then to resume without much ado—All last summer and during a part of the autumn I was kept in a state of anxious expectation, which actually affected my health. The Board of Visitors, who have the appointing power for the University of Virginia, deferred their action for two or three months[1]—and during the whole time I sat imprisoned in Richmond, working away desperately at a course of lectures—not knowing whether I should ever have an audience. About the middle of September the illustrious conclave met and I was elected by a "very flattering majority" that is with one dissentient vote—to the new[2] Professorship of the Greek language and literature in the University of Virginia and here I am and here I have been since the end of September. Now as you are doubtless beyond the reach of the conversations-lexikon,[3] I will preserve a very pardonable degree of ignorance in you—much more pardonable than my supposed want of acquaintance with the "Life of Christ"[4]—and will consequently proceed to enlighten you on the subject of the University of Virginia. The U. of Va. was founded Anno something or other—1819 I believe[5]—by the immortal Jefferson—author of our Declaration of Independence and so on. It was organized on a scale of extraordinary liberality for those times—and the first corps of professors was composed of European gentlemen of high reputation.[6] The buildings were erected at a vast expense—after M[r]. Jefferson's own outrageous architectural notions—every professor's house being a Greek temple and as Greek temples have no chimneys—so our houses have but one apiece. I will not edify you by a description of the Rotunda and the pavilions and the terraces and the Arcades and the lawn. They are all "grossartig" [imposing] says the authority above-cited and if the conversational lexikon does not know—who does? Certainly, not I. The distinguishing feature of the constitution of the University is its voluntary character—and the perfect independence of the professors. We are not subject to the tyranny of a president[7]—we have no board of trustees to prescribe text-books or interfere with our method of instruction, and while we are free the students are free likewise—There is no curriculum—no prescribed course of study—and the only obligation inferred is that of attending three schools[8]—but even this may be dispensed with at the wish of the parent or guardian and is not binding if the student be of age. It would amuse you to see the queer combinations of tickets on the catalogue—but the course is notwithstanding tolerably regular—Ancient Languages, Modern Languages and Mathematics for the first year then Moral Philosophy, <u>Natural</u> /"Physik"/ Philosophy and Chemistry.

The system has worked its way /through/ very effectually! At first the numbers were not large[9]—and just as they commenced to increase the murder of a professor by one of the students brought the whole institution into such bad repute that its best friends began to shake their heads.[10] But for the last 10 years it has been going steadily forwards.—The faults of our old traditional collegiate system—by which nothing except residence is required as a condition of graduation—nothing or next to nothing—these faults and the recent increase of bad feeling between the North and the South have given especial prominence to this institution and we now number more than 620 students in the three departments—Academical, Juristic and Medical. In my own school there are about 150 students. As for the compensation—I am almost ashamed to mention it or I should rather say vexed—because my European experience has taught me how much can be procured for a sum of money which only secures me a handsome livelihood. The State gives us $1000 per annum.—allows us to keep $2000 of our fees—($3000) and provides a house or allows /pays/ $300 for house-rent. But the expenses of living are enormous—we must buy our own books—and the married professors are growling for another slice from their fees which amount in some instances to more than $5000.[11]—So I am here—with a competence and a duty—three months holiday and an expectation of visiting Europe in 1858.—For the first few years I must devote all my energies to the organization of the school—to the practical application

of what I have learned and shall learn myself—and as I have been divorced
in a measure from philological studies for the last three years ~~I~~ as Greek
never was my <u>forte</u>—I shall have quite enough to do. <u>Then</u> I shall follow
your good advice—and try whether something can be done even in these
~~Trans~~ /Cis/ atlantic wilds.—

And now—my dear Hübner—enough and more than enough[12] of myself
and my work. While I was writing of myself, I ~~have been~~ /was/ thinking of
you—following you in thought through your beloved Italy; which must also
be my beloved Italy one of these days—imagining how pleasant it would
have been to hear your eloquent interpretations of those classic monuments in the presence of the monuments themselves instead of sitting here
in my lonely study with ~~the a~~ /the/ thermometer below the power of
Réaumur[13] and ~~the~~ /a/ most terrific snow-storm raging out-of-doors. And
again I find myself forming plans of a future meeting—but to what end? If
I am ever permitted to tread the soil of Germany once more—I shall doubtless find that the author of "Die römischen Heeresabtheilungen in Britannien"[14] has just left for Africa on a special mission for the government—
and who will there be to revive the memory of our "Ananasbowlen"[15] and
our innocent "Spritzen?".—We who live at the opposite ends of the earth
cannot be very accurate about dates—and therefore although it is the 18$\underline{th}$
of Jan$^y$ it cannot be too late to wish you from the bottom of my heart a
'Happy New Year'—and quite as fervently—the same kind feeling towards
~~your~~

Your sincere friend
Gildersleeve

P.S. Address University of Virginia—
We are blessed with a Post-Office of our own

1. The vote was supposed to have been taken in June, but was delayed because of "personal prejudice." The lone vote against him was cast by the rector, Andrew Stevenson (1784-
1857), because Gildersleeve "did not bear a Virginia name." See No. 165.

2. The number of students in the School of Ancient Languages had grown from 33 in
1843 to 259 in 1855-56. Consequently, Gessner Harrison (No. 2, n. 16; No. 5, n. 9), five times
chairman of the faculty in addition to his enormous teaching load, asked for assistance. On
26 May 1856 the board of visitors voted to divide the chair of ancient languages into a chair of
Latin and a chair of Greek and Hebrew. Harrison chose the Latin chair. See, further, W.
Briggs, "Basil Lanneau Gildersleeve at the University of Virginia," *Briggs-Benario*, 10-11.

3. Works like *Allgemeines deutsches Conversations-Lexicon,* 10 vols. (Leipzig: H. Reichenbach, 1834-37) and a supplement in 2 vols. (Leipzig: H. Reichenbach, 1842-44) were
popular with middle-class Germans of the age who wanted to appear cultured. See No. 49, n.
6. Gildersleeve is clearly being facetious.

4. David Friedrich Strauss (see preceding letter, n. 14), *Das Leben Jesu* (Tübingen: C. F.
Osiander, 1835-36), trans. as *The Life of Jesus* (only the earliest translations of 1843-45 were
titled *Life of Christ*) by Marian Evans (George Eliot) (London: Chapman Bros., 1846).

5. The university's charter is dated 15 January 1819; the university opened on 7 March 1825.

6. In the spring of 1824, Francis Walker Gilmer (1790–1826) was sent to England to acquire a faculty. George Blaetterman (1788–1850), a German resident in England, was the first appointment (in modern languages), followed by four others who were English and in their twenties. The three other original appointments were Americans.

7. Faculty governance was overseen by a chairman of the faculty.

8. Ancient languages, mathematics, and natural philosophy.

9. In the first session of 1825, 123 students matriculated.

10. Professor John A. G. Davis (1802–40) was trying to quiet a band of rowdy students on the night of 12 November 1840 when he was shot by a student from Georgia. He died three days later. The student population in that year was 179, but it declined to 128 by 1842–43 as a direct result of the incident. This was the climax of a history of student violence, and the Virginia students themselves worked hard to repair the situation by such measures as the honor code, established in 1842. By 1856 the total number of students was 645 (*Barringer*, 1: 149, 164). On the Davis incident, see Charles Coleman Wall, "Students and Student Life at the University of Virginia 1825 to 1861" (dissertation, University of Virginia, 1978), 173–76 and 87–132.

11. Gildersleeve was allowed 60 percent of student fees. See No. 35, n. 5. For the situation twenty years after his arrival, see No. 19, nn. 1–2.

12. Hor. *Epd*. 1.31; 17.19: *satis superque*.

13. René Antoine Ferchault de Réaumur (1683–1757), a French scientist, developed a thermometer that takes the freezing-point of water as 0°, the boiling-point as 80°.

14. *RhM* 11 (1857): 1–57.

15. A punch of light hock flavored with pineapple slices.

## 7 To: EMIL HÜBNER
### *Berlin*

University of V.ª Feb. 7. 1858

My dear Hübner—Your welcome letter reached me a few days ago and awoke the old love of travelling, which had been lying dormant for some time under the pressure of daily toil. The recollections of Germany—the anticipations of Switzerland roused me fully from my lethargy and every interval in my taskwork is filled up by bright dreams of the past and of the future. And that future is I hope no distant future. Indeed I have been telling all my acquaintances so long that I intended visiting Europe next summer that for shame's sake I should be obliged to go; how much warmer a feeling than shame impels me thitherward I need not say to you, who have made the discovery of a living man under my wooden exterior.— Oddly enough, I said five years since when I returned to America that I expected to visit Europe about every five years—the time is drawing nigh— and so is the fulfillment—or at least the prospect is near. You urge me to be <u>tenax propositi</u>:[1] my resolution has not wavered for a moment: a few thousand miles is a holiday-jaunt for an American—for we are accustomed to enormous distances at home—and unfortunately accustomed to finding very little at either end of our trips.—Our cities have few—nay—no attractions for me and were it not for the Ocean I should visit Europe every year. But that herring-pond, as we call it, is an ugly feature of the question—not so much for the danger—as I am tant soit peu fatalistic—nor for the sickness—as I am a good sailor—but for the length of the voyage out and back. It is very hard to resign 20-25 days of one's dearly bought vacation.—τῆς τύχης![2] Once it was the money—and now it is the time.—I shall try to obtain a short furlough in addition to my legitimate holiday—but at most I cannot have more than 10 weeks to spend in Europe. Of these I shall devote 6 to Italy—a little more than a fortnight to Switzerland and the brief residue will be divided among England—Germany—and France! Of course I shall try to make the best use of my time, but whether I shall be able to be as diligent as you advise, is more than doubtful. I am obliged to regard my vacation as a season of recreation after 9 months of incessant toil and I should rather see a little well than a great deal hurriedly. Which would you advise me to attack first—Switzerland or Italy? Is not the climate of Italy rather exhausting in the summer months? True, I am a Southerner by birth and in my early youth I was accustomed to a high temperature but my constitution has changed and I may not be physically able to follow your advice.—Let me hear from you as soon as possible with regard to this point—for on your opinion it will in a great measure depend whether I shall go from London to Basle or from London to Berlin.—So much then for the future. As for the present—I have little to report.—I am working at my vocation with all diligence—hardly knowing what success rewards my attempt to fuse /into one/ the different courses of instruction pursued in Germany. Quartaner—Tertianer—Secundaner and Primaner unterricht are all huddled together in a couple of years.—I have to lay the foundation and put on the capstone at the same time. Our university is the finishing school of this section of the country—and consequently it is necessary for me to hold forth on history—literature—structure of the language—syntactical theories, and what not—and at the same time to correct exercises—scold at monstrous forms—and teach the sublime principles of the most simple constructions.—Hence there is a great danger of my becoming ein eingefleischter Schulfuchs [an eternal student]—and of never accomplishing anything independent.—Still I am not without my pet projects.—One is an artistic translation of Herodotus in Lange's manner:[3] this would satisfy my harkening after belles lettres (a Ferienarbeit): another is a life of Julian the Apostate,[4] which would suit my strong biographical turn: and to this end let me beg you for your edition of Ammianus Marcellinus,[5] a worthy whom I admire very much and shall doubtless admire much more when he comes purified from your hands.—I /have/ commenced the collection of literature on the subject of Julian—and have written a lecture on him—intended for a literary society—and that is all that I have done outside of my regular avocations. Other minor plans and projects crowd upon me.—but metaphorically as well as literally I am shortwinded and doubt my power of accomplishing much.—Many thanks for your suggestions, which I shall duly consider.—Homer frightens me—I see a new book advertised in the English papers—Homer in three volumes by Gladstone[6] who may turn out to be a Grote in his way. Odd people, those English! This union of philological studies with practical politics is exceedingly ruinous—Cornewall Lewis—Grote and now Gladstone.[7]—You know how dear the Romans were to me—and /Just/ fancy my grief at being almost divorced from them. I have scarcely time to look into my pet authors—Mommsen's history[8] has been standing on my shelves I do not know how long and I have only had time to dip into it here and there.—My spare moments are devoted to Hebrew—which I tacked on to my present department because—for sooth—the charter of the University requires that Hebrew is to be taught—and the number of students does not warrant the appointment of a separate professor!—Every four or five years two or three stony theological students learn the alphabet—and some of the forms—become disgusted and give it up—and to satisfy this pressing necessity I have /to/ devote [myself] to a study interesting enough in itself—the little time that I might spend more profitably on Roman Antiquity.—Of course my own Hebrew is of the most elementary description. Tell it not in Geth—publish it not in Askelon[9]—that is—do mention to Bernays[10] that I am a professor of Hebrew. By the way give my best regards to him and assure him that I shall never forget his kindness to me in Bonn.—

Our library is miserably furnished.—We take in 3 philological periodicals (besides Aufrecht u. Kuhn's Ztschrft.—Philologus—Rheinisch. Museum—u.—Jahn's Jahrbüchen[11]—I shall try to get an appropriation for a full set of the last two—and I shall add the Bollettini[12] to the list. The yearly appropriation for Latin and Greek is almost $500 a year only and we can do little more than buy the principal new works—as they appear—By means of the catalogues I manage to keep up with the news of the recent literature—but I am sometimes at a loss, when a new name appears—one that has no past guarantees.—I anticipate great pleasure in reading up my Hübner-literatur—although no Römischer Eigenname[13] can ever give me so much joy as the /your/ German name at the foot of a letter to me.——I am afraid that I have been verifying the quotation you used to make in our Bonn days from Lord Chesterfield—l'anglais c'est /la/ langue pour le babillage[14]—and certainly I have chatted away about myself as unconstrainedly as /if/ we had been sitting over our beer /wine/ at Plittersdorf or over our Krammetsvögel at Altenahr.[15] I have had no object in doing so—and therefore I will not follow the example of many, who rationalize their own actions—afterwards.—But let me hope that I have shown you

thereby how heartily I reciprocate your interest in my welfare and how desirous I am to follow you in all your course.—Indeed—my dear Hübner—
so far from feeling any diminution in the warmth of my regard for you—I
~~find~~ /am sure/ that time and distance have only strengthened the bonds of
our union.—I share fully that confidence which you express at the beginning of your letter—I know that the letter—which I drop into the box will
bear its fruit—sooner or later—that kind words—good words—instructive
words—will come over the water in reply; and I do not object to the occasional sly thrusts and the occasional shade of irony for these remind /me/
of the former times—when you were wont to ~~sfrom~~ excite ~~by~~ my more slug-
gish nature by such appliances.—But—this time—be a little more
prompt—At all events write to me before the middle of May—in order that
I may make up my mind about the priority in time of Switzerland and
Italy.—Greet your relations in Berlin and in Dresden in my name—I owe
them some pleasant hours:—and let us hope that we shall meet again in
good old Germany—fight over our old battles—and express in winged
words new wishes for each other's welfare—And for the present

       Adieu

                    Yours sincerely
                    B. L. Gildersleeve

I write so much for myself and so seldom to others that my handwriting is
becoming worse and worse from year to year.[16]—Therefore ☞ unnecessary
caution.—Take this letter in broken doses.

1. Ovid *Met.* 10.405: *propositique tenax* ([Myrrha's nurse is] persistent in her purpose);
see also Hor. *Carm.* 3.3.1.
2. "Curse the luck" as at Eur. *Hec.* 425: Ὦ τῆς ἀώρου, θύγατερ, ἀθλίας τύχης (What
unforeseen, wretched luck, daughter).
3. Samuel Gotthold Lange (1711-81), with Immanuel Jakob Pyra (1715-44) and others,
introduced ancient meters into German poetry. His most famous work may be *Thirsis und
Damons freundschaftliche Lieder* (co-authored with Pyra) (Halle: C. H. Hemmerde, 1749),
but he published a translation, *Quinti Horatii Flacci odarum libri V et de arte poetica liber
unus (Des Quintus Horatius Flaccus Oden Fünf Bücher und Von der Dichtkunst Ein Buch
Poetisch)* (Halle: J. J. Gebauer, 1752), which ran afoul of Lessing (1729-81), who ultimately
destroyed Lange's limited status as a translator and poet. For Gildersleeve on Herodotus, see
No. 141, n. 32.
4. "The Emperor Julian," *Southern Review* 3 (January 1868): 179-209 ( = *E&S* 355-98).
5. Possibly *Ammiani Marcellini quae supersunt*, ed. C. G. A. Erfurdt, 3 vols. (Leipzig:
Weidmann, 1808).
6. William Ewart Gladstone (1809-98) was elected M.P. for the University of Oxford in
1847 and served as prime minister twice (1868-74, 1880-85). Gildersleeve refers to his *Homer
and the Homeric Age*, 3 vols. (Oxford: Clarendon Press, 1858). For Gildersleeve on this and
others of Gladstone's Homeric studies sixty years later, see *AJP* 40 (1919): 333. See H. Lloyd-
Jones, "Gladstone on Homer," *Times Literary Supplement*, 3 January 1975, 15-17 ( = *Blood
for the Ghosts* [Baltimore: Johns Hopkins University Press, 1982], 110-125).
7. Sir George Cornewall Lewis (1806-63), had been financial secretary to the Treasury
(1850), then, while editor of the *Edinburgh Review* (1852-55), wrote an attack on Barthold

Georg Niebuhr, *An Inquiry into the Credibility of the Early Roman History*, 2 vols. (London: J. W. Parker and Son, 1855). Previously he had published translations of works by August Boeckh (*The Public Economy of Athens* [London: J. Murray, 1828]) and Karl Otfried Müller (*The History and Antiquities of the Doric Race* [Oxford: J. Murray, 1830] and *A History of the Literature of Ancient Greece* [London: n.p., 1840]). He ultimately became home secretary under Lord Palmerston in 1859. George Grote (1794-1871) served in the House of Commons (1832-41) and published *A History of Greece, from the Earliest Period to the Close of the Generation Contemporary with Alexander the Great*, 10 vols. (London: J. Murray, 1846-56).

8. Theodor Mommsen, *Römische Geschichte*, 3 vols. (Berlin: Weidmann, 1854-56). See *AJP* 6 (1885): 483-86 and No. 61, n. 4.

9. 2 Kings 1:20.

10. Jacob Bernays (1824-81) was a student of Ritschl's (No. 23, n. 2) at Bonn and received his Ph.D. in 1848. He was professor in a Jewish seminary in Breslau (1853-66) and university librarian and extraordinarius at Bonn (1866-81). His work on Scaliger (No. 5, n. 17) is classic. At Bonn, Gildersleeve took Bernays' courses on Aristotle's *Poetics* (summer semester 1852) and Thucydides and Cicero's *Epistles* (winter semester 1852-53) and Bernays suggested his dissertation topic (*AJP* 32 [1911]: 360 [ = *SBM*, 232]). Of him, Gildersleeve said, "As a scholar, he never achieved any work of great bulk, but what he did was marked by classic perfection. He had keen insight and a fatal command of sarcasm" (*Professorial Types*, 7-8). See also *AJP* 5 (1884): 340 and *Sandys*, 176-79.

11. *Zeitschrift für vergleichende Sprachforschung auf dem Gebiete der indogermanischen Sprachen*, begun in Berlin in 1852 by Theodor Aufrecht (1822-1907) and Adalbert Kuhn (1812-81). *Jahrbüchen für Philologie und Paedagogik* begun in Leipzig in 1826 by Johan Chr. Jahn (1797-1846). In 1831 it became the *Neue JPP*, ed. Jahn and Gottfried Seebode (1792-1868).

12. The *Bollettino archeologico napoletano* was founded in Naples in 1842 and after 1861 was called the *Bollettino archeologico italiano*. The *Bollettino archeologico sardo* was published from 1855 to 1864 in Cagliari.

13. Possibly Hübner's "Beiträge zu den römischen Inschriften in Britannien," *PhM* 14 (1859): 347-66.

14. In his "Miscellaneous Pieces," Chesterfield advises his son about the value of badinage, and this may be what Gildersleeve refers to. The quotation in question cannot be found.

15. Plittersdorf is a small village outside Godesberg, on the Rhine five miles SE of Bonn; Altenahr, with its tenth-century castle, is fifteen miles WSW of Remagen and was generally the terminus of the popular excursions into the Ahr Valley. The Krammetsvogel is the fieldfare, a type of thrush.

16. A concern throughout his life; see No. 191.


8 To: **William Dwight Whitney**
*Yale-Whitney*

University of Virginia, March 6, 1858

My dear Whitney—

Fortune or fate or providence has cut me off from all my old associates of the German period and it rejoices my inmost heart to receive the assurance that I am not wholly forgotten by my commilitiones [comrades-in-arms] of the Friderica Guilelina.[1] In my modest obscurity I have watched

your career and knew in what part of the intellectual firmament to find
you; but to tell the truth, I lacked the courage or better perhaps the energy
to write and lo! you have put me to shame.—Many thanks then for your
kind letter and to show how much I appreciate your remembrance, I do not
hesitate to inflict on you the memorials of my last five years. I returned
from Europe in July 1853, and went to Richmond, where I remained for a
year.[2]—My first serious occupation was a severe attack of sickness, which
relieved me of all the superfluous health I had gained abroad. I then continued my studies after a fashion[3]—wrote a couple of review-articles[4]—
"prospected" for places—which were not worth having or which I did not
get[5] and finally accepted the position of a tutor in a wealthy family of the
South.—I spent a winter in the swamps of South Carolina—a summer in
the mountains of North Carolina[6]—grew weary of teaching "the beggarly
elements"—shook the dust of the Rip Van Winkle state from off my feet—
and returned home—with my savings—wrote a couple of review-articles
and an unpublished novel of the most nondescript character, in which I
tried to embody my German adventures.[7] Fortunately for my reputation an
opening in the University of Virginia closed my career as a novelist. I entered the lists—was elected in September '56[8]—and since October of that
year I have been Professor of Greek in this institution.—In comparison
with other colleges the salary is good—(between $3000 & $4000.)—but the
work is proportionately heavy[9]—to say the least.—I have no leisure and
our 9 months session is a season of almost unremitting toil.—But I am
anchored—for the present—perhaps finally—"Inveni portum: spes et fortuna valete.—"[10] My pretensions diminish with every year. I faintly hope
that I am useful and that is the utmost bound of my ambition.—I have
been lately nursing the idea of a trip to Europe next summer in order to
revive my spirits.[11] If you are in New York next June, be on the lookout for
me; I generally stop at the Brevoort-House.[12]—

The oriental society has or ought to have more than a general claim on
me—for I am ex officio teacher of Hebrew.[13] True my knowledge of that
interesting idiom is as limited as the number of my scholars—(not much
demand for the article as you may suppose)—but I am adding to my little
stock from year to year and expect to accost the Arabic in the course of
time. Unfortunately Sanskrit is too far above me—and you are too far from
me and so I leave the beautiful guṇa's and anusvâra's[14] and all the other
lovely changes in sound to those who have more time and opportunity. Of
late I have become more reconciled to comparative philology—and am ap-
propriating the results as far as Greek is concerned but very cautiously—
Benfey's Wurzellexikon is my horror.[15]—Pray tell me when you write
again, what rank he holds among Sanskrit scholars?—For my purposes
Geo. Curtius[16] is worth a dozen such as he—Alas and alack a day! how
hard it is to sink the shop, when one has no other home.—And of me that is

literally true. Here I sit in my office from early morning till midnight and the mould is growing over me.—a premature old bachelor of 26!—So you see I can sympathize only remotely with your paternal fondness for the new edition[17]—and you must conceal the fact of your acquaintanceship with such a horrid, tobacco-smoking wretch, from Mrs. Whitney,[18] whom I esteem most highly for your sake.—

My best regards to our common acquaintances in your region of the world and many, many thanks for your kind letter to

Yours sincerely
B. L. Gildersleeve

I enclose the $1.50 due[19]—
$1 in coin 50c. in postage stamps—

1. Gildersleeve and Whitney were among the five Americans (the others were Henry W. Carr of Charleston, Ludwig F. Billings, and Elias J. Hall) to register at the Royal Friedrich Wilhelm University in 1850, all with the faculty of philosophy. Whitney stayed for three semesters, Gildersleeve only one. On Whitney and his German experience, see Carl Diehl, *Americans and German Scholarship, 1770–1870* (New Haven: Yale University Press, 1978), 119–30.

2. For a similar account, see *Formative Influences*: 615–16, written some thirty-three years later.

3. See No. 3.

4. "Modest Critique of 'A Sketch After Landseer,' " *Southern Literary Messenger* 20 (1854): 118–20; "The Necessity of the Classics," review of *Grundriss der Griechischen Litteratur* by G. Bernhardy, *Southern Quarterly Review*, 26 (n.s. 10): 145–67.

5. See No. 3, n. 10.

6. Ibid., n. 9.

7. "Henry Stephens," review of *Essai sur la vie et les Ouvrages de Henri Estienne* by Leon Feugère, *Quarterly Review of the Methodist Episcopal Church, South* 9 (1855): 1–21, and "Theodore Agrippa d'Aubigné," review of *Mémoires de Theodore Agrippa D'Aubigné* by Ludovic Lalanne, ibid. 10 (1856): 78–107; "Nicodemus Frischlin," review of *Leben und Schriften des Dichters und Philologen Nicodemus Frischlin* by David Friedrich Strauss, ibid. 10 (1856): 348–82. On Gildersleeve's novel, see No. 4, n. 8.

8. On his appointment, see No. 6.

9. See *Formative Influences*: 616.

10. Janus Pannonius *Epigrammata* 160 (translation of *Greek Anthology* 9.49): *Inveni portum: Spes et fortuna valete / Sat me lusistis; ludite nunc alios* (I have found my haven: Farewell hope and fortune / You have toyed with me enough; now toy with others).

11. He went to Europe in the summer of 1860 (*Southerner*: 334) and visited Ritschl at Bonn (see No. 23, n. 2, and *AJP* 5 [1884]: 340).

12. The Brevoort House on Fifth Avenue at 8th Street was a quiet comfortable hotel conducted on the English system, where meals from a first-class French cuisine were not included in the room charges. See Ivan D. Steen, "Palaces for Travelers: New York City's Hotels in the 1850's," *New York History* 51 (1970): 285.

13. The American Oriental Society was founded in 1842 by the Boston businessman John Pickering; its classical section began in 1848. Whitney served the AOS as president for six years, librarian for eighteen, and corresponding secretary for twenty-seven. The classical sec-

tion became the APA in 1869. See, further, Lucius Shero, "The American Philological Association: An Historical Sketch," *PAPA* 94 (1964): x-l.

14. Guṇa is a regular Sanskrit vowel-change most often involved in Sanskrit derivational and inflectional morphology. Anusvâra is the sound of *m* or *n* made without entirely closing the mouth, used for final *m* or *n* before a variety of word-openings. See Whitney's *Sanskrit Grammar* (Boston: Ginn, 1891), 24. On Gildersleeve's inabilities with Sanskrit, see "Oscillations and Nutations of Philological Studies," *JHU Circulars*, no. 151 (April 1901): 48.

15. Theodor Benfey's (1809–81) *Griechisches Wurzellexicon*, 2 vols. (Berlin: G. Reimer, 1839–42) was the first systematic study of Greek etymology. See, further, *Sandys*, 206. He was at Göttingen, but Gildersleeve took no courses from him.

16. Georg Curtius (1820–85), was professor at Leipzig (1861–85) and champion of the comparative method that brought scientific linguistics to philology. He had published *Die Sprachvergleichung in ihrem Verhältnis zur classischen Philologie* (Berlin: W. Besser, 1848). His great works, in addition to his Greek grammars, were *Grundzüge der griechischen Etymologie*, 2 vols. (Leipzig: B. G. Teubner, 1858–62) and *Das Verbum der griechischen Sprache* (Leipzig: S. Hirtzel, 1873–76). See, further, E. Curtius, "Georg Curtius," *Unter drei Kaisern: Reden und Aufsätze* (Berlin: W. Hertz, 1889), 216–33, idem, *Ausgewählte Reden und Vorträge von Georg Curtius* (Leipzig: B. G. Teubner, 1886), vi–xxviiii, and *Sandys*, 207–8.

17. Edward Baldwin Whitney, who became assistant attorney general in the Garfield administration, had been born the previous year on 16 August.

18. Elizabeth Wooster Baldwin, daughter of Roger Sherman Baldwin (1793-1863), a former Connecticut senator and governor.

19. The annual assessment for the AOS was $5.00 with a like initiation fee. Gildersleeve's $1.50 is unexplained.

## 9 To: Socrates Maupin
### *UVa-Maupin*

Camp near Hamilton's Crossing[1]
Sept. 10, 1863

My dear Friend,[2]

So little has occurred to break the monotony of camp life since I joined my brother[3] on the 21st of last month[4] that I have not thought it worth the while to trouble my friends with barren letters. Still it is in some sort my duty to report to you from time to time so that you may know that I have not been seduced by the charms of military life so far as to renounce all allegiance to the University. It was my intention, as you are aware, to return home immediately after I had brought my brother his fresh horse but I found after I had set out that his brigade was so much further off than I supposed, and after I had reached camp that his mare was in so much better /plight/ than had been reported that I determined to remain with him and ride one of his horses instead of taking the dull, hot, dusty trip twice in immediate succession. Fitz Lee's brigade has been unusually quiet since I joined.[5] Our occupation consists in watching the Yankees on the other side of the Rappahannock and so long as they manifest no disposition to cross, we shall probably remain quiet. On the 28th of Aug. we moved down to Bowling Green[6] in anticipation of a raid on the Central r.r. but the next day we came back, covered with dust if not with glory and replete with watermelons if not with enthusiasm. Caroline Co. has not suffered to the same extent as Spotsylvania.[7] The farmers actually seemed to retain some kindly feeling for the soldiery,[8] a feeling which is utterly extinct in the greater part of our border territory. Unless these gentry come up more fully to the help of the cause, they will find the Jonah of our vessel, the unmitigated negro, thrown overboard. This is one of our weakest points and the Yankees know it.[9] At the beginning of the war the white heat of patriotic fervour kept all classes fused into a homogeneous mass; if we cool down too suddenly, there will be a line of severance between the slaveholders and the non-slaveholders.[10] Mechanics and professional men will tire of the war first. Then the speculators—Jew and Gentile—who will have invested all their gains in real estate + will complete the ruin of the currency in their own interest and be ready for peace on any terms which will secure their title-deeds. When our currency becomes utterly worthless, and class is arrayed against class, the chances of our independence will be very slender indeed. If more could realize, as you and I do, the horrors of Yankee rule, there would be a universal determination to submit to any privation, to run any risk, to wait any time rather than to yield to the dictation of /our/ enemies[11] but the masses do not understand the position; it is to them a sectional squabble rather than a national war and most men fancy that if the Yankees were victorious they could return to their homesteads under ~~toler~~ tolerable conditions—and that the good old times would gradually come back again.[12] Everybody in the army and out of the army is horribly sick of the war—Bad enough for the passengers to be seasick in a storm—but still that is not dangerous—but when the crew is sea-sick and the officers are sea-sick, and men lie about the deck so overcome with nausea that they care not whether they live or die, God be our pilot for vain is the help of man.[13]—~~As~~ For ~~myself~~ /my part/ I will not allow myself to regret the outbreak of the war. I have no scruples with regard to the justice of our cause. We are in the right—and that solves all questions for me as to my personal duty. But I must confess that I look forward with deep concern to the future of our country and of our state, whether we are successful in this struggle or not. If the war should stop now and peace be proclaimed before next spring, we should find the reorganization of society a Herculean task. If the war should be prolonged three or four years Chaos would come again, and the very elements require a new creation.—You may think that I am desponding—but the fact is that I have had lately too much time to think /in/ ~~quietly~~ and ~~alone~~ /solitude/ on the state of affairs and those meditations have not led to any very cheerful conclusions.—It is fortunate for our cause that military organization makes machines of men.

Our soldiers all wish the war over—almost all declare that /if/ they could
get out of it—they would not get into it again, and yet they fight as cheerfully as ever and keep up their spirits wonderfully in their wearisome camp
life.[14]—From all sides I hear encouraging reports of the condition of our
enemy. They men are well-fed, well-clad, well-shod. In this brigade we do
not fare as well as the infantry and yet my brother's rations form an abundant provision for us both. The horses do not get quite enough to keep
them in high order but still they are not suffering, and I have no doubt that
when we are called to move against the enemy we shall show that we have
profited by our long rest. How much longer that rest will last we cannot
tell—not long I think. It is no secret that Longstreet's corps has been withdrawn from this position of the line[15] and if the Yankee cavalry is in such
force as is represented, we should have to retreat and that not very slowly
before their advance. But no one seems to anticipate a forward movement
until after the great battle in Tennessee which promises to be the Arma-
geddon of the war. I shall not prolong my stay beyond the last week in
Sept.—Meanwhile I hope to receive an answer to this letter—addressed to
Co. D 1st Regt. Va. Cavalry—Fitzhugh Lee's Brigade.—I suppose my
place is suffering somewhat, intrusted as it is to the care of eye-servants,[16]
please give them a hint of my speedy return—for I do not wish to catch
them napping.—Ben requests me to send you his best regards. We are
both in excellent health, camplife agreeing with me almost as well as with
him.—

Present me kindly to Mrs. Maupin and the members of your family—
and give my regards to my other friends at the University

As ever—

Yours sincerely
B. L. Gildersleeve

1. A knoll overlooking the crossing of Old Mine Road and the tracks of the Richmond,
Fredericksburg, and Potomac railroads at the southern end of the 1862 Fredericksburg battlefield,

2. Gildersleeve translates "Mein lieber Freund," a phrase presumably reserved for close
professional colleagues; otherwise, he would have written the more English "My dear
Maupin." See, e.g., Nos. 8 and 11.

3. Benjamin Gildersleeve (1834–1921), enlisted 14 May 1861, was held prisoner from 2
January 1862 to 6 January 1863, and mustered out following Appomattox as a private. Shell-
shocked after the war, he never really recovered and returned to Abingdon, Va., to live in a
genteel poverty. Gildersleeve's two other brothers both enlisted as privates. John Robinson
Gildersleeve (1843–1918), a medical man, became an assistant surgeon, and Gilbert Snowden Gildersleeve (1847–1919) rose to captain of cavalry under J. E. B. Stuart.

4. See Creed: 75.

5. After Gettysburg, R. E. Lee brought his weakened army ("Lee's Miserables") down
across the Potomac into Virginia to rest, re-group, and face the exhausted troops of Gen.
George Meade, which were ranged along the Rapidan and Rappahannock Rivers from

Culpeper to Fredericksburg. Neither army was in any hurry to engage in action, and each was content to survey the other for several weeks, while a portion of Meade's troops went to New York to help quell the anti-draft riots. Lee's nephew, Brig. Gen. Fitzhugh Lee (1835–1905), one of the two commanders of Confederate cavalry divisions, was posted to Fredericksburg from 14 July to 9 October. When R. E. Lee maneuvered Meade away from the Rapidan, Fitzhugh's brigade held the line while the main army attacked the Federal flank (see n. 15 below).

6. Twenty-five miles to the south, in Caroline Co., Va.

7. See *Southerner*: 334, and G. W. Redway, *Fredericksburg: A Study in War* (New York: Macmillan, 1906).

8. On the farmers' plight, see *Southerner*: 340.

9. On slavery, see *Creed*: 85-86.

10. On Southern unity, see *Creed*: 79.

11. "To us submission meant slavery, as it did to Pericles and the Athenians; . . . and the bitterest taunt in the vocabulary of those who advocated secession was 'submissionist'" (*Creed*: 79).

12. "The rank and file were, to begin with, in full accord with the great principles of the war, and were sustained by the abiding conviction of the justice of the cause" (*Creed*: 81).

13. Ps. 60:11; 108:12.

14. On camp life, and the exchange of "rough jests with enemy pickets," see *Creed*: 80.

15. Lt. Gen. James Longstreet (1821-1904) was ordered on 9 September to take two divisions, about 12,600 men, as aid to Gen. Braxton Bragg in preventing the advance of Gen. William Rosecrans into Georgia. The full attack by Bragg's forces was originally scheduled for 10 September but for a variety of reasons was postponed for ten days. It finally took place at Chickamauga Creek and was a resounding, if short-lived, Confederate victory. Following Bragg and Longstreet's success, Lee moved on 9 October against Meade. See Archibald Gracie, *The Truth about Chickamauga* (Boston: Houghton Mifflin, 1911), and Glenn Tucker, *Chickamauga: Bloody Battle in the West* (Dayton, Ohio: Morningside Bookshop, 1972).

16. "*Arch.*, one who does his duty only when under the eye of his master or employer" (*OED*).

10 To: Benjamin Johnson Barbour
*UVa-Barbour*

University of Virginia Oct. 1865

Hon. B. Johnson Barbour,
Dear Sir,

Learning that Mr. A. Dallas Bache Courtenay, Son of Edward H. Courtenay formerly for many years Prof. of Mathematics in this Institution,[1] is a candidate for the place of cadet in the West Point Military Academy, we take great pleasure in recommending him for that situation.[2] He is a youth of fine abilities, exemplary morally, & possesses great aptitude for scientific pursuits. His appointment will be particularly gratifying to us, and will serve to lessen the debt of gratitude due his distinguished father for his valualable [sic] services to this Institution & the South as Professor & author.

Chas. S. Venable
 Prof. Math.
Francis H. Smith
 Prof. Nat'l Philosophy
J. L. Cabell
 Prof. Phys$^y$ & Surgery
M. Schele De Vere
 Prof. Mod. Languages
S. Maupin
 Prof. Chemistry

John B. Minor
 Prof. of Law
J. S. Davis
 Prof. Anat. & Mat. Med.
B. L. Gildersleeve
 Prof. of Ancient
 Languages
W. H. McGuffey
 Prof. Moral Philosophy
H. Howard M.D.
 Prof. of Medicine

1. Edward Henry Courtenay (1803–53), a native of Baltimore, graduated first in his West Point class (1821), served in the Corps of Engineers (1821–29), taught at West Point (1829–34), and the University of Pennsylvania, 1834–36, and, after eight years as an engineer in New York and Boston, succeeded J. J. Sylvester (see No. 30, n. 2) as professor of mathematics at the University of Virginia (1842–53). His posthumously published lectures, *Treatise on the Differential and Integral Calculus, and the Calculus of Variations* (New York: A. S. Barnes, 1855) remained a textbook at the university for many years (*Barringer*, 1:354).

2. This remarkable attempt to resume the tradition of Virginians at West Point (R. E. and Fitzhugh Lee, Stonewall Jackson, J. E. B. Stuart, and many others), signed by the complete professorate of the university with the exception of the historian George F. Holmes, was unsuccessful. Two Virginians each year had been admitted to West Point in 1859 and 1860, but all four either resigned or were dismissed in April 1861. Between 1861 and 1869 eleven cadets were appointed from the Virginia quota. Five were from Union-held parts of the state (Arlington, Wheeling, Fortress Monroe, Clarksburg, and Catlettsburg); one each from Washington, D.C., and Mississippi; and four were taken by Union appointees from New York, Michigan, New Jersey, and Ohio. Virginians from Confederate areas were not appointed to West Point until 1870, when five were admitted. This was the same year that the first postwar appointments were made from Mississippi; Alabama sent two cadets each in 1868 and 1869, the year Georgia sent its first four cadets. But despite the readmittance of Southern cadets, the bitterness of the Northern cadets against them did not fully end until after the Spanish-American War. See, further, J. L. Morrison, "The United States Military Academy, 1833–1866: Years of Progress and Turmoil" (Ph.D. diss., Columbia University, 1970), and W. S. Dillard, "The United States Military Academy, 1865–1900: The Uncertain Years" (Ph.D. diss., University of Washington, 1972).

### 11 To: Emil Hübner
*Berlin*

University of V$^{\underline{a}}$
April 21$^{\underline{st}}$ 1873

My dear Hübner,

You must have received by this time a copy of the revised edition of my Latin Grammar,[1] which I directed my publishers to send you. The first edition—published in 1867—was so wretchedly printed and in every way so immature that I did not venture to submit /it/ to the inspection of German scholars; and although I have revised the book with a good deal of care and it has had a certain success in this country, I am not by any means easy about it. The fact is, for the last seventeen years I have devoted nearly all my time to the study of Greek and in my Latin Grammar I have done little more than apply my Greek categories to the little I know about Latin;[2] and doubtless your practised eye, if indeed you think it worth while to look through the book, will notice not a few distortions that may be traced to Greek influences.

Although our correspondence has been interrupted so long, I still hope that you hold in pleasant remembrance the days, which we spent together in Bonn and for my part I can assure you that I have watched your career with the greatest interest and that your rapid rise and your well earned eminence in your chosen field of labor have filled me with joy and pride.

To show you how faithful I am to that happy /past/ I send you a little essay on Platen,[3] which I wrote some summers ago merely because the writing would recall at every line our rambles among the seven mountains, which Degenkolb[4] and yourself used to make vocal with Platen's ringing anapests; but you must regard the essay like the grammar as a token of goodwill rather than as a specimen of my literary ability and keep your judgment in suspense until I gather up the results of my Greek studies. That work will I trust be worthier of my old teachers and my old companions.

Maupin,[5] when he was with you, told you doubtless all of my personal history, that would be likely to interest you. An active and enthusiastic teacher, if nothing more, I have at all events been fortunate in securing the regard and affection of many of my pupils and this I am content to accept as the great reward of much hard work, prosecuted under disadvantages, of which scholars in Germany can form no adequate conception.

Of late years the cares of a family—I have a wife and two children[6]—have sobered me somewhat but the old spirit comes back again at times with the memories of Godesberg, Königswinter, Rolandseck and the Ahr.[7]

Yours faithfully<br>B. L. Gildersleeve

Prof. E. E. Hübner
Berlin

1. *Latin Grammar* (New York: Richardson, 1867; rev. ed., New York: University Publishing Co., 1872) and *A Latin Exercise-Book* (New York: University Publishing Co., 1871; rev. ed., 1873).A reader and primer followed in 1875.

2. Gildersleeve had originally intended a Greek syntax, but adapted the plan for his *Latin Grammar*. See *Syntax*, iii, and R. L. Fowler, "The Gildersleeve Archive," *Briggs-Benario*, 71.

3. See No. 3, n. 15.

4. See No. 4, n. 11.

5. Chapman Maupin (1847-1900), the son of Gildersleeve's University of Virginia mentor, Socrates Maupin, had been Gildersleeve's student (1861-67), with an interruption for the Civil War. After successfully running a private school in Ellicott City, Md., he taught English and Latin at Baltimore City College, and Gildersleeve would suggest him for a position in Latin at Johns Hopkins. Maupin helped Gildersleeve revise his *Latin Primer* in 1882 and taught two of his collaborators, Gonzalez Lodge and C. W. E. Miller (see "Correspondents"). Maupin's wife, Margaret Lewis Taliaferro (1846-1930), a great-granddaughter of John Marshall, was a distant cousin of Betty Gildersleeve's.

6. See No. 12, nn. 9 and 10.

7. Godesberg, a favorite summering-place with a fourteenth-century castle; Königswinter, where excursions to the Seven Mountains began; and Rolandseck (No. 5, n. 12) are all on the Rhine, SE of Bonn; Gildersleeve and Hübner visited Altenahr on their excursion in the Ahr Valley (No. 7, n. 15).

## 12 To: PAUL HAMILTON HAYNE
### *Duke*

University of Va
May 20ᵗʰ 1873

My dear Hayne,

It gives me unfeigned pleasure to get a letter from you. Of course I know that you are still singing as the bird sings, more sadly perhaps, more musingly, and your noble service to Timrod's memory has found its echo throughout the country[1] so that I am not ignorant of what you are doing but that is very different from the direct personal communication which awakens more immediately all the recollections of those happy days which I spent with my friends in Charleston. I recall your sweet home,[2] I breathe again the perfumed air of your garden, I sit again in the charmed seclusion of your dwelling—I refuse to think of all that lies between.—

As for me—the story of the last eighteen years has been eventful as such a lapse of time must be eventful to every man who thinks—My path is thickly strewn with abandoned projects, with hopeless failures; here and there a trivial success, all along, I may say, ~~with the~~ traces of honest effort. I started life with the fancy that I too had something of the poet in me[3] but my attempts at song found no response and in due time I subsided into plain prose and not much of that.[4] From the time when I entered on my professorship in 1856 to 1863, all my writing was done for my own culture or for my University work.[5] I then began to write for the press, and from that time on I have written more or less every year a few things for the Southern Magazine (The New Eclectic)—more for the Southern Review[6]— besides my school books which are slowly making their way[7]—Impatient in most things, I have not been impatient of my obscurity. If I live long

enough, I hope to do something for my proper sphere of work. If I do not—
I am content.

The close of the war left me poorer by four years—I had not much else to
lose—and a broken leg.[8] Of course while I was wounded I had nothing
better to do than to become sentimental, when I began to convalesce I fell
in love and in 1866 I was married.[9] I have two children living[10]—a boy four
years old and a baby girl—which is not the same thing as a girl baby, as I
need not tell a poet.——

Browne[11] was kind enough to send me your notice of my article soon
after it appeared. I felt all the time that some personal friendship colored
the review—though I could not divine the source—I am glad to have the
explanation—for after all abatement on the score of partiality—it is a pleasure to find out that there is here and there someone who understands my
aims.—

The names which you mention in your letter have an especial meaning
for me—even Timrod's, although I knew him but slightly.[12]—Thompson
was much our senior[13]—for on reading ~~your~~ about you the other day as I
did quite accidentally in Duykinck [sic],[14] I found that you and I must be
close contemporaries—but add ten years to our present age and it would
not seem to be so very much longer to live.—Ramsay's death was a severe
blow to me[15]—He was my most intimate friend.—Neither Lord[16] nor the
Dingles[17] have I seen since '58.—When I was in N.Y. last I hunted up
Barnard[18] and was received with the utmost expansion. He has aged very
much but his manner is unchanged—and the talk I had with him—to say
nothing of the dinner—unhinged me so that I was utterly unfit for proof-
reading that afternoon—

Why can't you stop on your way to N.Y.[19]—We are very little off the
highway—nay—we are on it[20]—if you come up through Tennessee—At
any rate let me know when you will make your Northern trip—as I shall
probably spend some time in the North this summer.—

It is odd that my thoughts should have been busy with you a day or two
before I received your letter—a day or two before I stumbled on that article
in Duykinck [sic].—

Does not this line occur in one of your early poems
  "The glaring eyeballs of the dread simoom"
It haunts me as the "Wolf's long howl on [sic] Oonalaska's shore" did
Campbell[21]

                                    Yours faithfully
                                    B. L. Gildersleeve

P. H. Hayne Esq.

1. When his friend and former schoolmate, the poet Henry Timrod (1828-67), died,
Hayne decided to present a selection of his poetry along with an affectionate memoir as a

means of introducing "the poet laureate of the Confederacy" to the world. *The Poems of Henry Timrod, Edited, with a Sketch of the Poet's Life* (New York: E. J. Hale, 1873) quickly became such a critical and popular success that the publication in January 1873 was followed by an expanded edition the following April.

2. After 1840 Hayne lived with his widowed mother and the family of his uncle, Col. Arthur P. Hayne, at 8 Alexander Street in a wealthy neighborhood of East Charleston, with a view of the Ashley River. On the house and its gardens, see Herbert Ravenal Sass, "Wild Life in a City Garden," *Atlantic* 107 (February 1911): 226-33, esp. 227, and Alice Huger Smith, *The Dwelling Places of Charleston* (Philadelphia: Lippincott, 1917; reprint, New York: Diadem Books, 1974), frontispiece and 221-22.

3. Gildersleeve's first publications were in 1842-43, "The Violets" and "Ode to Ashley," in *The Bouquet*, a children's weekly newspaper, edited by Edwin Heriot and published by B. B. Hussey in Charleston from 1841 to 1843. He subsequently composed "hymns to be sung at the meetings of the Juvenile Missionary Society" (*Formative Influences*: 612). He had gone to Princeton wanting to be a poet ("College in the Forties," *Princeton Alumni Weekly* 16, no. 16 [26 January 1916]: 376) and later published "Occidental Ghazels," *Southern Literary Messenger* 20 (1852): 173, "War Verses," *Central Presbyterian*, in 1863 (see A. C. Gordon, Jr., *Fugitive Writers of Virginian Verse* [New York: J. T. White, 1923], 299), "Matilda Guggenheimer: A Ballad" under the name "Sackville Dulcimore," *Southern Literary Messenger* 38 (1864): 232-33, and "Prayer in Anticipation of Battle before Richmond: May 25th, 1862," *New Eclectic Magazine* 5 (1869): 682-83. "All my early verses were as bad as they well could be; but I persevered in metrical composition for many years until I gained a useful command of the form, and to this day [1891] the Muse can tickle my brain as I lie asleep—otherwise not" (*Formative Influences*: 612). In the same place Gildersleeve calls himself "cursed with a poetic temperament, and unblessed by poetic power." With the end of the war, he ceased original composition and in middle age expended his efforts on translations. In his eighties, when his eyes failed him and books were useless to him, he devoted himself to poetic composition, almost exclusively in the sonnet form. See Nos. 183-84.

4. Gildersleeve's freelancing career may have been spurred by his contact with what he called "the Hayne Set" (n. 12 below; others called it "the [William Gilmore] Simms Circle") in Charleston in 1854, following his depressing winter of private tutoring (No. 4, n. 5). From that year to 1856, he published one short and three lengthy reviews and one article (No. 8, nn. 4 and 7).

5. Chiefly his 1863-64 editorials for the *Richmond Examiner*; see *Southerner*: 341, and "contributions, including war verses" to his father's newspaper, the *Central Presbyterian* (*SBM*, xxxi). For the *New Eclectic Magazine* (which became the *Southern Magazine* in 1873): "Classical Study," 5 (1869): 385-94; "Lord Lytton's Horace," 6 (1870): 471-81 (collected in 1890 in *E&S* [see No. 14, n. 4; No. 72, n. 5]); "On the Steps of the Bema: Studies in the Attic Orators," 12-13 (1873): 395-404, 559-69, 664-71; 4-22, 129-37, 272-83.

6. For the *Southern Magazine* see preceding note; for the *Southern Review*: "The Legend of Venus," 1 (April 1867): 352-82; "Xanthippe and Socrates," 2 (July 1867): 172-200; "The Limits of Culture," 2 (October 1867): 421-48; "The Emperor Julian," 3 (January 1868): 179-209; "Maximilian: His Travels and His Tragedy," 3 (April 1868): 476-505; "Apollonius of Tyana," 4 (July 1868): 94-125; "Platen's Poems," 4 (October 1868): 434-65; "Lucian," 6 (October 1869): 389-426. All were reprinted in *E&S*.

7. See No. 11, n. 1.

8. While carrying orders for Gen. John B. Gordon at the skirmish at Weyer's Cave (twelve miles south of Harrisonburg, Va.) on 25 September 1864, Gildersleeve had his "thigh-bone broken by a Spencer bullet" (*AJP* 22 [1901]: 468 [ = *SBM*, 75]). His leg was nearly amputated. "I lost my pocket Homer, I lost my pistol, I lost one of my horses, and finally I came very near to losing my life by a wound which kept me five months on my back"

(*Formative Influences*: 616). Although he refers to "my short and desultory service in the field" (*Southerner*: 334, see also No. 141), he was persistently identified with the heroic, but broken, Southern nobility (e.g., *Bruce* 3: 310). As one former student recalled, "[He] had shown that he could emulate the courage of the heroes of Hellas as successfully as he could expound the intricacies of their beautiful language" (R. H. McKim, *A Soldier's Recollections: Leaves from the Diary of a Young Confederate* [New York: Longmans, Green, 1910], 233). See also J. B. Gordon, *Reminiscences of the Civil War* (New York: Scribner, 1905), 422; and "The Dead Grammarian," *NY Times*, 11 January 1924: 16. Legends about his war activity grew with his general reputation. See Hayne, "Ante-bellum Charleston," *Southern Bivouac*, 4 (n.s. 1) (November 1855): 329, *Baltimore Sun*, 22 May 1915: 3, and Kathryn A. Jacob, "The Hopkins Four," *JHU Magazine* 25, no. 4 (July 1974): 24.

9. Gildersleeve was taken to "Hillandale," the nearby estate of Raleigh Colston in Albemarle County. There he was nursed by Elizabeth Fisher Colston (1846–1930), the eldest daughter of Raleigh (1821–1901) and Gertrude Powell (1826–1901) Colston of Richmond, and there they were married on 18 September 1866. See *Culbreth*, 398.

10. Raleigh Colston (1869–1944) and Emma Louise (1872–1954). Basil Seymour was born 10 March 1871 and died 2 October 1871. On Benjamin Fisher, see No. 13, n. 1.

11. William Hand Browne (1828–1912) a native of Baltimore, co-founded in that city the *Southern Review* (1866), and the *New Eclectic (Southern Magazine)* (1867–75). He later became professor of English literature at Johns Hopkins. For Gildersleeve on Browne, see No. 148, and *JHU Circulars*, no. 252 (February 1913): 19–21.

12. Contrary to some published statements (E. W. Parks, *Southern Poets* [New York: American Book Co., 1936], 100, and R. S. Moore, *A Man of Letters in the Nineteenth Century South* [Baton Rouge: Louisiana State University Press, 1982], 5, 146 n. 3), Gildersleeve was not a classmate of Timrod's. On 12 March 1909 he wrote to C. W. Kent, "I saw him occasionally when we were boys together but we did not go to the same school. . . . There was much talk of him in our set—the Hayne set, when I was in Charleston in 1854 . . . though a real poet, [he] was not a poet of supreme achievement." See *French*, 207–10.

13. John Reuben Thompson (1823–73) had just died. Born in Richmond to wealthy Northern parents, he edited the *Southern Literary Messenger* (bought for him by his father) from 1847, a decade after Poe had been its editor, until 1860. He made it the leading Southern journal of its time, with a more nationally representative group of authors than any other Southern journal. Gildersleeve published two pieces in Thompson's *Messenger*, "Occidental Ghazels" (see n. 3 above and No. 3, n. 16) and "A Modest Critique of 'A Sketch after Landseer,'" (No. 8, n. 4). See, further, No. 75. After the war, Thompson was until his death literary editor of the *New York Evening Post*. See the biographical introduction to *The Poems of John R. Thompson*, ed. J. S. Patton (New York: Scribner, 1920), and W. G. McCabe, "John R. Thompson," *UVa Alum. Bull.*, 3d ser., 11 (April 1918): 151–67.

14. *Cyclopedia of American Literature*, ed. Evert A. Duyckinck and George L. Duyckinck (New York: Scribner, 1866). The article on Hayne is at 2: 722. Many of the articles on Southern life and literature were written by the Charleston literary lion William Gilmore Simms (1806–70).

15. Major David Ramsay (1830–63), a descendant of Henry Laurens and the historian David Ramsay (1749–1815), was Gildersleeve's and G. W. Dingle's (n. 17 below) roommate at Weenderstrasse 59 in Göttingen from Easter term 1851 to Easter term 1852. He went on to Berlin and in 1852 took a J.U.D. with highest honors from Heidelberg. On his departure, Gildersleeve wrote in his diary (12 December 1852) "At 11:00 at night David took the steamboat—I weeping and throwing the overcoat after him." Ramsay served in the South Carolina legislature from 1858 to 1862 while practicing law in Charleston and was mortally wounded 18 July 1863 replacing a fallen Confederate flag during the successful Confederate defense of the second assault on Battery Wagner on Morris Island in Charleston Harbor. "The most

intimate friend I ever had, who fell after heroic services, was known by all our circle to be utterly at variance with the prevalent Southern view of the quarrel, and died upholding a right which was not a right to him except so far as the mandate of his State made it a right; and while he would have preferred to see the 'old flag' floating over a united people, he restored the new banner to its place time after time when it had been cut down by shot and shell" (*Creed*, 79). Gildersleeve's version is reflected in contemporary accounts such as J. Johnson, *The Defense of Charleston Harbor* (Charleston: Walker, Evans and Cogswell, 1890), 107; *Charleston Mercury*, 20 July and 5 August 1863; and *Charleston Courier*, 6 August 1863; but see E. Milby Burton, *The Siege of Charleston, 1861–1865* (Columbia, S.C.: University of South Carolina Press, 1970), 163.

16. Samuel Lord, Jr. (1830–99), W. D. B. Dingle (see n. 17 below) and Ramsay all matriculated together at Göttingen the year before Gildersleeve. An 1849 graduate of the College of Charleston, Lord became a prominent Charleston attorney and was associated with the Simms circle. With Simms, he helped erect a monument to Ramsay in the cemetery of the Circular Church, Charleston.

17. Gabriel Wesley "Jay" Dingle (1826–93), the 1845 valedictorian of the College of Charleston, registered in law at Göttingen for Easter 1848, and next at Berlin, where he roomed at Dorotheenstrasse 91 with George M. Lane (No. 22, n. 1), whose relationship with Gildersleeve began at this time. He took his J.D. from Heidelberg in the winter term 1852, was admitted to the South Carolina Bar in 1853, and became a prominent Charleston attorney, magistrate, and, in 1882, alderman. His brother, William D. B. "Billy" Dingle, also studied law at Göttingen, Easter 1850–Michaelmas 1851 and Easter–Michaelmas 1852 (see above, n. 15), although he had not graduated from college. On his return to Charleston he was admitted to the Bar and appointed notary public on 30 July 1855, the same day that Ramsay was made magistrate. He was elected sheriff in 1860 and served as deputy in 1875–78. Billy Dingle and Ramsay occur often in Gildersleeve's diary of 1850–53: "Billy is like a sexton, he dingles all the belles" (26 April 1851), and Gildersleeve stayed with G. W. Dingle in Paris in June 1853 (No. 2, n. 4) before touring France with both brothers.

18. Horace Barnard (1829–97) was born in Charleston, and attended Yale and Harvard Law School after his family returned to Hartford, Conn., whence Barnard's grandfather Horace (d. 1797) had emigrated to Charleston, as had many another "codfish aristocrat" (Benjamin Gildersleeve, Sr., had likewise left Connecticut but enjoyed no such social position). Gildersleeve's friend became a prominent attorney in New York and lived at 26 East 35 St. (*NYTimes*, 9 November 1897: 7). The meeting took place in 1872. See No. 14.

19. The success of the Timrod book enabled Hayne to make a long-postponed Northern excursion, principally to certify his royalty accounts with J. B. Lippincott. Following the trip to New York, Hayne became widely published and sought after for occasional verse, but his health continued to worsen and he died 6 July 1886.

20. Gildersleeve initially lived at Pavilion I (his brother Benjamin lived with him as a student in 1858–59) on the West Lawn next to the Rotunda at the university and kept it as a formal address for receptions (see *Culbreth*, 398–99), but at some point after his marriage, a brown frame house called "Oakhurst" was built for him on land tangential to the campus that may have been owned by Betty's cousins the Minors (No. 32, n. 5). Oakhurst burned on 19 February 1917, and the site today is known as "Oakhurst Circle," which gives off a lane called "Gildersleeve Wood." Hayne would have taken the Washington City–Virginia Midland–and Great Southern Rail Road from Lynchburg through Charlottesville to the North.

21. "The wolf's long howl from Oonalaska's shore" is from Thomas Campbell (1777–1844), "The Pleasures of Hope," 1.66. The Scottish poet was especially popular with Hayne and his friends for having favorably reviewed Simms' poem "Atalantis" in his *London Metropolitan* (January 1834): 12.

13 To: JOHN HAMPDEN CHAMBERLAYNE
*Virginia Historical Society*

University of Virginia
July 27th 1874

My dear Chamberlayne—

Your kind note ought to have been answered before and I can not tell why I did not acknowledge it immediately, as is my wont. But your kind expressions have been present to my mind all the time—and I thank you from the bottom of my heart for all your affectionate attention/s/ to me.

My wife bears up under her sorrow better than I could have expected.[1] The little one suffered so much that she was in some measure prepared to consign him to a higher guardianship.—Still the grief is poignant.—My dear friend, I hope you may never know the full significance of Tertullian's words: Liberorum amarissima voluptas—[2]

My best regards and warmest affection for your dear mother[3]—whom I have learned to revere and love even in the few days that I had the honor of knowing her—

Yours faithfully,
B. L. Gildersleeve

J. Hampden Chamberlayne Esq.

1. Benjamin Fisher Gildersleeve had been born 12 January and died 20 July 1874. On the death of an earlier son, Basil Seymour, see No. 12, n. 10. Both infants are buried next to their parents and brother Raleigh and his wife in Plot 58 of the University Cemetery, Charlottesville.

2. Tertullian *Ad uxorem* 5.1: *Addicunt quidem sibi homines causas nuptiarum de sollicitudine posteritatis et liberorum amarissima voluptate* (Further reasons for marriage which men allege for themselves arise from anxiety for posterity, and the bitter, bitter pleasure of children).

3. Martha Burwell Dabney Chamberlayne (1802–83). Chamberlayne's father, Dr. Lewis Webb Chamberlayne (1798–1854), was a professor at the Medical College of Virginia.


14 To: PAUL HAMILTON HAYNE[1]
*Duke*

June 5, 1875

My dear Hayne:

Ever since I received your kind letter of May 23d I have been trying to find time to answer it. Ordinarily I reply to all letters immediately but yours was not one that could be answered in my usual laconic style and I see that I must filch time, if I can not find it, to show my appreciation of the warm greeting which you send me over such an interval of time and space. It is not likely that I shall ever forget those golden days of Charleston memory and I am glad to find that others remember them as gratefully as I do. It is sometimes hard to bring oneself to believe that the best part of life in almost every sense is past—that the great joys as well as the great toils are over. When I am quite well I feel no diminution of the power of work. My pursuits make little drain on the imagination and what I can do, I can do perhaps better than before. But for the last few weeks I have been out of sorts physically and much more disposed to taste the salt wave in the air to which you allude so pathetically. But it is really laughable for you or me to talk about age—I am just between 43 and 44. There is a very respectable plateau of naked skin on my skull and a considerable sprinkling of grey hairs in my beard—but as soon as my liver gets right again I will try to laugh you out of your gloomy view of things.—I have at least half a dozen books to write—two of which are to be on a great scale and insure me imperishable renown warranted to last for two years.[2] Why don't you begin an Epic and resolutely live until it is finished?

To judge by your letter one would think that I had chosen the better part. Perhaps you never knew that I had up to my early manhood an earnest longing to write myself 'poet' and that the intimate conviction that I was not 'called' was one of the severest disappointments of my intellectual life[3]— And you, whose name is a household word, wherever the tender and delicate in American poetry is appreciated, dare to talk to me of the solid fame of the digger of Greek roots, the manufacturer of Latin school books! What little scholarly work I have done lies buried in the Southern Review and the Southern Magazine and I shall never have the courage to bid it rise in more permanent /form./[4] Persius is a vacation study—undertaken simply for the purpose of replenishing a lank purse[5]—After I got fairly started the old element of self love, self respect or whatever you may choose to call it—/came in./The author is a difficult one; je me [sic] suis piqué de force[6] and I hope that the result has not been altogether bad.—

The reference of the lank purse reminds me to tell/you that/ I have long been married[7]—nine years ago nearly—Two of my children—boys as lovely in my eyes as your ideal in the "Address to my Daughter"[8]—are not to be vexed by the problems of this life. Two are left me—a sturdy boy of six—a sonsy maid of three—to make some provision for them and for their dear mother is all my worldly ambition.—Neither poetry nor scholarship is over abundant in our land—but poetry finds an echo wherever there is a human heart and scholars can live only in a land of scholars. So you go on from perfection to perfection while I must needs deteriorate—unless I cling to far off ideals—

And so you would like to have me criticise your poems. I took the dainty little volume[9] in my hands and read a stanza and a poem here and there. It is the most I can do even for a dear friend in this crush of the closing ses-

sion. Perhaps I shall be more receptive when the calmer vacation comes—
though I see even there the grimy form of the printer's devil and the massive tomes of Patristic literature through which I have to wade for my new
book.[10]— My mental mirror is so disfigured by all manner of scholastic
scratches that I am afraid I am less competent to ~~judge~~/reflect / your work
that [sic] I was twenty one years since [?]. A man must be more or less a
poet to understand a poet and the poet in me is buried beneath
Gildersleeve's Latin Series.—

I have no photograph at hand that my wife, who is unselfishly desirous
of obliterating the wide interval between our years,[11] will allow me to
send.— You shall have one, however, before long, if you will promise me
yours.

I dined with Horace Barnard three years ago in N.Y. and we talked
much of Sam Lord and his wife.[12]—

Almost the last verses I ever wrote were on Ramsay. He was one of my
dearest friends[13]—

"Omittance is no quittance"[14]—I will come back to the Mountain of the
Lovers some other time—

Yours faithfully
(but furtively)
B. L. Gildersleeve

1. This letter bears some resemblances to Gildersleeve's letter to Hayne two years earlier
(No. 12).

2. One was certainly the Greek syntax, planned along the lines of the Latin grammar. He
tells us elsewhere: "My monument was to have been the Greek Life of the Second Century
after Christ" (*AJP* 25 [1904]: 357).

3. See No. 12, n. 3.

4. Ibid., nn. 5 and 6. In fact, the pieces for the *Southern Review* were collected and
published in *E&S* in 1890.

5. *The Satires of A. Persius Flaccus* (New York: Harper and Bros., 1875).

6. Properly "Je m'en suis piqué de force" ("Naturally I prided myself on it"). Possibly a
play on La Rochefoucauld, *Max.* 203: "Le vrai honnête est celui qui ne se pique de rien."

7. No. 12, n. 9.

8. Hayne's poem "My Daughter," in *Legends and Lyrics* (Philadelphia: Lippincott,
1872), describes a father's grief for his dead daughter: "And yet she only lives for me / In
golden realms of fantasie, / A creature born of air and beam, / The delicate darling of a
dream."

9. *The Mountain of the Lovers; With Poems of Nature and Tradition* (New York: E. J.
Hale and Son, 1875).

10. *The Apologies of Justin Martyr, to which is appended The Epistle to Diognetus* (New
York: Harper and Bros., 1877).

11. Elizabeth Gildersleeve, at twenty-nine, was fourteen years Gildersleeve's junior. No
likeness seemed to match her natural beauty. See No. 191.

12. No. 12, nn. 16 and 18.

13. Ibid., n. 15.

14. *As You Like It* 3.5.133.

# ❦ 3 ❧

## *DIKAIOSYNE*: FOUNDING THE JOHNS HOPKINS UNIVERSITY AND THE *AMERICAN JOURNAL OF PHILOLOGY*, 1875–1879

In seeking faculty for the new Johns Hopkins University, its first president, Daniel Coit Gilman (see "Correspondents"), visited Harvard, Yale, Princeton, Michigan, and Cornell. In the spring of 1875, he visited Cornell, Swarthmore, and the University of Virginia, and although his stay in Charlottesville was so short that some of the faculty felt overlooked,[1] he clearly had his eye on Gildersleeve: "I may be forgiven for bringing forth my treasured remembrance of the hour when we first met in old academic home, and when, all unsuspected by me, he was taking my measure for the office I was destined to fill."[2]

Gilman's first choice for the chair of Greek was the Harvard Hellenist William Watson Goodwin (1831–1912) (No. 50, n. 5), who had taken his Ph.D. from Göttingen in 1855, two years after Gildersleeve. Many of Gilman's first choices were from Harvard, partly because he did not want to raid his alma mater, Yale, and partly because some brilliant men, such as Francis J. Child (No. 21, n. 1), George Lane (No. 22, n. 1), and Goodwin, were not free to do their research at Harvard. Goodwin seemed especially amenable, since President Eliot was threatening to remove the Greek requirement for Harvard freshmen. On 27 October 1875 he formally declined, however, with the suggestion that Gilman try Gildersleeve. Following the interview in Washington (No. 16, n. 1), Gilman wrote Lane and Whitney (see "Correspondents"), both of whom had trained in Germany with Gildersleeve, and the Yale Latinist Thomas A. Thacher (1815–86). All three warmly endorsed him.[3]

Two features of Hopkins made Gildersleeve the ideal candidate. First, the entire university was founded on the German model and required not only familiars but advocates of the German system to make it work. Gildersleeve's published work showed him to be both.[4] Second, Johns Hopkins' will made special provision for the needs of Southerners (No. 18, n. 1). Gilman was eager to have an eminent Southerner so that the new university, situated in a Civil War border state, might have representation from both sides of the Potomac.

Circumstances in Gildersleeve's life also conspired to make him ripe for a change. He was certainly overtaxed with tedious undergraduate work (Nos. 29, 22). In his last year at the University of Virginia, Gildersleeve taught three levels of Greek, four hours per week of senior Greek, three hours each for juniors and intermediates, all involving "lectures (systematic and exegetical), examinations, written and oral exercises" in addition to "a private course of parallel and preparatory reading. . . also prescribed for each class." He also conducted the post-graduate department[5] and was obliged to teach Hebrew upon demand.[6] As a student said, it was "Socrates set to trundling a baby carriage,"[7] or as he himself put it,

> Diotimus, poor grammarian!
> If my heart hath pitied e'er a one,
>   It is he,
> Who, an almost centenarian,
> Perched upon "a peak in Darien,"
> Teaches little Jack and Mary Ann
>   A B C.[8]

Twenty-two years after receiving his Ph.D., his scholarly output consisted of his Latin series, which he called "decided failures" (No. 104), and his edition of Persius, which he called a "vacation study" (No. 14). Although professor of Greek, he had published nothing of book length on Greek subjects.

His personal life was altering in significant ways. Already forty-four, he had a growing family to support: Raleigh was six and Emma three. His salary had declined (No. 19, n. 2) because of vacillating policies that led to considerable insecurity from year to year (No. 35, n. 5). Moreover, on 20 June, his father died in Tazewell, Va., at the age of eighty-four, bringing Gildersleeve a sense of emergence from his father's shadow that he later described to his friend Hübner (No. 62). He was ready to turn to another strong father figure, albeit one of his own age. Gilman would guide his professional growth (Nos. 118, 131) as his father had formed his education.

Despite early conflicts with students and colleagues,[9] Gildersleeve was much loved and admired at the University of Virginia, and his poignant farewell shows his feeling for the school:

On Commencement Day [1875], . . . after the diplomas had been distributed and Dr. Harrison [see "Correspondents"] was about taking his seat, a wild cry for Gildersleeve rang throughout the Hall—an appeal that brought forth a sad response including these sentences: "In this Hall years ago I sat and heard Gessner Harrison [No. 5, n. 9] read his farewell because he could not trust himself to speak it, and even then he scarcely could proceed for the blinding tears. I thought at that time how glorious it must be for a man to stand as he then stood, with such an audience sobbing at his departure; but I little dreamed that I too would one day stand on the same spot and say good-bye to the same audience; I had not thought of saying farewell to you till I should bid the world good-night. Here to me love, labor and sorrow have found their keenest expression, while friendship for these colleagues around me has become the strongest—as between brothers—and the thought of separation saddens my heart. I may have spoken many ill-advised words since coming here, but have spoken naught in malice. I think I may say without fear of contradiction that I have striven faithfully to do my best; I hope some of my old pupils are not altogether ashamed of their preceptor; for them, at least, my heart swells with pride, and if I have turned out in the twenty years of my professional career only the one noble scholar who is to succeed me [No. 19, n. 4], I shall not think my life a failure. To the University I shall give my allegiance, her fame is mine, and her lofty standard of morals, her unswerving adherence to truth and purity, and all high and noble learning shall be my standard forever."[10]

With this goodnight, he once again moved north, leaving the pastoral simplicity of Charlottesville for the urban complexity of Baltimore, the "absolute independence" (No. 118) of Jefferson's old ideal for Gilman's ambitious notion of a university, which, according to Gildersleeve, "was the same as the Presbyterian's idea of heaven, namely, 'a place where meetings ne'er break up and congregations have no end.' "[11]

Getting the enterprise under way meant recruitment of faculty (Nos. 17, 25, 24) and students (Nos. 18, 20, 23, 26, 28–29) and fitting out offices (No. 27). Gildersleeve was Gilman's trusted confidant throughout the long and often trying process. Filling the Latin chair was one of the most perplexing problems; there were twenty applications, more than for any chair at the university,[12] but Gilman's first choice, Gildersleeve's Bonn and Göttingen classmate George M. Lane, did not come (Nos. 22, 25). Charles D'Urban Morris (1827–86) agreed to come as instructor for undergraduates and was an enthusiastic participant in the development of an English-style collegiate section at Hopkins, aided in teaching Latin by John M. Cross, the first registrar.

Gildersleeve also tried to secure a professor of English, but despite his efforts there was no English Department at Hopkins for the first three years of its life, although Gilman offered professorships to Henry Sweet (No. 45, and n. 7), William Dean Howells (No. 174, n. 2), and Edmund Gosse (1849–1928). By 1888 there was still no professor of English and the death of its lecturer Sidney Lanier in 1881 deprived the university of one of its best-known figures (No. 129). The English Department had centered around Albert S. Cook (see "Correspondents"), who was let go in 1881 in anticipation of Sweet's arrival, and Henry Wood (1849–1925), who became a Germanist in 1884. Gildersleeve's friend William Hand Browne (1828–

1912), who had no formal training in the field, but considerable experience as an editor (No. 12, n. 11), became lecturer in 1882 and then professor of English Literature in 1893.[13]

But the fledgling university felt its way cautiously forward, despite the real or imagined resentment of its competitors (No. 28, n. 1), who felt themselves Gilman's trout pools, much as Gildersleeve's personal enterprise, the *American Journal of Philology* (Nos. 36–38), was thought to compete with *Transactions of the American Philological Association* (No. 54, n. 4; No. 76).

The *American Journal of Philology* at first must have seemed to Gildersleeve a partial fulfillment of his adolescent dreams of becoming a journalist: again he worked, as he had for his father in 1845–46, as clerk and bookkeeper, putting together a publication; he came as close to being both a journalist and a classicist as he could, not only contributing to popular magazines such as the *Nation*, but ultimately writing a regular column, "Brief Mention." He wrote Walter Hines Page (see "Correspondents"), "If I had not been a philologian, I should have been a journalist and I can understand the fascination of the life. One can hardly be both— as I know by sad experience."[14] However keen his early enthusiasm for the *Journal*, he could scarcely have imagined at this date that he would edit what he called his "perpetual ball and chain" for forty years.[15]

1. *Hawkins*, 31.

2. "Address," *Daniel Coit Gilman: First President of the Johns Hopkins University, 1876–1901* (Baltimore: Johns Hopkins Press, 1908), 34.

3. Lane to Gilman, 6 December 1875; Thacher to Gilman, 13 December 1875; Whitney to Gilman, 12 December 1875.

4. "Necessity of the Classics," *Southern Quarterly Review* (Charleston) 26 (n.s. 10) (July 1853): 145–67; "Classical Study," *New Eclectic Magazine* 5 (October 1869): 385–94.

5. See Richard J. Storr, *The Beginnings of Graduate Education in America* (Chicago: University of Chicago Press, 1953), 157 and n. 45, and Mary B. Pierson, *Graduate Work in the South* (Chapel Hill: University of North Carolina Press, 1947), 34–35, 46, 57–59.

6. *University of Virginia Catalogue, 1875–1876*, 27–28; Nos. 7 and 8.

7. Felix Morley, "Basil Lanneau Gildersleeve," *Nation* 118 (23 January 1924): 84.

8. *H&H*, 14; see "St. Basil of Baltimore," *NYTimes*, 21 October 1923: section 2:6.

9. See introduction to chapter 2.

10. *Culbreth*, 400–401.

11. N. M. Butler, *Across the Busy Years* (New York: Scribner, 1939), 9.

12. Gilman to BLG, 29 March 1876.

13. See *Hawkins*, 49, 53, 73, 106, 163.

14. BLG to Page, 12 June 1883 [Houghton].

15. See No. 130.

15 To: DANIEL COIT GILMAN
*JHU-Gilman*

{University of Virginia}
Dec. 11th 1875

President D. C. Gilman
My dear Sir:
Accompanying this note you will find my formal letter of acceptance.
Let me say to you that your generous appreciation of my work as a teacher
has afforded me the greatest gratification—To such confidence as you
have reposed in me my whole nature responds with all its earnestness and I
shall enter upon my new duties with heightened interest because my success will be in a measure yours.

I shall begin at an early day to forecast my course. Some of it I can
prepare in perfect consonance with my present obligations. Much, however, will necessarily be left for the vacation, which I hope to be able to
devote to the service of the University untrammelled by other engagements.

Yours faithfully
B. L. Gildersleeve

16 To: DANIEL COIT GILMAN
*JHU-Gilman*

University of Virginia
Dec. 11th 1875

President D. C. Gilman
Johns Hopkins University
Sir:
Our full and free conference in Washington[1] removed any hesitation I
may have felt as to a change in my sphere of work and I now desire to state
in form that I find myself in perfect accord with your plans, and that under
the conditions which you propose I could give myself up without reserve to
the promotion of the important undertaking in which you have asked my
coöperation.

For the kind and cordial manner in which you communicated to me the
desires of the Executive Committee I renew my most sincere thanks.

I am
with high esteem
Yours very truly
B. L. Gildersleeve

1. In his eulogy of Gilman, Gildersleeve speaks of "my treasured remembrance of the
long consultation in Washington [8 December] when he invited me to share his work, and,

contrary to his wont, for he kept early hours, pursued until the night waxed old, the high theme of the University that was to be" ("Address," *Daniel Coit Gilman: First President of the Johns Hopkins University, 1876-1901* [Baltimore: Johns Hopkins Press, 1908], 34).

17 To: DANIEL COIT GILMAN
*JHU-Gilman*

University of Virginia
Dec. 20, 1875

My dear Sir:

Whatever overestimate you have made of my attainments you will find, I trust, that you have made no miscalculation as to my love of my work.

It is gratifying to me to learn that Latin scholars of eminence consider me competent to take charge of the Latin department but for the last twenty years Latin has been with me a subordinate study[1] and apart from my personal preferences I can do you more service in Greek—Perhaps when the University expands—it may be well to throw down the unnatural barriers between Latin and Greek of which Madvig complains so sorely[2] and let the professors interpret authors outside of their specific courses—

There is no question about Roby's eminent qualifications for the Latin Professorship as far as knowledge is concerned.[3] His name would be to the scholarly world a warrant of the high aims of the University. Of his didactic power I know nothing. For American young men, I should insist largely on intellectual alertness and most Englishmen turn slowly.

I have been thinking a great deal about my course, a little about the books, illustrations and the like. I will submit my views about the course before long in writing. The other subjects we can get at better by a talk, for which I will make memoranda.

The law requires me to tender my resignation here three months in advance. I should like to do this in April so that the Board of Visitors may be able to fill my place at the end of the session and my successor[4] may have time to prepare for his work. But if I do this, I shall forfeit my claim to the salary here from July to October, which I can not readily spare in existing circumstances. It would therefore be desirable to ascertain before the first of April, when my engagement is to begin. Of course I shall consider myself pledged to active work as soon as I enter formally into the engagement and I think I can turn the vacation to very good account.

At your request I send a memorandum of my expenses to Washington.

I am

with high regards
Yours faithfully
B. L. Gildersleeve

President D. C. Gilman

1.  Gildersleeve had been endorsed by Lane and Thacher (see introduction to this chapter) and was of course known principally for his Latin series (see No. 11, n. 1), but once having finished his edition of Persius, he concentrated on Justin Martyr.

2.  Johan Nicolai Madvig (1804–86), professor of Latin at Copenhagen (1829–86), twice minister of education and often Speaker of the Danish Parliament, was one of the most eminent textual critics of his time. For his views on Latin and Greek, see P. J. Jensen, *J. N. Madvig*, trans. André Nicolet (Odense: Odense University Press, 1981), 108–42. See also U. von Wilamowitz-Moellendorff, *History of Classical Scholarship*, trans. A. Harris (London: Duckworth, 1982), 132–33; H. Nettleship, "Johan Nicolai Madvig," in his *Lectures and Essays*, vol. 2, ed. F. Haverfield (Oxford: Clarendon Press, 1895), 1–23; and *Sandys*, 319.

3.  Henry John Roby (1830–1915), master at Dulwich College (1862–65, professor of jurisprudence, University College, London, 1866–68, had published his *Elementary Latin Grammar* in 1862 and followed it with his *Grammar of the Latin Language from Plautus to Suetonius* (1871–74), significant for being the first (and perhaps *only*) original grammar of Latin in English—i.e., one not based upon or translated from another (see No. 5, n. 15). But his great interest was school reform and he served on the Endowed Schools Commission from 1869 to 1874, after which he went into the sewing-cotton business and was ultimately elected to Parliament in 1890 (*DNB 1912–21*, 473–75). Roby had been suggested by George M. Lane (Lane to Gilman, 22 December 1875), but having been contacted by Lane on Gilman's behalf, declined consideration (Lane to Gilman 31 January 1876).

4.  For Thomas Randolph Price (1839–1903), see No. 19, n. 4 and No. 70, n. 3.


### 18 To: DANIEL COIT GILMAN
### *JHU-Gilman*

Dec. 30th 1875

My dear Sir:

On my return from Richmond I found your letter of the 22nd, inclosing a cheque for $12.[50]. Accept my thanks for your kind consideration.

Latin addresses itself to so wide a circle of students that I hope you will be able to get a strong man for that department. But in any case I will do my best for the University.

In order to get students from Virginia and North Carolina—especially from Virginia—some little pecuniary help would be desirable in addition to the relief from fees—enough, say, to outweigh the difference between living in a village and living in Baltimore.[1] These scholarships should, of course, be given for attainments. The examinations might be made local and in the case of good schools or colleges be left with the principals.

In this way I think we can attract some good material especially from the valley and lower tidewater Virginia—The Baltimore and Ohio R.R. ought to enable us to command West Virginia without difficulty.[2] Only there is not much material there.

As I understand my new work, my lowest level is to be the upper tier of my present Senior class in which I am doing some real University work. It will take two or three years of earnest effort to get our material up to that point. After that time I should not despair of fair success in the University part of our scheme.

I am, my dear sir,

Yours very truly

B. L. Gildersleeve

President Gilman

I have a strong impression that Wilhelm Wagner of Hamburg, who seems to be bilingual, would be a good man for your purposes.[3] He has edited Terence, Plato's Phaedo &c.—besides being a first-class man in other directions—

1. Johns Hopkins' will stated that free scholarships should be given to "such candidates from the States of Maryland, Virginia, and North Carolina as may be most deserving of choice." The trustees set ten scholarships of $500 for candidates "from any place" in philology, literature, history, ethics and metaphysics, political science, mathematics, engineering, physics, chemistry, and natural history. When a total of 152 applications were received by June 1876, the trustees doubled the number of scholarships and admitted twenty-one fellows for the first year, based, as in the English system, on merit, unlike Harvard's scholarships, which were based on need. See *French*, 40; *Franklin*, 11, 79–93.

2. Of the original twenty-one, two came from the University of Virginia (Joshua W. Gore, mathematics, and Alexander Duncan Savage [see "Correspondents"], philology) and Walter Hines Page (see "Correspondents") came from Randolph-Macon, but these were the only Southern schools represented.

3. Wilhelm Wagner (1843–80), professor of Latin at the Johanneum (gymnasium) in Hamburg, produced for the publishers Deighton, Bell these texts with English commentary: *Terence: Comoediae*, in the "Cambridge Greek and Latin Texts" series (Cambridge: 1869; reprinted 1878, 1883, 1885, 1892); *Plato: Phaedo* (London: 1870; Boston: J. Allyn, 1873); and Plautus's *Aulularia* (London: 1866), *Trinummus* (London: 1872), and *Menaechmi* (London: 1878). He may be best remembered for editing Richard Bentley's *Dissertations upon the Epistles of Phalaris, Themistocles, Socrates, Euripides, and upon the Fables of Aesop*, (Berlin: S. Calvary, 1874). See J. Glucker, "Professor Key and Doctor Wagner," *Pegasus* 12 (June 1969): 21–41.

19 To: JOHN HAMPDEN CHAMBERLAYNE
*Virginia Historical Society*

{University of Virginia}
Jan$^y$ 6$^{th}$ 1875 [1876]

My dear Chamberlayne:

If in removing to Baltimore I had to give up my Virginia friends, I should not accept any offers of ease or emolument but to some of them, as to you, I shall be nearer in space, to none of them, I trust, more distant in heart. The flower of my life, and flower it has been, has been consecrated to Virginia, and no such friendships can bloom for me elsewhere.

I leave the University simply because my position is untenable. I cannot live here without doing drudgery inside the school and outside,[1] which would rapidly use up what resources of mind and body I have left. It is far from certain that I shall better my pecuniary condition much by the change to a large city even with a considerable increase of salary,[2] but I shall at least be relieved from teaching the bare elements of my department and I shall have leisure to gather up and systematize the results of my work here. "Pelf and praise" I do not expect. I have a singular inaptitude for making or saving money and an utter repugnance to the ordinary means of acquiring reputation. I have lived well so far if bene qui latuit bene vixit[3] is true, and I am content to live well to the end. But to such recognition as yours of my work as a teacher all the titillable surface of /my/ heart is open and your letter has given me much more pleasure than scores of 'complimentary notices' could do.

I hope that Price[4] will be unanimously elected. If he is not to be my successor, I shall feel that my work at the University ends with me.

My wife thanks you for your kind remembrance of her.

Present my best regards to the ladies of your household.[5]

Yours faithfully,
B. L. Gildersleeve

1. In No. 22 Gildersleeve lists the advantages of Johns Hopkins, which manifest his sense of overwork and frustration in Charlottesville (see introduction to this chapter), but elsewhere (No. 118) he speaks of "the absolute independence" he enjoyed at the University of Virginia.

2. The figure was $5,000 (*Hawkins*, 129). He made $3,000–4,000 at the University of Virginia in 1857 (see No. 6), but sank to $1,905 in 1866–67. From 1870 to 1876, the maximum salary was $3,000. Of the other four original Hopkins professors, Sylvester managed to talk Gilman into a salary of $6,000, while Remsen and Rowland were given $3,000 each. On Sylvester's salary, see No. 30.

3. Ovid *Tristia* 3.4.25: "He has lived well who has lain well hidden."

4. Thomas Randolph Price (1839–1903), a classmate of his fellow Richmonder Chamberlayne's at the University of Virginia (1858), was elected and left Randolph-Macon to serve as professor of Greek from 1876 to 1882, when he went to Columbia. See, further, No. 70, n. 3.

5. Chamberlayne married Mary Walker Gibson (d. 1905) of Petersburg. His sister, Lucy Parke Chamberlayne (1842–1927), married the Virginia humorist George W. Bagby (*Va. Hist. Mag.* 36 [1928]: 228).

20 To: DANIEL COIT GILMAN
*JHU-Gilman*

University of Virginia
Jan<u>y</u> 8<u>th</u> 1875 [1876]

President D. C. Gilman:
My dear Sir—

As you seem to be in no haste about a Professor of Latin, I will make inquiries about Wagner,[1] although I am not sanguine of obtaining such information as I should desire. Of Wagner's attainments there can not be a moment's question and his reputation is a very wide one. I should only wish to satisfy myself as to his capacity as a teacher and his character as a man.

Your circular[2] suggests so many points of discussion that I am afraid of waxing prolix, if I trim them all up. How many of the twenty scholarships would you give to Virginia and North Carolina? Six to each? If the bill now pending in the Virginia legislature to make the University of Virginia a free school for Virginians should pass,[3] it would be hard to attract Virginians to Baltimore by free scholarships, and I hope you will succeed in getting the scholarships further endowed by private liberality. I take for granted that the Trustees, with the practical sagacity that has marked their whole administration, have looked into the matter of securing lodging and board for students at reasonable rates.[4] I understand that Berlin regained its lost ground last year by the establishment of a cheap refectory and now leads Leipzig handsomely.

I should not have the least objection to visiting Richmond, Staunton and Raleigh for the purpose of holding examinations.[5] Only I would suggest Winchester and Lynchburg as better points than Staunton. Perhaps, however, it would be best to make no formal announcement through the papers. At the next meeting of the Educational Association of Virginia with which I have been more or less prominently connected for the last seven years, I could find out the best young men at the various schools and could feel my way toward valuable connections for the University. Our experience here is not very encouraging as to competitive examinations. Of the eleven University scholarships offered not one has ever been taken, at least to my knowledge, and we have seldom had an application.[6] The best plan would be to give a general scheme of the examinations and intrust the details to the teachers—with the proviso that the teachers are to submit the papers to the representatives of the University for approval in advance of the examinations so as to secure a sufficient standard. But many of the best schools of Virginia I would trust implicitly—

My plan of work for the summer would involve a visit to the important points of Virginia, Tennessee and Kentucky, where I could hope to exercise personal influence, in a quiet way. I should travel not as a /professed/ agent but /simply/ as a professor on vacation—but, of course, if the subject of the new University should come up, as it would, I could not be churlish enough to withhold any information that I might possess. If we can offer an honest college course leading up to higher University instruction, I do not see why we might not make a respectable beginning even though we may have to work with rather unpromising material. For my part I should be disinclined to publish an ambitious University programme, which might fall through as at Harvard for lack of students.[7] By far the best plan would be the one which you suggested—pick out the best material that offers and organize that for University work. The rest must be ground through the college mill.[8] Of course the University classes would necessarily be very small—but the lower courses might be so arranged as to bring every student into personal contact with the presiding professor—In a few years by a system of cooperation with the colleges, we might gradually dispense with the more elementary classes. In this connection I would mention that I am much concerned to learn from my friend and pupil Prof. Maupin[9] of the Baltimore City College that a move is making against the salaries of the Professors in that institution. Such a step would drive away competent men like Maupin and deprive us of an important feeder.

Other points I will reserve for future letters—

I am

with great respect

Yours sincerely

B. L. Gildersleeve

1. No. 19.

2. The first of the *JHU Circulars* was an octavo describing the curriculum and faculty of the university. In December 1879 the *Circulars* took quarto form in imitation of the Cambridge *University Reporter* (*Hawkins*, 110).

3. In the winter of 1875–76, the General Assembly of Virginia granted every student from Virginia above the age of eighteen admission to the university without tuition fees, provided that the candidates passed admission tests designed by the faculty. These examinations were given all over the state, and though the first in 1878 were not well attended, the number of applicants grew in the ensuing years (*Bruce*, 3: 383).

4. There was no provision for student living accommodations in the early days. Since the depression of 1873 followed upon the effects of the Civil War, there was no shortage of homes willing to take in student boarders. The most popular area was north of the university in the area known as the "Latin Quarter," two blocks of McCulloh Street, where respectable rooms could be had for $6 per month; board was under $4 per week (*French*, 76–77).

5. Examinations were not held, and admission was strictly through application and the composition of essays on one's specialty (see No. 26).

6. The board of visitors established the eleven university scholarships in 1871, apportioning "five to the academic department, and two each in the departments of law, of medicine and of industrial chemistry, civil and mining engineering, and agriculture" (*University of Virginia Catalogue*, 1871–72). These scholarships were given up when free in-state tuition was declared by the General Assembly (*Bruce*, 4: 20–21).

7. In January 1870 Harvard announced eighteen series of lectures in two courses, philosophy and modern languages and literatures, as a means of teaching postgraduates. There were required readings and examinations for the students and a fee of $150 (the same as undergraduate tuition), but in the first year only nine students enrolled, despite such lecturers as Ralph Waldo Emerson on the "Natural History of the Intellect" and William Dean Howells on the "New Italian Literature." In 1872 thirty-five series of lectures were announced with fees as low as $3, and no fees for undergraduates, with similarly low enrollment. The lectures were done away with and the Harvard Graduate Department, later the Graduate School of

Arts and Sciences, was established in 1872. The first graduate courses appeared in 1875–76 (S. E. Morison, *Three Centuries of Harvard* [Cambridge, Mass.: Harvard University Press, 1946], 332–34). For C. W. Eliot on Harvard's weak graduate school and its debt to Hopkins, see *Franklin*, 389.

8. As early as 1871, Gilman had envisaged a graduate university only, and this idea seems to have persisted until January 1875. But by the time he took office, he realized that in the interests of public service, examinations and degrees for non-students, and reaching the public and professionals with its publications, the university required a collegiate section (Gilman, "Hopkins Inaugural," *Addresses at the Inauguration of Daniel C. Gilman as President of the Johns Hopkins University, Baltimore, February 22, 1876* [Baltimore: Johns Hopkins University Press, 1876], 34–35; *Hawkins*, 65–66). Gildersleeve was from the first freed from undergraduate teaching.

9. See No. 11, n. 5.

### 21 To: Henry Elliott Shepherd
### *JHU-BLG*

University of Virginia
Feb. 23ᵈ 1875[6]

Prof. H. E. Shepherd:
Dear Sir:
Several months ago I promised my influence, such as it is, to another candidate for the Chair of English Literature in the Hopkins University and took active steps to further the interest of that gentleman;[1] and, while I recognize your high attainments and your eminent fitness for such a position, I cannot, consistently with my engagements, do any thing that might seem to interfere with the prospects of the candidate, to whom I refer.

I am
With great respect
Yours truly
B. L. Gildersleeve

1. It is likely that Gildersleeve means his friend Francis James Child (1825–96) (No. 97), who studied at Berlin and attended Göttingen one year earlier (Michaelmas 1850–Easter 1851) than Gildersleeve and received his degree one year later (1854). He was teaching elementary courses and grading "themes" at Harvard when he was offered the chair of English at Hopkins in 1875 (Child to Gilman, 19 December 1875; see *Franklin*, 235–36). Like W. W. Goodwin (No. 50, n. 5), he was somewhat disaffected by the new trends at Harvard (see Goodwin to Gilman, 3 July 1875; *Hawkins*, 49–50) and seemed to hold out the promise of coming to fill the Hopkins chair, but after four months of agonizing and conferring, Child declined the permanent offer.

22 To: Daniel Coit Gilman
*JHU-Gilman*

University of Virginia
Feb͟ 29͟t͟h͟ 1876

Prof. D. C. Gilman:
My dear Sir—
.  I have written a long letter to Lane.[1] Bearing in mind his communication to you, I have made my approaches from the basis of my own case, which is in many respects parallel with his and I have emphasized these points:
1. Relief from the drudgery of elementary instruction.
2. Relief from the necessity of outside employment for bare subsistence.
3. Consequent opportunity for work on a higher plane.
4. Liberal views of the trustees both for institution and professors.
5. The pleasure of coöperating with such a man as our President.
I also dwelt somewhat on
6. the social aspects of Baltimore life
7. the library question
As Lane lives near a large city and knows the details of city life, he will be able to calculate for himself what the difference of emolument will amount to <u>practically</u> and I have not ventured to make any positive statement on a subject, which still keeps my own mind somewhat exercised—Indeed I have avoided throughout all exaggeration, which would not fail to reach. Of course my letter was unaffectedly cordial as I have a sincere affection for Lane despite our long separation and his long silence—

Very truly yours
B. L. Gildersleeve

1.  George Martin Lane (1823-97), a native of Boston, graduated in the Harvard Class of 1846 with Child and Norton and was a "Charlestownian" among the Charlestonians at Göttingen, where he lived with G. W. Dingle (see No. 12, n. 17) at Dorotheenstrasse 91 in 1849-50. In 1851 he lived in the same rooming-house in Bonn as Gildersleeve and in the same year took his degree from Göttingen. He also took courses at Berlin and Heidelberg. Succeeding Carl Beck (1798-1866) as professor of Latin at Harvard (1851-94), he combined the English literary taste with the exactitude of German scholarship. He is best remembered for his *Latin Grammar*, finished by his student M. H. Morgan in 1898 (New York: Harper and Bros.), and his contributions to Lewis and Short's *Latin Dictionary* (*Sandys*, 456-57). Lane had been a trusted adviser of Gilman's since he first suggested Gildersleeve for the Greek chair, and when Roby did not accept (see No. 17, n. 3), Gilman wrote Lane and received the encouraging response that the salary and opportunity to join Gildersleeve were tempting (Lane to Gilman, 15 February 1876). See, further, Nos. 24-25. In June 1898 Lane's son, Gardiner Martin Lane (see "Correspondents"), married Emma Louise Gildersleeve (Nos. 107, 108). See further *AJP*

19 (1898): 344; W. W. Goodwin, "Memoir of George Martin Lane," *Publ. Col. Soc. Mass.* 6 (1900): 97-105; and M. H. Morgan's "Memoir of George M. Lane, with portrait," *HSCP* 9 (1898): 1-12.

### 23 To: DANIEL COIT GILMAN
*JHU-Gilman*

March 23, 1876

Prof. D. C. Gilman:
My dear Sir—

Mr. E. T. [sic] Sihler[1] of Fort Wayne Ind. wrote to me several months ago and submitted testimonials from Ritschl[2] and Hübner,[3] which show that he is an honest, earnest, thoroughgoing student of unusual attainments for his years and absorbing devotion to philological pursuits. He now writes that he would like to be made a fellow of the Johns Hopkins University and I think that he would not be a bad appointment.[4] Indeed it was in my mind to mention his case when I was in Baltimore but in the multiplicity of things to be discussed Mr. Sihler was passed over.

I take him to be a very unworldly young man and he is clearly defective in aesthetic finish but he may ripen into something good and I hope you will take his case into kind consideration.

Yours faithfully
B. L. Gildersleeve

1. Ernest Gottlieb Sihler (1853-1942) studied at Berlin and Leipzig (1872-75). In 1878 he received the first Ph.D. in Greek given by Hopkins. He was named professor of Latin at New York University in 1892 and held the post until his retirement in 1923. His chief works include *A Complete Lexicon of the Latinity of Caesar's Gallic War* (Boston: Ginn, 1891), *Cicero of Arpinum* (New Haven: Yale University Press, 1914; 2d ed; 1933), and *Hellenic Civilization* (with G. W. Botsford) (New York: New York University Press, 1915; reprt. New York: Octagon Books, 1965). He summarized articles in *Hermes* for *AJP*, vols. 1-14, but Gildersleeve voiced his displeasure about him more than once to Hübner. See his autobiography, *From Maumee to Thames and Tiber: The Life-Story of an American Classical Scholar* (New York: New York University Press, 1930).

2. Friedrich Wilhelm Ritschl (1806-76), left his post at Breslau in November 1836 and went to Milan, where he struggled to decipher the Ambrosian palimpsest of Plautus, returning home on 2 August 1837. See Gildersleeve's "Friedrich Ritschl," *AJP* 5 (1884): 349-50. Like Gildersleeve, Ritschl was a "parson's son" who was given elementary instruction by his father and who "radiated love and kindness," but was also "a pugnacious, high-tempered man." Gildersleeve calls him "the greatest master of his time" and kept a bust of Ritschl on his desk all his life. See also *Professorial Types*: 8, and "Personal Reminiscences of Friedrich Ritschl," *PAPA* 8 (1877): 14-15. Ritschl was the more personable, Boeckh was aloof; see R. L. Fowler, "The Gildersleeve Archive," *Briggs-Benario*, 62. The chief biography is Lucian Mueller, *Friedrich Ritschl: Eine Wissenschaftliche Biographie* (Berlin: S. Calvary, 1877).

3. See "Correspondents."

4. In Hopkins' first year, Sihler gave three lectures on "Attic Life and Society" and a course on Aristophanes' *Acharnians* to two undergraduates (Sihler [cited n. 1 above], 103).

24 To: Daniel Coit Gilman
*JHU-Gilman*

University of Virginia
March 25ᵗʰ 1876

President D. C. Gilman:

My dear Sir—

I hope Mr. Sihler's case[1] is a sample of the kind of men who will desire the fellowship of the Johns Hopkins. Like you, I am a firm believer in young men and ten earnest fellows in love with their work will constitute a far more important element of true success than men of routine, who have lost their spring, though much better known. If I were choosing professors for a University I should be very slow to consider the claims of experienced schoolmasters, as such.[2]

Of Mr. Thomas Davidson I know little.[3] He has written one or two very elaborate commendations of the Allen and Greenough Series[4] which the Ginns print very conspicuously in their advertisements so that I suppose they attach a good deal of importance to his opinion but I have never seen anything else of his except two of his pupils from the St. Louis High School who were in my junior class last session.

I shall try to come to some conclusion as to the address before the National Association by the end of next month—but the other address, which you expect of me, is so much more important that I shall sacrifice the nation to Baltimore remorselessly, if need be.

I still incline to Sept. as the best time for the scholarship examinations. Sept. may be pleasant, but July will certainly be disagreeable and at Richmond we shall find every body out of town. On the other hand I appreciate the evils of postponement. How would it answer if I should write confidential letters to the leading teachers of the state and inquire what promising boys of theirs would like to go to Baltimore. In this way we might possibly secure candidates both at Richmond and at Staunton and I must confess I should be unwilling to fail of having applications for our scholarships. This part of our plans requires the most careful handling as what part does not?

Lane is still silent.[5] I look forward to his decision with great anxiety.

Yours faithfully
B. L. Gildersleeve

1. See preceding letter.

2. Presumably he means Davidson (see following note), but he may also refer to Charles D'Urban Morris, who became collegiate professor of Latin at Hopkins in 1876, or Saintsbury (No. 73, n. 11).

3. Thomas Davidson (1840-1900) distinguished himself as a classical student at Aberdeen and for a time (1860-66) taught Greek and Latin first in his native Scotland, then in England. After teaching and administering in the progressive St. Louis public school system headed by the Hegelian W. T. Harris, he returned to Boston in 1875, where William James endeavored to find him a place in the Classics Department at Harvard. Davidson was chosen to serve on a committee to study the condition of classics at Harvard, but his report (see his "The Study of Greek at Harvard," in the *Atlantic* 39 [January 1877]: 123-28, and his letter on the reaction, ibid. [March 1877]: 386-88) cast the department in a poor light, and his application for a Harvard post was rejected. Gilman was advised by others against him (*Hawkins*, 55 and n. 68), and although Davidson failed to secure a post in America, he was an enthusiastic early contributor to *AJP*, providing six notes, four reviews, and two reports on other journals to vols. 1-5 (BLG to Davidson, 9 August 1879, 8 October 1879). In 1883 he founded the Fellowship of the New Life in London, which in the next year developed into the Fabian Society. *DAB*, 3: 95-97; *NatCAB*, 23: 311-12.

4. See No. 126, n. 2.

5. See following letter.

<br>

25 To: DANIEL COIT GILMAN
*JHU-Gilman*

University of Virginia
April 1, 1876

Prof. D. C. Gilman:

My dear Sir—

Your letters of the 29th and 30th all reached me at the same time.

So far as my part of the programme is concerned, I think it would be better to announce twenty lectures beginning in October, three a week.[1] These twenty lectures will occupy every spare moment of my time for the next six months and I doubt whether I should be able to give them the requisite literary finish even in that time.[2] The interval of a day between the lectures would be a welcome breathing spell. I suppose 'show lectures' of this kind would be expected only once a year. In the latter term I should choose some scientific subject, which would not require so much on the form.[3]

My subject for October will be 'Greek Lyric Poetry'.

I will form a class in Thucydides, as this author will enable me to adapt my instruction to my material.[4] If I am fortunate enough to get good men, I can confine myself to the speeches; if the students are not so well prepared, I can still reach them at some points.

You were /so/ kind as to promise me to consider any applications I should make for the books necessary to prepare for my work next autumn and I will send you in a few days a list of such ~~recent~~ works on Lyric poetry and Thucydides as ought to be in our library. The complete list of the 'working library' in Greek I hope to have ready in time.

I hardly dared hope for any other answer from Lane and yet so much of my usefulness, to say nothing of my comfort, depends on the hearty cooperation of my Latin yoke fellow, that I hoped against hope.[5] As to the candidates on your list, I should have no trouble with Blair[6] or with Packard[7] (the Princeton man?). Greenough[8] I know only by his connection with the Allen series—which I can hardly judge impartially. Humphreys[9] we discussed in Balt.

If I am to deliver an inaugural, give me fair warning.[10]

Yours faithfully

B. L. Gildersleeve

1. The twenty lectures on Greek Lyric Poetry began 4 October (*JHU Reports* [1877] [ = *JHU Circulars*, no. 7 (February 1877): 73]).

2. Gildersleeve believed the subject matter of a lecture required "the living, plastic forces of personal research and personal communion with the sources" (*E&S*, 75).

3. In the second semester, Gildersleeve gave one lecture per week "On the Syntax of the Greek Verb" to nine students and, beginning in March, two lectures a week on Pindar. His Philological Seminary with six students met once a week after 6 December.

4. The Pedagogical Seminary on Thucydides had eight meetings with nine students.

5. On Lane, see No. 22, n. 1. Gilman to Gildersleeve, 29 March 1876: "Lane's letter came today—'declined with thanks'—So we go. Among other names to be thought of now will be Davidson/Blair/Humphreys/Packard/Nash/[Dr. Julius] Sachs &c &c &c. I feel great solicitude in the matter, & shall listen with great interest to your suggestions."

6. Walter Blair (1835–1909), an 1855 graduate of Hampden-Sydney, was hired as tutor there in the year of his graduation and by 1859 was professor of Latin. From 1859 to 1862 he studied in Germany but left without a degree to join the Richmond Howitzers, in which he served until the end of the war. He resumed his post at Hampden-Sydney after the war until 1896, when poor eyesight obliged him to resign. His *Latin Pronunciation: An Inquiry into the Proper Sounds of the Latin Language during the Classical Period* (New York: A. S. Barnes, 1873) and several essays on the topic aided Gildersleeve's campaign to introduce European theories of Latin pronunciation to the South (see No. 5 and n. 9). *NatCAB*, 16: 142.

7. An odd candidate for the Latin post, Lewis Richard Packard (1836–84) was professor of Greek at Yale (1863–84) and, with J. W. White (No. 50, n. 9), planned a "College Series of Greek Authors," but he died suddenly from a virus contracted in Athens and T. D. Seymour (see "Correspondents") assumed his editorial responsibilities. Packard's essays were posthumously collected and published as *Studies in Greek Thought* (Boston: Ginn, 1886), and he was president of the APA in 1880–81 (*Sandys*, 463–64).

8. Having failed to acquire Lane, Gilman suggested his colleague, James Bradstreet Greenough (1833–1901), who, after practicing law in Michigan, was tutor (1865) in Latin at Harvard, then assistant professor (1873), and finally professor from 1883 to 1901. Greenough attempted to do for Latin what Goodwin's *Syntax of the Moods and Tenses of the Greek Verb* had done for Greek. His *Analysis of the Latin Subjunctive* (Cambridge: J. Wilson, 1870), became the basis of his *Latin Grammar Founded on Comparative Grammar* (with the Rev. Joseph Henry Allen, D.D. [1820–98]), which came out the same year (Boston: Ginn, 1872) as

the revised edition of Gildersleeve's *Latin Grammar* (see No. 11, n. 1). He gave the first lectures at Harvard on Sanskrit and comparative philology (1872-80), produced texts of Caesar, Cicero, Horace, Livy, Ovid, Sallust, and Virgil for "Allen and Greenough's Latin Series," and was instrumental in founding *HSCP* (G. L. Kittredge, *HSCP* 14 [1903]: 1-16; *Sandys*, 458-59; *DAB* 4: 588-89).

9. Milton Wylie Humphreys (1844-1928) interrupted his studies at Washington College (now Washington and Lee University) to join the Virginia Light Artillery in 1862. He returned to Washington College in 1866 and graduated valedictorian in 1869. He remained to teach ancient languages as assistant and adjunct professor until 1875, with two years out for study in Leipzig, where he took the Ph.D. in 1874. He took particular interest in new schools and in September 1875 became the first professor of Greek at the new Vanderbilt University, where he stayed until he was called to be professor of Latin and Greek at the new University of Texas (1883-87). He followed Gildersleeve, T. R. Price, and J. H. Wheeler as professor of Greek at the University of Virginia, serving twenty-five years (1887-1912). A frequent contributor to *TAPA* and *AJP* on metrical and linguistic matters, he produced notable editions of Aristophanes' *Clouds* (Boston: Ginn, Heath, 1885), Sophocles' *Antigone* (New York: Harper and Bros., 1891), and Demosthenes' *On the Crown* (Smyth series) (New York: American Book Co., 1913). Gildersleeve speaks at *H&H*, 114, of "his exact command of all the canons of literature and science." See, further, *DAB* 5: 377-78.

10. There were no inaugural lectures by Hopkins professors.

### 26 To: Walter Hines Page
#### *Houghton*

University of Virginia
June 9th 1876

Prof. Walter Page
Dear Sir:

The essay, which you have submitted, however creditable to you as a writer of English, can hardly be considered such a proof of philological attainments as the Board expects.[1] One of our candidates for a fellowship has sent in two elaborate essays—one in Latin—on the traces of parody in the Attic comic poets;[2] another has been pursuing Sanskrit studies for several years.[3]

I would advise you to select some philological subject within the compass of your reading and do your best at it. Prof. Price,[4] who knows your course of study, will no doubt take pleasure in indicating the scope of your thesis.

I will return your papers when I hear from you again.

Yours truly
B. L. Gildersleeve

1. No sooner did Page receive this judgment than he asked Gilman to be released from consideration. His name had already been published on the list of fellowship winners, however, and Gildersleeve was obliged to ask him to write a second essay. Gildersleeve clearly

placed high value on Price's recommendation and, trying to give his seminar "quite a national air," with Sihler from the West (Indiana) and Wheeler and Lanman from the North, he was keen to have a Southerner, and especially one of literary ability. Page, at twenty-one the youngest of the fellows, was entirely educated by Southern denominational schools and had never traveled north of Ashland, Va. He reluctantly accepted the fellowship in August. See John Milton Cooper, *Walter Hines Page: The Southerner as American, 1855-1918* (Chapel Hill: University of North Carolina Press, 1977), 29-30.

2. Sihler had spent the previous winter preparing a monograph, *The Historical Aspect of Old Attic Comedy*, an abridgment of which he submitted to Hopkins (along with his Leipzig dissertation, *De parodiis comicorum Graecorum*) and read at the 1876 meeting of the American Philological Association before an audience containing March, Whitney, Goodwin, and Gildersleeve (Sihler [No. 23, n. 1], 91).

3. Charles Rockwell Lanman (1850-1941) received his A.B. (1871) and Ph.D. (1873) from Yale, where he was a student of Whitney's, and had spent 1873-76 at Berlin and Tübingen, where he studied under Whitney's teacher, Roth. After receiving a Ph.D. from Leipzig in 1875, he became associate in Sanskrit at Hopkins (1877-80) and then professor of Sanskrit at Harvard (1880-1926). For Page's portrait of Lanman's work and living conditions at Hopkins, see *Hawkins*, 84. See, further, *DAB* Suppl. 3, 444-45.

4. For Price, see No. 19, n. 4; No. 79, n. 3.


27 To: DANIEL COIT GILMAN
*JHU-Gilman*

University of Virginia
June 23$^{\underline{d}}$ 1876

My dear Sir:

I return Hewett's[1] letter. He may be worth considering in the later development of our plans.

Sihler is going in with great enthusiasm—proposes to study Plato's literary art for the first part of the year and to lecture on A.'s Wasps in the spring.[2] I inclose his letter as the shortest way of showing you his spirit.

His modest list of books is approved and I will supplement it at my earliest leisure. I think S. will be a useful coadjutor in the 'Greek Bureau of Observation', which I propose to establish at the J.H.—

The scholarships will not go begging. /I have/ got two more letters on the subject in the last two days and I am confident that many are looking forward to a course at the J.H. as the crown of their academic studies.

You were kind enough to say something about furnishing my office in Howard St.[3] with shelves while the carpenters are still at work. I shall need some 120 feet of shelving for my private library and for such university books as I shall have in use—the shelves from 9 inches to 12 apart with a small section for folios. Will any provision be made for /other/ office furniture?

My present plan is to go on to Staunton at 4:45 A.M. of the 30$^{\underline{th}}$. If you could come to this point on Thursday, we could go up together.[4] I should be delighted to have you under my roof—although I can not make you as comfortable as I might hope to do at a less crowded period of the session.

Yours faithfully
B. L. Gildersleeve

President Gilman

1. Waterman Thomas Hewett (1846–1921) received his A.B. from Amherst in 1869 and studied at Heidelberg for one year before taking a position at Cornell in the Department of North European Languages (1870–77). Failing to be considered at Hopkins, he studied further at Leipzig, Berlin, and Leyden for another year and received his Ph.D. from Cornell in 1879, where he remained as professor of German from 1883 to 1910. He was chiefly known for his *Poems of Uhland* (New York: Macmillan, 1896) and his *Cornell University: A History*, 4 vols. (New York: University Publishing Society, 1905). See *DAB* 4: 603–4.

2. Sihler gave three lectures on "Attic Life and Society" and a course in Aristophanes' *Acharnians* to "two advanced undergraduates from Kentucky" in 1876–77 (Sihler, [see No. 23, n. 1], 103–4).

3. In 1875 the trustees had purchased two buildings for $75,000 on the west side of North Howard Street whose backyards fronted Little Ross Street as a "temporary" site, which continued in use for nearly thirty years. The two houses were joined under one roof during the course of renovations costing over $1 million. Gildersleeve's office and *seminarium* were on the second floor of 181 North Howard St.

4. Gilman met Gildersleeve in Charlottesville early in the morning of Friday the 30th. They went on together to Staunton, where they interviewed "several callers" in the morning and in the afternoon visited the site where Gildersleeve had been wounded in the Civil War. From there they went by night to Richmond to meet the next day with the governor, the superintendent of schools, and other dignitaries (Gilman to Elizabeth Gilman, 2 July 1876, quoted in *Franklin*, 410–11).

### 28 To: DANIEL COIT GILMAN
*JHU-Gilman*

University of Virginia
July 8th 1876

President D. C. Gilman
My dear Sir:

Your letter or rather your envelope inclosing your cheque for $30 was received yesterday shortly after I reached home. My expenses will be covered by three dollars ($3).

I hope that my visit to Richmond was not without good results although the meeting of the Educational Association was so thin that I could not reach as many as I could have wished. My address on the subject of German universities and the Johns Hopkins was purely extemporaneous but, I have been assured, not the less effective on that account. Unfortunately when called on by the representative of the Enquirer for a synopsis of my remarks I found that much had faded out of my memory and I was obliged to make anew the most important part of the discourse and sat up until one o'clock in the morning to see it safely through the press.[1] I have had two copies sent to you—There is but one slight error of the press—'professional' career—instead of 'professorial.' From what I can gather this statement will disarm all animosity against the University and prepare the way for the friendly relations, which you know so well how to establish and strengthen.

I hope I have not gone beyond my lesson in any essential particular.

On the train from Weldon to Richmond, I fell in with Senator Ransom of N.C.[2]—father of one of my pupils—a very bright young man. In the course of conversation the plans of the J.H.U. were brought up quite naturally and he seemed to be much delighted with our scheme and expressed the intention of sending his son next winter. The father and son are worth the trip to N.C.—

As soon as I am a little recovered from the strain of the last three weeks I shall go to work on the organization of the Greek department.

Yours faithfully

B. L. Gildersleeve

1. The Virginia State Educational Association had met in Richmond 5–7 July. At the meeting on the 6th, Gildersleeve had been asked by the president at the public meeting to speak on the subject of the new university. The front-page account in the *Richmond Enquirer*, 7 July 1876, reads in part: "[Hopkins] does not enter into competition with any college, or with any university which aims at a general, liberal education. . . . If these men can be gathered from the different colleges in the country and brought together under the guidance of teachers who have devoted their lives to special studies, a nucleus will be formed from which nothing is to be feared for the success of other institutions, everything to be hoped for the advancement of the higher learning in this country."

2. Matt Whitaker Ransom (1826–1904), a Democratic senator, was first elected in 1872 and served until 1895. His son, Matt Whitaker Ransom, Jr., attended the University of Virginia for one year, 1873–74, but did not attend Hopkins.

29 To: ALEXANDER DUNCAN SAVAGE
*UVa-Savage*

Crawford's Springs[1]
Pond Gap, Augusta C° V<u>a</u>.
Aug. 7, 1876

A. Duncan Savage Esq
My dear Sir:

Your letter and telegram were directed to the Johns Hopkins. Hence this delay. Mr. Gilman writes me that he has offered you the fellowship and I am glad to learn that you have resolved to cast in your lot with us. Members of the Board with whom I have conversed are favorably impressed with your renunciation of lucrative employment in order to pursue your studies and I hope that the fellowship will prove a stepping stone to something better than you have given up.

I know no one whom I could recommend for the position which you have relinquished.[2] Few students leave the University with an adequate knowledge of French and German for conducting higher instruction in those languages.

Hoping to see you in a few weeks

I am

Yours faithfully
B. L. Gildersleeve

1. Crawford's Springs is unknown today. It may have been one of the Variety Springs, a series of fountains containing alum, chalybeate, and several other salts, in Augusta County, Va., seventeen miles SSW of Staunton and approximately four miles from Pond Gap, on the ridge of Little North Mountain. See J. J. Moorman, M.D., *Mineral Springs of North America: How to Reach, and How to Use Them* (Philadelphia: Lippincott, 1873), 151.

2. Savage was teaching school in Kingston, N.Y.

30 To: DANIEL COIT GILMAN
*JHU-Gilman*

[Aug. 7, 1876]<br>Pond Gap, Augusta C<u>o</u> V<u>a</u>

My dear Sir:

I have written to Savage and to Page. If Page can take a hint, he will understand from my tone that we should prefer a postponement of his acceptance.[1]

The draft of the circular was sent to you yesterday.

Mr. Sylvester is an illustrious man and I shall not undertake to criticize the action of the Board in his case but, if peculiar circumstances are to influence the maximum and new professors are to be added to the corps under more favorable conditions, I, for one, shall feel that my tenure is precarious, as self-respect may at any time compel me to relinquish a work to which I pledged myself with the understanding that my rank was to be equal to that of any other professor.[2]

Yours very truly
B. L. Gildersleeve

1. Page caught the hint but did not take it and wrote Gildersleeve his acceptance on 11 September 1876.

2. James Joseph Sylvester (1814–97), a brilliant but eccentric English mathematician, had taken high honors from Cambridge in 1837 but had later been denied a post because he

was a Jew. He taught at the University of Virginia (1841–42), but left amid controversy (*Bruce*, 3: 73–77; Wall [No. 6, n. 10], 108–9), and was professor of mathematics at the Royal Military Academy at Woolwich from 1855 to 1870. He had been so strongly recommended that the trustees offered him a salary of $5,000 per year on 27 November 1875, making him the first faculty member to whom a concrete offer was tendered. Sylvester demanded that he be paid in gold; that the university provide him with a residence; and that all his students' fees accrue to him. When the trustees demurred, Sylvester cabled them: "Untried institution uncertain tenure favorable home prospects stipend crowning career inadequate against risk incurred regret thanks decline." On 15 February 1876 the trustees offered Sylvester an extra $1,000 per year, a salary double Remsen's and more than three times Rowland's, who, with Gildersleeve, made up the original "Hopkins Four." Sylvester accepted. Gildersleeve may have learned of Sylvester's arrangement from George Lane, to whom Gilman communicated the terms in a letter of 18 February as part of his effort to induce Lane to join the Hopkins faculty (*Hawkins*, 42–43). Sylvester founded the *American Journal of Mathematics* in 1878 and resigned in 1883 to become Savilian professor of Geometry at Oxford. See also No. 41 and *JHU Circulars* no. 130, (June 1897): 53–57, and, on Sylvester's "Laws of Verse," "Grammar and Aesthetics," *Princeton Magazine* 59 (1883): 307. In general, see *DNB* 19: 258–60.

31 To: JAMES FRANCIS HARRISON
*"Collegiana," Virginia University Magazine 15, No. 1*
*(October 1876): 98–99*

Johns Hopkins University
Baltimore, November 8th, 1876

Prof. James F. Harrison,
Chairman of the Faculty of the
University of Virginia:[1]

My Dear Sir,—Your kind letter, enclosing the resolutions of the Faculty of the University of Virginia, was received yesterday. Let me beg you to convey to the gentlemen of the Faculty the assurance that I shall always consider this expression of their good opinion as the crowning honor of my long connection with the University; and if, in reviewing my career, the sense of my many shortcomings does not suffer me to accept their favorable estimate of my services as my due, there is nothing to diminish the gratification which I feel at the cordial friendship which has prompted this testimonial of regard and these wishes for my usefulness and prosperity in the time to come. Whatever good I may accomplish in my new field of work will be owing, in a large measure, to the spirit which I have caught from the traditions of the University of Virginia, and whatever personal success the future may have in store for me, I shall never cease to wish the companionship of the friends and brothers who were once my colleagues.

The welfare of the University of Virginia, I need not say, will always be near my heart, and I shall always rejoice in the increasing success to which your great school is destined.

With many thanks to you personally, Mr. Chairman, for the hearty good will of your letter,

I am yours, faithfully,
B. L. Gildersleeve

1. As chairman of the faculty (1873–86), James Francis Harrison, M.D., professor of Medicine, sent to Gildersleeve resolutions on 4 November voted by the faculty on 1 November that "while regretting the circumstances which induced Professor Gildersleeve to transfer his zeal, his energies and his high and varied acquirements to another scene, . . . [the faculty is confident] he will diffuse something of the glow of his own enthusiasm for the highest culture, and will effectually enlarge the range and elevate the grade of scholarship in the community by which he may be surrounded."

## 32 To: JOHN BARBEE MINOR
*UVa-Minor*

{Johns Hopkins University, Baltimore}
Feb 23ᵈ 1878

My dear Mr. Minor: I hope that you agree with me in thinking that an active correspondence is not necessary to the maintenance of old friendships. If not, I am afraid you have thought hard thoughts of me all these months. At all events, I shall not risk the appearance of coldness or indifference now that I am really delighted to learn of your convalescence from a long and distressing sickness.[1] Messages have been going backwards and forwards between the Maupins[2] and our house so that we have been kept apprised of your condition from time to time and it was with the greatest joy that we received the good news that you were on your way to complete restoration. I would urge you to take care of yourself, if I did not know that all such urging will be in vain and so I must hope that your grand powers of work, which I envy you more and more, will carry you through the labors you are sure to plunge into as soon as you get well. For all that get well as soon as possible and pay us a visit to show how well you are.

My work here has become more definite and consequently more satisfactory. The release from the drudgery of junior classes is a great blessing[3] and although the feeling of increased responsibility is not welcome to a man who /is/ constitutionally averse to responsibility, the modest success I have had thus far makes me hopeful of the future—and while I find that it requires good management to meet the demands of city life with my income, I am not so much worried as I was in my old home and consequently I have been able to indulge in an increase of flesh—which the ungodly will doubtless attribute to terrapin and oysters—

I am glad to hear that you are prospering at the University—No danger

of any successful competition with you in your line of work. Any diminution of your influence would be a calamity for the South and for the country
and I hope that the legislators who has [sic] just disgraced Virginia[4] will
not proceed to lay hands on the organon which is to effect one day, I trust,
her restoration to honor.

Give my best love to Mrs. Minor[5]—who is as dear to me as if she were
my own blood, to Miss Mary[6] and to the children—

Yours faithfully<br>
B. L. Gildersleeve

1. Minor suffered from a carbuncle in the winter of 1878.

2. On Socrates Maupin, see "Correspondents."

3. See No. 19, n. 1.

4. The Funding Act of 1870 proposed settling the $45 million war debt by a bond issue,
but was resisted by the Conservative governor James L. Kemper until 1875. In that year the
state began honorably to "pay the debt" caused by reparations and free public school (the
latter mandated by the 1869 Underwood Constitution), in part by reducing public expenditures, particularly those for public education. The popular reaction against the Conservatives
gave the impetus for formalizing the Readjuster Movement as a party, led by Gen. William
H. Mahone. Surprisingly, the colleges united with the religious press (of which Benjamin
Gildersleeve was a prominent member) in placing the value of honor above the "luxury" of
educating the masses, apparently secure that the university's free tuition plan (see No. 20, n.
3) would not be cut off. See, further, C. C. Pearson, *The Readjuster Movement in Virginia*
(New Haven: Yale University Press, 1917; reprint, Gloucester, Mass.: Peter Smith, 1969),
60–4; R. H. Pulley, *Old Virginia Restored: An Interpretation of the Progressive Impulse,
1870–1930* (Charlottesville: University Press of Virginia, 1968), 33–35; C. Vann Woodward
*Origins of the New South, 1877–1913* (Baton Rouge: Louisiana State University Press, 1951),
92–96.

5. Minor married Anne Jacqueline Fisher Colston (1827–83), the aunt of Gildersleeve's
wife Elizabeth, following the death of his first wife, Martha Macon Davis Minor, daughter of
his University of Virginia law professor, John A. G. Davis, in whose home he was a tutor while
in law school. After Anne's death, he married Ellen Temple Hill. See J. B. Minor (Jr.), *The
Minor Family of Virginia* (Lynchburg, Va.: J. P. Bell, 1923).

6. Mary Lancelot Minor (1840–1905) was one of Minor's three children by his first wife.
By Anne he had five children, including Raleigh Colston Minor (1869–1923), who succeeded
him in the chair of law at the University of Virginia.

33 To: WALTER HINES PAGE<br>
Houghton

March 22, 1878

W. H. Page Esq.
My dear Sir:

I am sorry to learn that you will not be able to resume your studies at the
University as soon as you expected when you went home.[1] The Greek
seminarium will not be kept up longer than April and as your studies have

been carried on almost wholly in private, there can be no pressing reason for returning to Baltimore, when the only channel of active working in common with the others will be closed. I am much concerned to think that ~~your~~ /this academic/ year should have yielded /you/ so much less satisfaction than the last and hope that your essay will be an ample vindication of your private studies and that you will find in your future career that your connexion with the Johns Hopkins has been after all of some service to you.

With best wishes for your success.

       I am

Yours sincerely

B. L. Gildersleeve

1. Upon his return from a tour of Germany in 1877, Page could not take much interest in parsing Greek. "In strict truth I ought not to hold the place I do here," he wrote his mother, "I am not working in the line that it requires and ought to require." February 1878 found him back in North Carolina, where he had fled from Baltimore, pleading ill health. Gildersleeve had given him permission to complete his written work, "the collection and comparison &c of the metaphors and comparisons in the orators," there, but Page explained to him on 6 May, "A disorder of the liver keeps me continually incapable of application," adding "my lack of preparation [at Hopkins] weighed heavily on me always, and the confining private work I did in consequence is what is now telling on my health." Within a day or two of writing this, Page took a post teaching English in the summer school at the University of North Carolina at Chapel Hill, where he lectured for six weeks in June and July, and in the fall of 1878 took a "professorship" at the Boys' High School in Louisville, Ky. See, further, J. M. Cooper, *Walter Hines Page: The Southerner as American, 1855-1918* (Chapel Hill: University of North Carolina Press, 1977), 32-43.

34 To: Jonas Marsh Libbey

*New York Public Library-BLG*

Dec. 12, 1878

Jonas M. Libbey Esq.

My dear Sir:

I am much gratified to learn that you desire my further assistance in the work of the Princeton Review, which has taken so high a rank under your guidance and commands the services of so many illustrious writers.[1]

As to the subject of another article: a man generally writes with more vigor, if not always with better judgment when he has a direct personal interest in a theme and in Colleges and Classics (p. 90) I foreshadowed an essay on the special province of the Classical Philologian in America.[2] This essay I prepared immediately after the other and it formed the staple of my President's Address before the American Philological Association last summer.[3] The meeting was attended by only twenty-five members—and no more publicity was given to the essay than if it had been read in a private parlor. No report of it reached the press beyond a few lines of summary[4] and as it is not customary to print the President's address,[5] I did not yield to the solicitations of the prominent members of the association who thought that an especial exception ought to be made in favour of an essay which seemed to them to have more than a passing interest and importance—first because I did not wish to suffer an invidious distinction to be made—and then because in preparing the essay I hoped to find some wider channel of usefulness than is afforded by the dry bed of a volume of transactions—By recasting the essay and giving it the higher finish that the reputation of the Review demands, I think the article would be at least as worthy of admittance to your pages as the former one and could easily be brought within the compass which you seem to think judicious—

Of course if the subject appears to you too narrow and special I can take up some of the wider themes which lie near enough to every teacher—but I am afraid they would require a little more canvas.—

The kind tone of your letter encourages me to make a little confession—such as I hinted at in one of my earlier letter communications, my heart's desire is to devote all the time I can spare from strictly professional studies to the exploration of the Renaissance of the second century and I should be very much pleased, if in the course of next year I could plant a little article on that subject.—[6]

With many thanks for your kind expressions and warmest congratulations on the great success you have achieved

> I am
>
> > Yours very truly
> > B. L. Gildersleeve

1. The magazine, founded at Princeton in 1825 as *Biblical Repertory*, was "one of the greatest religious quarterlies of the times" (F. L. Mott, *A History of American Magazines* [Cambridge, Mass.: Harvard University Press, 1957], vol. 1, *1850–1865*, 533). In 1869 the journal moved its offices to New York and shifted its focus from the purely theological, with little success. In 1878 Libbey was made editor and it became a bimonthly of general interest, publishing, among others, P. G. Hamerton, Simon Newcomb, Francis A. Walker, Charles W. Eliot, and J. Brander Mathews. This incarnation was unsuccessful and publication ended in 1884. See Mott, *History of American Magazines* vol. 2, *1741–1850*, 529–35; "Retrospect of the History of the *Princeton Review*" in the index volume of 1871.

2. "Classics and Colleges" *Princeton Review* 54 (July 1878): 67–95 ( = *E&S*, 43–84). On p. 90 Gildersleeve says, "so long as the texts of the ancient authors themselves are accessible, there is enough to do in the way of investigation into the grammatical and rhetorical usages of various writers, into the historical development of the classic languages, into the attitude of the antique mind toward the great problems of politics, of religion, of art, enough in all conscience to keep us busy."

3. Gildersleeve had joined the American Philological Association when he moved to Hopkins in 1876. He became vice-president the next year, when the meetings were held in Baltimore, and was elected president for 1877–78. His address was *University Work*.

4. Gildersleeve had predicted the worst in a letter to Gilman of 1 July 1878: "Saratoga will, I fear, be a failure. Our secretary undertook to make the arrangements by mail and telegraph. . . . I wrote to him frankly that I was afraid that many of the members would be frightened off by the Grand Hotel and $4 a day—although Saratoga need not be a dear place." The meetings were held 9–11 July, and the *New York Times* chose instead to report on a conference of white lead manufacturers on 11 July and a meeting of railroad men on the 12th.

5. Presidential addresses had previously been summarized and/or excerpted in the *Proceedings*, but not printed in full. Gildersleeve's address, given 10 July 1878, was printed in *PAPA* 9 (1878): 21–23.

6. His third and final contribution to the *Princeton Review* was "Grammar and Aesthetics" 59 (1883): 290–319( = *E&S* 127–57). For his projected work on the "Renaissance of the second century," see No. 82 and n. 11.

### 35 To: JOHN BARBEE MINOR
*UVa-Minor*

255 St. Paul St. Baltimore
March 2, 1879

My dear Mr. Minor:

I am much obliged to Aunt Nanny[1] for stirring up your pure mind—is that a legal fiction?—by way of remembrance. Else I am certain that I should never have received an answer to my affectionate letter and then I should have gone down to my grave with a worse opinion of mankind in general. As for my opinion of you in particular, that is a subject I dare not touch on, for the last few years of my residence at the University, I ~~considered~~ /valued/ myself chiefly as a means of grace to you and I shudder to think of the decline in your state since my salutary counsel was withdrawn—to say nothing of my inspiring example. Who looks after your hats now? Who advises you not to put too much sugar in your liquor, not too much pepper in your temper now? What wholesome leaven of frivolity lightens your massive morality now?—I am astonished you do not miss me more—and in spite of your ample apology for your long and shameful neglect, I intend to punish you for your shortcomings by withholding my ghostly counsel in this my answer.—

But this is Sunday night and I ought to be grave—and surely if anything were needed to make a Virginian grave, it would be the knowledge that a pack of wretches are trifling with the fair name of the old commonwealth[2]—filibustering as they call it—to prevent a settlement on the liberal terms—too liberal, if anything, proposed by the long-suffering creditors of the state—I have been watching the signs of reaction in the state with the most intense interest. Naturally despondent, I feared the worst at one time—and yet I could not bear the thought that Virginia should be put in the same category as Tennessee.[3]—For I am passably honest, even if I did live for twenty years within a mile and a half of Charlottesville[4]—After the question of the state debts is honorably settled—then, perhaps, I shall help you to abuse the Board of Visitors—because I shall be in a good humour and be prepared to denounce (except in my own case) the principle of compensation by fixed salaries.[5] You know that I never was fully in accord with you as /to/ that matter but I think that we might compromise on the basis of very high salaries and very (or shall I say rather) small fees—the salaries representing the bread and butter of life—the fees the terrapin and champagne. For what makes life worth having is not mere bread and butter but the other little things, and I am honestly convinced that, so far as stimulus is concerned, small fees would stir a man effectually enough—the little sums that I pick up occasionally outside of my salary are very pleasant morsels to my palate—in spite of my sublime views as to science for science' sake—but at the same time I should not like to have the food and raiment of my family dependent on a run of custom.—

The Johns Hopkins is developing slowly but satisfactorily in the main. The Trustees will in all likelihood appoint several new professors next summer[6]—and we shall emerge more and more out of our provisional condition. A University professor here has in some respects an ideal time and, so far as I am concerned, I could not reasonably desire anything better. Still the University classes must in the nature of things be small and the very indefiniteness of the duties of my post makes the responsibility of the professorship so much the greater.—With a certain definite round of work to do a man may take comfort in the thought that he has done his duty according to the measure of poor feeble humanity; and I never did trouble myself much about success. But here duty is so hard to formulate and success so important as a gauge of usefulness and so difficult to ascertain that the problem of life becomes more ~~difficult~~ /complex/ to me than I allowed it to be in times past, even though the material conditions of it are much easier.—

I am glad to learn that the University is holding its own this year so well. It is a great deal to do in these times. The Charlottesville Chronicle keeps me fairly informed as to current events in the neighborhood so that if I should ever revisit the glimpses, I shall not harrow up the feelings of the citizens by asking after those who have died insolvent. Of your social life at the University we have only glimmerings now and then; but we look for a full revelation when Miss Mary[7] comes on.—

I hope Mrs. Minor's[8] health is definitely reëstablished. Betty has been very uneasy about her—for she loves her aunt with a tenderness which even such a tough sinner as myself can understand. Give her my most dutiful love and tell her that we still think of spending a part of next summer in Virginia and in that case shall not fail to visit our old home—so that the two ladies may have a good cry over each other—The children are suffering with colds—Raleigh especially whose elongated palate gives him a genuine churchyard cough—but their general health is good— —Betty, you know, is so unstable that it is not worth while to report on her—She has been—I believe—decidedly better this winter than she was last.—At all events she is capable of looking fresh and young at times—

Give my best love to all your household—

Do you want the assurance of my distinguished consideration? I am afraid that would involve my not writing again—at least not writing such a letter and being so weak a brother as I am—I shall content myself with a less stately phrase

Yours faithfully
B. L. Gildersleeve

1. See No. 32, n. 5. Minor answered Gildersleeve's letter of 23 February 1878 on 8 November 1878.

2. The question of Virginia's honor formed the core of the policy of the increasingly retrenched Conservative government of 1879, which bucked the popularity of readjustment (see No. 32, n. 4), by proposing repudiation of the West Virginia debt and lowering interest rates. Minor summed up the Conservative view in his letter to Gildersleeve of 8 November 1878: "My wrath and indignation against the parricides who would thus destroy the morals, the good name, and the permanent industrial prosperity of Virg[a], have absorbed and diverted the sentiments with which otherwise I should have regarded the sneaking fraud of the silver bill, the cowardly succumbing to the supposed popular cry for more paper-money, the mean following in the wake of a perverted and corrupt public sentiment, after the manner of the sycophants and parasites of royal courts, instead of giving wise and brave counsel to the people, are the contemptuous indifference to the permanent and serious interests of the country, in the eager quest of party-triumph and personal emolument." See, further, Pearson, *Readjuster Movement in Virginia* (cited No. 32, n. 4); A. W. Moger, *Virginia: Bourbonism to Byrd 1870-1925* (Charlottesville: University Press of Virginia, 1968), 21-75; J. P. Maddex, Jr., "Virginia: The Persistence of Centrist Hegemony," in *Reconstruction and Redemption in the South*, ed. O. H. Olsen (Baton Rouge: Louisiana State University Press, 1980), 147-48.

3. The Tennessee legislature, under the influence of former president Andrew Johnson, suspended payment of interest on its debt in 1873, and an 1879 referendum on settling the debt found most voters in favor of the dishonorable road of repudiation rather than a shift in tax base from property owners to businessmen.

4. See No. 12, n. 20.

5. As early as 1854, Minor had proposed that student fees accrue to the professors and not the Library Fund. In 1856, Gildersleeve's first year, the minimum salary was set at $2,000, with each professor getting a different percentage of his students' fees, from 90 percent (medicine) to 45 percent (mathematics). Gildersleeve, as professor of Greek, received 60 percent; after the war, expecting fewer students, the board of visitors returned all fees to the professors. The inequity of this system soon became apparent as the man who had been longest at the university, Cabell in physiology and surgery, made only $767, while Venable in mathematics, who had been at the university for only one year, made three times that figure, and Minor made six times as much. (In 1865-66 Gildersleeve made $2,492, Minor $4,528; in 1866-67, under the new system, Gildersleeve made $1,905, while his Latin counterpart, Peters, in his first year, made $3,820.) When Venable sought a return to a fixed salary, Minor

proposed a compromise between fixed sums and a pro rata assessment from each college. In 1870-71 the maximum salary was $3,000, with all fees accruing to the university. Finally, in June 1876, the faculty proposed that nearly all fees go to a general fund from which the faculty salaries were drawn, with law professors (Minor included) receiving a $1,000 maximum salary and all fees. With the free tuition bill (No. 20, n. 3), the General Assembly gave broad powers to equalize salaries, so the board returned to the plan of 1870. See *Bruce*, 3: 98, 100–101, 317; 4: 41–50.

6. On 2 December 1878 the Hopkins trustees received a report calling for expansion of the university, and a search was begun. Gildersleeve was sent to Europe in the summer of 1880, and board members Thomas and King went in 1881, but neither trip resulted in an appointment, and the number of professors remained at the original six, with an abundance of associates and lecturers appointed in the meantime (*Hawkins*, 132–33).

7. See No. 32, n. 6

8. Ibid., n. 5. She had gone to Lynchburg, Va. to convalesce.


## 36 To: WILLIAM DWIGHT WHITNEY
### *Yale-Whitney*

March 17th 1879

Prof. W. D. Whitney:

My dear Whitney

The kind letter which you made time to write me last summer would have been answered immediately, if it had not been for the pressing duties of the Philological Association and after the meeting was over, it was too late. Your absence, I need not say, was deeply regretted; and while I obeyed your injunctions and made no public use of your letter, the numerous inquiries about you gave me occasion to explain to everyone why you could not be present.

I hope that your year in Germany will be of great service to you both for your health and your work; but we on this side are very forlorn without you and I especially at this time when I am about to enter upon an undertaking which a good word from you would go far to make a success; and while I should not despair of that good word, if you were here and I could talk with you freely, there is no telephonic communication between Baltimore and Berlin and I must trust to your general estimate of my working powers.

I have been urged to carry out myself what I have long thought to be a desideratum—the establishment of a philological journal which should serve at once as a repertory of the results of current philological work all over the world and as a means of intercommunication among American philologians. But an American Philological Journal without the support of the man, whom we all with one accord consider our foremost representative would have serious difficulties to contend with from the start and I hope you will let me know frankly at your earliest convenience how you are disposed towards the project and whether I should be authorized to avail myself of your opinion, if it should be possible.[1]

With best regards to Mrs. Whitney and heartiest wishes for your complete restoration to health and continued success in all your work

I am

Yours faithfully
B. L. Gildersleeve

1. Whitney responded favorably with the promise of an article and Gildersleeve used his name in the prospectus.

37 To: BOARD OF TRUSTEES, JOHNS HOPKINS UNIVERSITY
*JHU-BLG*

June 4th 1879

Gentlemen:

In response to the inclosed circular I have received favorable answers from a large number of representative men interested in the advance of philological studies; and I have a reasonable confidence that with a guarantee of partial support from the authorities of this university I might venture upon the undertaking with a fair prospect of success.[1] I would therefore respectfully ask for a subscription on the part of the University to one hundred (100) copies of the proposed journal (in all $300)[2] with the hope that this periodical will fill an important gap in the philological literature of the country[3] and prove to be another signal evidence of the wise liberality of the Board of Trustees.

I am, very respectfully,

Your obedient servant
B. L. Gildersleeve

To the Board of Trustees
Johns Hopkins University

1. Gildersleeve had sent out some 2,000 copies of the prospectus dated May 1879 announcing a journal composed of "original communications in all departments of philology, . . . condensed reports of current philological work, and . . . summaries of the chief articles in the leading philological journals of Europe, while a close watch will be kept over the fragmentary and occasional literature to which the isolated American scholar seldom has full access." By October he was able to send out another brochure listing some 217 charter subscribers.

2. The board was reluctant to own the Hopkins journals outright, and their practice was to subsidize a substantial subscription and let the library exchange the copies for the journals of other universities. Even with this limited support, beginning with 1879, nearly one journal a year was begun, starting with Remsen's *American Chemical Journal*, then *AJP* in 1880, Herbert Baxter Adams' *Johns Hopkins University Studies in History and Political Science* in 1882, Arthur L. Frothingham's (see No. 96, n. 6) *American Journal of Archaeology* in 1885

(Frothingham took the journal to Princeton with him the next year), *Modern Language Notes* in 1886, and G. S. Hall's *American Journal of Psychology* in 1887. See *Hawkins*, 107–10.

3. Gildersleeve reiterates his view from *University Work*: 518–19 ( = *E&S*, 98): "It certainly betokens great supineness on the part of our scholars that a country which boasts a Journal of Speculative Philosophy should not have even a solitary periodical devoted to a science which counts its professed votaries by hundreds, if not by thousands, and that our professors and teachers should be satisfied with consigning an occasional paper to the slow current of a volume of transactions or exposing a stray lucubration to struggle for notice amidst the miscellaneous matter of a review or the odds and ends of an educational magazine." This article was an expansion of his APA presidential address; see *PAPA* 9 (1878): 20 for the same thoughts.

### 38 To: James Morgan Hart
#### *Cornell*

June 6, 1879

Prof. Jas. M. Hart:
My dear Sir:

I am much obliged to you for your kind reception of my circular especially when I see how much you fear lest the professor of Greek should turn the projected periodical into a Journal of Classical Philology. The country is not ready for that yet, still less, I fear for a Journal of English Philology. Professor Garnett[1] an enthusiastic worker in English told me only last night that Sweet[2] had written to him in response to some inquiries, that it would not be feasible to carry on such a periodical as the Anglia[3] in England—which is a bad omen for America, though, I grant you, not decisive. I shall honestly set apart a due portion of my space for English Studies and I should be delighted to secure your help on the whole Germanic side.[4] With your familiar knowledge of German you do not appreciate perhaps the difficulty with which many teachers, who nominally read German, wade through the crabbed and prolix dissertations of German philological journals even when they have access to them and it is not every one who can find [time] to keep au courant of the world of literature. If there is any particular journal you would like me to keep my eye on, please let me know—One friend has promised a regular summary of the Anglia[5] and I should /be/ very much pleased if you could undertake a referat of some journal or any other special line of work.[6] If I am sustained by philologians of all arms, the contributors will find it worth their while to help. At the outset I must appeal to their love of the good cause—the same spirit which has prompted me to what Whitney calls a hazardous enterprise. Thus far the response has been very hearty.

Yours sincerely,
B. L. Gildersleeve

1. James Mercer Garnett (1840–1916) was a student of Gildersleeve's at the University of Virginia, from which he took an M.A. in 1860 at the age of nineteen. A member of the University of Virginia student military corps, he rose to be captain of artillery and probably encountered Gildersleeve during Early's Valley Campaign of 1864, although he does not mention him in his diary of the time (*Southern Historical Society Papers* 27 [1899]: 1–16). He studied philology at Berlin and Leipzig (1869–70), was principal and professor of history and English at St. John's College, Annapolis, Md., (1870–1880), and professor of English at the University of Virginia (1882–1896). He is best remembered for publishing the first American translation of *Beowulf* (Boston: Ginn, Heath, 1882), which followed his *Elene; Judith; Athelstan, or the Fight at Brunanburh; and Byrhtnoth or the Fight at Maldon: Anglo-Saxon Poems* (Boston: Ginn, 1889; 3d ed., 1911), and his edition of *Macbeth* (Boston: Leach, Shewell and Sanborn, 1897). He collaborated on *Barringer*.

2. On Sweet, see No. 45, n. 7.

3. *Anglia: Zeitschrift für englische Philologie* (Tübingen: M. Niemeyer), founded in 1877 and first edited by R. P. Wülker and M. Trautmann. The *Journal of Germanic Philology* (later *Journal of English and Germanic Philology*) was founded at the University of Illinois, Urbana, in 1897, followed by *Monatshefte für Deutschen Unterricht, Deutsche Sprache und Literatur* at the University of Wisconsin in 1899.

4. While Gildersleeve admitted in the editorial note to *AJP* 1, no. 1 (p. 2) that "the Greek element may seem suspiciously preponderant," he spoke of his "earnest desire to represent as fairly as may be the whole cycle of philological study." This volume featured two articles on German, one each on French, Romance languages, Semitic, Celtic and German, and English, with one essay on language by Whitney, two articles on Latin and nine on Greek. By vol. 10 (1889) there was one article each on English, French-Canadian, Sanskrit, Pennsylvania German, Anglo-Saxon, and Paleography, two on linguistics, three on Latin and six on Greek. By vol. 20 (1899) there were one each on Gâthas, Sanskrit, paleography, metre, linguistics, Irish-Latin, and Tennyson and Virgil, nine on Latin, and five on Greek. *AJP* continued through its first fifty years with non-classical articles; see H. T. Rowell, "Seventy-Five Years of the 'A.J.P.,'" *AJP* 75 (1954): 339.

5. Garnett provided reports on *Anglia* for *AJP* 1–7, James W. Bright for *AJP* 8–11.

6. Hart contributed "Keltic and Germanic" to *AJP* 1 (1880): 440–52; "A Peculiarity of Keltic (Irish) Ritual" and reviews of K. I. Schröer's *Faust*, and T. Zahn's *Cyprian von Antiochien und die deutsche Faustsage*, to *AJP* 3 (1882): 461–63, 220–23, 470–73 respectively; and a review of H. Zimmer's *Keltische Studien* to *AJP* 6 (1885): 217–20.

## 39 To: DANIEL COIT GILMAN
*JHU-Gilman*

University of Virginia
Aug. 6, 1879

My dear Mr. Gilman:

I have been here among my old friends since last Wednesday[1] and shall probably remain a few days and then settle for the rest of the vacation in some quiet corner of the mountains. After leaving Newport[2] I went to Providence where I spent a day with Harkness[3] who overwhelmed me with kindness. He has a son, who has just graduated with distinction at Brown and has given proof of unusually high tone.[4] I was very sorry not to see him, as a young man who declines the first honor in his class on account of his connexion with the faculty is not an everyday character. Harkness wishes him to devote himself to classic study—which indeed is the young man's own bent—but did not consider him mature enough for our vacant fellowship, about which I had already spoken to him. I urged him to communicate with you. If young Harkness could spend a year or two with us profitably, it would be a good thing and a pleasant thing for all of us.— In New York I had a pleasant talk with young Libbey of the Princeton Review[5] and think that I should be able to establish good relations with that organ—so that my future communication will not be circumscribed by his notions but be directed by my own studies. He is so much pleased with my former articles that he intends to republish them in pamphlet forms in a series of selections from the Princeton Review.[6] I told /him/ that I thought the project would be received with favour by our University.—Subscribers come straggling in for the Journal and my mind is at ease on the score of pecuniary support but I am rather depressed as to the prospect of getting out a crack first number in the autumn: and it may be better to postpone the publication until Jan. 1—that is to say nominally. The number might be printed and issued towards the end of November but bear date Jan.$^y$ 1880.—To begin with the calendar year would have many advantages; but I shall be guided by your advice.[7]

My wife was all ready to leave Baltimore on Friday 18$^{th}$—when she discovered that our little girl had an attack of diphtheritic sore throat—the same malady which distressed us so much before. Fortunately the disease yielded very readily to prompt and active treatment and I did not hear of my child's illness until she was well. But this deranged our plans and shortened my wife's stay in Richmond.[8] She is with me here in good health and spirits and the children are delighted to be in the country among their old playmates. If I did not intend to move on the 1st of October, I should return to Balt$^o$ without them—but I am afraid that my wife would not trust me with the work, even though our handful of goods and chattels is to be carried only a few steps. But I shall not fail to report my further movements to you from time to time.

My wife unites in kindest messages to Mrs. Gilman and yourself and to the young ladies, if they are with you.

Yours faithfully
B. L. Gildersleeve

1. 30 July 1879.

2. The Gildersleeves stayed at the Aquidneck Hotel in Newport for the last two weeks of July.

3. Albert Harkness (1822–1907) graduated as valedictorian from Brown in 1842 and received his Ph.D. from Bonn in 1854. Although he was professor of Greek at Brown (1855–92), the vast majority of his publications were a series of Latin schoolbooks that were a Northern

counterpart of Gildersleeve's Latin series. His *Latin Grammar for Schools and Colleges* (New York: D. Appleton, 1865; rev. ed., 1881) was last published in 1909. He was a founder of the APA and its president in 1875. He was also a member of the original managing committee of the American School of Classical Studies at Athens from 1881 to his death. See, further, *DAB* 8: 265–66.

4. Albert Granger Harkness (1856–1923), like his father, graduated first in his class at Brown (1879; A.M. 1882) and studied in Germany (1879–83) before returning to Brown. Unlike his father, he was a Latinist, taught at Madison (now Colgate) University (1883–89), and was annual professor at the American Academy, Rome (1902–3). His chief publications are "Age at Marriage and at Death in the Roman Empire," *TAPA* 27 (1896): 35–72; "Skepticism and Fatalism of the Common People of Rome as Illustrated by the Sepulchral Inscriptions," *TAPA* 30 (1899): 56–88; and "The Relation of Accent to Elision in Latin Verse, not Including the Drama," *TAPA* 36 (1895): 82–110. *NatCAB*, 19: 413.

5. See "Correspondents" and No. 34.

6. A series of sixteen 5-cent reprints were issued in 1879, of which no. 6 was Gildersleeve's "Classics and Colleges" (see No. 34, n. 2).

7. The first number was put together in October and November 1879, went to press in December, and was dated January 1880.

8. See following letter.

## 40 To: Daniel Coit Gilman
### *JHU-Gilman*

Stribling's Springs[1]
Augusta C° V<u>a</u>
Aug. 15<u>th</u> 1879

My dear Mr. Gilman

Many thanks for your cordial letter and the kind greetings from your household. I was very much tempted to follow your example and settle for the summer in one of your lovely New England villages but my wife very naturally desired to see her mother[2] and was especially solicitous about the health of a favorite aunt[3] and once in our old home we find it too troublesome to transport ourselves and our children to a distant part of the world—as Massachusetts seems to the true Virginian's eyes. So we have followed my wife's mother—Mrs. Colston—into this mountain retreat—some twelve miles from Staunton—one of the oldest and most quiet of Virginia watering places. The primitiveness of these resorts is doubtless familiar to you by report—and you know that people come to such place[s] in order to be uncomfortable and to enjoy the two Southern luxuries of idleness and talk. But if our cabin would be considered very rough by you Sybarites and Mrs. Gilman would be in despair at an apartment without wardrobe or chest of drawers, we who have fought through several summers like to this, stand it tolerably well. The air is cool—the sulphur water reasonably strong—the fare abundant after the old Virginia type—and the company made up of pleasant people—chiefly from Richmond—and Kentucky.—How long we shall stay I cannot tell—probably not long after the 1st of September. I should like to be back in Baltimore as early next month as possible and may precede my wife and children. This summer I have done very little and these last two weeks of vacation must be devoted as far as possible to preparation for next session which promises to be for me a year of very arduous work. A trunk of books supplies me with ample material for all manner of lucubrations and I hope to make my fortnight here tell.

We are all in fair health. My wife sends her love to Mrs. Gilman—and kind regards to you, and Emma is much gratified at Lizzie's[4] remembrance of her.

With best regards to Mrs. Gilman and all your household.

I am

Yours faithfully
B. L. Gildersleeve

1. Stribling's Springs, founded in 1817 by Dr. Erasmus Stribling of Staunton on 1,400 acres thirteen miles northwest of that city, was one of the most elegant of the Virginia resorts, boasting three springs: alum, sulphur, and chalybeate. Stribling's lost its former status under Chesley Kinney, who was obliged to sell out in 1878, but new owners began to refurbish the hotel and grounds, and by 1915 it had nearly regained its former eminence. Stribling's Springs (also known as Augusta Springs) no longer exists. See, further, Stan Cohen, *Historic Springs of the Virginias* (Charleston, W.Va.: Pictorial Histories Publishing Co., 1981), 109–10, and J. J. Moorman, M.D., *Mineral Springs of North America: How to Reach, and How to Use Them* (Philadelphia: Lippincott, 1873), 151–53. For an illustration, see Edward Beyer, *The Album of Virginia; or, The Old Dominion Illustrated* (Richmond: Enquirer Book and Job Printing Office, 1857).

2. Gertrude Powell Colston (1826–1901).

3. For Anne Jacqueline Fisher Colston Minor, see No. 32, n. 5.

4. Gilman had married Mary Ketcham in 1861 at the age of thirty, and had two daughters, Alice (1863–1945) and Elisabeth (Lizzie) (1867–1950). Mary died in 1869, and in 1877 he married Elisabeth Dwight Woolsey, who survived him by two years, dying in 1910.

# ᚳ 4 ᚴ

# EUROPE, 1880

As Jefferson had sent an agent to England to find faculty for his new university (No. 6, n. 7), so a legation of Hopkins trustees had gone to Europe in 1874 seeking faculty, and Gilman had followed in the summer of 1875.[1] Now Gildersleeve found himself "unexpectedly called upon to make preparations for a European trip" (BLG to J. M. Hart, 9 April 1880 [Cornell]) to find both new faculty (particularly a Latinist and an Anglo-Saxonist) and European contributors to the fledgling *AJP*. "In 1880, . . . I went abroad for the Journal, and for the first time I came into personal relations with English classicists; and the early numbers of the Journal shew that I had succeeded in enlisting the help of Oxford and Cambridge scholars of mark."[2]

From his arrival in Dublin on 8 May, Gildersleeve sought out the best classicists of Europe, finding Mahaffy and Palmer in Dublin, Tulloch in Edinburgh, Greenwood in Manchester, Verrall and Postgate at Cambridge, and Bywater, Butcher, and Robinson Ellis at Oxford. But his timing was bad: he arrived after the end of term both in Britain and Germany and so missed Jebb at Glasgow (he found him at Cambridge), Sellar and Blackie at Edinburgh, Liddell and Jowett at Oxford, and Windisch at Leipzig. At London he stayed for nearly a month at the Athenaeum and had access to prominent clubs (No. 46), where he met E. H. Palmer, and Sayce (No. 48). At Strassburg he interviewed Studemund and ten Brink, at Freiburg von Holst, at Heidelberg Wachsmuth, and at Berlin G. Curtius and Hübner, but not, of course, Wilamowitz, who in any case was not in town.

All but the truly exceptional, such as Jebb and Bywater, disappointed him in his search for that special blend of intelligence, industry, sensitivity, and attractiveness that made the ideal candidate; for above all he was seeking a teacher (Nos. 44, 49). He also examined salaries and libraries (No. 43) for comparison with Hopkins.

After Berlin, he refreshed himself with a trip to Italy (No. 51), which retained all the charm and magic it had held for him in 1853 (No. 4). At length his anxieties about Gilman's expenditures for his trip were allayed;

he had secured British contributors and European distributors for *AJP*, he had made himself and his institution more widely known and respected abroad, and he had established contacts that would serve him amply in the years to come. He had found neither a classical nor an English philologist who would join the ranks at Baltimore, but he had confirmed his judgment that the great scholars were not the best people to train young men and that the American character may be best for combining the needs of science and teaching in one personality.

1. *Hawkins*, 14, 33.
2. *AJP* 34 (1913): 495. For an account of the whole trip, see *AJP* 40 (1919): 444-48.

### 41 To: Daniel Coit Gilman
### *JHU-BLG*

Steamer Bothnia
April [May] 7, 1880[1]

My dear Mr. Gilman:

I have nothing to report except a safe and smooth voyage but that is something as it will assure you that your package[2] is likely to arrive in good condition. With the exception of one day we have had summer seas—very little rain—everybody on deck. The Bothnia is very roomy and comfortable, if not very fast—and I should not object to trying her again.[3] I found that I had chanced upon a much worse stateroom in my effort to oblige Mr. Sylvester but my illustrious friend and colleague has been 'bon prince' the whole way and there has not been a ripple in our relations.[4] The storm that preceded the Bothnia seems to have made the sea smooth for us and perhaps the same thing may apply 'in a figure' to my room mate, who has given me several letters and much good advice. I have not mapped out any careful itinerary, but as a general rule I shall not allow myself any considerable détours for matters foreign to the great object of my visit. We shall probably reach Queenstown about 11°30' A.M. and I expect to start for Dublin to-morrow—Two days will probably suffice for that point and from there I shall proceed to Glasgow—Edinburgh—Manchester—London. I will send you rough notes from each point, which you may read or not without wounding my susceptibilities—They may serve to guide a more formal report on my return.[5] However this trip may result—and I very much fear that I lack the quick observation and ready economy of time to make it as profitable as it would be for one better endowed, I shall always be grateful for the opportunity and if I can show that gratitude in no other way, renewed zeal and redoubled industry will prove that I have not been favored in vain.

Present my kindest regards to Mrs. Gilman—

Yours faithfully
B. L. Gildersleeve

1. As she sailed from New York on April 28, Gildersleeve's date is wrong.

2. He means himself.

3. She was a relatively new (built in 1874) 3,000-ton, 422-foot single-screw barque of the Cunard Line, sailing out of Liverpool.

4. On Sylvester, see No. 30 and *AJP* 41 (1920): 402: "I cannot say he honoured me with his friendship. Even his acquaintance was a perilous privilege. So explosive was he that I consider it the greatest achievement of my social life that I managed to cross the ocean with him as my room-mate with not even an approach to personal difficulty."

5. No formal report (see also Nos. 45, 50) exists.

42 To: Daniel Coit Gilman
*JHU-BLG*

{St. Enoch Station Hotel Glasgow}
May 12, 1880

My dear Mr. Gilman:

In conformity with my promise or threat, whichever you may consider it, I send you these tidings of my whereabouts and my progress. I landed at Queenstown on Friday last[1]—remained at Cork, not omitting the usual drive to Blarney Castle, until the early train of the next day which left at the very uncomfortable hour of six and reached Dublin about one. By a series of contretemps, which were curious but hardly worth relating at length, my letters did not take effect until Sunday night so that I had a rather doleful time in my lonely rambles about Dublin. Still I found Mahaffy[2] on Sunday night and from that hour on, my visit to Dublin was an unmixed pleasure. I spent several hours in the library—examined the museum—talked with men right and left on all manner of university themes—and have reason to think that after all my trip will be of real advantage—I think I shall be able to get help from some of the younger men on my journal—and I have promised in return for help in Latin to do some Greek work for the Hermathena[3]—Monday night I dined in Hall with Dr. Salmon[4] and had a very pleasant talk with some of the bright men of the college.—Their chief Latin man at least the chief one whom I saw—is a good scholar but narrow—Palmer,[5] another promising Latinist, I did not see—Think of it— both these Latinists know little or no German! Mahaffy, of course, knows

everything. He was born in Switzerland and speaks a very Swiss German. I
can't answer about his French—He received me royally and I have from
him a pocketful of cards to men in Edinburgh—Oxford—Cambridge—
London—I failed to see Dowden[6]—I am certain that he can be had for a
course of lectures on English literature—and I should not be surprised, if
he would come altogether, if wanted. Mahaffey [sic] is by no means disinclined to give a course of instruction on History and Archaeology—but this
you know as well as I do. I told him of course that I had no authority in the
matter but was glad of any information as to the sources from which we
may eventually look for help. I availed myself of an interval between the
two boats from Belfast to Glasgow and dined with my friend Dr. Porter of
Queen's College.[7] I think I made good use of my two hours and a half in
Belfast—the college buildings are well arranged and the liberality as to
library refreshing—Porter says that Tulloch[8] will almost certainly come to
America the next autumn and I shall follow your instructions and telegraph to St. Andrews—The Scotch colleges are, I believe, virtually dis-
banded and I do not expect to accomplish much more here now in Edinburgh. I shall take Manchester on my way to London where I expect to
arrive in a few days—

Yours faithfully<br>
B. L. Gildersleeve

1. Friday, 7 May 1880.
2. Sir John Pentland Mahaffy (1839–1919) was born at Chapponnaire, near Vevey, Switzerland, and graduated as first senior moderator in classics and logic from Trinity College,
Dublin, in 1859. In 1860 he was elected as first professor of ancient history. By the time
Gildersleeve met him, he had published *Social Life in Greece from Homer to Menander* (London: Macmillan, 1874), *Rambles and Studies in Greece* (London: Macmillan, 1876; 2d ed.,
1878), both with "improvements and corrections" by Mahaffy's student Oscar Wilde, and his
*History of Classical Greek Literature* (London: Longmans, 1880). For Gildersleeve on his
works, see *AJP* 9 (1888): 255 ( = *SBM*, 3); *Nation* 55 (4 August 1892): 89–91; *AJP* 13 (1892):
383 ( = *SBM*, 13). Mahaffy became provost of Trinity College, Dublin, in 1914 and was
knighted in 1918. For Gildersleeve's meeting with him, see *AJP* 40 (1919): 447–48, and W. B.
Stanford and R. B. McDowell, *Mahaffy: A Biography of an Anglo-Irishman* (London:
Routledge and Kegan Paul, 1971), 44–45, and in general, *DNB 1912–1921*, 363–66.
3. *Hermathena: A Series of Papers on Literature, Science, and Philosophy by Members
of Trinity College, Dublin*, edited by the members, began publication in 1873.
4. George Salmon (1819–1904) attended Trinity College, Dublin, on a classical scholarship and graduated with a first in mathematical moderations in 1838. His most important
publication, *A Treatise on Conic Sections* (Dublin: Hodges and Smith, 1848), remained a
standard textbook through the end of the century. He was Regius professor of divinity at
Trinity College (1866–88) and wrote an *Introduction to the Study of the Books of the New
Testament* (London: John Murray, 1885), which ran to seven editions. See, further, *DNB
1901–1911*, 251–54. On Gildersleeve's meeting with Salmon, see *AJP* 40 (1919): 446–47.
5. The Canadian Arthur Palmer (1841–97) had just been elevated from fellow to professor of Latin at Trinity College, at which he had been Berkeley medalist in 1862 and senior
moderator in classics in 1863. His *P. Ovidi Heroides XIV* (London: G. Bell, 1874) was re-

viewed by his friend A. E. Housman, *CR* 13 (1899): 172 ( = *Classical Papers of A. E. Hous-man*, ed. J. Diggle and F. R. D. Goodyear [Cambridge: Cambridge University Press, 1972], 471); of those who had edited the poems, Housman wrote, "first place belongs to Bentley, the second to Palmer, the third to Madvig." He also edited *Sexti Propertii elegiarum libri IV* (London: G. Bell, 1880), and his *Satires of Horace* (London: Macmillan, 1882) ran to six editions. See, further, *Sandys*, 436–37.

6. Edward Dowden (1843–1913) was professor of English literature at the University of Dublin from 1867 and had produced *Shakspere: A Critical Study of His Mind and Art* (London: H. S. King, 1875), *Poems* (London: H. S. King, 1876), and *Studies in Literature* (London: H. S. King, 1878); he would go on to publish *Essays, Modern and Elizabethan* (London: Dent, 1910) and several editions of Shakespeare's plays. See, further, *DNB 1912–1921*, 162.

7. Josias Leslie Porter (1823–89) was born in County Donegal, Ireland, educated at Glasgow, Edinburgh, and Free Church Divinity College, Aberdeen. After a decade of missionary work in Syria, he was appointed professor of biblical criticism in the Presbyterian College, Belfast, and in 1879 was made president of Queen's College, Belfast. How he became Gildersleeve's "friend" is not known. See, further, *DNB* 16: 187–88.

8. John Tulloch (1823–86), educated at St. Andrews and Edinburgh, was appointed principal and professor of divinity in St. Mary's College, St. Andrews. He is best known for *Rational Theology and Christian Philosophy in England in the Seventeenth Century* (Edinburgh: W. Blackwood, 1872). In an article on "American Colleges" in his series, "America and the Americans," *Good Words* 16 (1875): 641–48, 705–11, 773–776, 816–824, he devoted a long footnote (p. 774) to an enthusiastic account of his interview with "President Gillman" [sic]. Shortly afterwards, Gilman met him at St. Andrews and was further encouraged (*Franklin*, 210, *Hawkins*, 32). On Tulloch, see (Mrs.) M. O. W. Oliphant, *A Memoir of the Life of John Tulloch* (Edinburgh: W. Blackwood, 1889), 348–62, 367–70, and *DNB* 19: 1234–37. On his editorship of *Fraser's Magazine* in 1879–80, see the following letter.

## 43 To: DANIEL COIT GILMAN
### *JHU-Gilman*

Edinburgh May 17, 1880

My dear Mr. Gilman: My last letter was written in better spirits perhaps than my actual success justified but to have done anything at all in the beginning seemed a good omen and I was somewhat elated by my kind reception in Dublin after I got at the men. I did not expect much in Scotland, as I wrote you, and yet though fully prepared for failure, I am just now a little more down hearted than is reasonable. At Glasgow I found nobody. Jebb[1] was gone. I shall probably find him at Cambridge. Sir Wm. Thompson [sic][2] was in London. These were the men to whom I had letters. Ramsay,[3] the professor of Latin, whom I should have approached without an introduction, had also vanished. The Hunterian Museum interested me very much and I had a talk with a stray student and an interview with the librarian or the man in charge,[4] who was civil and obliging but not bright or enthusiastic. The best mss. were under glass in the Hunterian Museum and if there were treasures in the library he failed to show them. The room was fine but the shelves were unnecessarily rough and the whole thing had a wretchedly provisional look. The regulations as to the use of books, 125,000 volumes, are liberal enough. Rare volumes cannot be taken out— but otherwise students are allowed to have two books at a time or more upon special application. The annual appropriation for the library is small—£1000 and the professors do not seem to depend wholly upon it or even mainly—Jebb is said to have a fine private collection and well he may—for the professors in Scotch universities make money, if nothing else.[5] For five months work Jebb receives some £1200,[6] Ramsay very much more—the emoluments depending on the number of students, naturally large in Latin and Greek. The students pay 3 guineas each per annum and are counted by hundreds. The fixed salary is small— —though in some cases it forms a respectable nucleus. The largest I have heard of is the Sanskrit professor's in Edinburgh who receives £450 but he has only 4 students in Sanskrit and 12 in comparatively [sic] philology. The great inequality, which results from this system, is borne with more philosophy than might be supposed though there must be heart burnings as I know from my own experience under a similar system at the University of Virginia.[7] As Tait[8] said to me at Edinburgh, "We know what we are coming to when we are candidates for the place"—a consideration which does not weigh with the average American. Dr. Dickson,[9] professor of botany, to whom I brought a letter, teaches for three months and receives £1700 and as he is a man of large landed estates besides, is a bachelor and lives with his mother, he can hardly be puzzled to make both ends meet. I mention these points particularly to shew the difficulty, indeed the impossibility of moving anybody from these older seats of learning—even those who have only prospects [of] having better prospects than we can hold out. Then so many of the professors seem to be men of independent means—But to return to my narrative.—At Edinburgh I missed again the men whom I most desired to see—Blackie[10] had flitted to his home in the Highlands just two or three days before my arrival. He is doubtless worth seeing as a curiosity but hardly a sufficient inducement to make the trip to Oban[11] and back— especially as the time is short—Sellar[12] is travelling on the continent with his young wife—very clever—but supremely lazy at least—works only as the fit seizes him—and is utterly ignorant of the course of study on the continent, according to the account given by Eggeling,[13] the professor of Sanskrit. What surprises me is that men whom Tait represents as given up to cards and chess and all manner of extraneous studies and amusements should still accomplish so much more in the way of authorship than our own American professors, who stick more closely to their work—Still I don't think that Scotland will ever do much for us in the classical line— The Scotch import their classical men or have them trained in England[14]— The instruction is elementary and hurried. Tait—with whom I spent last evening—says that in the session he does nothing but the most simple class work—and he has no time for experiment except in the holidays—which, however, are sufficiently long—although his physical laboratory is still going on. As a rule—no postgraduate work. Occasionally Tait says he can get an assistant who is capable of following the higher range—and he was rubbing his hands at the prospect of having their new man, Crystal [sic],[15] author of Electricity in the Encyclopedia Britannica, to study and work with him this summer. He was much interested in Rowland,[16] of whom he thinks highly and wanted to know more about Hall[17] than I could tell him. It seems that he had lighted upon something of the same sort twelve or fourteen years ago but had been frightened out of it by Clerk Maxwell.[18] I found Tait a very interesting man, brusque and downright. I was at my ease with him in half-a-second and I learned more about matters in general than I shall trouble you with now. In fact my days are so full that I am ready to drop with fatigue by bedtime and I am now availing myself of a wakeful half hour before breakfast to write what I am afraid you cannot read and will hardly be worth reading, if you could.— —

Warned by my failure here and in Glasgow I telegraphed to St. Andrews Friday last and found that Tulloch[19] would be at home on Saturday. The entire day was spent on the trip of 45 miles and back. That is to say—I started at 9°00'—reached St. Andrews at 12°30', stayed there until 6°15' and did not get back to my hotel until 11 o'clock. It is an awkward place to get at and then the 15th of May is term-day[20] and all the ~~domestic~~ /servant/ world is upside-down—the train is crowded with ~~servants~~/flitters/[21] and their luggage—I was sorry to inflict myself so long on Tulloch—who, however, excused himself with as much grace as a Scotchman is capable of—He is not coming to America next autumn, partly because he is not an enthusiastic Panpresbyterian,[22] chiefly because he is editor of Fraser's magazine. Still he is not disinclined to give us a course of lectures /at/ some time and would like to hold the matter in abeyance.[23] After a good deal of talk he began to thaw and when after luncheon he took me to see Baynes,[24] the Encyclopedia Britannica man, he was much more flexible, thanks to our combined efforts and in our final talk became much more interested in our plans and needs. Baynes and I were more sympathetic. He laughed where the Principal only chuckled and was disposed to help me in every way. Only he could not tell me of any rising young Latinists and instead of ~~talking~~ pointing out sources of enlightenment in true editor fashion asked me whether I could not help him on the classical side of the Encyclopedia Britannica /myself/[25] and get him some good American contributors in other departments.—I must not forget to mention that Tulloch sent you sundry kind messages and thanked you for your reports which he hopes to receive regularly.—Yesterday I dined with Professor Dickson and, as I mentioned, spent the evening at Tait's where I met Crum Brown[26] the chemist and Eggeling, the Sanskrit professor—some of whose remarks

I have already anticipated. To-day is a holiday[27] throughout England and to make sure of finding Greenwood[28] at Manchester I telegraphed him yesterday but have not yet received an answer. If he is not at Manchester I shall probably go to York to-day and the day after to London. Thence after looking about me for a day or two I shall go to Cambridge.

I have been much disappointed in missing Robertson Smith[29] who has gone on to Aberdeen—His trial takes place this week here and I doubt whether this would be a good time to approach him at any rate. From what I can gather he would be available for a course of lectures—but I have an undefined suspicion that he is too eccentric for our purposes as a worker on the staff.

In conclusion I must say that Scotland is not very promising soil for the rearing of the kind of men we want. The best are themselves exotics or natives largely grafted on. In England I am afraid there is too little independent work in the classics but I will not prejudge—

With best regards to Mrs. Gilman

    I am

                          Yours faithfully
                          B. L. Gildersleeve

1. For Jebb, see No. 45 and n. 4.

2. Sir William Thomson, first Baron Kelvin of Largs (1824-1907), at twenty-one was made professor of natural philosophy at Glasgow, a post he held from 1846 to 1899. He made his mark with his work on electrodynamic qualities of metals, most notably in laying the transatlantic cable (*DNB 1901-1911*, 508-17). Gilman had contacted him while in Scotland seeking faculty in 1875, because Thomson had created the first laboratory of physics in Great Britain and his complaints (echoed by other Glasgow professors) about the university's new Gothic buildings may have raised Gilman's hopes of gaining him for the faculty (*Hawkins*, 33). In 1884 Thomson gave a series of twenty lectures (to twenty-six students) at Hopkins *On Molecular Dynamics and the Wave Theory of Light* (Baltimore: Johns Hopkins Press; London: C. J. Clay and Sons, 1904).

3. George Gilbert Ramsay (1839-1921), son of Sir George Ramsay and nephew of William Ramsay, professor of Latin at Glasgow, was professor of humanity at Glasgow (1863-1906). He is best known as a translator, particularly of the Loeb Juvenal and Persius (Cambridge, Mass.: Harvard University Press, 1950) (see *AJP* 40 [1919]: 332-34), and also for *The Annals of Tacitus* (London: J. Murray, 1904-9) and *The Histories of Tacitus* (London: J. Murray, 1915).

4. John Young, M.D. (1835-1902), was from 1866 to 1902 professor of natural history, Honeyman Gillespie lecturer on geology, and keeper of the Hunterian Museum, the repository of manuscripts and rare books at the University of Glasgow.

5. On teaching Greek at Glasgow in the 1890s, see Jebb's successor, G. Murray, *An Unfinished Autobiography*, ed. J. Smith and A. Toynbee (London: George Allen and Unwin, 1960), 93-103.

6. At the fixed exchange rate of $4.76 to the pound, Jebb's income equaled around $5,700, Dickson's $8,000, compared with Gildersleeve's $5,000.

7. See No. 35, n. 5.

8. Peter Guthrie Tait (1831-1901) was professor of mathematics at Queen's College,

Belfast (1854–60), and professor of natural philosophy at Edinburgh (1860–1901). *DNB 1901–1911*, 471–74.

9. Alexander Dickson (1836–87) was professor of botany at Dublin (1866–68), Glasgow (1868–79), and Edinburgh, where he was also Regius keeper of the Royal Botanic Garden (1879–87). *DNB* 5: 946.

10. John Stuart Blackie (1809–95), after a brief stint at the law (1834–39), was appointed first Regius professor of humanity at Marischal College, Aberdeen (1839–52), then professor of Greek at Edinburgh (1852–82). Better known for his politics and poetry (particularly the hymn "Angels holy, high and lowly" in his *Lays and Legends of Ancient Greece* [Edinburgh: Sutherland and K., 1857]) than for his scholarship, he produced the successful translations *The Lyrical Dramas of Aeschylus* (see the modern Everyman edition: London: J. M. Dent, 1930) and particularly *Homer and the Iliad*, 4 vols. (Edinburgh: Edmonston and Douglas, 1866). See, further, A. M. Stoddart, *John Stuart Blackie: A Biography*, 2 vols. (Edinburgh: W. Blackwood, 1895).

11. The port, yachting center, and resort in Argyll on Oban Bay, Sound of Kerrera, sixty air miles northwest of Glasgow.

12. William Young Sellar (1825–90) was a fellow of Oriel College (1848–53), assistant professor of Latin at Glasgow (1851–53), assistant (1853–59) and professor (1859–63) of Greek at St. Andrews, then professor of humanity at Edinburgh (1863–90). His chief works are still in profitable use by students and critics: *Roman Poets of the Republic* (Edinburgh: Edmonston and Douglas, 1863; 3d ed., Oxford: Clarendon Press, 1889), *Roman Poets of the Augustan Age: Virgil* (Oxford: Clarendon Press, 1877; 3d ed., 1897), and the posthumous *Roman Poets of the Augustan Age: Horace and the Elegiac Poets* (Oxford: Clarendon Press, 1892). In 1851, at twenty-six, he married Eleanor Mary Dennistoun, twenty-two, his only wife; Gildersleeve's reference to his "young wife" is ironical or erroneous. See E. M. Sellar, *Recollections and Impressions* (Edinburgh: Blackwood, 1907) and *DNB* 17: 1164.

13. Julius Eggeling (1842–1918), was born in Anhalt, Germany, educated at Breslau and Berlin, and was professor of Sanskrit at Edinburgh from 1875 to 1918. His chief publication is his translation of the *Satapatha-Brâhmana* (Oxford: Clarendon Press, 1882–1900).

14. For example, of all the nineteenth-century classicists who were native Scots, only W. D. Geddes (1828–1900) of King's, Aberdeen, and James Pillans (1778–1864) were trained exclusively at Scottish universities; J. C. Shairp (1819–85), Sellar (n. 12 above), Campbell (No. 45, n. 12), and J. Burnet (1863–1928) of St. Andrews were trained at Balliol; G. G. Ramsay (n. 3 above) and D. K. Sandford (1798–1838) of Glasgow also at Oxford; W. Ramsay (1806–65) and R. C. Jebb (No. 45, n. 4) of Glasgow were trained at Cambridge; Blackie (n. 10 above) of Aberdeen and Edinburgh was trained in Germany; and George Dunbar (1774–1851) of Edinburgh had no university training. E. L. Lushington (1811–93), an Englishman from Cambridge, and Gilbert Murray, an Australian from Oxford, were the only non-native classics professors. See M. L. Clarke, *Classical Education in Britain, 1500–1900* (Cambridge: Cambridge University Press, 1959), 152–59.

15. George Chrystal (1851–1911), professor of mathematics at Edinburgh. His article is in the ninth edition (1875–89), 8: 3–105.

16. Henry Augustus Rowland (1848–1901), professor of physics at Hopkins (1876–1901), and one of the "Hopkins Four." See No. 30, n. 2.

17. Probably Lyman Beecher Hall (1852–1935), the brightest young member of Remsen's chemistry seminar. With a Ph.D. from Göttingen (1875; A.B. Amherst, 1873), he received one of the first chemistry fellowships and went on to be professor of chemistry at Haverford College (1880–1917). Two articles may have attracted Chrystal's attention, "On the Oxidation of Mesitylene-Sulphonic Acid," written with Remsen for *JHU Notes from the Chemical Laboratory* 1 (1877), and "On the Oxidation of Substitution Products of Mesitylene," also with Remsen, ibid., 10 (1878).

18. James Clerk Maxwell (1831-79), professor of natural philosophy in Marischal College, Aberdeen (1855-60), professor of natural philosophy at King's College, London (1860-65), and professor of experimental physics at Cambridge (1871-79). See L. Campbell and W. Garnett, *The Life of James Clerk Maxwell* (London: Macmillan, 1882; rev. ed., 1884).

19. On Tulloch, see previous letter, n. 8, and below.

20. Whitsunday (always May 15 by law in Scotland) and Martinmas are the chief term-days—i.e., days in the quarter of the year when rents are due and servants are engaged for the winter or summer half-year.

21. I.e., people changing dwellings.

22. The Second General Council of the Pan-Presbyterian Alliance was to meet in Philadelphia, 28 September-2 October 1880 (*NYTimes*, 3 October 1880: 12).

23. In 1879-80 Tulloch assumed the editorship of the once progressive monthly *Fraser's Magazine for Town and Country*, which had published *Sartor Resartus* but was now suffering a decline owing to the lingering influence of Carlyle. Tulloch's last issue was January 1881; *Fraser's* died in October 1882, and Tulloch never came to Hopkins. See, further, *The Wellesley Index to Victorian Periodicals*, 1824-1900, ed. W. E. Houghton (Toronto: University of Toronto Press, 1972), 2: 303-521.

24. Thomas Spencer Baynes (1823-87) was professor of logic and metaphysics at Edinburgh (1851-55) and editor of the *Edinburgh Guardian* (1850-54) and *Daily News* (1857-64). From 1864 to his death he was professor of logic, metaphysics, and English literature at St. Andrews. He edited the ninth edition of the *Encyclopedia Britannica* from 1873 to 1887 and wrote the article on Shakespeare. He is also known for his translation of A. Arnauld's *Port-Royal Logic* (Edinburgh: Sutherland and Knox, 1851).

25. Gildersleeve did not contribute to the *Encyclopedia Britannica*.

26. Alexander Crum Brown (1838-1922), professor of chemistry at Edinburgh (1869-1908).

27. The Whitsunday bank holiday.

28. Gildersleeve would have been particularly interested in seeing Joseph Gouge Greenwood (1821-94), who trained at University College, London (B.A. 1840) and served Owens College, Manchester as professor of ancient and modern history (1850-54), professor of Latin (1850-69), professor of Greek (1850-85), and principal (1867-89). Like Hopkins, Owens was a new university founded through the largesse of a wealthy industrialist. Greenwood, a classicist, had guided the college through some desperate years to become the leading university of applied science in Britain. Moreover, Gildersleeve had spoken favorably of Greenwood's *seminarium* in *University Work*: 111-12, and no doubt favored his curriculum, which stressed the role of language and literature in this scientific environment. When Owens became Victoria University, Manchester, Greenwood was its first vice-chancellor (1880-86). His best-known work was *The Elements of Greek Grammar Adapted to the System of Crude Forms* (London: Walton and Maberly, 1857; 4th ed., 1873). See Joseph Thompson, *The Owens College* and H. B. Charlton, *Portrait of a University, 1851-1951* (both Manchester: Manchester University Press, 1886 and 1951 respectively).

29. The case of William Robertson Smith (see "Correspondents") naturally attracted the attention of everyone in Scotland, and not least Gildersleeve, since it seemed likely that Smith would soon need employment and might be happy to leave Scotland. The eight articles Smith wrote for the ninth edition of the *Encyclopedia Britannica* covered much of the scientific analysis of the Bible, done principally by Germans (and thus unfamiliar to the British), since the eighth edition (1853-60). His article "Bible" claimed a section of Deuteronomy (containing the "Deuteronomic Code") was not contemporaneous with the rest and thus not written by Moses, since it contains precepts that elsewhere in the Bible are proved to have been revealed at a later date. This view was denounced by the authorities of the Free Church as leading the reader to believe "the Bible does not present a reliable statement of the truth of

God, and that God is not the author of it." Smith was removed from his professorial, but not ministerial, duties in 1877, and he requested a trial for libel before the General Association, which postponed a final decision for four annual meetings from 1877 until it finally agreed to vote on the case on 20 May 1881. See, further, No. 48, n. 5, and No. 53.

44 To: Daniel Coit Gilman
*JHU-Gilman*

Cambridge May 28, 1880

My dear Mr. Gilman:

I have been very busy in the last ten days and while several half-finished letters to you attest my desire to show that I am doing what I can, I have not found time to digest the multitude of impressions and experiences gained since I last wrote you. I now send you a brief itinerary, promising myself to make a day for a more careful report.—I had a pleasant and I hope profitable day in Manchester with Greenwood[1] who was kindness itself. I saw the best men there in my line of work[2]—but the great scientific luminaries were out of place.[3] In London I did little more than look about me and study the ground for future operations. The only business I accomplished there was to see the Macmillans.[4] On Saturday last I came to Cambridge. The town has been full of strangers and the regular work of the University has been much interfered with;[5] but the opportunity of seeing certain sides of the life here will always be of indirect advantage to me and after all I have been able to see and talk with most of the men who are likely to be useful to me. Of course I have made it a point to hunt up the more promising young men—I can't say that I am much impressed with the force or grasp of those whom I have seen. The peculiar constitution of the English universities is almost necessarily fatal to the development of those qualities which we want in a classic. The scientific men are much more alert—more like ourselves. Skeat[6] and Sweet[7] might be good names for us—if we wanted names. The men themselves would not be forces in America. I don't know whether they can be had, but when I say that Skeat has the aspect of a tired and discouraged teacher of a girl's school and that he has no literary faculty that I can learn, and that Sweet, though a very young-looking man of his years, seems to be largely employed in the study of his spectacles, has no vivacity—no go, /You can understand why/ I should very much hesitate before attempting to transplant them to our soil. At the request of Martin's[8] friend, Dew-Smith,[9] I inspected Haddon,[10] a candidate for a demonstratorship of biology in the J.H.U. His manners are not the most engaging in the world but he is frank and full of life and there is nothing that I could discern which would prevent his abilities which must be considerable from being available for our purposes—

Latinists are hard to find here. Two of the younger men who are well-spoken of as classics,—Verrall[11] and Postgate[12]—will not answer. The first would be a laughing-stock on account of his peculiar mode of speech—and then he is specifically Greek. Postgate is ambitious but very green. While the boys here are very charming and straightforward, the continuance of schoolboy life, if I may say so, into maturer years breeds a certain ineptness for dealing with our problems and the best scholar in the world who has not diversified his life more than some of the specimens I meet here, would be singularly unfit for organizing a new department. After the new scheme of classical studies has had time to bear fruit we may hope for help from England.[13] Until then I am afraid we shall have to look elsewhere and that without disparagement to the capacity of our cousins or the elegance of their scholarship—without disparagement, I say, and yet I am afraid, if I were to go into details, you would accuse me of my old sin of fault-finding. As I said before, I have met most of the men whom I desired to meet. Jebb is now lecturing at Oxford, whither I go today.—

If I am not doing much for the University directly, I am tolerably sure that I shall accomplish something for the Journal which excites quite as much interest as I could have hoped.

Excuse the extreme scratchiness of this letter—It is a beautiful day but shivery and I am writing under great disadvantages. In a day or two I hope to make a more readable report.

Present my kindest regards to Mrs. Gilman.

Yours faithfully
B. L. Gildersleeve

1. On Greenwood, see preceding letter, n. 28.

2. These include the professor of Latin, Augustus Samuel Wilkins (1843-1905), editor of *M. Tulli Ciceronis de oratore libri tres* (Oxford: Clarendon Press, 1892) and *The Epistles of Horace* (London: Macmillan, 1892) and translator (with E. B. England) of G. Curtius's *Principles of Greek Etymology* and *The Greek Verb* (both London: J. Murray, 1875 and 1880 respectively).

3. For example, Henry Enfield Roscoe and Carl Schorlemmer in chemistry, W. C. Williamson in botany, Balfour Stewart and T. H. Core in natural philosophy, Arthur Schuster in physics, and Osborne Reynolds in engineering. Two of Manchester's greatest "scientific luminaries," J. P. Joule (1818-99) and John Dalton (1766-1844), had no connection with the university. See, further, R. H. Kargon, *Science in Victorian Manchester: Enterprise and Expertise* (Manchester: Manchester University Press, 1977).

4. The publishing firm founded by Daniel (1813-57) and Alexander (1818-96) Macmillan, originally in Cambridge, at this time in London at 29 and 30 Bedford Street, The Strand, was the British distributor of *AJP*. See C. Morgan, *The House of Macmillan (1843-1943)* (New York: Macmillan, 1944).

5. A three-day cricket match between the Gentlemen of England and the Cambridge Cricket team took place from the 24th to the 26th.

6. Rev. Walter William Skeat (1835-1912), the noted dialectician, founder of the English Dialect Society, and Elrington and Bosworth professor of Anglo-Saxon, Cambridge, from 1878. He was a close friend of J. A. H. Murray's (see No. 47, n. 9), whom he greatly supported in the early days of the *Oxford English Dictionary*; see K. M. E. Murray, *Caught in the Web of Words: James A. H. Murray and the Oxford English Dictionary* (New Haven: Yale University Press, 1977), 83-86. *DNB 1912-1921*, 495-96.

7. Henry Sweet (1845-1912), comparative philologist, phonetician, Anglicist, at this time was without a university position (having taken a fourth in *Literae Humaniores* at Balliol), despite the publication of his *Anglo-Saxon Reader*. The original of G. B. Shaw's Professor Higgins, Sweet had few friends, as he was, in K. M. E. Murray's words, "a most difficult, cross-grained man" (Murray [cited n. 6 above], 77). Luring him to Hopkins was one of the prime purposes of Gildersleeve's trip. By 1881 Gilman was so certain that Sweet would come to Hopkins that he dismissed A. S. Cook (see "Correspondents"). Despite the offer of a professorship at the usual starting rate of $5,000 per annum, Sweet declined (*Hawkins*, 163). He ultimately became university reader in phonetics at Oxford in 1901. *DNB 1912-1921*, 519-20.

8. Henry Newell Martin (1848-96), an Irishman and student of Thomas Huxley's, was the first to take a D.Sc. in physiology at Cambridge. In 1874 he was made a fellow of Trinity College, Cambridge, and in 1876 became professor of biology at Hopkins. *DAB* 12: 337-38.

9. Albert George Dew-Smith (1848-1903), a graduate of Cambridge (1873; M.A. 1876), was connected with the Cambridge Scientific Instrument Co. and the Cambridge Engraving Co.

10. Alfred Cort Haddon (1855-1940), educated at Cambridge, became professor of zoology at the Royal College of Science, Dublin (1880-1901), university lecturer in ethnology at Cambridge (1900-1909), and reader in ethnology at the University of London (1909-26).

11. Arthur Woolgar Verrall (1851-1912) was fellow of Trinity College from 1874, barrister, Lincoln's Inn, 1877. For Gildersleeve on Verrall, see *Nation* 61 (22 August 1895): 136-37; *AJP* 14 (1893): 398 ( = *SBM*, 20-21); 16 (1895): 261 ( = *SBM*, 31-32). When Gildersleeve came to notice Verrall's passing (*AJP*, 35 [1914]: 491-92), his attitude towards the man both as a scholar and particularly as a teacher had changed little since 1880, when Gildersleeve was most interested in finding a man who could teach well. On Verrall, see M. A. Bayfield, "Memoir," in A. W. Verrall, *Collected Literary Essays, Classical and Modern* (Cambridge: Cambridge University Press, 1913), ix-cii, and R. Ackerman, "Verrall on Euripides' *Suppliants* 939ff," *GRBS* 14 (1973): 103-8.

12. John Percival Postgate (1853-1926), professor of comparative philology, University College, London (1880-1908), professor of Latin at Liverpool (1909-20), editor of *Corpus poetarum Latinorum*, 2 vols. (London: Bell, 1894-1905). He contributed "Etymological Studies" to *AJP* 3 (1882): 329-39; 4 (1883): 63-70. For favorable comments on his *Select Elegies of Propertius* (London: Macmillan, 1881), see *AJP* 4 (1883): 208n, and for Brief Mentions, *AJP* 5 (1884): 542; 32 (1910): 241; 39 (1918): 110.

13. The Universities of Oxford and Cambridge Act of 1876 initiated reforms, part of which were intended to raise the level of scholarship by employing intracollege lectures, allowing professors to lecture on their specialties rather than on general topics. Further benefits of improved teaching did not immediately accrue until the college tutors, of whom E. C. Wickham of New College was the model, gave increased attention to individual instruction. See, further, M. L. Clarke, *Classical Education in Britain, 1500-1900* (Cambridge: Cambridge University Press, 1959), 111-27, and W. R. Ward, *Victorian Oxford* (London: Frank Cass, 1965), 303ff.

45 To: DANIEL COIT GILMAN
*JHU-Gilman*

Oxford June 1, 1880

My dear Mr. Gilman:

I am afraid that my last letter by the wildness of its chirography and the incoherence of its expressions, has made you seriously uneasy as to the effect of my trip on a too excitable brain. Indeed I have myself been meditating whether it would not be better for me to withdraw to Colney Hatch[1] or some such quiet retreat and allow my perturbed intellect to gather itself up before writing to you again. In all seriousness most of my ~~work~~ /writing/, in fact all of it, for many years has been done in perfect seclusion and it is very hard for me to do anything off-hand and en route. I am constantly reviewing in my mind what I have done and what I have failed to do, and at the end I may be able to make an intelligible report[2]—which will at all events have the merit of frankness.

At Cambridge, as I wrote you, I had a pleasant, if not a very profitable, time and at least gained an insight into the working of an English University which I could not have got from books. If you wish to test my judgment of men ask Martin[3] how he thinks Verrall and Postgate would suit our American conditions, and yet everywhere Verrall and Postgate are spoken of as the most promising young classical scholars in Cambridge. I have already given you a hint as to my estimate of Skeat and Sweet—not as to their attainments, of course, but as to their availability.—In Oxford I have met several men whom I wanted to see for various reasons. Jebb[4] I found at last. He is an excessively nervous man and all the time he is lecturing tries to make a double spiral twist out of his legs and casts from side to side an agonized stare at his auditors. His voice is highpitched, fashionable English style, though not so disagreeable as most readers[5] of that persuasion make it. And his utterance is broken every few minutes by a distressing hysteric cough. When he translates poetry, he lets his voice fall into the lower ranges, which are not unpleasant, only you wonder which is /his/ own voice. Of course the language is elegance itself and the literary judgment in the main sound.[6] I had a very pleasant talk with him after his lecture and while his manner is nervous, he was by no means the shrinking creature I had heard him described—He urged me very much to spend some days with him in Cambridge before my departure and actually volunteered to write for the Journal,[7] a favor which, in my modesty, I should hardly have dreamed of asking. As Jebb is one of the most prominent Greek scholars in England, I was especially interested in him and so have been betrayed into a bit of description, though, of course, he is out of our range. The man who impressed me most in my line as a man of learning and keenness and practical sense is Bywater[8] and if there were a man in

Latin at all like him, he would be worth all the compassing of sea and land which I have undertaken. But Robinson Ellis![9] If by any mischance we ~~shoud~~ had invited him, he would have come for he seems to be poor[10] and complains of small emoluments,—a strain far less common here than in the professional class in America—but a more awkward, ungainly, unworldly, blundering man it is impossible to conceive. His books are printed so superbly that somehow one fancies, absurdly enough, that the author was somewhat after the same pattern, but head, face, voice, gait, manner everything about the man is irredeemably absurd. Ridiculous stories about him without end are current in University circles and he is perfectly childlike in trotting out his weaknesses for inspection.[11] I shall have much to tell you about him for the amusement of your leisure moments, if you ever have any.—Lewis Campbell,[12] the editor of Sophocles, if not a very strong man, is bright and enthusiastic and his speaking face is a pleasant contrast to the wooden visages one encounters on every hand. Butcher,[13] the successful translator of the Odyssey, is a handsome young fellow with a marvellously interesting and intelligent countenance, but he is, by birth, I believe, an Irishman. Both Scotch and Irish by their fire are more likely to do good with us than the average Englishman—our Englishmen, of course, have fire enough.[14]

The grandees I have not seen yet, nor do I care much to see them. Liddell[15] was not at home and I am only afraid that I shall have to repeat my visit. Jowett,[16] the master of Balliol, is a laughing stock among Greek scholars for his inaccuracy, his strength lying simply in the elegance of his style. Max Müller[17] I have no excuse for calling on. Sayce[18] thinks I should do well to come back in vacation when all these men are more accessible than now when the tide of commemoration is beginning to rise.[19]

The Journal excites much interest and the /plan/ is warmly approved. I shall certainly have some prominent English names on my contributors list—Jebb, Campbell, Mayor, Ellis[20]—That is something to have achieved, something that I could hardly have achieved by sitting quiet in Baltimore. And that as so much else I owe to you—

Yours faithfully
B. L. Gildersleeve

1. Village in North London, site of a mental hospital opened in 1851.

2. See No. 41, n. 5.

3. On Martin, Verrall, Postgate, Skeat, and Sweet, see preceding letter, nn. 8, 11, 12, 6, and 7.

4. Sir Richard Claverhouse Jebb (1841–1905), professor of Greek at Glasgow (1875–89), Regius professor of Greek at Cambridge from 1889, lecturer at Johns Hopkins in 1892; knighted in 1900. He was a friend of Tennyson's and editor of *Selections from the Attic Orators . . .* (London: Macmillan, 1880), Sophocles in seven vols. (Cambridge: Cambridge University Press, 1883–96), and *Bacchylides* (Cambridge: Cambridge University Press, 1905).

Gildersleeve reviewed his *Homer: An Introduction to the Iliad and the Odyssey* (Boston: Ginn, 1887) in the *Nation* 44 (19 May 1887): 429, and others of his books at *AJP* 10 (1889): 123–24; 15 (1894): 118–19; 28 (1907): 479; 17 (1896): 390 (see also 30 [1909]: 226). See also Gildersleeve's memorial notice of him, 26 (1905): 491: "Grammarians, it is true, do not spare grammarians,—such is the savagery of our tribe,—but I am literary man enough not to invite a disastrous comparison with such spiritual insight, such artistic faculty, such unerring taste." See also "Professor Jebb's Great Work," *JHU Circulars*, no. 187 (May 1906): 104–5 (reprinted from the *Baltimore News*, 9 December 1905). Jebb's wife, the former Caroline Lane Reynolds of Philadelphia, wrote his life: *Life and Letters of Sir Richard Claverhouse Jebb, O.M., Litt. D.* (Cambridge: Cambridge University Press, 1907), with a chapter by Verrall on Jebb as a scholar (427–87).

5. I.e., "lecturers."

6. For a similar view of Jebb's lecturing, see A. S. F. Gow, *Letters from Cambridge, 1939–1944* (Oxford: Clarendon Press, 1945), 240.

7. Nevertheless, Jebb contributed to the *AJP* only a correspondence on *Antigone* at 12 (1891): 256–58.

8. "A fine morning . . . fine in every sense of the word, was the morning [in 1880] I spent with Ingram Bywater in his rooms at Exeter, part of the time pacing up and down the 'hortus conclusus' of the college and talking of Dion Chrysostomos, who was engaging my attention at the time. . . . Bywater was so much more than the prince of Aristotelians that he was" (*AJP* 36 [1915]: 476–77). On Bywater, see "Correspondents."

9. Robinson Ellis (1834–1913), professor of Latin, University College, London (1870), Latin reader, Oxford (1883–93), Corpus professor of Latin literature from 1893. "To the world at large he was the great editor of Catullus, though he edited so much else. To me he was a sympathetic friend and a generous helper in giving the American Journal of Philology the professional stamp. . . . Of the classical men whom I met during that summer, Robinson Ellis gave me the most cordial welcome, shewed the deepest interest in my project, and proved to be the most conspicuous and steadfast contributor to the work" (*AJP* 34 [1913]: 494–96; see also 36 [1915]: 231, 476). Ellis contributed at least one article per year to the first sixteen volumes of *AJP*; Gildersleeve reviewed his edition of Ovid's *Ibis*, *AJP* 3 (1882): 86–89, his *Correspondence of Fronto and Marcus Aurelius*, *AJP* 25 (1904): 357–58 ( = *SBM*, 115–16): on his Phaedrus lecture, see the *Nation* 35 (8 June 1882): 487–88, and *AJP* 15 (1894): 520–21 ( = *SBM*, 28–29).

10. Ellis was in fact very rich.

11. He was absent-minded to a fault and cursed with terrible eyesight, which led to the many stories. See Albert C. Clark, "Robinson Ellis 1834–1913," *Proceedings of the British Academy* 6 (1913–14): 517–24.

12. Rev. Lewis Campbell (1830–1908), born in Edinburgh, was professor of Greek at St. Andrews (1863–1902) and best known for his work on Sophocles and his chronology of the Platonic dialogues based on stylistic analysis. Associated throughout his career with Jowett, he completed his mentor's edition of the *Republic* (see n. 19 below) and collaborated with E. Abbott on *The Life and Letters of Benjamin Jowett, M.A.* (London: J. Murray, 1897). See *Memorials in Verse and Prose of Lewis Campbell*, ed. F. P. Campbell (London: W. Clowes, 1914).

13. Samuel Henry Butcher (1850–1910), born in Dublin, lecturer, University College, Oxford (1876–82), then professor of Greek at Edinburgh (1882–1903), M.P. (U.) Cambridge (1906–10), and president of the British Academy of Letters (1909). His translation, done with Andrew Lang, *The Odyssey of Homer Done into English Prose* (London: Macmillan, 1879), was praised by Gildersleeve in *AJP* 1 (1880): 466–68. See also Gildersleeve's reviews of other books of Butcher's: *AJP* 12 (1891): 521–22; 25 (1904): 482–83; *Nation* 60 (1895): 364–65; as well as Gildersleeve's memorial notice of him, *AJP* 32 (1911): 122: "Thirty-one years ago I

made for the first time the personal acquaintance of some of the lights of English classical scholarship. . . . Butcher, many years my junior, was then in the first flush of achievement. My heart went out to the young scholar. Whose heart was ever closed to him? . . . Vigilant care for the original, kind consideration for the interpreter—this is the spirit in which we ought all to work, a spirit of which Butcher was a shining example." Butcher was also one of the early visiting lecturers at Hopkins.

14. I.e., Martin (preceding letter, n. 8) and Sylvester (see No. 41, n. 4).

15. The Very Rev. Henry George Liddell (1811-98), dean of Christ Church, Oxford, had produced his *Oxford Greek Lexicon* (with Robert Scott) in 1843 (to the 7th ed. [1882] of which Gildersleeve contributed articles on ἔστε, ἵνα, πρός, οὐ, μή, and πρίν; see *JHU Circulars*, no. 33 [February 1883]: 59), followed by his popular students' textbooks, *A History of Rome from the Earliest Times to the Establishment of the Empire* (London: n.p., 1855) and *Life of Julius Caesar* (New York: Sheldon, 1860). See H. L. Thompson's *Henry George Liddell, D.D. Dean of Christ Church, Oxford* (London: J. Murray, 1899), 65-82.

16. Benjamin Jowett (1817-93), Regius professor of Greek at Oxford from 1855, master of Balliol College from 1870. In addition to his translations of the whole of Plato in four volumes (Oxford: Clarendon Press, 1868-71), Thucydides (Oxford: Clarendon Press, 1881), and the *Politics of Aristotle* in two volumes (Oxford: Clarendon Press, 1885), he conceived an Oxford edition of the chief Platonic dialogues, to which he (with Lewis Campbell) contributed an edition of the *Republic* in three volumes (Oxford: Clarendon Press, 1894). In reviewing his *Politics* in *AJP* 7 (1886): 125, Gildersleeve politely explained the reasons for the scholarly attacks on Jowett: "Dr. Jowett's translations, by reason of his peculiar conception of his task, withdraw themselves from philological criticism, and belong rather to the domain of English literature, which they undoubtedly adorn. He recasts his author rather than renders him, and there is no effort to reproduce the stylistic effect in English." Harsher criticisms by others were sufficient to make corrections take up one-third of the text of the third edition of his Plato (see *AJP* 13 [1892]: 259-60, and Paul Shorey's review, ibid., 349-72). Jowett's answer to a student who pointed out one of the "many slight but indisputable errors in the first edition" was: "It is not that I do not know these elementary things: but the effort of making the English harmonious is so great, that one's mind is insensibly drawn away from the details of the Greek" (L. Campbell, "Obituary," *CR* 7 [1893]: 475). See G. Faber, *Jowett: A Portrait with Background* (Cambridge, Mass.: Harvard University Press, 1958).

17. Rt. Hon. Friedrich Max Müller (1823-1900), born in Dessau, Germany, was Taylorian professor of modern languages, Oxford (1854), fellow of All Souls (1856-68), Corpus professor of comparative philology from 1868. Principal among his publications were *Ancient Sanskrit Literature* (London: W. H. Allen, 1849-74; 2d ed., 1890-92), *Lectures on the Science of Language* (London: Longmans, 1861), his edition of the *Rig Veda* in 5 vols. (London: Trübner, 1869), *Chips from a German Workshop* (London: Longmans, 1867-75), and *Sacred Books of the East* (Oxford: Clarendon Press, 1879). See *My Autobiography: A Fragment by the Rt. Hon. Professor F. Max Mueller*, ed. W. G. Max Müller (London: Longmans, Green, 1901), and *The Life and Letters of the Right Honourable Friedrich Max Müller*, ed. by his wife, 2 vols. (London: Longmans, Green, 1902).

18. Rev. Archibald Henry Sayce (1846-1933) was tutor at Queen's College, Oxford, until 1876, when he became Max Müller's deputy in the chair of comparative philology; he was professor of Assyriology from 1891 to 1919. His principal publications were *Assyrian Grammar for Comparative Purposes* (London: Trübner, 1872); *Babylonian Literature* (London: S. Bagster and Sons, 1877); *Introduction to the Science of Language*, 2 vols. (London: C. K. Paul, 1880); and an edition of Herodotus 1-3, *The Ancient Empires of the East*, 2 vols. (London: Macmillan, 1883). See, further, his *Reminiscences* (London: Macmillan, 1923).

19. I.e., Commemoration balls and the Encaenia were scheduled for the next week (see No. 46, n. 1).

20. Gildersleeve made a similar promise (adding Nettleship's name) in *AJP* 1, no. 3. For Jebb's contribution, see n. 7 above. Campbell contributed "Notes on the *Agamemnon* of Aeschylus" to *AJP* 1 (1880): 427–39, and correspondence in 3 (1882): 128–29. J. B. Mayor never contributed to the journal, and for Ellis's bibliography, see n. 9 above. For the only other English contributor, Nettleship, see following letter, n. 9.

46 To: Daniel Coit Gilman
*JHU-Gilman*

(London)
~~May~~ 9, 1880
June

My dear Mr. Gilman:

When I was at home I used to come to you with my troubles far more frequently than I ought to have done; and now that I have had the misfortune of missing the last train which would have taken me to Oxford in time to see the <u>encaenia</u> and Sylvester's glorification,[1] I naturally turn to you and find some consolation in telling you about it. I know that I ought not to have postponed the matter so long, but to the very last I was doubtful about going and it only became startlingly evident to me that it was a thing by all means to be done when I found that it was too late.—The reaction from the excitement in which I have lived during the past few weeks has left me in a depressed unenergetic mood, and if I were to expand now, I should produce a wrong impression as to the result of my trip so far. In every new place to which I come a certain period of waiting seems necessary and then the fruit ~~comes~~ /drops/, as it were, of itself. In London it is hard for me to see what I am accomplishing, for while Sylvester has had me made an honorary member of the Athenaeum,[2] which adds greatly to the comfort of my life here, I do not find that I am making much headway in forming acquaintances with men who would be useful to me. Meantime I am trying to do some work in the British Museum.

In looking back on the last month, the gain that I can discern is chiefly in the matter of the Journal. I have not only fair words and fair promises but articles in course of preparation by men of eminence.[3] Indeed I may say that I have enlisted most of the best men to be had and I am confident that the University cannot do more in the way of making itself felt throughout the world of science and letters than by keeping up its publications. Of course, I consider the facilities afforded me for making this trip a direct contribution on the part of the University to the Journal and gratefully accept the favor, hoping that it may not be necessary to ask for any other subvention than that already accorded, but if the case should arise, I hope to have your influence in behalf of an enterprise which promises to reward so richly in a higher sense all the troubles and, I may say, anguish it has cost.—At the same time I would suggest that a wider distribution of our circulars would not be amiss. Scientific and mathematical men are well aware as to what is doing at the Johns Hopkins, but there is not so much knowledge as to the organic working /of the institution/ as might be desired. It is true that our ~~force~~ /strength/ is almost wholly on the scientific and mathematical side,[4] but the plan of our historical and philological studies deserves some attention and might attract new forces. As to that part of my mission—the acquisition of first rate help—I am not by any means in the best spirits. As I wrote before—it is something not to have been betrayed by mere reputation into inviting men, who would have been sadly out of place. An error of that sort is even graver than delay can be. I have spoken confidentially to some men who know the situation and have no desire to join us themselves. They lament the dearth of men. Jebb thinks that Greek studies are going to ruin in England,[5] Bywater said he thought we should find better and broader men in America, having heard very good accounts of Wheeler[6] from Usener[7] and Buecheler[8]—Nettleship[9] declares that there isn't a suitable man except Pelham,[10] and Pelham is rich besides having switched off to the historical side. The grooves here are so deep that it is almost impossible to lift men out of them; and this is especially true of the classical ~~side~~ /people/. The scientific men can work as easily among us as in England. They are the only Americans among the English.[11] London may yet offer something. The type here seem to be much more like our own and I hope in a few days to get at some of the prominent members of the Savile Club,[12] who will enlighten me.

How long I shall stay in London depends on the way in which matters open—perhaps not longer than the end of next week—

As soon as I received your note of the 22[d], I wrote to Greenwood[13] thanking him and promising if possible to be present and if I am in England, I shall not repeat the blunder of to-day.

The respite from my ordinary work has made /me/ already eager to be at something more definite; I realize and realize most painfully that the heyday of life is over and I must gather up results with all speed. Perhaps this enormous pressure may result in something commensurate with the generosity on the /one/ part and the anxiety on the other—for now as during my whole life I ~~have been~~ /am/ haunted by the ghost of failure, which I can only banish by gazing at duty. If the duty were only clearer! I earnestly hope that you will find time to make suggestions as to my future course.

Yours faithfully<br>B. L. Gildersleeve

1. Sylvester (No. 36, n. 2) was awarded the honorary degree of D.C.L. at the Oxford Encaenia on 9 June 1880. The same summer he was also awarded the Copley Medal by the Royal Society of London.

2. The foremost literary and scientific club in London, founded in 1824 by Sir Walter

Scott, Thomas Moore, and others. See F. R. Cowell, *The Athenaeum Club and Social Life in London, 1824-1974* (London: Heinemann, 1975).

3. See preceding letter, n. 20.

4. Gilman on the one hand stressed a balance of science and literature at Hopkins, but on the other, as a graduate of the Sheffield School, keenly felt the neglect of science prevalent in American schools. Despite Remsen's Commemoration Day speech of 1878, which expressed fear at the consequences of imbalance, and despite Gilman's report in 1879 that there was a balance "so far as I can judge," the disadvantage under which the languages and literatures operated was clear: of the first four appointments to the faculty, three were in the sciences. On the growth of science and mathematics at Hopkins, see *Hawkins*, 138-51 and 294-308.

5. See his 1889 address, "On the Present Tendencies in Classical Studies," in R. C. Jebb, *Essays and Addresses* (Cambridge: Cambridge University Press, 1907), 545-59, esp. 554-58, in which he worries about the "love of technicality" and over-specialization: "In our generation, and more especially in this country, that noble old conception of classical studies which is implied in the term 'humanities' has rather fallen into the background" (557).

6. John Henry Wheeler (1850-87) was educated at Harvard (A.B. 1871, A.M. 1875) and was one of Gildersleeve's first Greek fellows (1876-77). He took his Ph.D. at Bonn (1879) with Usener, and was professor of Latin at Bowdoin College (1881-82) and professor of Greek at the University of Virginia (1882-87).

7. For Usener, see "Correspondents."

8. Franz Buecheler (1837-1908) was professor of Latin at Freiburg and Greifswald, and finally at Bonn (1870-1908). A close friend of Usener's, he was known for his editions of Frontinus, the Latin verse inscriptions, and Petronius, as well as the *Homeric Hymn to Demeter*. He also did epigraphical and dialectological work of importance. See *AJP* 29 (1908): 247, and *Sandys*, 481-82.

9. Henry Nettleship (1839-93), Corpus professor of Latin at his college, Christ Church, Oxford (1878-93), edited Conington's *P. Vergili Maronis*, 3 vols. (London: Whitaker, 1858), Mark Pattison's *Essays* (Oxford: Clarendon Press, 1889), and wrote *Ancient Lives of Virgil* (Oxford: Clarendon Press, 1879). He was a stout early supporter of *AJP*, contributing articles at 1 (1880): 253-70; 2 (1881): 1-19; 342-44; 3 (1882): 1-16, 170-92; 4 (1883): 75-76; 391-415; and 7 (1886): 496-99. See *DNB* 14: 236-38, *Sandys*, 435-36.

10. Henry Francis Pelham (1846-1907) was fellow and tutor at Exeter College, Oxford, and professor of ancient history and fellow of Brasenose from 1897. His *Outlines of Roman History* (London: Percival, 1893; 5th ed., London: Rivington's, 1920) was very popular, and his volume of *Essays*, ed. F. Haverfield (Oxford: Clarendon Press, 1911), was published posthumously. See *DNB 1901-1911*, 96-97, and *Sandys*, 441-42.

11. I.e., the only ones with the American characteristics.

12. Begun as the "New Club" in 1868, with Jebb among the original members, the name was changed when the club moved to 15 Savile Row. Devoted to cheap, plain cuisine, simple furniture, and variety of membership, it formed a contrast with the more luxurious Athenaeum. See *The Savile Club, 1868-1923* (privately printed, n. p., 1923).

13. For Greenwood, see No. 43, n. 28.

### 47 To: DANIEL COIT GILMAN
### *JHU-Gilman*

London, June 25, 1880

My dear Mr. Gilman:

I have now been in London some three weeks and although I fear you are tired of my frequent letters, I must at all events give some signs of life.

If my stay has not been productive of as much direct benefit as I had hoped, still it has enabled me to form connections which will /be/ of service to my work in the future. A brief experiment convinced me that it would be impracticable to work at the British Museum, unless I could be at it continuously, which was, of course, out of the question. Everybody who consults the Museum only now and then has the same complaint to make. I had to wait as long for a book as I should have had to wait at the Peabody,[1] perhaps longer; it /is/ only when one is an habitué that the profit begins.—Mr. Sylvester's kindness in having me made an honorary member of the Athenaeum has made my stay in London much more pleasant than it would otherwise have been but the tone of the place prevents one from forming acquaintances rapidly; and I shall go away without having had any serious talks with certain men whose names are in every-body's mouth and whose thoughts are in everybody's mind. Still it is something at all to have talked with the men who are prominent here and while my uniform experience has been that the work is the best part of the writer, one understands or thinks he understands Browning or Matthew Arnold better from even a brief interview.[2] Grove[3] I have seen a couple of times. He is a manner of Stanley indicator[4] and half warned me against going to see the Dean[5]—a hint which was quite sufficient to a man, who is not very forward at any time. I have not come into any close relations with the leading philologians here but I have made myself sufficiently well-known to them to render a better acquaintance possible. So I have had long talks with A. J. Ellis,[6] Rich^d Morris,[7] Mark Pattison[8] of Oxford, and Murray,[9] Editor of the Philological Society's Dictionary and /have/ made a visit to the last named at Mill Hill, where I saw the process going on. From Mill Hill I went with Sweet to Hampstead,[10] where I dined with him and had a long interview. He develops after a while and if you want a name he would do better than I supposed at first. Still he would not be magnetic, and he has scarcely any experience as a teacher. From some chance expressions I judge that he can be had. He is living in rooms at Hampstead, does not come to town often, does not believe in vast libraries and works out his salvation with a selection of good books on his special line. By the way Murray, the editor of the Dictionary, thinks that Brandt's article is very good[11] and Sweet is disposed to encourage his proposition to translate his /(S's)/ Phonology into German.[12] Cook's review of Skeat seems also to be considered just in the main.[13] Indeed I think we have reason to be fairly satisfied with our younger men and the danger is that Lanman's recent elevation will turn their heads as it has turned his.[14] There is no more hope of a professor of Latin in England than there is in America and the complaints of utter deadness are as rife here as they are there. It is a pity to have no better report to make than that—but it is the simple truth. What Germany may offer, I cannot tell. France, of course, cannot be expected to furnish us with much. As to lectures, I cannot help thinking that with the usual inducements held out we might get any man who is not too much tied down by business engagements—so that you can make your selection on the other side better than I can here.

In the matter of influencing the press, I have been able to form relations with contributors to the Academy and the Saturday Review, but I have not succeeded in getting at the editors.[15] I think both journals are well-disposed towards us; and the Spectator gave a very fair notice of my first number.[16] The Savile Club[17] to which Martin introduced me is made up /largely/ of rising men—who are to dominate the next twenty years and I trust I have not known some of them in vain.—

The other day I ~~added~~ /had/ a pleasant visit to Eton and got a further glimpse of English public school life.

I shall not trouble you with mere social matters and experiences, all of which I trust to pass through my philological alembic.

I expect to spend Sunday next in Cambridge—return to London and wind up definitely, proceeding to Paris towards the close of next week.

With kind regards to Mrs. Gilman and your daughters

I am

Yours faithfully
B. L. Gildersleeve

1. The library of the Peabody Institute in Baltimore served Hopkins' needs in its early years. Its 60,000 (in 1876) carefully chosen scholarly volumes, along with the coolness afforded by its high ceilings, made it an attractive "refuge," particularly in the summer. Nevertheless, obtaining books from Philip Reese Uhler (1835-1913), the man C. S. Peirce called "the jailer of the Peabody library," could be tedious (*Hawkins*, 118-20). Uhler had left Harvard in his last year to become assistant librarian at the Peabody. In 1863 he was made assistant in the Agassiz Museum of Comparative Zoology at Harvard (1863-66), but he returned to the Peabody and in 1876 was made an associate in natural sciences at Hopkins. *NatCAB* 8: 251.

2. There is no record of Gildersleeve actually meeting Browning or Arnold. On the former, see No. 179, n. 6, and *AJP* 32 (1911): 482-85 ( = *SBM*, 237-40); on the latter, see *AJP* 34 (1913): 487 ( = *SBM*, 295). He did meet Oscar Wilde at about this time (*AJP* 32 [1911]: 358 [ = *SBM*, 229]), but whether he did so in England or during Wilde's tour of America in 1881-82 (though Wilde did not lecture in Baltimore) is not known.

3. Sir George Grove (1820-1900), after training as a civil engineer, wrote analyses of musical programmes at the Crystal Palace from 1886, and after assisting on *Smith's Dictionary of the Bible* (1857-63) and editing *Macmillan's Magazine* (1868-83), he produced the first edition of his *Dictionary of Music and Musicians* ( A.D. 1450-1880), vols. 1-3 (London: Macmillan, 1879-89, 1890). See, further, C. L. Graves, *The Life and Letters of Sir George Grove* (London: Macmillan, 1903), and *DNB Supplement*, 794-96.

4. Although there are many kinds of "indicators" in scientific investigation, for the purposes of Gildersleeve's joke (and judging by his use of "alembic" at the close of the letter), we should probably understand a play on a chemical indicator—i.e., a reagent that reacts to a chemical's properties (e.g., acidity or alkalinity), as, for instance, the Sorensen Indicator. Here he means someone who reflects the disposition of Dean Stanley.

5. Arthur Penrhyn Stanley (1815–81), the dean of Westminster (1863–81), had been secretary to the Oxford Commission in July 1850 and authored most of its 1852 report. Among his many books are *The Life and Correspondence of Thomas Arnold, D.D.* (London: B. Fellowes, 1844) and *Lectures on the History of the Jewish Church* (London: J. Murray, 1863–76). See, further, Rowland E. Prothero, *The Life and Correspondence of Arthur Penrhyn Stanley, D.D.*, 2 vols. (London: J. Murray, 1893), and *DNB* 18: 931–35.

6. Alexander John Ellis (1814–90), philologist and mathematician, president of the Philological Society (1872–74, 1880–82), member of the Council of the Royal Society (1880–82), and author of *Essentials of Phonetics* (London: F. Pitman, 1848) and *The Alphabet of Nature* (Bath: J. and J. Keene, 1844–45). See, further, *DNB Supplement*, 605–7.

7. Richard Morris (1833–94) edited *The Poetical Works of Geoffrey Chaucer* (London: Bell and Daldy, 1866), and, with Skeat, *Specimens of Early English* (Oxford: Clarendon Press, 1867; 3d ed., 1872). See, further, *DNB Supplement*, 1068.

8. Mark Pattison (1813–84), rector of Lincoln College (1861–84), author of *Isaac Casaubon, 1559–1614* (London: Longmans, 1875; 2d ed., Oxford: Clarendon Press, 1892), *Milton* (London: Macmillan, 1879), *Sermons* (London: Macmillan, 1885), and *Essays*, 2 vols. (Oxford: Clarendon Press, 1889). See *Memoirs by Mark Pattison*, ed. Mrs. Pattison (London: Macmillan, 1885; reprint, Fontwell: Centaur, 1969), and *DNB* 15: 503–8.

9. Sir James Augustus Henry Murray (1837–1915) was master at Mill Hill School (1870–85) when appointed editor in 1879 of what would be known as the *Oxford English Dictionary*. In 1885 he moved to Oxford to devote himself to the dictionary full time. See K. M. E. Murray, *Caught in the Web of Words: James A. H. Murray and the Oxford English Dictionary* (New Haven: Yale University Press, 1977), and *DNB 1912–1921*, 397–400. For Gildersleeve's account of his trip to Mill Hill, see "The Philological Society's Dictionary," *Nation* 30 (24 June 1880): 44, and "The Hazards of Reviewing," *Nation* 101 (8 July 1915): 50.

10. On Sweet, see No. 44, n. 7. See *H&H*, 61–64, for Gildersleeve on Sweet's spelling reforms.

11. Hermann Charles George Brandt (1850–1920) studied at Göttingen, Freiburg, and Strassburg, was associate in German at Hopkins (1876–82), then returned to his alma mater, Hamilton College, as assistant professor (1882–1920), where he translated Lessing's *Nathen der Weise* (New York: Holt, 1895) and wrote a number of textbooks, including a popular *Grammar of the German Language for High Schools and Colleges* (New York: Putnam, 1884). See No. 60. The article in question is "Recent Investigations of Grimm's Law," *AJP* 1 (1880): 146–60. He also contributed seven reviews and three reports to *AJP* 1 and 2. *WhAm 1*, 131.

12. Sweet translated his *A Handbook of Phonetics* (Oxford: Clarendon Press, 1877) into German (with the stylistic aid of Wilhelm Scholle) as *Elementarbuch des gesprochenen Englisch (Grammatik, Texte und Glossar)* (Oxford: Clarendon Press, 1885).

13. On Albert Stanburrough Cook (1853–1927), see "Correspondents." His review of Skeat's *Etymological Dictionary of the English Language* is in *AJP* 1 (1880): 203–6.

14. On Lanman, see No. 26, n. 3.

15. *The Academy and Literature* reviewed vol. 1, no. 1 (17 [15 May 1880]: 368), particularly applauding the abstracts of German journals; no. 2 (18 [9 October 1880]: 262): "scarcely up to the level of the first"; and no. 4 (19 [26 March 1881]: 230). The *Saturday Review* gave no notice.

16. *Spectator* 53 (5 June 1880): 728 contains a one-page summary of the contents of the first issue.

17. Savile Club, see preceding letter, n. 12.

48 To: DANIEL COIT GILMAN
*JHU-Gilman*

Athenaeum Club
Pall Mall S.W.
June 30, 1880

Dear Mr. Gilman:

I am still in London. My friends in Cambridge wrote to me that this was the very emptiest week /there/ in the whole year[1] and advised /me/ to postpone my visit until next week, and this counsel was confirmed by all the Cambridge men I saw at the clubs. So I resolved to remain here instead, where I have opportunities almost every day of making acquaintances of men of note and of getting important hints. If I had taken a room in the neighborhood of the British Museum and gone to work at my orators,[2] I might have done more in one sense, but I can't help thinking that I can do all that nearly as well in Baltimore, while the acquaintance of living men is not to be had for the asking but is only to be made by watching and waiting. Of course I chafe somewhat at the want of definite employment but every now and then I am rewarded by some new acquaintance, some new discussion that seems to make amends for what otherwise would be set down as time lost. I already know—after a fashion—many more people of mark in England than I ever saw in all the rest of my life and I expect abiding results from some of these new connections. The coffee-room and the smoking room are my trout pools. The Englishman is a great luncher and the most accessible Englishman is often a smoker. So I have learned to lunch and have relearned how to smoke. Day before yesterday I met at the Savile E. H. Palmer,[3] the great Arabic and Persian scholar, who after some little talk invited me to lunch with him at his house,—miles away in the N.W.—That is the trouble about such invitations—Each of them costs half a day—but the time is not ill-spent. His wife is a German and we all spoke German, so that I had a little foretaste of the next few weeks. If you should like to have a course of lectures on Arabic literature, he would be most happy to come for a few weeks. He recommended to me in the strongest terms that strange person about whom we had some correspondence, one M. Baker surnamed A(braham) J(ohn) Muaṭṭar[4]—with whom I have just had an interview. I am very much afraid that the learned Persian would be surnamed Mulatto by our boys. He is certainly a most remarkable person—doubtless one of the best scholars in England—but utterly impractical, a religious enthusiast who can't talk five minutes without introducing his peculiar notions of Islamo-Christianity and a thorough Oriental in his want of personal cleanliness. The good people of the Athenaeum must have been a little scandalized at the appearance of my visitor. In order to put an end to the interview, I told him that I had no authority to make any arrangement with him and gave him your address, to which he might send Palmer's letter. I am afraid that we cannot make any use of him, but no one can help taking a deep interest in this earnest, sincere, tender-hearted fellow. He speaks English very well indeed and his manners are not unpleasantly oriental, but I forebear to speak of his dress as Mrs. Gilman is always present to my mind, when I write to you, whether officially or not.—I told Baker that I did not know whether we should develop the Semitic side or not, and if he writes to you, it will be an easy matter to close the affair, if you think fit.— —Yesterday afternoon Sayce told me that if I dined at the Savile, I should in all likelihood meet Robertson Smith. In fact, he would bring about an acquaintance. You know that he has come out of the controversy victorious and there is no hope of him.[5] Still one never knows what may turn up and as I went to Scotland in the hope of seeing him, I did not lose an easy opportunity. He is to all appearance a very young man for the stir he has made—a thorough Scotchman, as you might suppose, not a bad type, by any means, outspoken, resolute, rather Celtic face, as I understand /it/, a little man physically and hence prone to assert himself. I was somewhat disgusted to learn in the course of conversation that the Harvard people had opened negotiations with him in the event of his failure[6] in the great struggle through which he has passed triumphantly and which has left him perhaps a little more exalted and self-confident than is exactly pleasant to an onlooker. He would have been a great accession to us, however, and I am sorry not to have anyone approaching him to propose. It is indeed doubtful whether he would have come in any event. Our absurd tariff would have forced him to pay a heavy duty on his library[7] which must be considerable, and he emphasized especially the difficulty of getting books—The Johns Hopkins has certainly roused Harvard to great activity and I must confess that I am somewhat concerned at this new evidence of her aggressiveness. I wish the other colleges all prosperity, but I am not Christian enough to rejoice at being thwarted. You take a different view, I know, and I rejoice that we have a philosophic mind at the helm.

In England my course has been very much guided by the acquaintances I have made and the opportunities that have offered themselves; and in looking back I do not see that I could have done much more, if I had planned the whole thing out carefully. But I think it is high time for me to look at matters on the other side of the Channel, and there I shall require somewhat more system. I do not see that I can effect much in Paris unless I were to make up my mind to settle there for study—and at present I do not expect to stay there more than a week. Thence in all likelihood to Bonn for a couple of days— to Berlin and Leipzig. After Leipzig I shall consider where it would be best for me to spend the month of August, and by that time considerations of various kinds will make it necessary for me to keep quiet. If you wish me to see certain persons as for instance von Holst[8] at Freiburg—or if Strasburg should offer any inducements I could take those places on my way back.—August is no month for Italy or Greece, still something will depend on the heat of the summer. So far we have had nothing that we should call hot in America and I have not yet laid aside my winter underclothing. The Londoners are overjoyed at this beautiful weather. Think of three sunshiny days in succession! But I am chatting. Please let me hear from you now that you are in some measure relieved of official work and give me your counsel as to my further plans.

Yours faithfully,<br>
B. L. Gildersleeve

1. The Cambridge term ends the week beginning on the third Sunday in June, the Magna Comitia (admission for next year) would have been on Saturday the 19th and Tuesday the 22nd, and the once-popular Midsummer Fair (or Pot Fair) was June 22-25.

2. Probably preparing "On ΠΡΙΝ in the Attic Orators," *AJP* 2 (1881): 465-83.

3. Edward Henry Palmer (1840-82) was sizar (1863-65), scholar (1865-67), and fellow (1867-82) of St. John's College, Cambridge, and Lord Almoner's professor of Arabic (1871-82), but became bored with academics and in his last years was a journalist in London. He was killed by Bedouins while on a secret service mission in Egypt. In his brief, but highly adventurous, life, he wrote, among many works, *A Grammar of the Arabic Language* (London: W. H. Allen, 1874), *A Concise Dictionary of the Persian Language* (London: Trübner, 1876), and *The Desert of the Exodus: Journeys on Foot* (Cambridge: Deighton, Bell, 1871). On his German-Polish wife, who he claimed was of noble birth and whom he married in the summer of 1879 following the death of his first wife, see W. Besant, *The Life and Achievements of Edward Henry Palmer* (London: J. Murray, 1883), 212-16, and for Palmer in general, *DNB* 15: 122-26.

4. Mírzá Muḥammad Báqir of the Bawánát district in Fárs, Persia (modern Iran), surnamed Ibráhím Ján Mu'aṭṭar, was a poet and teacher. See Edward G. Browne, *The Press and Poetry of Modern Persia* (Cambridge: Cambridge University Press, 1914), 168ff., and *A Year amongst the Persians* (London: A. and C. Black, 1893), 12-15, esp. p. 14: "[He had] been successively a Shi'ite Muḥammadan, a dervish, a Christian, an atheist, and a Jew, [and] he had finished by elaborating a religious system of his own, which he called 'Islamo-Christianity.' . . . He was in every way a most remarkable man, and one whom it was impossible not to respect and like, in spite of his appalling loquacity, his unreason, his disputatiousness, his utter impracticability."

5. The General Assembly of the Free Church of Scotland finally met (see No. 43) on 29 June to vote on Robertson Smith's case. The original twenty-four charges had been reduced to but one: contradicting the Confession in regard to the historical authority of the Book of Deuteronomy as a historical record. By a vote of 299 to 292, the assembly voted to admonish Smith but allow him to keep his chair. There was general rejoicing at the verdict, but within a year, Smith was given a vote of want of confidence, and he was obliged to resign his post at Aberdeen. He went on to edit the last twelve volumes of the *Encyclopedia Britannica* (1881-88), was fellow of Christ's College, Cambridge (1885-94), chief librarian of Cambridge (1886-89), and Adams professor of Arabic (1889-94).

6. On 15 July 1880 he wrote Gilman from Paris: "Sayce . . . put the Robertson Smith matter in a somewhat different light. He said that Smith would have declined the call to Harvard at any rate because the position postulated too much drudgery and intimated that he would perhaps listen to us a year hence, now that he has vindicated his rights."

7. Gildersleeve errs. The tariff on new books was 25 percent ad valorem by the revised statute of 22 June 1874, but those "printed and manufactured more than twenty years at the date of importation" and individual libraries were duty-free (U.S. Congress Senate Finance Committee, *The Existing Tariff on Imports into the United States, Etc., and the Free List Together with Comparative Tables of Present and Past Tariffs and Other Statistics Relating Thereto*, 48th Cong., 1st sess., 1884, S. Rept. 12).

8. For von Holst, see following letter, n. 6.

## 49 To: Daniel Coit Gilman
*JHU-BLG*

Leipzig July 31, 1880

My dear Mr. Gilman:

When I wrote to you last from Paris[1] I had almost decided not to go to Strassburg but further reflection convinced me that it was a point of too much importance to be neglected and the night of the 17th of July found me there after a hot and dirty ride only paralleled in my recent experience by the Housatonic roads.[2] I was very kindly received by Studemund,[3] Warren's[4] teacher, who gave himself up to me the next day and put me in possession of many points of importance for us. In going to Strassburg I had my eye especially on Ten Brink,[5] who is one of the foremost men in the English department anywhere and I purposely conversed with him in English so that I might judge of his practical command of the language. He speaks slowly but fairly—The expression of pain is a mere play of feature as he looks troubled even when he speaks German, which is a second mother tongue to him. A Dutchman, married to a German wife of rather narrow views, hampered by a deaf and dumb son whom he adores, and for whose sake he has already refused an invitation to Vienna—These are the external points. He is not a strong lecturer—and I was sorry that I had to hear him in a line where show would have been out of place—so that I could not judge how far he would be quickened by the literary element in which he takes great delight and in which he has distinguished himself so much. But I will not go into particulars, unless you desire it. He is a strong man, in the prime of life, could hardly be tempted to leave his present field, but he is worth knowing, worth thinking about and he might be captured by your superior address.—Once in Strassburg I thought it would be well to make the little run to Freiburg and see how matters stand with von Holst.[6]—I think that he is sorry and I know that his wife is very sorry that he could not come. His trouble is not a derangement of the functions of the kidneys but as he explained it to me a displacement. He looks as well as he did when he was in America, indeed better, but he walks with some difficulty and is hypochondriacal to boot. His nature is very tense and he will inevitably wear himself out before long.—At Heidelberg which was my next stopping place I was much with the distinguished philologist and historian Curt Wachsmuth,[7] who married a daughter of my old teacher Ritschl[8] for whose sake I was received very warmly—and I had a long talk with our man Sewall,[9] who has developed a good deal since he has been abroad. He will probably never have much form but he begins to see the need of it—and that is something.—At Bonn where I remained several days I had long talks with the leading scholars of the University and found my intercourse with them very suggestive and instructive—In fact the wealth of the last two weeks I find is almost as bewildering as the whirl of my first experience of English life. The great leaders dwindle somewhat as one gets nearer to them but the characteristics come out more sharply and thus [?] the facility of subsequent communication will be of immense importance in my future work. Wheeler[10] made a very strong impression in Bonn and I have never known an American who left such a cultus behind him.—His fellow students adore him. Whether he owes his success there to the very qualities which /might/ impede his progress here /in America/ remains to be seen. He will undeniably be a useful man anywhere and is /still/thoroughly in love with Baltimore. At Bonn I also met Goodwin[11] who spoke his mind freely about the 'philological boom', as you called it, at Harvard. Like myself he is a little old-fashioned and does not like to see the department of philology narrowed down to phonetics or linguistics— and that would undoubtedly be the tendency of the new development.— Carolus Primus[12] is a vigorous ruler but there is no little wincing in consequence.—I have spent the last two days here[13]—have succeeded in making arrangements for the wider diffusion of the Journal and have had interviews with some of the leading men—besides attending lectures and making observations—Bloomfield[14] is here and doing well solemnly—Miss Thomas[15] and Miss Gwinn[16] have switched off from Classical philology and comparative philology to English—They seem to be working very happily here and are now much interested in finding out where they can get a degree—'Ohne Schuh' geh' ich nicht heim'[17], as the old German song has it, and they will not be satisfied with anything short of a title. I suppose they must be considered very lucky as the German authorities have shut down on lady students and while vested (or petticoated) interests are not to be disturbed, no new students of the contrary sex are to be admitted.— — —To-day I go to Berlin and shall remain there until the middle of next week and then turn my face southward. I do not know whether I shall get as far as Vienna. The universities will all be closed and my tour of observation may be considered at an end. My aim will be to find some quiet and cool retreat near a great library where I can digest my experiences and make some little preparation for next session—The word 'libraries' reminds me that Studemund has organized a very fine working library for his seminarium—he has some 4000 volumes—and some 500 Thalers a year to

keep it up[18]—He counts on a much larger percentage of loss than I should
have thought necessary—but he considers books as so much sulphuric
acid—made to be used—in fact, takes exactly the same view that you have
always advocated.—Before the plan can be realized with us, we shall need
more room—but the time is not far/distant/, I hope. Michaelis[19] of Strassburg has kindly volunteered his services, if we should ever need a collection
of casts—or rather if we should ever have the money to buy them for we
need them sadly. His experience will be worth a great deal as he has made
the whole collection at Strassburg personally—If Mr. Garrett[20] had given
his money to such a scholar, we might be better off at the Peabody—but I
[s]hall not prejudge the matter.—Michaelis's exposition was very interesting—and his help eventually will be of great importance—especially as he
has studied the question in regard to the formation of smaller collections
which are afterwards to be expanded. And all this, you observe, from sheer
love of the department. So to come back to the library, Studemund has
promised me a catalogue of his working library for the philological seminary—which would be of great service to us—certainly would save the head
of the department no end of time.—In this and other ways, then, I am
trying to make my stay in Europe of actual or eventual avail to the University—The two months for which provision was made I shall spin out to
more than four in the hope that there will be as much result as could have
been achieved by a man of greater tact, energy and resolution. So far my
health has been perfect and I trust at all events that I shall come back with
an appetite for work which may tell in the accumulated provisions that
await me.

 With best regards to Mrs. Gilman and wishes for a pleasant summer
  I am

Yours faithfully

B. L. Gildersleeve

1. On 15 July from the Hôtel de Lille et d'Albion.

2. The name of a town, river, and mountainous area in far western Massachusetts and
Connecticut. The Housatonic railroad, which at this time made a milk run that carried
100,000 quarts a day, ran from Bridgeport, Conn., to Pittsfield, Mass. "A century ago, the
vista from the railroad was one of mine shafts, iron forges, denuded hills and smoldering
charcoal pits" (*NYTimes*, 6 October 1985: sec. 10: 19).

3. Wilhelm Studemund (1843-89), whom Gildersleeve calls "my charming Strassburg
host of 1880" (*AJP* 34 [1913], 104 [ = *SBM*, 271), was a Plautine scholar who, in his *Fabu-
larum reliquiae Ambrosianae codicis rescripti Ambrosiani apographum* (Berlin: Weidmann,
1888), upheld the scientific textual analyses of Ritschl and provoked controversy with his
Ritschelian writings on Latin grammar and accent. He is also known for *Gai institutionum
commentarii quattuor* (Leipzig: Hirzel, 1874). See, further, *Sandys*, 142.

4. Minton Warren (1850-1907), after graduating from Tufts (1870), received his Ph.D.
from Strassburg in 1879 and was associate (1879-83), associate professor (1883-92), and professor (1892-99) of Latin at Hopkins, then professor of Latin at Harvard (1899-1907). He
published no books but contributed three articles to *HSCP* and three to *AJP*, including a

version of his dissertation, "On the Enclitic -Ne in Early Latin," *AJP* 2 (1881): 50-82, and over thirty-five reviews. He was particularly inspiring as a teacher, and his course on Terence encouraged H. R. Fairclough to edit the *Andria* and translate the *Phormio*. See Fairclough, *Warming Both Hands* (Stanford: Stanford University Press, 1941), 80.

5. Bernhard Egidius Conrad ten Brink (1841-92) was professor of modern languages at Marburg (1870-73) and English at Strassburg (1873-92), and author of *Geschichte der Englischen Litteratur*, 2 vols. (Berlin: R. Oppenheim, 1877-93) and *Chaucers Sprache und Verskunst* (Leipzig: T. O. Weigel, 1884).

6. Hermann Eduard von Holst (1841-1904), professor of history at Strassburg (1872-74), Freiburg (1874-92), and Chicago (1892-99), originally came to New York in 1866, and by 1869 was assistant editor of *Deutsch-Amerikanisches Conversations-Lexikon*. As a German academic who specialized in American history, he was highly sought after by Gilman (whom von Holst had advised in 1875) for the Hopkins faculty (*Hawkins*, 170-71). Among his works are: *Verfassungsgeschichte der Vereinigten Staaten von America* (Freiburg: C. Lehmann, 1867), translated as *The Constitutional and Political History of the United States*, 8 vols. (Chicago: Callaghan, 1876-92) (vol. 3 trans. J. J. Labor and P. Shorey [see "Correspondents"]), *The Life of John C. Calhoun* (Boston: Houghton Mifflin, 1882), and *John Brown*, ed. F. P. Stearns (Boston: Cupples and Hurd, 1888).

7. Curt Wachsmuth (1837-1905) was professor at Marburg, Göttingen, Heidelberg, and Leipzig and is best known for *Ioannis Stobaei anthologia*, ed. with O. Hense (Berlin: Weidmann, 1884), and *Die Stadt Athen im Alterthum* (Leipzig: B. G. Teubner, 1874-90). See Bursian, *Biogr. Jb. Alt. K.* 136 (1907): 164-97, and *Sandys*, 229.

8. For Ritschl, see No. 23, n. 2.

9. Henry Sewall (1855-1936) received his Ph.D. in physiology from Hopkins in 1879 and was fellow (1879-82) and associate (1880-82) in biology. He went on to the University of Michigan as professor of physiology (1882-89) and was ultimately chairman of medicine at the University of Colorado (1911-18). He was the first to discover the principle of acute immunity (1887) following innoculation with rattlesnake venom.

10. On Wheeler, see No. 46, n. 6. He had been at Bonn in the summer semester of 1878 and winter semester 1878-79.

11. On William Watson Goodwin (1831-1912), see No. 50, n. 5. On the Harvard programme, see No. 20 and n. 7.

12. Charles William Eliot (1834-1926) graduated from Harvard (1853), taught mathematics and chemistry there (1858-63), and was professor of chemistry at M.I.T. (1865) and president of Harvard (1869-1909). Under his administration, Harvard added graduate schools in arts and sciences (see No. 20), applied sciences, and business administration, vastly increased its endowment, reformed its administration, liberalized the discipline of students, and introduced an elective system for undergraduates. See his *Educational Reform* (New York: Century, 1898) and H. James, *Charles W. Eliot, President of Harvard University, 1869-1909*, 2 vols. (Boston: Houghton Mifflin, 1930).

13. Leipzig, where *Anglia* was edited (No. 38, n. 3), was the foremost continental European university in English literature and language studies.

14. Maurice Bloomfield (1855-1928) received the first Hopkins Ph.D. in Sanskrit (1879) and remained there as fellow (1879-80), associate (1881-83), associate professor (1883-91), and professor (1891-1928) of Sanskrit. He is the author of *Hymns of the Atharva-Veda* (Oxford: Clarendon Press, 1897), *The Religion of the Veda* (New York: Putnam, 1908), and he contributed nineteen articles and ten reviews to *AJP*. On his lecturing, see *H&H*, 65.

15. Martha Carey Thomas was studying at Leipzig (1879-82), which would not grant women degrees, was denied admission to Göttingen, and finally took a Ph.D. in philology *summa cum laude* from Zürich in November 1882. See, further, "Correspondents."

16. Mary Mackall "Mamie" Gwinn (Hodder) (1861-1940) was, like her childhood friend Carey Thomas, the daughter of a Hopkins trustee (Charles J. M. Gwinn [1819-94]), but,

although several years younger, was saturnine while Thomas was energetic and curious. The two spent 1879–83 studying in Europe (see preceding note), but Gwinn took no degree. She took the first Ph.D. from an American women's college (Bryn Mawr) in 1888, and Thomas immediately made her associate in English. They lived together in the Bryn Mawr deanery until Gwinn eloped in 1904 with a man Thomas called "that degenerate [Alfred] Hodder" (1866–1907), a professor of English at Bryn Mawr (1895–98) who became secretary to the district attorney of New York and published in philosophical journals and the *Nation*. After her husband's death, she moved back to Baltimore for six years and spent the remaining twenty-seven years of her life in Princeton. See *Martha Carey Thomas: The Making of a Feminist: Her Early Journals and Letters*, ed. M. H. Dobkin (Kent, Ohio: Kent State University Press, 1979), 155–287, 314, and C. Meigs, *What Makes a College? A History of Bryn Mawr* (New York: Macmillan, 1956).

17. "Without my shoes I won't go home," from an early nineteenth-century Bavarian folksong, see *Der Zupfgeigenhansl*, ed. Hans Breuer (Leipzig: F. Hofmeister, 1913), 130.

18. The silver thaler, the unit of money for Berlin and northern Germany, was replaced by the mark in 1873. One old thaler equaled three new marks, and so 500 thalers amounted to $357.

19. Adolf Michaelis (1835–1910), professor of archeology at Strassburg and author of *Ancient Marbles in Great Britain*, trans. C. A. M. Fennell (Cambridge: Cambridge University Press, 1882) and *Kunstgeschichte des Altertum*, vol. 1 of A. H. Springer's *Handbuch der Kunstgeschichte* (Leipzig: E. A. Seeman, 1898).

20. John Work Garrett (1820–84) was named president of the Baltimore and Ohio Railroad by its largest individual stockholder, Johns Hopkins, and made it a great and profitable company. One of the twelve original trustees, he broke with Johns Hopkins University in 1883. See *Hawkins*, 4–5.


## 50 To: DANIEL COIT GILMAN
### *JHU-BLG*

Dresden Aug. 8, 1880

My dear Mr. Gilman: Your last two letters reached me on Thursday and Friday respectively and I cannot thank you enough for your expressions of confidence although with my native tendency to extract sourness from sweetness I am very much frightened at the thought of the great expectations which the trustees have formed as to the result of my prolonged trip. During the remaining weeks I shall try to formulate my observations, such as they are. Would you advise a systematic report or a personal narrative?[1] As I said in my last letter, irrespective of the /professional/ advantages of my recent experience, I think that enough will have been gained by the University to justify the outlay and yet so much more might have been accomplished by greater energy, tact, and perseverance that I am by no means satisfied with myself. So your last letter suggests more extended and detailed inquiries as to American students who are working in Germany than I have made for other departments than my own. What I could learn in Strassburg from Ten Brink about students of English was not very satisfactory and much that I have seen confirms my suspicion that American students are /too/ prone to acquire the undesirable sides of German work and become more German than the Germans in their mode of presentation, in the cumbrousness of their apparatus, in the thinness of conclusions as compared with the thickness of material, in a certain routine criticism, which well-known models have made a mere mechanical process.[2] These strictures, of course, indicate a follower of the old ideal school in which I was brought up—but in my judgment no other school can do anything for classical philology in America for we lack the basis which sustains the present German wearisomeness and if we dissociate classical philology from our general life, it has no hope of a future. But I don't intend to bore you with a review article and will only add that I think it entirely unnecessary to sacrifice real scientific progress in the effort to maintain the lines on which men like Boeckh and others worked.[3] Harvard has gone in distinctly for a course, which cannot be a real success in our country[4] and I prophesy a return to earlier principles in Germany itself.—Goodwin is much troubled at the prospect of the new development.[5] Nothing would seem to me more clearly to indicate the dearth of first class men than the appointment of Seymour to the chair of Greek in Yale.[6] Allen[7] asked me in a letter whether I did not think S. a splendid Greek scholar? I did not answer the question—because some of S's papers had proven to me that he was sadly lacking both in accuracy and reach. I would rather have Wheeler[8] any day—and that is not paying W. a high compliment.—White[9] has made an excellent impression every where. Without knowing him personally, I should think that his excellence lay in his earnestness and his enthusiasm—both leading to the bottom of things, if possible. A fine grain he can hardly have. I was amused to find how much Goodwin gives in to him. The robuster element is too much for Goodwin's quieter nature—though Goodwin in other cases yields only at the moment.—But I am wandering even more than usual and I think I can see you with pencil in hand bringing me to book.—Of the men I have seen and heard of here among the Americans I think our men Wheeler and Bloomfield[10] are best worth being kept in view. I was sorry that I could not see Windisch[11] and ask his opinion about Bloomfield but I think there can be no mistake about his ability and I am sure that he will develop more constructive power than Lanman.[12] When I go to Munich I will make inquiries about Elliott[13] who remains as much a riddle to me now as he was four years ago.—As to recommendations and the like, my trip has given me an immense advantage—I shall be able henceforth to consult confidentially so many leading men that it will not be necessary to rest satisfied with formal testimonials. Certainly /Berlin,/ Leipzig, Strassburg, Bonn will give up their secrets.—

My visit to Germany has been so full of interest and profit that I regret more and more that I lingered so long in Paris—but perhaps the regret is vain. The time of my sojourn in Berlin was dictated to me by my friend,

Prof. Hübner,[14] who arranged my visit so as to strike a period of exceptional brilliancy—when I could come into contact with the great men of the University—and the whole of my trip was arranged with reference to that—so that my stay in Leipzig was shorter than I had expected.—Still, as I reported, I did something for the Journal there, got the promise of all Teubner's[15] new publications and secured Brockhaus[16] ~~for~~ /as/ my German publisher. A long interview with Georg Curtius[17] gave me much to think about and I dined with the foremost Latinist there, Ribbeck,[18] and / had/ a full and free conversation with him, also.—Berlin which I reached Saturday week (July 31) was almost too brilliant with its grand celebration at the Museum and University[19]—but still Hübner was right—I saw men and talked with men, whom I might have hunted for in vain for months—I will not trouble you with a list of celebrities only you will be gratified to know that such men as Hoffmann[20] and G. Kirchhoff[21] are well acquainted with the work of the John Hopkins University and that Remsen's and Rowland's[22] names and achievements are familiar to them. Zeller[23] was kind enough to propose my health at a <u>farewell dinner</u> given to the great Slavonic scholars of Berlin who have accepted an invitation to St. Petersburg—and this festivity must be accepted as a set off against my failure to attend the Manchester banquet, where I should hardly have been seated between a Müllenhoff[24] and a Weber.[25]

I left Berlin Friday afternoon and came to Dresden in company with Hoffmann. Yesterday was spent chiefly in the gallery and with German friends. To-day is a day of rest. To-night or to-morrow I go to Munich. From there I hope to make a short Italian tour, so as to be able to concentrate on Rome and Naples, if I should ever be so fortunate as to see their side of the water again.

With best wishes to Mrs. Gilman

I am

Yours faithfully

B. L. Gildersleeve

1. See No. 41, n. 5.
2. See *AJP* 37 (1916): 494-504 ( = *SBM*, 364-76).
3. Phillip August Boeckh (1785-1867), whom Gildersleeve called "the greatest living master of Hellenic studies [of his time]" (*H&H*, 42) was professor of Greek at Heidelberg (1809-11) and Berlin (1811-67) and was known for his historical approach to a wide range of ancient authors and topics. Gildersleeve took two courses from him in the winter term 1850–51: Demosthenes' *De corona* and a survey of Greek literature (*AJP* 36 [1915]: 108-9 [ = *SBM*, 317-18]). "Boeckh I worshipped, ignorantly, no doubt" (*AJP* 28 [1907]: 117 [ = *SBM*, 141]). See also *Professorial Types*: 4-5; "A Novice of 1850" *Johns Hopkins Alumni Magazine* 1 (November 1912): 7; *AJP* 28 (1907): 232-34 ( = *SBM* 142-45); M. Hoffmann, *August Boeckh: Lebensbeschreibung und Auswahl aus Seinem Wissenschaftlichen Briefwechsel* (Leipzig: B. G. Teubner, 1901); and Bernd Schneider, *August Boeckh: Altertumsforscher, Universitätslehrer und Wissenschaftsorganisator im Berlin d. 19 Jh.* (Wiesbaden: Reichert, 1985).

4. On the Harvard programme, see No. 20, n. 7.

5. William Watson Goodwin (1831-1912) graduated from Harvard (A.B. 1851) and, after receiving a degree from Göttingen in 1855, returned to Harvard as tutor (1856-60) and Eliot professor of Greek literature (1860-1901). He wrote *Syntax of the Moods and Tenses of the Greek Verb* (Cambridge, Mass.: Sever and Francis, 1859; rev. ed., 1889; see No. 78 and n. 11), *An Elementary Greek Grammar* (Boston: Ginn, 1870), and numerous textbooks, including his *Greek Reader*, ed. with J. H. Allen (Boston: Ginn, 1871). He was the first director of the American School of Classical Studies at Athens (No. 67, n. 1) and twice president of the APA (1871-72, 1884-85). Gildersleeve gave him the lead article in vol. 1 of *AJP*, his only contribution to the journal. See H. W. Smyth's (see "Correspondents") memorial notice, *Proc. Am. Phil. Soc.* 52 (1913): iii-ix and *DAB*, 7: 411-13.

6. Gildersleeve's opinion, probably based on Seymour's articles "On the Composition of the *Cynegeticus* of Xenophon," *TAPA* 9 (1878): 69-83, and "On the Date of the Prometheus of Aeschylus," *TAPA* 10 (1879): 111-24, obviously improved, for when Seymour died, Gildersleeve called him "America's leading Homerist" (*AJP* 29 [1908]: 118; see also 123-25). See further "Correspondents."

7. Frederic De Forest Allen (1844-97) graduated from Oberlin (1863), taught at the University of Tennessee (1866-68), received his Ph.D. from Leipzig (1868-70), and taught at Cincinnati (1874-79) and Yale (1879-80) before being named professor of Greek at Harvard, where he remained until his death. He was president of the APA (1881-82) and is remembered for his edition of *Medea*, revised by C. H. Moore (Boston: Ginn, 1900) and *Remnants of Early Latin* (Boston: Ginn, 1880). See Gildersleeve's notice, *AJP* 18 (1897): 247, and J. B. Greenough, "A Memoir of Frederic de Forest Allen," *HSCP* 9 (1898): 27-36.

8. On John Henry Wheeler, see No. 46, n. 6.

9. John Williams White (1848-1917) graduated from Oberlin (B.A. 1868) and Harvard (Ph.D. 1877) and was professor of Greek at Harvard from 1884. Like Gildersleeve, he became a Schmidtean (No. 158) and translated Schmidt's *Leitfaden in der Rhythmik und Metrik der classischen Sprachen* (Leipzig: F. C. W. Vogel, 1869) as *An Introduction to the Rhythmic and Metric of the Classical Languages* (Boston: Ginn, 1878). His great work is *The Verse of Greek Comedy* (London: Macmillan, 1912), and he also produced *The Scholia on the Aves of Aristophanes* (Boston: Ginn, 1914) and *Index Aristophaneus* (Cambridge: Cambridge University Press, 1932). He was also the first chairman of the managing committee of the American School of Classical Studies at Athens (1881-87) and editor of the "College Series of Greek Authors." For his influence on James Loeb (see No. 70, n. 4), see W. M. Calder III, "Ulrich von Wilamowitz-Moellendorff to James Loeb: Two Unpublished Letters," *ICS* 2 (1977): 315 ( = *Selected Correspondence*, 213), and, in general, *DAB* 20: 112-13.

10. On Bloomfield, see preceding letter, n. 12.

11. Ernst Wilhelm Oskar Windisch (1844-1918) received his Ph.D. from Leipzig in 1867 and became professor of Sanskrit there. He edited G. Curtius's *Kleine Schriften* (Leipzig: n.p., 1886) and wrote *Geschichte der Sanskrit-Philologie und Indischen Altertumskunde* (Strassburg: K. J. Trübner, 1917-20).

12. On Lanman, see No. 26, n. 3.

13. Aaron Marshall Elliott (1846-1910) was a Quaker from Wilmington, N.C., who graduated from Haverford (1866) and studied at Harvard (1866-68) and at Paris, Florence, Madrid, Munich, Tübingen, Berlin, and Vienna (1868-76) without taking a further degree (he received an honorary Ph.D. from Princeton in 1877). Named an associate in Romance languages at Hopkins in 1876, he established a model department, teaching Italian, Spanish, Persian, and French, but was not considered a candidate for a professorship by Gilman. As the Johns Hopkins Executive Committee had recently agreed to expand the Romance languages department, Gildersleeve made inquiries of Elliott's Munich professors. He helped found the Modern Language Association in 1883 and was made associate professor in 1884, professor in 1892. "There was something almost romantic about this new recruit we called

Elliott. . . . He lived the life of the peoples he studied, and there is no real mastery of a language unless you know the life of the people" (*JHU Circulars*, no. 231 [January 1911]: 9). See *DAB* 6: 93-94, *Hawkins*, 160-61.

14. See "Correspondents."

15. Benediktus Gotthelf Teubner (1784-1856) founded B. G. Teubner in 1824 to produce low-priced Greek and Latin classics, then extended his business to popular publications in many fields. The classics series continues to grow and flourish.

16. Friedrich Arnold Brockhaus (1772-1823) founded his publishing company in 1805 at Amsterdam primarily to publish reference books. In 1817 he moved to Leipzig and published the encyclopedia that became *Der Grosse Brockhaus* in 20 vols (1928-35).

17. For Georg Curtius (1820-85), see No. 8, n. 16.

18. Otto Ribbeck (1827-98) studied at Berlin and Bonn and was professor of Latin at Bern and Basel (1856-62), Kiel (1862-72), Heidelberg (1872-77), and Leipzig (1877-98), where he was Ritschl's successor. He edited Virgil in five volumes (Leipzig: B. G. Teubner, 1894-95) and wrote the three-volume *Geschichte der römischen Dichtung* (Stuttgart: Cotta, 1887-92). See E. Ribbeck, *Otto Ribbeck: Ein Bild seines Lebens aus seinen Briefen, 1846-1898* (Stuttgart: J. G. Gotta'sche, 1901), and *Sandys*, 188-89.

19. On 3 August 1880 the fiftieth anniversary of the founding of the Berlin Museum was celebrated with a great public ceremony at which the crown prince of Germany spoke. See "My Sixty Days in Greece," *Atlantic* 79 (May 1897): 632.

20. Heinrich Hoffman-Donner (1809-94), Frankfurt physician and poet.

21. Gustav Robert Kirchhoff (1824-87), professor of physics at Berlin (1874-87), was one of the founders of astrophysics and discoverer (with Bunsen) of spectrum analysis (1860).

22. Ira Remsen, (1846-1927), professor of chemistry (1876-1913) and president (1901-13), and Henry Augustus Rowland (1848-1901), professor of physics (1876-1901) at Johns Hopkins.

23. Eduard Zeller (1814-1908) professor of philosophy at Heidelberg (1862-72) and Berlin (1872-1905), best known for *Grundriss der Geschichte der Griechischen Philosophie* (Leipzig: Fues's Verlag, 1886), trans. as *Outline of the History of Greek Philosophy* by S. F. Alleyne and E. Abbott (New York: Holt, 1886), which ran to thirteen editions, the last in 1955. He also wrote *Platonische Studien* (Tübingen: C. F. Osiander, 1839), *Geschichte der christlichen Kirche* (Stuttgart: Franckh'schen, 1847), and *Geschichte der deutschen Philosophie seit Leibniz* (München: R. Oldenbourg, 1873). See W. M. Calder III, "Wilamowitz to Zeller: Two Letters," *GRBS* 19 (1978): 177-84, esp. n. 5., and *Sandys*, 477.

24. Karl Victor Müllenhoff (1818-84), professor of Germanic Philology at Berlin (1858-84), best known for *Deutsche Altertumskunde*, 5 vols. (Berlin: Weidmann, 1870-1900). *ADB*, 22: 494-96.

25. Albrecht Friedrich Weber (1825-1901), professor of Sanskrit at Berlin (1856-1901), known for *Indische Studien*, 18 vols. (Berlin: F. Dümmler, 1850-63; Leipzig: F. A. Brockhaus, 1865-98).

51 To: EMIL HÜBNER
*Berlin*

253 St. Paul St.
Baltimore Oct. 31, 1880

My dear Hübner:

Most of my letters come to my office and I gave you the number of my house so that I might receive news from you at home. I could 'make believe' then that I was receiving a visit. And so I was much rejoiced when the postman brought your letter of the 12ᵗʰ just as I was at breakfast—faced by my wife and flanked by my boy and my girl. 'Why here is a letter from Hübner!' and they had heard enough about my Berlin friend and my Berlin friend's wife and his children to know that it was a 'red letter' day. How gladly I would have put a leaf in my table and made you all sit down with us but as that could not be I transported myself in thought to your /hospitable/ board and called up each kind face and all the pleasant chat. Yes—you are right. We must not let the old ties grow slack and I cannot help hoping that we may transmit our friendship to our children—for my children, if they are spared to me must cross the water and of your three boys[1] one at least must come to America. My wife has taken quite a fancy to Heinz—with his poetic face—Uz's photograph was taken at so tender an age that it is not characteristic of him now—but you have changed so little that I could show my people what manner of man had received me with such brotherly kindness. I hope the other members of the family will join those that are here in effigy.—My wife has steadily refused /for several years/ to have her photograph taken—; her face which in nature is bright and sunshiny becomes rather wobegone in a photograph but I hope to overcome her objections for my sake and yours.[2] The only decent likeness of my recent self is rather large but you shall have a copy before long—and the boy and girl also in good time—Since my return I have been busy but not so much busy as distracted. For one reason or another I have found it almost impossible to get into a regular course of work; and scarcely had I begun to see my way to a resumption of old habits when Baltimore went mad over her sesquicentennial. The town was born in 1730[3] and 150 years is a long time in our history, so we had parades and processions and illuminations and ado generally, which lasted an entire week, indeed more. Say now that we are a prosaic people! Although it must be acknowledged that the artistic side of it, the pageants and the decorations were largely due to the foreign residents—chief of whom are the Germans, who went into the celebration with great enthusiasm. From the 11ᵗʰ to the 19ᵗʰ of this month, then, I had to struggle with all the incidental confusion and only in the last week or so have I had any stretches of honest work.—Besides I will not deny that I have come back seriously disorganized by my trip—full of ideas, of plans, of aspirations, it is true, but still so much under the spell of my travels that I readily slip from work to vision. All this will of course give way to the dire necessity of teaching my classes and editing my journal and making myself generally useful—but just now the revelation is too new and the music too recent to be shut out. I know I did not make the best use of my time everywhere because I did not fall into hands like yours—but I try to follow your wise advice and not fret about what I failed to see and failed to accomplish. It was a summer of unparalleled undreamed of richness for me. You ask for the details of my last month in Europe—That last month begins with my entrance into Italy on the 11$\underline{th}$ of August and my heart beats faster at the recollection. I saw the lakes as I saw Milan twenty years ago when I ought to have been more susceptible and I still remember the days I spent on Como Maggiora and Como as among the most beautiful of my life—but there was no such intoxication as I felt last summer. Perhaps it was because I was travelling all alone and could give myself up to my impressions—Whatever was the reason, I was as a man walking in a wonderful dream. All Europe is to an American of culture and reading fairy land. I remember how I felt when I first ~~came~~ went to Berlin in 1850—but Italy is a country apart—and as I came back to France I almost resented the difference. How much depends on the order of a trip. A friend had urged me to go from Venice to Naples by Foggia and then come up to Rome and Florence. It would have been a great mistake—After Rome and Naples I was in no mood to stop anywhere and I was almost ready for the translation to another world, which the proverb recommends.[4] Of course in some respects it was not a good time to visit Italy. So in Rome some of the great galleries were absolutely inaccessible—but to one who rejoices in color, nothing could have been more beautiful, than to see Italy in her midsummer splendor—What was the heat or even the <u>tafani</u>[5] in comparison with the exuberance of that life? The hotels were desolate but the streets were not—and as for the landscape—here and there I passed over roads along which the foliage had been dredged with dust but in the main the greenery was lovely.—A cynical friend who knows Italy well told me that it was a fortunate thing for my enthusiasm that I only had three weeks for the country. However that may be, I shall always be happier for those three weeks and that suffices. You asked for an itinerary and I gave you a rhapsody—In fact I am not an accountable person when I get on that subject— I thought I wrote you before that I spent one day in Verona—three days in Venice—a day in Bologna—three days in Florence—a week in Rome— four days in Naples—a morning in Pisa—and a day in Genoa. I slept in Turin and satisfied myself with a glimpse of the city in the morning. My time was short and I preferred wisely or unwisely the scenery of the Mt. Ceniz to Turin. It was a long and fatiguing ride to Paris where I staid two days chiefly spent in making purchases for the household— —two days in London—and thence to Liverpool[6]— —Heinz and Uz will be glad to know that there was a gale or a half gale one night, just enough to heighten the enjoyment of the latter part of the voyage which was beautiful. I am a good sailor for a landsman and did not suffer from seasickness. On board I found some old friends who helped me to pass the hours which are more or less weary on shipboard—and, as I wrote before, I arrived safe and sound in New York on the 22$\underline{d}$ of Sept. and two hours afterwards was speeding home.—Tell the dear boys that I have not forgotten their stamps but my son wants to make a collection for them himself to show his appreciation of their kindness. I send a small instalment now.

Present my kindest regards to your wife[7]—surely a 'gnädige Frau'[8] to me—and to your children—I am much obliged to Friedländer[9] for remembering me—and I cannot trust myself to speak of the goodness of our friends at Loschwitz[10]—for I shall become sentimental—

Yours faithfully

B. L. Gildersleeve

1. Hübner had four children, Rudolf (affectionately called "Pausanias" for guiding Gildersleeve around Bonn in 1880; 1864-1945), who became a historian of the law, Heinrich ("Heinz"; 1869-1945), who became a portraitist, Ulrich ("Uz"; 1872-1932), who became an artist, and a daughter, Marie. *NDB* 9: 717.

2. For another poor reproduction of Betty, see No. 191.

3. See H. E. Shepherd (see "Correspondents"), *History of Baltimore, Maryland* (Uniontown, Pa.: S. B. Nelson, 1898).

4. "Vedi Napoli, e poi muori" (See Naples and die).

5. I.e., "gadflies."

6. He embarked from Liverpool on 11 September.

7. Marie Hübner (1839-96), daughter of Berlin historian J. G. Droysen (1808-84).

8. Literally, "merciful wife," but more regularly in address, "Madam."

9. The great numismatist Julius Friedländer (1813-84) originally intended a career in medicine, but on a trip to Italy in 1838, he suffered an illness that affected his hearing, leading in his old age to total deafness (see BLG to Hübner, 24 April 1884 [Berlin]). In 1840 he became an assistant in the Royal Coin Collection. His father's great collection of coins served as the basis of his dissertation, written at Kiel under Hübner's father-in-law, J. G. Droysen (see n. 7). He was assistant (1840), head of the ancient section (1858), and, in 1868, the first director of the Royal Coin Collection in Berlin, making it the equal of those at the British Museum and Paris. He increased the number of documented ancient Italian coins during a trip to Italy with Mommsen in 1844–47. His work *Die Ital. Schaumünzen des 15. Jahrhundert (1430–1530)* (1882) is still valuable. Gildersleeve inserted a notice of his death in the *New York Evening Post*, 23 April 1884: 2. See, further, *NDB* 5: 453.

10. Hübner's home in Dresden.

# ❦ ILLUSTRATIONS ❧

Gildersleeve in his early years at the University of Virginia

*Below:* Pavilion I, University of Virginia

128

Gildersleeve at the time of the founding of
the Johns Hopkins University

*Below:* The Chimneys

129

University of Virginia
Dec. 11th 1875

President D. C. Gilman
Johns Hopkins University

Sir:

Our full and free conference in Washington removed any hesitation I may have felt as to a change in my sphere of work and I now desire to state in form that I find myself in perfect accord with your plans, and that under the conditions which you propose I could give myself without reserve to the promotion of the important undertaking in which you have asked my coöperation

For the kind and cordial manner in which you communicated to me the desires of the Executive Committee I renew my most sincere thanks.

I am, with high esteem
Yours very truly
B. L. Gildersleeve

Gildersleeve to Daniel Coit Gilman, 11 December 1875

130

Emil Hübner

William Dwight Whitney

Daniel Coit Gilman at the time
of the founding of the Johns
Hopkins University

Hermann Usener

Benjamin Lawton
Wiggins

Benjamin Ide Wheeler

Thomas Dwight Goodell

Herbert Weir Smyth

H. Rushton Fairclough

Joseph Edward Harry

135

Gonzalez Lodge

Daniel Coit Gilman at
the time of his retirement
from the Johns Hopkins
University

Thomas Day Seymour

Paul Shorey

Charles Forster Smith

Charles William Emil
Miller

138

Gildersleeve in his study

# ❦ 5 ❧

# WIDENING SPHERES, RISING FORTUNES,
# 1880–1896

As Gildersleeve turned fifty, he found himself fashioning a second career after turning from provincial collegiate instructor to international university professor. As a scholar, feeling his career was "not a success" (No. 57), he planned editions of Pindar, which he completed (No. 68), and Aristophanes' *Frogs*, which he did not (No. 71), and a work on Greek syntax with his assistant, C. W. E. Miller (No. 82). As a teacher, he finally solidified the program at Hopkins (No. 63) and took pride in the accomplishments of his students, particularly Smyth (No. 66). But clearly the bulk of his time was devoted to his "ball and chain" (Nos. 71, 82), the "Sisyphus stone" (No. 140) of the *AJP*, with its "unremunerative tasks of bookkeeping, proofreading, and the correspondence." He had imagined he would edit the journal for about ten years to get it well off the ground, but at the end of that time no successor appeared (No. 72, n. 7) and Gildersleeve continued a job that would be his for forty years. In 1890 *AJP* lost some of its international character with the founding of the British journal *Classical Review*, to which many of his English contributors defected (BLG to Smyth, 16 October 1890 [Harvard]).

He readily accepted many of the duties, if not the title, of doyen of American classics. Having served as president of the APA (1877–78), he was offered the directorship of the American School of Classical Studies at Athens (Nos. 67, 68) and was given honorary degrees by Sewanee (D.C.L. 1884) and Harvard (LL. D. 1886). Nevertheless, America seemed hopelessly behind Europe, and APA meetings began to depress him more and more (No. 55), until he was led to the conclusion that "American philology is naught" (No. 56; see also No. 60).

One of the happier features of his "long years of work and the manifold disappointments" (No. 82) was his capacity for warm and loyal friendships. In this period he became close to two men, B. L. Wiggins and B. I. Wheeler. His development of a summer school at the University of the South, Sewanee, Tenn. (No. 65), where he visited for four summers (1883, 1884, 1886, 1887), in large part grew from his friendship with Wiggins. There he had his first contact with C. F. Smith, who would become an abiding friend, and there he was able to contribute to the education of some of the finest young men of the South.

Another friendship of even longer duration involved Wheeler, who regularly sought Gildersleeve's students for his staff at Cornell (Nos. 74, 85, 86), with whom he toured the Peloponnesus (No. 169) and stayed in Heidelberg, where the two planned a Gildersleeve-Wheeler Series of Greek texts for Harpers (No. 88).

This period closed with a signal event: in his sixty-fifth year, this great American Hellenist made his first trip to Greece, after seventeen previous crossings of the Atlantic. He had planned the trip as early as 1890 (No. 73), but it was not until 1896, "after much vacillation," that he decided finally to go. The first modern Olympics scarcely diverted him; but two excursions in Greece with the great archaeologist Dörpfeld (see *60 Days*, written for his student, the editor of the *Atlantic*, Walter Hines Page [see "Correspondents"]) affected him profoundly for the remaining quarter century of his life.

## 52 To: HERMANN USENER
### Bonn

Baltimore Dec. 3, 1880

My dear Professor Usener:

A few weeks ago Wheeler[1] wrote me that you complained of my faithlessness in failing to meet you at Paris and I determined to make a clean breast of it and confess my sin but before I could muster courage to write to you, here came your letter with its bitter reproaches, and if I could sink into the earth before you in atonement, I would gladly go further down than the deepest mud of that Lutetia[2] from which I failed to rescue you. The English language does not suffice to express my grief and confusion of face and you have frightened me so much that I dare not use German. After Wheeler recovers from his honeymoon and is restored to the ranks of rational beings,[3] I will beg him to intercede for me and perhaps you will 'ladle out' forgiveness to your guilty ingrate. The fact is, my dear friend, that when I got down to Munich I was seized with a fever which did not leave me until I had been some weeks at home. It was perhaps a metaphorical fever but a fever for all that. I was Italy-mad and when I got back to Paris after my three weeks in Italy, I was no more an accountable being than one of the Lotus-eaters and then I was in Paris a very short time, and every hour was occupied by the hateful business of shopping for the women of my family. I did not know where you were though to be sure, I might have found out from Bonnet,[4] if I had not made excuses. I am miserable enough at the thought of having missed you—and, what is worse, I shall never be able to think of those happy hours in Bonn, which I owe to you, without self-reproach. Still I gather some crumbs of comfort from your writing to me at all and I am glad that you have not dismissed /me/ from your memory with silent contempt.

Accept my best thanks for your information about Harkness,[5] who has been very friendly to me—and whom I shall be glad to vindicate. I must confess, however, that I thought the Bonn gentlemen were /more/ severe in the year of grace 1854 than they seem to have been; and I am afraid that you are much more harsh now than your predecessors were in that pleasant vacation.

A few days since, I received the copy of Diels' dedication to you.[6] Of course 'me' for 'mihi' was a mere slip of the pen and it was corrected in all but a few copies. I shall make the proper explanation in the next number of the Journal.[7] Perhaps the first notice was ill-judged but most American scholars are so superstitious in their admiration of everything German that your friend Diels might have found imitators even in his bad grammar. You know, as well as I do, that of late years there has been a good deal of scandalously bad Latin published; and that persuadere with the acc. is not incredible you may convince yourself by reading the first page of Blaydes's Lysistrata.[8]

A man cannot take a five months' vacation with impunity and I have had my hands full since my return. The conditions of our work are so very different from yours that I am afraid you would not consider my activity as truly philological in the higher sense. Still I trust that I am doing something for the good cause. If you care to see the Journal I will send it to you regularly. Wheeler is to write the summary of the Rh. Museum hereafter and it will be done carefully and lovingly.[9] The poor fellow has got himself entangled in an alliance which will enable him to interpret Euripides more sympathetically than ever. He seems to be very proud of his choice and very much excited over his approaching bliss.

Your essay on St. Palagia interested me deeply.[10] It crossed the track of some feeble studies I made many years ago and as soon as I can find time I hope to put your results into an English dress—not a translation exactly but a variation with all acknowledgments due. I only wish I had some opportunity to give expression to my grateful sense of your kindness. Cut off so long from active intercourse with German scholars, I must have seemed to you sadly behind the times and yet you never let fall a word that could by any possibility have mortified me and I shall never cease to think of you most affectionately and even more if I am no better than the frogs of Leutsch's lecture—still remember that frogs may have some sentiment in their πομφολυγοπάφλασματα.[11]

At any rate don't ruin me in the opinion of your wife,[12] who must never know that she wasted her goodness on me. Rather teach her to be sorry for my privations, for the old homesickness which comes over everyone who has learned to love European life is often strong upon me now.

Yours faithfully<br>B. L. Gildersleeve

Prof. H. Usener

1. Neither Usener's nor his student Wheeler's (No. 46, n. 6) letters survive.

2. Lutetia (*Luteus* = "muddy") Parisiorum was the ancient name for the site of Paris.

3. For the appeal Wheeler's wife made to Gildersleeve after her husband's death, see No. 71, n. 17.

4. Alfred Max Bonnet (1841–1917) received his Ph.D. from Bonn in 1872. He edited *Gregorii Turonensis opera*, with W. Arndt, B. Krusch et al. (Hanover: Hahn, 1884–85) and *Acta apostolorum apocrypha* (Leipzig: Mendelssohn, 1891).

5. On Albert Harkness, who was beginning his term on the managing committee of the American School of Classical Studies at Athens, and who had received his Ph.D. from Bonn in 1854, see No. 39, n. 3.

6. *Doxographi Graeci*, ed. Hermann Diels (1848–1922) (Berlin: G. Reimer, 1879). The dedication contained two sentences employing the accusative (*me*) with *persuadere*, which normally takes the dative (*mihi*). See *AJP* 1 (1880): 241.

7. *AJP* 1 (1880): 514.

8. *Aristophanis Lysistrata*, ed. F. H. M. Blaydes (1818–1908) (Halle: Orphanotrophei Libraria, 1880). The *argumentum* has *cives* as the object of *persuadere*. See preceding note.

9. Wheeler wrote reports on *RhM* for vols. 2–7.

10. H. Usener, *Legenden der Pelagia* (Bonn: A. Marcus, 1879).

11. "Noises made by rising bubbles"; see Ar. *Frogs* 249.

12. Lily Dilthey (1846–1920), whom Usener married in 1866, was the sister of the philosopher Wilhelm Dilthey (1833–1911).

53 To: WILLIAM ROBERTSON SMITH<br>Cambridge University Library

June 13, 1881

My dear Professor Smith:

I thank you most cordially for your "Old Testament and the Jewish Church"[1] which I received from you some time since through your American publishers and which I have read with the deepest interest. It gave me sincere pleasure to be thus assured that in the heat of your conflict[2] you remembered our talk of last summer and I consider myself fortunate to have had even a slight personal acquaintance with /one/ whose writings are so full of light and power. I am not a theologian nor a Biblical critic and cannot speak with authority—but as a student not unfamiliar with philological methods, I am at a loss to see how we can refuse at this time of day to apply those methods to historical documents and as a man earnestly desirous of a religious basis for his higher life, I cannot feel that my reverence for the divine in the word is impaired by the studies that you are making. Indeed for some you are saving the spiritual value of the Old Testament. But I have no right to encroach on time which is so full of noble employment. Your work and your conflict are watched with eager eyes from this side of the Atlantic and you will pardon me for not confining myself to a simple acknowledgment of your courtesy.

I am

With high regard

Yours sincerely

B. L. Gildersleeve

Professor W. Robertson Smith

1. *The Old Testament in the Jewish Church: Twelve Lectures on Biblical Criticism* (Edinburgh: A. and C. Black, 1881). These were lectures delivered by Smith in January–March 1881, while charges were still pending against him.
2. On the trial, see No. 43.


54 To: JAMES MORGAN HART
*Cornell*

June 17, 1881

My dear Professor Hart:

I shall be glad to give you five pages in no. 3 and 5 pages in no. 4 for the reviews.[1] Your cordial cooperation has always been a great comfort to me in the thankless work of the Journal. The undertaking was not exactly forced on me but the moral obligation was very strong and if I have lost much of the peace and comfort of my life, I have the grim satisfaction of showing practically what the troubles of philological life in America are. I judge from the tone of some of my correspondents that /they think/ the editor's office is a lucrative one![2]—I could easily write a string of philological articles and earn some hundreds of dollars by 'potboiling' work[3] besides in half the time that I spend on the unremunerative tasks of bookkeeping, proofreading and correspondence.—Still I am not the least soured by it, perhaps because I was soured before.

My circular seems to have stirred up those who least needed stirring up.[4] However I am glad of anything that elicited your kind letter.

Yours faithfully

B. L. Gildersleeve

1. For Hart's contributions, see No. 38, n. 6.
2. Writing to Charlton T. Lewis (1834–1904) on 21 April 1881 [Yale], Gildersleeve lamented his "expenditure of much coinable time" and said that, while contributors could not be paid, "I hoped there would be a little surplus at the close of the first year to divide among my helpers," but there was not. See No. 171.

3. E.g., his "potwalloping job" as "sub-editor" (*AJP* 38 [1917]: 222) of *Johnson's Cyclopedia* (see No. 80, n. 1).

4. The fear was that the *AJP* would reduce the number of papers submitted to the APA, but such was not the case: "I was interested to observe by the Proceedings of the Philological Association that the papers were more numerous than usual—quite a different result from that which was predicted on the establishment of the Journal" (BLG to Whitney, 13 May 1881 [Yale]).

### 55 To: Daniel Coit Gilman
*JHU-Gilman*

July 16, 1881

My dear Mr. Gilman:

I returned last night from Cleveland. The meeting of the Philological Association was pleasant but miserably unfruitful of papers. We failed to make the connection at Pittsburg[h]—a very common accident, it seems and I got to Cleveland only in time to hear the last sentences of Packard's address,[1] which turned on Greek mythology and Greek religion—Toy's paper may have been good.[2] Whitney's was a subacid essay on mixture in language,[3] in which Max Müller came in for his share of verjuice. Seymour produced a halting and jejune affair about the aorist participle—as poor a piece of grammatical work as I ever desire to see.[4] The other papers were slight or inconclusive or unmethodical or wild and I was never in all my life more out of heart with my profession.—I took a paper with me, one which I had just finished for my Journal and read it to fill up a doleful blank.[5] As I have told you often, there is no satisfaction in reading scientific papers before people who either can't or won't criticise. The gathering in of a certain amount of complimentary remarks is a poor reward.—I should not have gone except on account of the Journal for which I secured some help in the way of contributions. Whitney seems to be pleased whenever I /go to the meetings and/ pay that tribute to his creation[6] and he promises me a review and an article for the Sept. number[7] which is going to be the best as the July no. is the poorest that I have issued yet.—I took Price with me to the Association and put him in the line of promotion.[8] The contact with other men will give him courage and develop him—though there is some trouble about his temperament and his health. The more we encourage good men elsewhere, the better for us, as our work will be more truly appreciated. If you have room in your course for a series of lectures on literature, English, Romance, or Norse, it would be well to think of J. A. Harrison of Washington and Lee.[9] He has a History of Spain and a French grammar in press. If the latter turns out to be a good book philologically, we ought to try to get him. He is in many respects a wonderful fellow and possesses a number of literatures as no man of his age in this country does.

His imagination is perfervid but he is a man of increasing power. By the way they are thinking of him at Columbia.—Goodwin[10] has written me a long—relatively long—and actually cordial letter from California. He accepts for one week in February. Wheeler has gotten his Bowdoin professorship, to my infinite delight.[11] One less to provide for.—When I think how I chafe under my growing correspondence, I blush as I compare your mountains of letters—and resolve never to vex you by writing unnecessarily or at too great length.—Still when I get to the Sweet Springs,[12] if I ever get there, I will send you a note from time to time that you may know that I have not fretted myself to death, which I shall do long before sixty-five. With kind regards to Mrs. Gilman

I am

Yours faithfully

B. L. G.

D. C. Gilman Esq.

I find that I have closed my letter without referring to the upsetting of my plans for the summer. My wife's old cook was seized with a malignant sore throat just a day or two before my wife and children were ready to start for Narragansett. We lost our rooms there as it was impossible to leave an old servant in such a plight. While I was away another servant fell sick and as it is too late in the season to get good rooms at the sea side and the doctor thinks that the mountain air is what Emma needs most, we have determined to go to the Sweet Springs in W. V$\underline{a}$.—by far the most comfortable of Virginia watering places—where I expect to do no end of work. If I find myself getting jaded, I can take a run Northward just before the beginning of the session—

B. L. G.

1. Lewis R. Packard (see No. 25) delivered the presidential address, "The Morality and Religion of the Greeks" at 8:00 P.M. on Tuesday, 12 July 1881.

2. Crawford W. Toy of Harvard had spoken in the afternoon on "The Home of the Primitive Semitic Race," published in *TAPA* 12 (1881): 26-51.

3. "On Mixture in Language" (ibid.: 5-26). He attacked Max Müller's "axiom," enunciated in *Lectures on Language*, that mixed languages cannot exist.

4. "On the Use of the Aorist Participle in Greek," (*TAPA* 12 [1881]: 88-96), given Thursday morning, 14 July, before Gildersleeve's paper. See No. 50 and n. 6.

5. "On ΠΡΙΝ in the Attic Orators" (see No. 48, n. 2).

6. The APA; see No. 8, n. 13.

7. "What is Articulation?" *AJP* 2 (1881): 345-50, another paper given by Whitney at the Cleveland meeting, and a review of *Nubische Grammatik* by R. Lepsius, ibid.: 362-72.

8. On Price, see No. 69, n. 3. Price was elected to the 1881-82 Executive Committee, on which Gildersleeve served.

9. James Albert Harrison (1848-1911) studied Latin and Greek with Gildersleeve at the University of Virginia (A.B. 1868), studied at Bonn and Munich (1868-1870), was professor

of Latin and modern languages at Randolph-Macon (1871–76), and Washington and Lee (1876–95), and professor of Romance and Teutonic languages at the University of Virginia (1895–1911). Gildersleeve refers to his *Spain* (Boston: Estes and Lauriat, 1881) and *French Syntax* (Philadelphia: J. E. Potter, 1882). His great work was *The Complete Works of Edward Allan Poe*, 17 vols. (New York: Crowell, 1902). He also wrote *The Story of Greece* (New York: Putnam, 1885) and *Anglo-Saxon Prose Reader*, ed. with W. M. Baskervil (New York: A. S. Barnes, 1898). He gave ten lectures at Hopkins 12 February–2 March 1880 and returned in 1882 to lecture on Anglo-Saxon poetry. Gildersleeve nominated him for membership in the National Institute of Arts and Letters (No. 145, n. 5). See, further, *DAB* 8: 343–44.

10. Gildersleeve seems astonished that Goodwin (No. 50, n. 5), who recommended him to Gilman (No. 15, n. 1), would be cordial. Their meeting in Bonn (see No. 49) was apparently agreeable, and such of their correspondence as remains is friendly, if businesslike.

11. On John Henry Wheeler, see No. 46, n. 6.

12. See following letter, n. 1.

### 56 To: Daniel Coit Gilman
*JHU-Gilman*

Sweet Springs, Monroe C$^{\underline{o}}$ W.V$^{\underline{a}}$[1]
July 23, 1881

My dear Mr. Gilman:

The President of the University of Vermont[2] informs me that 'he can find a hundred good scholars where he failed to find one man of sterling worth.' Perhaps you would do well to write to him about a professor of English. I know that we can't boast of any similar success.[3] For a good English scholar I should be willing to abate a little in my demands of sterling worth. Indeed I should allow my man to be a little immoral now and then, provided he did not shirk the proprieties of social intercourse. Seriously professors of the right kind are very hard to find—so hard that I have been asked if I would like to be principal and professor in a projected university at Austin, Texas[4] with the 'large and liberal' salary of $5000 a year[5]—but out of regard to your tribulations I think I shall decline. American philology is naught and, as I wrote you before, Cleveland took away any lingering hope I might have had. Somehow the utter barrenness of the land revealed itself to me more completely than ever. Wells[6]—our new Fellow—was listened to with profound respect more profound than Brandt would have shown. I never saw March[7] in better plight—He said that he was sunburnt and attributed his healthier appearance to the exposure but I thought he had more vitality than I had ever discerned before in him. If he could get rid of his spelling reform mania! As compared with Corson[8] and Lounsbury,[9] he is of course easily the best—and has good work left in him. But will he come? Lafayette will not let him go, if he can be held and he has an enormous family, which he can hardly maintain in Baltimore on the maximum salary, if my experience is worth anything. But that is a matter for him to decide.—Of the three mentioned, I should without hesitation vote for March.—

We are settled here probably for the summer. The air is sweet, the scenery mildly beautiful, the temperature most of the time charming. I arrange to work several hours every day and hope to return 'forehanded' for the severe tests of next session. My little girl blooms in the mountain air and the rest of us are well—

With kind regards to Mrs. Gilman and yourself from me and mine

    I am

Yours faithfully
B. L. Gildersleeve

D. C. Gilman Esq.

1. One of the most elegant of the springs, located on the Virginia border, fifteen miles south of White Sulphur Springs, W. Va. and eighteen miles SSW of Covington, Va. See, further, F. Logan, *The Old Sweet: Biography of a Spring* (Roanoke, Va.: n.p., 1940).

2. Matthew Henry Buckham (1832-1910), had been professor of English (from 1856), Greek (from 1857), and rhetoric (from 1863) at the University of Vermont before becoming its eleventh president (1871-1910). While he more than tripled the number of faculty during his administration, he lamented the lack of well-rounded men. See his posthumous *The Very Elect* (Boston: Pilgrim Press, 1912). On Buckham, see *NatCAB* 2: 42.

3. See No. 21.

4. The University of Texas, originally enacted in 1858, was not begun in earnest until after the Civil War, when the constitution of 1866 provided for a university fund. A board of regents was authorized in March 1881, and in September Austin was chosen as the site. Founded on the University of Virginia model, there was no president in the early years and the first chairman of the faculty, Ashbell Smith (1805-86), a former Texas surgeon general and secretary of state, worked diligently to recruit the best scholarly faculty possible. The first professor of classics was Milton Wylie Humphreys (see No. 25, n. 9). See M. C. Berry, *The University of Texas: A Pictorial Account of Its First Century* (Austin: University of Texas Press, 1980), 3-8.

5. In 1885 professors at Columbia earned $5-7,000; at Hopkins $5,000; at Harvard $4,000; Yale $3,500; Princeton $3,000 and housing; the University of Virginia $3,000 and housing and six acres of land; Cornell $2,750; Michigan $2,200. M. Bishop, *A History of Cornell* (Ithaca, N.Y.: Cornell University Press, 1962), 237 n. 6.

6. Benjamin Willis Wells (1856-1923) received his A.B. (1877) and Ph.D. (1880) from Harvard, studied at Berlin (1877-79), and was accepted for a fellowship at Johns Hopkins. He gave Johns Hopkins as his affiliation at the 1881 APA meeting, but his article in that year's *Proceedings* ("History of the a-Vowel from Old Germanic to Modern English," 12 [1881]: 68-88) gives "Friends' School, Providence R.I.," where he taught from 1881 to 1891, when he took a position at Sewanee and became a founding editor of *The Sewanee Review*. He left Sewanee in 1899 to edit *The Churchman* in New York City, retiring in 1912. He contributed articles on English philology to *TAPA* each year from 1881 to 1887 and wrote more than twenty school texts in French and German, including *Modern German Literature* and *Modern French Literature* (Boston: Roberts, 1895 and 1896 respectively).

7. Francis Andrew March (1825-1911) graduated from Amherst (B.A. 1845; M.A. 1848)

and practiced law from 1849 to 1853, when illness forced him to retire. In 1855, after a year in a private school, he joined the faculty of Lafayette College, Easton, Pa., and was made the first professor of English language and comparative philology in America in 1858. He held the chair for forty-nine years, teaching in addition French, German, Latin, Greek, political science, philosophy, botany, and other subjects. He is generally credited with introducing the application of *exegesis* to classroom studies of English literature, and he had great influence. His great work was *A Comparative Grammar of the Anglo-Saxon Language*, but he is also known for his *Introduction to Anglo-Saxon*, and *Method of Philological Study of the English Language* (New York: Harper and Bros., 1870, 1840, and 1865 respectively). He supervised American contributors to the *OED* (see Murray [cited No. 44, n. 6], 266-67) and was president of the APA twice (1873-74, 1895-96) and the MLA once (1891-93). His "enormous" family had nine children, the eldest of which was the lexicographer Francis Andrew March (1863-1928). *DAB* 12: 268-70.

8. Hiram Corson (1828-1911) received no college education, but after seven years as a private tutor in Philadelphia (1859-65) was named professor of rhetoric and English literature at St. John's College, Annapolis, Md. (1866-70) and professor of English literature at Cornell (1870-1903). He wrote *An Introduction to the Study of Shakespeare* (Boston: D. C. Heath, 1889), *A Primer of English Verse* (Boston: Ginn, 1892), and *The Aims of Literary Study* (New York: Macmillan, 1895). He gave a popular series of lectures at Hopkins in 1884. *DAB* 4: 453-54.

9. Thomas Raynesford Lounsbury (1838-1915) received his A.B. from Yale in 1859 and was professor of English (1871-1906) and librarian (1873-96) at the Sheffield Scientific School. He wrote *A History of the English Language* (New York: Holt, 1879), *Studies in Chaucer: His Life and Writings* (New York: Harper and Bros., 1892); and *English Spelling and Spelling Reform* (New York: Harper and Bros., 1909). Gilman described his ideal English professor as "the man who has both literary & philological aptitude—a future Child or Lounsbury" (*Hawkins*, 163). *DAB* 11: 429-31.


57 To: EMIL HÜBNER
*Berlin*

253 St. Paul St. Baltimore Md.
Oct. 23ᵈ 1881

My dear Hübner:

This is my fiftieth birthday and I feel an irresistible inclination to have a chat with my old friend. We Americans as a rule do not observe such anniversaries with as much ceremony as the Germans do and the very quiet of the day reminds me by contrast of the way in which we celebrated my coming of age just twenty nine years ago. I have still and shall keep to the end the seal which you gave me on that occasion. Sealing wax is out of fashion now on this side of the water but kind feeling will never be, I trust.—I received your kind letter of July 10ᵗʰ in the mountains of Virginia whither I had betaken myself with my wife and children for the summer months.[1] Our summers in the cities of the Atlantic seaboard are so oppressive that it is necessary for the health of my family to migrate in July and we do not return until the middle or end of September, my work beginning about the first of October. And this was an exceptional summer. It was not only very warm but there was a long continued drought, which in this section of the country has not been broken yet. The heavens seem to be of brass;[2] unfortunately our skies are not and the mosquitoes, a great pest of our climate, are lively still.—I took to my summer resort a pile of books but accomplished very little except to spoil my holiday somewhat. My little girl, who is not very strong, was much benefitted by her stay at the watering place, where we spent the summer and by the use of the baths; and we all derived some advantage from the sweet air of the mountains. As usual I have nothing to complain of in the matter of health except a slight affection of the throat which is, I hope, yielding to remedies. Life is lapsing into its old ways with me. I have a handful of college graduates to prepare for higher work than is ordinarily done in America. My own life has not been a success from the philological point of view but I think I can do something towards helping the new generation to better things.— My young men are working at Plato now and in conformity with my own tendencies are studying the grammatical, stylistic and rhetorical side.[3] I find that the Journal still gives me no little work to do and what with minor articles for the press,[4] what with my outlines of Greek syntax and my projected edition of Pindar,[5] I do not lack employment, which is after all the main thing. I cannot help hoping that after I have cleared off some scores I shall have another opportunity [of] going abroad— —perhaps to Athens for some months. Of course I shall not fail to take Berlin on my way. I belong henceforth to you and yours. In any case I do not intend to let you forget me. My boy is growing apace and is making fair progress in his studies although he is far behind German boys of his age in the classics.[6] He has not much fancy for Latin or Greek but he has a good clean mind and so far as I can judge he has a kind of legal acuteness. In that case, indeed in any case, I should wish him to study some three years in Germany and stranger things have have [sic] happened than the fulfillment of your promise to look after him when he enters the University of Berlin.[7]—But I have given you three solid pages about myself and I must stop my egotistic ramblings.

Sooth to say—public affairs have not furnished a very pleasant theme for correspondence. The assassination of the President though the freak of a half cracked creature is a bad sign.[8] Then we have been going too fast lately and I am afraid that there are breakers ahead.—I should be delighted to have you on this side but the risk would be too great. If one of your boys should like to try his fortunes in America you can count on me.— Your pamphlet "über mech. Cop. von Inschriften" came safely to hand.[9] I have received nothing from Friedländer.[10] Best thanks for your kind remembrance of me. Everything that you write is of deep interest to me,

Present me most affectionately to your wife and dear children and thank Friedländer especially for his good will. He is a man I should have liked to know better.—I will not be such a laggard in writing again.

Yours faithfully

B. L. G.

1. See No. 56, n. 1.

2. Deut. 28:23: "And the heavens over your head shall be brass, and the earth under you shall be iron."

3. Gildersleeve had twelve students studying the *Symposium*, including Eben Alexander (see No. 91, n. 11) and Edward Henry Spieker (see No. 114, n. 1).

4. Gildersleeve wrote reviews of Campbell's *Sophocles* and Zangemeister and Wallenbach's *Exempla codicum Latinorum litteris maiusculis scriptorum* for the *Nation* (32 [1881], 425, 460–61), as well as the articles "Remus and Romulus" (ibid., 460) and "The Dark Side of German Professional Life" (*Nation* 33 [1882]: 410–11 (none listed in Miller's bibliography in *SBM*).

5. See No. 68.

6. Raleigh was twelve years old.

7. See No. 71.

8. President James A. Garfield (1831–81) was shot on 2 July 1881 in a Washington railway station by a frustrated office seeker named Charles J. Guiteau. Garfield died on 19 September 1881.

9. *Über mechanische Copieen von Inschriften* (Berlin: Weidmann, 1881) originally appeared as *Mechanische Copieen von Inschriften* in *Jahrbücher des Vereins von Alterthumsfreuden im Rheinlands* (Bonn: C. Georgi, 1870).

10. See No. 51, n. 9.

58 To: JOHN RANDOLPH TUCKER

*UNC-Tucker*

June 19, 1882

My dear Mr. Tucker:

Sir William Jones's wellknown [sic] lines[1] are an expansion not a translation of a famous fragment of Alcaeus (23 Bergk[2]): ἄνδρες πόληος πύργος ἀρεύϊοι 'Brave men are the tower of a state.' This commodious commonplace has attracted many literary squatters in ancient as in modern times. See a similar sentiment in Soph. Oed. Tyr. 56,[3] Thuc. 7.77.[4] The rhetorician Aristeides has preserved the substance of the passage of Alcaeus and Sir William Jones has drawn from that also (I 555 Jebb 821 Dindorf)[5]—'not houses well roofed nor stones of walls well built nor sheets and (naval) arsenals form the city'[6] So again 'not stones nor timbers nor the craft of craftsmen'[7]—Alcaeus was an aristocrat and reactionist. Hence his heretical views. Duty constitutes a state—especially a duty on ship building materials, which prevents one having a navy.[8] This reminds me to

thank you for your last document which I read greatly to my enlightenment.[9]

Betty unites with me in kind regards.

Yours faithfully

B. L. Gildersleeve

Hon. J. R. Tucker

1. Actually, "An Ode in Imitation of Alcaeus," from *Poems Consisting Chiefly of Trans-lations from the Asiatick Languages* (London: W. Bowyer and J. Nichols, 1782), has for an epigraph not this line of Alcaeus', but the synopsis of Alcaeus' theme by Aristeides mentioned by Gildersleeve (see n. 6 below):

Οὐ λίθοι, οὐδὲ ξύλα οὐδὲ
Τέχνη τεκτόνων αἱ πόλεις εἰσιν,
'Αλλ' ὅπου ποτ' ἂν ὦσιν ῎ΑΝΔΡΕΣ
Αὐτοὺς σώζειν εἰδότες
'Ενταῦθα τείχη καὶ πόλεις.

(Not stones, nor timber, nor the art of building constitute a state; but wherever there are men who know how to defend themselves, there is a city and a fortress.)
Jones' poem begins:

What constitutes a State?
Not high-rais'd battlement or labour'd mound,
Thick wall or moated gate;
Not cities proud with spires and turrets crowned; . . .
No:—MEN, high-minded MEN, . . .
Men, who their *duties* know, . . .

2. T. Bergk, *Poetae lyrici Graecae*, vol. 3 (Leipzig: Rechenbach, 1843) ( = E 1.10 in *Poetarum Lesbiorum fragmenta*, ed. E. Lobel and D. Page [Oxford: Clarendon Press, 1955]).

3.                       ὡς οὐδέν ἐστιν οὔτε πύργος οὔτε ναῦς                       56
ἔρημος ἀνδρῶν μὴ ξυνοικούντων ἔσω.

(Since neither walled town nor ship is anything, if it is empty and no men live with you within.)

4. ἄνδρες γὰρ πόλις, καὶ οὐ τείχη οὐδὲ νῆες ἀνδρῶν κεναί (Men make a state, not walls nor unmanned ships). See also Aesch. *Pers.* 349; Her. 8.61; Eur. fr. 825; Plut. *Ly-curg.* 19; Dem. 18. 299; Dio Chrys. 56.5.3; Cic. *Ad Att.* 7.11.

5. *Aelius Aristides opera omnia Graece et Latine*, ed. Samuel Jebb, 2 vols. (Oxford: Sheldon Theatre, 1722-30); and *Aelius Aristides opera*, ed. W. Dindorf (Leipzig: Weid-mann, G. Reimer, 1829) ( = *Orat.* 3.298 in *P. Aelii Aristidis opera quae exstant omnia*, ed. C. A. Behr [Leiden: E. J. Brill, 1976]).

6. Aristeides *Orat.* 25.64 (Behr) ( = Lobel-Page Z 103), quoted in n. 1 above.

7. Idem, 23.68.

8. Tucker was particularly interested in tariff reform, serving on the Tariff Bill Con-ference in the 2d session of the 47th Congress (1882); hence this joke.

9. Possibly his speech in the House of Representatives on 5 May 1882 on the effect of importation of British steel and cotton. See "Speech on Tariff and Tax Commission," *Appendix to Congressional Record* 13 (47th Cong. 1st sess.), 275-91.

59 To: DANIEL COIT GILMAN
*JHU-Gilman*

July 5, 1882

Dear Mr. Gilman:

Harris[1] is evidently a bright man but makes no pretensions, I believe, to critical Greek studies after the German pattern. His proper business is mathematics; his recreation the study of mysticism especially in its Greek forms. He seems to be conscious of the limitations of English university life. Whether he has earnestly tried to free himself from those limitations is another matter. If there were room for him in the University, I should personally like to have him work with us but a temporary appointment is always a dangerous experiment. The fascination of the Johns Hopkins is phenomenal so that perhaps even Brandt[2] will withstand the call to Hamilton. By the way Brandt came to my room the other day and frankly begged pardon for his conduct in the Burgess affair[3] and said much harder things against himself than I should have exacted. He is a useful man despite the infirmities of his temper and we should miss him. If he goes, we ought to try for a strong modern languages man and let him set that whole department straight, the hardest, by the way, to get straight in the whole scheme.

Mr. Sylvester[4] has returned to Baltimore and seems to stand his summer in America very well so far.

We expect to leave Baltimore next Monday. If Martha's Vineyard does not answer our purposes, I shall be tempted to try Berkshire again.

Yours very truly,
B. L. Gildersleeve

President D. C. Gilman

1. James Rendel Harris (1852–1941) was third wrangler at Cambridge (1874) and lecturer in mathematics at Clare College (1875–82). He was hired as lecturer to teach New Testament Greek at Hopkins in 1882 but also taught physics in the absence of C. S. Hastings, and, in his second year, philosophy. He published *New Testament Autographs* (Baltimore: I. Friedenwald, 1882), but in 1885 he attacked the practice of vivisection, which seemed indirectly to criticize Henry Newell Martin's (No. 44, n. 8) experiments on dogs. Harris interpreted a notice from the executive committee as a limitation on his freedom of speech and declined reappointment to his chair for 1885–86. He became professor of biblical languages and literatures at the Quaker Haverford College (1885–92) and returned to Cambridge in 1893 as lecturer in paleography. In 1918 he was appointed curator of Eastern manuscripts at the John Rylands Library in Manchester. He returned to Hopkins to lecture in 1894–95 and 1909–10, and in 1887 he published his edition of *The Teaching of the Apostles* with the Johns Hopkins Press. See *AJP* 41 (1921): 94 ( = *SBM*, 400); *Hawkins*, 152–54; *DNB 1941–1950*, 360–62; and T. R. Glover, *Cambridge Retrospect* (Cambridge: Cambridge University Press, 1943), 69–74.

2. On Brandt, see No. 47, n. 11.

3. Edward Sandford Burgess (1855–1928) had received his B.A. (1879) and M.A. (1882)

from Hamilton and was a fellow in botany at Hopkins in 1881–82. He was not hired by Hamilton and returned to Hopkins as instructor in botany for one year (1885). He received his Ph.D. from Columbia in 1899 and was professor of anthropology at Hunter College from 1895 to his death. His specialty was asters, the subject of his dissertation and *A History of Pre-Clusian Botany in its Relation to the Aster* (New York: Torrey Botanical Club, 1902).

4. No. 30, n. 2.

## 60 To: DANIEL COIT GILMAN
*JHU-Gilman*

62 Narragansett Ave
July 27, 1882

My dear Mr. Gilman:

I didn't answer your last letter immediately because I wished to think over the situation, although my first thoughts are often my best thoughts[1] and meditation muddles rather than clarifies. The more I see of the leading philologians of the country the less confidence do I feel in the future of the department in America. The older men are revolving in circles, the younger men are parroting their European teachers. No freshness, no initiative anywhere. The value of Brandt was that he dared to think for himself but he had got himself into the text-book line,[2] which is always dangerous for a University teacher—and his return to Hamilton may be the end of him. But that is the dead past which you justly accuse me of resurrecting and burying again all to no purpose.—Raddatz[3] is a good man and would in all likelihood fill Brandt's place better than anyone I know. He has very respectable attainments in the scientific line of Germanic philology.—He will do the Middle High German very well—and with greater leisure would develop into a University teacher—The appointment would be popular among our German friends, from whom we are to draw much of our support in future. He is modest. If he is ambitious, he conceals his ambition admirably. He knows how to manage American youth and he is not likely to make enemies. If he is appointed, he will stay and we ought to expect him to stay and have his position thoroughly defined from the beginning— Imported Germans are as a rule, insufferably conceited and arrogant, and the advantages of their method and learning are often more than counterbalanced by bad manners and unspeakable peculiarities.—As to Stickney[4] I am very much at a loss what to say. He is doubtless an accomplished man but he has next to nothing to show in the way of scientific works. His paper on the subject of instruction in modern languages[5] did not impress me as the production of a strong man. To choose him would be in a certain sense to acknowledge the principal of expediency—whereas we have declined to consider mere availability thus far.—A younger man or a man of more spring would be desirable—and yet in the dearth of professional talent in the country I should hesitate to protest against Stickney or any other fairly endowed man. I must frankly say that Stickney's ability to keep up a handsome establishment is not necessarily a recommendation in my eyes. What might be gained in one direction would be lost in another. Nothing is clearer to me than the prospect of a large and permanent increase in the cost of living in Baltimore.—Those of us who are wholly dependent on our salaries find it very hard to keep up a decent appearance. Remsen tells me that he overran his salary last year. My own experience makes me gloomy and apprehensive. To introduce into our number a rich man whose style of living would remind us at every turn of our narrower means might be a source of trouble instead of strength, unless the fortunate man were at the same time a person of commanding power in himself. Our President might be as rich 'as the dreams of avarice'[6]—That position is exceptional, naturally exceptional and no one who has observed with as much admiration as I have the large and liberal way in which you have interpreted your social obligations could have any other wish for you than the most ample means for carrying out your views[7]—but I am not at all certain that rich professors are as desirable as rich Presidents. So in my judgment that element is not in Stickney's favor—at least not unconditionally so— —

You have forgiven my candor so often, I hope you will forgive it once more.

Yours very truly<br>B. L. Gildersleeve

President D. C. Gilman

1. A play on Eur. *Hipp.* 436: αἱ δεύτεραί πως φροντίδες σοφώτεραι ([For mortals,] second thoughts are often wiser).

2. Brandt did not actually publish a textbook until 1884, but he published little else in his career at Hamilton. See No. 47, n. 11.

3. Charles Frederick Raddatz (1838-1941), instructor in German at Baltimore City College, was appointed temporary instructor in German at Hopkins (1882-86), contributed reports on *Germania* to *AJP*, and wrote a report on German orthography for the National Education Association in 1877.

4. Austin Stickney (1831-96), took his A.B. from Harvard in 1852 and was professor of Latin at Trinity College (1858-64, 1870-71). Wealthy enough both by marriage and inheritance to work no more than he wanted to, he spent sixteen years abroad (1863-79) traveling and writing. He returned to New York in 1879, but held no formal academic position thereafter. His chief publication was a translation of G. F. Schoemann's commentary on Cicero's *De natura deorum* (Boston: Ginn and Heath, 1881). *NatCAB* 15: 351-52.

5. "On the Single Case-Form in Italian," *TAPA* 8 (1877): 87-93.

6. "I am rich beyond the dreams of avarice," Edward Moore, *The Gamester* (1753), 2.2.

7. The trustees offered Gilman a starting salary of $8,000, or $7,000 and a house. See *Hawkins*, 21.

61 To: Emil Hübner
*Berlin*

253 St. Paul St. Baltimore
Oct. 15, 1882

My dear Hübner: I received your last letter while I was summering far away from Baltimore and I have carried it in my pocket since as a talisman. Seldom have I felt such good counsel take so immediate effect. Rather prone by nature to melancholy brooding with intervals of spasmodic work I am sure that if I had been so fortunate as to have your cheering companionship all these years, I should have accomplished much more than I have done and so should have been much happier. Since I came to Baltimore /to live/ I have been distracted by so many engagements that I have not been able to finish any big piece of work. Now I have set my teeth and bearing your admonition in mind, I hope to finish my school edition of Pindar's Olympians and Pythians and to put into shape my collections on Lyric Syntax before next summer.[1] Then I shall feel as if I were entitled to a real holiday. I am glad to learn that you are working in my favorite field. If you will only get out a Grundriss that will save less energetic mortals the trouble of hunting up the literature![2] This brings me to my Journal. Do you see /it/ now since you have given up the <u>Hermes</u>?[3] It will be a pleasure to me to send it to you—one of the few pleasures incident to the editorial work.—To my innocent eyes Mommsen seemed great enough until his library burnt and now that the sympathy of the scholarly world has turned his head, he seems small enough.[4] You have your self respect and your happy temper—both greater blessings than an association with an arrogant and opinionated old man, whatever his distinction.—

I too spent my holiday at the seaside but my holiday was much longer than yours. We left home on the 10th of July and did not return until the 14th of September. Baltimore is usually very hot in the summer and I always migrate with my family for eight or ten weeks. This time we chose for our summer sojourn an island off the coast of Massachusetts which bears the quaint name of Martha's Vineyard—You see we Americans are accustomed to great distances and it doesn't seem strange to us when we go five or six hundred miles for our summer stay. I don't know the exact distance of Martha's Vineyard from Baltimore but it is more than 24 hours' travel by rail and boat.[5] Many of my friends go to Mt. Desert off the coast of Maine for the summer, others to Nova Scotia. Martha's Vineyard is a droll place, droll even to our American eyes—For many years it has been a famous camp meeting ground and the Methodists congregated there in great numbers. Then a town sprang up of cottages built in the fantastic, sugar cake style—with abundance of jigsaw ornamentation—little wooden boxes packed close together—with walks and drives laid in asphalt.[6] After a while a watering place (Oak Bluffs) arose outside of the camp meeting grounds but the type of architecture is essentially the same although the cottages have more room. Cottage City has become a noted place for all manner of conventions and experiments of the Yankee type. So we had a Martha's Vineyard Summer Institute where all the new fancies in education were expounded by the space of five weeks—There was a session of the Women's Christian Temperance Union where numbers of female orators held forth. There was always some absurdity or extravagance or excitement going on—and we could sit in our cottage and look on at the current of this queer life and so amuse ourselves with our Yankee brothers—who are very unlike the people of my section. The climate is heavenly, neither too warm nor too cold, the bathing, though not surf bathing, was delicious—There were excursions without end—Amusements for the children, boating, fishing, 'rinking'[7]—I read my Aristophanes, collected statistics for Pindar—heard my boy his Latin and so made believe that I was working. The truth is, I was very idle and gazed at the sea with the revived love of my boyhood. We are better and stronger—and that is something. While I was there I had my little cottage photographed—and to make it look more natural we four sate in the porch. By the help of a strong glass you will be able to make out sundry human figures—

Raleigh grows apace. I am afraid that he will never care for Latin and Greek—but for all that he must know something of German life and German 'Wissenschaft'—and he knows /already/ about his German home. Indeed you and yours are constantly mentioned in my household.

I inclosed a few stamps for the great collection[8]—

With kindest regards to the 'gnädige Frau' and affectionate remembrances to your children—

Yours faithfully
B. L. Gildersleeve

1. See No. 68.

2. Hübner wrote a series of *Grundrisse* published by Weidmann in Berlin: on Roman literature (1869), classical philology (1876), and Latin Grammar (1860), but Gildersleeve here refers to his *Grundriss zu Vorlesungen über die griechische Syntax* (Berlin: W. Hertz, 1883). See No. 68, n. 5.

3. Hübner had edited *Hermes*, under the guidance of R. Hercher (1821–78), A. Kirchhoff (1826–1908), and later J. Vahlen (No. 164, n. 6), with Mommsen (see following note) overseeing all, from its founding in 1866. By 1881 Mommsen began to consider his protégé Hübner lazy and inaccurate, largely based on Hübner's sloppy collection of inscriptions in Spain and Portugal for vol. 2 of the *Corpus inscriptionum Latinorum* (*CIL*), which Mommsen edited. In 1881 Hübner and his co-editors at *Hermes* were summarily removed by Mommsen and replaced by Georg Kaibel (1849–1901) and Carl Robert (1850–1922), allies of his son-in-law, Wilamowitz. See W. M. Calder III, "B. L. Gildersleeve and Ulrich von

Wilamowitz-Moellendorff: New Documents," *AJP* 99 (1978), 9-11 ( = *Calder, Selected Correspondence*, 149-51).

4. Following legal training at Kiel, Theodor Mommsen (1817-1903), was given a grant by the Danish government to visit Italy, where he began his life's work of studying inscriptions. He was made extraordinarius in civil law at Leipzig in 1848, but, as a result of supporting the monarchy in 1848, was removed from his post in 1850. While professor at Zürich (1852-54), he began his great history of Rome (No. 7, n. 7). In 1854 the Berlin Academy made him chief editor of the *CIL* and, following a stint at Breslau (1854-58), he was elected professor at Berlin (1858-1903). He wrote on nearly every aspect of antiquity including literature, epigraphy, numismatics, and textual criticism. In 1902 he was awarded the Nobel Prize in Literature. See, further, Lothar Wickert, *Theodor Mommsen: Eine Biographie*, 4 vols., (Frankfurt-am-Main: Klostermann, 1960). On the evening of 12 July 1880, Mommsen fell asleep with a lighted pipe on his desk, and the resulting fire destroyed most of the library in his home in Charlottenburg. Among the losses were several ancient manuscripts on loan from libraries. Although scholars of many nations contributed to rebuilding Mommsen's library, the one enduring result of the blaze was that libraries ceased loaning ancient manuscripts to individuals. See Wickert, 4: 42-45, 263-65, and W. M. Calder III, "Wilamowitz' Call to Göttingen: Paul de Lagarde to Friedrich Althoff on Wilamowitz-Moellendorff," *SIFC*, 3d ser., 3, no. 2 (1985): 151-52.

5. Gildersleeve would have traveled about 365 miles from Baltimore to Martha's Vineyard.

6. To the north of present-day Edgartown was Cottage City, incorporated in 1907 into Oak Bluffs. See Charles Edward Banks, M.D., *The History of Martha's Vineyard, Dukes County, Massachusetts* (Boston: George H. Dean, 1911), 2: 11.

7. I.e., roller skating or possibly lawn bowling.

8. See No. 52.

## 62 To: EMIL HÜBNER
### *Berlin*

Nov. 28, 1882

My dear Hübner:

The tidings of your father's death brought to me a sense of bereavement such as I have never felt at the loss of one whom I had seen so seldom.[1] But I was privileged to be twice at his home[2] and it seems to me as if the long interval of twenty seven years between the two visits had been filled with the kindness which he felt and showed to all and especially towards the friends of his sons. Whenever I think of my last visit to Germany I think of his sweet and noble old age and the charm of his Loschwitz home, where his beautiful life was closed. He could well say, as he said a few years since, that the ring of Polycrates[3] had no warning for him for the end seems to have been calm and peaceful. You will feel, my dear friend, as I felt some years ago, when my father was taken away that a new solemnity is added to life.[4] So long as the father lives, the son is not in the front and the whole aspect of life is strangely altered when the headship is changed.

To have known your father and your mother is to know you better, is to understand better your own sweet home life. To be remembered by you at such a time as this is a new proof that I have beyond the seas /friends/ who count me among those nearest to them and admit me to a share in their holiest sorrow.

Please assure your mother of my deepest sympathy. With kind regards to all your household whose grief is my grief.

I am

Yours faithfully
B. L. Gildersleeve

Professor Emil Hübner

1. Hübner's father (No. 2, n. 18) died 7 November 1882.
2. Nos. 2 and 51.
3. Polycrates was famed as the most fortunate and most cruel of Greek tyrants. When his ally, Amasis, king of Egypt, felt that Polycrates' unbroken good fortune would arouse the jealousy of the gods, he advised him to throw away his dearest possession. Polycrates threw a particularly beautiful signet ring with an inset emerald into the sea, but in five or six days it turned up in the belly of a fish that the tyrant was about to eat. This proved to Amasis that this good fortune was unnatural, and he broke off his alliance. The story, told by Herodotus 3.40–45, is treated by Grote in his *History* (see No. 7, n. 6), 4: 323, as a fictitious account of the break, which he contends was made by Polycrates, not Amasis.
4. Gildersleeve's father died 20 June 1875 in Tazewell, Va. His will was probated in October, and on 8 December, Gildersleeve met with Gilman in Washington.

### 63 To: Daniel Coit Gilman
*JHU-BLG*

Feb. 6th 1884

In admitting a student to an examination for the degree of Doctor of Philosophy I have always considered the time of study an important element. A certain amount of leisure is necessary for survey, for consolidation. In my department less than three years of University work as distinguished from college work would not suffice a student for the proper digestion of the material and methods offered here. Of course study at any other university centre will count but not the /teacher's/ work of ~~the class-rooms~~ a teacher in an ordinary classical school.

The thesis must show an ability to investigate if not on the higher lines that lead to new results at least on the lines that lead to sharp, clear, systematic presentation of what is known. Original work is a much abused phrase, few men after all are capable of doing more than getting material together for the thinker who is to come. Careful collation, clear arrangement, sober criticism may be expected of all. The difference between the highest and lowest here can not be measured by any fixed rule.

Of every candidate for the degree of Dr. of Philosophy in the department of Greek—a knowledge of Latin is required. If Latin is the minor subject the examination is entrusted to the Latin department. If it is not, the candidate must show his knowledge of the language by translating a piece of prose Greek into Latin.

The formal examination consists usually in

1) Translation from Greek into English of selections from the different departments and different ages of Greek literature. The selections are of average difficulty and are taken from less familiar authors, so that in the majority of cases this exercise shows the ability of the student to read Greek at sight.

2) A classic passage is given (with the critical apparatus)—or a selection of passages—on which the student is to write a commentary giving his views of the various readings with substantiations of that same

3) As a test of grammatical and lexical familiarity with Greek the candidate is required to write without grammar or dictionary a Greek thesis— based on some familiar passage of Greek history or literature

4) An examination on the history of Greek literature covering the Classical period—the portions studied in the university being treated with more details—

5) The examination before the Board—as has been agreed on is considered a test of general bearing, facility of expression, readiness of resource /rather/ than a test of special knowledge—

## 64 To: KARL BRUGMANN
*Staatsbibliothek Preussischer Kulturbesitz*

Feb. 26, 1884

Dear Sir,

President Gilman has informed me of the position of the negotiations with respect to the professorship in the Johns Hopkins University tendered to you some time since.[1] As I had been instructed to open the correspondence, it seems right that I should explain the part I took in the Matter. When Mr. Wheeler informed me that he found you would be obliged to return to the work of a gymnasial teacher and that he thought it possible you would accept an honorable call to America which should secure leisure for scientific work, I was delighted at the opportunity of securing for our university the services of a man, who so fully represents the advanced thought and work of comparative grammar. Philologians—classical philologians especially—on this side of the water understand perfectly what your special line of work is, but it so happens that we felt it especially necessary to have a man who should organize and control the higher work in Germanic Languages, and as Dr. Bloomfield[2] said that you had lectured in Germany on that portion of the subject which would have been expected of you here, I ventured to emphasize that side. It seems there has been some misunderstanding on the subject and this I deeply regret.

You have no warmer admirers anywhere than in America, and in the whole field of knowledge that you command there is no one for whose opinion I have more respect, and the failure of the negotiations will not be due to any want of appreciation on my part of the great work you are doing.

With the material conditions I had, of course, nothing to do. After I had given what I considered due emphasis to the importance of your scientific activity, I had to leave the details in the hands of the authorities, the Trustees of the University. As a professor, dependent on my salary for a support and with a family to provide for, I understand the importance which attaches to a provision for those whom we may be called to leave behind. But as no such provision is made in America, and as we are a more adventuresome people than the Germans, the American professor, if he has no outside means, adapts himself to the situation, and trusts to the current of things, or if he is exceptionally prudent insures his life and thus provides for the immediate future of his family, if he should be taken away. We cannot expect those who have been accustomed to the stable order of German university organization to adapt themselves readily to the conditions of our life, and we can only hope in exceptional circumstances to secure the services of distinguished German scholars. If I thought that such exceptional circumstances had presented themselves in your case, you must forgive my agency in the matter on the ground of my sincere admiration of your work and of my conviction that in a short time the professorship tendered you would have become such as one would not willingly exchange for any one in the United States.

> I am,
>> with sincere respect
>>> Yours very truly
>>> B. L. Gildersleeve

Professor Karl Brugmann

1. When Hermann Charles George Brandt (No. 47, n. 11) returned to his alma mater, Hamilton College (Nos. 59-60), in 1882, German instruction was left to Henry Wood and James Wilson Bright, both in English, and C. F. Raddatz (No. 60, n. 3) to fill in as they could. B. I. Wheeler (see "Correspondents") was in Germany from 1881 to 1885, principally at Heidelberg, where he learned (perhaps from Brugmann's collaborator Hermann Osthoff) of Brugmann's situation at Leipzig and promptly informed Gildersleeve. Gilman decided to

ask Brugmann, through Wheeler, if he "would be willing to accept a Professorship of Comparative Grammar combined with instruction in Gothic and Old High or Middle High German and the directorship and control of the Modern Language Department" (BLG to Wheeler, 4 April 1883). Brugmann did not accept, and Wood, who had a Leipzig Ph.D., was made associate professor of German in 1885. See, further, *Hawkins*, 162.

2. No. 49, n. 14.

## 65 To: BENJAMIN LAWTON WIGGINS
### *Sewanee*

June 14, 1884

My dear Professor Wiggins:

Last Thursday I had a long and most pleasant interview with my old friend and college mate Richardson Miles[1] of Charleston, who seems to take the deepest interest in Sewanee and was kind enough to express a great desire that I should carry out my project of visiting you this summer.[2] I asked him what would be the best time to go and he said August but you are the best judge of that. Our work here is over, in fact has been over for more than a week and I hope to get the notes to my Pindar printed[3] and the next no. of the Journal ready by July 1—It is important that I should make plans for the family during my stay at Sewanee, if I have to relinquish the thought of taking them with me.— — You know that I have cherished the hope of building up a summer school at Sewanee not only for Greek but also for Latin and other branches—I am sure that you could concentrate enough force there for the two summer months to be of service to the southern states and to your own institution.—My visit I consider as an experiment in that direction—Miles talked to me freely about the situation and now that I understand the circumstances more fully I can appreciate the efforts you have made—and are making. It gives me great pleasure to know that you value my coöperation so highly. It would be a great favor, if you would let me know what part of my courses you would like to have.

Yours very truly
B. L. Gildersleeve

Professor B. L. Wiggins

1. Charles Richardson Miles (1829–93), graduated from the College of Charleston in 1849, sharing first honors with Sam Lord (No. 12, n. 16). He represented Charleston in the South Carolina General Assembly (1878–80) and was attorney general for the state in 1882 and 1884–86.

2. Gildersleeve loved the University of the South, a private school for the Southern elite, run by men of religious background. It was convenient to the Virginia springs where his family regularly vacationed, and his summer earnings paid his summer expenses. He visited Sewanee from 28 July to 17 September and planned a summer school of ancient languages "to bring the teachers and advanced students into more intimate contact with the great educa-

tional movement in Germany and England." The plan was approved by the Sewanee trustees in 1885. From 19 July to 18 September 1886 he devoted two hours per week to critical interpretation of the *Symposium* in seminary fashion, two to the "Syntax and Literature of the Language," and two to "popular lectures on Homer's Odyssey" for nine students, five of whom were Sewanee faculty (*University of the South Papers*, ser. B, no. 20 [1886]). On the 1887 session, see No. 71, n. 3. C. F. Smith (see "Correspondents") attended the lectures.

 3. See No. 68, and n. 4.

<br>

## 66 To: Martha Carey Thomas
### *Bryn Mawr*

Johns Hopkins University
Baltimore Oct. 7, 1884

My dear Miss Thomas:

 Your letter has been received and I will give the matter my best thought. I was favourably impressed with Mr. Smyth[1] and what work he has done seems to me good. He is doubtless an earnest and well-equipped lover of Greek and I am very glad that he has turned his attention to dialectology which has been too much neglected by American Hellenists. Whether he may not go too far in following the lead of Fick,[2] of whom he is a devoted disciple, is another matter. If Mr. Smyth will take the position of an associate professor you can hardly do better. No name among my own men occurs to me just now for either the higher or the inferior office. Sterrett,[3] as you say, is dangerously ill and in any case is clearly meant for the career on which he has been arrested, I hope only for a time.

Yours very truly
B. L. Gildersleeve

Miss M. Carey Thomas

 1. Herbert Weir Smyth (1857-1937) was teaching German and Sanskrit at Williams (1883-85). He was lecturer and reader in Greek at Hopkins from 1885 to 1888, when he went on to Bryn Mawr. See, further, "Correspondents."

 2. August Fick (1844-1916), as professor of comparative philology at Göttingen (1876-88), taught Smyth. He is best known for *Vergleichendes Wörterbuch der indogermanischen Sprachen* (Göttingen: Vandenhoeck & Rupprecht, 1870-71) and his work on Homeric dialect, *Die homerische Odyssee in der ursprünglichen Sprachform wieder hergestellt* (Göttingen: R. Peppmüller, 1883), in which he argued that Homeric dialect contains Ionic elements owing to the Ionians having translated the Homeric poems into the Aeolic dialect; when they were translated back from Aeolic, some untranslatable words were retained and these are clearly the work of an "Ionic Homerid" and thus indicate passages that are not genuine. Smyth reviewed Fick's *Die homerische Ilias . . .* at *AJP* 7 (1886): 232-36.

 3. John Robert Sitlington Sterrett (1851-1914) was a student of Gildersleeve's at the University of Virginia (1868-72) who studied at Leipzig, Rome, Berlin, and Munich (Ph.D. 1880) and was at this time a student (1882-83) and later secretary (1883-84) of the American School

of Classical Studies at Athens. After his return to America he was professor of Greek at the Universities of Miami (Ohio) (1886–88), Texas (1888–92), and Amherst (1892–1901), and head of the Greek Department at Cornell (1901–14). His dissertation had dealt with the Homeric Hymns, but his stay in Athens interested him in epigraphy. He wrote *The Wolfe Expedition to Asia Minor* (Boston: Damrell and Upham, 1888) and *A Plea for Research in Asia Minor and Syria* (Ithaca, N.Y.: Journal Printing, 1911). *DAB* 17: 594–95.

67 To: Daniel Coit Gilman
*JHU-Gilman*

Johns Hopkins University
Baltimore Dec. 4, 1884

Sir:

Last year without any motion of mine I was designated Director of the American School of Athens for the year 1885–1886. The position was promptly declined.[1] I could not see sufficient reason for abandoning my work here even temporarily to engage in an experiment which lacked in my judgment the prime conditions of success. Recently the first director of the school[2] wrote me an urgent letter which I inclose herewith in which he is kind enough to express his conviction that my services are much needed at Athens and to beg my reconsideration of the refusal to accept the position. After conference with you I determined to abide by my previous decision and the position has since been filled for the next two years.[3]

While my conviction remains unshaken that there was not sufficient reason for an application to the Board of Trustees for a leave of absence which would involve a virtual suspension of University work in Greek for an entire year, I am not insensible of the great advantages that would accrue to the department if an opportunity should be given me of gaining a personal acquaintance with Greece and the seats of ancient Greek life. In order to accomplish this, it will not be absolutely necessary to break the continuity of my work at the university for a whole session. By increasing the number of the lectures in the first half session I might cover the ground sufficiently to warrant me in leaving America in the early spring and a return in the month of November would not be so late that I could not overtake arrears. In this way there would be no important break in my service and I should be more free for study and travel than if I were limited to Athens for seven or eight months and perplexed by the problems of a new sphere of activity.

In this whole matter I have tried to consult not my own inclinations but the interests of the University to which I have devoted my best energies from the beginning of its active life and in whose service I hope to spend whatever is left to me of time and strength.

In my circumstances, it is necessary to lay plans far in advance and I should be glad if you could present these considerations to the Executive Committee and ascertain how far my views meet their approval.

Yours respectfully,
B. L. Gildersleeve

President Gilman

1. Gildersleeve was elected director for the fourth year of the American School (1885-86), and he was clearly prepared to go to great lengths to serve. Despite declining the office, he was an original member of the managing committee and the board of trustees from their incorporation in 1886 (with Goodwin, James Russell Lowell, C. E. Norton, J. W. White, and others) until his death, contributing "the immense prestige of his name" rather than active participation (he attended only one meeting of the committee). See, further, L. E. Lord, *A History of the American School of Classical Studies at Athens* (Cambridge, Mass.: Harvard University Press, 1947), 5, 23, 40.

2. William Watson Goodwin, see No. 50, n. 5.

3. James Cooke Van Benschoten (1827-1902) of Wesleyan University was the third director (1884-85) and Frederic De Forest Allen (No. 50, n. 7) of Harvard was the fourth (1885-86).

68 To: Emil Hübner
*Berlin*

253 St. Paul St. Baltimore
Jan.ʸ 18, 1885

My dear Hübner:

The pretty cards reached us yesterday. I had to interpret the kind messages to my wife and Emma but Raleigh reads German a little and managed to make out your good wishes for the New Year. We are all much pleased at being remembered by our friends on the other side. Nor did we forget you when Christmas came but knowing as I do that you belong to a family of artists[1] I could not trust my taste in the selection of cards and so I sent instead a book that I thought might interest you somewhat being out of the ordinary run. The author is Harris who has great celebrity as the author of 'Uncle Remus'[2]—His negro books are a great delight to us for we are Southerners and know the dialect and the race as Northern people cannot know them and my wife who was brought up on a plantation reads the rabbit stories admirably.—In Mingo[3] Harris has tried a new dialect vein and as the book may not be as well known to you as the others which are very popular among your English friends, I have sent it at a venture.— In a few weeks I expect to present you with my edition of Pindar's Olympian and Pythian Odes[4]—It is intended for beginners and I cannot hope that it will receive any serious, much less any favorable notice at the hands of German scholars. I have had no time to work at it except at night when I was tired out or in the hot early summers and I am afraid that the book betrays my fatigue as well as other things. But it is done—and I draw a long breath at last—It will be a pretty book to look at, I think, and not a very small one (cxv + 395).—I shall next attack my long neglected Greek syntax—in which your book[5] will be invaluable to me—and and [sic] expect to spend four or five years at that—if so much life be granted me.—

My plans for Europe are somewhat misty. Raleigh goes to the Johns Hopkins next autumn and will have to study there for some time before going abroad for his University work, but we keep Berlin steadily in view for him.— The Directorship of the American School at Athens has been offered to me twice and the last time urged upon me but on conference with the authorities of our university I determined not to accept.[6] My courses here are followed by some eighteen or twenty enthusiastic students[7] and I do not like to break the continuity of work that promises so well.—It would do me a great deal of good to run over for a few weeks next summer but I do not see my way to it yet. My dream is to go to Greece in March of next year—to have my family meet me in July somewhere in England and take a run on the continent with them afterwards. But many obstacles rise between the dream and the realization.[8]—After Raleigh is once settled in Germany as a student I may persuade my wife to spend the winter there with my daughter—but she is very domestic and very American. Still I cannot help hoping that if life and health are spared we shall pass many months of an old age in Europe.—Haven't I poured out my soul to you just as I used to do in the old Bonn days? I verily believe that if I were not a dreamer I should not consent to live, for I do not work as joyously as you do and chafe under the limitations that nature has imposed on me. But however discontented I am with the imperfections of my work, I have much to live for in my little family and among my dreams is the fair one that you and yours will one day be to them living presences and not names—familiar names it is true but still names.—[9]

At the present writing we are all well and though I am a little 'abgespannt' [weary] I hope to be ready for new undertakings in a week or two—

With best wishes for the New Year and kindly greetings to all your household and especially to the 'Gnädige'[10]

Yours always faithfully<br>B. L. Gildersleeve

Professor Emil Hübner

1. On his father, Julius, see No. 2, n. 18, and on his uncle, E. Bendemann, see ibid., n. 19. Two of Hübner's children, Heinrich and Ulrich, became artists (see No. 51, n. 1).

2. Joel Chandler Harris (1848-1908), a native of Georgia, worked on newspapers, chiefly the *Atlanta Constitution*, where in 1879 he published his "Tar-Baby Story," which introduced Uncle Remus, a wise old plantation negro who told animal fables. The character became extremely popular, and four Uncle Remus books followed, which preserved the regional

rural dialect of blacks of the era. See, further, Julia Collier Harris, *The Life and Letters of Joel Chandler Harris* (Boston: Houghton Mifflin, 1918). For Gildersleeve on Harris, see *AJP* 40 (1919): 337 ( = *SBM*, 393).

3. *Mingo, and Other Sketches in Black and White* (Boston: J. R. Osgood, 1884) represented a change from the "Uncle Remus" stories. A collection of four pieces, the first compares two Southern types: a middle-class white woman, whose pride has been wounded by a rude aristocratic lady, and Mingo, a former slave, who is her servant and displays deep understanding of mankind; the second treats Southern "moonshiners"; the third a runaway slave; and the fourth a greedy landowner.

4. *Pindar: The Olympian and Pythian Odes* (New York: Harper and Bros., 1885) was published in April and announced in the May *JHU Circular*, no. 39 (1885): 80.

5. See No. 61, n. 2.

6. See preceding letter.

7. In 1884-85, Gildersleeve had one of his best groups: seventeen students in lyric poetry; eighteen in his seminary; nineteen in history of Greek oratory; and twenty in Greek syntax. Among these students were William Muss-Arnolt (No. 72, n. 8), George Willis Botsford (1862-1917), the publisher-to-be Charles Albert Doubleday (b. 1859), Gonzalez Lodge, C. W. E. Miller (see "Correspondents"), Moses S. Slaughter (1860-1923), and George Meason Whicher (1860-1937).

8. He did not get to Greece until 1896 (see Nos. 90-91).

9. Hübner was the unofficial guardian of Gildersleeve's family from 1889 to 1890, when Raleigh was pursuing advanced work at the Technische Hochschule in Charlottenberg and Betty and Emma were living in Berlin.

10. No. 51, n. 8.


## 69 To: Emil Hübner
### *Berlin*

Winchester, Virginia
Aug. 5, 1885

My dear Hübner:

You have long since received my acknowledgement of your beautiful present, which Reimer sent by the slow and inexpensive way of the Smithsonian Institution.[1] I am very proud of the book; such a token of friendship reconciles me with myself, the person with whom I am most at variance in this world, and in the time of my deepest depression it will help to lift me out of my self-distrust. My long career as a teacher has not been without influence and in that respect I have in my own country quite as much reputation as I deserve. As a writer I am too fanciful, too impetuous and make slips of which I am afterwards so vividly conscious that I am miserable for months and in fact bear about myself always a huge burden of blunder.[2]—Of course my Pindar is no exception to the rule of my literary work and there are things in it that I repent of daily and it is almost a pity that I have a vacation in which I am free to torment myself.—From what you write I gather that the agent of the Harpers failed to send the presentation copies as ordered and that the Harpers /themselves/ have made good the omission. I have no objection to the use you desire to make of the extra copy. If it were only worthier of the destination!—

I remained in Baltimore until July 18$\underline{\text{th}}$ hoping to get the second no. of Vol. VI of the Journal off the press—so that I might be free of the annoyance of proofsheets for at least a month but I did not succeed and I am still followed by the shadow of the printer's devil. This week, however, I shall be through with it and I expect to set out on Monday next for a trip along the Atlantic coast as far as Maine,[3] returning here towards the close of the month. The last ten days of July were phenomenally hot and all that I could do was to sit still at a little watering place in the mountains of West Virginia.[4] Now I am with my family in a little town of the Valley of Virginia, which has a remarkable history especially in connexion with the late war, when it was taken and retaken scores of times.[5] I am writing in sight of hills which I have seen wreathed with the smoke of artillery—and I look down on streets along which I have ridden in advance and retreat—while whizzing bullets and screaming shells filled the air instead of the singing of locusts. It is a sleepy old Virginia town, where I meet at every turn my own friends and the kindred of my wife—I have some new books to read and I am really more contented than I have been for months.—Give my best greetings to the Gnädige[6]—It is a great pleasure to me that anything I have said, done or written should have found favor in her sight—for she is to me the embodiment of all that is good and gracious.—

Please excuse the huge envelope. I haven't anything better at hand for inclosing the photograph of my son Raleigh, whom I herewith introduce to my friends and his, the dear household in Ahornstrasse.[7]

> Yours faithfully
> B. L. Gildersleeve

Professor E. Hübner

1. *Exempla scripturae epigraphicae Latinae a Caesaris dictatoris morte ad aetatem Iustiniani consilio* (Berlin: G. Reimer, 1885). Gildersleeve had sent a letter of thanks on 27 June 1885.

2. See, e.g., on the Second Pythian, *AJP* 33 (1912): 490 ( = *SBM*, 269-70).

3. Gildersleeve visited Gilman at Mt. Desert (No. 147).

4. Perhaps the Sweet Springs of No. 57, n. 1.

5. The Second Battle of Winchester (Gildersleeve was not in service for the first, on 25 May 1862) took place on 19 September 1864. The Union general, Sheridan, was blocking the offensive movements of Gen. Jubal Early (No. 141, n. 25) and driving the Confederates from the Valley of Virginia. Fighting had raged back and forth around the town as the two forces alternately pursued one another up and down the valley. Finally, with reinforcements and expert use of his cavalry, Sheridan forced a Confederate retreat south through Winchester to Fisher's Hill, Va. (see *Creed*, 76). Six days later (25 September), Gildersleeve was wounded at Weyer's Cave (see No. 12, n. 8).

6. See No. 51, n. 8.

7. Hübner lived at Ahornstrasse 4, in the Thiergarten. For an account of the seminars he conducted there, see E. G. Sihler, [cited No. 26, n. 1], 62-63.

70 To: HOUGHTON MIFFLIN Co. [H. E. Scudder]
*Houghton*

Sewanee, Tenn. Sept. 8th 1886

Gentlemen:

Some time ago I wrote a provisional answer to your letter of the 10th ult. and I now desire to add the results of my further thinking on the subject.

The "bifurcation"[1] is there. We have now in this country more exact technical knowledge and truer appreciation of Greek than ever, we have more earnest and more widespread desire to know about Hellenism than ever. The intermediate class of college bred smatterers is growing smaller and the classics will not recover their hold until the teachers of the classics better that hold by a higher literary culture. Such at least is my conviction and I think that your proposed movement to meet the wants of the wider class, to stimulate in the direction of literature proper the narrower class of American Hellenists, too much given to arid specializations, and so to prepare the way for a wider use of Greek in the scheme of education, I think that such a movement will be attended with success, if you can find the men to conduct it. But, as I have already hinted, our best technical scholars are not literary men in the true sense and our literary men are not as a rule scholarly enough to meet the demands now made of everyone who undertakes to deal with Greek. Harvard seems to me to have greater resources for the combined work than any other American institution and I am not surprised to find that your list includes so many Harvard men. Such men as Palmer[2] and Dyer[3] are literary men as well as classical scholars and there are doubtless younger men there who would do good work. My friend Price[4] of Columbia is an accurate scholar and full of the literary sense, if he were not so fastidious as never to finish anything.—He could do the Theocritus, for instance, exceedingly well. So I might find here and there in the country men who might be fairly equal to the proposed task. But on the whole it may as well be frankly acknowledged that we have no men equal to the best Englishmen in the combination of accurate knowledge and literary skill. We have no man that, all things considered, is the peer of Jebb and many English scholars, inferior to some American scholars in range and accuracy of knowledge, are vastly superior to the great majority of our professors in the art of literary expression. Still the thought seems to be good and timely and in spite of all drawbacks it may be well to keep the plan steadily in view. In no case can it be carried out without long preparation and full inquiry and if I can do anything to further an enterprise, which if successful, will redound greatly to the honor of American letters, I shall be happy to do so and in any case consider myself honored by your desire that I should cooperate in the work.

My own scheme, the one to which I referred in my first answer, the one which I have borne in mind for many years without any definite hope of realization is an Encyclopaedia of Greek Literature—something after the pattern of Chambers' Encyclopaedia of English Literature to which I owed so much in my boyhood. So much of Greek Literature is an absolutely unknown country even to classical scholars that I have thought that such a work would be of value and interest even to professed students of Greek. Brief historical and critical introductions, followed by the best translations or new translations—one edition for English readers—one for classical scholars with the Greek original facing the English. Not in the clumsy royal octavo two-column form but a neat 12mo of which the model could be found in some of your own admirable publications.[5] Two volumes would suffice for the epic—one for lyric—three for the drama (Aeschylus and Sophocles one—Euripides one—Aristophanes one) history two—philosophy two—Oratory two—with a final volume for retrospect—which I should prefer to introduction—and for indexes. Under proper management such a work would be, in my judgment, a substantial if not a brilliant success and would not require so much native talent as your plan postulates. At all events I have thought it right to make the suggestion.—

Personally I have my hands full of work—part begun, part promised. Still in all matters belonging to Greek I am willing to spend and be spent and I have much material accumulated, that can be utilized in any scheme that has for its object the furtherance of Hellenism.—

I hope you will pardon the fullness with which I have written as well as the vagueness especially as you seem to look to me for a more precise formulation of your plans rather than an expansion of the principles on which your plans are based.

I wind up my summer course the end of this week. From here I go to the Alleghany Springs Virginia[6] for a week and thence to New York for a few days—If anything further suggests itself to you, address me at the Alleghany.

Yours very truly<br>B. L. Gildersleeve

Messers. Houghton, Mifflin & Co.
Boston Mass

1. On the "bifurcation," see "Classics and Colleges," *Princeton Review* 54 (July 1878): 87 ( = *E&S*, 72).
2. George Herbert Palmer (1842-1933), tutor in Greek, Harvard, 1870, moved by President Eliot to the philosophy department in 1872, full professor from 1883. Gildersleeve reviewed his *The Odyssey of Homer I-XII* (Boston: Houghton Mifflin, 1884) in the *Nation* 39 (16 October 1884): 335-36. He also translated *The Antigone of Sophocles* (Boston: Houghton Mifflin, 1899). His other books are *The New Education* (Boston: Little, Brown, 1887), *The*

*English Works of George Herbert*, 3 vols. (Boston: Houghton Mifflin, 1905), and *Formative Types in English Poetry* (Boston: Houghton Mifflin, 1918).

3. After graduating from Harvard in 1874, Louis Dyer (1851–1908) entered Balliol College, Oxford, where he remained until 1877, gaining a degree in absentia in 1878. He was tutor and then assistant professor of Greek at Harvard from 1877 to 1887. In 1893 he returned to Balliol as lecturer in German and Italian from 1893. He contributed to the *Nation* and the major classics journals (except *AJP*) and was the author of *Plato's Apology and Crito* (Boston: Ginn, 1890), a very popular edition, as well as of *Studies of the Gods in Greece at Certain Sanctuaries Recently Excavated* (Lowell Institute Lectures) (London: Macmillan, 1891) and *Machiavelli and the Modern State* (1899 Royal Institution Lectures) (Boston: Ginn, 1904).

4. Thomas Randolph Price (1839–1903) was a student of Gildersleeve's and an 1858 graduate of the University of Virginia. He studied in Berlin in 1859 with Boeckh (No. 50, n. 3) and G. Curtius (No. 8, n. 16) and returned from his studies in Paris in 1862, running the Union blockade on Christmas Eve to join the staff of J. E. B. Stuart. After the war he assisted with Gildersleeve's *Latin Grammar* (1867), was professor of Greek and Latin at Randolph-Macon College (1869–70), Gildersleeve's successor as professor of Greek at the University of Virginia (1876–82), and professor of English at Columbia from 1882. He produced no books; his most prominent classical piece was "The Color-System of Virgil," *AJP* 4 (1883): 1–20. He also wrote "King Lear," *PMLA* 9 (1894): 165–81, and "Troilus and Criseyde," *PMLA* 11 (1896): 307–22. See Gildersleeve's speech on the dedication of the Price Library at the University of Virginia, *UVa Alumni Bulletin*, n.s., 5 (January 1905): 2–6; Thornton's (see "Correspondents") sketch at *Barringer*, 1: 432–35; Gildersleeve's memorial notice, *AJP* 24 (1903): 239; and BLG to Hübner, 22 January 1899 [Berlin]: "The best friend I have in America."

5. Classicists will recognize the format of the Loeb Classical Library, endowed by the philanthropist James Loeb (1867–1933) in 1910. On 30 August of that year, Loeb wrote to Gildersleeve from his home in Murnau asking his advice upon the "suggestion . . . that it would be both serviceable and timely to publish an edition of Greek & Latin authors accompanied by an English translation." The undated draft of Gildersleeve's reply states "The general plan proposed in your circular is one that I have advocated in public and private for over half a century." See, further, P. Shorey, "The Loeb Classics," *Harvard Graduates' Magazine* 36 (1928): 333–43, and W. M. Calder III, "Ulrich von Wilamowitz-Moellendorff to James Loeb: Two Unpublished Letters," *ICS* 2 (1977): 315–32 ( = *Selected Correspondence*, 213–30).

6. Located in Montgomery Co., Va., the Alleghany advertised waters that cured dyspepsia. Betty and Emma stayed at the Alleghany while Gildersleeve was at Sewanee in 1884, 1886, and 1887 (see No. 71, n. 4).

## 71 To: Benjamin Lawton Wiggins
### *Sewanee*

1017 St. Paul St.[1] Baltimore
Nov. 4, 1887

My dear Wiggins:

I saw by the newspaper that the Bishop and Mrs. Quintard[2] had returned in safety but my pleasure would not have been complete without your personal assurance that you had them once more—It is the next best thing to seeing them. I am sorry that their way houseward did not lie through Baltimore and now I am afraid you will not let them go far away for some time so that my hope of getting an account of the European adventures at first hand is very slight.—Give them both my best love and congratulations and assure them how much nearer I have felt myself to them ever since I was privileged to be one of the household at the Hall.[3]

The first few weeks of the session the pull of the world was very heavy—I fancied that I had fairly recovered my elasticity before I returned to Baltimore[4] but I was mistaken and I am just beginning to get used to the double burden and leave off the sad refrain 'Issachar is an ass bowed down.'[5]—My graduate course is one that is especially oppressive and as I put much vehemence into teaching younger pupils, my undergraduate work is a strain on my nerves as well as a drain on my time.[6]—Then I have the perpetual ball and chain of the Journal. To be sure, I have had to resign outside work.[7]— My ed. of the Frogs hibernates[8] and only now and then do I steal a moment for this or that.—So in the dearth of papers for our Philological Society I am preparing a screed on the Participle to be read at our next meeting[9]— And as if this were not enough I have been active in the organization and equipment of the University Club of which I have been made President.[10]—You will understand therefore, my dear, dear friend, why I don't sit down and work at a catalogue of the Classical Library for Sewanee.— Such a catalogue would require weeks and weeks of hard work and work that would be all the harder because I have no bibliographical aptitude, no bibliographical taste. Nor do I know in the least what you have.—It would be easy enough to say—Get a full set of the Teubner Classics[11]—the Didot Classics[12]—the Haupt and Sauppe[13] series—Stephanus' Thesaurus[14] and half a dozen other sets that might occur to me but I could not discharge my conscience on such easy terms—You will have to make out your list yourself with such help as you can get from such catalogues of classical works as Westermann's[15] and Macmillan's[16] and when you have made it out I will look over it if I can find time. It is one of the penalties of knowing and loving people that one can do so little for them.—Poor Wheeler died the other day[17]—and now his widow writes to ask me—at his dying request— that I look after his collation of Longus and edit the book—There is something to take with me to Europe and spoil my much needed trip withal.— But I must not make up a letter out of grumblings and indeed I do not intend to grumble but only to show you how impossible it is for me to do what you would naturally expect of me on the matter of those books.— —

My wife has thus far retained what she gained at the Alleghany Springs and my daughter is in fair health—They both remember Sewanee with much pleasure and always associate the members of your household with what was brightest in that summer.[18]—Raleigh is in his last year in the Collegiate Department and is looking forward with eagerness to his emancipation! The session is fairly on its way—the machine moves forward without a hitch and, barring accidents, there will be nothing to record for the rest of the academic year—my thirty second!—

Give my best love to Mrs. Wiggins.[19] How I should like to see Catherine's[20] bright face again!

Yours faithfully and affectionately
B. L. Gildersleeve

Professor B. L. Wiggins

1. Gildersleeve had not moved. Owing to Baltimore's northward expansion, city houses were renumbered in 1886.

2. Charles Todd Quintard (1824–98) of Connecticut, Wiggins' father-in-law, was professor of physiology at Memphis Medical College, but was ordained an Episcopal deacon in 1855, and in 1865, after serving as chaplain and surgeon in the war, was elected bishop of Tennessee. He took a guiding role in the founding of the University of the South (Sewanee), was its first vice-chancellor (1867), obtained endowments in England, and saw its first academic department opened before his retirement in 1872. See, further, *DAB* 15: 313–14 and M. Guerry, *Men Who Made Sewanee* (Sewanee, Tenn.: University Press, 1932), 37–48.

3. Fulford Hall, Bishop Quintard's home on the Sewanee campus.

4. A gift of $500 by an alumnus, Rev. J. A. Van Hoose of Birmingham, Ala., defrayed Gildersleeve's expenses in giving three courses of lectures from 6 August to 10 September 1887: ten public lectures on "Aristophanes and his Times," ten before a seminary on "Thucydides' Story of Plataea," and ten on "Outlines of Hermeneutics." (These lectures have not survived.) After resting at Alleghany Springs (see No. 70, n. 5) with his family from 11 September until the end of the month, he returned to Baltimore.

5. Gen. 49:14.

6. Beginning Fall 1884, Gildersleeve taught a course of sixteen "conferences in Greek grammar" for eight to ten undergraduates. The course was dropped within a few years.

7. Although Miller's bibliography lists no contributions to any non-academic journal from 1887 to 1891, *Poole's Index* credits him with a review of Jebb's *Introduction to Homer* (*Nation* 44 [19 May 1887]: 429) and an article on "The Teaching of Latin" (*Nation* 45 [7 July 1887]: 8).

8. "For years I worked at an edition of the Frogs that was to have been illustrated by parallels from the annals of literary persiflage" (*AJP* 37 [1916]: 373 [ = *SBM* 357]). His three years' work was "pigeonholed" when the Harper's Classical Series was discontinued in 1890, and Gildersleeve claimed he was "not disconsolate" (BLG to Wiggins, 21 January 1890 [Sewanee]). In any case, he had not made much progress to judge by a draft notebook in the Hopkins Archives, despite the inscribed projected completion date of 1891. See R. L. Fowler, "The Gildersleeve Archive," *Briggs-Benario*, 67.

9. "On the Stylistic Effect of the Greek Participle," read 18 November to the University Philological Association, published in the *JHU Circulars*, no. 7 (January 1888): 23–24, as "Studies in the Stylistic Use of the Greek Participle," and published in *AJP* 9 (1888): 137–57 under the original title.

10. In 1876 the fellows had loosely organized a *Kneipe* after the German fashion, which soon became a "German Club." In the fall of 1887 the University Club for faculty and fellows formalized this social arrangement, with Gildersleeve as its first president (see *Hawkins*, 89, 275–76). H. W. Smyth wrote his mother an account of an evening at the University Club with Gildersleeve presiding (8 November 1887, Smyth papers at Harvard).

11. On Teubner, see No. 50, n. 15.

12. Ambroise Firmin Didot (1790–1876), descendent of François Didot (1689–1757),

who founded the Parisian printing and bookselling firm in 1713, edited *Bibliothèque grecque* in sixty-seven volumes with two atlases (Paris: Didot, 1839–90).

13. Moriz Haupt (1808–74), professor of Latin at Berlin from 1853 to his death, edited school texts of Ovid *Met.* 1–7, Catullus, Tibullus, Propertius, and Virgil (see *Sandys*, 135–36) in the series he co-edited with Hermann Sauppe (1809–93), professor of classics at Göttingen (1856–93), who contributed *Plato. Protagoras*, trans. J. A. Towle, (Boston: Ginn, 1892). On Sauppe, see *Sandys*, 163, and W. M. Calder III, "Ulrich von Wilamowitz-Moellendorff to Hermann Sauppe: Two Unpublished Letters," *Philologus* 129 (1985): 286–98.

14. Stephanus, the Latin name by which Henri Estienne (1531–98) is known, published his *Thesaurus linguae Graecae* in five folio volumes in 1572. (His father Robert [1503–59] had produced a *Thesaurus linguae Latinae* in 1532, which was reissued as late as 1734.) There were two nineteenth-century editions, one at London by Valpy (1815–25), the other at Paris by Didot (1831–63). On the Thesaurus, see *Quarterly Review* 44 (January 1820): 302–48. On Henri Estienne, see Gildersleeve, "Henry Stephens," *Quarterly Review of the Methodist Episcopal Church, South*, n.s., 9 (January 1855): 1–21, and Mark Pattison, *Essays*, ed. H. Nettleship (Oxford: Clarendon Press, 1889), 1: 67–123.

15. Georg W. Westermann (1810–79), whose brother Anton (1806–69) published a *History of Eloquence in Greece and Rome* (Braunschweig: Westermann, 1833–35), devoted his publishing firm to school-texts and maps and began publishing a *Monatshefte* in 1856. See T. Mueller, *Der Verleger Georg Westermann, 1810–79* (Braunschweig: Westermann, 1965) and *100 Jahre Westermanns Monatshefte, 1856–1956* (Braunschweig: Westermann, 1956).

16. On Macmillan's, see No. 44, n. 4.

17. On John Henry Wheeler, see No. 46, n. 6. His notes on Longus were never published.

18. Gildersleeve and C. F. Smith (see "Correspondents") had been Wiggins' houseguests during the 1887 session.

19. Clara Quintard Wiggins (1851–1915) was the daughter of Charles Todd Quintard (n. 2 above).

20. The Wigginses had two daughters, Katherine (1888–1916) and Elizabeth (1893–1959), and one son, Charles Quintard Wiggins (1890–1944).

## 72 To: EMIL HÜBNER
### *Berlin*

Baltimore May 7ᵗʰ 1890

My dear Hübner:

Many thanks for your cordial greeting from over the seas. If everything goes right, I hope in less than a month to see your kind face again and to receive a welcome from your own mouth.[1] Raleigh has doubtless told you that instead of my sailing on the 28ᵗʰ of this month the day has been changed to the 21st and in a fortnight hence, if nothing happens, I shall be making my way towards Germany once more. The Karlsruhe is a superb new steamer of 6000 tons,[2] as large as the Saale but she is not fast and I cannot expect to be in Bremen before the third of June or in Berlin before the fourth. Of course I shall stay long enough to celebrate Raleigh's twenty first birthday which falls on the sixth[3]—Thence to Vienna, where I am to meet my wife and daughter.[4] Further than that I have no plans. I may take

a long run onto distant countries or I may content myself with a quiet summer in the Tyrol or in the Salzkammergud. In any case I am glad that I am
to have a long surcease from regular work for I need a rest. Last winter I
suffered much from insomnia, which was doubtless aggravated by the publication of the fat book which I sent you the other day.[5] I had been urged by
my friends over and over to collect my educational essays and literary studies, which had originally been published under very unfavorable auspices
and which in their judgment deserved a better fate than the oblivion that
had overtaken them. Any serious revision was out of the question, but the
collection of the things, the preparation for the press, the correction of the
proofs and the haste with which the enterprise was carried out wrought on
my nerves and kept me in a half feverish state for a couple of months. The
book was intended chiefly for my personal friends as a manner of memorial
volume and my friends have so regarded it for of the 600 copies to which
the edition was limited no less than 500 were subscribed for before publication. Of the few copies reserved for presents very few will go to Germany,
for very few Germans would not be offended by my freedom of speech—
and even you will find it hard to forgive some of my utterances. But I hope
you will overlook much in the old comrade who has kept 'Platen's Poems'
in the volume because it gave him an opportunity to lay claim to your
friendship.[6]

The tenth volume of the Journal is happily completed[7] and the index is
not altogether unworthy of German painstaking.[8] The work on my Aristophanes has been suspended for the present owing to some trouble with
the publisher[9] and I am engaged instead in a Short History of Greek Literature, a little school book which I hope to have off my hands some time
next year.[10] Of course I still take an interest in grammatical work.
Goodwin in his new Moods and Tenses has made a handsome acknowledgement of his obligations to my researches[11] but if it had not been for
your prompt recognition of my efforts I am sure that German scholars
would not have taken much notice of me and that Goodwin himself would
hardly have studied my essays so carefully. As it is, I feel that my work has
not been all in vain and I am sure that what I have yet in reserve is not
worse than what I have done thus far.

Give my kindest regards to Mrs. Hübner and the household.

My next greeting I will deliver in person, God willing.

Yours faithfully and affectionately
B. L. Gildersleeve

Professor Emil Hübner

1. Gildersleeve arrived at Bremerhaven on the 3rd of June and Berlin on the 4th. He left
for Vienna on the 7th.
2. The ship served the Norddeutscher Lloyd Line out of Bremen.

3. Gildersleeve and his son celebrated the birthday "by a little dinner in the Zoological Gardens" (BLG to Gilman, 6 June 1890).

4. See following letter.

5. *Essays and Studies Educational and Literary* (Baltimore: N. Murray, 1890). Hübner reviewed it at *DLZ* 12 (25 July 1891): 1093-95.

6. See Nos. 3 and 11.

7. Gildersleeve seems to have expected to be released from the *AJP* after a decade, for he wrote to Gilman on 12 May 1890: "My successor has not revealed himself yet and I have begun the eleventh volume, if not cheerfully, at least resolutely."

8. The indices to vols. 1-10 appeared in *AJP* 10 (1889): 515-58, prepared by William Muss-Arnolt, fellow in Greek (1883-91) and instructor in New Testament Greek (1891-93). He also compiled the individual indices to vols. 11-14, but subsequent ten-year indices listed only contributors.

9. See preceding letter.

10. See No. 82, n. 9.

11. In the preface to his *Syntax of the Moods and Tenses of the Greek Verb* (Boston: Ginn, 1889), viii-ix, Goodwin expresses his indebtedness to Gildersleeve's grammatical articles, saying, "He has discussed almost every construction of the Greek moods, and he has always left his mark" (viii).

### 73 To: DANIEL COIT GILMAN
#### JHU-Gilman

Vienna, Rathhausstr. 20[1]
June 16, 1890

My dear Mr. Gilman:

Your note of June 10 reached me a day or two ago in this place where my wife and daughter are refitting after a long respite from the plague of tailors and dress makers. I have not been in Vienna since 1853[2] and find very little to remind me of the old city—though from certain points of view such as the Belvedere[3] I can discern the old in the new. The weather is cold, windy and showery and in other circumstances I should be tempted to speed to a warmer climate.

Saturday evening I met a few of the Viennese professors at Dr. Scaife's[4] and in response to an invitation received there I attended /this morning/ a lecture on Persius by Professor Schenkl[5] and was conducted by my learned colleague over the buildings of the university which far transcend anything that I have ever seen in magnificence and convenience—and yet I have the the [sic] Technische Hochschule at Charlottenburg[6] fresh in memory. The coming benefactor of the Johns Hopkins[7] ought not to overlook the University of Vienna in making his plans for the great academic building that is to bear his name. The philologians and archeologists together occupy a special section and the plan of having special rooms for study and special libraries for seminary use reminds me very much of home and very Hopkinsian indeed as to want of means for the increase of the library. The work of the Johns Hopkins is well known and duly appreciated in the University of Vienna and on making the round of the building I was very warmly received by several men of the highest position in the philological and archeological world such as v. Hartel[8] and Benndorf.[9] To-morrow night I am to sup with a number of scholars at the Hotel de France[10] and so my visit to Vienna will not be without a certain professsional interest.

Since I last wrote I have considered carefully the problem of a visit to Greece and have come to the conclusion that the project must be abandoned so that I shall not need your good offices with the trustees. My duty to the University and my duty to my family alike demand the renunciation. If better days bring the readoption of my dream, well— If not, I am not unfamiliar with the arts of self-denial. Many thanks for your kindly interest—

You have undoubtedly a knotty question before you and as my mind is constructed to see knots and not to devise solutions, I am afraid that I can be of little service. Saintsbury[11] is an accomplished man but I don't think that his style is careful enough for one who ought to be a model of English composition. Moulton[12] might be of temporary service and as he is coming to America at any rate it might be well to experiment with him. The other man you mention I do not know at all.

Now that I have given up Greece I expect to spend a quiet uneventful summer, partly on the Salzkammergut and the Tyrol, partly in Switzerland. I have a book in hand which I shall work at by fits but my main object will be to recover the spring that I need for what must necessarily be a very hard year.

Yours very truly<br>
B. L. Gildersleeve

President D. C. Gilman

1. The Pension Pohl operated by Frau Röhrich in the Innere Stadt, on the east side of the Rathaus.

2. See No. 2.

3. An imperial chateau built for Prince Eugene of Savoy in 1693–1724, now an art museum.

4. Walter Bell Scaife (1858–1936) received his A.B.(extra ord.) from Hopkins in 1887 and was the first American to receive a Ph.D. from Vienna (also 1887). He was reader in American historical geography at Hopkins (1889–90) and lecturer in modern history at the University of Pennsylvania (1891–92) before passing "the greater part of his life traveling in search of a favorable climate and studying when his health permitted" (*WhoAm*, 4: 831). He wrote *Florentine Life during the Renascence* (Baltimore: Johns Hopkins Press, 1893).

5. Karl Schenkl (1827–1900), professor at Innsbruck, Graz, and finally Vienna (1875–1900), is known as a founder (with von Hartel, see below) of *Wiener Studien*, as editor of *Xenophontis libri Socratici* (New York: Harper and Bros., 1883) and *D. Magni Ausonii:*

*Opuscula* (Berlin: Weidmann, 1883), and for a series of Greek and Latin texts for schools and Greek-German/German-Greek lexicons (Leipzig: Teubner, 1873). *Sandys*, 160.

6. Raleigh was studying architecture at the Technische Hochschule.

7. Gildersleeve must refer to the executor of the estate of John W. McCoy, a local merchant who as first president of the Baltimore branch of the Archaeological Institute of America took a great interest in Johns Hopkins and at his death on 20 August 1889 willed the university his library of 8,000 volumes, his house at 1300 Eutaw Street, which became the president's house, and an unrestricted residuary estate of nearly half a million dollars. So as not to disadvantage the humanities departments in the face of the growth of the sciences, the trustees decided in 1891 that the bulk of the money should be put into a spacious humanities building named for McCoy. Gildersleeve recommended the Tuscan Renaissance-style quadrangle shape, containing offices, classrooms, and a library, of the University of Vienna, designed by H. von Ferstel and built (1873-85) on the Franzenring, adjacent to the Rathhauspark. McCoy Hall was built in four stories of red brick on the block between Monument and Little Ross Streets, an area 100' × 175', with administrative offices, meeting rooms and an auditorium on the first floor, department libraries, offices, seminary, and classrooms on the second and third floors, and the library on the fourth. It was opened in October 1894, and Gildersleeve moved from his cramped office on Howard Street to the "spacious new building . . . where I have a bright, simple, and in every way comfortable study [office no. 14] with an adjoining seminary room" (BLG to Wiggins, 11 December 1894 [Sewanee]). Abandoned in the move to the Homewood campus in 1916 (No. 173, n. 6), McCoy Hall was consumed by fire on 27 November 1919. See *French*, 62-63; *Hawkins*, 321; *JHU Circulars* no. 327 (November 1920): 3-4.

8. Wilhelm von Hartel (1839-1907), the epigraphist, was extraordinarius at Vienna (1869-1907) and known as a founder, with Schenkl, of *Wiener Studien*, author of *Homerische Studien* (Berlin: F. Vahlen, 1873), editor of the Vienna series of Latin Fathers, rector of the University of Vienna, and Austrian minister of education. He also edited *Festschrift Johannes Vahlen* (see *AJP* 22 [1901]: 229-30 [ = *SBM*, 66-67]). *Sandys*, 479-80.

9. Otto Benndorf (1838-1907) was professor of archaeology at Zurich, Munich, Prague, and Vienna, was involved in three major excavations, including Ephesus with Heberdey and Wilberg. His publications include his Bonn dissertation, *De anthologiae Graecae epigrammatis quae ad artes spectant* (Leipzig: B. G. Teubner, 1862), *Griechische und sizilianische Vasenbilder* (Berlin: I. Guttentag, 1869-83), and *Philostrati maioris imagines*, ed. with K. Schenkl (Leipzig: B. G. Teubner, 1893). *Sandys*, 226.

10. A fine hotel at Schottenring 3, in the Innere Stadt.

11. After teaching in schools from 1868 to 1876, George Edward Bateman Saintsbury (1845-1933) established himself in London as a man of letters with essays in *Macmillan's Magazine*, the *Pall Mall Gazette*, and especially the *Saturday Review*. By the time of this letter, he had produced *Dryden* in the "English Men of Letters Series" (1881) and *A History of Elizabethan Literature* (London: Macmillan, 1887). In 1895 he was appointed Regius professor of rhetoric and English literature at Edinburgh. His later works include *A History of Criticism and Literary Taste in Europe from the Earliest Texts to the Present Day*, 3 vols. (Edinburgh: W. Blackwood, 1900-1904) and *A History of English Prosody*, 3 vols. (London: Macmillan, 1906-10). *DNB 1931-1940*, 775-77. He praised Gildersleeve's 1868 essay on "Maximilian: His Travels and his Tragedy" (see No. 149).

12. Richard Green Moulton (1849-1924) visited the United States in 1890. He had great success as a lecturer in the University Extension Scheme in England from 1874 to 1892 and helped organize the American Society for the Extension of University Teaching. He was professor at the University of Chicago from 1892 to 1919. His works include *Ancient Classical Drama* (Oxford: Clarendon Press, 1890), *The Literary Study of the Bible* (Boston: D. C. Heath, 1895), and *The Modern Reader's Bible* (New York: Macmillan, 1895-98). *DAB* 16: 291-92.

74 To: BENJAMIN IDE WHEELER
*California*

{ University Club
1005 North Charles Street }
CONFIDENTIAL                                                    Baltimore March 14, 1891

My dear Professor Wheeler:[1]

Your letter of the 9th was not one to be answered on the spur of the moment and I happen to be very busy just now so that you must excuse the delay.

Let me say in advance that I think you are fortunate in having so many good men to choose /from/ and in being safe from a serious mistake, if your choice falls on any one of the list. I will also with equal frankness say that my personal interest is very much engaged in behalf of Emerson,[2] whom I have known well for years and whom I esteem for his moral worth as well as for his scholarly aspirations. He has had, as you know, unusual advantages, long residence abroad, a good training in the school of Heinrich Brunn,[3] familiarity with Greece and other classic lands, experience in archaeological work. He has, it is true, more artistic and literary sensitiveness than power of artistic and literary expression. His language is full of odd twists and hidden humors and his ways of presentation will, I fear, be always more or less exotic but the soul of the matter is in him and though while he was associated with me he never showed any sympathy with what he is perfectly capable of calling my grammatical 'goniobomby-cinism,'[4] he has a good knowledge of Greek /a knowledge/, that is, in my judgment, equal to any range of archaeological research, though he would not claim to be an accomplished epigraphist. His strength lies rather in the Archaeology of Art. I wish he could have the opportunity of giving a few lectures at Cornell so that you might judge for yourself what hold he is likely to gain on the students. If I know Cornell aright, it will be a good school for him and he might come into closer touch with the American mind in a sphere where sympathy would not be lacking on the part of his colleagues.

Sterrett's[5] work as an epigraphist does not need any comment from me. I knew him when he was a boy at the University of Virginia and whenever I have met him of late years—despite his distinctions—he seemed to me to have lost little of his awkward and embarrassed manner but these may be the survival of old times. Indeed he has told me that he never feels at his ease with me. Courage he has, as his work has shown. As to his scholarship, I am inclined to think that considering the drawbacks incident to his mode of life he is superior to some of his carping critics—and men who have watched him as a teacher and men who are competent to judge rank him very high.

Tarbell[6] you know better than I do. He is an unusually good man who rises every year in my esteem.

Fowler's[7] great foible is his vanity but while he can never get rid of it, he has turned out so much better in every way than I expected that I have, what I once thought impossible, a very kindly feeling towards him.

J. R. Wheeler[8] is a pleasant man to deal with—but his lectures here lacked perspective and the man himself does not hold his audience.

All this in the freedom of perfect confidence and in the warmth of my interest in Cornell.

Are you going to work at the ᾿Αθηναίων πολιτεία—and if you are, could you not be tempted to give me a review for the Journal?[9]

My kindest remembrances to Mrs. Wheeler—

Yours faithfully,
B. L. Gildersleeve

1. Since coming to Cornell in 1888, Wheeler had presided over a rapid growth in classics, even as other branches of the humanities were languishing. President White had wanted the university to have a fine arts and archeological gallery, and the gift of the Fiske-McGraw mansion in 1889 gave him a place to house it. With an additional bequest from Henry W. Sage, he was able to hire a classical archaeologist and entrusted Wheeler with screening candidates. See M. Bishop, *A History of Cornell*, (Ithaca, N.Y.: Cornell University Press, 1962), 241–42, 279, 327.

2. Alfred Emerson (1859–1943) developed his interest in archaeology while living in Europe as a boy. He received his Ph.D. at Munich under Brunn (see following note) and after a postgraduate course at Princeton, he was fellow (1882–84), instructor in archaeology (1884–85), and fellow by courtesy (1885–86) at Hopkins, where he shared a house with his lifelong friend Woodrow Wilson. He was professor of Latin at Miami University, Oxford, Ohio (1887–88), and professor of Greek at Lake Forest (1888–91). Called to Cornell (1891–97) with the specific charge of creating the Museum of Casts of Classical Sculpture with the Sage funds, he opened the museum in McGraw Hall on 31 January 1894. He was professor of archaeology at the American School of Classical Studies at Athens from 1897–99, was assistant director of the Art Institute of Chicago, and with J. Thacher Clark made excavations in North Africa and Italy. He contributed "On the Conception of Low Comedy in Aristophanes" to *AJP* 10 (1889): 265–79 and helped provide the illustrations to *Pindar*.

3. Heinrich Brunn (1822–94) received his Ph.D. at Bonn in 1843 and for twenty-one of the next twenty-four years lived in Rome, returning in 1865 to be professor of archaeology at Munich, where he served until his death. His first major work was his *Geschichte der griechische Künstler*, 2 vols. (Braunschweig: C. A. Schwetschke und Sohn, 1853–59). *Sandys*, 221–22.

4. Herodicus Babylonius, *ap.* Ath. 5.222a, refers to grammarians as γωνιοβόμβυκες, a favorite word of Gildersleeve's to describe himself. He translates it "corner-hummers"; for the epigram, see "Grammar and Aesthetics," *Princeton Review* 59 (1883): 310; *AJP* 13 (1892): 383 ( = *SBM*, 14); 37 (1917): 338 ( = *SBM*, 382); and No. 178.

5. On Sterrett, see No. 66, n. 3.

6. Frank Bigelow Tarbell (1853–1920) received his A.B. (1873) and Ph.D. (1879) from Yale, where he was tutor in Greek (1876–82) and assistant professor of Greek and instructor in logic (1882–87). He was the first annual professor (1888–89) and secretary (1892–93) of the American School of Classical Studies at Athens and instructor in Greek at Harvard (1889–92). Upon his return from Athens in 1893, he was appointed associate professor of Greek

(1892–93), and then professor of Greek (1893–1918), at the new University of Chicago. He edited *The Philippics of Demosthenes* (Boston: Ginn and Heath, 1880) and wrote *A History of Greek Art* (Meadville, Pa.: Flood and Vincent, 1896; reprinted through 1936). He contributed two articles to *AJP*. *DAB* 19: 306.

7. Harold North Fowler (1859–1955) received his B.A. from Harvard in 1880 and was the first student registered for membership at the American School of Classical Studies at Athens (see L. E. Lord, [cited No. 67, n. 1], appendix 1, 273–77), where he studied in the school year 1882–83. He received his Ph.D. from Bonn in 1885, was instructor in classics at Harvard (1885–88), professor of Latin at Phillips Exeter Academy (1888–92), and professor of Greek at the University of Texas (1892–93) and at the College for Women (later Flora Stone Mather College), Western Reserve University (1893–1929). He was annual professor at the American School at Athens in 1903–4 and 1924–25, and research professor in 1929. For ten years (1906–16) he edited the *American Journal of Archaeology*. He wrote numerous school texts, including *Thucydides Book V* (Boston: Ginn, 1888), as well as a *History of Ancient Greek Literature* (New York: D. Appleton, 1902; rev. ed., 1923), a *History of Roman Literature* (New York: D. Appleton, 1903; rev. ed., 1928), and a *Handbook of Greek Archaeology*, with J. R. Wheeler (see following note) (New York: American Book Co., 1909). He also translated the first four volumes of Plato and the tenth volume of Plutarch's *Moralia* for the Loeb Classical Library. He was president of the APA in 1913. *NatCAB* 44: 341–42.

8. James Rignall Wheeler (1859–1918) received his B.A. from the University of Vermont (1880) and, while a postgraduate student at Harvard, joined the first class of students at the American School at Athens. He received his Ph.D. in 1885 and after two years of travel and study in Europe, returned as reader at Hopkins (1887–88), then lecturer at Harvard (1888–89). From 1889 to 1895, he was professor of Greek at his alma mater, and in 1895 was appointed professor of Greek and archaeology at Columbia, where he remained until his death, serving as dean from 1906 to 1911. The signal feature of his career was his service to the American School at Athens as annual professor (1892–93), secretary (1894), and chairman of the managing committee (1901–18). His publications were few, including *Lectures on Science, Philosophy, and Art, 1907–1908* (New York: Columbia University Press, 1908), two studies of Athenian topography in *HSCP*, his contribution to the inscriptions in *The Argive Heraeum*, ed. Charles Waldstein et al., vol. 1 (Boston: Houghton Mifflin, 1902), and ten articles in *TAPA*. See *DAB* 21: 49 and Nelson G. McCrea's memorial notice, *AJP* 39 (1920): 110–11. On Wheeler's chairmanship of the American School, see Lord (n. 6 above), 99–129.

9. B. I. Wheeler produced no work on Aristotle's *Constitution of Athens*, Papyrus CX-XXI of the British Museum, ed. F. G. Kenyon (London: British Museum and Longmans, 1891) in January of that year. G. Kaibel and U. von Wilamowitz-Moellendorf's edition (Berlin: Weidmann) appeared later in the year, and editions by F. Blass (Leipzig: B. G. Teubner, 1892) and J. E. Sandys (London: Macmillan, 1893) soon followed.

## 75 To: Benjamin Johnson Barbour
### UVa-Barbour

Johns Hopkins University
Baltimore May 19, 1891

My dear Sir:

My memory is none of the best and my habits in the matter of preserving letters and papers are of the worst; and I am afraid that your hope of recovering poor Thompson's[1] verses through me is doomed to disappointment. From your letter I gather that your communication was made prior to Dec.

1884 and a search through such letters as I have preserved from 1881 to 1884 inclusive has not revealed the paper to which you refer. Before 1881 when I began to keep files of letters or accounts of the journal of philology everything is in wild disorder.

Just now I am undergoing the miseries of the close of the session and a further search is impossible. Whether vacation will bring me the needful leisure is more than doubtful, for three summers in Europe have left me heavy arrears to make up.

Needless to say, I sympathize with you deeply in your pious task but the new generation of the South looks down with pity on the men of our time and their ideals of literary art,[2] and will find 'no work nor desire nor knowledge nor wisdom in the grave'[3] of the antebellum period. Still the duty of keeping alive the memory of such a man as Thompson was is imperative and I am glad that you have undertaken it.

My wife desires her kind remembrances.

Yours sincerely
B. L. Gildersleeve

B. Johnson Barbour, Esq.

1. On Thompson, see No. 12, n. 13. Thompson's most often anthologized poems are the war lyric "Lee to the Rear," the dirges "General J. E. B. Stuart" and "Ashby," the lyric "The Window-Panes at Brandon," and the humorous "On to Richmond," called by Edwin Mims in the *Cambridge History of American Literature* (New York: Putnam, 1918), 2: 305, "one of the marked achievements of the period." See, further, J. B. Hubbell, *The South in American Literature* (Durham, N.C.: Duke University Press, 1954), 521–28.

2. "It has grown into a habit among too many of the periodical writers of our day to elevate 'the New South', at the expense of the 'Old' in all matters pertaining to literary and intellectual enlightenment. They are not content to represent this section as undergoing, in their opinion, a sort of esthetic "*renaissance*," but declare that for the *first* time may we really claim to have any genuine culture whatever," wrote Paul Hamilton Hayne (see "Correspondents"), "Ante-Bellum Charleston," *Southern Bivouac* 1, no. 4 (September 1885): 196. Several champions of the "New South" were among Gildersleeve's correspondents and students—for example, C. F. Smith, who wrote: "He who compares Southern literature as it is, in any line, with Southern literature as it was before 1860, must lack patriotism if his heart does not swell with pride in what is and augur brighter things still for years to come" ("Southern Dialect in Life and Literature," *Southern Bivouac* 1, no. 6 [November 1885]: 351). See, further, Gildersleeve's friend Thomas Nelson Page's, *The Old South: Essays Social and Political* (New York: Scribner, 1892).

3. Eccles. 9:10.

76 To: THOMAS DWIGHT GOODELL
*Yale-Goodell*

July 18, 1891

My dear Sir:

As a member of the Executive Committee I am in duty bound to say that the Association has the first right to the MSS of all papers read before that body and that it is necessary to secure the general consent in order to have any particular paper printed elsewhere than in the Transactions.[1] Some of the papers read before the Association were meant originally for the Journal and these were ceded without difficulty. As to the others you can understand that I should not like to appear as using my position in order to enrich the Journal at the expense of the Transactions. Still as there was an unusually large crop of papers at our late meeting, it is more than likely that the Secretary[2] will not object to the transfer of one or two and the matter might be arranged through correspondence with him. At the same time it is but fair to add that the supply of matter for the Journal is such that the publication of your paper, if found in every way desirable, might be retarded and not forwarded by the transfer to the Journal.

Yours very truly<br>B. L. Gildersleeve

Prof. T. D. Goodell

1. Goodell's paper, "Aristotle on the Public Arbitrators," given on the afternoon of 7 July 1891 at the APA meeting at Princeton (abstract in *TAPA* 22 [1891]: xii–xv), was published in *AJP* 12 (1891): 319–26. Deleterious effects of *AJP* on *TAPA* had been very much a live issue since Gildersleeve first sent out his prospectus in 1879. On 13 May 1881 [Yale], he wrote to Whitney, "I was interested to observe by the Proceedings of the Philological Association that the papers were more numerous than usual—quite a different result from that which was predicted on the establishment of the Journal."

2. H. W. Smyth (see "Correspondents") was secretary-treasurer of the APA from 1889 to 1904.


## 77 To: HORACE ELISHA SCUDDER
*Houghton*

The Cliff House[1]<br>Kennebunkport Maine<br>Aug. 10, 1891

My dear Mr. Scudder:

Your invitation[2] is tempting as every invitation must be to set one's self right; for I have often been forced to observe that even the most charitable of my Northern friends find it difficult to understand how a Southerner could have gone into the conflict with a clean conscience and whenever a reference is made to the war there is a certain reticence among wellbred people as if the Southern interlocutor had fallen into some heinous sin. Of course, stump speakers have much to say about the reconciliation of the Blue and the Gray and magnanimous concessions are made to the motives that activated the champions of the Lost Cause but apart from the insincerities of public oratory there abides in the hearts of the survivors of the band of soldiers that Harvard sent out[3] the conviction that nothing but passion could have silenced the conscience of the Southern man. They cannot understand the serenity of our confidence in the justice of our cause. The intellectual aspect of the question as it presented itself to the Southern mind has been ably set forth by Mr. Ropes in the article which you had the kindness to send me,[4] but I doubt very much whether the average Southerner could have formulated his political principles with so much distinctness as Mr. Ropes has done. The prevalent Southern theory of the government has long been incorporated into our daily life. It had become what is called a faith and where there is faith there is conscience.

But however tempting the theme, I am afraid that I am not the man to handle it, in fact I know that I am not the man to handle it, if it is to be treated philosophically and historically. As a representative of the student class—familiar with the views and aspirations of the best of our Southern young men, I might be able to put into shape some of the recollections of the impending struggle, I might be able to show how plain the faith was that stretched before our feet. The cause was one for which I wrote, prayed, fought, suffered but in the long agony I never was haunted by a doubt as to the righteousness of the course which we followed and even if there had been a doubt as to the justice of our cause, the command of the State would have sufficed. Since the war I have not troubled myself much about public affairs except when great questions demanded at least the quiet protest of a vote but I have not on the other hand missed the passions of the war. My son promises to be as national as his father was provincial— if that is the right word—;[5] and perhaps he will find it as hard to understand my position /of/ thirty years ago as I should find it to explain that position to the sons of Harvard.

Now, if after this frank confession, you think that anything I could write on the subject would be of interest to the readers of the Atlantic Monthly, I shall be glad to make the attempt—leaving you entirely free to reject my work—if it is not what you want. Should you still think favorably of the plan, please give me some notion of the space I am expected to occupy.

A few weeks ago I was about to ask you whether you could make any use of a study of a far different subject and it is a little odd that you should have thought /of/ me in connexion with a theme which I have not touched since I wrote for the Richmond Examiner during the war.[6]

Yours very truly<br>B. L. Gildersleeve

Horace E. Scudder Esq.

1. A summer hotel built in 1881 in this town on the south coast of Maine, about eighty-five miles NE of Boston.

2. Scudder had written to Gildersleeve on 6 August 1891: "I should be very glad if you

[find] . . . an opportunity to make more intelligible to the educated man of the North . . . those springs of conduct that sent the young Southerner into the field with untroubled conscience and high sense of duty." Of the article Gildersleeve wrote, "Once in my long career I overleaped the bounds of my classical paddock, and . . . I wrote an article begun as mere literature and finished under the pressure of strong emotion. It was entitled "The Creed of the Old South" and was widely noticed. This is what the *Nation* had to say of it: 'A poetical view of the Southern cause in the Civil War.' I made no protest against the criticism. I make none now. Perhaps, after all these years, poetry may appear more philosophical than history" ("The Hazards of Reviewing," *Nation* 101 [8 July 1915]: 50). See also the "Notes" to *Creed*.

3. Gildersleeve may refer to the corps of Harvard students formed to guard the Cambridge Arsenal after the attack on Fort Sumter. Harvard sent 938 alumni to the war, of whom 117 died; the University of Virginia sent over 2,500, of whom 503 died (R. H. McKim, *A Soldier's Recollections* [New York: Longmans, Green, 1910], 5). In the words of S. E. Morison, "College life went on much as usual, and with scarcely diminished attendance. Public opinion in the North did not require students to take up arms. . . . No fear of being charged with cowardice, no public compulsion or worked-up propaganda, compelled these men to serve on either side" (*Three Centuries of Harvard, 1636–1936* [Cambridge, Mass.: Harvard University Press, 1936], 303). On the University of Virginia, see, further, C. C. Wall, Jr., *Students and Student-Life at the University of Virginia, 1825–1861* (diss.; University of Virginia, 1978), 282.

4. John C. Ropes, "A Few Words about Secession," *Harvard Monthly* 4 (1887): 85–95.

5. Gildersleeve sees the same generational difference in Pindar, following the Persian War: "The man whose love for his country knows no local root, is a man whose love for his country is a poor abstraction; and it is no discredit to Pindar that he went honestly with his state in the struggle. It was no treason to Medize before there was a Greece and the Greece that came out of the Persian War was a very different thing from the cantons that ranged themselves on this side and on that of a quarrel which, we may be sure, bore another aspect to those who stood aloof from it than it wears in the eyes of moderns, who have all learned to be Hellenic patriots" (*Pindar*, xii).

6. On his contributions to the *Examiner*, see No. 12, n. 4, and No. 139, n. 2.

### 78 To: BENJAMIN LAWTON WIGGINS
*Sewanee*

Baltimore Nov. 22, 1891

My dear Professor Wiggins:

Ordinarily I am a most exact person in the matter of correspondence and to make sure of answering letters of importance I usually put them in a little pocket book and keep them there until answered. And so when you made your recent grave charge against me I opened my pocket book and found— if not your letter, the envelope of the letter, the letter itself having been filed. I am, therefore, without defence except that my wife was ill at the time and I was in great turmoil and trouble. If I remember right I had written that there was no prospect of my going to Sewanee and that if any change in my plans took place I would let you know. My wife had answered Mrs. Wiggins's kind letter and had declined her invitation and of course her answer carried mine with it but she says that I had promised to write and in any case I ought to have been more explicit. But I am sure you would forgive me freely, if you could see how much disturbed I am by this revelation of my forgetfulness.

I am glad to be so fully informed as to the fortunes of the People of the Mountain—whom I shall always remember with peculiar affection and gratitude; and the 'gossip' of your letter was very welcome. In return I am afraid I have little to offer except a brief account of the doings of the family. My wife and I spent what was left of the summer at Kennebunkport,[1] a little watering place on the Maine coast, the attractions of which have revealed themselves of late years to a pleasant set of Baltimore people. Kennebunkport combines the charms of sea and river and land—no one element in extraordinary force but all harmonizing in a way that gains on the sojourner the longer he stays. The air has a delicious tone and my wife who was suffering greatly when she reached her destination began to walk a day or two afterwards and left K. in unusually fine health. A week in Boston passed very pleasantly. A day or two in New York gave us an opportunity of seeing our boy who has found work in a young architect's office and seems to be contented and happy in his new home.[2] Since our return to Baltimore we have had much tribulation in making our preparations for housekeeping but after many provoking delays we finally established ourselves at 1002 Belvidere Terrace (N. Calvert St.)[3]—a sunny little house, where we hope to see you very often, if you should gladden our hearts by coming to Baltimore this winter, as you propose to do.

My daughter spent the summer and most of the autumn in Virginia and her first season at the White Sulphur[4] was 'bliss'—the only word for a débutante at the White—and she enjoyed thoroughly her sojourns at Lexington,[5] Lynchburg and Richmond. She is with us now and we hope to keep her for the winter but when the spring comes, she will doubtless be flitting again.

The work at the University is going on steadily with largely increased numbers. Some of the men in my class are unusually mature[6] and I hope for good results. The authorities have given me as an assistant D[r]. C. W. E. Miller,[7] whose business it is to do the detail work of my Greek Syntax. The preliminary work consists of an elaborate index to the five Ms. volumes that you have seen. This will be finished before long and will be followed up by the registration of examples. I aim at a complete catena of Greek usage from Homer to Aristotle—not a complete statistic, that would take too much time, but a complete catena.[8] But the attempt to make a catena has already revealed curious gaps and the filling out of these gaps will lead to statistical research here and there. Interesting results have been reached already and Miller has in hand a paper on the imperative in the orators,[9] which will be a pretty chapter in aesthetic syntax. I will send you before long a specimen blank I have got out for the purpose of registration. Even if I should not be spared to see the work completed, I shall have the satisfaction of laying down the lines on which the work is to be done. Perhaps when your burden of teaching is lightened, you will be able to render me substantial help.

There will be no difficulty in securing the courtesy of the University for Mr. Nauts.[10] I will speak to Mr. Gilman about it at the earliest opportunity—and I hope that Mr. Nauts will like Baltimore as well as you seemed to do.

My wife joins me in kind remembrances to Mrs. Wiggins and hopes that you will continue in the same frame of mind towards our household.

Hoping to see you before long.

   I am

          Yours affectionately
          B. L. Gildersleeve
Professor B. L. Wiggins

1. See preceding letter, n. 2.

2. After completing his course at the Technische Hochschule in Berlin, Raleigh returned to New York, where he lived from 1890 to 1915, when he designed for Princeton Upper and Lower Pyne (1896) and McCosh Hall, then (1906) the largest building on the campus. He later became president of Phillips Manor Co. and of Survey Investors (both 1915–44).

3. With his family in Europe for two years, while Raleigh was in Berlin and Emma was being social, Gildersleeve sold his former residence at 1017 St. Paul Street and tabernacled for most of 1891 at the Mount Vernon Hotel in Baltimore. Belvidere Terrace, occupying the block on the west side of N. Calvert Street between Eager and Chase Streets, was built in 1880. The *Baltimore Sun* of 25 November 1923 called it "a section of fashionable and representative Baltimore homes" (see ibid., 17 February 1963). The three-story row house on N. Calvert Street, which still stands, was within easy walking distance of Gildersleeve's office in McCoy Hall, and he lived in it with his family for the rest of his life.

4. All of the Virginia Springs were great gathering-places for eligible young aristocrats of both sexes. The White Sulphur, now home of the Greenbrier, was among the elite and was immortalized as a place of romance in a play, *White Sulphur Springs*, by one John Selden. See P. Reniers, *The Springs of Virginia* (Chapel Hill: University of North Carolina Press, 1941), 75–87.

5. Home of Washington and Lee University and the Virginia Military Institute.

6. Among his students in 1891–92 (date of Ph.D. and chief place of employment in parentheses) were W. W. Baden (1892; Ursinus), W. L. De Vries (1892; canon and chancellor, Washington Cathedral), W. A. Harris (1892; University of Richmond), J. H. T. Main, (1892; Grinnell: president and dean), A. M. Carroll (1893; George Washington), W. R. Grey (1893; Davidson); Alfred Gudemann (Ph.D. Berlin, 1887; Pennsylvania), George M. Bolling (1896; Catholic University and Ohio State), L. L. Forman (1894; Cornell).

7. See "Correspondents."

8. For Gildersleeve's original intention for the syntax, see R. L. Fowler, "The Gildersleeve Archive," *Briggs-Benario*, 70–72.

9. "The Limitation of the Imperative in the Attic Orators" was read 13 July 1892 at Charlottesville (*TAPA* 23 [1892]: xxix–xxxix) and published at *AJP* 13 (1892): 399–436.

10. William Boone Nauts (1860–1931), a Sewanee graduate (1882), became first assistant at the Sewanee Grammar School (1883–1893), attended Gildersleeve's 1886 summer lectures at Sewanee, and was at Hopkins in 1891–92 before returning to his alma mater as professor of ancient languages (1893–1900), then Latin (1900–31). He also served Sewanee as acting dean (1911–12), commissioner of buildings and lands (1916–21), and registrar (1926–31).

79 To: UNIVERSITY COLLEGE, LONDON
*Testimonials in Favour of Alfred Edward Housman . . .*
(Cambridge: Cambridge University Press, 1892)

The Johns Hopkins University, Baltimore,
March 21, 1892

Mr. A. E. Housman's[1] critical work in Greek and Latin shows remarkable insight, range and resource, and I have pleasure in giving expression to the high opinion I have conceived of his scholarship and ability.

### B. L. GILDERSLEEVE

    1. Alfred Edward Housman (1859–1936) seems to have contacted Gildersleeve in advance of advertising his candidacy on 19 March 1892. The curtness of Gildersleeve's recommendation may be due in part to the fact that his former student Henry Clarke had applied for the same post and was using a recommendation previously written (31 May 1888) by Gildersleeve. Another reason may relate to the latter of Housman's two publications in *AJP* ("On Certain Corruptions in the *Persae* of Aeschylus," 9 [1888]: 317–25, and "The Oedipus Coloneus of Sophocles," 13 [1892]: 139–70). Because of a press deadline, Housman was not allowed to see proofs of his article and a one-page list of extensive corrigenda was published (ibid., 398). Gildersleeve's apology is tipped into the front of the number and one senses the repayment of a debt behind this letter. Gildersleeve later reproves Housman's "mordancy" at 27 (1906): 487 n. 1: "In [his *AJP* articles] the Pramnean wine of his criticism is not unduly tart. Fortunate are those in whom the bitterness of life does not generate bitterness of temper." See also 28 (1907): 114. Housman's references to Gildersleeve are only incidental; see *The Classical Papers of A. E. Housman*, ed. J. Diggle and F. R. D. Goodyear (Cambridge: Cambridge University Press, 1972), 850, 854, 865.

80 To: BENJAMIN LAWTON WIGGINS
*Sewanee*

The Johns Hopkins University
Baltimore June 6, 1892

My dear Professor Wiggins:

    Once upon a time I used to pride myself on being one of the promptest of correspondents but of late years I have fallen into the bad habit of putting letters that require elaborate answers into my pocket book and then I seem to have discharged a solemn duty and go lightly on my way until the pocket book becomes unwieldy. Looking over these reserved letters to-day I find that one of yours bears an ancient postmark March 17 and I am smitten with confusion. Can it be possible that I have not written at all or have I written a brief note—reserving fuller details for the letter that was evidently never sent? Whichever the case may be I hope you will forgive me as freely as your own generous heart will dictate. More I can not expect, though I must add that up to within a few days I have been busy enough to inspire pity. For the replenishment of my purse and the punishment of my sins I have undertaken to edit the Greek literature department of John-son's Cyclopedia[1] and to my great surprise the publishers came down on me for a tale of bricks[2] to be delivered May 15.— It was done but not without a considerable strain. Now I am free—comparatively—My stu-dents have scattered, the examinations are over. I can quietly organize my summer work and answer my letters.—

I found great pleasure in having Nauts[3] with me. He seemed to sympa-thize fully with the work of the department and his kindly ways made him friends so that I am sure he will not regret his stay in Baltimore. It was a real grief to me that you could not join him—but I can understand that you are much too important a person to dispose of your time in that way.

My plans for the summer are yet unformed except that I shall stay here until the second week of July—when I have promised to go to the meeting of the Philological Association at the University of Virginia[4]—Sewanee is not in the range of possibilities—I am sorry to say—and I am afraid that my eyes have looked their last on the Delectable Mountain[5]—but I hope and my wife hopes that we shall not lose our friends there and we both join in cordial thanks to Mrs. Wiggins and yourself for your kind invitation.

Yours faithfully<br>
B. L. Gildersleeve

Professor B. L. Wiggins

1. Gildersleeve was one of thirty-six editors who worked under the general direction of Charles Kendall Adams (1835–1902) on *Johnson's Universal Dictionary*, 8 vols. (New York: D. Appleton and A. J. Johnson, 1893–97). He was told the whole eight volumes would be printed in eighteen months at most, and by 22 August 1894 [California] he was complaining to B. I. Wheeler that after two years vol. 5 was not yet out. For Gildersleeve's estimate of his contributions, see No. 141 and n. 33.

2. Exod. 5:18.

3. No. 78, n. 10.

4. On the meeting, see the following letter.

5. This nickname for Sewanee comes from the site in Part 2 of Bunyan's *Pilgrim's Progress*, from which Heaven may be seen after the Pilgrim reaches middle age: "The Delectable Mountains, where Christian and Hopeful refreshed themselves with the Varieties of the Place" (284 Wharey).

## 81 To: HERBERT WEIR SMYTH
### Harvard

{ University Club<br>
1005 North Charles Street }<br>
Baltimore June 6, 1892

My dear Dr. Smyth:

I send you inclosed notes to Dew-Smith and Postgate of Cambridge,[1] to Ellis[2] and Munro[3] of Oxford. Dew Smith is not a classic but to my mind the most delightful man I met at either university. I could multiply letters but once introduced you will get on swimmingly. You will doubtless meet Adam of Emmanuel, Armitage Robinson of Christ's, Verrall of Trinity, Henry Jackson and J. S. Reid[4]—all of whom I know more or less and you may remember to reciprocate any kind mention they make possibly make [sic] of me.

As to the meeting of the Philological Association I may give an informal talk on my plans for a Greek syntax but I can not and will not promise anything.[5] It is too bad that you are not able to be with us in Virginia[6] though I am considered a renegade for having deserted the University and under the embarrassing circumstances may not develop as much cheerfulness as I have done at other meetings.

With best wishes for a pleasant and successful trip

     I am

                              Yours faithfully
                              B. L. Gildersleeve

Professor H. W. Smyth

1. For Dew-Smith and Postgate, see No. 44, nn. 9 and 12.

2. For Robinson Ellis, see No. 45, n. 9.

3. John Arthur Ruskin Munro (1864-1944), excavator on Cyprus, fellow of Exeter College, and rector of Lincoln College, Oxford.

4. James Adam (1860-1907), the great Platonic scholar (see A. M. Adam, "Memoir," *ap.* J. Adam, *The Religious Teachers of Greece* [Edinburgh: T. and T. Clark, 1908], i–lv); Joseph Armitage Robinson (1858-1933), fellow and dean of Christ's, Cambridge, Norrisan professor of divinity (1893-97) and dean of Westminster (1902-11), author of *A Study of the Gospels* (New York: Longmans, Green, 1902) and *St. Paul's Epistle to the Ephesians* (London: Macmillan, 1909); for Verrall, see No. 44, n. 11; Henry Jackson (1839-1921) succeeded Jebb as Regius professor of Greek at Cambridge in 1906, edited the *Journal of Philology* (1879-1920) and *Aristotle's Ethics, Book 5* (Cambridge: Cambridge University Press, 1879) (see R. St. John Parry, *Henry Jackson, O.M.* [Cambridge: Cambridge University Press, 1926]); James Smith Reid (1846-1926), fellow of Gonville and Caius College, was the first professor of ancient history at Cambridge and is known for *M. Tulli Ciceronis academica* (London: Macmillan, 1885) and *The Municipalities of the Roman Empire* (Cambridge: Cambridge University Press, 1913) (see *DNB 1922-1930*, 713-14).

5. The APA met in Charlottesville, 12-14 July 1892. Gildersleeve gave no paper, but discussed the papers of W. G. Hale, R. S. Radford, C. P. G. Scott, and M. Humphreys (see *PAPA* 23 [1892]: xxviii, xxxix, xliv, lxiii) and was elected to the executive committee. C. F. Smith recalled in his memorial article, "Basil Lanneau Gildersleeve: An Intimate View," *Sewanee Review* 32 (April 1924): 168, that a young scholar, probably Radford, attacked Hale in his paper. Hale, although in the room, did not respond. Gildersleeve defended him so impressively that the speaker, although he already had a Ph.D. (Radford's was from the University of Virginia in 1891), enrolled at Hopkins that fall and took a second Ph.D. there (as Radford did in 1895).

6. Smyth served as secretary-treasurer from 1889 to 1904, when he was elected president, but he was, as the letter shows, abroad in 1892.

## 82 To: BENJAMIN LAWTON WIGGINS
*Sewanee*

{University Club,
Madison Square}
Sept. 15, 1892

Dear Professor Wiggins:

Your most interesting letter of Aug. 28 was received as I was about to leave Narragansett Pier[1] and I postponed answering it until I had a comfortable place where I could write with like fulness even if I could not hope to rival the charm of your narrative. D[r]. Gailor's[2] letter I answered at once for it was but fair to him that he should not be kept in suspense as [to] the material for the first number of the new review.[3] The joy and enthusiasm of your work fill me with admiration and yet at the same time with unspeakable sadness. Once—and that not so long ago [—] there would have been something like an emulative response but the long years of work and the manifold disappointments that have crossed each stage of my career have told on my powers of imitation and for the rest of my days I must be content to finish the work that I have already blocked out—and as there is enough of it for twenty years I shall not be idle, even if I cannot be hopeful.— My Syntax has been resumed. My assistant Miller has completed an index to the five volumes that you know and we have made a preliminary survey of the ground.[4] The gaps that reveal themselves are discouraging— and I see that there is no hope of an exhaustive treatment of the whole subject—Still I may look forward to an outline of the work that has been done and that remains to be done and I am under bonds to publish something before very long. Miller has just completed under my direction an interesting study of the imperative in the Attic orators[5] and Bishop will furnish for the Journal an exhaustive statistic of the use of -τέον.[6] A great concordance of the Attic orators is in progress[7] and so if I can not add much myself to the sum of that which is known, I can stimulate and direct others.— The demands on my resources are so great that I am obliged to do a lot of hack work that interferes seriously with such labors of love as the Sewanee people propose. So, for some months I have worked almost daily for an hour or so on the Greek articles in Johnson's Revised Encyclopedia[8]— I should not have undertaken the job, if the work had not been in the line of my contract with Holt for a short History of Greek Literature.[9] The preparation of these articles will aid me materially in getting up this little book, to which I committed myself more than two years ago and for which I have collected a good deal of stuff.— Then I ought to superintend the revision of my Latin series[10]—and if I do any purely literary work at all I ought to begin seriously my Greek Renascence of the second century[11]— which I should like to publish in chapters. All this is outside of my classes, which are more and more exacting and of the Journal which is an ever present ball and chain. By this you will see that whether I have lost my elasticity or not, I have enough work on me and before me to satisfy reasonable requirements of professional and literary activity—and that I should be justified in declining any new ventures in periodical literature—especially in view of the sad failures of my earlier career.—Whenever you are ready to publish your booklet on the Greek play,[12] you are perfectly welcome to command my services—and there must be no question of pecuniary consideration—I am bound to you as I am to no one else in Sewanee and you must let me do for you whatever I can. It will be little enough.

When President Gilman reads of all that you have /done/ for giving life to Greek studies at Sewanee, he will doubtless wonder why I have not done something of the sort at Baltimore—but the practical ability that has been vouchsafed to you in so abundant measure has been denied to me—and and I must be content to admire your success without emulating it—

Yesterday's paper told us that the cholera had made its appearance in New York[13]—where I am lingering with wife and daughter on my way home. Wife and daughter expected to spend some six weeks in Virginia but the news of malarial fever at the University gave them pause and as our quarters in New York are pleasant we determined to remain here despite the excitement at quarantine. And even now that the disease has declared itself in the city, we shall not be frightened into going at once—Baltimore can hardly be a pleasant sojourn at present. The streets are all torn up for laying the cables of the improved roads—and there is less danger from the cholera here than there would be from malaria there—So we are in a strait betwixt two. In any case, however, I must return before long to put my study in order for the new session—

Accept my best thanks for your interesting letter and all the new evidence of your affectionate regard for

Your faithful friend<br>B. L. Gildersleeve

Professor B. L. Wiggins

1. A summer resort in Washington County, R.I., thirty miles south of Providence, on the west shore of Narragansett Bay, with hotels, large and elegant summer cottages, and a fine beach. It was always particularly popular with Southerners.

2. See "Correspondents."

3. The *Sewanee Review* was raised from the ashes of the short-lived (April–December 1890) *University of the South Magazine* by William P. Trent, a biographer of the Charlestonian William Gilmore Simms (1806-70), who aimed at the English kind of review that Simms had successfully edited. Thus, the prospectus announced that "the *Review* will conform more nearly to the type of the English reviews than is usual with American periodicals." See, further, Mott, (cited No. 34, n. 1), 733-40. Gildersleeve never contributed to the *Sewanee Review*.

4. Gildersleeve had planned a Greek syntax while still at the University of Virginia and had used his plan for his *Latin Grammar* (1867) (*Syntax*, iii). In 1882 he had planned a syntax of Pindar and even wrote an introduction to it (No. 78, n. 8). Originally his syntax to Pindar

was to be followed by a volume on orators; one on historians; another on the philosophers; and a final volume on comedy, tragedy, and epic. A notebook dated 1874 with additions and the note "begin here May 24 98" exists in the Hopkins Archive.

5. See No. 78, n. 9.

6. Charles Edward Bishop's "The Greek Verbal in TEO" appeared in *AJP* 20 (1899): 1–21, 121–38, 241–53. Gildersleeve was currently publishing his "Verbals in -τος in Sophocles" (13 [1892]: 171–99, 329–42, 449–62).

7. Gildersleeve may refer to Forman's *Index Andocideus, Lycurgeus, Dinarcheus* (No. 85, n. 2) or a concordance made from his notes. If the latter, it does not exist.

8. See No. 80, n. 1.

9. The Holt project fell through, perhaps for reasons given by M. W. Humphries (No. 25, n. 9) in his memorial notice, *UVa Alumni News* 12 (January 1924): 133: "A publishing house once obtained his consent to write a book on Greek literature. In their announcement of this work they said it would do away with the need of studying Greek. The book was never forthcoming."

10. He means the *Latin Grammar*, which he revised and enlarged, with Gonzalez Lodge (New York: University Publishing Co., 1894). The only other revised work of the series was his *Latin Primer* of 1875, revised with Chapman Maupin (No. 11, n. 5) (New York: University Publishing, 1882).

11. Presumably the same project he mentions to J. M. Libbey (No. 34).

12. Never published.

13. The Indian cholera epidemic of 1891 in the following year was brought to Europe by pilgrims returning from Mecca. The ensuing epidemic, which killed Tchaikovsky among others, was principally confined to western Russia, but the disease, brought by immigrants and other transatlantic voyagers, reached New York in the summer. The *NYTimes*, 14 September 1892: 2, said, however, that no new case had been reported that day.


### 83 To: Edmund Clarence Stedman
*Columbia*

1002 N. Calvert St.
Baltimore Nov. 7, 1892

My dear Mr. Stedman:

I am happy to have your book,[1] proud to know that you retain a kindly remembrance of one of your most devout listeners. The printed page is bright with its web of thought and fancy but I am so fortunate as to recall at every turn the voice and the presence of the critic and the poet so that the criticism and the poetry vibrate as well as shine. To read your book is to renew the charm of /your/ visit to our workshop, is to forget "Wood St."[2] and all the other wooden things with which my daily life has to deal.

Accept my best thanks for this new expression of your regard and believe me

My dear Mr. Stedman
as ever

Yours faithfully
B. L. Gildersleeve

Edmund Clarence Stedman Esq.

1. Stedman (see "Correspondents") was chosen to inaugurate the Turnbull lectureship in poetry at Hopkins in 1889, but had to postpone his appointment for a year because of the demands of the *Library of American Literature* (see No. 139, n. 6) and medical advice. In the spring of 1891, he delivered eight lectures on "The Nature and Elements of Poetry," which he repeated at Columbia and the University of Pennsylvania in 1892, published serially in the *Century*, and then published collected (Boston: Houghton Mifflin, 1892), a copy of which he sent to Gildersleeve, the occasion of this letter.

2. Possibly from Wordsworth's "The Reverie of Poor Susan," 1-2:

> At the corner of Wood Street, when daylight appears
> Hangs a Thrush that sings loud, it has sung there for years.

The thrush gives Susan, working in the city, a momentary reverie of her youth as a milkmaid in the country. Stedman mentions Wordsworth frequently in the lectures, but not this poem.


### 84 To: Thomas Frank Gailor
*Sewanee*

The Johns Hopkins University
Baltimore Feb.ʸ 28, 1893

My dear Dr. Gailor:

Your letter of the 25ᵗʰ was received yesterday. I had been made aware of the kind intentions of the Faculties and the Trustees of the University of the South by a letter from Professor Wiggins and had already considered most carefully the highly honourable invitation which you have conveyed to me.[1] It is one of the signal distinctions of my life and if I could recognize in myself any reasonable fitness for the services demanded I should be tempted to comply with your request. But while I have worked too long in the domain of letters to disclaim the style and title of scholar I have never laid any claim to oratory and my performances in public functions of the kind have not been such as to inspire /me/ with any confidence in my fitness for such work. And even if I could manage to get through an address with tolerable credit I am not the man for that special occasion. You want someone who has been thoroughly identified with the institution from the beginning, who knows every stage of its history and is /in/ closest sympathy with its mission not only in the state but also in the church. No one but a Churchman could adequately represent the University of the South on its great day.

There are other considerations fatal to my acceptance. For instance during the present session I have been repeatedly drawn off from the work of my life by outside calls[2] and I must concentrate my energies on certain things that I have to do while it is called to-day and the acceptance of your invitation would break up a summer of work devoted to the making up of lost time.

But I will not weary you with a recital of my perplexities and troubles. With many thanks to the Faculties and Trustees for the honour they have done me and to you for the kind words with which you have reinforced their invitation.

I am

Yours sincerely

B. L. Gildersleeve

Rev. Thos. F. Gailor S.T.B.
Vice-Chancellor of the University of the South

1. Both Gailor's and Wiggins' letters are lost, but they probably refer to the twenty-fifth commencement, which occurred in the university's thirty-sixth year. The university had been founded in 1857 by the planting of a cross on the plateau of Sewanee Mountain in the Cumberland Mountains of Tennessee, and with an endowment of $3 million, but the war came and the first classes were not held until 18 September 1868, when the faculty, composed of Southern generals (Robert E. Lee was the first choice for president, but he went to Washington College [now Washington and Lee] and the honor fell to Josiah Gorgas) and churchmen, built the first classrooms.

2. He may refer to his continuing work for *Johnson's Cyclopedia* (No. 80, n. 1), two reviews for the *Nation*, and "Professorial Types," for the Hopkins student yearbook, *The Hopkinsian* 1 (1893): 11–18. The current "work of [his] life" was the revision of *Latin Grammar* and the resumption of his *Syntax* (No. 82, n. 4).

## 85 To: BENJAMIN IDE WHEELER
*California*

June 11, 1894

My dear Professor Wheeler:

I think that I have a man who will do good work in the very line that Laird[1] has left. His name is L. L. Forman.[2] He was formerly an instructor in the University of Pennsylvania under Lamberton[3] and studied with me two years, taking his Ph.D. degree last spring. Some years ago he made special studies in Germany especially with regard to the work of the gymnasium and he is perfectly at home in the use of German authorities. This practical mastery of Greek is unusual and his translation—largely extemporaneous—of the introduction to Froude's Caesar[4] was much better work than I ordinarily get from my candidates. You can confide to him all the tiresome, yet indispensible exercise business. He is accurate, painstaking, and extremely neat in all his work.— and a literary man in his taste and style.

D<sup>r</sup>. Forman wants to make a beginning in a University career and although he is a mature man and a married man he would not object to taking a subordinate position with a moderate salary,[5] which is all you have to offer. He is fully alive to the advantages of Cornell as a place for study and development and indeed he is so much impressed with the importance of the position for him that he would be willing to run up to Ithaca and let you look him over, if my recommendation should lead you to consider him seriously.—It may save trouble if I were to add, that like myself he makes no pretensions to attainments in comparative grammar.

Yours faithfully
B. L. Gildersleeve

Professor B.I. Wheeler

1. Arthur Gordon Laird (1868-1951), educated at Dalhousie, Cornell, and Leipzig, taught briefly at Stanford and Cornell before following Charles Kendall Adams, who left the presidency of Cornell to be president of the University of Wisconsin in September 1892. Laird taught at Wisconsin from 1894 to 1938, co-edited (with C. F. Smith) *Herodotus VII and VIII* (Smyth Series) (New York: American Book Co., 1908), and was associate editor of *Classical Journal*, to which he contributed numerous articles and reviews, from its founding in 1905 until 1908.

2. Lewis Leaming Forman (1857-1933) taught at the University of Pennsylvania for one year (1890-91) after receiving his A.M. there. He arrived at Hopkins at the advanced age of thirty-three, causing Gildersleeve to write in a follow-up letter to Wheeler of 15 June 1894 [California]: "He came into my classes against my protest because I hate to have about me in statu pupillari men who have made up their mind on almost every topic I have to touch." He was instructor of Greek at Cornell (1894-1900, 1902-11), then moved to Europe. When World War I broke out, he worked for two years in a British munitions factory, donating his pay to the Institute for the War Blinded. Back in America in 1916, he organized the American Rights Committee, whose goal was American involvement in the war. In 1917 he returned to England to help maintain at his own expense some forty French war orphans. On the death of Charles E. Bennett in 1921, he returned to Cornell, declining a professorship in favor of an instructorship, and taught until 1924, when he moved to France, where he lived and studied for seven years. His best work may be in the linguistic commentary in his *Selections from Plato* (London: Macmillan, 1900, 1906). He wrote *A First Greek Book* (New York: Harper and Bros., 1899), compiled *Index Andocideus, Lycurgeus, Dinarcheus* (Oxford: Clarendon Press, 1897), and *Aristophanes Clouds* (Smyth Series) (New York: American Book Co., 1915), see *AJP* 37 (1916): 114-15 ( = *SBM*, 342).

3. William Alexander Lamberton (1848-1910) had been fellow by courtesy at Hopkins (1887-88), instructor in mathematics at the University of Pennsylvania from 1867 to 1878, then of Greek and Latin (1878-80), and finally of Greek (1880-1910). He wrote *The World's History and Its Makers* with E. Sanderson and J. McGovern (Philadelphia: T. Nolan, 1907) and edited *The Sixth and Seventh Books of Thucydides* (New York: Harper and Bros., 1886) and *Thucydides II and III* (Smyth Series) (New York: American Book Co., 1905). *WhAm* 1: 700.

4. The 18-page introduction to James Anthony Froude's (1818-94) *Caesar: A Sketch* (New York: Scribner, 1879; reprinted through 1937), was a favorite piece for turning into Greek.

5. Forman was independently wealthy.

86 To: BENJAMIN IDE WHEELER
*California*

Sept. 24, 1894

Dear Professor Wheeler:

The only name I can think of at the moment who might serve your purpose as a temporary substitute for Bristol[1] is J. N. Anderson,[2] a Master of

Arts of the University of Virginia, who has studied in Germany and who took the degree of Ph.D. here this year. He has an excellent practical knowledge of Latin and Greek, has read a great deal and has done something in the way of prose and verse composition. He is said to be an excellent teacher—A man of refined nature, of quiet manners and prepossessing appearance. I should not call him 'incisive' or 'inspiring', but he respects himself and would in all likelihood make others respect him and would, I think, keep his pupils interested.

Best thanks for information about the Cyclopaedia.[3]

Address                                   Yours faithfully
Dr. J. N. Anderson                        B. L. Gildersleeve
Williamston S.C.

Professor B. I. Wheeler

   1. George Prentiss Bristol (1856–1927) was educated at Hamilton College (A.B. 1876, A.M. 1883) and was a student at Hopkins (1879–80) and Heidelberg. He was assistant professor of Greek at Hamilton (1883–88) and rose from assistant professor (1888) to professor of Greek (1898–1927) at Cornell. He edited *Cornell Studies in Classical Philology* beginning in 1891, published *Ten Selected Orations of Lysias* (Boston: Allyn and Bacon, 1892) and wrote *The Teaching of Greek and Latin in Secondary Schools* (with C. E. Bennett) (New York: Longmans, Green, 1906). *WhAm* 1:140 and *Cornell Alumni News* (26 May 1927): 416. Bristol's place was taken by Frank Louis Van Cleef, who had been at Wisconsin since 1892. Van Cleef graduated with honors from Harvard and received his Ph.D. from Bonn (1890). He edited *Index Antiphonteus* (Boston: Ginn, 1895) and published the lectures of Frederic De Forest Allen, *Lectures on Greek Literature* and *Introduction to Homer* (both Cambridge, Mass.: F. L. Van Cleef, 1888).

   2. James Nesbitt Anderson (1864–1945) received his A.M. in 1887, was at Harvard (1887–88), Berlin (1889–90), and Heidelberg (1890). After taking his Ph.D., he was professor of Greek and Latin at the University of Oklahoma (1894–96), then professor of ancient languages (from 1905), dean of the College of Arts and Sciences (1910–30), and dean of the Graduate School (1930–38) at the University of Florida. He edited *Selections from Ovid* (Gildersleeve-Lodge Series) (New York: University Publishing Co., 1899). *WhoAm* 2: 25.

   3. No. 80, n. 1.


87 To: HERBERT WEIR SMYTH
*Houghton*

Oct. 13, 1894

Dear Professor Smyth:

   The Nation people sent me your great book[1] a week or so ago and asked me to notice it briefly. I told them that it was not a book to be noticed briefly, that it deserved a long critical review by the best man to be found, that I was not that best man and had no pretensions whatever to be a dialectologist. In spite of my protest they insisted that I would write a readable notice /and/, that they did not want anything technical and in a moment of weakness I yielded. If there is any/thing/ especially foolish in my notice[2] I hope you will not bear too heavily on an old fellow who has tried in his time to do good work on his own line and who has been guilty of this Pfuscherei [scamped work] in order to express his admiration for an achievement that is utterly beyond his powers.

But whom can I get to review it for the Journal?[3]

Yours faithfully<br>B. L. Gildersleeve

Professor H. W. Smyth

    1. *The Sounds and Inflections of the Greek Dialects: Ionic* (Oxford: Clarendon Press; New York: Macmillan, 1894).
    2. "It has been reserved for an American scholar . . . to give the world a book on the Ionic dialect which, by fulness of detail, by command of the documents, by painstaking research, by acuteness and suggestiveness, deserves to rank with the most memorable achievements of the closing century in the domain of Greek studies," Gildersleeve wrote in the *Nation* 59 (8 November 1894): 346. On the limitations of Smyth's book, see W. Schulze, *Kleine Schriften*, 2d ed., ed. W. Wissmann (Göttingen: Vandenhoeck & Ruprecht, 1934; supplement, 1966), 682–92, for a review of Smyth's "The Vowel System of the Ionic Dialect," *TAPA* 20 (1889): 5–138.
    3. Hans (later Hanns) Oertel (1852–1952) of Yale reviewed Smyth's book at *AJP* 15 (1894): 497–501.

88 To: BENJAMIN IDE WHEELER<br>*California*

Oct. 24, 1894

My dear Professor Wheeler:

Will your engagements leave you time to review Smyth's Ionic Dialect[1] for the Journal? You are the man to do it and if you fail me I do not know on whom to call. My regard for Smyth is such that I would strain a point to take the thing in hand myself. Only I am not equal to anything except a feeble summary of contents and nothing short of a critical review would be commensurate with the importance of the book.

Newson[2] was here yesterday and it seems that he has not abandoned his scheme and looks to you still as the Atlas who is to carry the Greek series[3]—Oddly enough he thinks or thought that the main obstacle in your mind is the difficulty of collaboration.—I calmly informed him that it was my deliberate conviction that the main trouble with you as with me was that you did not see how it would pay. I told him it was all nonsense to guarantee /us/ $500 apiece on the series—the $500 apiece must mean on the books that we accepted as part of the series—and our own contributions must be left out altogether.—I said furthermore that I could not take a very active part in the enterprise—/and that/ my share would be limited to the production of a small Greek syntax—of some 300 or 400 pages and eventually of an Elementary Greek Grammar the forms to be done by you and the syntax by myself—The selection of the men, the outlining of the plan, the reading of proof—I should be willing to undertake /or rather to help in/ —no more.—If you take hold of the scheme vigorously I think it will be a success so far as Greek things are ever a success; but you know I am not over sanguine and may be a weight on you—So I shall go overboard cheerfully with my singing robe about me.[4] When you see Newson, it should be made plain to him that while he is a pleasant fellow and gives very good lunches, we must have something tangible in the way of honorarium and that our income is to begin with the engagement of our helpers.

I have [been] busy and half sick since my return home and have not had time to examine Higgins's paper[5]—There will be in any event little chance to make room for it in any early number—and the Latin form is against it—some of my experiences in publishing Latin articles have been doleful in the extreme. One makes oneself partially responsible for such dreadful things—though I have do not doubt [sic] Higgins is more careful than Hanssen . . .[6]

B. L. G.

1. See preceding letter.

2. Henry D. Newson (1854–1929) was at this time director of the educational department of Harper Brothers. He later formed the H. D. Newson Company, which produced the Aldine Series of elementary school texts.

3. Harper's was the leading textbook publisher in the country for much of the nineteenth century, especially known for its Geography Series and Readers. Its first series was begun in 1835 by Charles Anthon (1797–1867), Jay professor of Greek and Latin at Columbia, and grew in thirty years to over thirty volumes of reference works and texts, nearly all of which were in print at the turn of the century. See, further, Eugene Exman, *The House of Harper* (New York: Harper and Row, 1967), 163–70. Gildersleeve was well known to the Harpers, having contributed his edition of Persius (1875) to their Classical Series, *Justin Martyr* (1877) to their Douglass Series of Christian Greek and Latin Writers, and *Pindar* to the New Classical Series, under the editorship of Henry Drisler (1818–97), Jay professor of Greek at Columbia. The New Classical Series failed in 1890 (No. 71, n. 8), and the firm now wanted to initiate a Gildersleeve-Wheeler Series, for which see No. 114.

4. See the story of Arion, Her. 1.24.

5. Leonidas Raymond Higgins (1859–1955), was educated at Brown (B.A. 1884), received his Ph.D. (under Wheeler) from Cornell in 1898, and was instructor in Greek at Northwestern (1895–97). He taught in Chicago schools from 1898–1901 and then became instructor in Latin at Cornell College, Mt. Vernon, Iowa (1901–2). In 1902 he was appointed professor of Greek and Latin at Grand Island College, Grand Island, Nebr., and, later, at Ottawa University, Ottawa, Kans., until his retirement in 1929. His submission treated some synonymous Greek verbs, and when Gildersleeve got around to reading it, he found it only serviceable for "a general history of ἐθέλω and βούλομαι" (BLG to Wheeler, 2 October 1894 [California]). Higgins resubmitted a paper on βούλομαι, but it was not printed in *AJP*.

6. "Miscellanea Graeca" by F. Hanssen of Santiago, Chile (*AJP* 13 [1892]: 437–48) required nine corrigenda at 14 (1893): 262. The ellipsis is Gildersleeve's.

89 To: HENRY RUSHTON FAIRCLOUGH[1]
*Stanford*

Dec. 2, 1895

Dear Prof. Fairclough:

The candidate for Ph.D. in Greek has to present an essay in Greek (8 or 10 foolscap pages) on some theme to be agreed on—The topics of examination are:

1. History of Greek Literature—Minutiae not required for the post-Aristotelian period

2. Translation of a number of unseen passages—generally selected from the wide range of post-classic literature

3. A critical exercise—consisting usually of a commentary on selected variants.

The oral examination takes up points in the history of literature and grammar—For this there is no regular scheme—

Yours sincerely
B. L. Gildersleeve

Professor H. R. Fairclough

1. Fairclough (1862-1938) was lecturer in Greek and ancient history at his alma mater, Toronto, from 1887 to 1893. He went to Hopkins for graduate work, as would other Toronto men such as W. J. Alexander, Gordon J. Laing, W. P. Mustard, and J. C. Robertson. He had spent the year 1886-87 at Hopkins and was awarded a fellowship for the following year (along with Augustus Taber Murray, a recent graduate of the Quaker Haverford College), but in April 1887 Canada federalized her universities, creating an immediate need for instructors, and Fairclough was nominated as lecturer in Greek and ancient history at his alma mater. Since 1893 he had been teaching Greek and Latin at Stanford with his former colleague Murray, the only Ph.D. (Hopkins, 1890) on the Stanford classics faculty, and he felt obliged to complete the dissertation he had begun ten years earlier. Because of his status at Toronto, Fairclough was allowed to write an essay in lieu of an examination in Greek prose composition and complete his degree with only limited residence in Baltimore. Following his degree, he returned to Stanford, where he taught, with interruptions, until his death. See, further, "Correspondents."

90 To: DANIEL COIT GILMAN
*JHU-Gilman*

Hotel Trinacria, Palermo
April 5, 1896

My dear Mr. Gilman:

To you next to my own family was due the announcement of my safe arrival at Naples but the rush has been so great that I could not find a quiet moment in which to write and remembering that you sent me one or two tokens of your good will from Sicily[1] I found a certain propriety in writing you my first letter from Palermo which I reached early this morning. Sicily is a part of Greece and I have always desired to approach Athens in the legitimate way, not by the back door of Brindisi and Corfu but by her own port.[2] So I expect to leave Catania on Wednesday afternoon after a peep at Syracuse and if the weather is fair, at Taormina, so that if all goes well, I shall be in Athens next Friday.[3] Wheeler[4] has secured rooms for me and everything promises well for my plans.

The trip to Naples might well be called a halcyon trip.[5] It was a little rough one night but that was all. Very few of our passengers were sea-sick and I enjoyed the perfect rest and freedom from all bodily and mental troubles—The company was composed of Americans almost wholly and Americans of the better class and that means they were staid and quiet people so that our life was not full of excitement and gossip. Some pleasant acquaintances I made and some renewed. New Haven was especially well-represented—the two daughters of President Porter[6]—Mr. Day,[7] the banker and Mrs. Day, Mrs. Eaton[8] and her cousin Miss Van Winkle. Mrs. Eaton received me kindly on account of your introduction and we became, I venture to say, good friends, and when we parted, she sent by me to you and yours many kind messages. The Princeton boys with young Robert Garrett at their head did their college credit by their steady behavior on board and yet though I am a Princeton man I was not so much interested in their success as to accompany them to Athens[9]—I staid in Naples long enough to see the Museum[10] again with its priceless masterpieces and to revisit Pompeii, which one can never study too often, especially on account of the <u>domus vettiorum</u> exhumed last year[11]—a marvel beyond description and worth much more to me than any mock Olympic games. Saturday was a cold and rainy day and the run to Palermo was not unpleasant and to-day the rain has interfered a good deal with the sunshine but I have been more than delighted with Palermo and wonder how Kaiser Wilhelm, who is on one of the German men of war under my window, stands affected towards Panormus.[12]

When I am fairly established in Athens I will try to make amends for this hasty scrawl written by the light of /the/ two composition candles of this excessively German inn. The Germans summer in Italy, as you know—and carry their nationality about with them quite as much as our British cousins.

Give my best regards to Mrs. Gilman and your daughters and believe me

      As ever
                Yours faithfully
                <u>B. L. Gildersleeve</u>

President Gilman

My companion, Scott,[13] I ought to add is very well and full of enthusiasm. His <u>bonhomie</u> seems to make friends for him everywhere and I am sure he is much better liked than I am.

1. A photograph of August von Platen's (Nos. 3 and 11) monument at his grave in the Greek theatre of Syracuse and a postcard from Segesta; see *E&S*, 450n., and BLG to Gilman, 12 May 1890. After completing his work on the organization of the Johns Hopkins Hospital, Gilman was given a leave of absence by the trustees for the school year 1889–90.

2. For Gildersleeve on the Piraeus road, see *60 Days*: 209.

3. Gildersleeve left on the *Birmania* of the Florio-Rubattino line in the early evening of Wednesday the 8th (*60 Days*: 206) and arrived in Athens on the 10th.

4. B. I. Wheeler was professor of Greek literature at the American School of Classical Studies at Athens, 1895–96, and spent the summer at his alma mater, Heidelberg. He accompanied Gildersleeve on the first of Dörpfeld's tours to Tiryns, Mycenae, Epidaurus, Olympia, and Delphi.

5. *60 Days*: 205. He had boarded the *Fulda* for Naples at New York on 21 March.

6. Noah Porter (1811–92), president of Yale. His wife died in 1888.

7. Possibly Wilbur Fisk Day (1871–1914), banker and auditor of Yale.

8. Perhaps the wife of Daniel Cady Eaton (1837–1912), professor of history and the criticism of art at Yale.

9. The head of the American Olympic Committee for the revived games of 1896 was William Milligan Sloane (1850–1928), professor of French history at Princeton, who brought four juniors, Herbert B. Jameson, Francis A. Lane, Albert C. Taylor, Robert Garrett, and their trainer, "Scotty" McMaster, to Athens. A five-man delegation from the Boston Athletic Association, four of whom were Harvard graduates, along with four others from Boston not affiliated with the B.A.A., comprised the Boston delegation. Both groups traveled first class on the *Fulda*, the Princeton team working out twice a day on deck, the Boston team once. See R. D. Mandell, *The First Modern Olympics* (Berkeley and Los Angeles: University of California Press, 1976), 114–18, and *60 Days*: 205. Robert Garrett (1875–1961), grandson of the wealthy Baltimore banker and Hopkins trustee John Work Garrett (No. 49, n. 20), underwrote the Princeton team's costs on the journey and, much to the dismay of the Greeks, won the discus throw (*60 Days*: 212). His discus is still on display in the main gymnasium at Princeton. For an account by a contemporary classicist, see Eugene P. Andrews, "A First-Hand Account of the First of the Modern Olympic Games," *Cornell Alumni News* (December 1972): 22–24.

10. The Museo Nazionale houses a famous collection of ancient frescoes and sculpture from Pompeii, Herculaneum, Stabiae, and other sites.

11. The House of the Vettii (named from the seals of two freedmen found there) on the Vicolo di Mercurio in the northern section of Pompeii, contained magnificent frescoes in the atrium, original marble ornaments in the peristyle, and a magnificent Cupid series in one of the main rooms. "What must the external glory of antique civilization have been when an insignificant corner of it could yield such wealth of art? . . . This is the lesson of Pompeii" (*60 Days*: 205).

12. The Latinized Greek name of Palermo.

13. On Scott's (see "Correspondents") trip with Gildersleeve (Scott left him on 17 May), see *PAPA* 56 (1925): xxvii–xxviii and the following letter.

91 To: DANIEL COIT GILMAN
*JHU-Gilman*

{ Hôtel Grande Bretagne
Athènes le} 18 Mai 1896

My dear Mr. Gilman:

Your kind letter of April 30 met me Saturday[1] when I returned from the island trip, as it is called, the second of Dörpfeld's[2] excursions which I have taken. The first or Peloponnesian trip lasted sixteen days and this ten so that since my arrival in Athens on the 11th of last month[3] I have spent twenty six days in outside travel and have seen much that is denied to the ordinary traveller and that under unparalleled guidance. You know Dörpfeld and it is not necessary for me to characterize him. He [is] a most remarkable man not only for his wonderful power of combination and his rare gift of exposition but for the sweetness and wholesomeness of his nature and his management of men and things. At the last dinner on board the Theseus I was deputed to make the speech for the company and I said among other things that I had never appreciated so fully before the truth of Thomas à Kempis' saying (I hope I am quoting correctly): Bonum est sub praelato vivere[4] and I only wish I could be under similar guidance the rest of the summer, though it must be said that our leader worked his followers very hard at times. To have studied Tiryns, Mycenae and Epidaurus under such a master, to have spent three days in Olympia[5] with him and to have been introduced by him to Delphi is an inestimable privilege.—The trip from which I have just returned was a voyage through a region of waking dreams—Aegina, Calauria,[6] Delos, Sunion, Eretria, Marathon, Thermopylae and Samothrace are the points that marked our route which ended in the Troad, where we had the good fortune to see not only Hissarlik but its former rival Bunarbashi.[7] I say its former rival for the explorations and excavations of 1893 and 1894 have put a new face on the matter and he who has seen Mycenae must believe in the Hissarlik of to-day. The island trip was less fatiguing on the whole than the Peloponnesus trip but early hours and long walks and uncomfortable rides were not lacking and I reached Athens quite ready for a little rest though I shall doubtless be equally ready for pastures new after a few days.—My general health is very good though my weak leg is an uncertain quantity[8]—and though I was the oldest man of the company and hampered by my stiff knee with the exception of the three days' ride through Arcadia which I thought it prudent to give up, I went nearly everywhere with the youngest and most active of the party. Everyone was very kind and considerate and help was often eagerly offered when help was unnecessary. The two trips brought me into contact with some of the younger members of the American school and I have been able to draw my conclusions more surely than if I had watched their work formally. As you may imagine, I have laid up many things in my head.

The rush of impressions has been bewildering and I suffered at first from insomnia owing to the constant excitement[9] but now the vision is becoming clearer and I am sure that your prophecy as to the value of the trip for my future work will be fulfilled. As yet I have not been able to put down much in black and white and my projected letters to the Sun and the Nation have come to naught.[10] My methods of literary work are not compatible with rapid travelling, but something tangible, something printable will come out of it all, I am sure. I have one or two articles in mind that will be out of the common run and I should be glad to prepare in the quieter months of the summer one or two lectures based on my trip. The scheme presented in your Peabody list is interesting and novel and I think I should be able to give a talk on Athens bringing the modern element into the foreground but Olympia and Delphi seem to me as much set apart now as they were two thousand years ago.[11] Still I shall be glad to try my hand as I shall have to wake up from this dream before long to face the fundamental question.

I arrived at Athens in the midst of the hurly burly of the Olympic games and on my return from the Peloponnesus trip I spent my time in studying the city—Still I have made a few acquaintances. Our minister Mr. Alexander[12] invited me to dinner and night before last I dined at Mrs. Schliemann's[13]—Wheeler[14] and his wife have been all kindness and I hope that we shall be able to have him at the Hopkins for some talks on epigraphy which he knows how to make interesting. To be sure the sight of the stones themselves is the thing that stirs the blood—

My plans are not very definite—I am meditating a trip to Sparta and one to Thessaly and there is some talk of a leisurely voyage among the Greek islands—but after all I have seen and felt, it seems /sometimes/ as if it would be a good thing to have my study at the Hopkins for quiet digestion—for I am, ~~per~~ as you know, a man of books—Scott left me yesterday[15]—He is a faithful soul and I have a high opinion of his Christian character and his single minded enthusiasm—I am sure he will give a good account of himself—

Present my best regards to Mrs. Gilman and the young ladies—and pardon this long letter that I have allowed to run on regardless of the manifold engagements that will encompass you when you get it.— Yet I must add that I have been invited by Seymour to inaugurate the new classical building at Yale—with an address.[16] It is a signal honor and I suppose I shall have to accept for the sake of the Johns Hopkins as well as on my own account.

Yours faithfully
B. L. Gildersleeve

1. May 16.
2. Wilhelm Dörpfeld (1853-1940) was trained in architecture at the Berlin Bauakademie, where he attracted the attention of Friedrich Adler, who subsequently became his

father-in-law. Adler arranged for him to assist the German excavation at Olympia in 1877, where Dörpfeld developed the techniques (especially studies of building materials) that made him one of the great pioneers in archaeological method. Indeed, Schliemann was so impressed by his method that he asked Dörpfeld to join him permanently, but he was already committed to the Deutsche Archäologische Institut, which he served as secretary for twenty-five years during the great period of German archeological discovery. He went to Troy as Schliemann's adviser, and in the year of Schliemann's death (1890), Dörpfeld uncovered a likely candidate for the Homeric Troy Schliemann had so long sought (see below). He continued to live in Athens and give tours and lectures of the Greek sites, and when he tried to retire in 1909, the German Foreign Office protested so vehemently that he postponed his retirement for three years. His chief works are *Troja 1893* (Leipzig: F. A. Brockhaus, 1894), *Das griechische Theater* (Athens: Barth & von Hirst, 1896), *Alt-Ithaka* (Munich-Gräfelfing: R. Uhde, 1927), *Alt-Olympia* and *Alt-Athen und seine Agora* (both Berlin: E. S. Mittler & Sohn, 1935 and 1937 respectively). The later works advocated theories of his own, and won few (or no permanent) converts. For Gildersleeve on Dörpfeld, see "Classical Studies in America," *Atlantic* 78 (December 1896): 735–36, and *AJP* 27 (1906): 360. The standard biography is P. Goessler, *Wilhelm Dörpfeld: Ein Leben im Dienst der Antike* (Stuttgart: W. Kohlhammer, 1951) (cf. the review of A. von Gerkan, *Gnomon* 24 [1952]: 166–68, who stresses the laudatory basis of the book).

3. He was in Palermo on 5 April (see previous letter) and arrived in Athens on the 11th.

4. *Imit. Chr.* 1.9: *Valde magnum est, in obedientia stare, sub praelato vivere et sui juris non esse* (It is of great importance to live in obedience, to be under a superior, and not to be at our own disposing).

5. See *60 Days*: 635ff. The tour of the Peloponnesus ran from 22 April to 7 May. They toured Olympia May 2–5. The island tour ran from 12 to 22 May. For the complete itinerary, see *AA* 11 (1896): 148–49.

6. See *AJP* 33 (1914): 363–65.

7. In 1893 a fortress was discovered on the mound of Hissarlik, a spur between the main Scamander valley and its eastern tributary (known as the Simois in antiquity) about three and a half miles from the Hellespont, laying to rest any doubts about Hissarlik as the site of ancient Troy. Bunarbashi, whose hot and cold springs were thought to be those that lay outside the gates of Troy, is more than a mile away from Hissarlik. Schliemann's conclusions from the excavations of the site in 1872–74 drew heavily on comparisons with his finds at Mycenae and discerned nine levels at Hissarlik, of which the sixth, distinguished by Dörpfeld in 1882, is thought to be Homeric Troy. Dörpfeld confirmed and supplemented these findings in 1894. See H. Schliemann, *Troja* (Leipzig: n.p., 1884); W. Dörpfeld, *Troja 1893* (n. 2 above) and *Troja und Ilion* (Athens: Beck & Barth, 1902); and, secondarily, A. C. Lascarides, *The Search for Troy, 1553–1874* (Bloomington, Ind.: Lilly Library, Indiana University, 1977), and M. I. Finley, *Schliemann's Troy: One Hundred Years After* (London: Oxford University Press, 1975) ( = *PBA* 60 [1974]: 1–22).

8. See *60 Days*: 630.

9. Ibid.

10. He wrote *60 Days* for the *Atlantic* instead.

11. Gildersleeve lectured with slides at McCoy Hall on 9 October, and at the University Club on "Athens" on 13 November.

12. Eben Alexander (1851–1910), graduate of Yale (A.B. 1873), was professor of Greek at the University of North Carolina (1886–93), when President Cleveland named him envoy extraordinary, minister plenipotentiary, and consul general for Greece, Romania, and Serbia, a position he held until August 1897. He returned to North Carolina as professor of Greek (1897) and dean (1900–1910). *NatCAB* 12: 266; *WhAm* 1: 14; *CJ* 6 (1910–11): 136.

13. Sophia Engastromenos Schliemann (1852–1932) was seventeen years old when she became Schliemann's second wife; she was his widow at thirty-eight. From 1878 to 1880 he built her a palatial three-story house, called Ilíou Mélathron, or the "House of Ilium" (now

the seat of the Areopagus, the Greek Supreme Court), on University Street in Athens, where she regularly received visiting scholars and dignitaries. It was natural that Dörpfeld would bring his tourists, particularly one so prominent as Gildersleeve, to meet her. On the house, see L. and G. Poole, *One Passion, Two Loves* (New York: Crowell, 1966), 215–18, and 256 for a picture.

14. See preceding letter, n. 4.

15. Ibid., n. 13.

16. T. D. Seymour (see "Correspondents") brought Gildersleeve to the dedication of Phelps Hall on 16 October 1896. Gildersleeve's speech was reprinted as "Classical Studies in America" (see n. 2 above).

## 92 To: DANIEL COIT GILMAN
*JHU-Gilman*

{ American College for Girls,
Constantinople. }
(Scutari) June 15, 1896

Dear Mr. Gilman:

Some weeks ago while I was in Athens revolving the problem 'What next?' I was overpersuaded by Miss Patrick of the College for Girls at Constantinople to make the college a visit of some days and to deliver the commencement oration on the 19th inst. I had missed seeing Constantinople on the island trip and the inducement to make good my failure at other people's expense was tempting at the moment. Repentance came too late and I am here. I arrived last Wednesday the 10th and have managed to see the principal sights of Constantinople after a fashion and I count myself richer by a number of interesting experiences—Still it was not a wise thing to do but I cannot have your counsel at every turn as I have at home. A day or two after my function is discharged I shall set out for central Europe but I have not decided yet where I shall settle down though I incline to Heidelberg where the Wheelers are summering.

I am under the impression that I wrote to you about Dörpfeld in my last letter. Can't we manage to have him in Baltimore for one or two lectures.[1] His terms are not high and it would be an injury to the University to fail to recognize a man of his singular merit. His German is remarkably simple and limpid and almost anyone who can read German can follow him;[2] and his personality is, as you know, full of charm. I feel very keenly on this matter. Dörpfeld has shown me especial kindness and I would do anything in my power to bring about the desired result.

I have heard the report,[3] I have not seen it in print yet that you have been invited to take charge of the whole educational system of the state of New York. The invitation is not surprising but I must refuse to believe that you will accept it. The Johns Hopkins University needs you more than it has ever done and your name and fame are bound up with the University. You are responsible for your creation. Of course, your withdrawal would be a stunning blow to me—the culmination of all the troubles of this year.[4]

My general health is good—although I cannot sleep as I ought to sleep and my weak leg refuses the service which it yielded cheerfully at the beginning of the trip.[5]

Letters recently received show me that a great deal of work awaits me and I am afraid that very little of it can be done on this side.

With kind regards to Mrs. Gilman and the young ladies

> I am
>
> Yours faithfully
> B. L. Gildersleeve

President Gilman

1. See No. 96, n. 1.
2. Reporting on his lectures in New York, the *NYTimes*, 13 November 1896: 5, said, "He spoke so deliberately and with such perfection of accent and pronunciation that it was not difficult for one who knew a little about that language to follow him."
3. The initial endowment of the Johns Hopkins University had been common stock of the Baltimore and Ohio Railroad, and although dividends had been paid in stock rather than cash as early as 1878, the university remained financially sound until earnings dropped to 8 percent in 1886, 4 percent in the spring of 1887, and zero from then through 1890. A variety of gifts (including McCoy's, see No. 73, n. 7) produced an emergency fund of $100,000 that saw the Hopkins through the next five years, but the financial stress reached a crisis again in 1896, when Gilman called for a relief fund of a quarter-million dollars in his *Annual Report*. At the same time, Gilman let it be known that he had been offered the post of city superintendent of the schools of New York, a job many felt him likely to take. Within days of the *Report*'s publication, the fund was fully subscribed, and Gilman stayed at the helm. For Gilman's letter of 27 May 1896 to the trustees, see *JHU Circulars*, no. 126 (June 1896): 96, and, further, *Franklin*, 307–19. On 1 January 1897, a luncheon was given by the trustees and professors for those who had contributed to the fund. For Gildersleeve's speech, "The University and the City," see *JHU Circulars*, no. 128 (February 1897): 20.
4. He means the university's troubles; Gildersleeve had suffered no misfortunes recently.
5. See preceding letter, nn. 8–9.

### 93 To: Daniel Coit Gilman
*JHU-Gilman*

Heidelberg, June 29, 1896

My dear Mr. Gilman:

When I last wrote, I did not know how perilously near we were to losing you.[1] Since then I have received fuller information and even now I have not quite recovered from the postliminary fright. You need no assurance from me how I feel in this matter. Apart from the loss to the University, which, at this crisis, would have meant ruin, my own happiness and usefulness, which have been so largely determined by your wisdom and goodness, were at stake. Under no other chief could a man of my temperament have served so cheerfully, so hopefully. In fact I have never thought of working under any other President without serious disquietude. In my not infrequent hours of depression I have gone to you for comfort and have never failed to return with new heart and vigor to my work. . . . no new field is possible for me.[2] I should have missed you inexpressibly. Many problems remain which you alone will be able to solve and I hope that as long as I am connected with the Johns Hopkins University I shall have the inestimable privilege of your friendship and your counsel.

As to the financial crises, the gravity of which I find was not overestimated by pessimists like myself, I suppose the University is safe for five years but I am glad to see that its friends are devising more liberal things than mere safety and I hope we shall see a new and vigorous expansion.— Last night when I was witnessing the illumination of the castle from Professor Ihne's[3] house on the other side of the river, I fell into talk with one of the professors of the University of Heidelberg, who seemed to be deeply interested in our affairs and I am sure that any disaster to the Johns Hopkins would be felt the world round.

As you have seen by the date on this letter I am back again on familiar ground or rather more familiar ground—for Heidelberg has developed very much in the last six years—to say nothing of the forty-two years that have elapsed since I first saw the famous town. My little discourse at the college for girls in Scutari[4] went off very well as I have been told and was listened to devotedly by an audience of some three or four hundred, among them representatives of the Turkish government, of the Greek and American churches, of the Philological Syllogos of Constantinople. America was represented by our Chargé d'affaires[5] and altogether I had a sufficiently dignified audience outside of the Faculty itself and the Robert College[6] people. The Levant Herald[7] gave a fair abstract of the address and a synopsis of it has appeared, I believe, in one of the Armenian papers. The whole visit of nearly a fortnight was a droll episode in my life as well as in my trip and if I did not see Constantinople so well as I might have done, if I had gone there a month before, still I have learned many things that I could have learned in no other way. The ladies of the school were kindness itself and carried out their notions of hospitality into the most minute particulars. From the time I left Athens to the time I reached Vienna I was at no expense whatever except for a few independent ventures of my own and I must say that I have been spoiled by this experience so that for the last three or four days I have resented very much the necessity of putting my hands into my own pockets. I left Constantinople last Tuesday, the 23d, and took the new Constanta or Kûdtendjê [sic][8] route by steamer as far as the Roumanian seaport on the Black Sea—thence via Bucharest and Budapest to Vienna. The railway journey is much more interesting than the route taken by the Orient Express, and as I was personally conducted by the President of the College, Miss Patrick,[9] I had very little trouble with the necessary change of cars and inspection of luggage. At Vienna I staid a couple of days making up my mind what next to do. The season is too early for St. Moritz—and as my general health is suspect I hesitated to go in for a cur at Carlsbad[10] simply because my legs were not all they were ten years ago and so I determined to join my friends the Wheelers at Heidelberg[11] and work up my Greek notes—what I have seen and heard and thought for the last three months will keep me busily employed for many a day and when my university mail finds me, as it will in a few days, I shall have no reason to complain of lack of occupation.

Pardon this long letter and present my best regards to Mrs. Gilman and the young ladies.

Yours faithfully as ever

B. L. Gildersleeve

President Gilman

1. See preceding letter, n. 3.

2. The corner of this page is torn, taking with it the first word(s) of this sentence.

3. Joseph Anton Friedrich Wilhelm Ihne (1821–1902), professor at Heidelberg, is best known for his *Römische Geschichte*, 8 vols. (Leipzig: W. Engelmann, 1868–90), translated by the author as *The History of Rome*, 5 vols. (London: Longmans, Green, 1871–82). His *Early Rome* (London: Longmans, Green, 1876) ran to more than seven editions.

4. The American College for Women (later Constantinople Woman's College) opened as a high school in 1871 at Scutari (Usküdar) on the Anatolian side of the Bosphorus by the Woman's Board of Missions, the auxiliary of the American Board of Commissioners for Foreign Missions. It received a college charter from the Commonwealth of Massachusetts in 1890. See n. 7 below and Mary Mills Patrick, *A Bosporus Adventure: Istanbul (Constantinople) Woman's College, 1871–1924* (Stanford: Stanford University Press, 1934).

5. The minister to Turkey, Alexander Watkins Terrell (1827–1912), was in Washington from 15 April through 10 July, and in his absence, the secretary of the legation, John Wallace Riddle (1864–1941) was chargé d'affaires.

6. Robert College was founded by Americans in 1863 as a liberal arts college for men. Originally chartered in the state of New York, it was nationalized in 1971 and is now Bogaziçi Üniversitesi (University of the Bosphorus).

7. "He told in an entertaining way of his recent visit to the Trojan plain, and how he reproached himself for returning to Athens without a visit to Constantinople" (*Levant Herald and Eastern Express*, 22 June 1896: 313). His address was "Spiritual Rights of Minute Research," which he had given at the Bryn Mawr commencement the preceding June. "He dwelt on the contrast between the new suburb of Philadelphia and ancient Byzantium" (ibid.).

8. Constanta (Rumanian Küstanjê) is Rumania's outlet to the Black Sea, 149 mi. SE of Bucharest, near Tomi, where Ovid was exiled. It was founded by Constantine the Great (274–337 A.D.) in honor of his sister, Constantia.

9. Mary Mills Patrick (1850–1940), originally from New Hampshire, was appointed as a teacher at an American mission school in Turkey and in 1875 joined the American School. She helped develop the school into the American College for Women, and in her summers she studied abroad, receiving a Ph.D. from Bern in 1897 with her dissertation, *Sextus Empiricus and Greek Scepticism* (Cambridge: G. Bell, 1899). She became sole principal of the school in

1899 and retired in 1924, returning to the United States. Her books include *Sappho and the Island of Lesbos* (Boston: Houghton Mifflin, 1912), *The Greek Sceptics* (New York: Columbia University Press, 1929), and her autobiography, *Under Five Sultans* (New York: Century Co., 1929). *DAB*, suppl. 2: 516-17.

10. The sulphur waters of Karlsbad (modern Karlovy Vary in Czechoslovakia) were famed for easing liver ailments. For a contemporary view, see Titus Munson Coan, "Carlsbad Waters," *Harper's Magazine* 67 (1883): 116-28. Gildersleeve returned there in 1907 (No. 137).

11. No. 90, n. 4.

### 94 To: Daniel Coit Gilman
*JHU-Gilman*

Heidelberg, July 6, 1896

Dear Mr. Gilman:

Your kind letter of June 5 reached me day before yesterday having travelled from Baltimore to Athens, thence to Constantinople, to London, and so here. Your communication to the New York people is so explicit that my mind is entirely easy and the Baltimore subscription will secure the University against detriment for the next five years;[1] and really the twentieth century must take care of itself. How happy I am to know that you are still to guide the fortunes of the University—I need not tell you. In my last letter I tried to give expression to my deep feeling on the matter and I am sure you understood me then and understand me now.

As to the Peabody course let me thank you for [your] generous and considerate offer.[2] Athens I shall be glad to take and on looking over my photographs I am fairly confident that I have ample material for illustration. But Delphi and Olympia are embarrassing. The French are very jealous about Delphi[3] and will not allow a note book or a Kodak on the ground and there is little to be said of Olympia to-day unless I take up the monuments. I have several views of the scenery of Delphi, a marvellously impressive place: but of Olympia I have comparatively little.[4] Perhaps I shall be able to get something more from Athens and I believe that the Peabody has a good deal of material that might be utilized for slides freely and renounce the attempt to make it fit closely into the general scheme. Perhaps you would have the goodness to ask Mr. Uhler[5] to order for the Peabody Library the new edition of Murray's Greece[6] which appeared just before I left Athens. It would help him materially in completing the Peabody list of books on Greece in advance of the lectures.

I came here from Vienna about a week ago in order to have a conference with Wheeler as to a scheme which we have /had/ on hand for a year or so and matters are maturing.[7] Then I want to write up my notes of travel and make a number of sketches to be elaborated next winter. I was sorry to leave Greece so abruptly but it seemed impossible for me to make arrangements for further travel /in Greece/ and I needed repose after the long strain. In addition to all the other things that I have in hand I have been invited to make an address at Yale on the opening of the Phelps Hall Oct. 16th.[8]—and that weighs on my mind somewhat as I shall have a very critical audience.

With your example before me I ought to meet all these obligations in a cheerful spirit but I have neither your resources nor your buoyancy and just now I lack the encouragement of your presence.—Still I hope to pull through respectably.

I shall be here a week or so longer and expect then to turn my face southward, as I have engaged passage by Kaiser Wilhelm II which sails from Genoa, Aug. 27.

With best regards to Mrs. Gilman and the young ladies

      I am

                Yours sincerely
                B. L. Gildersleeve

President Gilman

1. No. 92, n. 3.
2. No. 91, n. 11.
3. Delphi, occupied by the modern village of Castri, was bought by the French government in 1891; excavation began in 1892. Periodic reports on the excavations appeared in *BCH*. A complete description of the sites of Delphi and Olympia may be found in the *Princeton Encyclopedia of Classical Sites*, ed. R. Stillwell (Princeton: Princeton University Press, 1976), 264–67 (Delphi) and 646–50 (Olympia). See also L. E. Lord, (cited No. 67, n. 1), 58–62, on why the French did not want Americans taking pictures at the site.
4. The lecture on Olympia and Delphi (16 pp.) exists in the Hopkins Archive. It stresses the importance of the religious aspects of the games. See *60 Days*: 638.
5. The notorious "jailer of the Peabody library," Philip R. Uhler (No. 47, n. 1).
6. *Handbook for Travellers in Greece*, 6th ed. (London: J. Murray, 1896).
7. See following letter.
8. See No. 91, n. 16.

## 95 To: BENJAMIN IDE WHEELER
*California*

                { Hôtel Engadiner-Kulm
                      St. Moritz}
                      Aug. 16, 1896

My dear Wheeler:

Your letter of the 6th from Oxford and the note from Newson[1] reached me yesterday. I am glad to learn that you are pleasantly situated in Oxford and are working out your programme with your wonted steadiness. Trochilos, Amarusia and Poulakion[2] all moving on each in a several orbit of authorship, Wheelwomanship and dentition.

As soon as I could I sent you a post card from Lucerne announcing my arrival. Nothing more definite was possible as I myself was innocent of any fixed plan. I only knew that I was making or rather butting my way towards Italy. Lucerne would, I thought, be as cheerful a sojourn for a solitary wayfarer as Heidelberg and so it would have been, if it had not rained every day for the eight days of my stay and sometimes all day. I was out on the lake only once and as I had descended the Rigi[3] twice I did not think it worthwhile to go up on the only tolerable morning available. Between the showers I strolled through the town, looked into the shop windows and inspected the forlorn tourists who went through the programmes as religiously as if the sun were shining in the sky. The Hotel [sic] de l'Europe[4] where I stayed was crowded but I made few acquaintances. Our touring countrymen are not always the best specimens. My reading alternated between Pausanias and Zola, about as disparate as the Odes of Pindar and Luther's Table Talk between which that old German index-maker[5] divided his time. Every now and then I was cheered by the sight of a familiar face and I had a long talk with my old student Fay,[6] whose methods are not exactly yours; but while I consoled myself with the reflection that if rain was dearer at Lucerne than at Heidelberg, it was cheaper [than] that at St. Moritz yet I broke away from Lucerne as I had done from Heidelberg and Wednesday last went to Chur.—Here my luck changed. The weather improved vastly and the drive over the Alber pass to St. Moritz[7] was one of the interesting experiences of the summer. 'Interesting' is just the word for the Engadine—which cannot compare in sublimity with the Bernese Oberland or the Zermatt region or the valley of Chambéry and yet has a charm of its own. Elliott[8] has found a room for me at the Kulm Hotel—a horribly dear establishment by the way[9]—and here I am for a matter of ten days—What social life there is in the Dorf centres in this hotel—I have met one friend at least and a number of acquaintances and in the hundreds of guests there are several people worth knowing—At all events, it is a preparation for the American world whither I am going. The climate is very bracing but I am tempted to take longer walks than I ought to take though I hardly expect to rival my tramp to Wolfsbrunnen[10]—

It is a short and easy run /from here/ to Genoa which I expect to reach about the twenty-fifth.—If the beautiful weather which glorifies the lake and mountains should change I can go down to the lake of Como for a few days and so I have become reconciled to the Southern route after all—

I return Newson's note herewith. He writes confidently but I imagine we shall both eat Sunday luncheons at his expense before the enterprise is launched. For one I am not going to submit to his hospitality without charging him for it and I have serious thoughts of making him pay for Knauff, Haussmann and my Wildbad experiences[11]—Kurtheater and all—The more I think of what he gave me to eat the more convinced I am that my gout has been seriously aggravated by his injudicious selection of meat and drink.

Give my best regards to Frau Amarusia and Poulaki—with his beautifully phonetic Giddersleeve and believe me

As ever

Yours faithfully
B. L. Gildersleeve

Professor Benjamin Ide Wheeler

1. No. 88, n. 2.

2. Gildersleeve has given the Wheelers Greek names: τροχίλος means "sheave" or "little wheel," hence an approximation of "Wheeler" (the word also means "wren"); "Amarusia" may be Gildersleeve's formation from ἀμαρύσσω meaning "sparkle," "twinkle" (Amarousion is also an area of Athens) and echoes the first name of Wheeler's wife, Amey Webb Wheeler (1853–1935); πουλάκι μου means "darling," [lit. "my little bird"] and is applied to Wheeler's son, Benjamin Webb Wheeler (1893–1980), later professor of history at the University of Michigan.

3. The south slope of the Rigi mountains consists of broad terraces and easy slopes looking out over a vista of Lake Lucerne, making it one of the favorite Swiss resorts of Gildersleeve's day.

4. A first-class hotel on the right bank of the Reuss.

5. Unknown; possibly Boeckh (No. 50, n. 3), editor of *Index Lectionum*. For Gildersleeve, a Pindarist, reading the Table-Talk, see *H&H*, 85.

6. Edwin Whitfield Fay (1865–1920), one of America's most original and prolific Sanskritists after Whitney, was a native of Louisiana, received his M.A. from Southwestern Presbyterian University (1883), was fellow in Greek at Hopkins (1888–90), where he received his Ph.D. in Sanskrit. After a year at Michigan and another at Texas, Fay taught at Washington and Lee (1893–99) and then returned to Texas (1899–1920). He wrote *The History of Education in Louisiana* (Washington, D.C.: U.S. Printing Office, 1898), an edition of the *Mostellaria* (Boston: Allyn and Bacon, 1902), and thirty-two articles and nine reviews for *AJP*. *DAB* 6: 304; *NatCAB* 24: 328–29.

7. Known for its baths and walks, St. Moritz is the highest of the Engadine villages.

8. On A. M. Elliott, see No. 50, n. 13.

9. "An extensive pile of buildings at the upper end of the village" (*Baedeker's Switzerland* [Leipzig: Karl Baedeker, 1906], 447), whose rooms cost between 4–12 fr. ($1–2) as opposed to the Hôtel de l'Europe in Lucerne, where Gildersleeve paid 3–6 fr. A number of Baltimore socialites, including the businessman Richard Janney White were at St. Moritz at the time (BLG to Gilman, 17 August 1896).

10. About 1.5 mi. east of Heidelberg.

11. Gildersleeve accompanied Wheeler to Wildbad, where Mrs. Wheeler was spending a large part of the summer taking the alkaline waters as a treatment for her gout.

## 96 To: DANIEL COIT GILMAN
*JHU-Gilman*

{ University Club
Baltimore. }
Sept. 10, 1896

My dear Mr. Gilman:

Your two letters, one of Aug. 30, one of Sept. 4, were handed to me by Miller on my arrival at the University this afternoon.

Dörpfeld will reach New York[1] next week and a formal invitation ought to be sent him as soon after his arrival as possible. He will, I understand, go to Ithaca first where he will be the guest of our friend Wheeler. Of course, when I see him at Yale I shall urge him to come but the invitation must proceed from the head of the University. The evening of Nov. 4 would be fatal to any lecture but the election will not matter much as to the afternoon. I shall be very happy to join Dörpfeld at dinner, as you propose, but I am very desirous of doing something for him myself and I am sorry that my house is too small to allow me the privilege of inviting him to stay with me.

I arrived in New York last Tuesday after a delightful voyage. Two slight showers and a couple of hours of fog were the only drawbacks. The Kaiser Wilhelm II is a very comfortable boat, I had a good stateroom and a pleasant room with M[r.] Nancrede[2] of Ann Arbor. The Jacobis[3] and Miss Emerson,[4] friends of my Athenian days were at the same table as were Fox of New Haven[5] whom I had long known and Arthur Frothingham[6] who kindly showed me some of his antique treasures he is bringing in from Italy—In fact the voyage was one of the most pleasant of my fourteen crossings of the Atlantic and I should have been sorry when it was over had I not looked forward to meeting my people in New York. The mountains of Maryland and the seashore of New England had done wonders for our invalid and I hoped to find Emma even better than she was when I saw her but I am sorry to say that New York undid some of the good work that had been wrought and I hastened to send her back to the mountains again. So we came down from New York to-day. My wife and Emma went on to Monterey[7] and I remain here to straighten out matters. Fortunately the two Millers have made my work comparatively easy and I expect to get off again on Saturday to remain in the mountains until the University forces reassemble. Just now the buildings are very lonely but Mr. Murray[8] has got back and that is always the dawn of returning life.

With best regards to Mrs. Gilman and the young ladies

     I am

                        Yours sincerely
                        B. L. Gildersleeve

President Gilman

1. Dörpfeld (No. 91, n. 2) lectured in German at Hopkins on "The Acropolis of Athens" and on "Troy" on 4 and 7 November, then at Columbia University on "Troy and the Homeric Citadel," "Olympia," "Greek Theatre," "Recent Excavations in Greece," "The Acropolis," and "Tiryns and Mycenae" (10–19 November). The first two lectures on the Columbia campus were so crowded that the remaining four were given downtown at the Academy of Medicine.

2. Perhaps Charles Beylard Guérard de Nancrede (1847–1921), chair of surgery at the University of Michigan from 1889 to 1921. See *DAB* 14: 379–80.

3. Abraham Jacobi (1830-1919), a native of Westphalia, received his Ph.D. from Bonn in 1851 and moved to New York in 1853. He was professor of children's diseases at New York Medical College (1860-64), New York University Medical College (1865-70), and the College of Physicians and Surgeons (1870-1919), and married Mary Corinna Putnam (1842-1906), daughter of the publisher George P. Putnam and one of the first female members of the American Medical Association. See *DAB* 10: 563-65.

4. Mary Alice Emerson (1865-1922), the first woman granted seminar privileges at Oxford, served in a number of schools before becoming dean of women and professor of English at Carleton College (1907-11) and then professor of English at Boston University. In addition to religious plays and pageants, she wrote most of *Composition and Rhetoric* with Sara E. H. Lockwood (Boston: Ginn, 1901). *NatCAB* 20: 146.

5. George Levi Fox (1852-1931) graduated from Yale in 1874, taught at Hillhouse High School in New Haven (1877-85), was rector of Hopkins Grammar School (1885-1931), and from 1896 was lecturer on comparative municipal government at Yale. *NatCAB* 4: 555.

6. Arthur Lincoln Frothingham (1859-1923) was born and educated in Rome, received his Ph.D. from Leipzig (1883), and was fellow in Semitic languages (1882-85) and lecturer in Babylonian and Assyrian art and archeology at Hopkins (1883-86). He then became professor of archeology and the history of art at the College of New Jersey (now Princeton) (swapping ancient history for history of art), where he stayed until his retirement in 1905. He founded the *American Journal of Archaeology* in 1885 and edited it until 1896 (No. 37, n. 2). From 1895 to 1896 he was associate director of the American School of Classical Studies in Rome. Among his works are *The Monuments of Christian Rome from Constantine to the Renaissance* (New York: Macmillan, 1908), *Roman Cities in Italy and Dalmatia* (New York: York, Sturgis and Walton, 1910), *A Text-Book of the History of Sculpture* (with Allan Marquand) (New York: Longmans, Green, 1896), and *Stephen Bar Sudaili the Syrian Mystic and the Book of Hierotheos* (Leyden: E. J. Brill, 1886). See, further, *DAB* 7: 42-43 and A. A. Donohoe, "One Hundred Years of the *American Journal of Archaeology*: An Archival History," *AJA* 89 (1985): 3-30.

7. Monterey, at Blue Ridge Summit, Pa., is just over the Pennsylvania state line, fifteen mi. WSW of Gettysburg, Pa., and about twenty mi. ENE of Hagerstown, Md. See two letters following.

8. Nicholas Murray (1842-1918), librarian at Hopkins, older brother of Thomas C. Murray (1850-79), the first Hopkins librarian. Nicholas, after attending Williams (A.B. 1862) and Columbia (LL.B. 1867), came to Hopkins in 1879 as secretary to Gilman and was made librarian and manager of the Publication Agency (later Johns Hopkins Press). One of his nephews was Nicholas Murray Butler, president of Columbia. *French*, 211-12.

## ❦ 6 ❧

# FRUSTRATIONS AND HONORS, 1896–1905

Gildersleeve rose to a position of eminence in the classical world comparable to that of W. W. Goodwin of Harvard (No. 50, n. 5). Both were famous syntacticians, both were president of the APA twice, together they received honorary degrees from Yale (No. 120), but Gildersleeve's Oxford and Cambridge degrees (No. 131) came no fewer than fifteen years after Goodwin's. Goodwin had no journal to rob him of free time (No. 128), and he enjoyed the benefits and resources of the Eliot professorship of Greek from the age of twenty-nine. But he was not so identified with the literature (No. 129) and ethos (No. 124) of his region as Gildersleeve, who, for his literary contributions as well as his scholarship, was elected to the National Institute and later the American Academy of Arts and Letters, as Goodwin was not.

With his growing reputation came some deep frustrations as Gildersleeve realized his career at Hopkins would not turn out exactly as imagined. There was no substantial relief from the drudgery of the *AJP*, and the advance of age made him reluctant to begin projects of interest (Nos. 114, 128). He still had dreams of getting out a Greek grammar (No. 101) and had reluctantly given up on editions of the *Frogs* and *Symposium*. (No. 71, n. 8; No. 128) His great work of the period was the summation of his career as a teacher, the *Syntax*, which moved agonizingly slowly (Nos. 103, 108). He had high hopes for the Gildersleeve-Wheeler Series, partly because of his affection for his collaborator, but the series was never substantially realized, despite Gildersleeve's considerable efforts (Nos. 98, 103, 114).

But the failure of the Gildersleeve-Wheeler Series was offset by the success of the Gildersleeve-Lodge Series (Nos. 104, 113, 126), which brought his Latin books back into use, and by the beginning of the Smyth Series (No. 114). He was increasingly called on for advice (Nos. 105, 113) and found disciples among those he had never had as students (No. 104). But in the very year in which he was praised by the Oxford orator for the editorship of the journal (No. 131 and n. 6) that put American classical scholarship on the world stage, two new journals that were clearly rivals of *AJP*

(No. 132), despite protestations from their editors, were begun, and Gildersleeve became anxious over the future quality of his creation.

His personal life changed as well. Friends such as Child (No. 97), Usener, Lane, and especially Hübner (No. 117) died. Gilman, to whom he felt he owed so much, retired as president (Nos. 112, 118) and Gildersleeve felt bereft. If he imagined his "world were coming to an end" with the marriage of his daughter Emma (Nos. 107–8) in 1898, the loss was restored a year later by the arrival of Katharine Ward Lane, who taught him what he called *l'art d'être grandpère*.

### 97 To: ELIZABETH ELLERY SEDGEWICK CHILD
*Houghton*

Blue Ridge Summit
Franklin Co. Penn.[1]
Sept. 14, 1896

My dear Mrs. Child:

As one of your dear husband's[2] oldest friends and associates I venture even in the hour of your fresh grief to send a word of sympathy. Although I had seen him so rarely of late years the old tie abode as strong as ever and his affectionate greeting made me feel at each interview that there was no change in him since we were both young men in Germany. In the high distinction which he won, in his great achievements in the world of letters I took a personal pride and nothing gave me more pleasure than when I found that his warm heart received into the circle of his friends those who were nearest and dearest to me so that my wife had a place in his affection and knows how to measure my sorrow. There are many in Baltimore who learned to know him and to love him when he was lecturing at the Johns Hopkins University and it is a sad pleasure to remember how he seemed to enjoy his visits to our quiet home.

My wife joins me in messages of tender sympathy and we both hope that you will continue to count us among your friends.

I am

Yours sincerely
B. L. Gildersleeve

Mrs. F. J. Child

1. See preceding letter, n. 7.
2. On Francis J. Child, see No. 21, n. 1.

98 To: BENJAMIN IDE WHEELER
*California*

Monterey, Blue Ridge Summit[1]
Franklin Co. Penn. Sept. 26, 1896

Dear Professor Wheeler:

Though I have no direct evidence I take for granted that you and yours are once more at Cornell and under your own roof tree. Your Oxford letter for which you have my best thanks reassured me as to the success of your visit to England and I hope that your usual good fortune followed you across the Atlantic.

For my own part I had one of the smoothest and most pleasant passages on my record and I had the great good fortune of finding my family in New York and my daughter in much improved health. During my short stay in New York I saw Newson,[2] who seemed to be satisfied with our progress in the matter of the series. By the way, I have just received a letter from Newhall,[3] the man whom I had thought of in connexion with the Plato part of the scheme. He tells me that he has finished his school-edition of the Charmides and Lysis—two dialogues which he has been studying for the last six months at my suggestion—Of course I had to answer that he must be patient if he is desirous of having his work appear in our series. I do not know whether you have his name on our list. He is Barker Newhall, formerly instructor in Brown University, now headmaster of the classical department of an Academy in Monson, Mass. He made his Ph.D. some years ago at the J.H.U. and his dissertation dealt with the mimetic features of Plato's Gorgias, if I remember aright.

Finding that my presence was not urgently needed in Baltimore and that No. 66 of the Journal was closed, I came up here after a day or two of work at the University.—The climate is delicious at this season—almost too delicious for work—but I have managed to get together a number of paragraphs that will have to pass muster for an address on Oct. 9th.[4]—

Monday the 28th I return to Baltimore and take up the burden of life in sober earnest.

Did you find time to write that review of Thumb while you were in Oxford?[5]

Give my best to Dörpfeld,[6] if he is in your reach. Mr. Gilman promised to send him a formal invitation to Baltimore.—which I will reinforce when I see him at Yale.—

My humble service to Frau Amarusia and affectionate messages to Poulaki,[7] whose phonetic transmutation of my name is a philological feat worthy of permanent record.—It seems so strange that I am going back to a life in which there is to be no Spitz Merlin,[8] no Hotel u. Pension Lang[9] and all that these names imply.—

      Goodbye

               Yours faithfully
               B. L. Gildersleeve

Professor B. I. Wheeler

1. No. 96, n. 7.
2. No. 88, n. 2.
3. Barker Newhall (1867–1924) received his A.B. from Haverford in 1887 and his Ph.D. from Hopkins in 1891, having been fellow in Greek that year. He was instructor in Greek at Brown (1892–94), returned to Hopkins as fellow by courtesy (1895–96), and after his year in Monson was professor of Greek at Kenyon College from 1897 to 1924. His dissertation was entitled *The Dramatic and Mimetic Features of the Gorgias of Plato*. He published *The Charmides, Laches and Lysis of Plato* (New York: American Book Co., 1900) and *The Barker Family of Plymouth Colony and County* (Cleveland: F. W. Roberts, 1900).
4. On 9 October, Gildersleeve spoke in McCoy Hall, probably either on Athens or on Olympia and Delphi. William Henry Welch of the Medical School was also on the program.
5. Wheeler's article, "The Question of Language-Standard in Modern Greece," *AJP* 18 (1897): 19–25, is essentially a review of Albert Thumb's *Handbuch der neugriechischen Volkssprache: Grammatik. Texte. Glossar.* (Strassburg: K. J. Trübner, 1895).
6. No. 91, n. 2.
7. No. 95, n. 2.
8. Spitz is a pension on Schlierbach Road on the right bank of the Neckar in Heidelberg.
9. A private hotel on Rohrbacher-Strasse in Heidelberg.

## 99 To: Benjamin Ide Wheeler
*California*

               1002 N. Calvert St. Baltimore
               Oct. 31 1896

My dear Wheeler: The blue prints have not turned up and I am becoming superstitious about the illustrations to my lectures. However, I shall have enough for Athens and if your man sends me the Zappeion for which I sent him the photograph day before yesterday there will be no sensible lack. For Olympia and Delphi I am badly off and I am sending Mr. White[1] by this mail a few photographs. Surely he can get up the slides by the end of the week.

I shall open my mouth wide on the third of November and the Lord will fill it[2]—I hope it is the Lord—with McKinley, the most nauseous dose I ever swallowed[3]—but this state is too close at least in my judgment to allow the sentimentality of voting for Palmer. You are a lucky man.

Does it not seem absurd for an old creature like myself to be making

phrases about Athens and showing lantern slides on the very night when
the future of everything and everybody is trembling in the balances? Again
I say you are a lucky man for you are in the fight.[4]

Yours faithfully<br>
B. L. Gildersleeve

Professor B. I. Wheeler

    1. Unidentified man who converted photographs to slides for Gildersleeve.
    2. Psalm 81:10: "I am the Lord your God, who brought you up out of the land of Egypt, /
Open your mouth wide and I will fill it."
    3. The presidential election of 1896 was waged on the question of the gold standard, the
plank supported by the eventual winner, William McKinley (1843-1901), Republican of
Ohio, opposed by William Jennings Bryan (1860-1925), Democrat of Nebraska, who favored
unlimited coinage of silver. A group of renegade conservative Democrats who favored the
gold standard ("Gold Democrats") nominated their own candidate, John M. Palmer (1817-
1900) of Illinois. The Maryland vote was not as close as Gildersleeve predicted: the state went
54.7 percent for McKinley to 41.6 percent for Bryan and 1 percent for Palmer. The national
plurality for McKinley was only 51 percent. Gildersleeve, as staunch a fiscal conservative as
he had been during the war, wrote Wheeler on 6 November [California]: "We are all rejoicing
in the sound money victory with the one reserve, that is with unabated hostility to the other
planks in the Republican platform. I was never nearer becoming an active politician."
    4. Wheeler had been an active Democrat since 1880, when he helped form a committee to
reform Rhode Island politics. He was active in Grover Cleveland's second campaign (1888),
but in spite of his Democratic sympathies, he formed an enduring friendship with Theodore
Roosevelt, and he was Theodore Roosevelt professor at the University of Berlin in 1909-10.

100 To: Henry Rushton Fairclough<br>
Stanford

Nov. 14 1896

Dear Professor Fairclough:

    I should like to keep your dissertation[1] by me a little longer partly for
the pleasure of going over it more carefully, partly in order to read the
Introduction and the chapter on Euripides before the Johns Hopkins Philological Association which meets next Friday. But I have not forgotten that
you want the proof back as early as possible so that your publishers may
bring it out this month and it has already been in my hands what you will
doubtless consider an unconscionable time and then I have no express permission from you to make the desired use of it and so the dissertation is on
its way back to California.

    A criticism of a treatise like yours to be worth anything would require
careful meditation and ever since my return to Baltimore I have been under pressure that prevented anything like prolonged reflection on other

people's work. But I am confident that your dissertation will do you great credit and while the Johns Hopkins University has had very little part in your training I am glad to have so thoughtful and attractive a paper go out from our school. To the list of authorities I have nothing serious to add and my eyes have detected few typographical errors. One or two you will find noted on the margin.

With best wishes for the happy continuance of your work on the study of Greek Literature

I am

Yours faithfully
B. L. Gildersleeve

Professor H. R. Fairclough

1. Fairclough's dissertation, *The Attitude of the Greek Tragedians toward Nature*, was published in Toronto by Rowsell and Hutchinson in 1897.

101 To: Benjamin Ide Wheeler
*California*

1002 N. Calvert St.
Baltimore May 21, 1897

My dear Wheeler:

Your proof reached me this morning and shortly afterwards Newson[1] came in all anxiety about the series. The Larger Syntax is at last getting into type and I have before me the first batch of 20 pages. It will be pushed as fast as possible but the progress during the summer will necessarily be slow. Still the 750pp. to which I shall limit myself will be set up in the course of the next year and the syntax of the grammar—our grammar— can be made pari passu. If you can prepare the inflexions meanwhile we can have that cornerstone ready among the earliest of the books. Now that this beginning has been made, the contract ought to be put into final shape and Mrs. Wheeler's fortune assured.

I see that you are continuing to enlighten the world on things Greek.[2] Our friends have certainly made a deplorable mistake—which anyone could have seen in advance—and my favorite non tam turpe fuit vinci quam contendisse decorum est[3] hardly applies. Scudder writes me that you are to have an article in the June Atlantic[4] to which I look forward with eagerness.

Last Monday I returned from a week's lecturing at Northwestern[5]—

good houses and kind words—I felt the strain somewhat but as you remarked when we were in the Peloponnesus together[6]—I am tough—
With best regards to Frau Amarousia and Poulaki[7]

> I am

> > Yours faithfully
> > B. L. Gildersleeve

Professor B. I. Wheeler

1. No. 88, n. 2.
2. "The Modern Greek as Fighting Man," *North American* 164 (May 1897): 609-16,
described from a historical perspective the character of the Greek military in light of Greek
encroachments on Crete in 1897 that precipitated the Graeco-Turkish War of that year, a
quick and humiliating defeat for the Greeks, as Gildersleeve predicts in the next sentence.
[3]Ovid *Met.* 9.6: "It was not so shameful to be conquered as it was proper to have con-
tended." See *AJP* 34 (1913): 493 ( = *SBM*, 302) and cf. 35 (1914): 234.
4. "Greece and the Eastern Question," *Atlantic* 79 (June 1897): 721-33. On Scudder, see
"Correspondents."
5. Probably invited by J. A. Scott (see "Correspondents"), Gildersleeve gave six lectures
at the First Methodist Church on: "A Grammarian's Spectacles" (Greek and Roman influence on English), "An Evening with Odysseus" (concluding with his reading of "The Ballad
of the Swineherd," his translation of the Eumaeus song, published in *The Pathfinder* at Sewanee [July 1907], 2-9), "An Hour with Sappho," "A Talk with Aristophanes," "Poet and
Potter" (the similarities of influence and development of literature and the plastic arts in
Greece; this lecture of fifty-nine pages, survives in the Hopkins Archive as "Evanston Lecture
VI"), and "Hellas and Hesperia" (the survival of Greek ideals in America). He also addressed
students informally at chapel on scholarship and methods of study and spoke to the Twentieth Century Club of Chicago on "Athens as I Saw It in 1896" (*Northwestern* 17, no. 25
[20 May 1897]: 1-3.
6. No. 90, n. 4.
7. No. 95, n. 2.

102 To: ARMISTEAD CHURCHILL GORDON[1]
*UVa-Gordon*

1002 N. Calvert St.
Baltimore May 26, 1897

Dear Sir:
I have not met you since the old days but I still feel a certain proprietary
right in those whom I knew as students in the University of Virginia and
still feel a special pride in those who like yourself have nobly fulfilled the
promise of their youth. And this must be my excuse for addressing you on a
matter that concerns the institution with which you have so responsible a
connexion.
Your Board is about to select a President. It is a new departure, a break

with tradition and much depends on the wisdom of your choice. The President of today is preeminently a man of affairs, a man who knows the world and the things of the world. Scholarship of a certain order is desirable to give finish and grace, to the ready wit, to the offhand speech and the frequent letters but there must be no pedantry, no display of recondite learning. The President must be in touch with every department and not entangled in any one. You want a Southern man who is in sympathy with your past and yet not hampered by it—a teacher who is familiar with the problems of education, a business man above all who knows the way to administer and to increase your revenue, a man who has moved much in society and possesses the gift of arousing interest and enthusiasm. Such a man you have to hand in Gordon McCabe.[2] The office would be the fit crown to a long career of educational work and I am sure that he would throw himself into the duties of the position with entire devotedness.—I have just answered one letter of inquiry from a member of the Board and have expressed myself to the same effect and I hope that you will but look upon the matter as I do.

Yours very truly<br>
B. L. Gildersleeve

Hon. Armistead C. Gordon

1. Armistead Churchill Gordon (1855-1931), Gildersleeve's student while at the University of Virginia (1873-75), was the university's rector (1897-98; 1906-18). At Gordon's instance, the board appointed a three-man committee with himself as chair in June 1896 to study the question of appointing a president for the university to facilitate the chaotic communication between the board and the chairman of the faculty. On 12 May 1897 the majority report of the committee favored appointing a president but retaining a chairman of the faculty, and Gildersleeve assumed the presidential search was on. But some faculty who felt they had not been adequately consulted on the matter from the outset, along with various conservative alumni groups, opposed the change, with the result that a president was not chosen until 1904, when Edwin A. Alderman (see "Correspondents"), then president of Tulane, accepted the position. See *UVa Alumni Bull.* 4 (August 1897) for the reports and *Bruce*, 5: 15-38.

2. William Gordon McCabe (1841-1920) received his B.A. from the University of Virginia (1861) and A.M. from William and Mary (1868) and Williams (1889). He rose from private to colonel in the Confederate Army and after the Civil War he established a university school at Petersburg (which employed Bain and Thornton [see "Correspondents"], among others), moving to Richmond in 1895. He was president of the Virginia Historical Society in 1903 and served on the University of Virginia board of visitors for eight years. A noted writer, he published a variety of books, including *The Defence of Petersburg* (Richmond: G. W. Gary, 1876), *Aids to Latin Orthography*, and *Ballads of Battles and Bravery* (both New York: Harper and Bros., 1876 and 1879 respectively). He reviewed Gildersleeve's *Persius* in the *Boston Evening Transcript*, 25 June 1875. When it appeared that a president would be appointed in 1897, McCabe, who was to receive a Litt.D. from Yale in that year, was the leading candidate, (*Bruce*, 23-28). See A. C. Gordon's *Memories and Memorials of William Gordon McCabe*, 2 vols. (Richmond: Old Dominion, 1925). For McCabe on Gildersleeve, see his "Theodore Sandford Garnett 1844-1915," *UVa Alumni Bull.*, 3d ser., 9, no. 3 (July 1916): 409.

103 To: BENJAMIN IDE WHEELER
*California*

June 7, 1897

My dear Wheeler:
The oral examinations for Ph.D. are over and I am free to consider the matter of the series.

The Larger Greek Syntax is going forward. Some thirty pages are actually in type and I hope that the composition will move on steadily but taught by old experience, I don't expect to see the book printed before the winter of '98. When do /you/ wish to get the smaller grammar out?

I am still under the impression that when we were in Heidelberg we made out a provisional list of names. Forman[1] and Bristol[2] were among them. We ought to secure C. F. Smith[3] of Wisconsin; and among southern scholars Addison Hogue[4] of Washington and Lee would do good work on Attic lines—

Whenever a name or scheme occurs to me I will write.

When I read your pronouncement in the North American[5] I congratulated myself that I curtly refused to discuss the same theme. I knew nothing about the matter, it is true but that little circumstance does not always keep me back.

Your Atlantic article is, I suppose, a vaunt-courier[6] of your Alexander.[7] What a trenchant writer you are! There is no sense in wishing you more power to your elbow. After reading you I seem to myself, what I am, a dawdling old gentleman—

Best regards to Frau Amarousia and to Poulaki.[8] My knee has been giving me some trouble and I am ready to join the Wheelersche Kleeblatt, Trochilus, Trochile and Trochilidion[9] of Wildbad.

Yours faithfully
B. L. Gildersleeve

Professor B. I. Wheeler

1. No. 85, n. 2.
2. No. 86, n. 1.
3. See "Correspondents."
4. Addison Hogue (1849–1942) graduated from Hampden-Sydney College in 1869 and was one of Gildersleeve's early postgraduate students at the University of Virginia (1869–72). He became professor of Greek at Hampden-Sydney (1872–86), did further postgraduate work at various German universities (1883–85), and was named professor of Greek at the University of Mississippi (1886–93). In 1889 he published his only scholarly book, *Irregular Verbs of Attic Prose* (Boston: Ginn, 1889), and in 1894 he became professor of Greek at Washington and Lee, where he remained until his retirement in 1921. He also wrote *The Best Way to Teach Greek to Beginners* (Boston: Allyn and Bacon, 1900).
5. No. 101, n. 2.

6. *King Lear* 3.2.1: "[Ye Winds,] Vaunt-couriers to oak-cleaving thunderbolts."

7. See Ibid., n. 4. Wheeler wrote a series of articles on Alexander the Great for the *Century* 57–58 (n.s. 35–36) (November 1898–October 1899): 1–24, 202–19, 354–73, 554–71, 678–91, 818–31; 24–38, 230–44, 396–409, 525–39, 764–78, 900–911, from which came *Alexander the Great: The Merging of East and West in Universal History* ("Heroes of the Nations" Series) (New York: Putnam, 1900).

8. No. 95, n. 2.

9. Gildersleeve uses the masculine, feminine, and diminutive of his formation for "Wheeler" (see No. 95, n. 2).

## 104 To: Charles Wesley Bain
### *UNC-Bain*

June 7, 1897

Dear Sir:

In reply to your letter of the 1st inst. I desire to say that my part in the projected Gildersleeve-Lodge series will be very small.[1] I cannot undertake to read MSS.—and though I have made an exception in your case I have not time to point out the details that have disturbed me and as to the plan I renounce all pretensions to an opinion. My own elementary books have been decided failures—if I may judge by results and my attempts to give a semblance of life to disjointed phrases are a horrible memory, recalled most vividly by the contemplation of the difficulties under which you have labored in constructing a book and of the meagre vocabulary, which is all that present methods allow. I make no doubt that your book is better composed to the end in view than anything that I could excogitate but I have no passion for elementary teaching, no especial fitness for it, and I leave the whole thing in D$^r$. Lodge's[2] hands and am willing to abide by his decision—From my talk with him I gathered that he was willing to take your book into the Series but not as a substitute for the Primer for which he has other plans.

Do you think that Mooney's use of my L.G., to which he does not refer once, is legitimate?[3] He seems to have presumed the confidence of a number of my particular friends and I must confess that I was at first somewhat incensed to find that he helped himself to whatever suited him in terminology, examples, and translations.

Many thanks for your kind offer to help in proof-reading. My assistant D$^r$. Miller[4] is an admirable proofreader and while I should value another pair of fresh eyes I cannot spare the time that would be lost in the transmission of proofs. When we reach the stage of the plateproofs, I shall bear your generous proposition in mind.—[5]

Hoping that when D$^r$. Lodge returns matters will adjust themselves to the satisfaction of all concerned

I am

Yours sincerely

B. L. Gildersleeve

Chas. W. Bain Esq.

1. The University Publishing Company, founded in 1868 with support from Horace Greeley and August Belmont of New York, the firm of Robert Garrett and Sons (No. 90, n. 9), and Johns Hopkins of Baltimore, aimed at producing textbooks by the best scholars of the South. "A Northern business man who had published an *Army and Navy Journal*, or something of the sort, during the war, when he found his occupation gone, tried to exploit the local patriotism of the South by getting up a series of Southern textbooks, with results that will not be forgotten by those who invested their money or their time in the venture" ("Hazards of Reviewing," *Nation* 101 [8 July 1915]: 49). Jefferson Davis was an early stockholder, and the director and long-time vice-president was Gildersleeve's old commander, Gen. John B. Gordon of Georgia (see Allen P. Tankersley, *John B. Gordon: A Study in Gallantry* [Atlanta: Whitehall Press, 1955], 320-22). Among its first offerings were a revision of Gildersleeve's *Latin Grammar* (1872) and M. F. Maury's *Physical Geography* (1873). In 1892 the company was reorganized by C. L. Patton and the Gildersleeve-Lodge Latin Series was announced in 1899, under the supervision of Gildersleeve and Gonzalez Lodge (see "Correspondents") of Bryn Mawr (later Columbia), with the cooperation of Moses S. Slaughter (1860-1923) of Wisconsin (later Texas) and Thomas Fitz-Hugh (1862-1957) of Texas (later Virginia). There were four initial offerings in the Preparatory Series: a school edition of Gildersleeve's *Latin Grammar* (three-fifths the size of the larger grammar and edited by Lodge), Bain's *First Book in Latin*, J. N. Anderson's *Selections from Ovid* (No. 86, n. 2), and *Cicero's Orations* by R. W. Tunstall (1851-1917), with a Caesar promised by Bain and an *Aeneid* promised by Fitz-Hugh. There were seventeen offerings in the Collegiate Series. When the company liquidated in 1906, the Gildersleeve-Lodge Series was sold to D. C. Heath Co. See, further, John Tebbel, *A History of Book Publishing in the United States*, vol. 2, *The Expansion of an Industry, 1854-1919* (New York: R. R. Bowker, 1975), 586.

2. See "Correspondents."

3. W. D. Mooney, *A Brief Latin Grammar* (New York: American Book Co., 1897).

4. See "Correspondents."

5. Bain in fact did read the proofs and Gildersleeve acknowledges his help in the preface.

## 105 To: ALBERT STANBURROUGH COOK
### *Cornell*

Nov. 13, 1897

Dear Professor Cook:

You have asked me a number of hard questions in the last few years and I reflect with sorrow and mortification that I have never answered even one—either to your satisfaction or to mine and yet it seems that you have kept the hardest until now.[1] So few of our American classical scholars are professedly literary men or even literary critics that I should have to go into matters of personal impression if I were to make out a list of those "whose taste and judgment, whose esthetic sense and perception of essential values have not been impaired by their erudition." And to make my judgment a matter of personal impression rather than of documentary evidence would be highly invidious. American classical scholars have done very well on German lines of work but they do not seem to me to have excelled so much on the literary and aesthetic side. There is not one that can measure with English or French scholars. Most of them have not even tried. See the American Journal of Philology <u>passim</u>.[2] It is a sad state of affairs and I assure you that my own career to which you refer in such kind terms has been a very wobbling and unsatisfactory one to the man who has run it and has run it—in the course of nature—nearly to an end.

Yours faithfully
B. L. Gildersleeve

Professor Albert S. Cook

1. Cook's letter is lost, but Yale was presumably seeking a classicist to replace Whitney (see "Correspondents"), who died in 1894. Cook may also have wanted a replacement for Carleton Lewis Bronson (1866-1948), who had been trained at Yale (B.A. 1887, Ph.D. 1897), had been instructor in Latin (1889-90), tutor in Greek and Latin (1892-96), and instructor in Greek (1896-97). Charles William Leverett Johnson (1870-1954), a student of Gildersleeve's (B.A. 1891, Ph.D. 1896), became instructor in Greek (1897-1900). Cook may also have been seeking a candidate for the recently established (1894) Emily Sanford professorship of English literature, awarded to Charlton Miner Lewis (1866-1923), who held the chair from 1899 to 1923.

2. Gildersleeve refers to the fact that among the early contributors to *AJP*, the English tended to provide most of the literary articles, whereas American contributions tended to be more scientific. For his later views on English and French scholarship, see *AJP* 37 (1916): 494-504 ( = *SBM*, 364-76) and 30 (1909): 231.

106 To: Martha Carey Thomas
*Bryn Mawr*

1002 N. Calvert St.,
Baltimore, Nov. 14, 1897

My dear Miss Thomas:

I have just returned from the meeting held at the University in commemoration of your beloved and lamented father.[1] The review of that large, untiring, beneficent, loving activity made the ordinary life which so many are content to lead seem inexpressibly narrow and mean. What a heartsearching for those who have to look back on a career of like length unilluminated by a spirit like his! But, after all, that spirit was a special endowment. It is not to be purchased by a forthputting of will. A shining light—that is possible. A burning light—No!

Everyone that has ever known him even slightly will miss him but the consolation of a rounded and triumphant career abides. It is what every man who has aught in him of the higher life would wish for himself. But I cannot think of this consolation when my thoughts turn to you for I divine the depths of a sorrow that can not be fathomed. You inherit so much from your father that you are for me his representative and I owe you both more than I have ever told for the quick intellectual sympathy with my work which ardent man and aspiring girl showed in those earlier Baltimore days. I rejoice in all your success as I love to think of your almost daughterly kindness to me and I claim the privilege in this hour of your bereavement, the sad privilege of sorrowing with you.

Yours faithfully and affectionately,
B. L. Gildersleeve

Miss M. Carey Thomas

1. James Carey Thomas (1833–97), one of seven Quakers on the first board of trustees, was the only physician. A descendant of seventeenth-century Maryland landowners, he had served on the board of managers at the Quaker Haverford College, and was trustee of Hopkins from 1870 until his death. As early as 1876 he had pressed the board to admit women on a full-time basis. In 1889 he secured the gift of $100,000 (provided by various wealthy women) for the medical school, providing it would admit women on an equal basis with men. Of his value to Hopkins, Hawkins (p. 5) says, "[His] good deeds defy enumeration, and the promotion of education was one of his chief activities." See also E. Finch, *Carey Thomas of Bryn Mawr* (New York: Harper and Bros., 1947), 67; Gilman's memoir in *JHU Circulars*, no. 133 (December 1897): 37; and A. B. Thomas, *The Story of the Baltimore Yearly Meeting from 1672 to 1938* (Baltimore: Weant, 1938), 97–98, 111.

107 To: BENJAMIN LAWTON WIGGINS
*Sewanee*

1002 N. Calvert St.
Baltimore Feb$^y$ 20, 1898

My dear Vice-Chancellor:

The other day I was looking through D$^r$. Hoffman's[1] Baccalaureate sermon and my eye lingered on the photograph of Fulford Hall[2] with the good Bishop musing on the porch. I little thought that I was so soon to receive the intelligence that I was poorer by one friend in a world that does not hold many such friends. I knew that his health was not robust but his sudden departure was a sad surprise. So many of my companions and contemporaries have died in the last year or two that I feel the loneliness of old age coming over me and find myself spending more and more time with my memories. The Bishop was all goodness and loving kindness to me from the first time I met him and he was so intimately associated with the months I passed at Sewanee that in reviewing those interesting episodes of my life, I shall often have occasion to think of him. Present my sincere condolence to Mrs. Quintard and to your wife. Mrs. Wiggins' devotion to her father touched another chord on my heart—and made me love and admire her doubly. My thoughts will be much with your darkened household.

Professor Piggott[3] whom I met a few days [ago] told me that you expected to stop in Baltimore about this time or I should have written to you ere now about a matter on which I am sure you will take an interest. My daughter's engagement will be announced in a day or two and you ought to have the news before the press brings it to you. She is to marry, probably next June, M$^r$. Gardiner M. Lane[4]—son of an old friend and comrade of mine the late Professor Lane of Harvard.[5] I have known the younger Lane from his boyhood[6] and liking him for his father's sake have learned to like /him/ for his own—He was a leading scholar at Harvard but gave up the classics for business in which he has had a successful career. He was at one time Vice-President of the Union Pacific and is now a member of the banking house of Lee, Higginson & C$^o$ of Boston—He is a man of marked ability, of the highest character and of the sweetest disposition. I do not know any man to whom I could couple my only daughter so hopefully—And yet I dare not think of the loss to us—Our daughter has been the light of our house[7] and we have lived very much for her during the last ten years—Friends bid us be thankful that we have kept her so long[8] but she is still young and this change makes us old.

My wife joins me in messages of sympathy to you and to your household.

Yours faithfully and affectionately
B. L. Gildersleeve

Vice-Chancellor B. L. Wiggins

1. Eugene Augustus Hoffman (1829–1902), dean of the General Theological Seminary, New York.

2. Fulford Hall was the home of Bishop Quintard (see No. 71, n. 1), who had died on 15 February.

3. Cameron Piggott (1861–1911) received his M.D. from the University of Maryland, did graduate work (1882–86), and was an assistant (1886–87) in chemistry at Hopkins before becoming professor of chemistry and geology at Sewanee (1887–1911).

4. On Gardiner M. Lane, see "Correspondents."

5. No. 22, n. 1. Lane had died the year before, on 30 June.

6. Gardiner Lane visited Gildersleeve in April 1878, presenting a letter from his father that read in part, "I wish he could be under your instruction, + perhaps some day he may be" (Lane to BLG, 9 April 1878).

7. Cic. *Fam.* 14.5.1 calls his daughter Tullia *lux nostra* (our light); see *AJP* 20 (1899): 460.

8. Emma married Gardiner Lane in Christ Church, Baltimore, on 8 June 1898, a week before her twenty-sixth birthday.

108 To: BENJAMIN IDE WHEELER
*California*

1002 N. Calvert St. Balt°
Feb<sup>y</sup> 20, 1898

My dear Wheeler:

Your letter was received day before yesterday, Forman's MS.[1] yesterday. I will examine the latter as soon as I can make time. It is very natural that he should be somewhat impatient to get his book out as the GW series has been in a state of suspended animation for two years. After long haggling the Harpers sent me a form of contract for my Larger Syntax which I signed in a fit of desperation. The terms seemed to me rather hard but I wanted to get the book printed as a legacy to my students and I fancied that the charges for changes of copy would be met by the income from the other contract. But the other contract has not been signed. After printing 65 pp. of the syntax I received a notification that $100 of the $300 allowed had been exhausted and I found that I could not afford to treat the proof as so much copy—I should have /been/ willing to spend a good part of my $500 per ann. on the Larger Syntax but I could not face the prospect of paying $1000 /cash/ for the privilege of having the Harpers print my book. The proof reader alone drives me wild—It has therefore become necessary to prepare the copy carefully so as to avoid unnecessary expense and the book is moving on or rather crawling on at the snail's pace of 4 or 5 pp. a week. By the end of the year we shall have between 250 and 300 pages in print—/not/ more than a third—This third can be abridged in a few weeks and the outline of the remaining two thirds got ready so as to make up the smaller syntax, of say 120 or 130 pp, so that the GW grammar could be put on the market before the end of the school year 1898–1899, which is the date contemplated on one of the various contracts that we have had under consideration—Perhaps it may be thought advisable to publish Part I of my syntax simultaneously but I am not exercised about that—The book will /as I said/ be more of a legacy to my old students than anything else. There ought to be some vitality in the Smaller Grammar but I must confess that I have more confidence in your management than in my work—

Forman's MS seems to be a copy and I suppose I can keep it by me for some time—He was an excellent scholar before he came to the Johns Hopkins and I always thought that he overrated his indebtedness to me.[2] But one's students get over that feeling after a while—I have no doubt that he has made a very good book and I do not see why it might not be published by the Harpers independently and afterwards incorporated into the Series. The changes in the plates would not be very expensive—and actual use would be a very valuable test.

My trip to Greece was an inspiration that carried me over the hard work

of last session most nimbly. The current session has been a drag. In consequence of the failure of the contract to go into effect I have had to undertake extra work for which I have no relish so that I am in a somewhat
resentful mood.— —My daughter who is the sunshine of our house is going to withdraw her light from us next June when she expects to marry
Gardiner Lane[3]—whom you know—a fine fellow—whom I like extremely
but it is a breaking up after all—and I feel as if the world were coming to
an end.

My wife joins me in kind remembrances to Mrs. Wheeler and yourself.

Yours faithfully<br>B. L. Gildersleeve

Professor Benj. I. Wheeler

1. *A First Greek Book* (New York: Harper and Bros., 1899). On Forman, see No. 85,
n. 2.

2. Forman's book was dedicated to "my best friend," George Prentiss Bristol (No. 86,
n. 1), but Gildersleeve is thanked in the preface.

3. For the expression, see preceding letter, n. 7; for the marriage, see ibid., n. 8.

109 To: CHARLES ELIOT NORTON[1]
*Houghton*

1002 N. Calvert St.<br>Baltimore May 22 1898

Dear Mr. Norton:

As the greatest of Pindar's editors has declared that the dark saying of
N. 3.74[2] became darker to him the more he studied it,[3] the least of Pindar's
worshippers might decline the problem without dishonour. But you are
more than welcome to my view.

The first trouble is with the text. Are we to read ὁ θνατὸς αἰών or ὁ
μακρὸς αἰών? The weighty authority of Aristarchus[4] is in favour of ὁ θνατὸς αἰών but ὁ μακρὸς αἰών is so seductive that the latest editor of Pindar, Christ,[5] a sensible man, has yielded to it. The article of ὁ μακρὸς
αἰών to which an English editor of some note objects[6] is just what we ought
to find. ὁ μακρὸς βίος is used of <u>that</u> extreme old age, so longed for before
it comes, so hateful after it comes and ὁ μακρὸς αἰών would give quite in
Pindar's implicit manner the fourth step. ἐλᾷ is not clear. Does it /mean/
'drives' as one drives a team or 'drives' as one drives a furrow?[7] Are we to
think of the four virtues abreast in the τέθριππον with φρόνησις as the
dominant mare (ἀρετὰς) or are we to think of the four virtues in succession, with φρόνησις as the last in the τετράγυον of life (Od. 18,374)?[8] I
incline to the latter view—to the interpretation that makes φρόνησις the
culminating, not the controlling element.[9] Plato's four virtues are tempt-

ing[10]—all the more so because they doubtless go back to Pythagoras and Pindar was under Pythagorean influences. But we need not follow Plato closely. Pindar gives us the popular Dorism Plato an idealized Dorism.[11] σωφροσύνη is the virtue of boyhood—especially Doric boyhood, beset as it was by lovers—ἀνδρεία is the virtue of manhood—δικαιοσύνη for which Aegina was famous, Aeacus being a great judge[12]—belongs to maturer years, the age of Shakespeare's justice,[13] and ὁ μακρὸς αἰών with its old experience brings φρόνησις brings σοφία brings resignation and Goethe's philosophy of die Forderung des Tages[14] (τὸ παρκείμενον). These four virtues make up the τετράγωνος ἀνήρ and each is brought to the test by trial διάπειρά τοι βροτῶν ἔλεγχος[.] (O 4.18) Aristokleides has the potentialities of them all and by the grace of god he may like Damophilus show them all— P 4,281: κεῖνος γὰρ ἐν παισὶν νέος, ἐν δὲ βουλαῖς πρέσβυς ἐγκύρσαις ἑκατονταετεῖ βιοτᾷ. Surely ἑκατονταετεῖ βιοτᾷ will satisfy the conditions of ὁ μακρὸς αἰών. As for the correspondence to the other fourfold state I am not certain that I can satisfy either of us. The genealogy is mixed as I have noted on O 13.10[15] to which add the remark in Herodotus 8.77: δῖα Δίκη σβέσσει κρατερὸν Κόρον, Ὕβριος υἱόν—but it might be said that ὄλβος demands σωφροσύνη lest it beget κόρος—ἀνδρεία checks κόρος—δικαιοσύνη quells ὕβρις and φρόνησις is the truest guard against ἄτη.

This is the way the passage looks to me now. Perhaps more reflection will make it appear still darker.

But what is perfectly clear to me is that no memory of my delightful week in Cambridge is more delightful than that of dinner at Shady Hill,[16] the charming home, the gracious hostess and all your own kindly appreciation of my work in the domain which you have subdued.

Yours faithfully

B. L. Gildersleeve

Professor Charles Eliot Norton

1. This letter has been published with full apparatus and discussion by the editor at *GRBS* 25 (1984): 233-42.

2. *Nemean 3* is a hymn on the victory in the pancration by Aristocleides, an Aeginetan. Youths stand on the banks of the Asopus waiting for the Muse to arrive with their victory song (1-8). The Muse is to sing of Zeus Nemeanus and Aegina, whom the victor has ennobled by his triumph (9-26). There is a digression on the Aeacids, Peleus, Telamon (31-42), and the young Achilles (43-63). The song of these exploits beseems Aristocleides, for testing one's mettle proves one's abilities at all stages of life, and Aristocleides has the four virtues necessary for victory (64-76). Though Pindar sends his poem late (76-79), the eagle nevertheless can strike upon his prey from afar (80-82), and the victor's glory ranges from Nemea to Epidaurus to Megara (83-84).

The portion in question is this:

ἐλᾷ δὲ καὶ τέσσαρας ἀρετὰς
⟨ὁ⟩ θνατὸς αἰών, φρονεῖν δ᾽ ἐνέπει τὸ παρκείμενον

3. The *explicationes* to the *Nemeans* (and *Isthmians*) in A. Boeckh's (see No. 50, n. 3) edition, *Pindari opera quae supersunt* (Leipzig: Weigel, 1811–21), are by L. Dissen. In 2: 378 he says, "Et haec quidem Boeckhius, qui ultro fatetur sibi hunc locum, quo eum diutius consideret, eo obscuriorem fieri: nunc his accuratius expositis certe hoc effectum est, ut status controversiae liqueat."

4. Gildersleeve prefers the old reading, last read by an editor (Christ) in 1896 and read only twice since 1855. No editor since 1898 has read with Gildersleeve.

5. W. Christ, *Pindari carmina* (Leipzig: B. G. Teubner, 1869, 1891).

6. J. B. Bury, who says (*The Nemean Odes of Pindar* [New York: Macmillan, 1890], 60) that R. Y. Tyrrell opined "that ὁ was introduced by some one who thought that the fourth virtue corresponded to a fourth age, attained only by those who lived long."

7. Liddell-Scott-Jones' *Greek-English Lexicon* cites this instance as meaning "plant, produce" (s.v. ἐλαύνω, III.3). For driving a furrow, see Hes. *Works* 443 and Pind. *Pyth.* 4.228. Gildersleeve may be thinking of Arist. *Ach.* 995 (ὄρχον ἐλάσαι μακρόν, "plant a long vine row") or Plato *Rep.* 433b, where justice allows the other virtues to "take root" (ἐγγενέσθαι, καὶ ἐγγενομένοις).

8. Odysseus answers the mocking offer of Eurymachus to work on a farm with the wish that they might compete with one another in ploughing the four-acre spread.

9. The scholion is actually a combination of these views. It draws from Aristarchus this interpretation, in the words of Bury: "Each of the three ages of man, childhood, early manhood, and elder age, has a proper excellence of its own; and besides these there is another excellence not confined to a particular time of life, namely wisdom" (42).

10. The three virtues mentioned by Gildersleeve plus φρόνησις appear together at *Phaed.* 69c and *Laws* 631c.

11. Gildersleeve's interpretation seems to derive from note K (pp. 254–62) of *Platonis Phaedo. The Phaedo of Plato*, ed. W. D. Geddes (London: Macmillan, 1885), which deals with "The Platonic Division of the Virtues." See Briggs (n. 1 above): 240.

12. On the justice of the Aeacidae, see *Ol.* 8, *Pyth.* 8, *Nem.* 8, *Isth.* 5, and fr. 1, but particularly *Nem.* 8.7–12.

13. The fifth age of seven, following the soldier's, "And then the justice, in fair round belly with good capon lin'd, with eyes severe and beard of formal cut, full of wise saws and modern instances" (*As You Like It*, 2.7.153–56).

14. "Was aber ist deine Pflicht? Die Forderung des Tages" (*Maximen und Reflexionen*, 443).

15. At *Ol.* 13.6–10, Law, Justice, and Peace, the daughters of Themis, repel hubris, "the bold-tongued mother of Excess." "Theognis reverses the genealogy, v. 153: τίκτει τοι κόρος ὕβριν ὅταν κακῷ ὄλβος ἕπηται, but that makes little difference as, according to Greek custom, grandmother and granddaughter often bore the same name. It is a mere matter of ῞Υβρις—Κόρος—῞Υβρις" (*Pindar*, 229–30).

16. "Shady Hill" was the Norton family's nine-acre estate in Cambridge, demolished by Harvard president Nathan Pusey shortly before his retirement in 1971.

110 To: JOSEPH EDWARD HARRY
*JHU-BLG*

Jan^y 13, 1900

Dear Professor Harry:

It would be foolish in me to raise the hue and cry of 'Stop thief!' every time that a younger scholar brings out something that he has picked up in my lecture room.[1] I myself find on every hand anticipations and coincidences and I am not always careful to ticket my property. Your acknowledgement of obligation was not aptly worded; for when an old student of mine says that he owes me much indirectly, no reader will gather from that the direct use of grammatical formulae and when my views have been published, it would have been graceful to indicate the context in which these formulae appear. Most of the notes in which I recognize my hand will be found in my Justin Martyr, my Pindar, and in the American Journal of Philology and you must have thought me strangely constituted, if you imagined that I objected to Professor Blake's painstaking study of my grammatical work. I was glad to have one diligent pupil more.

My Brief Mention note meant simply what it said. I have reached the late afternoon of life and I am quite resigned to the effacement which overtakes all individual contributions to the work of the world and I have no reclamations to make. Scaliger's law[2] is worth more than most discoveries and yet Bishop in the Journal[3] referred to Curtius[4] and not to Scaliger—wherefore a German scholar[5] cried aloud and spared not.[6]

If you get a year off, I should advise you to devote your time to Archaeology: Paleography and Epigraphy.

Guthrie[7] is a clever man but he may make lapses for which a classical scholar would not like to be responsible.

Yours sincerely<br>B. L. Gildersleeve

Professor J. E. Harry

1. In a letter to Gildersleeve of 6 January 1900, Harry worries about Gildersleeve's "Brief Mention" at *AJP* 20 (1899): 354, regarding his *Hippolytus* and Robert William Blake's (1864-1921) *The First Two Books of the Hellenica of Xenophon* (Boston: Allyn and Bacon, 1892) (see below), in which "Both the editors have expressed themselves as indebted to my work and both the editors have made large use of my formulae—BLAKE with almost painful scrupulousness of reference, whereas HARRY has not thought it worth while to particularize, except in a few instances." Harry recalls Gildersleeve's remarks about "Blake's overloading his book with references" and pleads that as his book was being published, "I was obliged to cut some of these [references] out to reduce the size."

2. For Joseph Justus Scaliger's (1540-1609) etymological "law," see his note on p. 266 of C. A. Lobeck's *Phrynici eclogae nominum et verborum Atticorum* (Leipzig: B. G. Teubner, 1820). Basically the law states that εὖ and negative prefixes are compounded not with verbs but with nouns, thus εὐάγγελος (in Phrynicus Atticistus 235, which probably refers to Plato *Rep.* 4320 or *Tht.* 144b) is correct, and the verb is εὐαγγελέω, not εὐαγγέλλω. Gildersleeve refers to it at *AJP* 29 (1908): 370 ( = *SBM*, 168) ("a discovery not to be overestimated in its reach") and 37 (1916): 237 ( = *SBM*, 355). See also J. A. Scott, "Gildersleeve the Teacher," *PAPA* 56 (1925): xxvi.

3. See No. 82, n. 6.

4. No. 8, n. 16.

5. Since Gildersleeve does not refer to a scholar of German descent in his *BM*, he must refer to himself.

6. Isa. 58:1: "Cry aloud, spare not, lift up your voice like a trumpet."

7. William Norman Guthrie (1868–1944), author of *Songs of American Destiny: A Vision of New Hellas* (Cincinnati: Robert Clarke, 1899), had asked Harry to collaborate on translations of Sophocles' *Oedipus Tyrannos*, *Oedipus Coloneus*, and *Antigone*. Harry declined the offer.

### 111 To: Herbert Weir Smyth
*Harvard*

1002 N. Calvert St.
Baltimore April 20, 1900

Dear Professor Smyth:

The dedication of your admirable Greek Melic Poets[1] to an old scholar reminds me of the Pindaric wish for that persistent veteran Psaumis: φέρειν γῆρας εὔθυμον ἐς τελευτάν.[2] It makes very little difference whether we combine εὔθυμον with γῆρας or with τελευτάν,[3] for old age is a manner of death but if anything could infuse cheerfullness into my atrabilious composition it would be such an honour as you have done me by associating my name with the most erudite and scholarly contribution that America has yet made to the exegesis of Greek Poetry. I feel for the first time as if perhaps I had won instead of losing the long game and that it is worth while to have been a pioneer.

You know my love of the Greek Lyric Poets and you may imagine how I have revelled in your book and with what joy I have welcomed all the light you have thrown on the facets and the settings of those jewels. My farthing candle[4] has not done much in the way of illumination and in the warmth of your friendship you have exaggerated your indebtedness to my work but every now and then I find something in your commentary that has a familiar colour and I rejoice.

I hope that your memorable year at Athens[5] will have a pleasant close and that you will return in good health and spirits to take up the work in America, which you are called to carry forward.

With best regards to Mrs. Smyth and kind messages from my wife

I am

Yours faithfully and gratefully
B. L. Gildersleeve

Professor Herbert Weir Smyth

1. London: Macmillan, 1900.

2. *Ol.* 5.51. He also quotes the line in a letter to C. F. Smith of 24 October 1908, printed in *Sewanee Review* 32 (April 1924): 175 and recounted by Smith in "American Greetings," *Proc. Class. Assn.* 18 (1921): 13.

3. I.e., whether the line is translated "may you bring a kindly old age to life's end" or

"may you bring old age to a kindly end." The scholia read the former, but in his commentary, Gildersleeve suggests Pindar may intend the latter.

4. Edward Young (1683–1765), "Satire VII," v. 56: "How commentators each dark passage shun, / And hold their farthing candle to the sun."

5. Smyth was visiting professor at the American School of Classical Studies at Athens, 1899–1900.


112 To: Daniel Coit Gilman
*JHU-Gilman*

Baltimore, Wednesday May 16, 1900

Dear Mr. Gilman:

Your letter of May 1[1] reached me day before yesterday and while I was revolving the news it contained Dr. Griffin[2] sent me the sketch of your tour from Paris to Bordighera. It was very interesting. One does not shut one's eyes to the scenery visible from a mourning coach but there is not the same light on the landscape and what you said to me was of more moment than the Paris exposition or the stop at Avignon. I was not unprepared for the news. You had repeatedly given me to understand that you would hardly do more than round out the twenty fifth anniversary of the working life of the University and that at three score years and ten you would seek a release from the labours and responsibilities of your high office. You are richly entitled to freedom from the pressure of official work and your active mind will find ample and congenial employment in gathering up the results of your thought and experience for the benefit of those who are to come after you.[3] The end must come some day and as you are wise above your fellows, I can not dispute the wisdom of your decision. How sad that decision is to me personally I need not say. I had hoped that as I had been blessed with your generous consideration from the beginning of my work at the Johns Hopkins, I should never know the rule of another chief. At my time of life it will be hard to follow the lead of a stranger, who does not know the history of our common work and can not make allowances for the peculiarities of temperament and other frailties that have found so indulgent a judge in you. If I were in a position to follow you in your withdrawal as closely as I followed you in your accession, I too should give up my remaining years to literary work of which I have enough in hand to occupy me for all the time that remains but I have made no provision for an old age of independent study and I expect to die in harness. As for the University, it is unthinkable without you and yet the problem must be thought out. It is a problem for others rather than for me as I shall live in memories rather than in hopes. Still I must do whatever is laid upon me and so a few hours after I received your letter, I put myself in communication with M[r]. M[c]Lane[4] and gave him your letter to read. We had a long talk about the situation and I have all confidence that the Trustees will not do anything without full consultation at every step with those whom you have designated as possessing your confidence.[5]

Everything seems trivial in comparison with this momentous change and yet important things have happened, the tragic solution of the Craig[6] problem, the impending, if not accomplished election of a new professor of Mathematics.[7] The work of the session is nearing its end. Thanks to your organization of the University everything is going on smoothly but we miss the benign presence of the head of the house.[8]

Yours faithfully<br>
B. L. Gildersleeve

President Gilman

1. Gilman had written from Bordighera: "There is one thing I wish to say to you, & not to anyone else at present. You must have surmised that I am ready to be released from the office that I hold; . . . I do not know when I shall write my official letter [of resignation],—but I am facing the beginning of my 70th year & so I think the inevitable cannot long be postponed. You have been such a constant, such a wise, such a helpful adviser,—& so dear a friend, that I take you first into my confidence." His letter of resignation was presented to the trustees on 17 November (see the *New York Evening Post* and *NYTimes*, 21 November 1900, the latter reporting [on p. 1] that although Gilman claimed "advancing years," the likely reason was the shortage of funds caused in part by the lack of support by Marylanders). The formal resignation, effective 1 September, took place on the Hopkins Commemoration Day, 22 February 1901, the twenty-fifth anniversary of the opening of the university. Gilman delivered no valedictory, only a short announcement. For Gilman's letters of resignation, see *JHU Circulars*, no. 150 (March 1901): 31–32, and for Gildersleeve's Commemoration Day address to Gilman, see *Franklin*, 386–87. Gilman left Baltimore in June; see No. 118.

2. Edward Herrick Griffin (1843–1929), professor of the history of philosophy and dean of the college faculty from 1889 to 1915.

3. He wrote an account of the early years of Hopkins, *The Launching of a University* (New York: Dodd, Mead, 1906).

4. James Latimer McLane (1834–1923), lawyer and financier, was president of the Western Maryland Railroad (1871–73), a member of the Maryland legislature (1879), and for many years a member of the Baltimore City Council. A Hopkins trustee from 1891 to 1902, he was president of the board of trustees in 1900–1901 and thus head of the special committee to search for a new president. See *French*, 142–43. Despite his prior wishes and expectations, Gilman served on the search committee.

5. See Gilman's letter (n. 1 above): "But I trust that they [the trustees] will advise with you and Remsen and Griffin, & with Welch or Howell or representatives of the Medical faculty." Gildersleeve and Remsen were the final choices of the trustees, but Gildersleeve, at sixty-nine, was considered too old, and Remsen, at fifty-four, was elected on 3 June 1901.

6. Thomas Craig (1855–1900) was educated at Lafayette (A.B. 1875) as a civil engineer but, desirous of studying under J. J. Sylvester (see No. 29, n. 2), entered Hopkins as one of the first fellows in mathematics (1876–79; Ph.D. 1878). After a stint with the U.S. Coast and Geodetic Survey (1879–81), he rose to professor of mathematics at Hopkins (1892–1900). He edited the *American Journal of Mathematics* (1894–99). Towards the end of his life the weakness of his heart limited his academic activities, obliging his colleagues to undertake more and more of his responsibilities in addition to their own. *DAB* 4: 496.

7. Frank Morley (1860–1937), of King's College, Cambridge (A.B. 1883, A.M. 1886,

D.Sc. 1898), was called from Haverford, where he had been professor of pure mathematics since 1888. He edited the *American Journal of Mathematics* (1901-29) and was president of the American Mathematical Society (1919-20). *DAB Suppl. 2*, 473-74.

    8.  The term is used in England for the master of a college.


## 113 To: Gonzalez Lodge
### *JHU-BLG*

May 21, 1900

Dear Professor Lodge:

Laing[1] dropped in the other day and told me that you had accepted the position at Bryn Mawr[2] and Fay[3] in a letter received Saturday informed me that Miss Thomas[4] had offered him your place at Bryn Mawr so that I was not surprised this morning at receiving the official announcement from Russell,[5] who seems to think that I have done him a good turn in bringing about a conference between the Dean of the Teachers College and the Professor of Latin and Greek elect.[6] Q.F.F.F.Q.D.O.M.E.T.[7]

I have thought over the situation.[8] All things considered—Kirk[9] being out of the question—Smith[10] is the best Hopkins man available. If Sutphen[11] had mellowed somewhat, he would be a good man. Wilson[12] would like to have the place and Kirby Smith[13] would like to see him prominent elsewhere than here.—But Steele[14] who is looking out for a change, is a thoroughly endorsable man and will keep up the scientific reputation of Bryn Mawr.

Carter's work is very slight[15]—I am just comparing [h]is performance with Rothstein's[16]—whom he copies and abridges—I delight in sending Propertius[17] and if I were not so busy, I should be glad to annotate freely—but the U.P.Co. is crowding me with proof while I am up to my eyes in university work. I have given them to understand that there can't be any hurry about the book. It is impossible that there should be any money in it.

More when we meet

Yours faithfully
B. L. Gildersleeve

Professor Gonzalez Lodge

    1.  Gordon Jennings Laing (1869-1945) was educated at Toronto (A.B. 1891, D. Litt. 1923) and received a Ph.D. in Latin from Hopkins (1896, LL.D. 1938). He was reader in Greek at Bryn Mawr (1897-99), then rose from instructor to professor of Latin at the University of Chicago (1899-1935), where he was also dean of humanities (1931-35) and alumni dean (1940-43). In 1921-23 he was professor of classics and dean of the faculty of arts at McGill. He was annual professor at the American School of Classical Studies in Rome (1911-12), managing editor of *Classical Journal* (1905-8), associate editor of *Classical Philology* (1905-21; 1923-45), and president of the APA (1924-25). His principal publications are: *Masterpieces of Latin Literature* (Boston: Houghton Mifflin, 1903); *Selections from Ovid*

(New York: D. Appleton, 1905); *The Phormio of Terence* (Chicago: Scott, Foresman, 1908); *Survivals of Roman Religion* (New York: Longmans, Green, 1931). He also helped Paul Shorey revise his *Horace Odes and Epodes* (Boston: B. H. Sanborn, 1910). *WhAm* 2: 209; *CJ* 41 (1945–46): 36–37; *NYTimes*, 3 September 1945, 23.

2. Gildersleeve means Columbia; Lodge was leaving Bryn Mawr.

3. No. 95, n. 6.

4. See "Correspondents."

5. James Earl Russell (1864–1945), in his first year as head of the psychology department at Teachers College (1897), was instrumental in retaining the school's ties with Columbia and was named dean in the same year. Later he became Barnard professor of education (1904–27). Under his leadership, Teachers College grew from 169 students in 1897 to over 5,000 at his retirement in 1927. *DAB Suppl. 3*, 676–78.

6. Lodge wrote Gildersleeve on 20 May 1900: "I owe the New York place to you."

7. I.e., *Quod felix faustum fortunatumque detur omen mihi et tibi* (May this be a good omen for me and you), a formular expression.

8. In the same letter (n. 6 above) Lodge wrote: "We are having a hard time to get a successor. Please tell me what you can of Steele. Fay has declined. . . . Anybody that you can suggest will be carefully considered—but not Kirk."

9. It is not clear why William Hamilton Kirk (1857–1947), educated at Hopkins (A.B. [extraord.] 1893, Ph.D. 1895) and instructor in Greek at Vanderbilt (1895–1900), was "out of the question." Educated largely by his father, John Foster Kirk, editor of *Lippincott's Magazine* (1870–90), Kirk never attended college and first taught at Episcopal Academy, Philadelphia (1880–92), with no degree. In the year of this letter he was named professor of Latin at Rutgers, where he served until his retirement in 1934, helping establish a classics program at the New Jersey College for Women (now Douglass College). Kirk published his dissertation, *Demosthenic Style in the Private Orations* (Baltimore: Friedenwald, 1895) and five articles in *AJP*. He also contributed to *Studies*.

10. Charles Sidney Smith (1867–1951) was educated at Princeton (A.B. 1888, A.M. 1891), where he served as instructor in Greek (1891–97). He did graduate work at Leipzig (1897–98) and Hopkins (1898–1900), then was called to be assistant professor of Greek and Latin at Columbian (now George Washington) University (1900–1906). He returned to Hopkins for his Ph.D. in Latin (1906), then returned to Columbian in 1907 as professor of Latin. He published *Selections from Valerius Maximus* (Boston: Leach, Shewell, and Sanborn, 1895) and his dissertation, *Metaphor and Comparison in the Epistulae ad Lucilium of L. Annaeus Seneca* (Baltimore: J. H. Furst, 1910).

11. Morris Crater Sutphen (1869–1901), another Princeton man (A.B. 1890, A.M. 1893) received his Ph.D. in Latin from Hopkins in 1899. He was instructor in Latin at Williams (1897–98) and at Hopkins (1899–1901), where he was secretary and treasurer of the editorial committee for *Studies*. He contributed an important article to *AJP*, "A Further Collection of Latin Proverbs," 22 (1901): 1–28, 121–48, 241–60, 361–92, before his early death by drowning. See K. F. Smith, *AJP* 22 (1901): 392; *JHU Circulars*, no. 157 (April 1902): 56.

12. Harry Langford Wilson (1867–1913) was educated at Queen's University, Kingston, Ontario (A.B. 1887, A.M. 1887, LL.D. 1903) and received his Ph.D. in Latin (1896) from Hopkins, where he rose from instructor to associate professor of Latin (1895–1906) and professor of Roman archaeology and epigraphy (1906–13). He was professor of Latin at the American School of Classical Studies in Rome (1906–7) and a foreign member of the Imperial German Archaeological Institute (1907–13). He published his dissertation, *The Metaphor in the Epic Poems of P. Papinius Statius* (Baltimore: J. Murphy, 1898), *D. Iuni Iuvenalis saturarum libri V* (Gildersleeve-Lodge Series) (New York: University Publishing Co., 1903), and contributed six articles, thirteen reviews, and five notices to *AJP*. *WhAm* 1: 1361; *NatCAB* 31: 481.

13. See "Correspondents."

14. Robert Benson Steele (1860-1944) was educated at Wisconsin (A.B. 1883, A.M. 1888) and received his Ph.D. from Hopkins in Latin (1890). He was professor of Latin at Antioch (1886-88), St. Olaf (1890-91), Illinois Wesleyan (1891-1901), and Vanderbilt (1901-38). Of his more than one hundred publications, twenty-one articles were for *AJP*. His grammatical studies of Livy were collected as *Livy* (Leipzig: F. A. Brockhaus, 1910-13), and he also wrote *Temporal Clauses in Livy* (Baltimore: Lord Baltimore Press, 1921). *WhAm* 5: 689; *NYTimes*, 14 December 1944: 23.

15. Jesse Benedict Carter (1872-1917) graduated first in his class at Princeton (1893) and studied at Berlin, Leipzig, and Göttingen. After teaching at Princeton for two years (1895-97), Carter returned to Germany and received his Ph.D. from Halle (1898). He then returned to Princeton, where he was assistant professor (1898-1902) and professor (1902-7) of Latin. He was annual professor at the American School of Classical Studies in Rome in 1904-7 and was named director of the school in 1907. In 1913 he was made director of the American Academy in Rome, of which the American School had become part. On his role in the American School, see L. and A. Valentine, *The American Academy in Rome, 1894-1969* (Charlottesville: University Press of Virginia, 1973), 66-75. His chief interest was Roman religion: *De deorum Romanorum cognominibus quaestiones selectae*, (Diss., Halle; Leipzig: B. G. Teubner, 1898); *Epitheta deorum quae apud poetas Latinos leguntur* (Leipzig: B. G. Teubner, 1902); *The Religion of Numa* (London: Macmillan, 1906); *The Religious Life of Ancient Rome* (Boston: Houghton Mifflin, 1911); he also translated C. F. Huelsen's *Roman Forum: Its History and Monuments* (Rome: Loescher; New York: G. E. Stechert, 1906). *DAB* 3: 539.

16. Max Rothstein, *Die Elegien des Sextus Propertius*, 2 vols. (Berlin: Weidmann, 1898); 3d ed. with title *Propertius Sextus Elegien*, 2 vols. (Dublin and Zurich: Weidmann, 1966).

17. In his letter (n. 6 above), Lodge had complained to Gildersleeve of having to enlarge the linguistic notes in Carter's commentary in *Selections from the Elegiac Poets* for the Gildersleeve-Lodge Series (New York: University Publishing Co., 1900, 1905, 1908); Gildersleeve had been reading the Propertius section.


114 To: HERBERT WEIR SMYTH
*Harvard*

1002 N. Calvert St.
Baltimore Oct. 28, 1900

Dear Professor Smyth:

I have sent to the author the page proof of Spieker's review of your Melic Poets, which is to appear in No. 83 of the Journal.[1] Spieker had been teaching the fragments and as he asked me every few weeks when your book would come out, I thought that he had the requisite knowledge and the necessary enthusiasm and assigned the Melic Poets to him for review. But who is competent to the work? For my own part I have kept your book by me at home for my special refreshment and never fail to learn something from it whenever I open it. My copy has pasted in an extract from Robinson Ellis's cordial letter about it;—But I have already expressed my joy in the book and my pride in the dedication of it to me.

A few days ago I received a letter from the A.B.C.[2] reviving the Harper's plan of a /Greek Series/ and asking me if I would not take charge again, at the same time intimating that they would like me to sound you as to your inclination to join in this scheme and get up a Gildersleeve-Smyth series instead of the projected Gildersleeve-Wheeler series. After some four years of negotiation I withdrew from the Gildersleeve-Wheeler scheme as it was evident that Wheeler's heart was not in the project—He is a εἷς κοίρανος ἔστω man.[3] And now Wheeler has begged to be released from his contract. All that remains of the series is Forman's book[4]—which was suggested by Wheeler and Newhall's Plato[5] for which I am in a sense responsible. My Larger Greek Syntax is outside the series and was provided for by a special contract which the A. B. C. has generously modified since to relieve me from the heavy pecuniary responsibility that rested on me. The contract for a smaller Greek grammar to be prepared by Miller and myself—though I was the only one named—was drawn up but fortunately never signed. I am too old for such schemes and have no further ambition in the text book line and your revision of Hadley[6] will answer all the purposes of a school and college Greek grammar for the next twenty years. In what remains of life I shall play with my little syntactical task[s]—though my interest in them has waned greatly, edit the Journal, cobble up futilities for Brief Mention and amuse myself with my adversaria—You know enough, are mature enough, strong enough, resolute enough, to give America and England a good Greek Series and you need no senior editor. If you want a collaborator who is accurate and painstaking and knows as much about syntax as I do, even if he has not committed himself to as many formulae as I have, there is my helper Miller. The Smyth-Miller series would command respect and deserve confidence. Of course, I am willing to help—call me consulting editor, if you choose.[7]—

I am eager to hear an account of your year in Greece from your own lips. At no distant date you will doubtless be translated to Harvard[8] and then perhaps the enthusiasm will be congealed. Don't wait too long before you come to see your old friend.

With best regards to Mrs. Smyth[9]

     I am

                   Yours faithfully
                   B. L. Gildersleeve

Professor Herbert Weir Smyth

1. Edward Henry Spieker (1859–1918) was educated at Baltimore City College and Hopkins (A.B. 1879, Ph.D. 1882), where he was assistant in Greek and Latin (1882–86), associate (1886–88), associate professor (1888–1915), and collegiate professor (succeeding C. D. Morris) (1915–18). The most devoted to undergraduate teaching of anyone in the department, he was one of the many "home-grown" Hopkins faculty members, including H. B. Adams in history, M. Bloomfield in Sanskrit, J. W. Bright in English, A. M. Elliott in Romance languages, M. Warren in Latin, and others (see *Hawkins*, 207). Spieker regularly taught four Greek courses per semester and taught a course on "Elegiac, Iambic, and Melic

Poets; Sophocles" in the spring terms 1896–1900. He published a notice and two reviews in *AJP*; the review in question is 21 (1900): 327–31. See *WhAm* 1: 1163–64.

2. In 1890 severe drains on the capital of the Harpers caused by the death or retirement of the second generation of Harper brothers made the firm insecure, and in May of that year the firm joined a consortium of A. S. Barnes and Co., D. Appleton and Co., and two others to form the American Book Company as an outlet for their textbooks. By 1896 the new conglomerate, headed by John W. Harper, was in trouble. The Harpers withdrew and tried to reorganize, but on 6 December 1899 went into receivership. See, further, Eugene Exman, *The House of Harper* (New York: Harper and Row, 1967), 171–83. Gildersleeve replied to the American Book Company's letter on 24 October 1900 [Harvard]: "I was sixty-nine years old yesterday and am in no mood for committing myself to any elaborate scheme of Greek textbooks. . . . My school books have yielded me little except labor and sorrow. Smyth has the learning, the vigor, the industry necessary to the undertaking. He is in the front rank of American Hellenists and you could not find an abler man to put at the head of the series. . . . But a Gildersleeve-Smyth series—no!"

3. *Il.* 2.204: "Let him be the sole commander."

4. No. 85, n. 2

5. *The Charmides, Laches and Lysis of Plato* (New York: American Book Co., 1900). On Newhall, see No. 98.

6. See Smyth, *A Greek Grammar for Schools and Colleges* (New York: American Book Co., 1916), vi.

7. Smyth edited the "Greek Series for Colleges and Schools," which listed twenty-three titles, including (among those mentioned in this volume) Spieker's *Greek Prose Composition* (1904), Harry's *Prometheus* (1905), Forman's *Clouds* (1915), C. F. Smith and A. G. Laird's *Herodotus* (1908), Sterrett's *Iliad 1–3* (1907), Heidel's *Euthyphro* (1903), and H. N. Fowler and J. R. Wheeler's *Greek Archaeology* (1909). Volumes announced but never realized included an *Agamemnon* by Shorey, an *Odyssey* by C. B. Gulick, a *Theocritus* by Fairclough and Murray, a *Thucydides* by Lamberton, and an *Anabasis* by C. W. E. Miller.

8. Smyth went to Harvard in 1901.

9. Eleanor Adt Smyth (1865–1955), whom he married in Baltimore in December 1887.


## 115 To: Gonzalez Lodge
### *JHU-BLG*

Nov. 20, 1900

Dear Professor Lodge:

Shannon[1] of Fayetteville, Ark. sends me a postal card in which you accept his correction of 501 with regard to Sallust and propose to substitute 'always' for 'never'.[2] You must have been bulldozed into such a concession—Jacobs Sall. Cat. 2.1[3] says igitur steht bei Sall. in Aussagesätzen immer zu Anfang und dann niemals in der schwachen Bedeutung unsers tonlosen 'also'; in Fragesätzen hat es die zweite [to which the passages cited by Shannon belong],[4] einmal, Or. Macr. 14, die dritte Stelle.—

The proper wording should be 'never except in interrogative sentences'.[5]

Shannon says he cannot understand what you write about ne̲ for

<u>necdum</u>[6] but I have declined to enter into that question. We must keep a united front.

Yours faithfully
B. L. Gildersleeve

Professor Gonzalez Lodge

1. Charles Henry Shannon's association with Fayetteville, Ark., is unclear. Educated at Emory and Henry (A.B. 1892) and Wisconsin (Ph.D. 1897), he held one-year positions at Vanderbilt, Emory and Henry, and Wisconsin before becoming assistant professor of Greek and Sanskrit at Tennessee in 1901, where he remained until 1916. He contributed "Etymologies of Some Latin Words of *Will* and *Desire*" to *PAPA* 31 (1900): xxiv–xxvi. His letter to Gildersleeve is lost.

2. Gildersleeve had written " 'never' for 'always' " and corrected by hand with a reversing loop. Para. 501 of the *Latin Grammar* deals with *igitur* used in illative sentences: "In CICERO it is usually post-positive, in SALLUST never."

3. R. Jacobs, *C. Sallusti Crispi de coniuratione Catilinae et de bello Iugurthino libri* (Leipzig: Weidmann, 1852), 18.

4. Gildersleeve's brackets

5. Lodge replied on 21 November, "What I meant by saying <u>always</u> instead of <u>never</u>, as my copy of Grammar has correction 'never (except in interrogative sentences)['] /(cf. H. III 3 D)/ just as you write, I can not explain except by a lapsus mentis."

6. Para. 482.5.R.2

116 To: Hermann Usener[1]
*Bonn*

Baltimore 12/II 1901

Verehrtester Freund und College:

Wenn ich in Ihrer schönen Heimath wäre, würde ich gewiss Deutsch mit Ihnen sprechen. Also sei es gewagt meinen Dank für den schönen Brief vom 22. v.M. auf Deutsch zu sagen.[2] Holperig aber herzlich.

Möge sich der günstige Eindruck den die ersten Seiten der Syntax auf Sie gemacht haben beim Weiterlesen bestätigen. Aber so viel mir auch an Ihrem wissenschaftlichen Urteil gelegen ist, kann ich mich doch im schlimmsten Falle mit dem Zeugniss [sic] Ihres unveränderten Wohlwollens trösten.

Seit einigen Jahren kommt mir das Rheinisches Museum regelmässig zu, aber erst durch Ihren Brief hab' ich erfahren dass ich die Sendung Ihrem gütigen Auftrage schulde.[3] Alles was von Ihrer Feder herrührt, lese ich, wie Sie wissen, mit tiefstem Interesse und aufrichtiger Bewunderung, und es macht mir eine besondere Freude Ihren Forschungen nachzugehen und wenn meine vielfachen Geschäfte es erlauben dem amerikanischen Publikum einen Bericht über Ihre Arbeiten zu erstatten.[4]

Meine herzlichen Glückwünsche zu dem schönen Bunde mit dem geistreichen und geistesverwandten Gelehrten, dessen Nekyia mich höchlich interessiert hat.[5]

Dem Gildersleeveschen Hause geht augenblicklich alles gut. Meine Tochter die sich vor drei Jahren mit einem Bostoner Bankier Herrn Lane, dem Sohne eines alten Freundes und Collegen vermählt hat,[6] ist die glückliche Mutter eines allerliebsten zweijährigen Mädchens[7] die mir l'art d'être grandpère sehr leicht gemacht hat und mein Sohn hat sich zu einer achtbaren Stellung in New York als Architekt durchgearbeitet.[8] Meiner Frau hat das verflossene Jahrzehnt wenig angehabt und ich selber bin noch rüstig und munter, trotz der 70 Jahre. Wir denken oft an die Bonner Tage und all' die Güte die Sie und Ihre reizende Gemahlin uns haben angedeihen lassen.[9]

Meine Frau lässt herzlich grüssen und obgleich sie meine Sehnsucht /nach/ dem zweiten Bande des Dionysius[10] nicht teilen kann, teilt sie doch in vollem Masse alle Wünsche für das Wohlergehen Ihres Hauses.

Ihr treu ergebener
B. L. Gildersleeve

Herrn Geheimrath Usener

## [TRANSLATION]

My dear Friend and colleague:

If I were in your beautiful homeland, I would certainly speak German with you. And so, let me dare to express my thanks in German for your fine letter of the 22d of the previous month. Clumsily but sincerely.

May the favorable impression which the first pages of the syntax made on you be confirmed in further reading. But no matter how much I am concerned about your scholarly judgement, I can, in the worst case, take consolation in the experience of your unchanged goodwill.

For some years now Rheinisches Museum has come regularly to me, but for the first time I have learned through your letter that I owe this to your kind instructions. I read everything you write, as you know, with the deepest interest and sincere admiration, and it gives me special pleasure to follow your research and, if my various occupations permit it, to render an account to the American public about your work.

My sincere congratulations on the fine alliance with the clever and congenial scholar, whose Nekyia has interested me greatly.

For the moment everything is well with the Gildersleeve family. My daughter, who 3 years ago married a Boston banker, Mr. Lane, the son of an old friend and colleague, is the happy mother of a lovable 2-year-old little girl who has made the art of being a grandfather very easy for me, and

my son has made his way to an honorable position in New York as an architect. The past decade has had little effect on my wife and I am myself still
vigorous and lively in spite of 70 years. We think often of the days in Bonn
and all the good things that you and your charming wife bestowed upon us.

My wife sends her best greetings, and though she cannot share my longing for the 2nd vol. of Dionysius, she shares completely in all wishes for the
welfare of your household.

Yours faithfully

B. L. Gildersleeve

1. This letter has been published by R. L. Fowler, "The Gildersleeve Archive," *Briggs-Benario*, 85. The present text retains Gildersleeve's punctuation and spelling.

2. The letter, dated 23 January, is also printed by Fowler, 83–85.

3. Usener was co-editor (with Franz Buecheler [1837–1908]) of *RhM*, the journal begun at Bonn in 1827 by August Boeckh (No. 50, n. 3), whose editors included Fr. Welcker (1784–1868), Ritschl (No. 23, n. 2), Bernays (No. 7, n. 10), and Ribbeck (No. 50, n. 18), among others. See *AJP* 27 (1906): 102.

4. Gildersleeve had reported on Usener's article "Beiläufige Bemerkungen," in his digest of *RhM* 55 (1900) and recently reviewed Usener's *Götternamen* (Bonn: F. Cohen, 1896) at *AJP* 17 (1896): 356–66 and *Die Sintfluthsagen* (Bonn: F. Cohen, 1899) at *AJP* 20 (1899): 210–15.

5. Usener's daughter Maria married Albrecht Dieterich (1866–1908), a philologist and historian of religion at Heidelberg, in March 1899. Following his studies at Leipzig, Dieterich had studied under Usener at Bonn. Gildersleeve refers to his *Nekyia: Beiträge zur Erklärung der neuentdeckten Petrusapokalypse* (Leipzig: B. G. Teubner, 1893; 2d ed., 1913). *NDB* 3: 669–70. Gildersleeve had sent a note of congratulation on the engagement 6 November 1898 (Bonn), which he may have remembered at the last moment, for he struck from an earlier draft (at the Hopkins Archive) at this point of the letter this sentence: "Obwohl ich von Ihren Verhältnissen nichts wusste, war ich im Begriff durch das Journal die Aufmerksamkeit meiner Leser auf das Buch zu lenken—aber es hat mir /an/ Zeit und Raum gefehlt" (Although I did not know of your relationship, I was about to call my readers' attention to the book through my journal, but I did not have the time and space). The notice was never printed.

6. On Gardiner Lane, see "Correspondents" and Nos. 107–8.

7. Katharine Ward Lane (1899–) became a well-known sculptress, specializing in animal figures. She was decorated Chevalier de l'Ordre National de Mérite (France), won the Widener Gold Medal of the Philadelphia Academy of Fine Arts, executed a famous frieze on the walls of the Institute of Biology at Harvard, and, like her grandfather, was elected to the National Institute of Arts and Letters (see No. 145). In 1947 she married F. Carrington Weems of New York. Her autobiography is *Odds Were against Me* (New York: Vantage Press, 1985).

8. See No. 78, n. 2.

9. Gildersleeve and Usener first met in Bonn in 1880 (see No. 46 and *AJP* 27 [1906]: 102); Gildersleeve visited him again in the rainy July of 1888, when he brought his family to Germany.

10. The second volume of Usener's edition of *Dionysii Halicarnassensis: De imitatione librorum reliquiae* (Bonn: C. Georgi, 1889) was completed by Ludwig Radermacher (Bonn: C. Georgi, 1904; 2d ed., 1929).

117 To: Emil Hübner
*Berlin*

1002 Belvidere Terrace
Baltimore March 3, 1901

My dear Hübner:

Your review of my book in the DLZ has given me great pleasure.[1] It is a monument to our friendship, which I will carefully preserve for those who are to come after me. How you would have hated the work if it had come to you as the performance of a stranger, I will not ask. I cannot help thinking that you would have found some good in it but you would hardly have turned the fair side out so persistently; and none but a loving hand could have traced my career with such an appreciation of my aims in life. In the few years that in the course of nature remain to me, I hope to be faithful to the ideals that have controlled me from my youth up and to be worthy of your friendship to the end.—The book is, as you have divined, a manner of legacy to my old students, who will read between the lines and reproduce my way of handling the phenomena, which I have simply registered as material for convenient reference.

Some time ago I was asked to deliver the chief address before the Philological Congress at Philadelphia during Christmas week.[2] I had made a number of notes in my semi-humorous fashion more for the sake of amusing myself than with the thought of bringing them out before a philological audience, composed in part at least of Philistines. Just as I was about to give myself up to serious preparation my daughter who was staying with me fell ill of typhoid fever[3] and I was utterly incapable of any work besides my routine preparation for lectures so that I had to use my notes as if they were the real address. To my great surprise, the thing was a success and I have allowed it to be printed for limited circulation. I will send you a copy in a few days and, of course, you will understand me, because you like 'Brief Mention' but it is an audacious performance.

My daughter is quite restored and is beginning to take her place in the social world again. My own health is excellent and I have resumed work on the Syntax—It will amuse me for the rest of my time. Kind messages as always from my wife

Yours faithfully
B. L. Gildersleeve

Professor Emil Hübner[4]

1. Rev. of *Syntax, DLZ* 22, no. 7 (16 February 1901): 410–14.
2. The address, subsequently printed as "Oscillations and Nutations of Philological Studies," *JHU Circulars*, no. 151 (April 1901): 45–50, was delivered on 27 December 1900.
3. Emma and her daughter Katharine (see preceding letter, n. 7) had come to visit on

15 November for a two-week stay. As she was about to leave, a mild fever developed into typhus, which required two nurses around the clock: one for Emma, another for Katharine. The fever broke after another two weeks, but she recovered so slowly that she was not able to return to Boston until 26 January. During that time she occupied the main bedroom on Calvert Street and the study was given over to the baby.

    4. Hübner had died on 21 February.

### 118 To: Daniel Coit Gilman
### *JHU-Gilman*

Baltimore, Friday, June 21, 1901

Dear President Gilman:

    On my return to Baltimore yesterday I found your letter of farewell awaiting me.[1] All that I have said and written and felt about the prospective severance of our official relations has come painfully true; and a final personal interview would have tried my self control, might have tried yours. For more than half of my long career as a teacher I have served under you and it was only under you that the personal element entered into my work. It was the confidence with which you inspired me that gave me the courage to renounce the absolute independence of my position at the University of Virginia,[2] and your generosity has never given me a moment's reason to regret the change. Indeed, whatever success I may have had was all the more welcome because it redounded to your honour, as my chief. Your sympathy and your appreciation have never failed me in all these years and I often linger in memory on the special acts of kindness with which you have brightened the current of a life, which has not been all sparkle and all smoothness. Henceforth I must face the loneliness of the survivor but the nature of things will see to it that the stretch is not too long and I hope that I shall justify your choice to the end. If I have not much goods laid up for many years, I have much work laid up for many years and that is better. And as for you, I know that there will be no remission of your activity in other spheres so that I shall take courage from your example as well as pride in the achievements of my former leader, if 'former' it must be.

    With cordial thanks for your assurances of personal friendship and with best wishes for your happiness in the new life upon which you are entering.[3]

    I am

Yours faithfully
B. L. Gildersleeve

President Gilman

¹Gilman's letter of June 16 reads in part:

My dear Gildersleeve
    I am sorry that I missed seeing you on Friday, and yet, if we had talked for an hour, I doubt whether we should have been the better for it. We should have inclined to the painful aspect of the Calendar + have failed to appreciate all the good things that the passing years have brought to us. But I should have been glad to tell you how much I rejoice in your accumulating honors. Chicago [LL.D. 1901] is good; Yale [see No. 120, n. 2] is better; best of all is the tribute of your scholars of which the public will hear when your birthday comes [see No. 121, n. 2].
    I lay down my office with a constant remembrance that <u>you</u> and <u>Remsen</u> have been my chief counsellors,—the one in all that pertained to science,—the other in all that pertained to letters. My hands have been strengthened by such strong, wise, independent + experienced counsellors. . . .

Ever faithfully yours
D. C. Gilman

2. For other aspects of the University of Virginia position, see No. 19 and n. 1.
3. Gilman became first president of the Carnegie Foundation (1901–4).


119 To: DAVID MARVEL REYNOLDS CULBRETH
*Culbreth*

[October 23, 1901]¹

Dear Mr. Culbreth:
    Nothing could be more gratifying to me in this season of good wishes than your assurance that you owe something to your old teacher. Few echoes come to the professor from those who have sat under his teachings. Only when a memorable occasion arises does he learn how his teachings have told on the world and his pupils. The completion of my seventieth year has brought out many expressions of good will and many kindly remembrances not only from those whom I have trained for my own calling but from those who think they owe more to the man than to the Hellenin. [sic] And if it be a weakness, let it be a weakness, for I prefer to be remembered as a personality than as a teaching machine of so and so many donkey powers. I have no quarrel with those who have not kept up their Greek studies, but those who will recognize the idealism of the School of Greek, I hold to my heart as I have ever done. I have read your letter to my wife who pronounces it beautiful and who unites with me in thanking you for your tribute to your old teacher, to whom you have ever shown a loyalty and affection that are exceedingly precious in a forgetful world.

Yours faithfully
B. L. Gildersleeve

1. Gildersleeve's seventieth birthday.

## 120 To: DANIEL COIT GILMAN
### *Yale-Gilman*

Baltimore Nov. 21, 1901

Dear President Gilman:

Your note has been affixed to the copy of the address which you have so kindly sent me.[1] It will reinforce the cordial words on the title page and serve in after times to shew how your regard has followed me beyond the term of our official connexion. The address with its wealth of facts and its sharp characteristics of the worthies of Yale is welcome on its own account but also as it recalls the scenes of the wonderful celebration with the honour that was shewn you and with the happy coincidence that made me an adopted son of Yale and your academic brother on my seventieth birthday.[2] Such a distinction was well worth waiting for.

Yours faithfully
B. L. Gildersleeve

President Gilman

1. *The Relations of Yale to Letters and Science: An Address Prepared for the Bicentennial Celebration, New Haven, Oct. 22, 1901* (Baltimore: privately printed, 1901).
2. On Wednesday, 23 October 1901 (coincidentally his seventieth birthday), Gildersleeve was one of 60 worthies, including Osler, H. S. Pritchett, and Remsen of Hopkins, W. W. Goodwin, C. E. Norton, F. L. Patton, B. I. Wheeler, G. W. Cable, S. L. Clemens (Mark Twain), R. W. Gilder, W. D. Howells, T. N. Page, H. L. Higginson, and Woodrow Wilson, who were given honorary degrees at the commemoration exercises of the 200th anniversary of the founding of Yale College. Gildersleeve and Betty stayed with the Seymours (see No. 128 and n. 14).

## 121 To: GEORGE LINCOLN HENDRICKSON
### *JHU-BLG*

April 1, 1902

Dear Professor Hendrickson:

You must work out your paper[1] to your own satisfaction. There is no immediate pressure for copy and if you can[,] get the first ready for the second number of the new volume.

I wish that you could have been with us on the 20th of last month.[2] Such honor I never expected to experience. It was an atmosphere of loving kindness few are privileged to breathe even once in a life time. Yet I do not deny that I missed [you] for though I can't lay claim to any decisive influence on your career, I can't afford to give you up as one of my men; and if you knew the esteem in which you are held by men who have a right to judgment, you would not withhold from [me] the satisfaction that I have in remembering that you were one of us

Your contribution to the volume is a grateful tribute to the

[End of draft]

1. "The Literary Form of Horace, *Serm*. I 6," *AJP* 23 (1902): 388–99.

2. In a ceremony at the University Club honoring his seventieth birthday (actually held on 20 February), Gildersleeve was presented with *Studies in Honor of Basil L. Gildersleeve* (Baltimore: Johns Hopkins Press, 1902), a collection of forty-four essays by friends and former students, edited by E. H. Spieker (No. 114, n. 1) and a committee comprising M. Bloomfield (No. 49, n. 14), K. F. Smith, C. W. E. Miller, and H. L. Wilson, with M. C. Sutphen serving as secretary. See *NYTimes*, 21 February 1902: 9, which calls the articles "personal sketches." Bloomfield was toastmaster at the banquet, and addresses were given by Sihler, F. G. Allinson (No. 142, n. 2), Miller, M. Warren (No. 55, n. 4), Edward H. Griffin of Hopkins, J. R. Wheeler (No. 74, n. 7), and Wiggins. See *Johns Hopkins University Celebration of the Twenty-Fifth Anniversary of the Founding of the University and Inauguration of Ira Remsen, LL.D. as President of the University* (Baltimore: Johns Hopkins Press, 1902), 159–67.

122 To: Lulu Gildersleeve Reed
*JHU-BLG*

April 14, 1902

/Reed/

Dear Miss ~~Gildersleeve~~:

The name Gildersleeve is not so very uncommon in New York and there was a large family connexion of that name in Huntington, L.I. from which I am descended. My father, Rev. Benjamin Gildersleeve[1] was the son of Finch G.[2]—an officer of the Continental Army and Finch the son of another Benjamin.[3] Mr. Willard Harvey Gildersleeve of Gildersleeve, Conn.—who takes much more interest in genealogical matters than I do,[4] tells me that he can trace my line and his back to Richard Gildersleeve,[5] the immigrant, who made his appearance in Wethersfield, Conn. about 1647. I do not know what the foundation of the Dutch origin is. There is a tradition to that effect in the family but it seems to be a myth. My father had three brothers Frederick,[6] William[7] and Thomas.[8] Some of the descendants of Frederick and William are living in the West. One of them, a grandson of Frederick I saw when I was in Chicago five years ago.

I should advise /you/ to write to Mr. Gildersleeve, mentioned above.

Yours very truly
B. L. Gildersleeve

Miss L. G. Reed

1. On Rev. Benjamin Gildersleeve (1791-1875), see chapter 1, introduction, n. 4.

2. Finch (1750-1812) formed a company of "Liberty Boys" (New York Minutemen) and served in the Continental Army (1776-81). He was with Washington at Valley Forge in the winter of 1778, and for his services to the state in the Revolutionary War, he was granted 1,200 acres of bounty lands at Cincinnatus and Scipio, N.Y. Finch and his wife Mary Seymour ("Polly") (1758-1850) had nine children. In 1800 he sent his son Frederick, aged seventeen, to survey the grant, and two years later Frederick settled there at "Military Tract," Scipio, Cayuga County, N.Y. See, further, W. Gildersleeve, *Gildersleeve Pioneers* (Rutland, Vt.: Tuttle, 1941), 240-42.

3. Born in Huntington, Suffolk Co., N.Y., Benjamin Gildersleeve (1724-94) was one of the ten children of Thomas Gildersleeve, a prominent local farmer, and grandson of Richard Gildersleeve (n. 6 below). An early signer of the Association (supporting the Continental Con-

## GILDERSLEEVE GENEALOGY

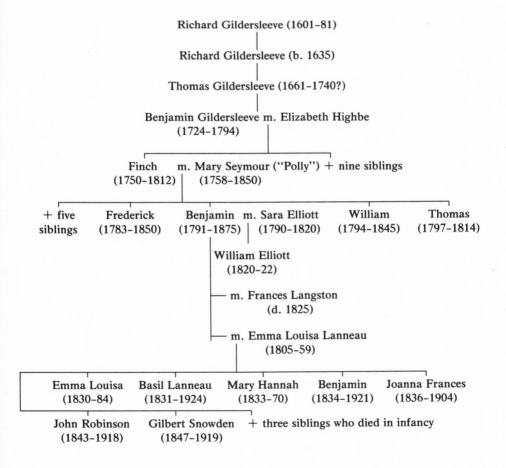

gress), he lost much of his holdings to the British in the Revolutionary War. *Gildersleeve Pioneers*, 236–40.

4. Born in 1886 (Gildersleeve probably did not know his genealogist was only sixteen years old), Willard Gildersleeve wrote *Gildersleeves of Gildersleeve, Conn. and the Descendants of Philip Gildersleeve* (Meriden, Conn.: Press of the Journal Publishing Co., 1914) and *Gildersleeve Pioneers* (n. 2 above). Between graduating from Wesleyan (B.S. 1908) and Columbia (M.A. 1923), he was football coach of Connecticut, New Hampshire, and Massachusetts state colleges, (1908–10), athletic director of St. Lawrence University (1909–10) and Westminster College (1911–13), and taught high school in Grand Island, Nebr. (1911), Meridien, Conn. (1913–15), Hyannis, Mass. (1916–18), and Hackensack, N.J. (from 1918).

5. On Richard Gildersleeve (1601–81), see Charles M. Andrews, "A Biographical By-Path through Early New England History," *New England Magazine* 13 (n.s. 7) (February 1893): 702–9, and *Gildersleeve Pioneers*, 15–133.

6. Frederick Gildersleeve (1783–1850) was the eldest son of Finch and Polly and was deeded part of the Scipio land in 1804. He remained on the farm when Benjamin went off for his schooling. Benjamin ultimately ceded his 100 acres to Frederick. *Gildersleeve Pioneers*, 241ff.

7. Rev. William Gildersleeve (1794–1845), like his older brother Benjamin, sold his interest in the family farm to Frederick. He attended Williams College (A.B. 1820) and received an M.D. from Yale Medical College, but failed as a physician. Licensed to preach by the Baptist Church in 1829, he devoted himself to missionary work first at two churches in Holland, Venango Co., Pa., then in Indiana and Sunbury, Delaware Co., Ohio. He had two sons and three daughters. *Gildersleeve Pioneers*, 249–51.

8. Dr. Thomas Gildersleeve (1797–1814). Another brother, John Robert (1796–ante 1822) died young. Benjamin's sisters were Lydia (1787–1870) and Betsy (1789–1831), and two siblings, Romulus and Drusilla, died in infancy.


## 123 To: Joseph Edward Harry
### *JHU-BLG*

Dec. 22, 1902

Dear Professor Harry:

If I have ever handled any of my students without gloves, I am pretty certain that you stand high in that class; and I cannot say that I am sorry for it, as you yourself recognize the salutariness of the discipline. There are certain qualities such as self assertion and determination that are not attractive in a pupil and yet promise better things than mere docility and sympathy. It was of your type that I wrote in my Pindar before I knew you: 'The jibbing pupils are sometimes the best and the teacher's fairest results are sometimes gained by the resistance of an active young mind.'[1] Well— The days of pupilage are long past; and it is very evident that you /have/ forgiven me. Your Prometheus[2] is doubtless an excellent piece of work and the dedication of it to me will be an honest tribute to an old teacher, which it would be worse than unmannerly to decline; though I confess it always costs me a pang to see how far short I fall of the stature given to me by the mists of memory.

Don't go into the Presidential business[3] until you have sucked your real life dry.

I shall be glad to see your young friend[4] and find out what you would not tell me about your work in Cincinnati.

Yours sincerely,
B. L. Gildersleeve

Professor Joseph E. Harry

1. *Pindar*, ix, of Pindar's reluctance to acknowledge those who influenced him.

2. *The Prometheus Bound of Aeschylus* (New York: American Book Co., 1905). Harry had written (12 December 1902): "May I ask the privilege of inscribing it to the greatest of all my teachers? How truly great your influence has been on my life becomes more and more apparent as graduation day recedes and enables me to get a better perspective. Others have helped me; but none have inspired me with a love of excellence in the best things except you; no other has ever left the Socratean sting that spurs to fruitful effort, has ever possessed that quality indispensable for the achievement of the highest results: savoir blâmer."

3. In February Harry had been asked to interview for the presidency of Swarthmore College. He had inclined to accept when the selection committee became sharply divided and a faction tried to reinstate the former president. Harry promptly withdrew his name. Gildersleeve's feelings about administration may have been pricked by his being recently passed over for the presidency of Johns Hopkins (see No. 112, n. 5).

4. One of Harry's graduate students who was passing through Baltimore had asked him for an introduction to Gildersleeve.

124 To: EDWIN ANDERSON ALDERMAN
*UVa-Alderman*

Baltimore Jan 31, 1903

Dear President Alderman:

The problems propounded in your letter of Jan 24 are beyond me.[1] I have never made a special study of American history and since Reconstruction days I have taken very little interest in politics and most certainly lay no claim to political forecast. For more than a quarter of a century I have lived in a border city, which may have been Southern once, which cannot be called distinctively Southern now and have worked in an institution manned almost entirely by Northern men or men with Northern sympathies. My vacations have been spent in the North or abroad and while I have not lost my sympathy with the South, the only South that I really know is the South of the past and I should be very much at a loss if I were asked to pick one half a dozen men of your generation in whom the Southern spirit 'incarnates itself'. What will abide in the future of what we Southerners were, I cannot divine. There was a charm, a potency about the old life that ought not to perish utterly. But I can't undertake to analyze that charm, that potency for myself or others. Still I was much struck by the concluding words of a little sketch by Owen Wister, 'Twenty Minutes for Refreshments'[2] in which he makes a dash at an analysis. 'What a pity' he says, 'that we shall [soon] have no more Mrs. Brewtons. The causes that ~~have~~ produced her—slavery, isolation, literary tendencies, adversity, game blood—that combination is broken forever'. I suppose that on the twenty-third of February you will tell us that although the combination is broken, something distinctive will remain.[3] Your address will be eloquent and no doubt as instructive as eloquent and I am sorry that I cannot make any contribution to the material that you will handle in your masterly a [sic] manner.

Yours sincerely<br>
<u>B. L. Gildersleeve</u>

President Alderman

    1. Alderman had written: "I am trying to study the contributions made by southern stock and southern civilization to our American character. . . . I want your judgement as to what these qualities are, and as to what men best incarnate them and show them forth." On the project and Alderman's speech, see D. Malone, *Edwin A. Alderman: A Biography* (New York: Doubleday, 1940), 154–57.

    2. *Harper's Magazine* 100 (January 1900): 235–44. It is the story of a sixty-year old woman of the Old South who, with her servant, accompanies Wister on a trip through the Southwest. The passage cited is on p. 244 (brackets indicate a word Gildersleeve has left out; the strike-through is a word he has added). Gildersleeve also quotes this passage in the introduction to "The Ballad of the Swineherd," *Pathfinder* 2 (July 1907): 2.

    3. Alderman spoke at Hopkins on Commemoration Day, 23 February 1903, on the contemporary South. For an abstract of the speech, see *JHU Circulars*, no. 162 (April 1903): 43–45.

125 To: HAMILTON BOWEN HOLT<br>
JHU-BLG

Feb<sup>y</sup> 6, 1903

Dear Sir:

    The subject you suggest for an article in the Independent does not appeal to me. To a man who for fifty years has been preaching and writing about ideals in classical study and in the teaching of the classics,[1] the theme lacks the charm of novelty. If, as your editorial writers seem to think, it is impossible to combine accurate scholarship with delicacy of literary taste and breadth of historical vision, those who have been working on the lines that I have followed so long are under a strong delusion. I only hope that the delusion will last for the few years that remain. In any case any plea I could make for the guild to which I belong would be construed as a vindication of my own career[2] and as to the world's judgment of that I give myself little concern. That is one lesson I have learned from Plato.[3]

Yours very truly<br>B. L. Gildersleeve

Hamilton Holt Esq.

1. Beginning with "my maiden review article," "Necessity of the Classics," *Southern Quarterly Review* 26 (n.s. 10) (July 1854): 145–67 (see *AJP* 37 [1916]: 496 [ = *SBM*, 366–67] [with excerpt]).

2. "I have often meditated on the future of traditional culture, but as anything I might write on the subject would be interpreted as a plea for the classics, I am content to die in my nest" ("The Hazards of Reviewing," *Nation* 101 [28 July 1915]: 50). See No. 185.

3. E.g., *Cri.* 47b: "Then a man should be afraid of the criticism and welcome the praise of the one qualified person, but not those of the general public." See also *La.* 184d-e, *Tht.* 170b ff., and the latter half of *Grg.*

126 To: GONZALEZ LODGE
*JHU-BLG*

Oct. 10, 1903

Dear Professor Lodge:

I answer your letter of the 10th. at the earliest practical moment.[1] Of course as your piety toward an old teacher got you into the scrape of the Latin Series I must do what I can to help you but really the whole text book business is nauseating in the extreme. Think of the new Allen and Greenough[2] and the dreadful Höllenbuch[3] grammar in which Hale persistently smudges over the valuable distinction between anticipatory and prospective[4] and so interferes with my Greek teaching. But nothing matters much now. Still I was amused to see that Paul Lejay in the Revue critique of August 12 calls our school grammar 'une petite grammaire latine d'une rare clarté,'[5] thus picking out as a characteristic of the book the very point which has been so rudely attacked.

A new ed. of the Latin Composition? What does that mean[?] Has that word machine the U.P. Co., actually disposed of 1000 copies by sale and gift in 4 years. Incredible energy! I can't say that I am much pleased with my part in the book[6] and I cannot say just now which of the continuous exercises I dislike most. One that must be turned out is 14C.[7] I could not bring out the double meaning of Quid agit?[8] in the English translation of Seneca and that gives the whole thing a hoist. Doubtless if I can make time to reread them I shall be thoroughly disgusted. What did you do with the book of exercises from which these were selected? If you did not return them you might pick out something better. In any case I will try to help though just now I dare not promise. From what Heidel[9] writes I suppose I shall have to reset his Lucretius this session and I groan in spirit.[10]

My health is excellent and I have come back to my work with the conviction that after all I am good for nothing else.

Yours faithfully

B. L. Gildersleeve

1. Gildersleeve had mentioned to Lodge in the spring that he was dissatisfied with some of the later exercises in their *Latin Composition*, and Lodge wanted his corrections before putting the revisions through the press for the second edition in 1904. Lodge had actually written on *4* October to say, "It has become necessary to issue another edition of this book—and a man at Oberlin named [Charles Nelson] Cole has gone over the thing completely from the results of practical teaching and has made corrections, additions to the Vocabulary, etc." Cole (1871–1945) was educated at Illinois Wesleyan (A.B. 1894), Illinois (A.M. 1897), and Harvard (Ph.D. 1901). He was instructor in Greek and Latin at the Preparatory School of the University of Illinois (1895–97), instructor in Latin at Cornell (1899–1902), and associate professor (1902–4), professor of Latin (1904–36), and dean of the college of arts and sciences (1911–36) at Oberlin. He published nothing of importance. *WhAm* 5: 143.

2. Joseph Henry Allen (1820–98) and James Bradstreet Greenough (1833–1901), *Allen and Greenough's Latin Grammar for Schools and Colleges* (Boston: Ginn, 1901), a shorter version of their *A Latin Grammar Founded on Comparative Grammar* (Boston: Ginn, 1872) (See No. 25, n. 8).

3. A pun on "Hale and Buck" ( = *A Latin Grammar* by William Gardner Hale [1849–1928] and Carl Darling Buck [1866–1955] [Boston: Ginn, 1903]) and the *Heldenbuch*. For Gildersleeve on Hale, see No. 81, n. 5, and "The Teaching of Latin," *Nation* 45 (7 July 1887): 8.

4. See also Hale's "The Anticipatory Subjunctive in Greek and Latin: A Chapter of Comparative Syntax," *Univ. of Chicago Stud. Class. Phil.* 1 (1895): 1–92.

5. Rev. of *Studies*, *RCHL*, n.s., 56 (12 August 1903): 134n.

6. "The senior collaborator has furnished the greater part of the material; for the remainder, as well as for the notes, the vocabulary, and the arrangement, the junior collaborator is responsible" (*Latin Composition*, iv). The "book of exercises" mentioned below provided the material.

7. The first part of *Latin Composition* comprises sixty sets of single-sentence exercises, while the second part comprises sixty passages of continuous prose "frankly translated or adapted from accepted Latin models." 14C (no. 115, p. 135 in both editions) is drawn from Seneca *Epis. Mor.* 51.1–4. The first three sentences drill on the formula *Quid* + *agere*, twice in indirect questions, once in a direct question. Gildersleeve eliminated these sentences, added five others from Seneca's passage, and sent Lodge the changes in December.

8. I.e., "What is he intending (up to)?"; "What is he doing?"

9. William Arthur Heidel (1868–1941) graduated from Central Wesleyan College (A.B. 1888, A.M. 1891), studied at Berlin (1888–90), and, after teaching at Illinois Wesleyan (1890–94), became a fellow in Greek at the University of Chicago, from which he received a Ph.D. in 1895. He was professor of Latin at Iowa (now Grinnell) College (1896–1905) and finally at Wesleyan University from 1905 until his retirement in 1936. From 1906 to 1941 he served on the managing committee of the American School of Classical Studies at Athens, and as associate editor of *Classical Philology*; he was also a fellow of the American Academy of Arts and Sciences. In addition to his fifty articles and sixty reviews, he published his dissertation, *Pseudo-Platonica* (Baltimore: Friedenwald, 1896; reprint, New York: Arno Press, 1976); *The Necessary and the Contingent in the Aristotelian System* (Chicago: University of

Chicago Press, 1896), *Plato's Euthyphro* (Smyth Series) (New York: American Book Co., 1903; reprint, New York, Arno Press, 1976), and *Hippocratic Medicine, its Spirit and Method* (New York: Columbia University Press, 1941). *NatCAB* 30: 274-75. He had written Gildersleeve on 6 October 1903 that he was at work on Lucretius, but wanted to change the format from endnotes to footnotes. He never completed the project, later (12 October 1922) writing J. Ilberg, "I had spent seven years on an edition of Lucretius, which I abandoned because I could not find an American publisher willing to undertake anything but a text-book for college students, in which I was not interested."

10. *Il.* 20.169: ἐν δέ τέ οἱ κραδίῃ στένει ἄλκιμον ἦτορ ([a lion's] brave spirit groans in his heart).

### 127 To: HENRY RUSHTON FAIRCLOUGH
*Stanford*

December 27, 1903

Dear Professor Fairclough:

ἐγὼ τόδε τοι πέμπω—ὀψέ περ.[1] Prompt in most things I am slow to acknowledge the receipt of books for I have got into the way of entering the new arrivals on the Journal record and that seems to be a manner of quittance. But the dainty little volume[2] that bears your name and Murray's[3] belongs to a different category and I have been intending to write your colleague and yourself a special /letter/ —nay actually indited two lines of a little poem to express my gratification at the kind words written on the fly leaf. Murray and you had the strong literary bent before you ever knew me so that I can not take your expressions of indebtedness too strictly. Still I began as a literary man and it is always a comfort to me when I find that I have not warped the generous nature of my pupils by my grammatical methods. There is nothing that reconciles me to a career that has been full of disappointments than the success of my men and success of the right kind. So with best New Year's wishes for you both, I put your ANTIΓΟΝΗ among the special treasures of my library.

Yours faithfully and affectionately
B. L. Gildersleeve

Professor Fairclough

1. Pind. *Nem.* 3.76-80: "I send this to you—though late."
2. *The Antigone of Sophocles*, trans. Fairclough and A. T. Murray (San Francisco: P. Elder and M. Shepard, 1902).
3. Augustus Taber Murray (1866-1940) was educated at Haverford College (A.B. 1885) and Hopkins (Ph.D. 1890) and attended Leipzig and Berlin. He was professor of Greek at Earlham College (1888-90), Colorado College (1891-92), and Stanford (1892-1932). See No. 89, n. 1. He was annual professor at the American School of Classical Studies at Athens (1922-23), and made his mark as a translator, with three contributions to the Loeb Series: *The Odyssey, The Iliad* (both London: Heinemann; New York: Putnam, 1919 and 1924-25 respectively), and *Demosthenes Private Orations* (London: Heinemann; Cambridge, Mass.:

Harvard University Press, 1936); and *Four Plays of Euripides* (Stanford: Stanford University Press, 1931). He also wrote *Greek Composition for Colleges* and *The Anabasis of Xenophon* (both Chicago: Scott, Foresman, 1902 and 1914 respectively). *NatCAB* 30: 167–68.

### 128 To: THOMAS DAY SEYMOUR
*Yale-Seymour*

Manchester, Mass.[1]
Sept. 15, 1904

My dear Seymour:

I have cleared off all the arrears of my summer correspondence except the answer to your letter, which I saved for the last—so that I might give myself free rein. That letter was dated June 21, the day I sailed for the other side in the Saxonie[2] so that it had been lying in Baltimore all these weeks, awaiting my return from a somewhat freakish trip. I emerged from the work of the session fresher than usual so that I began to think that I might well have accepted an invitation to lecture in California[3]—and /I/ made very light of the promise I had given Münsterberg[4] to hold forth at St. Louis. 'I shall have time for that /' said I '/ and much more besides'— But my family protested against the strain of the long journey and the inevitable excitement, to say nothing of the equally inevitable failure of my oratorical efforts. So I suddenly felt very old, begged off from Münsterberg and betook myself to the other side. I had no earthly scientific excuse—no investigations to make, no MSS to collate—I wanted to see Europe once more—and one corner in particular that I had never seen. At seventy-two + there isn't much margin for trips and I felt that it was now or never. My wife went with me to check my enterprising spirit and we had an outing which enlarged our experiences and deepened our former impressions. We had scarcely anything but sunshine for the nine weeks we were ashore, so that if we had been determined sightseers, our two months would have been equivalent to double that amount. Unfortunately it was very hot in England and during our stay there I felt an indescribable lassitude, which interfered with my full enjoyment of my surroundings. When I got to London I found that George Macmillan[5] had put me down for a speech[6]—So I was forced to pull myself together and managed to scramble through somehow. It was fortunate for me that I preceded White,[7] who made ample amends for his aged and frivolous colleague. I made some new acquaintances, revived some old ones, but I feel I was not up to my normal tension and so we went to France where the climatic conditions of the sea-coast were much better.—Rouen—Trouville—Dives—Caën—Bayeaux—St. Malo—Dinard—these were the stations of our little French trip. At Dinard, a moody, flirty French watering place—'flirty' being used in a figurative sense—we stayed nearly two weeks—making little excursions in the neighborhood—Thence to Mt. St. Michel—and from Mt. St. Michel to Paris—where we spent a fortnight—much of it in the shops—as a tribute to my wife's care of me during the trip.—Thence back to London & Liverpool and so back by the same Saxonie to Boston, where we arrived on the eighth of September in better condition even than when we set out—an utterly unambitious, loafing summer and I am glad of it— —And the first letter I opened was yours—with all its kind appreciativeness of what I have done—and all the gentle admonition of what remains to be done in the few years that are left me. I do not mean to say that I have absolutely renounced all the fine projects to which you seem to think I am committed—but surely it is high time to say 'spatio brevi spem longam reseces'[8]—So long as I hold my professorship—so long as I continue to edit the Journal I cannot hope to do much besides and really I sometimes think I can't be better employed. I have said everything I want to say about Greek Syntax—and other men can collect examples as well as I can. What are the few epigrams I could contribute to the History of Greek Civilization in comparison with Ouvré's book,[9] which is an astounding performance in the matter of 'smartnesses'.—As for Aristophanes—my plan of an edition of the Frogs was given up long ago[10]—and if I were to do the Symposium,[11] I should not be allowed to lie in consecrated ground. To keep myself out of a drowsy circle,[12] I have been enjoying the Nemeans and Isthmians—which I intend to substitute for the Fragments of the Greek Lyric Poets in next session's work. It is very odd—going back to Pindar after all these years— going back to him in earnest—There is a certain disillusionment about it— I can't get into the exalted mood I was in twenty years ago.

I write thus freely to you—for of all the scholars I know you have shown the truest sympathy—and I value your kind interest in my work and your generous appreciation of all that I have tried to do more than I dare attempt to tell.

I saw Scott[13] in Paris. We three—my wife, Scott and I recalled with joy the hours we spent under your roof at New Haven in 1901—[14]

My wife joins me in affectionate messages to your familiars.

Yours faithfully
B. L. G.

1. Gardiner Lane (see "Correspondents") bought a summer country house in West Manchester in 1899. The estate of over 100 acres originally belonged to the poet and critic Richard Henry Dana, Sr. (1787–1879), who bought the land in 1845 and in 1846 built a house on a promontory overlooking a cove of surpassing beauty ("Dana's Beach"). Lane had Dana's house torn down to replace it with "The Chimneys," a large white Georgian house designed by Raleigh Gildersleeve, with seven freestanding chimneys to accommodate his sister's frequent ill-health and love of fireplaces. On the other hand, Emma so disliked the sound of the surf that she had her bedroom in the front of the house, as far from the beach as possible. The house was finished in 1904, and Gildersleeve probably came up for the housewarming. The grounds feature a great formal Italian garden, terraces, wildflower garden, and paths de-

signed by Frederick Law Olmstead, son of the designer of Central Park. Gildersleeve composed the following on the gardens:

The Chimneys
A classic garden, woodland walks romantic
Screened by a forest belt from idle priers
Love's safe retreat and friendship's sanctuary.
The beach sings welcome to its Lord Atlantic
And lilies listen to celestial choirs.
This is no 'Chimneys,' T''is the land of Faerie!

The house is currently the residence of Gildersleeve's granddaughter, Katharine L. Weems (No. 116, n. 7). On The Chimneys, see Elsie P. Youngman, *Summer Echoes from the 19th Century Manchester-by-the-Sea* (Rockport, Mass.: Don Russell, 1981), 138-40.

2. A 600' Cunard steamer. For a picture, see Eugene W. Smith, *Passenger Ships of the World Past and Present* (Boston: George H. Dean, 1947), 822.

3. Wheeler had asked Gildersleeve to come out to Berkeley as early as 1901 and broached the subject again on 7 December 1903, inviting him to teach in the summer session (27 June-7 August) for $750. Eleven years later, Wheeler invited Gildersleeve to be Sather lecturer (see No. 168).

4. Hugo Münsterberg (1863-1916), who was under the influence of Wilhelm Wundt, received a Ph.D. in Psychology from Leipzig in 1885 and an M.D. from Heidelberg in 1887. Teaching first at Freiburg, he was invited by William James to Harvard. After three years there, he returned to Freiburg for two years, then in 1897 returned to Harvard, where he remained until his death, founding a laboratory devoted to experimental psychology. See, further, *DAB* 14: 337-39. He had invited Gildersleeve (and Wheeler) to speak in the department of the history of language/philology at the World's Congress of Arts and Science at the St. Louis Exposition of 1904.

5. George Augustin Macmillan (1855-1936), the second son of Alexander Macmillan (No. 44, n. 4), was director of Macmillan and Co., one of the founders (along with Sayce [No. 45, n. 18]) and honorary secretary of the Hellenic Society (1879-1919) and its honorary treasurer (1879-1934). He was also honorary secretary of the British School at Athens (1886-97) and chairman of its managing committee. *Who Was Who* [England], *1929-1940*.

6. Gildersleeve spoke at the twenty-fifth meeting of the Hellenic Society, of which Jebb was president, and dined with Jebb on 6 July; see *The Life and Letters of Sir Richard Claverhouse Jebb O.M., Litt.D.*, ed. Lady C. Jebb (Cambridge: Cambridge University Press, 1907), 400. On the society, see, further, G. Macmillan, *An Outline of the History of the Society for the Promotion of Hellenic Studies, 1879-1904* (London: R. Clay and Sons, n.d.) and P. T. Stevens, *The Society for the Promotion of Hellenic Studies, 1879-1979* (Oxford: n.p., n.d.).

7. John Williams White (1849-1917) was educated at Ohio Wesleyan (B.A. 1878), studied in Germany, traveled in Greece, published his edition of the *Oedipus Tyrannus* (Boston: Ginn, 1874), and was a tutor at Harvard for three years (1874-77) before receiving his Ph.D. there in 1877. He was elected professor of Greek (1884-1909) and was a close associate of C. W. Eliot's (see No. 49, n. 12) in the development of Harvard. With C. E. Norton and W. W. Goodwin, he founded the Archaeological Institute of America in 1879 and was its president for five years. He was the first chairman of the managing committee of the American School of Classical Studies at Athens, was professor of Greek in 1893-94, and in 1890 founded *HSCP* with J. H. Allen and J. B. Greenough (No. 25, n. 8). One of the earliest Americans to be seriously interested in Greek metrics, he translated J. H. H. Schmidt's (see "Correspondents") *Leitfaden in der Rhythmik und Metrik der classischen Sprachen* as *An Introduction to the Rhythmic and Metric of the Classical Languages* (Boston: Ginn, 1869) and later wrote *The Verse of Greek Comedy* (London: Macmillan, 1912). His other publications include

school texts, many studies of Greek metre, and *The Scholia on the Aves of Aristophanes* (Boston: Ginn, 1914). He contributed one review to *AJP*. Among the many undergraduates he drew to classics, the most important may have been James Loeb (see No. 70, n. 4). *DAB* 20: 113–14.

8. Hor. *Carm.* 1.11.6–7: *sapias, vina liques, et spatio brevi spem / longam reseces* (Be wise, prune the vine, and cut back any long hope for our short span of life).

9. Henri Ouvré (1863–1903), *Les Formes littéraires de la pensée grecque* (Paris: F. Alcan, 1900); see *AJP* 25 (1904): 233–34 ( = *SBM*, 110–11). Gildersleeve's copy exists in the Hopkins Archive.

10. No. 71, n. 8.

11. On 9 January 1905, Gildersleeve wrote Barker Newhall (No. 98 and n. 4), who was planning an edition of the *Symposium*: "Ask yourself what professor would undertake to have classes—not to say mixed classes in the Symposium?" Gildersleeve regularly taught the *Symposium* in the four-year cycle in his seminary (1881, 1885–86, 1897–98, 1901–3, etc.). For Gildersleeve on this dialogue, see "Studies in the Symposium of Plato," *JHU Circulars*, no. 55 (January 1887): 49–50.

12. Perhaps from Plato *Rep.* 404a on the unsuitability of the bodily habit (ἕξις) of athletes: Ἀλλ', ἦν δ' ἐγώ, ὑπνώδης αὕτη γέ τις καὶ σφαλερὰ πρὸς ὑγίειαν (No, I said, that is a drowsy habit and dangerous for one's health).

13. On Scott, see "Correspondents."

14. See No. 120, n. 2.

## 129 To: EDWIN MIMS
*Vanderbilt*

Nov. 5, 1904

Dear Professor Mims:

I have fulfilled my promise and jotted down a few words about Sidney Lanier.[1] My acquaintance with him was not very long nor very close. I have no letter of his, no note—nothing characteristic and I have to deal in vague generalities. It is hardly what you want but it is all that I can do.

Yours sincerely
B. L. Gildersleeve

Professor Mims

You have set me a hard task. To make a photograph by so dim a light requires a long exposure and, as you say, I am a busy man. I was a busy man when I first knew Sidney Lanier, busy with the problems of the new University, with my courses of instruction, with my research, with my publications. And Lanier was a busy man, busy with his lectures,[2] with his work as a literary man,[3] with his work in the Peabody orchestra.[4] Once, I remember, he came to a dinner given in his honour fresh from a lecture at the Peabody in a morning suit and with chalk on his fingers.[5] Came thus, not because he was unmindful of conventionalities. He was as mindful of them as Browning. Came thus because he had to come thus. There was no time to dress. The poor chalk-fingered poet was miserable the whole evening, hardly roused himself when the talk fell on Blake and when we took a walk /together/ the next day he made his moan to me about it. A seraph with chalk on his fingers. ~~The old story of Pegasus in harness.~~[6] Somehow that little incident seems to me an epitome of his life, though I have mentioned it only to show how busy he was. I have been a pot-walloper myself and know what it is, know the bitterness of it. He knew the bitterness of it but kept his sweet temper throughout. And so it came about that though for a time he was a near neighbor of mine, just across the street,[7] I saw comparatively little of him. We never became intimate and yet we were good friends and there was much common ground.[8] Our talks usually turned on matters of literary form. He was eager, receptive, reaching out to all the knowable, transmuting all that he learned. He would have me read Greek poetry aloud to him for the sake of the rhythmical, the musical effect.[9] Offenbach the frivolous, as I have read somewhere and quoted somewhere, called music an algebra.[10] A frivolous soul was Offenbach but he began his career as a composer of sacred music. I have often thought of that definition of music in connection with Lanier. The gate through which he looked into the celestial city of poetry was the five-barred gate of the musical staff. So he was, so he is, hardly to be apprehended by one, who like myself, is not musical. Still the laws of rhythm have a wide range and in all that pertains to the art of verse, the more subtle art of prose, we were both deeply interested. It was delightful to see how he rediscovered antique doctrines of composition. Not only delightful but comforting: for it showed that these antique doctrines were not mere figments of pedants, that they went back to the consciousness of true artists. And there never was a truer artist in theory, in practice, in poetry, in music, in the conduct of life than Sidney Lanier, nor a purer. His bust at the Johns Hopkins recalls his personality.[11] 'A noticeable man',[12] tall, thin, quick in his movements, at least in his stronger days, a long stride, a mobile face, the face of a man who had seen visions and yet was not ~~unsure~~ /unaware/ of the life about him. To me he was always something apart /even/ before the world understood how far apart he dwelt from the mob of rhymers—'the tuneful choir' in the public language of the eighteenth century.[13] It is this separateness that made it hard for me to characterize Lanier when he was here, that makes it almost impossible for me to help you to fix what has become floating to me by the lapse of time. 'Into the woods my master went.'[14] The only thing to do is to go into the woods of poetry with the master.

1. Having lost his health in the Civil War, Lanier (1842-81), a poet and musician from Macon, Ga., arrived in Baltimore in December 1873 as first flutist of the Peabody Orchestra. Both he and Gildersleeve were Confederate veterans, and both had been contributors to the *Southern Magazine*. They had mutual friends in Baltimore and were members of the Wednesday Club, an amateur musical and dramatic organization. See *The Centennial Edition of the Works of Sidney Lanier*, vol. 10, *Letters, 1878-1881*, ed. C. R. Anderson and A. H. Starke (Baltimore: Johns Hopkins University Press, 1945), li, 54. On the strength of his

work in Anglo-Saxon poetry, Lanier was appointed lecturer in English at Hopkins from 1879 to 1881 (see chapter 3, introduction). In 1878 he organized a course of lectures at the Peabody on Shakespeare, to which Gildersleeve contributed two talks, one on *Agamemnon* and *Macbeth*, the other on Lucian's *Timon of Athens* compared with Shakespeare's (*Lanier Letters*, 70). Mims' book (see No. 133) is *Sidney Lanier* (Boston: Houghton Mifflin, 1905).

2. Lanier's lectures at Hopkins were published as *The Science of English Verse* (New York: Scribner, 1880); see "Grammar and Aesthetics," *Princeton Review* 59 (1883): 307, n. 1 ( = *E&S*, 152–53).

3. *The Boy's Froissart, The Boy's King Arthur, The Boy's Mabinogion, The Boy's Percy*, and *The English Novel and the Principle of its Development* (New York: Scribner, 1879, 1880, 1881, 1882, 1883 respectively).

4. Lanier had written a cantata for the American centennial, *The Centennial Meditation of Columbia, 1776–1876*, in addition to his duties with the Peabody orchestra.

5. This and the next six sentences are quoted by Mims, p. 302.

6. Gildersleeve may refer to the story at Pind. *Ol.* 13.64ff.

7. Lanier lived at 180 St. Paul Street in 1879 when Gildersleeve was living at 255 St. Paul Street.

8. This and the next three sentences are quoted by Mims, p. 239.

9. Mims reads incorrectly as "the rhythmic and musical effect."

10. "Offenbach the frivolous has said: 'music is an algebra'. Poetry like music is made up of equations" ("Symmetry in Pindar," *JHU Circulars*, no. 25 [August 1883]: 138). See also "Grammar and Aesthetics," (cited n. 2 above): 310 ( = *E&S*, 157): "Music and architecture rest on mathematics."

11. The bust by Ephraim Keyser was placed in Donovan Hall at Hopkins and now resides in Special Collections in the Milton S. Eisenhower Library.

12. Wordsworth, "Stanzas Written in my Pocket-Copy of Thomson's 'Castle of Indolence' ": "A noticeable Man with large gray eyes" (3).

13. E.g., Thomas Gray, "Stanzas to Mr. Bentley," 1–2: "In silent gaze the tuneful choir among, / Half pleas'd half blushing let the muse admire," and Dryden, "Alexander's Feast; or, the Power of Musique: An Ode on St. Cecilia's Day," 20–21: "*Timotheus* plac'd on high / Amid the tuneful Quire."

14. Lanier, "A Ballad of Trees and the Master," written in Baltimore, 1 December 1880, published in the *Independent* 32 (23 December 1880).

## 130 To: T.D. SEYMOUR
### *Yale-Seymour*

Baltimore March 12, 1905

My dear Seymour:

Your appreciation of my work has helped me during all these years much more than you can ever know and I am honestly delighted that you like my latest escapade which landed me among the psychologists.[1] The paper was wrung from me by a New York man[2] who insisted that I ought /not/ to hide all this philosophy from the world and so I have put into print the substance of a private conversation. The thoughts such as they are have been familiar to me for years and I have aired them in my lecture-room and among friends but I should not have had the courage to bring /them/ out, if I had not been assured by specialists that they were worth while.

I can echo part of your letter.[3] If any one had told me twenty-five years ago that the Journal would be my best chance of being remembered, I should have been much chagrined. I had so much more important things to do, although in my salutatory I naturally magnified my new office.[4] But life shapes itself without regard to our planning and in the last few years since the quest of copy has ceased to worry me, I have taken a certain pleasure in getting up the little paragraphs in Brief Mention. I am at heart a feuilletoniste and ought to have stuck to the newspaper vocation, which has always attracted me. Poor old Wilson [sic] who was hanged for murdering D$^r$. Parkman was called Skyrocket Jack at Harvard.[5] Perhaps some day I may share his fate—metaphorically [—] and sometimes I dolefully compare my rocket stick with the well-squared timber of men whom I recognize as true scholars. It will be some comfort to me when I am turned off[6] that you were persuaded better things of me.

Why you should have any regrets as to your career I cannot see. Whatever you have published is structurally solid, could not have been /done/ by any man who did not know his business thoroughly. It is the kind of work that inspires respect and every professional teacher of Greek appreciates the influence you have exercised as an apostle of sanity. And yet you are so generous in your judgement of others who are not so sound.

My wife joins me in kind regards to Mrs. Seymour[7] and yourself.

Yours faithfully<br>B. L. Gildersleeve

Professor Seymour

1. "A Syntactician among the Psychologists," *Journal of Philosophy, Psychology and Scientific Methods* 2 (1905): 92–97; reprinted, with a prefatory note, *AJP* 31 (1910): 74–79. Seymour had written Gildersleeve on 10 March: "Seldom do I see—seldom have I ever seen—an article of five pages into which so much thought and sound learning are packed as in your article on 'A Syntactician' +c. I thank you for sending me a copy."

2. Frederick James Eugene Woodbridge (1867–1940), who had succeeded Nicholas Murray Butler as professor of philosophy at Columbia and in 1904 was named first Johnsonian professor of philosophy. He founded his journal (after 1920 called *The Journal of Philosophy*) with James McKeen Cattell in 1904 and edited it until his death. See, further, *DAB* suppl. 2, 734–35.

3. In the letter mentioned in n. 1, Seymour, after congratulating Gildersleeve on twenty-five years of *AJP*, said: "I should have been much hurt a quarter of a century ago if one of my friends had predicted that I should (in this time) do no more really scholarly work than I have shown" in addition to his pedagogical and administrative duties.

4. "Editorial Note," *AJP* 1 (1880): 1–3, esp. p. 3: "The Journal enters upon a career that is full of hope. To be found not wholly unworthy of this trust is henceforth one of the highest aims of my professional life."

5. Professor George Parkman (1790–1849), a noted Boston physician, and donor of the land on which the Harvard Medical School stands, was murdered in a college laboratory on 23 November 1849 by John White *Webster* (1793–1850), professor of chemistry and mineralogy and author of *A Manual of Chemistry* (Boston: Marsh, Capen, Lyon and Webb, 1839), who was hanged for the offense. See *The Trial of Professor John White Webster*, intro. by

George Dilnot (New York: Scribner, 1928). S. E. Morison, in *Three Centuries of Harvard* (Cambridge, Mass.: Harvard University Press, 1936), 282, called the affair "the gravest scandal in the history of the University."

6. I.e., "hanged."

7. Sarah Melissa Hitchcock Seymour (1846–1916), the daughter of Henry Hitchcock, president of Case Western Reserve, Seymour's alma mater, where he was professor (1872–80).

131 To: D.C. Gilman
*JHU-Gilman*

{The Norfolk Hotel,
Harrington Road,
South Kensington.}
July 13, 1905

Dear Mr. Gilman:

Your kind note of July 1[1] reached me to-day and I suspend my packing to thank you for the affectionate interest you have shewn in the recent distinctions that have fallen to my lot.[2] Like nearly all my honours, the Cambridge and Oxford degrees, having come late in my life, fail to affect the severity with which I have always judged my/self/[3] ~~feeling~~ and my dominant feeling is a desire to do something worthy of all the pleasant things that have been said publicly and privately about my work. So you must forgive me, my dear friend, if I shew a little nervousness about the eloquent tribute you have paid to my aims and my achievements. I feel almost ashamed of having imposed on so clearsighted a judge.

The memorable meeting in Washington to which you refer was the turning point of my life.[4] I have never stopped to ask myself what would have become of me, if I had not put myself under your guidance. I should doubtless have done some honest work, but without the Johns Hopkins I should never have edited Pindar, the thing that has made me more friends among English classical scholars than anything else I have done,[5] and without your suggestion and your aid I should never have established the American Journal of Philology, which according to the Oxford orator is the crowning achievement of my long career.[6] So that all I have done and been in the last thirty years is bound up with your work in Baltimore, and the recognition of my position in the world of classical scholars is at the same time a recognition of your greater achievement.

My wife and I are about to leave London for the Continent. She has never seen Belgium or Holland and we shall spend a fortnight there. After that we have no definite plans. I feel a certain longing to see my old university Göttingen again[7] and to renew my early acquaintance with Thüringen. A friend suggests the Dolomites—where you were so happy some years

ago[8] and old ties draw us to Lausanne and the Lake of Geneva. We expect
to reach Paris about the first of September and to sail for home on the
tenth from Cherbourg. I must confess that I have lost much of my old love
of touring and envy you the quiet sea side[9] with a shelf of books old and
new.

My wife joins me in best thanks for your letter of congratulation and in
all manner of kind messages to Mrs. Gilman.

Yours faithfully<br>
B. L. Gildersleeve

President Gilman

1. Gilman's note has not survived.
2. At 3 P.M. on 14 June 1905 in the Senate House, Cambridge, Gildersleeve was awarded
a doctorate of letters. Also honored were Lord Reay, president of the British Academy, S. R.
Driver, professor of Hebrew at Oxford, Father Francis Ehrle, prefect of the Vatican Library,
and Frederic Harrison. At 12 noon on 28 June Gildersleeve was made a doctor of letters at
the Encaenia in the Sheldonian Theatre, Oxford, along with the painter Holman Hunt and
Maj. Gen. Sir Francis Wingate.
3. For example, Gildersleeve had expressed his "invincible self-distrust" to Gilman at the
beginning of his career at Hopkins (BLG to Gilman, 10 June 1876).
4. See No. 16, n. 1.
5. For a thirty-year retrospective of his *Pindar*, see "Pindaric Notes," *JHU Circulars*, no.
287 (July 1916), 35–37. See also R. L. Fowler, "The Gildersleeve Archive," *Briggs-Benario*,
n. 117.
6. The oration, by W. W. Merry, was never published and no copy has survived.
7. See No. 157.
8. Gilman had toured Italy in 1900 (see No. 112, n. 1).
9. Gilman was summering at his cottage, "Over-Edge," on a cliff in Northeast Harbor on
the SSW coast of Mt. Desert, the island on which he had vacationed since 1881 (*Franklin*,
416–17).

132 To: WALLACE MARTIN LINDSAY
*St. Andrews*

Nov. 2, 1905

Dear Professor Lindsay:

When the Chicago people told me that they were about to get up a journal of classical philology, what could I say?[1] One man informed me that it
was intended to stimulate production in the West, another that it was
meant to provide a vehicle for the teeming wealth of the West,[2] a third that
it was to be largely given up to reviews of current philological literature,[3]
for which as I had often lamented, there was scant space in my Journal. Of
course, they have my best wishes, but it is not in human nature to be overjoyed at an enterprise, which will certainly draw away from me valued contributors and make my editorial work harder.[4] But as Wilamowitz wrote to
me some time ago in a noble letter 'Die Wissenschaft geht vor'[5] and I hon-

estly wish them all success and a maintenance of the scientific standard. Some of my best friends have gone into the enterprise[6] and your name will help them very much.

The German slip in quantity amused me greatly and reminds me that I wrote in my maiden essay 'Necessity of the Classics'[7] more than fifty years ago à propos of English scholarship 'Every lad in the rudiments learns to sneer at Paley's ⟨false⟩ quantity[8] and triumph over Pitt's short syllable in labenti' with a reference to Macaulay's Essays— Art— Thackeray's Chatham.[9] So I have put your letter in my own copy of the Journal Vol. XXIII p. 4.[10]

Let me congratulate you on the completion of your edition of Plautus— It is a boon to every Latin scholar. How I wish I could take up 'the hearty old Cock' as I did when I was a student in Ritschl's prime.[11]

But thanks for your note.[12] It really did require an answer because I was pleased to see that you recognized the friendly spirit of the Journal or what is the same thing of its editor.

Yours faithfully<br>B. L. Gildersleeve

Professor W. M. Lindsay

1. Lindsay was a member of the original board of *Classical Philology*, serving from 1906 to 1937. G. L. Hendrickson (see "Correspondents") of the University of Chicago wrote to Gildersleeve on 17 December 1904 asking his opinion of (and blessing for) the establishment of the journal by his department: "The thought of entering this field has I think come to us mainly from a realization that a good many young men who have shown promise by dissertation and otherwise go forth + fall victims to the depression of their environment + produce nothing more. . . . There is too here in the West a considerable amount of almost wasted effort going into petty 'series'. . . There is also the question of the effect which a new publication might have upon your journal." *CP*'s prospectus likewise acknowledged Gildersleeve: "The impetus given to research in classical philology by Professor Gildersleeve is due not less to the influence of *The American Journal of Philology* founded by him than to his instruction and example. In so far as CLASSICAL PHILOLOGY shall fulfill its object it may in fact be looked upon as an off-shoot of *The American Journal of Philology* and as a witness to its founder's influence upon American classical scholarship." Gildersleeve welcomed the first issue, published 1 January 1906, but others were not so charitable, e.g., Seymour, writing to Gildersleeve on 10 February 1906: "I think my colleagues here all agree with me in regretting the establishment of Classical Philology, and I believe all would prefer to publish articles in your Journal. We recognized your courtesy in giving a formal welcome to the new periodical, but in my opinion quite enough is published in our line, and the quality will not be improved by increasing the quantity."

2. E.g., Hendrickson: "It will be well for the cause of classical studies to provide a more abundant opportunity for publication, to collect what is now scattered, and if possible to stimulate new and greater activity." These are the main points of justification in the prospectus.

3. "In addition to formal articles stating the results of investigations, especial attention will be given to reviews of books and monographs. . . . It will be the aim of the editors to supply . . . a real need by the prompt publication of critical notices of American, as well as European, work" (Prospectus).

4. "The whole Chicago enterprise is a repetition of the Aaron Burr conspiracy. . . . It is a droll thing that an antique secessionist like myself should be called to support the national standard of an American journal" (BLG to Seymour, 20 February 1906).

5. Wilamowitz's letter is lost.

6. Original associate editors included Lodge, C. F. Smith, Wheeler, and J. W. White. On the editorial staff, Hendrickson and Laing were former students of Gildersleeve's, and F. F. Abbott, Paul Shorey, and Edward Capps, the managing editor, were friends and correspondents.

7. *Southern Quarterly Review* 26 (n.s. 10) (July 1854): 145–67. The quotation is from p. 158 ( = *AJP* 37 [1916]: 497 = *SBM*, 368).

8. See *AJP* 36 (1915): 360–61 ( = *SBM*, 335–36).

9. Pitt wrote some Latin verses on the death of George I. "All true Etonians will hear with concern that their illustrious school-fellow is guilty of making the first syllable in *labenti* short," Macaulay remarked in "William Pitt, Earl of Chatham," review of *A History of the Right Honourable William Pitt, . . .* by Rev. Francis Thackeray, reprinted in T. B. Macaulay, *Critical and Historical Essays Contributed to the Edinburgh Review*, vol. 2 (London: Longman, Brown, Green, and Longmans, 1844), 150. A note adds: "So Mr. Thackeray has printed the poem. But it may be charitably hoped that Pitt wrote *labanti*."

10. In "Problems in Greek Syntax," *AJP* 23 (1902), where he discusses "absurd lapses" in verse composition.

11. See *PAPA* 8 (1877): 14–15 and *AJP* 5 (1884): 339–55.

12. Lindsay's note is lost.


### 133 To: EDWIN MIMS
*Vanderbilt*

Baltimore Nov. 21, 1905

Dear Professor Mims:

Your Sidney Lanier[1] came to me yesterday during the hours that are sacred to my professional work. I do not know when I have ever laid aside my regular work for any thing else. But that day I played truant and read little or no Greek. Both the subject and the presentation [of] it interested me deeply and I congratulate you on the successful accomplishment of a difficult task. It is so hard to hold the balance between promise and performance where the promise is so largely the performance. But there is performance enough to give Lanier the poet a permanent place in the best American literature. True the life was the great thing as we all felt, who were privileged to watch the progress of that rare spirit through the every day world, as something apart. It is a gratification to me that you thought any words of mine worthy of association with his name and fame and his fragrant memory.[2]

Faithfully yours
Basil L. Gildersleeve

Professor Mims

1. See No. 129.
2. Ibid., nn. 5 and 8.

# 7

# EMINENCE, 1906–1915

In his sixth and final decade of teaching, Gildersleeve stood astride his profession. He had eclipsed Goodwin in importance. Students of his, such as Smyth, Allinson, Harry, Lodge, and Fairclough, were themselves important figures, and Bolling, Hendrickson, and J. A. Scott were among the best young men in classics (see No. 169, n. 1). Gildersleeve's "sphere of influence" included such men as Shorey and C. F. Smith. His views were solicited by Southern literary historians (Nos. 138–39), his "blessing" was sought by John Dewey for the fledgling AAUP (No. 165), and his opinions were quoted by journalists, both in articles (No. 152) and in the amusing and informative interviews he began to give. Since, as Shorey says, "by the maturing experience of long years, by varied travel and study and intercourse with the scholars of all nations, and it may be by the opportunities of his life work in the earliest of American universities . . . Gildersleeve developed into what it is pleasant to believe is the ideal type of cultured and scholarly American," and because *AJP* had shown his nation's scholarship (and its editor's) to be in many ways equal to or better than that of the Europeans, he was the first classicist elected to the National Institute of Arts and Letters and later to the American Academy of Arts and Letters. Further, the rapprochement with Wilamowitz (No. 146) had cleared the way for wider acceptance of his work in his beloved Germany.

Still, his natural modesty did not permit him to enjoy honors that he felt came to him too late in life to do him the good they once might have (No. 154), and he grew pessimistic about the future of the classics in America (No. 152). It was time to begin to sum things up. He followed his autobiographical articles *Formative Influences* (1891) and *Professorial Types* (1893) with "A Novice of 1850," *Johns Hopkins Alumni Magazine* 1 (November 1912): 3–9; "The College in the Forties," *Princeton Alumni Weekly* 16, no. 16 (26 January 1916): 375–79; and the inaugural Barbour-Page Lectures at the University of Virginia, *Hellas and Hesperia* (No. 143), which were "drawn mainly from my memories of life and books." He was an unofficial genealogist of his highly extended family (Nos. 144, 149).

Though Gildersleeve may have seen himself as a lame schoolmaster like

Tyrtaeus, or sympathized with the sufferings of crippled Philoctetes (No. 151) the rest of the American classical world began to view him in the way his students always had, as Zeus.

134 To: UNIVERSITY OF GLASGOW
*University of Glasgow*

Johns Hopkins University, Baltimore
August 27, 1906

My opinion of Mr RHYS ROBERTS'[1] equipment for the high position he is seeking does not rest wholly on his published work, with which the course of my studies has made me familiar; for a personal acquaintance has put me in a position to understand better than I could otherwise have done the scope of his educational activity, which seems to have been no less remarkable than his contributions to philological literature. These contributions have been received by the world of scholars with a rare unanimity of approval and admiration. The breadth of his views, the soundness of his scholarship, the fineness of his literary touch have been noted by all his critics; and the value of his initiative in a domain that has been too much neglected in Great Britain is recognised on all hands. As the study of ancient rhetoric forms a substantial part of my work as a teacher of Greek, I have welcomed most cordially each of Mr Roberts' additions to my apparatus, and have more than once given public expression to my sense of the debt that I owe to his labours.[2] I will allow myself to add that in the present crisis of Hellenic studies it is highly important that Greek should be represented at the great University of Glasgow by a man who, like Mr Roberts, is well furnished for the office of showing the formative influence of Hellenism and for the honour of maintaining the tradition of the Greek chair, a tradition consecrated by the life and the work of Sir Richard Jebb.[3]

BASIL L. GILDERSLEEVE

1. William Rhys Roberts (1858-1929) took a first place in the Classical Tripos in 1881 at Cambridge and received an M.A. in 1884 (Litt.D. 1900, Hon. LL.D., St. Andrews). After serving as professor of Greek at the University of North Wales (1884-1904), he joined the young classics department at the new University of Leeds, where he stayed until his retirement in 1923. Quickly realizing that he would be required to devote a great deal of time to extension work, however, he unsuccessfully applied for the chair at Glasgow. His publications include *The Ancient Boeotians*, his editions with translations of *Longinus On the Sublime*, *Demetrius On Style* (Cambridge: Cambridge University Press, 1895, 1899, and 1902 respectively), *Dionysius of Halicarnassus on Literary Composition* (London: Macmillan, 1910), *Aristotle: The Poetics; "Longinus": On the Sublime* (Loeb Classical Library) (London: Heinemann; New York: Putnam, 1927); and his translation, *Aristotle's Rhetoric* (New York: Modern Library, 1954). *The Times* (London), 1 November 1929: 18.
    2. See *AJP* 18 (1897): 493 ( = *SBM*, 47); 20 (1899): 228-29; 24 (1903): 101-6 ( = *SBM*,

90–94), esp. 92: "One hails with satisfaction the prospect of a new edition of the *De Composi-tione* [of Dionysius of Halicarnassus] by so competent a hand as Mr. Roberts."
   3. For Jebb, see No. 45, n. 4.

## 135 To: Thomas Day Seymour
### *Yale-Seymour*

{ The Chimneys[1]
Manchester, Massachusetts. }
Sept. 16, 1906

My dear Seymour:

It was a real charity to let me know that you like my outgivings in the last number of the Journal.[2] As I grow older, I feel more and more lonely and self distrustful; and I read and reread with dismay Rudyard Kipling's cruel indictment of the old man,[3] which I have copied on the fly leaf of my favorite performance, my Problems in Greek Syntax.[4] The jests, such as they are, still come readily enough, and as you say, I get a certain amusement out of my own fancies, but the personal note which appeals to some of those who know me and especially to such good friends as you are, may do more harm than good to the Journal, as a serious periodical. But I am too old to mend my ways and as I have sacrificed so much to the Journal, I hope it will survive me and looking down the years I say to myself mox sine cortice nabit.[5]

My general health is very good but I wrenched my sound knee in the early summer and I must renounce long walks—a great privation. Le temps, ce vieux Parthe, nous tue en fuyant[6] and I have some shooting pains to remind me of my uric trouble in my blood. My wife had a sharp spell of sickness in mid-summer but she has bloomed out again. We spent a month at the Warm Springs of Virginia[7] for the sake of my infirmity with no marked benefit. The bath was delicious and that is something to remember. A ten days' stay at my daughter's was followed by a sojourn of five or six weeks at my old resort—the Hawthorne Inn, E. Gloucester.[8] Since the twelfth of this /month/ my wife and I have been here—the most beautiful place for situation on the whole North Shore—the family being abroad. Of course we miss them sadly—but old people must learn the lesson of renunciation. We have had no discomfort from the heat the entire summer and may count ourselves fortunate.

My wife joins me in kind regards to Mrs. Seymour[9] and yourself and to your children whom we are glad to have seen so that our message means something.

Yours faithfully
B. L. Gildersleeve

1. For The Chimneys, see No. 128, n. 1.

2. Gildersleeve's Brief Mention at *AJP* 27 (1906): 359-61 ( = *SBM*, 132-33) dealt with V. Bérard's *Navigations d'Ulysse* (Paris: A. Colin, 1906).

3. "The Old Men" in *Five Nations* (London: Methuen, 1903), 49-51, reads in part: "This is our lot if we live so long and labour unto the end— / That we outlive the impatient years and the much too patient friend: / And because we know we have breath in our mouth and think we have thought in our head, / We shall assume that we are alive, whereas we are really dead."

4. *AJP* 23 (1902): 1-27, 121-41, 241-60 (reprinted Baltimore: Johns Hopkins Press, 1903).

5. Hor. *Sat.* 1.4.119-20, Horace is addressed by his father: *simul ac duraverit aetas / membra animumque tuum, nabis sine cortice* (As soon as age shall have strengthened your limbs and soul, you will swim without a float).

6. "Time, that old Parthian, kills us as he flees." Possibly composed by Gildersleeve.

7. The Warm Springs (said to be 98° F.) twenty miles north of Clifton Forge in Bath Co., Va., was one of the oldest of the Virginia springs and always far less formal than Hot or White Sulphur Springs. Fallen into decreptitude, it was bought in 1891 (along with Hot and Healing Springs) by a syndicate that included J. P. Morgan, George Bliss, and others. See P. Reniers, *The Springs of Virginia* (Chapel Hill: University of North Carolina Press, 1941), 270-71. The gentlemen's circular bath house, where Gildersleeve undoubtedly took the waters for his gout, alone of the nineteenth-century structures still remains in use. For photographs, see M. Fishwick, *Springlore in Virginia* (Bowling Green, Ky.: Bowling Green State University Popular Press, 1978), 262-64.

8. The Hawthorne Inn, built in 1891, was the social center of picturesque East Gloucester, Mass., some forty miles up the north shore of Massachusetts from Boston and eight from Manchester and The Chimneys. Situated on Wonson's Point, the inn held 450 guests and had a "permanent waiting list," despite mediocre food and its reputation as "a third-class hotel run for first-class people." See J. E. Garland, *Boston's Gold Coast: The North Shore, 1890-1929* (Boston: Little, Brown, 1981), 51-54.

9. See No. 130, n. 6.


### 136 To: Edward Fitch[1]
*Hamilton College Library*

January 2, 1907

Dear Professor Fitch:

Your letter[2] interests me deeply. Wilamowitz[3] is a wonderful man and not the least wonderful thing about him is his generosity, paired as it is with a caustic wit that burns to the bone. The only letter I ever received from him pertained to my comments on his Timotheos.[4] Nothing could have been more frank, more chivalric. —I do not swear by him—but there is nothing like him in the range of my studies[5] for suggestion,[6] for illumination.[7] From chance expressions of his, I gather that he thinks well of the spirit of American work and I am pleased to learn that he counts me as one of the agencies in the progress of the last quarter of a century.

I hope that you will bring your studies in oratio obliqua into an accessible form.[8] Don't postpone the publication too long.—I send you herewith a recent doctoral dissertation by one of my men[9]—which touches on the subject p. 30 foll. Ebeling[10] is a man for whom I have a sincere affection and it is a pleasure to know that you two are friends and together hold me in kind remembrance.

With best wishes to you both[11] for the New Year.

I am

Yours sincerely,

B. L. Gildersleeve

1. This letter, to Wilamowitz's only American doctoral student, has been published by W. M. Calder III, "B. L. Gildersleeve and Ulrich von Wilamowitz-Moellendorff: New Documents," *AJP* 99 (1978): 3-4 ( = *Selected Correspondence*, 143-44).

2. Fitch had written Gildersleeve on 1 January 1907 describing Wilamowitz's letter encouraging his interest in the history of indirect discourse. "This general topic led him to refer to you and to your services to classical philology in America; which he did with such evident cordiality that I am tempted to make this personal reference."

3. On Wilamowitz, see "Correspondents." Gildersleeve's appreciation developed over the years: "If any man desires to be avenged of a philological adversary he need only await Wilamowitz's leisure, for annihilation at his hands is merely a question of time" (*AJP* 12 [1891]: 387). Gildersleeve's favorite epithet for Wilamowitz was "Rough Rider"; see *AJP* 22 (1901): 232 ( = *SBM*, 69), at *Johns Hopkins University: Celebration of the Twenty-fifth Anniversary of the Founding of the University and Inauguration of Ira Remsen, LL.D. as President of the University* (Baltimore: Johns Hopkins Press, 1902), 162, "Oscillations and Nutations of Philological Studies," *JHU Circulars*, no. 151 (April 1901): 50, and "Pindaric Notes," *JHU Circulars*, no. 287 (July 1916): 36. See also BLG to Ebeling, 21 April, 8 May 1906, and 25 September 1907.

4. *Timotheos: Die Perser* (Leipzig: J. C. Hinrichs'sche Buchhandlung, 1903), reviewed by Gildersleeve at *AJP* 24 (1903): 222-36. This is probably the letter referred to in No. 132.

5. Calder adduces *AJP* 37 (1916): 500 ( = *SBM* 372): "Wilamowitz himself has no parallel, he has the range of Hermann, the vitality of Bentley and Verrall's sense of literature."

6. See *AJP* 22 (1911): 232 ( = *SBM*, 69).

7. See *AJP* 34 (1913): 111 ( = *SBM*, 280).

8. Fitch produced only the abstract "The Proprieties of Epic Speech in the *Argonautica* of Apollonius Rhodius," *PAPA* 33 (1902): lix-lxi. In the previous year Gildersleeve had written "Notes on the Evolution of Oratio Obliqua," *AJP* 27 (1906): 200-208.

9. G. W. Elderkin, *Aspects of the Speech in the Later Greek Epic* (Baltimore: Friedenwald, 1906).

10. Herman Louis Ebeling (1857-1945) was educated at Hopkins (B.A. 1882, Ph.D. 1891) and at Berlin, Bonn, and Göttingen (1894-95). He taught at Overlea Home School (1877-79), German Theological Seminary (1882-86), Miami University (Oxford, Ohio) (1891-99), Haverford (1901-3), Hamilton (1903-11), and Goucher College, Baltimore (1911-33). He published his dissertation, *A Study in the Sources of the Messeniaca of Pausanias* (Baltimore: J. Murphy, 1892); *Greek Thought: Selections from Homer to Menander* (Baltimore: privately printed, 1934); and regular reports on *Hermes* for *AJP*. *NatCAB* 33: 397.

11. Calder (n. 1, above), n. 18, thinks he refers to Fitch and his wife, but Fitch had closed his letter with a mention of his holiday dinner with Ebeling, "the sharer of all my philological hopes and misgivings" and does not mention his wife, so it seems Gildersleeve means Fitch and Ebeling by "you both."

137 To: BENJAMIN LAWTON WIGGINS
*Sewanee*

{Villa Victoria
Karlsbad}[1] June 19, 1907

Dear Vice-Chancellor:

Your letter of May 30th. did not reach me until this morning and by the time my answer arrives the great and notable day of Sewanee's Jubilee[2] will be over and the opportunity past of expressing even in some inadequate fashion my interest in the noble work you and your colleagues have done and are doing in your city set on a hill, my admiration of the lofty spirit of conseration [sic],[3] which animates your academic community and the pleasure I take in recalling the days,[4] when I was permitted to breathe your air, to share your activity and to enjoy the companionship of the chosen spirits, who made Sewanee a cherished memory for the remainder of my days. I am glad that President Remsen[5] is to be the representative of the Johns Hopkins on the great occasion for he is not unaware of the closeness of the ties that bind me to Sewanee, and if in the high tide of your celebration I should not be forgotten, he will not fail to report the evidence that I have not wrought at Sewanee in vain.

When Professor Swiggett[6] asked me to contribute something to the Jubilee Pathfinder,[7] the notice was too short and my work too engrossing to permit me to prepare anything worthy of such a time but I did not have the heart to decline outright and so on the impulse of the moment I offered him a characteristic extract from my lectures on the Odyssey.[8] I have had many misgivings since about the propriety of fixing in print such a burlesque as the 'Ballad of the Swineherd' but the 'Ballad of the Swineherd' was conceived in the spirit of the E.Q.B.[9] which used to brew the strongest punch known to my ancient experience in such matters. So I trust I shall be forgiven if I appear in motley at your grand jubilee.

I have recovered so rapidly in the last few weeks from my trouble of last winter[10] and am performing such pedestrian feats since I have been over here that I feel as if I had come to Karlsbad under false pretences and that I ought really to be roaming about the region of 'Peerless Tennessee' instead. My <u>kur</u> will be a very mild one as the doctor finds very little the matter with me but he thinks that my wife will be greatly benefited by the waters—which he considers a specific for her form of chronic indigestion. At all events the long rest will make me hungry for my usual work.

We both join in best regards to Mrs. Wiggins and your household and we both look forward with great interest to the accounts of the celebration which will assuredly redound to the glory of our great and good friend, the Vice-Chancellor.

Yours faithfully
B. L. Gildersleeve

1. On Karlsbad, see No. 93, n. 10.

2. Wiggins had written on 17 April inviting Gildersleeve to Sewanee's Semi-Centennial Jubilee on 20-27 June 1907, with the exercises held on the 26th and 27th. When Gildersleeve declined, Wiggins wrote again on 30 May asking for a letter to be read on 27 June, but Gildersleeve did not know that this letter would be published as an appendix to *Semi-Centennial of the University of the South* (Sewanee, Tenn.: Sewanee University Press, 1907), 121-22. Wiggins apologized in a letter of 21 March 1908.

3. In its published form (see above note), this word was read as "consecration." Minor punctuation changes were also made.

4. In three summers between 1883 and 1887 (he visited for one week only in 1885).

5. See No. 50, n. 22, and 112, n. 5.

6. Glen Levin Swiggett (1867-1961) was educated at Indiana University (A.B. 1888, A.M. 1890) and the University of Pennsylvania (Ph.D. 1901), in addition to graduate work at Hopkins in German (1889-90, 1892-93). After teaching at Michigan, Purdue, and Missouri, he was professor of modern languages at Sewanee (1903-12) and founded and edited the Sewanee *Pathfinder*, which lasted for five volumes (July 1906-11). Following his tenure at Sewanee, he became a consultant to the U.S. Bureau of Education and published eight volumes of sonnets. *Who's Who* 29 (1956-57): 2524.

7. "The Ballad of the Swineherd," *Pathfinder* 2 (July 1907): 2-9.

8. He read the ballad at Northwestern on Friday, 14 May 1897 (see No. 101, n. 5).

9. A literary and social club for the professors, officers, and gentlemen resident at Sewanee, organized in 1870 and meeting bimonthly. The name E.Q.B. derives from "Ecce Quam Bonum," the title of Psalm 133 and the motto on the pamphlet of the board of trustees meeting at Lookout Mountain in 1853. The name was suggested by General Josiah Gorgas, second vice-chancellor of the university.

10. Having wrenched his knee in the summer (No. 135), a "stiffness" (BLG to Ebeling, 2 October 1906) was aggravated by his chronic rheumatism.


### 138 To: EDWIN MIMS
*Vanderbilt*

Sept. 26, 1907

Dear Professor Mims:

Your letter of Aug. 9th.[1] reached me a few days ago after my return from Europe, where I spent nearly four months for the benefit of my health, which, I am happy to say, seems to be quite restored. The arrears of correspondence were heavy so that I have just come to your letter—which could not be dispatched in a few lines.

Some time ago the literary critic of the N.Y. /Sun/[2] rebuked [?] Trent[3] for mentioning me among the 'literary men' of the country—He granted that I was a scholar but my 'literary baggage' was of the slightest—Perhaps he was right—Yet in my long career I have written enough that might be called 'literature' to justify mention and even in my technical writing I have never forgotten that my original purpose in life was to be a man of letters.[4] The 'Brief Mention' of the American Journal of Philology is to some extent 'literary'—and if I were to collect my newspaper work,[5] my formal addresses, my fugitive poems[6]—to say nothing of my popular lectures—there would be matter enough for a number of volumes—But at my time of life I have learned to say: Spes et fortuna valete.[7]—Such literary faculty as I have has been of great service to me in my professional calling and every now and then some one who knows tells me that I deserve to be considered one of the fraternity of American authors[8]—Well—if you are inclined to take me seriously as an author, I know I shall be in kind hands and skilful hands—What more could any one want? It will be hard for me to help you because I am a very busy man—and much of the material outside of what you mention is not easily accessible—But when the stress of the opening session is over I will send you what I can lay hands on—In my 'Problems in Greek Syntax' (A.J.P. XXIII)[9]—a series that attracted a great deal of attention on the other side[10]—there is a 'suspirium grammatici'—which expresses my longing for the faire fields of literature[11] and my remonstrance against the decree of fate that made me what I am.[12] And yet really I do not repine. I might have been an essayist—I could never have been a novelist[13]—And of the poet I have only the temperament[14]—And my late afternoon has brought me many assurances of appreciation that would comfort me, if I needed comfort.

I am very human and /am/ extremely gratified that you should think me a proper person to figure in the list of Southern Writers you unroll. I knew them all personally except Haygood and Grady[15]—and I am sure that those whom I knew would not object to my company.

Yours sincerely,<br>
B. L. Gildersleeve

1. Mims was planning to collect a dozen " 'studies' of significant and prominent Southerners who have lived since the war," trying "to show the significance of a man and his work as an inspiration to Southerners and as a revelation to Northerners" (Mims to BLG, 9 August 1907). These Southerners included R. E. Lee, Dr. Bledsoe, P. H. Hayne, T. N. Page, W. H. Page, S. Lanier, J. Woodrow, A. G. Haygood, and H. Grady (see n. 14 below). His "A Great American Hellenist: Professor Basil L. Gildersleeve" appeared in the *Methodist Review* 64 (October 1915): 751–62, but the collection was never published.

2. Reviewing Trent's *A History of American Literature, 1607–1865* (New York: D. Appleton, 1903), an anonymous reviewer in the *New York Sun*, 24 June 1903, said, "There seems little reason for the inclusion of the names of scholars like Drisler and Anthon and Goodwin and Gildersleeve, whose purely literary baggage is of the slightest."

3. *Southern Writers: Selections in Prose and Verse*, ed. W. P. Trent (New York: Macmillan, 1905), 379: "Classical scholarship has its notable exemplar in Professor Basil L. Gildersleeve of Johns Hopkins, who is also an essayist worthy of being much better known."

4. See No. 127.

5. See No. 12, n. 5 and No. 139, n. 2.

6. See n. 8 below.

7. "Farewell, hope and fortune" (see No. 8, n. 10).

8. See Nos. 140, 141 (addendum). Two of his poems were published in *Virginian Writers of Fugitive Verse*, ed. A. C. Gordon, Jr. (New York: James T. White, 1923), 299–300, and his

speech on Gilman's retirement in *The Speech for Special Occasions*, ed. E. A. Knapp and J. C. French (New York: Macmillan, 1925), 88–96.

9. See No. 135, n. 4.

10. Among the reviews are *Ath* 3957 (29 August 1903): 282–83; *BIFC* 9 (1903): 260–61 (Zuretti); *CR* 17 (1903): 399; and 25 (1911): 228 (Richards); *DLZ* 2 (15 August 1903): 2026; *NPR* 19 (1903): 421–26; 555 (Weber); *REG* 16 (1903): 286–87 (Goelzer); *RFIC* 3 (1903): 522 (Levi); *WKlPh* 27 (1903): 738–40 (Vollbrecht); *IF* Anzeig. 16 (1904): 63; *IF* 16 (1904): 5–8 (Meltzer); *RCr* 57 (1904): 26–27; *RPh* 2 (1905): 167 (Martin); *ZöGy* 1, no. 50 (1905): 26–29. Gildersleeve had doubted he would get a good notice in Europe (see BLG to Hübner, 26 June 1893 [Berlin]).

11. E.g., Sidney, *First Eclogues* 7.99: "So faire a fielde would well become an owner." See also Spenser, *Shepheardes Calendar* "November," 188.

12. *AJP* 23 (1902): 3: "It is a droll fate that a man whose ambition for all his early years was to be a poet, or, failing that, to be a man of letters, should have his name, so far as he has a name at all, associated with that branch of linguistic study which is abhorrent to so many finely constituted souls. But when I renounced literature as a profession and betook myself to teaching, I found that there was no escape from grammar, if I was to be honest in my calling."

13. See No. 4, n. 8.

14. See No. 12, n. 3 and No. 14.

15. For Henry Woodfin Grady (1851–89), see *Library of Southern Literature* (New York: Martin and Hoyt, 1908–13), 5: 1957–86. For Atticus Greene Haygood (1839–96), see ibid., 2239–63.

### 139 To: EDWIN MIMS
### *Vanderbilt*

Oct. 25, 1907

Dear Professor Mims:

I send you under another cover a number of things that can hardly be called easily accessible. You can keep them all except those marked 'unica.'[1] My things are very much scattered. I could not get at my articles in the Examiner unless I were to go /to/ Richmond and consult the file for 1863–4 in the Valentine Library and pick out my property with the help of a list which I kept at the time.[2] Of my many occasional addresses I send a few characteristic specimens. For many years I prepared almost all the 'state papers' of the Johns Hopkins University[3] —resolutions on great occasions, tributes to deceased worthies, letters to other universities—I cannot undertake to collect these nor to run down my little essays in verse—the serious ones—and the would-be jocose ones—Just now I am very busy answering congratulatory letters[4] —and when that job is over I must work at my lectures and my Journal. A new number is about to be succeeded at a short interval by a newer number and Brief Mention is always a more serious problem than one would suppose from the form it presents. Sometimes many hours of reading go to the writing of one paragraph. Some of my too partial students have urged me to write my memoirs, as if I had anything to tell—for I have known very few interesting people.

Stedman once apologized to me for not having put me in his <u>columbarium</u> of American Literature[5] together with all the writers of trivial sketches and Poet's Corner verses—I smiled then—My smile is still broader at 76.—Newspaper men at a loss for a subject have sometimes taken me up in the silly season[6] but their articles have given me no pleasure—rather have they made me pity the writers and the subject. In the course of nature I am nearing the end. Sometimes I wonder what would have become of me, if I had persevered in the cult of the Muses, the service of letters pure and simple. I honestly doubt whether I should have made as much of myself as I have done by my analytical studies in their synthetical dress—My 'Problems in Greek Syntax' in the twenty-third volume of the Journal—afterwards reproduced in a thin book[7]—those are the studies that hold the sense of my life—Nothing that I have ever written has been so much noticed in the foreign press.[8] The title is not alluring but some of the best sentences I have ever penned are there.

Well, I intended to write a line, I have covered two pages with my minuscule writing. You have material enough for an article much longer than the importance of the subject warrants.

Yours sincerely,<br>
B. L. Gildersleeve

1. Probably "Formative Influences" and "Spiritual Rights of Minute Research"; see No. 141.

2. The list of sixty-three unsigned editorials exists in the form of a letter to Edward Valentine dated 28 April 1905 in the Valentine Museum, Richmond. Other lists are at the Virginia State Library, Richmond, and the Leonard L. Mackall Collection at Hopkins. On the editorials, see No. 12, n. 5.

3. Gildersleeve wrote to Mims on 26 October: "All I meant to say [by 'state papers'] was that I served very often as English Secretary to the University and I do not arrogate to myself any of the merit that attaches to the management." He performed similar functions to a more limited extent at the University of Virginia, see Thornton on McGuffey (No. 177, n. 2): 253.

4. "On October 1, 1906, he had been professor of Greek fifty years, an event allowed to pass unobserved until a year later—his seventy-sixth birthday, October 23, 1907—when he was accorded by his many educational friends a befitting golden jubilee" (*Culbreth*, 402–3). See *Baltimore Sun*, 22 October 1907, for testimonials from M. W. Humphries (No. 25, n. 9), Shorey, and Seymour (see "Correspondents" for both the latter).

5. *A Library of American Literature from the Earliest Settlement to the Present Time*, ed. E. C. Stedman and E. M. Hutchinson, 11 vols. (New York: Charles L. Webster, 1890). For Stedman, see "Correspondents."

6. E.g., the *NYTimes*, 17 May 1885: 5, and the caricature of Gildersleeve under the title "Some Well-Known Baltimoreans: A Grecian," *Baltimore Sun*, 18 April 1905. See also the *Sun*, 22 October 1907.

7. See No. 135, n. 4.

8. See preceding letter, n. 10.

## 140 To: CHARLES WILLIAM KENT
*UVa-Thornton*

Dec. 21, 1907

Dear Professor Kent:

I wish I could help you personally in the matter of Edward Coates [sic] Pinkney[1] but the subject lies quite outside my line of work and with the return of health comes a portentous accumulation of arrears. My class work is heavy. I have two books in hand[2] and there is the Sisyphus stone of the Journal. The man who /could/ do the Pinkney or could tell you some one to do it is William Hand Browne.[3] By the way, Browne himself ought not to be omitted from any list of notable Southern authors. His wide reading makes its fall in his writing—always limpid, always tactful, and withal shot through with delightful flashes of humour. Unfortunately I cannot suggest anyone to do Browne, unless it be the Baltimore poet Edward Lucas White.[4] He might be helpful in the Pinkney matter also. Of course, I am willing to approach Browne but the compliment would be much greater if the invitation came from you as if without any suggestion from me.

Surely I am thrice and four times blessed[5] to have such a chronicler as Thornton.[6] He has insight, he has sympathy so necessary to the deepest insight—and he is a past master in the art of characterization. What he wrote of Price[7] is worth all that has ever been said of him and by an odd coincidence in turning over some old papers at one o'clock this morning I lighted on his discourse about President Atkinson[8] and could not go to bed until I had finished it—His style has all the Roman gravitas combined with the elusive grace of the Greek.—

If any noteworthy lines come up to my mind, I will let you know but my memory is very capricious.

Give my best regards to Mrs. Kent[9]—who is associated with my early life at the University and like the rest of her family is never to be forgotten.

Yours faithfully
B. L. Gildersleeve

1. Kent had asked Gildersleeve to be a consulting editor for *The Library of Southern Literature* (hereafter *LSL*) (New York: Martin and Hoyt, 1908–13), of which he was literary editor (Edwin A. Alderman and Joel Chandler Harris were editors-in-chief) and most other consulting editors were presidents of Southern universities. On 8 August Gildersleeve accepted, but promised no biographies. Nevertheless, Kent asked him to write the biography of Edward Coote Pinkney (1802–28), which was ultimately written by Wightman Fletcher Melton (1867–1944), then head of the English Department at Baltimore City College (*LSL*, 9: 4063–78).

2. Gildersleeve may refer to his three-part review of Stahl (see No. 146, n. 3) and some other book he was to review, or he may have been referring to part 2 of his *Syntax of Classical Greek* published in 1911, and some other unrealized project, displaced by the call to the Barbour-Page Lectures (see No. 143).

3. Browne (see No. 12, n. 11) refused Kent's request (Kent to BLG, 27 December 1907).

4. Edward Lucas White (1866–1934) was educated at Hopkins (A.B. 1888) and taught Greek and Latin in various Baltimore private schools. His chief publications were his verse, *Narrative Lyrics* (New York: Putnam, 1908), his historical novels, *El Supremo* and *The Unwilling Vestal,* and his short stories, *The Song of the Sirens* (the latter three New York: Dutton, 1916, 1918, and 1919 respectively), and *Why Rome Fell* (New York: Harper and Bros., 1927). *NatCAB* 18: 297, *WhAm* 1: 1333.

5. Virg. *Aen.* 1.94: *O terque quaterque beati.*

6. For Thornton, see "Correspondents." His sketch of Gildersleeve appears in *LSL,* 4: 1795–99. See also following letter and Thornton's address, "Basil Lanneau Gildersleeve at the University of Virginia," *Johns Hopkins Alumni Magazine,* 13 (January 1925): 122–26.

7. For Thornton's notice of Thomas R. Price, see No. 70, n. 3.

8. "John Mayo Pleasants Atkinson, D.D.: A Memorial Address" (Petersburg, Va.: Mitchell Manuf'g Co., 1900), delivered at Hampden-Sydney College, 22 February 1900, at the unveiling of Atkinson's portrait. Atkinson (1817–83) was the fourteenth president of Hampden-Sydney (1857–83).

9. Eleanor Smith (Miles) Kent, daughter of Francis Henry Smith (1829–1928), professor of natural philosophy at the University of Virginia from 1853, and Mary Stuart Harrison Smith, daughter of Gildersleeve's Latin colleague at the University of Virginia, Gessner Harrison (1807–62). Kent was thus brother-in-law of William M. Thornton (see following letter, n. 10).

141 To: WILLIAM MYNN THORNTON
*UVa-Thornton*

February 15, 1908

Dear Professor Thornton:

Under the fresh impression of your visit, which gave so much pleasure to my wife and myself, I jotted down /and now inclose—in this envelope/ some things that I thought might be of service to you in preparing the pages that are to be set apart for me in the Library.[1] In a package which may reach you before this letter I have sent you sundry documents that may interest you as showing different phases of my literary work. Please return at your convenience Formative Influences[2] and the Spiritual Rights of Minute Research.[3] The others you can keep as souvenirs and my diploma likewise—one of a number sent me by the University of Göttingen for my Jubilee in 1903.[4] Latin lends itself admirably to eulogy and the author of its characteristic, one of the leading professors of the University,[5] has put in a few words that defy translation all that I could have wished to accomplish in my half century.—I do not look on anything I have done or lived with complacency but I worked faithfully for those twenty years at the University of Virginia and when I compare what I taught my boys in the two years or more they stayed with me /with what is done to-day/ I am not ashamed of my record as a teacher. And those twenty years prepared me for the work vastly greater in volume that I have done in Baltimore—much of it of a literary character. But a literary man must be judged by his literary output not by his unpublished lectures though as in my case they are perhaps better than what stares at the author in cold print. Think of Twenty Public Lectures on Greek Lyric Poetry—Twenty-four on Homer— a course in the tragic poets—ten lectures on Aristophanes—his Art and his Times—all more or less carefully styled[6]—To these add occasional speeches—Addresses and /the/ like and you will see that I have been fairly active outside of my professorial and editorial work.—

My teaching here has been much freer, much less systematic than at the University of Virginia—With a small class of specialists, I could let myself go—and sometimes I think I have 'indulged my genius' too much. But those of my pupils who have since amounted to more have forgiven me— and forty odd of them joined some years ago in a sumptuous memorial volume.[7]—All my honors and distinctions—almost without exception— have come to me late in life and it is well for my character that it should have been so. If I had put myself in the way of such things I might have had them earlier—but I have never raised my finger to secure these so called prizes. I pushed my candidacy for the Chair of Greek in the University of Virginia in 1856. But I was merely seeking a sphere of work. If that had been denied me, I should have turned to journalism for which I have always had a weakness. Since that remote date I have simply done my work regardless of appreciation. At the University of Virginia my students helped me by their evidence of sympathy. As for my colleagues—one star was not allowed to differ from another star in glory.[8]

Well, I have been garrulous about myself—the inevitable failing of old age.

Let me say once more that if I am to be counted among the literary men of the South, I am delighted to think that my chronicler is to be one of those who understood me best and one who not only shares my enthusiasm for perfection in literary form but has achieved a style that will adorn the story of a man who is sometimes tempted to say of style as Buffon said: 'Toutes les beautés intellectuelles qui s'y trouvent, tous les rapports dont il est composé sont autant de vérités aussi utiles et peut-être plus précieuses pour l'esprit public que celles qui peuvent faire le fond du sujet.'[9]

My wife joins me in all kind messages to 'Cousin Rosalie'[10] and to you.

Yours faithfully
B. L. Gildersleeve

[Addendum][11]

No man is a judge of his own writings.[12] You must decide for yourself what on the whole is the best long specimen but of course I am more than willing to help you by pointing out some things that have attracted attention and may therefore be considered characteristic. Of course The Creed of the Old

South is the only thing that ever had much vogue Atlantic Monthly Janry 1892.[13] Years after the publication William Archer in his America To-day called it "an essay—one might almost say an elegy, so chivalrous in spirit and so fine in literary form that it moved me well nigh to tears. Reading it at a public library I found myself so visibly affected that my neighbors at the desk glanced at me and I had to pull myself sharply together."[14]

The close of that article would furnish a fair extract p. 86—Only p. 87 1. 8 for 'Trojans' read 'brothers of Briseus'—

Essays and Studies

A grammarian's Confession of Faith
E. & S. p. 156

Apollonius of Tyana and Christ
E. & S. p. 294

Death of Julian
E. & S. 397
Early manner

Verse

The Ghazel E. & S. 406

Platen's little volume of Gaselen &c
p. 408 1.2 for 'find' read 'forge'

Maximilian and Julian E. & S. p. 494

'In a previous study' to end.
A passage lauded by Saintsbury[15]

My later articles are to be found in the Atlantic Monthly for Dec. 1896 February March May; Sept. 1897[16]

I like the passage beginning

Of my three days in Olympia p. 639 to end or perhaps 'It was my fortune' &c—p. 638

The close of The Southerner in the Peloponnesian War[17]—VI p. 339 might have some intrinsic interest—and shows my easier manner

Both the Creed of the Old South and The Southerner in the Peloponnesian War have been treated by Rhodes as serious historical documents[18] and they are.

One of my class room translations will be found in the March No. p. 303. Alcaeus[19]—

In Formative Influences I allude to my military service[20]—a very desultory affair—Summer of 1861 on Col. Gilham's[21] staff—under Gen'l Lee[22]—1863 private in the First Virginia Cavalry[23]—1864 aide-de-camp (Captain) on Gen'l Gordon's[24] staff—Valley Campaign under Early.[25] When Gordon's Reminiscences appeared, I was much pleased at his reference to me p. 432: 'He was a most efficient officer, and exhibited in extreme peril a high order of courage and composure. While bearing an order in battle he was desperately wounded and maimed for life.'[26] The 'efficiency' I question but I believe I succeeded in disguising any tremors I may have felt and did not disgrace my Revolutionary ancestors[27]—I wrote to Gordon that as the great Greek poet Aeschylus said nothing about his tragedies in his epitaph but only tells of what he did at Marathon,[28] so I a Greek professor was prouder of his praise than of any academic honors I had ever received.

Most of my writing if not /all/ is professional—and the best of it—So the Introduction to Persius[29]—The Introduction to Pindar[30]—In the twenty-eight volumes of the Journal there are many miniature essays, many aphorisms that have been quoted and referred to by the select few who really like my writings and as I told you—some of my best things, as I remember them, are interred in the Richmond Examiner 1864-5.[31] But I shall never have the time, even if I should muster up the courage to collect those scattered proofs that I was something more than an honest and fairly successful teacher of a language that seems to be going to the wall. Well— we know that wall is not the worst.—

The characteristic of Herodotus in the Herodotus volume of Appleton's Hundred Best Books[32] is in my judgment one of the best things I ever wrote—The articles on Greek literature in Johnson's Cyclopedia are mere pot boilers[33]—'Aristophanes' says a great deal in a small compass—'Euripides' and 'Hesiod' are among the better pieces.

1. Charles William Kent (see "Correspondents"), literary editor of the *Library of Southern Literature* (see preceding letter, n. 2) assigned his brother-in-law Thornton, a highly accomplished literary portraitist (see preceding letter), to write the biographical sketch of Gildersleeve that appears ibid. 4: 1795-99.

2. *Forum* 10 (February 1891): 607-17.

3. An address delivered at the Bryn Mawr commencement, 6 June 1895, which was subsequently published (Philadelphia: Alfred J. Ferris, 1895).

4. No notice of Gildersleeve's Jubilee was taken in this country until American Göttingen students met with him in Philadelphia in 1913, the sixtieth anniversary of his doctorate, and presented him with a loving cup, now in the possession of Dr. Benjamin Gildersleeve of Bowling Green, Ky.

5. Friedrich Leo (1851-1914), the Plautine scholar, had written for Gildersleeve's *Jubiläumsdiplome*: Artem grammaticam severe atque eleganter excolendo musis famulari et voluit et potuit studiorum Graecorum et Latinorum trans oceanum auctor et pater floruit floretque ingenii lepore copia sententiarum urbano sermone antiquorum in novo mundo exemplarium felix aemulus (As the founder and father of Greek and Latin studies across the ocean, he both wished and was able to serve the Muses by cultivating the grammatical science rigorously and elegantly; and he has flourished and continues to flourish in the charm of his wit, in the abundance of his ideas, in sophisticated talk, a successful rival in the new world of his old paragons).

6. Gildersleeve gave twenty lectures on Greek lyric poetry at regular intervals, beginning with his first term in 1876. He taught Aristophanes (seminary) and gave nine public lectures on Greek tragic poetry in 1879 and the tragic poets in spring 1880. He did not teach Homer (generally an undergraduate course taught by Morris, Nicolassen, or Spieker) until spring 1906.

7. See No. 121, n. 2.

8. 1 Cor. 15:41: "There is one glory of the sun, and another glory of the moon, and another glory of the stars; for star differs from star in glory."

9. *Discours sur le style* (1753); Buffon wrote "humain" where Gildersleeve has "public."

10. Thornton's first wife was Eleanor Rosalie Harrison (d. 1920), daughter of Gessner Harrison (see preceding letter, n. 9). There was no official family tie between Harrison and Gildersleeve.

11. An undated MS in the University of Virginia collection, obviously a companion to this letter.

12. For the phrase, see "The College in the Forties," *Princeton Alumni Weekly* 16, no. 16 (26 January 1916): 375. Thornton chose "Lucian" from *E&S*; "The Creed of the Old South"; pp. 49–50 of "Oscillations and Nutations of Philological Studies," *JHU Circulars*, no. 151 (April 1901): 45–50; and the "suspicium grammatici" Gildersleeve mentioned to Mims (No. 138), from "Problems in Greek Syntax," *AJP* 23 (1902): 3–5.

13. *Atlantic* 60 (January 1892): 75–87. Reprinted in book form with "A Southerner in the Peloponnesian War" (see n. 16 below) (Baltimore: Johns Hopkins Press, 1915).

14. W. Archer, *America To-Day: Observations & Reflections* (London: Heinemann, 1900), 121. Archer (1856–1924), the Scottish drama critic, playwright, translator of Ibsen, and friend of Gilbert Murray's (No. 156, n. 3) does not cite Gildersleeve or the essay by name; when he quotes from p. 77 of "Creed," (120–21), he attributes the passage only to "one of [the] survivors" (120) or "a scholar-soldier in the South" (121). See also 123–29, where he recounts an interview with Gildersleeve, whom he names.

15. Saintsbury reference unknown.

16. "My Sixty Days in Greece," *Atlantic* 79 (1897): 199–212, 301–12, 630–41; "A Southerner in the Peloponnesian War," ibid., 80 (1897): 330–42.

17. On Aristophanes and the Confederacy; part 6: 339–42.

18. See J. F. Rhodes, *History of the United States* (New York: Macmillan, 1904), 5: 350, 370 (where he also quotes Gildersleeve's anonymous editorial in the *Richmond Examiner* of 31 December 1863), and, later, *History of the Civil War* (New York: Macmillan, 1917), 369.

19. "My Sixty Days in Greece" (see n. 16 above), 303 gives a translation of Alcaeus Z 34 (Page).

20. "Formative Influences" (n. 2 above), 616–17.

21. Col. William Gilham (1819–72) graduated from West Point in 1840, where he was an assistant professor of natural and experimental philosophy (1841–44). After service in the Mexican War, he resigned to become commandant of cadets, instructor in infantry tactics (1846–61), and professor of physical sciences (1846–50), chemistry and mineralogy (1850–61), and scientific and practical agriculture (1846–61). He wrote *A Manual of Instruction for the Volunteers and Militia of the United States* (Richmond: West and Johnston, 1861) and *Authorized Cavalry Tactics* (Philadelphia: C. Desilver, 1861). Commissioned as inspector-general in April 1861, he served as colonel in the 21st Virginia Infantry throughout the war. For a picture of life in Gilham's regiment, see John H. Worsham, *One of Jackson's Foot Cavalry* (New York: Neale, 1912). See also *Ham Chamberlayne—Virginian*, ed. C. G. Chamberlayne (Richmond: Press of the Dietz Printing Co, 1932), 24. For Chamberlayne, see "Correspondents."

22. After an undistinguished career at West Point, Fitzhugh Lee (1835–1905), nephew of Robert E. Lee, began the war as a staff officer. Following the Manassas campaign, he was made lieutenant-colonel of the 1st Virginia Cavalry in August 1861, brigadier-general in July 1862, and major-general in September 1863, following the campaign Gildersleeve writes of to Maupin (see No. 9). On Lee, see Harry Warren Readnor, "General Fitz Hugh Lee, 1835–1915" (Thesis, University of Virginia, 1971).

23. See No. 9.

24. With no military experience, John Brown Gordon (1832–1904) rose through his courage and aptitude for strategy to the rank of brigadier-general in November 1862, less than two years after his enlistment, and finally to lieutenant-general by war's end. After the war he

served as senator from his native Georgia (1873 - 80) and was instrumental in organizing the University Publishing Co., which published Gildersleeve's *Latin Grammar* (see No. 104, n. 1). See, further, J. B. Gordon, *Reminiscences of the Civil War* (New York: Scribner, 1904), and Allen P. Tankersly, *John B. Gordon: A Study in Gallantry* (Atlanta: Whitehall Press, 1955).

25. Jubal Anderson Early (1816–94) enlisted early in the war and rose to the rank of lieutenant-general by war's end. In June 1864 he was given independent control of his corps in the Shenandoah Valley of Virginia in order to drive part of the Union forces westward across the mountains and away from Robert E. Lee's forces at Richmond. Early managed to cross the Potomac and by 11 July was ready to attack Washington. Stymied by delays and fresh Union defenders sent to Washington, he returned back down the valley and continued to raid and obstruct Union lines of supply and communication. A force of over 40,000 men under Sheridan was sent to stop him. Gildersleeve was with Early when Early routed the Federals at Kernstown (23–24 July) and when he was defeated at Fisher's Hill (22 September) (see No. 69, n. 5). The remainder of the war brought Early few successes and numerous disasters, and he was finally relieved of his command following the near-obliteration of his forces at Waynesboro in March 1865. He remained after the war the archetype of the unreconstructed Confederate. See Early's accounts, *Autobiographical Sketch and Narrative of the War between the States* (Philadelphia: Lippincott, 1912) and *A Memoir of the Last Year of the War for Independence, in the Confederate States of America, Containing an Account of the Operations of His Commands in the Years 1864 and 1865* (Lynchburg, Va.: C. W. Button, 1867); also Frank E. Vandiver, *Jubal's Raid: General Early's Famous Attack on Washington in 1864* (New York: McGraw-Hill, 1960).

26. *Reminiscences* (n. 24 above), p. 422. On the wound, see No. 12, n. 8.

27. Finch Gildersleeve (1750–1812), see No. 122, n. 2.

28. Paus. 1.14.5: "Aeschylus, who had won such renown for his poetry . . . recorded at the prospect of death nothing else, and merely wrote his name, his father's name, and the name of his city, and added that he had witnesses to his valor in the grove at Marathon and in the Persians who landed there" (trans. W. H. S. Jones [Cambridge, Mass.: Harvard University Press, 1918]). For the epitaph, see *Aeschyli septem quae supersunt tragoediae*, ed. D. Page, 2d ed. (Oxford: Oxford University Press, 1972).

29. *The Satires of A. Persius Flaccus* (New York: Harper and Bros., 1875), viii–xxxvii.

30. *Pindar, The Olympian and Pythian Odes* (New York: Harper and Bros., 1885), vii–cxv. See R. L. Fowler, "The Gildersleeve Archive," *Briggs-Benario*, 86–92.

31. He means 1863–64; see No. 12, n. 5, and No. 139, n. 2.

32. Introduction to *The Histories of Herodotus*, trans. H. Cary (New York: D. Appleton and Co., 1899), iii–xviii). On Gildersleeve's own translations of Herodotus, see No. 7 and *AJP* 30 (1909): 353 ( = *SBM*, 184–85).

33. See No. 80, n. 1. Gildersleeve quotes part of his Aristophanes article at *H&H*, 105.

<br>

### 142 To: INGRAM BYWATER
*Bodleian Library, Oxford*

Baltimore March 14, 1908

Dear Professor Bywater:

I thank you for your note of February 29. While it confirms my worst fears, it gives me the assurance that I have the right of a friend to share your sorrow.[1] No one could have seen you two together without understanding something of the harmony of thought and feeling that made life so happy for you both and to the Hellenist your common delight in the exquisite flower of Greek poetry was an intimate charm.[2] My wife, who cherishes with me the memory of her kindness as of yours joins me in this message of sincere sympathy.

Yours faithfully<br>B. L. Gildersleeve

1. Bywater's wife, Charlotte Cornish, a woman of great charm and learning, was originally married to Hans William Sotheby (1827–74), a fellow of Exeter College, Oxford (1851–64), and barrister. After his death she put herself under the tutelage of the Italian medievalist D. Comparetti (1835–1929) and became widely versed in Italian literature. She married Bywater in 1885. With a thorough reading knowledge of ancient Greek, she was most proficient in modern Greek, and at her death, on 17 February 1908, she left a bequest for the promotion and study of Byzantine and modern Greek at Oxford. See W. W. Jackson, *Ingram Bywater: The Memoir of an Oxford Scholar, 1840–1914* (Oxford: Clarendon Press, 1917), 114–19.

2. Gildersleeve expressed similar feelings about Francis G. Allinson (1856–1931), the second Hopkins Ph.D. in Greek (1880), and his wife (BLG to Allinson, 18 December 1913): "What a joy life must be to you both, mated as you are, moving in the same sphere of studies in such perfect harmony of vision and feeling."

143 To: EDWIN ANDERSON ALDERMAN<br>UVa-Alderman

Baltimore April 27, 1908

Dear President Alderman:

The cordial letter in which you have welcomed my acceptance of the invitation to give the initial course of the Barbour-Page lectures enhances my sense of the honour bestowed and the responsibility incurred.[1] Dr. Flippin[2] did not state definitely the number of lectures expected nor the date. The subject, I understand, is to be chosen from the lecturer's special range of study but I take for granted that technical lectures are not desired—such as a series of discourses on the value of grammatical and linguistic studies for the appreciation of literary form. Of course, in my long career I have emerged from my academic seclusion and given so-called popular lectures so that I know fairly well what would interest a cultivated audience without being too elementary for the few specialists in attendance and I am revolving some of these subjects now—doubtful whether to let the lectures turn on single authors such as Aristophanes—or ranges of literature—such as the Athens of the Greek orators—or general themes such as the persistence of the Greek Element in Modern Life. If I dared to go into more personal matters I might draw upon the experience of an old student and give a series on Scholarship and Life somewhat after the fashion of a French essayist I have in mind—La vie et les livres.[3] Of course I appreciate the difference there must be between lectures intended for delivery merely and lectures that are to be printed also and whatever material I have on hand, if used, will have to be recast.

But I am not going to trouble you with my meditations and my perplexities. Turn this letter over to Thornton who knows me and my public and ask him to answer it. Perhaps you will be more successful than I have been in my correspondence with him.

With all assurances of high esteem and with grateful appreciation of your kind expressions

      I am

Yours sincerely

B. L. Gildersleeve

1. Gildersleeve gave the three inaugural Barbour-Page lectures at the University of Virginia (published as *H&H*) on 19–21 November, entitled "The Channels of Life," "The Pervasiveness of the Greek Language and Literature," and "Hellas and Hesperia: Analogies of Ancient Greek and Modern American Life." The Barbour-Page Foundation, begun by a donation of $22,000 by Mrs. Thomas Nelson Page (her maiden name was Barbour) in 1907 and under faculty supervision, was "to be used in securing each session the delivery before the University of a series of not less than three lectures by some distinguished man of letters or of science" (*H&H*, 5). An initial lecture had been given by Dr. J. Adair Mitchell of Philadelphia. Following his wife's death, Page insisted the lectures be known as Page-Barbour, as they are today. On Gildersleeve's lectures, see *UVa Alumni Bulletin*, 3d ser., 2 (January 1909): 9–14 (with portrait).

2. James Carroll Flippin, M.D. (1878–1939), joined the faculty in 1902 as adjunct professor of bacteriology and rose to dean of the medical school (1924–39). As chairman of the faculty committee on jubilee celebrations he had written Gildersleeve on 10 April to offer him, on the basis of his "past association and connections with the University and other obvious reasons," the first lectureship for an honorarium of $500.

3. "These lectures have been drawn mainly from my memories of life and books, the life my own, the books, perhaps in undue measure, my own studies, published and unpublished" (*H&H*, 7). Gildersleeve may be thinking of Gaston Deschamps (1861–1931), *La Vie et les livres*, 5 vols. (Paris: A. Colin, 1894–1900).

144 To: Sophie Lanneau Hart

*Charles S. Norwood*

Baltimore Dec. 29, 1908

Dear Sophie:[1]

Many thanks for the graceful verses[2] in which you have retold the family myth of the Huguenot origin of my fine old grandfather,[3] of whose character and career his descendants have every reason to be proud. I never believed the story for the Acadians were devout Catholics and the fancy that he belonged to a Huguenot family in the midst of a Catholic community has been effectually dispelled by documents, copies of which were sent to me by Alfred Lanneau[4] summer before last. According to the Nova Scotia records—still in existence[—]our ancestor Pierre LaNoue[5] or de la Noue, if you choose, was born in France in 1647, years before the Revocation of the Edict of Nantes[6]—His son Pierre[7] was born at Port Royal, Nova Scotia, in 1682—and so the time goes on—all baptized into the Catholic Church with Catholic promptness. My grandfather Basile was born Nov. 23, 1746 and baptized the following day. Pierre,[8] his older brother—it is true—married a Protestant after he returned from exile but she also went over to the Catholic Church. According to Macready [sic][9] my grandfather was the only Acadian that remained in Charleston and it was not strange that he became a Protestant and an office bearer in the Huguenot Church—especially as his first wife—a Miss Thomas,[10]—was the descendant of a Huguenot family.— I am sorry to spoil your little romance but if you will write to Alfred, you will find that he has given up the claim so confidently made by some members of the family without any documentary warrant. But if I have spoiled your romance I have not spoiled your poetry and I thank you for the opportunity of wishing you all happiness for the New Year now so close at hand.

Your affectionate cousin<br>Basil L. Gildersleeve

P.S. My best regards to your sister[11] and her husband[12] in which my wife desires to join.

1. This letter is printed in S. R. Mowbray and C. S. Norwood, *Bazile Lanneau of Charleston, 1746-1833* (Goldsboro, N.C.: Hillburn Printing Corp., 1985), 34–36. See also the genealogy following No. 161.

2. Sophie had sent Gildersleeve a copy of *Fireside Musings; or, Grandfather's True Story*, a verse account in which she tries to make a connection with the Huguenot soldier François De Lanoe, called "Bras de Fer" for the iron arm he wore after losing his own in battle. Without the benefit of scientific genealogy, but relying on family tradition, Sophie made numerous historical errors apart from that of a Huguenot origin of the family: the La Noues were aristocrats, not peasants; she has her fictitious hero "Charles" go to Canada for a reunion with his brother, when in fact it was not the older brother but the younger, Gildersleeve's grandfather, Bazile Lanneau, who left and returned to find his brother; she credits two sisters of "Charles," but there were no female children born to René and Marguerite Lanneau; there was also no son and brother René. Sophie claims as a source an "eyewitness" of the reunion of the brothers in Canada; her father Charles Henry Lanneau had written an account from memory, "Recollections of my Father," which contains much the same misinformation and may have been the source not only of the stories, but also of the hero "Charles." On the Huguenot origin, see Mowbray and Norwood, 199.

3. Bazile Lanneau (1746-1833) was born in Balisle, Acadia (about sixty miles west of Halifax, Nova Scotia), of French stock. In 1755 his village was burned, and on 13 October, as a boy of eleven, he was put on a transport ship, which docked at Charleston on 20 November 1755. The Acadians were not allowed into the city until 9 December, and by that time, Bazile's entire family had died of smallpox. He was offered aid by Col. Henry Laurens (1724-92), a wealthy statesman, but Bazile made his way more or less independently. In 1781 he built a brick store and had established a sufficient business to own eleven slaves in 1830. He held many municipal offices in Charleston and was three times elected to the state General Assembly (1796-97; 1798-99, 1802-4). See Mowbray and Norwood and also Chapman J. Milling, *Exile without an End* (Columbia, S.C.: Bostick and Thornley, 1943).

4. Alfred Wright Lanneau (1846–1924), a bookkeeper at Lanneau's Art Store in Charleston, wrote a family history, "Bazile Lanneau—The Exile" (reprinted in Mowbray and Norwood, 213–20), describing the exile of the Acadians from Nova Scotia to Charleston in 1755. In a letter of 1907 to his cousin, Prof. John F. Lanneau of Wake Forest, he wrote: "You will see that our Acadian ancestors were intensely Catholic and that Bazile Lanneau was baptised into the communion of that church. His first wife, Suzanne Frizelle, was a French Protestant—Huguenot" (Mowbray and Norwood, 91). He must have written much the same to Gildersleeve.

5. Pierre La Noue was a well-to-do Huguenot born in Bogard, France. Obliged to renounce his Protestantism, he emigrated to Acadia (now Nova Scotia) in 1667, where he was listed in the First Nominal Census (1671) as a barrel maker. In 1681 he married Jeanne Gautrot in Port Royal, Acadia. P. Gaudet, "Acadian Genealogy and Notes," *Report Concerning Canadian Archives for the Year 1905*, vol. 2 (Ottawa, 1906), appendix B, 5–6.

6. After the Revocation of the edict on 18 October 1685 by Louis XIV, a million Huguenots fled France, mostly for England and Prussia. Sophie thought that "Charles" Lanneau had left France after Louis XV's edict of 1752.

7. Pierre La Noue II, who married Marie Granger in 1702, was the only son of Pierre I (ibid., 15).

8. Pierre La Noue IV (b. 1744) was exiled to Charleston at the age of eleven, where he was apprenticed to a physician. But after the treaty of Paris in 1763, he returned to his homeland, settling first in Liverpool, Nova Scotia, where he married a Protestant, Mary Doane, by whom he had four children. He died in Acadia sometime before 1793. Bazile brought Mary and two of her children back to live with him in Charleston. See No. 161, n. 3, and Mowbray and Norwood, 181.

9. Edward McCrady, *South Carolina under the Royal Government* (New York: Macmillan, 1899), 328n, quoting George Howe, D.D., *History of the Presbyterian Church in South Carolina* (Columbia, S.C.: Duffie and Chapman, 1870), 1: 303: "The Acadians in one way or another ultimately left the province. A few remained in the Colonies, some of whom recovered from their despondency and became useful citizens. Among these are the family of Lanneau in Charleston, who embraced the Protestant faith and have long been recognized for their devoted piety."

10. Suzanne Frizelle was a French Huguenot who arrived in Charleston in 1764. A letter describes her as "good and beautiful and the sister of Mr. Stephen Thomas's first wife" (Mowbray and Norwood, 10).

11. Louise Stephens Hart Norwood (1865–1934), with whom Sophia lived all her life, both as students in New York and Lexington, Mo., and in Charleston and Goldsboro, N.C., after Louise's marriage (Mowbray and Norwood, 143).

12. George Alexander Norwood (1863–1947) was in Johns Hopkins Hospital hospital for a stomach operation, and he and his wife were visited several times by the Gildersleeves.


### 145 To: ROBERT UNDERWOOD JOHNSON
*American Academy and Institute of Arts and Letters*

Baltimore April 27th 1909

Dear Mr. Johnson:

In my judgment Paul Shorey[1] of the University of Chicago is eminently worthy of a place in the Institute.[2] He is the only Grecian in the country who is distinctly a literary man. I should like to see the honor bestowed on a veteran of letters Dr. William Hand Browne,[3] of the Johns Hopkins Uni-

versity—who has a wonderful range of knowledge and is thoroughly im-
bued with the literary spirit. He is even older than I am—and the election
would be a deserved compliment.—I do not understand why James Albert
Harrison's[4] name is not on the list. His edition of Poe alone would seem to
entitle him to recognition and he has an array of books to his credit—some
of them of striking individuality—The English critics have recently attacked Hannis Taylor's[5] last book—but I do not know the merits of the
controversy [sic]) and his first secured for him a high position among
writers on constitutional subjects. The new President of Harvard Lowell[6] is
an exceptional man—but perhaps he will follow the example of his predecessor. As to the change of the name[7] I am willing to be guided by the
advice of those who are more intimately acquainted with the history of the
Academy than I am.—But if we call it the American Academy we ought to
let in the Canadians. It would have been better in my judgment to incorpo-
rate the Institute—the membership of which does not rouse sectional jeal-
ousies as did the membership of the Academy. But all that is already ancient history.

Yours faithfully

B. L. Gildersleeve

1. Asked for nominations to the institute, Gildersleeve names one classicist and three
Southerners along with Lowell. Shorey was elected to the institute in 1911 and the academy in
1918; Lowell to both in 1910. For Shorey, see "Correspondents."

2. The American Academy of Arts and Letters, founded in 1904 as an interior organization of the National Institute of Arts and Letters, was originally known as the Academy of
Arts and Letters. It drew its first 30 members from the 250 members of the National Institute
of Arts and Letters, itself founded by members of the American Social Science Association in
1898, and William Dean Howells (No. 174) was the first president. In March 1908 the academy grew from thirty to fifty members, with Gildersleeve elected as the 40th member (Gilman
was no. 34). Unlike European academies, the American academy (and the institute) made no
attempt to regulate language or dictate taste, but merely sought to promote American art,
literature, and music by recognition of excellence and sponsorship of symposia and public
addresses by its members. Charter members included Henry Adams, Mark Twain, W. D.
Howells, Henry James, C. E. Norton, and E. C. Stedman. Although an early member of both
the institute (1905) and the academy, Gildersleeve attended only two of their meetings and
was unable to contribute any public addresses (BLG to Johnson, 9 February 1915 [Am.
Acad.]). See *Proc. Am. Acad. and Nat. Inst. A and L*, 1 (1905-13), 1: 44-45.

3. No. 12, n. 11.

4. No. 55, n. 9. Harrison's 17-volume edition of Poe was completed in 1902.

5. Hannis Taylor (1851-1922), originally from North Carolina, practiced law in Mobile,
Ala. (1870-92), and was president of the Alabama Bar Association (1890-91). As minister to
Spain (1893-97) he successfully negotiated many difficult commercial agreements as the
Spanish-American War approached. He returned to Washington to practice law and write,
producing *The Origin and Growth of the English Constitution*, 2 vols. (Boston: Houghton
Mifflin, 1889-98), and *Cicero: A Sketch of his Life and Works* (Chicago: A. C. McClurg,
1916), among other books. Gildersleeve refers to his *The Science of Jurisprudence* (New
York: Macmillan, 1908), in which Taylor proposed the widely rejected view that Pelatiah
Webster (1725-95), a Whig economist, had taken a crucial role in writing the U. S. Constitution. Despite the hostile reception of his view, he reiterated and expanded it in *The Origin*

*and Growth of the American Constitution* (Boston: Houghton Mifflin, 1911). *DAB* 18: 326–27.

6. Abbott Lawrence Lowell (1856–1943), graduate of Harvard (A.B. 1877, LL.B. 1880), practiced law for seventeen years (1880–97) before accepting a part-time lectureship at Harvard in 1897. In 1900 he became professor of government, but taught only half-time so that he could continue his writing and lecturing. His great work was *The Government of England* (New York: Macmillan, 1908). In 1909 he was elected president of Harvard, and while he carried on many of his predecessor Eliot's programs, particularly the professional schools, he restricted the elective freedoms of the undergraduate curriculum in favor of more general introductory, but required, courses. See, further, Lowell, *At War with Academic Traditions in America* (Cambridge, Mass.: Harvard University Press, 1934) and *What a University President Has Learned* (New York: Macmillan, 1938), and H. A. Yeomans, *Abbott Lawrence Lowell, 1856–1943* (Cambridge, Mass.: Harvard University Press, 1948).

7. On 7 November 1908 the academy adopted a constitution calling itself the American Academy of Arts and Letters.

### 146 To: Ulrich von Wilamowitz-Moellendorff
### *Göttingen*

Baltimore, Oct. 30, 1909

Dear Professor Wilamowitz:[1]

Your letter of Aug. 8[2] crossed the ocean twice in search of me and finally found me in Paris on the eve of my return to America. Let me thank you for your kind reception of my Notes on Stahl,[3] which were written with the benevolent intention of saving those who are not specialists in Greek syntax the trouble of wading through the book. I could not prevail upon myself to finish the thing but the essential points have been made. Unfortunately few German classical scholars understand English as you do[4] and my interpretations of Stahl are apt to be misinterpreted.[5]

You may think it a poor return for your kindness in sending me from time to time your contributions to current philological literature, which I prize very highly, when you receive a little book of mine Hellas and Hesperia,[6] intended for an American public, in fact, a local American public. It is a cryptic autobiography,[7] the precipitation of a long life of study and effort. The space between the lines I have kept for myself. As for the rest, I must trust your charity. That charity will have a still further strain on it when I print my study on the seventh Nemean,[8] written soon after your memorable ~~memorable~~ paper[9] as an introduction to a summary of your results. But to understand everything is to forgive everything and it is not necessary to tell you that I am not to be taken too seriously.

With high esteem and sincere gratitude for your indulgent reception of my work and play[10]

I am

Yours sincerely
B. L. Gildersleeve

1. This letter was published by W. M. Calder III, "B. L. Gildersleeve and Ulrich von Wilamowitz-Moellendorff: New Documents," *AJP* 99 (1978): 4-6 ( = *Selected Correspondence*, 144-46).

2. Calder reads May, but the date is clearly August.

3. "Stahl's Syntax of the Greek Verb," *AJP* 29 (1908)8 257-79, 389-409; 30 (1909), 1-21 (reprinted as *Notes on Stahl's Syntax of the Greek Verb* [Baltimore: Johns Hopkins Press, 1909]), on J. M. Stahl, *Kritisch-historische Syntax des griechischen Verbums der klassischen Zeit* (Heidelberg: C. Winter, 1907; reprint, Hildesheim: G. Olms, 1965).

4. Wilamowitz may have spoken some English when Gildersleeve visited him in 1907, but it is more likely they conversed in German. Wilamowitz's wife Marie (1855-1936), the daughter of Theodor Mommsen, provided him with summaries of English scholarship (W. M. Calder III, "Ulrich von Wilamowitz-Moellendorff to William Abbott Oldfather: Three Unpublished Letters," *CJ* 72 (1976-77): 120 ( = *Selected Correspondence*, 248).

5. Calder (p. 145 n. 23) cites *AJP* 36 (1915): 242 ( = *SBM*, 332): "True, the points of my shafts have often failed to reach their mark because so few German critics are possessed of a knowledge of idiomatic English, or if that is too bold a word for an American, the kind of English in which I indulge; and German misinterpretation of American utterances would furnish a comic afterplay more suited to the character of *Brief Mention* than the grave reflexions to which I have given expression." See also No. 72.

6. See No. 143, n. 1. For a negative review, see *Nation* 89 (18 November 1909): 490, cited in "The Hazards of Reviewing," ibid. 101 (8 July 1915): 50.

7. See No. 143.

8. "The Seventh Nemean Revisited," *AJP* 31 (1910): 125-53.

9. Ulrich von Wilamowitz-Moellendorff, "Pindars Siebentes Nemeisches Gedicht," *SKPAW phil.-hist. Klasse* 15 (1908): 328-52 ( = "Pindaros und Bakchylides," *Wege der Forschung* 134, ed. W. M. Calder III and J. Stern [Darmstadt 1970], 127-58 = Wilamowitz, *Kleine Schriften*, ed. W. Buchwald [Berlin 1972], 6: 286-313). Gildersleeve's piece, according to p. 125 n. 1, was written early in 1909.

10. The epigraph of Gildersleeve's article is Plato *Phlb* 30e: "Playfulness is sometimes a relief from seriousness."


## 147 To: Kirby Flower Smith
### *JHU-BLG*

Aug. 7, 1910

Dear Kirby:

The postcards illustrating Chantecler[1] were a joy to me as they have been to other 'Sommerfrischler.' I have not been studying the play seriously but after reading it two or three times I have been jotting down the Aristophanic elements and perhaps something will come of it[2]—if I am at a loss for a review or Brief Mention—when the wretched printers clamor for copy as they will be doing shortly. Thus far this has been a very restful summer. Reading Aristophanes is fun—not work—and that is all I have done professionally. The rest is sheer loafing.—I have with me only a hat box of books—The catalogue would amuse you but I am /too/ lazy to copy it—Some of the books I shall probably never open on this trip but there is a certain comfort in contemplating the backs of them. Some times I wonder whether my brain has gone to sleep definitely but every now and then there is something that I mistake for a flash of light—and the fact is I suspect that I am breeding without the normal nausea—That will come later for others. I have received the half dreaded letter from Wilamowitz about the Seventh Nemean[3]—I do not undertake to read between the lines—It was a hard letter for him to write—but it is generous and kindly—Perhaps 'considerate' is the best word—One bears with an ancient creature like myself, thinking that it will not be for long.—But I have developed a toughness that is a surprise to me and indulgence may be misplaced—

I am sorry that you have had so much rain. That is one of the drawbacks of a European holiday which an American feels most. On this side we have so much sunshine that we cannot understand what the English call a fine day—which simply means the absence of rain.—On the other hand we have had to suffer from excessive heat—I say 'we'—but I do not mean my wife and myself for we have escaped—except for a few hot days in June—From the 21st of the month to July 5 we were with our daughter at her beautiful country place near Manchester, Mass[4]—thence we went to the Hawthorne Inn, E. Gloucester[5] where we stayed until the 29th and on the 30th we arrived here and are occupying two rooms in the cottage the Lanes have taken for the season. Mt. Desert is more beautiful than my memory pictured it—I was here twenty five years ago[6]—and the life with our dear children and our fascinating grand child[7] is sheer happiness—We shall be here until the end of the month. After that either to the White Mountains or back to Gloucester—where we were very comfortable.

Give my love to your wife[8]—my wife joins me in all kind regards and best wishes—

Yours faithfully

B. L. G.

1. *Chantecler* was the last finished play of Edmond Rostand (1869-1918). Produced in February 1910 with Lucien Guitry in the title role, it is an animal allegory whose characters are birds (mostly poultry) engaged in a struggle for supremacy in a barnyard. This play has obvious parallels with Aristophanes' *Birds*, although it is more poetic than dramatic and was considered too contrived and far-fetched by contemporary critics and audiences.

2. Nothing appears to have come of it except the remarks at *AJP* 32 (1911): 367 ( = *SBM*, 234) and 33 (1912): 227. Paul Girard published "A propos de 'Chantecler': Aristophane et la Nature," *Revue de Paris* 175 (October 1910): 531-56.

3. See preceding letter, n. 8. Of the Pindar article Wilamowitz wrote (1 July 1910): "Wir lieben den Dichter—das tun wenige, und seine Sprache ist uns lebendig—das gilt auch für wenigere. Ich wünschte, wir fühlten noch mehr gleich, aber es ist wohl ein Compliment für den Dichter, daß wir es nicht tun" (We love the poet—few do that—and his language is alive for us—and that is true of even fewer. I wish that we felt closer on this matter but it is probably a compliment to the poet that we do not). See R. L. Fowler, "The Gildersleeve Archive," *Briggs-Benario*, 76-77.

4. On "The Chimneys," see No. 128, n. 1.

5. On the Hawthorne Inn, see No. 135, n. 8.

6. He was probably visiting Gilman during his summer off from teaching at Sewanee (1885). On Mt. Desert, see No. 131, n. 9. For his activities in 1910, see following letter.

7. On Katharine Ward Lane Weems (1899–), see No. 116, n. 7.

8. Charlotte Rogers.


## 148 To: THOMAS DWIGHT GOODELL
### Yale-Goodell

Baltimore Oct. 9, 1910

Dear Professor Goodell: Yesterday I was thinking of you and wondering somewhat why I had had no word from you for months and by way of stirring up your mind to remembrance I was about to send you a reprint of my latest Brief Mention when your letter came together with your most interesting article on Greece as you saw it last summer.[1] It woke a longing in me which will never be stilled. My vacation though not so full of visions as yours was very delightful—much of it having been spent with my daughter and her family at beautiful North East Harbour on Mt. Desert—walking—driving—boating.[2] Those five weeks were the best because I was kept too busy to be haunted as I am always haunted on this side by the ghost of work. After three months' absence I came back with the feeling of a culprit. It does not seem to me that I have a right to let my mind lie fallow for so large a part of the time that is left me and yet I cannot manage to do anything that is worth while. I /do/ manage to read a little but I find myself unable to write away from my usual haunts and before the holidays are over I begin to despair of my mind. When I get back to my books I seem to be /as/ alert as ever—if I dare use that pretentious adjective of myself. So I have entered upon the fifty-fifth year of my professorate with my wonted jauntiness. You see the fact that I have a poor memory serves to keep me awake because I have forgotten so much that I taught four years ago.— My notice of Roberts's Dionysius,[3] to which I imagine you refer in your letter, was taken in good part by the author, who is a personal friend of mine and whose request for some mention of his book I had to grant. I did not have time for a close study of it and instead of a serious criticism I followed the line of least resistance and wrote what you have read. Honestly I was more pleased by the respect which he showed for your work[4] than by anything else in it. The fact that I don't agree with you at every point makes no difference. No dissidence in matters philological shall be allowed /to mar/ the delightful memories of our talks on the Zeeland.[5]—The paper on the Seventh Nemean haunted me for months after it was written and I printed it to get rid of it.[6] I remember counseling you about it and your gentle push helped me to make the plunge. I got a long letter—a long letter for him— from Wilamowitz. However imperious[7] he may be in his published work, he is generosity itself in his correspondence and whilst he makes no concessions, he makes up for whatever poor opinion he has of my penetration, by effusive expressions of delight at my presentation. He has said some nice things about my Hellas and Hesperia[8]—which was not intended for European consumption and which I have sent to only a few friends on the other side.—

I am interested to learn that you are going into Pindar[9] seriously for I hold your unbribable judgment in high esteem and perhaps you will let /me/ know whether you decide for Wilamowitz or for myself or perhaps against us both, though as you have intimated, Pindar is not so much at stake, and the essay is really a manner of intellectual blow-out.[10] I get frightfully tired of the conventionalities of our friends.

My wife joins me in best regards to Mrs. Goodell for whom as for you we both have a special niche in our gallery of personal memories.

Yours faithfully<br>
B. L. Gildersleeve

1. "Greece Revisited," *Nation* 91 (1 September 1910): 183–85.
2. See preceding letter, n. 6.
3. *AJP* 31 (1910): 234–38 ( = *SBM*, 200–204). On Roberts, see "Correspondents."
4. *Dionysius of Halicarnassus On Literary Composition*, ed. W. Rhys Roberts (London: Macmillan, 1910); for mention of Goodell, see pp. 18 n. 39, 25 n. 1, and 32.
5. A Red Star Line steamer sailing between Antwerp and New York. He and Goodell may have been shipmates on Gildersleeve's 1907 crossing (to meet Wilamowitz in Berlin) or, less likely, on his 1905 crossing (to receive degrees from Oxford and Cambridge).
6. On the article and Wilamowitz's letter, see the preceding letter.
7. This is the same word Wilamowitz found applied to him by Gildersleeve in contrast to the "imperial" Boeckh. U. v. Wilamowitz-Moellendorff, *Erinnerungen, 1848–1914*, 2d ed. (Leipzig: K. F. Koehler, 1929), 312. The comparison is in "Oscillations and Nutations of Philological Studies" (*JHU Circulars*, no. 151 [April 1901]: 45), which also uses his favorite epithet for Wilamowitz: "Rough Rider" (50); see No. 136, n. 3.
8. "Es [*H&H*] liegt noch auf meinem Arbeitstische, und ich greife gern danach, denke auch mit dieser Lektüre manchem Collegen eine Freude zu machen. Sie drücken jeder usserung so viel Persönlichkeit auf, und die Eigentümlichkeit des Urteils reizt eben so stark wie der Schliff des Ausdruckes, daß des künstlerischen Genusses fast noch mehr ist als der Belehrung" (It is still lying on my desk and I like to take it in hand and believe that this reading material is pleasurable to many of my colleagues. You put so much personality into each statement and the uniqueness of the judgment is as striking as the elegance of expression, so that the artistic enjoyment is almost more than the instruction) (Wilamowitz to BLG, 1 August 1910).
9. Goodell was to teach a graduate seminar in Pindar later in the year; he did not publish anything on Pindar.
10. I.e., "feast, entertainment."

149 To: MARY GILDERSLEEVE WYLIE
*JHU-BLG*

Baltimore, Nov. 21, 1910

Dear Mary Gildersleeve:

Your mother[1] writes me that you are the only one of her children to bear the old family name Gildersleeve. Doubtless as time goes on you will find it rather cumbrous and some naughty man will persuade you to drop it so as to make more room for his.[2] Meanwhile I have great pleasure in complying with your Mother's request and send you herewith a likeness of the oldest of your great uncles, who has carried without too much discomfort to himself his three syllables and twelve letters and without any material damage to the name that has come down to him through a long line of decent people, one of them, an officer in the Continental Army,[3] another, his father and your great-grandfather,[4] a servant of God and man whose memory is revered by all who knew him or his work.

Yours affectionately
Basil L. Gildersleeve

1. Louise Gildersleeve Pratt (1866–1958), wife of Richard Evans Wylie (1860–1936), daughter of Rev. Henry Barrington Pratt (1832–1912) and Joannah Frances Gildersleeve (1836–1904), Gildersleeve's youngest sister.
2. She married Dr. Allies Barksdale Gray (b. 1893) in 1930.
3. On Finch Gildersleeve, see No. 122, n. 2.
4. For Benjamin Gildersleeve, see chap. 1, introduction, n. 4.

150 To: GARDINER MARTIN LANE
*JHU-BLG*

Baltimore Feb$^y$ 15, 1911

Dear Gardy:[1]

I hold Professor von Wilamowitz[2] [who is indisputably the foremost Greek scholar in the world][3] in high esteem and our personal relations are very pleasant. In fact, I may consider him my friend. And it is just because of these relations that I should hesitate to approach him on the subject of coming to Harvard as exchange professor [if that is what you mean by asking me to help you]. Indeed I do not see how I could advise him to relinquish his wonderful work [as a writer and lecturer at home] for the sake of the classical department at Harvard [especially as I cannot say with conviction that it would be as fine a thing for your University as you think. Most of these great Germans are disappointing when they come to be embarrassed by an unfamiliar ~~language~~ /idiom/. Much of Wilamowitz's power resides in his full use of his mother tongue.] When he lectured at Oxford he lectured in German.[4] If he attempted English he would certainly fail of producing the effect of which I myself have been witness. [the effect he is accustomed to produce on his vast Berlin audiences.][5] So you see that I cannot give a hasty answer to your hurried note. I will think the thing over. Needless to say, if you succeeded in getting Wilamowitz, I shall do my best—As I have done in other cases—to make his sojourn in America pleasant.[6]—

My health continues good and I flatter myself that I am still able to do decent work both as a teacher and a writer.

Professor Robinson[7] of the Johns Hopkins, who has just returned from Harvard where he has been lecturing informs me that the impression is general there that I am merely a titular professor. Similar reports have come to me anyhow in the last ten years. I am not much disturbed by them, tho rather strengthened to /do/ my best while I am still in the land of the living.

With best love to Emma and Katharine.

Yours faithfully

B. L. Gildersleeve

1. Gardiner Martin Lane was chairman of the Committee of Overseers of the Harvard Classics Department and in 1903 had given funds for importing foreign classicists to speak at Harvard. In that capacity (as well as that of Gildersleeve's son-in-law), he wrote on 14 February 1911, "The Classical Department is anxious to get Mr. Willamöritz [sic] as exchange professor. Do you think that you could help accomplish this?" Of the three versions of Gildersleeve's reply that exist, two are so nearly identical that I have included only the expansion that went into the last and final copy.

2. On the relationship, see W. M. Calder III, "B. L. Gildersleeve and Ulrich von Wilamowitz-Moellendorff: New Documents," *AJP* 99 (1978): 1-11 ( = *Selected Correspondence*, 141-51), and idem, "The Correspondence of Ulrich von Wilamowitz-Moellendorff with Edward Fitch," *HSCP* 83 (1979): 369-96 ( = *Selected Correspondence*, 65-92). Relations had been strained early by Theodor Mommsen's (see No. 61, n. 4) sudden removal of Gildersleeve's great friend Hübner from the editorship of *Hermes* (see No. 61 and n. 3). The villain in Gildersleeve's eyes was Mommsen, but relations with his son-in-law Wilamowitz were understandably cool, because Wilamowitz thought Hübner had transferred his hatred of Mommsen to him and thus prejudiced Gildersleeve against him. But this is not reflected in any of Gildersleeve's letters to Hübner, which are all that survives of their correspondence. Gildersleeve's friend Usener was friendly with Wilamowitz (after an initial student-teacher flap at Bonn), who dedicated his *Antigonas* to him. But Usener seems to have given the one no entrée to the other, and it appears no thaw could occur until Hübner and Mommsen had died. By 1905 Wilamowitz had sent Gildersleeve offprints, and Gildersleeve speaks of receiving "a noble letter" sometime earlier (see No. 132), which is probably the letter on Timotheos referred to in No. 136. Finally in 1907 they met in Berlin, thanks to the intercession of Edward Fitch (see No. 188).

3. "Wilamowitz, the foremost Hellenist of our day" (*H&H*, 51). See No. 136.

4. *Greek Historical Writing* and *Apollo*, trans. G. Murray (Oxford, Oxford University Press, 1908). The lectures were delivered on 3-4 June 1908. On Wilamowitz's visit, see P. S. Allen in W. M. Calder III, "Ulrich von Wilamowitz-Moellendorff on Sophocles: A Letter to Sir Herbert Warren," *California Studies in Classical Antiquity* 12 (1982): 60 n. 39.

5. See Wilamowitz to Fitch, 12 June 1907, in Calder, *HSCP*, 379-80 ( = *Selected Corre-*

*spondence*, 75–76). Wilamowitz's lectures were delivered twice a week in the evenings to audiences of about four hundred, comprised both of students and local gentry. See W. Jaeger, "Classical Philology at the University of Berlin 1870 to 1945," *Five Essays*, trans. A. M. Fiske (Montreal: M. Casalini, 1966), 58, and Wilamowitz, *Erinnerungen, 1848–1914* (Leipzig: K. F. Koehler, 1929), 289ff.

6. Wilamowitz declined Harvard's invitation. He recalled later, "Dem Professorenaustausch mit Amerika habe ich ablehnend gegenübergestanden. Als ich von Harvard gewünscht ward, fragte das Ministerium daher nur telephonisch in einer Form an, der ich entnahm, man rechnete auf keine Zusage" (With regard to the exchange of professors with America, I took a negative view. When Harvard sought me, the ministry therefore asked only by telephone in such a way that I gathered that they thought I would say no) (*Erinnerungen*, 290).

7. David Moore Robinson (1880–1958), after receiving a Ph.D from the University of Chicago in 1904, had come to Hopkins as associate in classical archaeology in 1905 and rose to be Vickers professor of archaeology in 1920. His books include *Sappho and Her Influence* (Boston: Marshall Jones, 1924), *Greek and Latin Inscriptions* (with W. H. Buckley) (Leyden: E. J. Brill, 1932), *Pindar: A Poet of Eternal Ideas* (Baltimore: Johns Hopkins University Press, 1936), and *A Short History of Greece* (New York: Huxley House, 1936).


151 To: PAUL SHOREY
*Chicago*

May 15th, 1911

Dear Shorey:-

I am interested in So. Phil. 818, and without waiting to consult the commentators, none being accessible at my house, I studied out the problem with the following result:

"Jebb has interpreted πλέον φρονεῖς by the light of τί παραφρονεῖς αὖ;[1] and φρονεῖς by itself might be used here as elsewhere in contrast to madness,[2] but like you I balk at πλέον. φρονεῖν is notoriously tricky. We have it used here three times within a short space in ways that do not admit of a uniform translation—σαφῶς φρόνει, παραφρονεῖς, πλέον φρονεῖς.[3] When Philoktetes is in his senses, he speaks connectedly. Here, frenzied by a sudden access of pain, he ejaculates, so that ἄνω has to be interpreted by Neoptolemus, who is still holding the hand of Philoktetes (ἐμβάλλω μενεῖν) and refuses to let him go until he recognizes that the crisis has come as set forth by Philoktetes himself—ὀξεῖα φοιτᾷ καὶ ταχεῖ ἀπέρχεται— for like all chronic sufferers Philoktetes talks a great deal about the details of his affliction.[4] The ejaculatory μέθες is followed by a distinct remonstrance against the pain of the touch. The aorist προσθίγῃς intimates that Philoktetes has wrenched his hand free. Then Neoptolemus yields: καὶ δὴ μεθίημ᾽, τι δὴ πλέον φρονεῖς. If as is plain (δὴ) = since you know your own case so much better (τι) than I. πλέον φρονεῖς exactly as in Plato, Hipp. Min. 371 A.[5] It is precisely the language of a nurse to a patient who is to be humored".

I return to the University and find that Campbell[6] has the same interpretation of πλέον φρονεῖς down to the details, the quotation from Plato
and the nurse business. Your interpretation is the same as the Scholiast's,
ἀντὶ τοῦ, ὠφελιμώτερον ἐμοῦ. 'Male', says old Hermann, 'nisi legit εἴ τι
δὴ πλέον φρονεῖς,[']'[7] which is the accepted reading now.
I spare you my comments on the commentators.

Yours faithfully,<br>
<u>B. L. Gildersleeve</u>

1. The passage in question, 806–18, in the second episode of the play (730–826), occurs
when, in a paroxysm, Philoctetes prays for death and begs Neoptolemus to throw him into the
crater of a burning mountain near his cave. Neoptolemus is touched (806) and swears he will
not leave Philoctetes (810), who begs to be taken away (814), but when Neoptolemus reaches
for his hand, Philoctetes fears that a touch might kill him (818).

2. *Sophocles: The Plays and Fragments, Part IV, The Philoctetes*, ed. R. C. Jebb (Cambridge: Cambridge University Press, 1908), 133: "The mere touch of the youth's hands is
torture to the sufferer (817): and Neopt. releases him the moment that he seems to be recovering self-mastery."

3. 810, 815, 818.

4. Gildersleeve, when aching with the gout induced by his war wound, may well have felt
affinity with the Greek captain, whose foot was wounded by a snakebite while he was on his
way to battle at Troy.

5. Plato *Hipp. Min.* 371a: [Achilles] ὥστε καὶ τοῦ Ὀδυσσέως τοσοῦτον φαίνεται φρονεῖν πλέον ([Achilles] is seen to be so much more clever than Odysseus).

6. *Sophocles*, ed. L. Campbell, vol. 2 (Oxford: Clarendon Press, 1881), 429, and *Philoctetes* (Oxford: Clarendon Press, 1879) adduce Thuc. 5.29 in addition and explain: "Neoptolemus feels like an inexperienced nurse, and perceives that the sickness is beyond his treatment. He begins to think that the sick man must know what is best for his own state."
Campbell's translation "supposing that you must know best" is preferred to Jebb's "art more
sane" by J. C. Kamerbeek, *The Plays of Sophocles: Commentaries, Part VI, The Philoctetes*
(Leiden: E. J. Brill, 1980), 117–18, whereas T. B. L. Webster, *Sophocles Philoctetes* (Cambridge: Cambridge University Press, 1970), 119, agrees with Jebb.

7. *Sophoclis Tragoediae*, ed. K. G. A. Erfurdt, 7 vols.; vols. 5–7 ed. G. Hermann (Leipzig: G. Fleischer, 1811–25), vol. 6 (*Philoctetes*), 133.

152 To: ROBERT UNDERWOOD JOHNSON<br>
New York Public Library-Century

October 2, 1911

Robert Underwood Johnson, Esq.,
The Century Magazine,

Dear Mr. Johnson,
    Your invitation to contribute an 'Open Letter' to the series you are pub-
lishing in the Century[1] is a pleasant surprise, and I have been revolving the
rare compliment in my mind for some days.

But if there is any subject that has been discussed to death, and that I have helped to discuss to death since 1854,[2] it is the place of the ancient classics in education; and I cannot get up enough interest in the matter to undertake the commission which you offer me. For the wider question, the discussion of which the ancient classics form only a part, I have neither the equipment nor the courage. The truly deplorable tendency of today is to break with the past altogether. There is to be no such thing as literary tradition, nothing but a succession of new births; and those who come after us will need elaborate commentaries in order to understand the text of the men of my time, which is rapidly becoming a remote past.

With many thanks for considering me a possibility in what Matthew Arnold calls 'these bad times',[3]

I am

Yours sincerely,

B. L. Gildersleeve

1. The *Century*, of which Johnson was made editor in 1909, began publishing a series of informal "Open Letters" in vol. 81 (November 1910): 156-60.

2. "Necessity of the Classics," *Southern Quarterly Review* 26 (n.s. 10) (July 1854): 145-67, a review article of G. Bernhardy, *Grundriss der griechischen Litteratur*, vol. 1 (Halle: E. Anton, 1852). Gildersleeve quotes pp. 157-59 of "my maiden review article" at *AJP* 37 (1916): 496-97 ( = *SBM*, 367-69).

3. "To a Friend" (1849): "Who prop, thou ask'st, in these bad days, my mind?"

## 153 To: WILLIAM MYNN THORNTON
### UVa-Thornton

{Galen Hall
Atlantic City, N.J.,} July 2, 1912

My dear Thornton

It is not altogether my fault that I am not an alumnus of the University of Virginia. In 1846 the Presbyterians most tenacious of the sons of men[1] were not fully reconciled to the shade of Jefferson[2] and my Presbyterian father sent me to a Presbyterian college,[3] although I pleaded for the University. At any rate I am glad that the term alumnus has been stretched to include an old professor and in a spiritual sense I am an alumnus because I owe much of my training to the influences that surrounded me as a youthful teacher.[4] The beautiful medal[5] reached me today—beautiful in conception, in execution and it means as much to me as to any of the recipients. The day of the presentation I was bound to my duty to The Johns Hopkins but I read eagerly the accounts of the memorable scene and the impression was enhanced by Alderman's description of the gathering of the old soldiers—with whom I too could claim comradeship—for Alderman was here for a few days—and nearly all our talk was of the University, its men, its fortunes and its prospects. Your signature to the letter adds to the preciousness of the gift for I need not tell you how near you and yours are to my heart.

I have been here for the last four weeks and more for my wife's health. Ever since the end of October—She has been a semi-invalid and the treatment of this sanitarium[6] was recommended as calculated to aid her recovery—in all these months she has not suffered much but it is a great trial to a woman so alert and energetic to walk softly as she may have to do the rest of her days. She looks very well and it seems absurd to call her a patient but she has drawn heavy draughts on her nerve force for forty-odd years and must pay the penalty. She seems to be better—and perhaps to use the familiar phrase the good effects of the treatment will shew themselves after she leaves the place. On the 25th we expect to go to the Catskills—Onteora[7] near Tannersville—and after two weeks there we may revisit our old haunt, the North Shore of Massachusetts.

With best love to Rosalie[8] from us both and joint assurances of faithful friendship for you and your house

> I am
>
> Yours faithfully
> B. L. Gildersleeve

1. Ps. 45:2 "fairest of the sons of men."

2. Thomas Jefferson was not hostile to religion, but he wanted no impingement of the state upon religious freedom and thus had no professor of divinity or theology at his state-supported university. In 1829 some Episcopal church leaders believed that that year's typhus epidemic was divine retribution against the "godless" school (*Trans. Am. Phil. Soc.* 53, pt. 8 [1963]: 41–42), and in 1847 the influential *Southern Literary Messenger* (9 [September 1847]: 575) said that Jefferson had done more ill for religion than any other American in history. See also M. D. Peterson, *The Jefferson Image in the American Mind* (New York: Oxford University Press, 1960), 127–29, 242–43, and C. C. Wall, Jr., "Students and Student Life at the University of Virginia, 1825 to 1861" (diss., University of Virginia, 1978), 19–20.

3. On Gildersleeve's college career, see introduction to chapter 1.

4. He once told his student Walter A. Montgomery: "At the University of Virginia I learned what scholarship and toil meant in terms of growth and inner rewards." W. A. Montgomery, "My recollections of Basil Lanneau Gildersleeve" [two recordings at the University of Virginia], side 2. See also W. Briggs, "Basil L. Gildersleeve at the University of Virginia," *Briggs-Benario*, 9–20.

5. Alderman decided to invite all the living University of Virginia alumni who had served in the Confederate Army to attend special ceremonies at the 1912 commencement, 10–12 June, and receive bronze medals specially struck for the occasion. The 5.25 cm diameter medals depict a bust of Minerva surrounded by a laurel wreath. On the reverse are an unfolding scroll, the dates 1861–1865, and the legend, *Non ille pro caris amicis aut patria timidus perire* (Hor. *C.* 4.9.51–52: "That man was not afraid to die for his beloved friends or his country"). Gildersleeve was included among the 117 living veterans invited, but was not among the 80 who attended the reunion. His brother, John Robinson Gildersleeve, M.D. (1843–1918), did attend.

6. Galen Hall was a 276-bed private recovery sanatorium ("not for insane or objection-able cases," its advertising read), established in 1893 and providing a "First-Class Table" (*Polk's Medical and Surgical Register* 6 [1900]: pt. 1, p. 21).

7. Onteora Park, a cottage colony of over seven hundred acres, begun in 1887 by the Catskill Mountain Camp and Cottage Co., lay on the Eastkill Valley Road about sixty miles NNE of Poughkeepsie, N.Y. Patrons of Onteora (the original name of the Catskills) have been characterized thus: "[Nearby] Tuxedo Park people were very rich, those of Onteora were merely rich" (Alf Evers, *The Catskills from Wilderness to Woodstock* [Garden City, N.Y.: Doubleday, 1972], 537–44; quotation from 541).

8. No. 141, n. 10.

## 154 To: CHARLES FORSTER SMITH
### *Smith*

[Oct. 23, 1912]

I am far too analytical for my own happiness and I cannot recognize in myself many of those fine qualities of head and heart with which I have been credited in late years. The praise which might have lifted me up in the first half of my career[1] humiliates me now. I know that I have a fervent nature, a rather nimble wit and artistic sensitiveness, a certain power of expression—but there are many who have all these things—and such success as I have had in my allotted line of work has been due to the rarity of journalistic talent in our range of studies. One of my German critics has called me recently the Mark Twain of Greek syntax[2]—and as Mark Twain is immensely popular in Germany I ought to be pleased with the tag. A French reviewer says that the poet is not dead in me,[3] and I cannot help tracing that reference to Sainte-Beuve's memorable saying.[4] Well, to quote my favorite verse of V. Hugo, *J'ai fait ce que j'ai pu; j'ai servi, j'ai vielli* [sic].[5] ἱκόμην ἵν' ἱκόμην,[6] and if the world chooses to accept the estimates of my friends Charles Forster Smith and William M. Thornton,[7] I am not the only one who has had more than he has earned. I have had delight in my work and, as it seems, that delight has been contagious. I enjoy the acknowledgement when it comes from those who know that on the solemn verge of life I can honestly say that I never sought praise for praise' sake. But there abides that which cannot be analyzed—and that is the chief thing, after all. Nearly all my pupils are my friends, and this love has been won by no arts of mine, for I have been a rather hard task-master and an unsparing critic. Still, they may have recognized the fact that I am that good in my heart, and they know that I set myself hard tasks and criticize myself unsparingly. Somehow my sphere of influence seems to have taken you in,[8] and I am proud of the way in which you have upheld the standard of our common studies. Your published work has been more on literary lines than has mine. I have written reams of lectures and themes, but what I have written is now out of date. Still the literary spirit in me lives and I read with interest and profit what you put forth—as for instance your contribution to the volume of Columbia lectures,[9] the latest thing I have seen from your pen. I am a very busy man and cannot always take time to acknowledge lesser things my friends send me, but whenever I read anything of yours I read it in the light of our love for one another. Of this love let the long letter I have written you be a testimony. Of the hundreds of letters I write every year there are few so long as this—few that carry with each line such affection and such confidence.

1. Gildersleeve may be thinking of W. W. Goodwin (No. 50, n. 5), who was elected Eliot professor of Greek at Harvard at the age of 29.

2. Hans Meltzer, "Griechische Syntax, Bedeutungslehre und Verwandtes, 1904–1910," *BJ* 159 (1912): 310: "Man möchte ihn den Marc Twain der griechischen Syntax nennen; er ist ein Eigener und hat Eigenes zu geben" (One could call him the Mark Twain of Greek Syntax; he is a special person and has special things to offer). In the same journal (p. 13), S. Witkowski calls him the "naughty boy of Attic syntax." See "Paulus Silentarius," *AJP* 38 (1917): 42.

3. Henri Goelzer, reviewing *Problems* in *REG* 16 (1903): 287: "Il y a aussi 'un poète mort jeune' à qui le grammairien survit" (There is also a 'poet who died young' whom the grammarian survives), and A. Martin, *RPh* 29 (1905): 167: "Ce grammairien est cependant toujours un peu poète" (This grammarian is still always a little bit of a poet).

4. "Il se trouve, en un mot, dans les trois quarts des hommes, comme un poète qui meurt jeune, tandis que l'homme survit" (One finds, in a word, among most men, something like a poet who dies young, while the man survives) (*Revue des Deux Mondes* [1 June 1837]: 636 [ = *Portraits littéraires* 1.4.5]). See also Alfred de Musset, "À Sainte-Beuve," 4–5 (*Poésies Complètes* [Paris: Gallimard, 1957], 378–79): "Il existe, en un mot, chez les trois quarts des hommes / un poète mort jeune à qui l'homme survit" ("There exists, in a word, within most men / a poet who has died young, whom the man survives"), and *AJP* 6 (1885): 522 ( = *SBM*, 1).

5. "Veni, Vidi, Vici" (1848), in *Contemplations* (Paris: Hachette, 1922), 2: 389–91. The last word should be "veillé."

6. Soph. *OC* 273: "I've reached the point I've reached."

7. Smith wrote "The South's Contribution to Classical Studies" for *The South in the Building of the Nation* (Richmond: Southern Historical Publication Society, 1909), 7: 135–72 (on Gildersleeve: 140–44); for Thornton on Gildersleeve, see No. 141, n. 1.

8. Smith was not a student of Gildersleeve's; they first met at the APA meeting at Ithaca, N.Y., in 1886. In 1887 Smith attended Gildersleeve's summer lectures at Sewanee, and both were houseguests of Wiggins' (No. 71, n. 18). Shortly thereafter Smith began reporting on *Philologus* for *AJP*. Smith, "Basil Lanneau Gildersleeve: An Intimate View," *Sewanee Review* 32 (April 1924): 162, 167.

9. *Greek Literature* (New York: Columbia University Press, 1912).

## 155 To: Thomas Dwight Goodell
### *Yale-Goodell*

Baltimore, Nov. 10, 1912

Dear Professor Goodell:

If M⁽ʳˢ⁾ Goodell knew how much I enjoyed your letter, she would retract her reproach as to its length.[1] My letters are perforce short, I have to write so many of them; and then I am so full of repentances that when I read them over, I make all manner of changes so that they must needs be rewritten and for lack of time the rough drafts, as they turn out to be, are handed to my type writer.[2] So it comes about that I seldom write to my children and friends for a type written letter to one's nearest and dearest still seems to me a profanation—so old fashioned am I.

I am glad that you have had a pleasant summer and that you welcomed the reminder of me on your genealogical tour.[3] I have long known from Bardesley [sic][4] that Gyldensleeve occurs in the pre-American records of the Southern Counties of England so that the figment of a Dutch or Swedish origin of my family is naught.

Your paper on μή[5] is now in the hands of the printer as is my appended note,[6] which [is] simply a statement originally intended for Brief Mention of my incorrigibility. In the few reprints I intend to have made of the note I thought to let it go out together with your work, as it would be less intelligible alone. It is very generous of you to give me an additional chance to flourish my cup and balls[7] but the reprints will not appear for some time after the number of the Journal is issued so that you /can/ change your mind about circulating your copies with an appendix of scant scientific value.

I shall probably have a Brief Mention skit about White's big book.[8] As you know I have long since retired from the metrical field and am content to be οὔτ' ἐν λόγῳ οὔτ' ἐν ἀριθμῷ[9] in a domain in which I was after a fashion a pioneer for I preceded White by some years in advocacy of Schmidt's[10] schemes. Being an older man and stiffer in my intellectual joints, I have not been able to adapt myself to the New Metric and not being musical I could not set up as a champion of the system I had accepted, so I turned the whole matter over to my colleague, Miller, who, it seems, is willing to undertake the review, but I am afraid he will not finish it before 1915—the date fixed for the opening of the Panama Canal.[11] His deliberation and meticulousness are the real cause of the abrupt termination of our joint work on the Syntax.[12] I had hoped that you could do what I have done sometimes—write a semi-popular review for the Nation and a technical one for the Journal.[13] Perhaps you can manage that yet.[14]

As it is contrary to the tradition of the American Philological Association to publish Presidential Addresses in extenso, I have published more than one of them in the Journal[15] and unless you have in view some more remunerative or other/wise/ desirable vehicle than my lumbering machine, I should be proud to have the address for my summer number.

Thanks for the information about Tuttle.[16] I did not wish to be caught by an undergraduate.

My wife is resuming her social activities in some measure but she needs to be watched and sufflaminated. My daughter is much better and my hopes of seeing you in Washington[17] or on your way back are raised.

Both the Gildersleeves send kind messages to both the Goodells—of whom we often speak as you would have us speak

Yours faithfully

B. L. Gildersleeve

1. Goodell had written on 5 November 1912: "My wife laughs at me for writing longer letters than I receive. But then, a page from you is worth five from me."

2. His type writer at this time was a Miss O'Reardon, Miller's assistant. See *AJP* 34 (1913): 115 ( = *SBM*, 281).

3. Goodell had been "looking over parish registers and indexes of prelate records in Suffolk and Norfolk" when he found variants of the name Gildersleeve.

4. C. W. Bardsley (1843-98), *A Dictionary of English and Welsh Surnames with Special American Instances* (London: H. Frowde, 1901), 317, lists a Roger Gyldenesleve in Norfolk in 1273. He also lists the name in *English Surnames: Their Sources and Significations*, 4th ed. (London: Chatto and Windus, 1889), 404. See also P. H. Reaney, *The Origin of English Surnames* (London: Routledge and Kegan Paul, 1967), 244.

5. "Imagination and Will in MH," *AJP* 33 (1912): 436-46.

6. "Usque Recurret μή," ibid.: 447-49. See also "Encroachments of μή on οὐ in Later Greek," *AJP* 1 (1880): 45-57.

7. I.e., the children's game also called bilboquet. Gildersleeve sent Shorey (see "Correspondents") a sonnet entitled "Cup and Ball," in which he compared the octave to the ball and the sextet to the cup.

8. John Williams White, *The Verse of Greek Comedy* (London: Macmillan, 1912). Gildersleeve's "skit" appears at *AJP* 34 (1913): 104-9 ( = *SBM*, 271-78). On White, see No. 50, n. 9.

9. "neither in reckoning or account" (Suidas, s.v. "ὑμεῖς ὦ Μεγαρεῖς," quoting "Callimachus in his Epigrams"). Cf. Call. *Epigr* 25.6 (Pfeiffer).

10. See the "skit" on White (n. 8 above) and No. 158. Goodell was also a Schmidtean who had learned his metrics from Seymour (see "Correspondents") in a Pindar course. For the "New Metric" vs. Schmidt's metric, see Shorey's review of White, *CP* 8 (1913): 99-104 ( = *Paul Shorey: Selected Papers*, ed. L. Tarán [New York: Garland, 1980], 1: 98-103).

11. Miller never wrote the review.

12. For Miller's role in the *Syntax*, see No. 78.

13. "The Hazards of Reviewing," *Nation* 101 (8 July 1915): 49-50: "Sometimes I could manage to divide the matter of a review between the *Nation* and the *Journal*, as in my reviews of Robinson Ellis's "Ibis" [*Ovidii Nasonis Ibis* (Oxford: Clarendon Press, 1881), in *AJP* 3 (1882): 86-89 and *Nation* 34 (8 June 1882): 487-88] and Riemann and Goelzer's "Syntaxe Comparée" [O. Riemann and H. Goelzer, *Grammaire comparée du Grec et du Latin: Syntaxe* (Paris: A. Colil, 1899), in *AJP* 20 (1899): 231-32 and *Nation* 68 (18 May 1899): 380-81], the technical part falling to the *Journal*, the wider aspect being represented in the *Nation*."

14. Goodell, to whom White dedicated his book, declined to review it for the *Nation*. It was reviewed there by (M.?) Humphreys (96 [17 April 1913]: 391).

15. Goodell was president of the APA, 1911-12. Gildersleeve had published two presidential addresses: Bernadotte Perrin's "The Ethics and Amenities of Greek Historiography," *AJP* 18 (1897): 255-74, and Abby Leach's "Athenian Democracy in the Light of Greek Literature," *AJP* 21 (1900): 361-77. The *AJA* had published Merriam's address in 3 (1887): 303-21, and other addresses had been published in *HSCP*, *CJ*, and the *Atlantic*. Gildersleeve published his own (second) presidential address, "The Range and Character of Philological Activity in America" in *PAPA* 40 (1909): xxxviii-xxxix in abstract. On the *AJP*'s use of papers read at the APA meetings, see No. 76.

16. Edward Hotchkiss Tuttle (1879–1939), a student of Seymour's at Yale, took his B.A. there (1901) and, after European travel and education (1903–5), taught at Boys' Latin School in Baltimore (1907–16). He moved back to North Haven, Conn., where he devoted the rest of his life to the study of languages. The matter to which Gildersleeve refers is not known.

17. The APA met in Washington, 27–30 December 1912.

## 156 To: Thomas Dwight Goodell
### Yale-Goodell

Baltimore, January 6, 1913

Dear Professor Goodell:

Many thanks for the Yale Review[1] although I was disappointed in not finding among the contents your 'Critic of Life' which I had expected to find in the number.[2] There was much to interest me in the Review, which is a great credit to Yale. First and foremost, of course, that fascinating creature, Sir Gilbert Murray's Tradition in Greek Literature[3] for Sir Gilbert it is—[4] unless a notice received from the Hellenic Society, of which I am a member, is wrong and that is very unlikely, because the English are so very particular about titles. The Murrays are delightful people, great friends of my daughter and her husband. I do not understand the difficulty about titles to which you refer.[5] (Sir) Gilbert's wife, as the daughter of the Earl of Carlisle, is Lady Mary Murray. Sir James's wife is simply Lady Murray. Americans are always blundering in such things— Of course, if the ladies are both 'Mary Murray' the signatures might give some trouble.

I was about to ask /you/ whether after reading my comment on your article,[6] you might not prefer to leave off that trifling skit but my friends here assured me that it was a very innocent performance and I am glad to learn that you are of the same opinion so that we can go out to the world under the same cover.

I had a charming visit to Washington[7] and many old friends and pupils—and enjoyed the cordiality with which I was greeted everywhere. Lodge and his wife whom I did not meet there stopped over in Baltimore to see me and we had a pleasant time together. If the Goodells had only done the same, my joy would have been complete—but I could not extract[?] a positive promise from you.— I might say that I was glad to see you so buoyant and alert—but what else was to be expected of a young fellow like you?

My wife joins me in kind remembrances to you both.

Yours faithfully
B. L. Gildersleeve

1. *Yale Review* 2, no. 2 (January 1913).
2. "An Athenian Critic of Life," *Yale Review* 2, no. 3 (April 1913): 540–59.
3. "The 'Tradition' of Greek Literature," *Yale Review* 2, no. 2 (January 1912): 215–33;

reprinted as "The Tradition or 'Handing Down' of Greek Literature," in Murray's *Greek Studies* (Oxford: Clarendon Press, 1946), 87–105. George Gilbert Aimé Murray (1866–1957), Regius professor of Greek at Oxford (1908–57), had published *Ancient Greek Literature* (Oxford: Clarendon Press, 1897); the Oxford Classical Text of Euripides (1902–9); *Rise of the Greek Epic* (Oxford: Clarendon Press, 1907); and *Four Stages of Greek Religion* (Oxford: Clarendon Press, 1912; revised in 1925 as *Five Stages of Greek Religion*). Murray was a good friend of Gardiner Lane's, Gildersleeve's son-in-law (see "Correspondents"). See, further, Murray, *An Unfinished Autobiography* (London: George Allen and Unwin, 1960) and H. Lloyd-Jones, *Blood for the Ghosts* (Baltimore: Johns Hopkins University Press, 1982), 195–214. Gildersleeve reviewed his *Euripides and His Age* (New York: Holt, 1913) at *AJP* 36 (1915): 230–34 ( = *SBM*, 320–25).

4. Gildersleeve had erroneously referred to "Sir Gilbert Murray" at *AJP* 33 (1912): 485. He recanted at 34 (1913): 116: "I have become so accustomed to Sir Richard, Sir William, Sir John, Sir Sidney, Sir Frederick, that . . . Sir Gilbert slipped from my pen—doubtless a mere anticipation. Surely a priest of the Muses like Gilbert Murray is not too much honoured by a prefix once borne by Shakespeare's parsons, by Sir Topas and Sir Hugh." The notice from the Hellenic Society is a mystery, since *JHS* never listed Murray as a knight in its annual membership lists. Murray was not knighted, but received the Order of Merit in 1941.

5. Goodell had written Gildersleeve on 5 January 1913: "I'm told that there's a lot of inconvenient specifying made necessary in Oxford to distinguish between [Sir James Murray's] Lady Mary and the Regius Professor's Lady Mary." Murray's wife was Lady Mary Henrietta Howard (d. 1956), eldest daughter of the ninth earl of Carlisle; but James Augustus Henry Murray (see No. 47, n. 9) was at this time married to his second wife, Ada Agnes Ruthven (1845–1936), who is not known by the name Mary. Gildersleeve has explained the style correctly; see *Debrett's Correct Form* (London: Debrett's Peerage, 1970), 55, 72. Goodell must have misheard "Lady Murray" and "Lady Mary" as identical.

6. See preceding letter, n. 5. Goodell wrote in the letter cited in n. 5 above: "No expression of disagreement could be more friendly. I am proud to have your pages conjoined to mine."

7. See preceding letter, n. 17.

### 157 To: MAX PAUL ERNST SCHNEIDEWIN
### *JHU-BLG*

JOHNS HOPKINS UNIVERSITY,
Baltimore, Maryland,
March 25, 1913.

Dear Professor Schneidewin:

Your kind card of the third instant was a pleasant surprise. I had watched the career of 'little Max' for many years, and I have noticed his work from time to time in my Journal[1]—delighted to find that he was striving for the good cause, although on somewhat different lines from those in which his father had achieved such eminence—but I little thought that after sixty years the figure of the American youth of 1851–2 remained fresh in the memory of the son of the great scholar to whom I owe so much for guidance, inspiration, and loving interest.[2] I was in Göttingen a few years ago,[3] and lingered as I passed by the house where I had been so hospitably received; and thought of Lane's[4] story how you had fallen the whole long flight of stairs and were picked up half conscious, and how your father—anxious lest your brain had been injured—leaned over you and said: 'Max, lieber Max, was ist das Geschlecht von Ensis?' and how his face brightened when you answered, 'masculini generis'. Lane died in 1897, and did not live to see the marriage of my daughter to his son—a happy union. Goodwin died a few months ago.[5] I am the sole survivor of that gay Göttingen group of American students—an old, old man. But my health is good, and I am still in full activity. I have not lost my interest in my work, but, like all old men, my thoughts often revert to the distant past in which the romance of my life lies; and Göttingen is my dearest university, as your father was my dearest teacher.

I have not forgotten my German, but in my busy life I must take the shortest way—English and the typewriter.

With many thanks for all the kind thoughts of me revealed by your note, and with best wishes,

I am
In alter Treue
Yours sincerely,
[unsigned TC]

1. *AJP* 18 (1897): 242 ( = *SBM*, 41–42); *AJP* 20 (1899): 230–31 ( = *SBM*, 49–50).
2. "He was a man of prodigious memory and knew his Homer and Sophocles by heart, and impressed us by the subtlety of his acquaintance with the Greek tongue" ("Professorial Types": 7); "One of my favorite teachers was Schneidewin" (*AJP* 37 [1916]: 373 [ = *SBM* 356]); see also *AJP* 36 (1915): 360 ( = *SBM*, 335); *AJP* 37 (1916): 501 ( = *SBM*, 372–73).
3. In the summer of 1905, see No. 131.
4. George M. Lane, who had been with the Charlestonians at Berlin and Göttingen in 1849–51; see No. 22, n. 1.
5. 15 June 1912.

## 158 To: JOHANN HERMANN HEINRICH SCHMIDT
### JHU-BLG

June 18, 1913

Dear Professor Schmidt: Your Heidelberg letter of June 8 has been received.[1] If you had done me the honour of reading my review of Professor White's book more attentively, you could hardly have failed to discover that my so-called renunciation[2] of your system was not seriously meant. The principles I have learned from you have become part of my mental constitution[3] and it was only the lack of musical training that made me relinquish the treatment of metres to my assistant, Professor Miller, who is as good a Schmidtean as even you could desire.[4] Not long ago I was pleased to see that in an English work on Aristoxenos[5] the author made effective use of your schemes which he had learned from my Pindar. I have referred to you more than once of late years[6] and always in a different tone from that which you have seen fit to assume towards the work of my collaborators on the Journal.[7]

You complain that I have not published any formal review of your Griechische Synonomik.[8] There is little space in the Journal for reviews and the book does not lend itself to a short review. One of my pupils at my instance has been working for a number of years on a Dictionary of Synonyms based on your book but he has not yet succeeded in obtaining a publisher.[9] Of course, your book is steadily used in my Seminary.

I am glad to hear that you are in vigorous health and wish you all manner of success in your new undertaking.[10] The Civil War left me with one crippled leg[11] so that I cannot rival your pedestrian achievements[12] but I am thought to bear my eighty-two years lightly and though I am naturally as quick to resent injustice as you are, I have succeeded to some extent in cultivating the tolerance appropriate to our patriarchal age.

Yours sincerely,
B. L. Gildersleeve

1. Schmidt had written an intemperate eight-page letter in response to Gildersleeve's sending him the first number of *AJP* 34, which contained Gildersleeve's "skit" of White's *Verse of Greek Comedy* (see No. 155, n. 8), 104–9 ( = *SBM*, 271–78), in which he describes his indebtedness to Schmidt's theories and simultaneously admits that they have become passé. Schmidt had replied: "Auch Sie werden nicht glauben, daß die ganz evidenten Wahrheiten, die ich zutage gefördert habe, und für den wirklich studierenden, das gesagte in seinem Sinne würdigenden der Hauptsache nach durch erdrückende Beweise bewiesen habe, jemals untergehen können" (Even you cannot believe that the utterly obvious truths that I have brought to light and that I have overwhelmingly proved in the main points can ever be forgotten by one who has truly studied and appreciated what I have said).

2. Schmidt: "Sie also haben für sich 'meinem Systeme' entsagt. Natürlich, wie alle meine Feinde, ohne auch nur in einem einzigen Punkt meine Kunstformen zu widerlegen, oder widerlegen zu können" (You yourself renounced 'my system,' naturally as all my enemies do, without even in one point rebutting my Kunstformen [*Die Kunstformen der Griechischen Poesie und ihre Bedeutung* (Leipzig: F. C. W. Vogel, 1868–72), the collection of his four books of metrical theory; see "Correspondents"] or being able to).

3. Gildersleeve had been among the first to introduce Schmidtean schemes to America (see No. 5 and n. 9.), and he had mixed results. In "Oscillations and Nutations of Philological Study," *JHU Circulars*, no. 151 (April 1901): 47, he describes the metrical work of Dindorf, "whose handbook of metres was treated exactly as if it were a table of logarithms from which there was no appeal. It was a very blind proceeding. . . . Then arose Westphal, then came J. H. H. Schmidt and all was light." At the University of Virginia, Gildersleeve gave three lectures per week to his senior class, the Monday lecture concerned the class's compositions of the previous week, the Wednesday lecture the critical study of a work of literature, and the Friday lecture was devoted to Schmidtean analysis of Greek metre. See W. M. Thornton, "Gildersleeve the Teacher," *UVa Alumni Bulletin*, 3d ser., 17 (April 1924): 124–25. He used Schmidt's own notes in writing the metrical analysis for his *Pindar* and later decided that he

could not do a volume of the *Isthmians* and *Nemeans* because he was too wedded to the old (i.e., Schmidtean) ways (*AJP* 34 (1913): 104 [ = *SBM*, 271]).

4. I.e., he was trained by Gildersleeve.

5. C. F. Abdy Williams (1855–1923), *The Aristoxenian Theory of Musical Rhythm* (Cambridge: Cambridge University Press, 1911) cites Schmidt on pp. 2 and 8 and analyzes Pind. *Pyth*. 8 along Gildersleeve's lines, p. 113. See *AJP* 33 (1912): 232–33 ( = *SBM*, 249–50).

6. In addition to "Oscillations" (n. 3 above), see *AJP* 29 (1908): 502 ( = *SBM*, 178), 368–69 ( = *SBM*, 166–67); *AJP* 33 (1912): 232–33 ( = *SBM*, 249–50).

7. Schmidt: "Ich habe aber auch die Auktoren Ihrer Zeitschrift geprüft, und die öden Statistiken und Buchstaben-Etymologien deselben sattsam erkannt, so daß von solchen Leuten—ich meine aber nicht alle, kein würdiger, ja kein menschenwürdiger Fortschritt zu hoffen ist" (But I have also examined the "authors" of your journal and I have sufficiently recognized from the desolate statistics and letter-etymologies of same that from those people—and I am not talking of all people—no worthwhile progress is to be hoped for).

9. *Synonymik der griechischen Sprache*, 4 vols., and *Handbuch der lateinischen und griechischen Synonymik* (Leipzig: B. G. Teubner, 1876–86 and 1889 respectively). Schmidt: "Freilich auch von meiner Synonymik hat Ihre Zeitschrift nie eine Rezension gebracht, dagegen trostlose Silbenstechereien genug besprochen" (In fact, your journal has never published a review of my Synonymik either, but instead treated boring syllable-measuring). Gildersleeve had written an appreciative, if informal, notice of Schmidt's *Synonymik* at *AJP* 7 (1886): 406–7.

9. Unknown.

10. Schmidt: "Da ich an einem dreibändigen Werke arbeite und erst den zweiten Band vollendet habe, wärend [sic] nun der erste und dritte neu aus dem längst vorhandenen Manuskript erst in besserer Form neu zu schreiben ist. . . . In 2 bis 3 Jahren erscheint mein neues Werk, das wiederum völlig neue Bahnen eröffnet" (I am working on a tome of three volumes and have only finished the second, while the first and third have to be written over in a better form from the existing manuscript. . . . In two or three years my new work will be published, which is going to open completely new paths). According to *Sandys*, 158, n. 3, this was to have been an application of Schmidt's metrical principles to a new *nomos* of Timotheus and the *Odes* of Bacchylides. The work never appeared.

11. See No. 12, n. 8.

12. Schmidt: "Übrigens befinde ich mich außerordentlich wohl, und mache häufig, trotzdem ich bald den 80sten Geburtstag feiere (Jan. 1914), Fußwanderungen von 54 bis 62 Kilometer am Tage, arbeite auch wissenschaftlich mit alter Frische, ohne auch nur einen Tüttel von Alter zu fühlen" (By the way, I am extremely well and I very often go hiking for 54 to 62 kilometres a day, even though I will be celebrating my 80th birthday (Jan. 1914), and I am also working professionally with my old vigor without feeling my old age even a bit).

159 To: RICHARD THEODORE ELY
*State Historical Society of Wisconsin*

1002 N. Calvert St.
Baltimore, Oct. 24, 1913

Dear Professor Ely:

You belong to the early period of the Johns Hopkins University, a time when it was well worth while to live, a time of pioneer work, of enthusiasms.[1] I never meet anyone who was with us in those days that did not respond with fervour to the memories waked by the review of the actors and the activities of that day—when the staid citizens of Baltimore would shake their heads and tell me confidentially that they could not help thinking that man Richard T. Ely was a dangerous person. And that dangerous person has gone /on/ and acquired an international fame and the pillars of society are not yet in the dust. I did my appointed work faithfully to the best of my ability and had little thought of setting an example—and yet I have of late years been gratified to find that my individual influence has been for good, perhaps more good than what I have achieved in my special /line/. Your kind and cordial letter was a pleasant surprise.[2] Although we worked side by side so many years and our personal relations were always pleasant and your Southern connections brought you nearer to me,[3] I never dreamed that you were especially influenced by what I did or said. I look back on my work since I was fifty-nine—your present age—Twenty-three years of distinctive work—work that has been much doing—work that has overcome opposition and found approval—I am glad to learn that my course of life has given a man who has achieved as much as you have the courage to go forward.

Yours faithfully<br>B. L. Gildersleeve

1. Ely had been assistant professor (1881–82), associate (1882–87) and associate professor (1887–92) of economics at Hopkins before moving to the University of Wisconsin.

2. Ely's letter for Gildersleeve's eight-second birthday is lost.

3. Ely had married Anna Morris Anderson (d. 1923), of an old Virginia family, in June 1884.


160 To: CHARLES FORSTER SMITH<br>Smith

[October 26, 1913][1]

Your letters always move me to grave thoughts and your congratulations, welcome, if not deserved in anything like the full measure dealt out by your warm heart, have prompted a process of introspection such as I naturally avoid. The love shown me by my pupils is a strange thing to me, because, outside of classroom and consultation room I have had little intercourse with them, and I reproach myself very often with not doing more for them socially, though I am sometimes able to help them in their professional careers. I am absorbed in my work to a fault, even though my heart goes out to them and I am, I may say honestly, grateful for their affection. It is like every good and perfect gift—from above. It is simply the overflow of my own enthusiasm, and you know how so many students regard the dreams and visions of their teachers as mere *deliramenta*. Well, I am glad to be assured that my enthusiasm has been contagious—but that also is no merit of mine. As Goethe says, '*Alles ist als wie geschenkt.*'[2] That is the way the best things come, and among the best things I count the friendship you have shown me since we first met—a friendship that has been heartily reciprocated. My health is good and my work as an editor keeps me in constant touch with the present and suggests plans for a future which in the course of things cannot be long. I am trying to gather up my unpublished papers, but new aspects are constantly coming up—new aspects of old themes asserting themselves.[3] My old age is not torpid, whatever else it is.

1. Written in response to greetings on his eighty-second birthday.

2. "Ja, das ist das rechte Gleis, / Daß man nicht weiß, / Was man denkt, / Wenn man denkt; / Alles ist als wie geschenkt" (That is the right track, / that they do not know / what they think, / if they think; / Everything is, as it were, a gift) (*Zahme Xenien* 2). See also No. 168 and *AJP* 41 (1920): 402.

3. See, e.g., *AJP* 34 (1913): 232 ( = *SBM*, 282).


## 161 To: CHARLOTTE LANNEAU MEAD
### *JHU-BLG*

January 20, 1914

My dear Cousin Charlotte:

Your grandfather[1] was the great nephew of my grandfather.[2] His father, Peter,[3] was brought to Charleston by my grandfather, but he must have died before I was born. I knew /recall/ Cousin Peter,[4] son of Peter Fleetwood[5] and was his guest when I passed through Charleston in 1854.[6] His wife, Cousin Gracie, his children, Mollie (Whilden), Fleetwood, Gracia, Charles I remember also.[7] Charles[8] the doctor I saw in Charleston when I was there in 1892.[9] Your father, Jefferson Bennett,[10] I cannot recall. He was named after Jefferson Bennett, son of the Governor,[11] close friend and travelling companion of my Uncle John.[12] There is no doubt about the cousinship whatever. I have a number of nieces and nephews, great nieces and great nephews, but I am not much interested in genealogy; and if you desire further information, you can get it by a letter to Alfred W/r/ight Lanneau, Pitt Street, Charleston, S.C.[13]

At my time of life—I am in my eighty-third year—it is not likely that I shall ever go to California, though my health is very good; ~~and~~ /but/ as I am still of an enterprising nature, I may look in on you at the Broadview Apartments.

I have a number of photographs taken within the last ten or fifteen years. The photogravure of 1901 is after all my favorite, and I have much pleasure in sending it to you.

My handwriting is rather hard to read, and my signature must serve as the autograph desired.

With best thanks for your interest, and with best wishes for you and yours,

I am,

Yours faithfully
[unsigned TC]

1. Fleetwood Lanneau (1809-83) was a partner in the family grocery business, Lanneau, Smith and Whilden, on Hayne Street in Charleston. He represented St. Philip and St. Michael's Parishes in the South Carolina General Assembly (1848-49, 1852-53, 1858-59) and was tax collector for the Lower District. See Mowbray and Norwood (No. 144, n. 1), 182-83 (with portrait).

2. For Bazile Lanneau, see No. 144, n. 3.

3. Pierre (Peter) Lanneau V (1786-1834), was born in Liverpool, Nova Scotia, the son of Pierre La Noue IV (1744-?), who was the brother of Bazile. In 1793, Pierre IV's brother, Bazile, widowed and childless, returned to Nova Scotia to be reunited with his lost brothers (No. 144, n. 2), but found only his brother Amand (1737-1815) and Pierre's family. He adopted two of Pierre's four children, Pierre V and Sarah (1779-1835), and brought them back to Charleston with the intention of teaching Pierre the tanning trade. He became a mariner and in 1807 married Rebecca Armstrong of Charleston (1788-1871), by whom he had two sons, Fleetwood (n. 1 above) and Peter II (1812-1839). See Mowbray and Norwood, 181-82.

4. Gildersleeve means Fleetwood Lanneau II (n. 7 below), who was killed in the Civil War.

5. Gildersleeve means Fleetwood Lanneau (n. 1 above).

6. See No. 3.

7. Gracey Windsor Lanneau (1814-98) and her husband Fleetwood had seven children: Mary Stephens (1834-1916), who married Benjamin Franklin Whilden (1828-83); Gracia Jan (1837-1916); Fleetwood II (1839-62); James Caldwell (1844-58); Jefferson Bennett (1842-1901); Thomas Windsor (1852-98); and Charles Blum (1846-1937).

8. Charles Blum Lanneau (1846-1937) studied medicine at South Carolina Medical College, Göttingen, and Heidelberg. He practiced medicine in Charleston, Darlington, S.C., and Savannah, Ga.

9. Gildersleeve was invited to speak to the New England Society. Some of his remarks are included in his obituary in the *Charleston News and Courier*, 12 January 1924: 1.

10. Jefferson Bennett (1842-1901) served in the South Carolina Infantry in the Civil War. By his second wife, Charlotte Jane Griffith, he had three children, Charles Griffith (b. 1875), Fleetwood Lanneau (b. 1877), and the addressee of this letter, Charlotte Lanneau (b. 1879), who married Louis Durand Mead.

11. Washington Jefferson Bennett (b. 1808), was the son of Thomas Bennett (1781-1865), governor of South Carolina from 1820 to 1822, during which term a slave rebellion was quashed and the abolition movement suffered as a result. Bennett later served in the South Carolina Senate from 1837 to 1840. C. M. Bennett, "Family Records of Gov. Thomas Bennett, Jr.," *SC Hist. Mag.* 51 (1950): 51-54.

12. John Francis Lanneau (1809-67), third brother of Gildersleeve's mother, Emma Louisa, graduated from Yale, where he underwent a religious conversion, and theological seminaries at Princeton, N.J. and Columbia, S.C. In 1832 he began his mission in Jerusalem, Beirut, and Mt. Lebanon. In 1846 he returned to America and with his wife settled in Marietta, Ga. Mowbray and Norwood, 177-79.

13. See No. 144, n. 4.

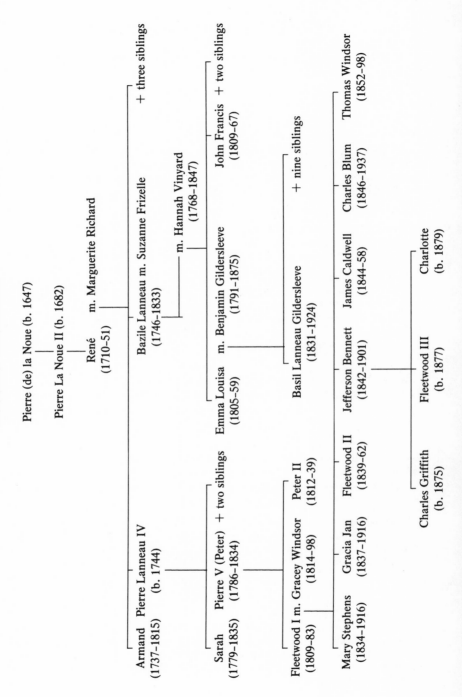

162 To: JOSEPH VILLIERS DENNEY
*JHU-BLG*

March 2, 1914

Dean J. V. Denney,
The Ohio State University,
Columbus, Ohio.
Dear Dean Denney:

In reply to your letter of inquiry of February 25, I have no hesitation in recommending for the vacant chair of Greek at The Ohio State University Professor George Melville Bolling,[1] a distinguished Doctor of Philosophy of this University (1896), for many years Professor of Greek in the Catholic University of America, Washington, D.C. The Washington post he relinquished last year in order to seek larger opportunities of development, and he is now holding one of the Johnston Scholarships[2] in the Johns Hopkins, which are bestowed on men who have given assurance of unusual achievement in their respective fields of work. Dr. Bolling's published contributions to Greek studies are all marked by scholarly care and insight, and some of his recent work in the American Journal of Philology[3] has elicited high commendation from foreign authorities—notably the eminent scholar Wackernagel[4]—and I myself have been so much impressed with his knowledge of matters Homeric that I have turned over to him my Homeric course announced for the present session. As a Sanskrit scholar Dr. Bolling is held in high esteem by Professor Bloomfield,[5] and he has made notable contributions to Sanskrit studies.[6] And as if in anticipation of your needs, he has been pursuing studies in art and archaeology under Professor Robinson.[7] His manner—somewhat reserved except among intimates—becomes animated in the work of the class; and he is an interesting teacher, as well as one who commands his subject. Dr. Bolling is a man of attractive appearance, vigorous health, well equipped physically as well as mentally for the arduous studies to which he is devoted. He is a gentleman by birth and breeding, belongs to one of the oldest Virginia families;[8] and the two Bollings, husband and wife—there are no children—would, I am sure, prove a welcome accession to the social life of Columbus. There is no university in the country that would not be a gainer by securing the services of such a man.

Yours sincerely
[unsigned TC]

1. George Melville Bolling (1871–1963) was educated in his native Baltimore at Loyola College (A.B. 1891) and Hopkins (Ph.D. 1896), writing his dissertation on the participle in Hesiod (see *Catholic U. Bull.* 111 [1897]: 421–71). He taught Sanskrit, Greek, and comparative philology at Catholic University (1895–1913) before becoming professor of Greek at Ohio State, where he remained for twenty-six years (1914–40). He was a founder and president of

the Linguistic Society of America (1932) and editor of *Language*. In 1920 he was given the Gold Cross of the Redeemer by Greece for his services as an adviser during World War I. Among his publications are: *The External Evidence for Interpolation in Homer* (Oxford: Clarendon Press, 1925), *The Athetized Lines of the Iliad* (Baltimore: Linguistic Society of America, 1944), and *Ilias Atheniensium: The Athenian Iliad of the 6th Century* B.C. (Lancaster, Pa.: APA, 1950). *NYTimes*, 3 June 1963: 29.

2. The three Johnston scholarships were university fellowships established by Mrs. Harriet Lane Johnston (1833-1923) in memory of her husband (Henry E.) and two sons (Henry E., Jr., and James Buchanan). Bolling held the Henry E. Johnston Scholarship.

3. Bolling had contributed to *AJP* "An Epic Fragment from Oxyrrhynchus," 22 (1901): 63-69; "The Beginning of the Greek Day," 23 (1902), 428-35; "Contributions to the Study of Homeric Metre," 28 (1907): 401-10; 33 (1912): 401-25; 34 (1913): 152-71; and "An Archetype of Our Iliad and the Papyri," 35 (1914): 125-48, along with five notes, and would contribute four more articles while Gildersleeve was editor.

4. Jacob Wackernagel (1853-1938), author of *Altindische Grammatik* (Göttingen: Vandenhoeck and Ruprecht, 1896) and co-editor with Wilamowitz (see "Correspondents") and others of *Die Griechische und Lateinische Literatur und Sprache* (Leipzig: B. G. Teubner, 1905).

5. No. 49, n. 14.

6. *Parisistas of the Atharvaveda*, ed. with J. von Negelein (Leipzig, F. A. Brockhaus, 1910-11); "The Relation of the Vedic Forms of the Dual," *JAOS* 23 (1902): 318-24; and "The Çântikalpa of the Atharva Veda," *JAOS* 33 (1913): 265-78.

7. On Robinson, see No. 150, n. 7.

8. The Bolling family dates from the seventeenth century in Virginia; see *Virginia Magazine of History and Biography* 22 (1914): 103-7, 215-17, 331-33, 441-46; 23 (1915): 94-96. Bolling's mother, Hannah Lamb, could trace her ancestry to Anthony Lamb, who died in York Co., Va., in 1700; see *William and Mary Quarterly* 7 (1898-99): 51-54, 109-12.


## 163 To: EMILY McKIM REED
### *Maryland Historical Society*

Oct. 23, 1914[1]

Dear Mrs. Reed:

You are—I verily believe—outside of my own family the very earliest of my acquaintances now living—I say acquaintances because in those far off days I came very near hating the malapert young girl, who delighted in crossing my courtship of Sally Taylor[2] and I see you now waving in mockery the gold-mounted manatee whip [?][3] that I brought that obdurate fair one from Cuba.[4] Dear me! What blows fortune has dealt us since—And yet we live and have what I might call a sneaking pleasure in life.—Of course, you will say speak for yourself. My enjoyment of life is still full—It is an interesting world. Well—if it is not an interesting world, it is a world that seems suddenly to be interested in me and I am writing notes at finger speed in reply to letters, telegrams, presents, flowers—and I must content myself with this scrawl to my former enemy, long since my friend and a good friend too.

Many many thanks for your delightful note and all your kind wishes, which breathe sincerity.

Yours faithfully and affectionately
B. L. Gildersleeve

As I am closing this note, I fish up one or two old acquaintances out of the depths of my memory but one must not tell women the truth. They are not used to it.

1. Gildersleeve's eighty-third birthday.
2. Unidentified.
3. Unclear in the MS. A manatee-whip was made from the very tough hide of the manatee, which inhabits the warm waters of the Atlantic coast. Such whips were fashionable with lady riders.
4. For a typical Charlestonian's excursion in the 1850s, see "A Trip to Cuba," *Russell's Magazine*, 2 (1857–58): 59–63; 116–23; 235–39; 322–27; 439–45, 536–43.

## 164 To: CHARLES FORSTER SMITH
*Smith*

[October 25, 1914]

I have been kept busy writing acknowledgments; and then there were letters from different parts of the country which could be dismissed in a few words. But some of these letters that came I put aside for repeated reading and more detailed answer—yours among them. I prize the love of my pupils and often wonder at it, because I am so jealous of my time that I have little intercourse with them outside the classroom, and yet there is no mistake in the genuineness of their affectionate expressions[1]—and I am happy to think that there must be an atmosphere of goodwill that pervades the home of our common studies, or in other moods I simply quote St. James' faulty hexameter.[2] Now you were never a pupil of mine, though you honored my auditorium at Sewanee all those years ago.[3] But I feel towards you as I feel towards only a few of the many who have followed my lectures, and I recognize the personal element in your estimate of my work and influence. In this 'narrow and funambulatory track of goodness,' as Sir Thomas Browne has it,[4] I find it best not to look at the spectators. My ears are as capacious as Cicero's for praise[5]—but I resolutely stop them, and chewing laurels upsets one's mental and moral digestion. I have figures, you see, that swear at each other, as they do in Brief Mention, to the disgust of my critics. Still the truth is there. Recognition came to me so late in life that I had time to observe how many men were spoiled by premature success.[6] I read all the pleasant things that are said of me—sample the süssigkeiten [sweetmeats], as Vahlen[7] called them in a letter he wrote me not long before his death—and turn to my work. It is the only salvation for a man of my susceptible nature. . . . but I appreciate and reciprocate all the affection that manifests itself in all that you write of me and to me— and I need it, for these are dark days with me. There was no festivity on my birthday. On the third of October I lost my son-in-law, Gardiner Lane.[8] You doubtless know his name as the Treasurer of the Archaeological Association. You may have seen some of the tributes paid to him in the press.[9] Boston is in mourning for him. My poor daughter—they were devoted to each other—is left to face a world of problems without his strong support. Perhaps it is better for her that she has so much to do; and then there is the child[10]—a charming girl of fifteen—for whom she will live. But the pity of it! Lane was one of the two strong stays of my old age. I looked to him as well as my son for the future of my wife when my time too should come— and now he is taken and I am left.

1. See No. 160.

2. James 1:17: πᾶσα δόσις ἀγαθὴ καὶ πᾶν δώρημα τέλειον ἄνωθέν ἐστιν (Every good endowment and every perfect gift is from above). See *AJP* 40 (1921): 337 ( = *SBM*, 393).

3. This was at the third summer session given by Gildersleeve at Sewanee, in 1887; Smith had met Gildersleeve the summer before at the APA meetings at Cornell. An editorial note to the article in which this letter is published, "Basil Lanneau Gildersleeve: An Intimate View," *Sewanee Review* 32 (April 1924): 162, erroneously gives the date of the Sewanee lectures as 1888, when Gildersleeve was in Europe.

4. *Christian Morals* (1716), sec. 1: "Tread softly and circumspectly in this funambulatory track and narrow path of goodness."

5. E.g., Cic. *Fam.* 5.12 and *Att.* 1.16.

6. See No. 131.

7. Johannes Vahlen (1830–1911), a fellow-student of Hübner's and Gildersleeve's at Bonn, became ordinarius at Berlin and was an editor of *Hermes* until he was purged by Mommsen along with Hübner in 1881 (No. 61, n. 3). He and Gildersleeve met again in Berlin in 1907 with Wilamowitz; see R. L. Fowler, "The Gildersleeve Archive," *Briggs-Benario*, 80–81. He edited *T. Macci Plauti Menaechmi* (Berlin: F. Vahlen, 1882), *Ennianae poesis reliquiae* (Leipzig: B. G. Teubner, 1928), and Karl Lachmann's (1793–1851) *Kleine Schriften* (Berlin: G. Reimer, 1876), but was principally interested in emending Latin authors; see his *Gesammelte Philologische Schriften* (Leipzig: B. G. Teubner, 1911–23).

8. Lane had taken his family to Europe in July 1914, in part to visit John Singer Sargent, whom he commissioned to paint a set of murals for the rotunda of the Boston Museum of Fine Arts, in part to visit the baths at Marienbad. The family was in Austria when war was declared and as they hurried to get home, Lane found his stomach cancer deteriorating. He was very ill when he arrived home on 12 September and died on 3 October 1914. See K. L. Weems, *Odds Were against Me* (New York: Vantage Press, 1985), 15–17.

9. Both the *Boston Evening Transcript* and the *Boston Globe* (evening edition) of 3 October 1914, put Lane's obituary on the front page. The *Transcript* devoted five separate articles to him (pp. 1, 4) and covered his funeral (5 October 1914) on the front page. Among the pallbearers were Harvard President A. Lawrence Lowell (No. 145, n. 6), Senator Henry Cabot Lodge, Charles Francis Adams II, and Henry L. Higginson. See also *NYTimes*, 4 October 1914: sec. 2, 14.

10. On Katharine Ward Lane, see No. 116, n. 7.

### 165 To: John Dewey
#### *JHU-BLG*

February 5, 1915

Dear Professor Dewey:[1]

It is recorded of my master, Friedrich Ritschl,[2] that when he went to Italy in quest of Plautine Mss., he was amazed and disgusted to find that his title of Professor—an honourable title in Germany, which cannot be assumed at will—carried with it scant distinction in his new sphere of work; so that he fell back on his initial 'Doctor', which was more highly esteemed in Italy than the more pretentious designation. In Germany the 'mailed fist' strikes down all pretenders to a title, which in that land of officialdom must have the sanction of the State. In the twenty years of my professorship at the University of Virginia, it was considered bad form to use the title in social intercourse, and this is, I believe, the case in other university circles. The chief reason is the easy assumption of the title in other lines of employment, though there is something unsubstantial in the designation itself; and it will be as hard to redeem it as it has been to re- deem the word 'sophist', which is its[3] equivalent in Greek culture.[4] But the object of your meeting—an object with which I am in perfect sympathy—is not so much to redeem the title as to guard the approach to the office as it is exercised in the American University.[5] The Association of University Professors has been formed, as I understand it, to insure better methods of election, so that the choice shall not be swayed by the prejudice, favorit- ism, whim of any individual. It is true that no matter how carefully guarded the avenues to promotion may be, mistakes will be made. Even in Germany, the consecrated land of professors, personal influence is abused.[6] The father-in-law is a potent figure.[7] Creed—political or reli- gious—may check promotion.[8] But the professorial chair of a German uni- versity cannot well be filled by a downright ignoramus, as was once the case in America, though insane men have been known to flourish even there. Now, my practical contact with college and university professors goes back more than sixty years, and the judgment of that earliest stage is not to be despised. It has been said that you can no more fool a school boy as to the capacity of his teacher than you can fool the Almighty, and if I did not stand in awe of my teachers, it was because they did not deserve re- spect. In a little article on professionalism of the Professorate, written many years ago, I claimed for the Johns Hopkins the beginning of a new era in professorial life, the institution of a regular career for a man who would aspire to a part in the higher ranges of educational work.[9] It is no derogation to the great names that illustrate the catalogues of the older universities of the country to say that they were happy accidents. In the early days the ambitious youth taught school while he was preparing for something higher—law, medicine, or divinity. The tutor who bloomed into a professor was usually a man without initiative. In our theological days the returned missionary and the 'stickit minister'[10] were often provided for by professorships. When a desirable vacancy occurred, the active canvass for the position was conducted without much regard to the qualifications of the candidate. There was no president of the University of Virginia in my time, and so the complaint, still so rife, as to the undue influence of the Presidency did not hold. The power was vested in the Board of Visitors, appointed by the Governor, and shifting every four years. When I myself was a candidate, the election was postponed for three months, because of personal prejudice, and I was left in racking suspense for all those weeks;[11] and when the time came and I sent in the testimonials of my German teachers[12] of whose good opinion I was inordinately proud, the testimonials would have been of no effect, if it had not been for the influence of two prominent members of the Board, one a friend of my father, another a man who was favorably impressed by a personal interview with the candidate. It is an amusing reminiscence that the Rector of the University, who cast the only vote cast against me, frankly said that he was influenced by the fact that I did not bear a Virginia name.[13]

My confidences will go no farther than my own appointment. The system established by Mr. Jefferson was well calculated to insure faithful work on the part of the teachers, no matter what the original equipment may have been, and I have publicly acknowledged my indebtedness to the Jeffersonian plan. But although the position at the University of Virginia was one of the best in the country, I regarded my professorship as only one stage in the course I set out to run; but the Civil War crossed all my plans, and I was doomed to be that meaningless thing—a dean. For my present professorship I was not a candidate. I was called, and the call was due entirely to the judgment of the first President of the Johns Hopkins University, who considered me, if not the best man, the best available man.[14]

In the development of the plan of the Johns Hopkins the choice of professors is made by the Trustees, upon the recommendation of the Academic Council—a small body of professors under the chairmanship of the President. The Academic Council, originally composed of the first full professors, was subsequently enlarged by cooptation.[15] A new method of supplying vacancies has been introduced, according to which the professorial body at large will be represented. The change has not had time to affect the work of the Council, nor does it affect the principle, which is the election of professors on the nomination of professors. Needless to say, the judgment of the President, who is *ex officio* Chairman of the Council, is an important element in the decision.

My own good fortune in my relations to University authorities has not lessened my interest in the endeavors of the confraternity after a better state of things. I am an old man, but not a patriarch, and instead of the 'benediction' you ask, I send you and your associates my cordial wishes for a successful issue of your deliberations.

Yours faithfully,<br>
Basil L. Gildersleeve

Professor John Dewey,<br>
Columbia University,<br>
New York City.

1. In 1914, at the instigation of a number of professors, many of whom were from Hopkins (particularly A. O. Lovejoy in philosophy), a meeting was called for 1–2 January 1915 to found the American Association of University Professors. As chairman of the organizational meeting, Dewey wrote to Gildersleeve on 4 December 1914 requesting that he speak to the six hundred academics who would assemble in New York on "the need of & possibilities of such an association." He went on, "I need not tell you how many of us regard you as the Doyen of American higher scholarship, and as an exemplar of the spirit which should animate the whole professorate." Gildersleeve declined to speak chiefly because of the strain of travel on a nearly blind eighty-four-year-old. Dewey wrote back on 22 December, asking for "at least a brief letter to be read at the meeting giving us, as it were, your benediction?" Although the letter is dated too late to have been read at the meeting, it would certainly have given Dewey ammunition for his attacks on recruitment and appointment practices. The letter was published in the *Johns Hopkins Alumni Magazine* 3, no. 3 (March 1915): 195–97.

2. For Ritschl, see No. 23, n. 2.

3. The printed version reads "its"; the TS reads "the." This text follows the printed version, as the TS contains many typist's errors. In the third-to-last paragraph of the TS, "confidences" replaces the struck-through "confessions."

4. The Greek word σοφιστής originally meant "master of one's craft," particularly as applied to musicians and poets. It was then applied to intellectuals such as the Seven Sages and became synonymous with "philosopher." At Athens, men who professed to make others wise, i.e., "professors of arts and sciences," called themselves "Sophists" and were lampooned for their pretension by Aristophanes in *The Clouds* and attacked by Socrates and Plato, so that the term ultimately came to mean "quibbler," "cheat" (LSJ, s.v. "σοφιστής").

5. The three principal areas of concern were "methods of appointment and promotion," "the recruiting of professors, and the effect thereon of the existing system of graduate fellowships and scholarships," and "the limits of 'standardization' in higher education, with especial reference to the standardizing activities of extra-academic corporations" (J. Dewey, "President's Address" *AAUP Bulletin* 1, no. 1 [1915]: 13). The first two are clearly in line with Dewey's views on democratizing the academic community, and he was chairman of the organizational meeting and the association's first president. As early as the first year of its life, however, the association found itself primarily concerned not with the way fellowships and positions are attained but rather with the way they are maintained through the system of tenure.

6. Gildersleeve is certainly thinking of Mommsen's (No. 61, n. 4) treatment of Hübner and his preventing the historian Julius Beloch (1854–1929) from getting a post in Germany. Gildersleeve may also have in mind the swift rise of Nietzsche (AJP 37 [1916]: 116 [ = *SBM*, 343]).

7. In addition to Mommsen (No. 61, n. 4), whose daughter had married Wilamowitz (see "Correspondents"; Mommsen himself was the son-in-law of his publisher, G. Reimer),

Ritschl (No. 23, n. 2) was the father-in-law of Curt Wachsmuth (No. 49, n. 7), as Droysen (No. 51, n. 7) was of Hübner.

8. For example, Mommsen's affiliations in 1848 forced him to take a post in Zürich (along with Otto Jahn [1813-69] and Moriz Haupt [No. 71, n. 13]). The only way for a Jew such as Gildersleeve's teacher Jacob Bernays (No. 7, n. 10) to become an ordinarius was to convert, as did Theodor Benfey (1809-81).

9. "On the Present Aspect of Classical Study," *JHU Circulars*, no. 50 (June 1886): 105-7: "Whatever we [at Hopkins] may have failed to do, we have assuredly not failed in rousing to greater vigilance and stimulating to a more intense energy in other parts of the wide field, and . . . our example has made for life and growth and progress" (105). See also "University Work in America and Classical Philology," *Princeton Review* 55 (1879): 511-36 ( = *E&S*, 87-123).

10. A minister licensed by the Presbytery to preach, but who cannot obtain a pastoral charge or gain a preferment. See S. R. Crockett's novel, *The Stickit Minister* (1893). The term could be applied to Gildersleeve's father.

11. See No. 6, nn. 1-2. The board of visitors at that time (terms in parentheses) comprised Andrew Stevenson (1845-57), Fleming B. Miller (1852-56), James Laurence Carr (1853-59), Sherrard Clemens (1854-56), William T. Joynes (1856-59), and John Randolph Tucker (1856-59), the latter being attorney general of Virginia. The secretary of the board was R. T. W. Duke (1853-64), the principal of Lewisburg Academy, later Confederate officer and member of Congress.

12. K.F. Hermann and F. Schneidewin of Göttingen had died; see No. 5.

13. Andrew Stevenson (1784-1857), former Speaker of the U.S. House of Representatives and minister to the Court of St. James, had assumed the rectorship after the death (on 5 February 1856) of his predecessor, Jefferson's closest associate in the founding of the university, Joseph C. Cabell (1778-1856). He died less than a year later.

14. See chapter 3, introduction.

15. The trustees had followed the German model, putting "the chief responsibility of guiding the internal affairs of the University" in the control of an academic council, specifically the right to name fellows and veto the appointment of associates. But the junior faculty were virtually disenfranchised and could only be appeased by the creation in May 1882 of the board of collegiate advisers to regulate undergraduate studies and subsequently, in October 1883, of a board of university studies, comprised of associate professors, to oversee graduate instruction.

# 8

# O MAKROS AIÔN: TWILIGHT,
# 1915–1924

The failure of his eyes and ears obliged Gildersleeve to retire in his eighty-fourth year, after sixty years of uninterrupted teaching. He continued to edit *AJP* through volume 40 (1919) and to write his "Brief Mention" until 1920 (No. 185). He found solace in the late years in composing sonnets, often in the insomnious hours of the early morning. They were shared with the friends they were written for (Nos. 183–84), and, although cherished by their recipients, were never collected.

The illness and death of family and friends took its predictable toll on his spirits, with the added intimation of his own mortality coming in the form of a heart attack (No. 172) from which his aging body was very slow to recover. Betty's health was still dubious, and his daughter Emma seemed, if anything, less strong after the death of her husband (No. 164).

Betty's sudden illness in December 1915 in fact prevented his undertaking the risky trip to California as Sather lecturer (No. 170), and indeed his days of travel farther from Baltimore than The Chimneys were over. But he had the deep satisfaction of being recognized as a literary figure (Nos. 167, 174, 187), and his birthdays brought him an abundance of good wishes from students and non-students old and young, at home and abroad (Nos. 168, 180, 189–91). The reconciliation with Wilamowitz (No. 188) was as much a comfort to this student of the old German school as the onset of World War I was a heartbreak.

Gilman had set as one of his last instructions, "Whatever you do, do not resign." Gildersleeve felt obliged to explain his resignation/retirement to his friends by means of a small, privately published pamphlet, "An Unspoken Farewell." In it he puts a close to his career as elegant and honorable as this long life had been:

A close contemporary of Mr. Gilman's, I might fittingly have withdrawn when he retired, and one of the younger men of that first generation took the helm. But I held on through the new administration, through the interregnum. . . . I am alone escaped to tell of the ravages of time. I can't say that I enjoy the rôle, but I am playing it philosophically . . . . The old archer Time has shot his arrows into the drums of my ears, and my manner of teaching requires physical as well as mental alertness. There remains enough work to do. At least I have mapped out enough to last for another sixty years. I am still to work for the University in the management of the American Journal of Philology, which has furnished so large a part of my employment for the last thirty-six years. I am gathering up the results of my researches. I am still pushing forward my favorite lines of investigation. When my time comes, I will not say with Cassandra, ἀρκείτω βίος,[1] 'Let life suffice', but with the unknown speaker of a fragment of Aeschylus, 'Life's bivouac is o'er'[2], διαπεφρούρηται βίος. These words of a warrior remind me of Victor Hugo's 'J'ai servi, j'ai veillé', 'I have served, I have watched'[3]—served as a teacher, watched as a critic; and of Landor's 'warming both hands before the ⟨bivouac⟩ fire of life.'[4] Διαπεφρούρηται βίος shall be my epitaph.[5]

1. Aes. *Ag.* 1314.
2. Aes. *frag.* 265 (Nauck).
3. See No. 154, n. 5.
4. "Dying Speech of an Old Philosopher": "I strove with none, for none was worth my strife: / Nature I loved, and, next to Nature, Art: / I warm'd both hands before the fire of life. / It sinks: and I am ready to depart."
5. It is the epitaph on his gravestone at Plot 58 of the University Cemetery in Charlottesville, but it is misspelled, with an English "V" in place of the upsilon. See also his memorial notice of Hübner, *AJP* 22 (1901): 114.

## 166 To: John Adams Scott
### *JHU-BLG*

May 26, 1915

Professor John A. Scott,
Northwestern University,
Dear Professor Scott:

My resignation,[1] which I have had in view for some years, was postponed on account of Smith's[2] absence from the country. The time is ripe. My health is good. I am not aware of any decline in my powers of assimilation and illustration, but my hearing has become dull, and I am not certain that I could any longer manage the Practical Exercises, which constitute a characteristic part of my teaching.[3] I might continue to lecture until the end, but lecturing is not teaching; and I am naturally desirous to sum up in book form the result of nearly sixty years of thought and research in my favorite domain—The Literary Significance of Greek Syntax. I have had all the material together for some time, but it is a subject one cannot work at in vacation, and during the session my class and the Journal keep me too busy. That is to be my main occupation for some time. The Trustees have made handsome recognition of my long service.[4] I am to retain my old and well-beloved quarters in the University,[5] and with God's mercy <u>Brief Mention</u> will still make its quarterly appeal to my friends. I have simply been myself, just as you in your turn have first and foremost been John Adams Scott.

Yours faithfully

[unsigned TC]

1. Gildersleeve's resignation was announced 21 May 1915. He had announced his intention to resign in March, and though the trustees had tried to persuade him to stay on, he had written Henry Holt on 10 May, "I have resigned my professorship." See also *Baltimore Sun*, 22 May 1915.

2. Kirby Flower Smith (see "Correspondents").

3. Each year at Hopkins, as he had at the University of Virginia, Gildersleeve taught a class in "Practical Exercises" (until 1883 called "Greek Composition and Translation"), required of all Greek students. See Scott's account, "Gildersleeve the Teacher," *PAPA* 56 (1925): xxii–xxviii.

4. He was allowed to retire at full pay.

5. 14 McCoy Hall; see No. 73, n. 7.

### 167 To: MARY ELIZABETH PHILLIPS[1]
*Phillips/Poe Museum*

[June 17, 1915]

[Poe was] A great celebrity, in the eyes of Richmond people, he was observed wherever he went. In 1843, I read 'The Gold Bug' . . . being a native of Charlestown, [sic] and familiar with Sullivan's Island, I was duly critical . . . and there were things in 'The Raven' to which I took objection in the *Watchman and Observer*—my father's paper . . . But I made concessions to his genius and through my friend Jno. [sic] R. Thompson, Editor of the *Southern Literary Messenger*, I procured Poe's autograph, diligently sought since then and never found. I remember seeing him as he came out of his hotel[2] *a modest establishment* on Broad Street-[and] watched him as he walked, *doubtless* towards the office of the *Messenger*,[3] a noticeable man[4] clad in black,[5] the fashion of the times,[6] closely buttoned up, erect, forward looking, something separate, in his whole bearing. I was to see him again, for he gave a reading in the Exchange Hotel, where he recited his 'Raven' and other poems to a small audience—chiefly of women . . . Pictures *are apt to* come *in* between a man and his memories, *and that is the trouble with family portraits. One's real mother's presence is usurped by a picture that is often faulty as a work of art and as a portrait.* But I can hardly be mistaken as to some points of his face, a beautifully poetical face. The eyes *were* fine. The forehead challenged *e*special attention for its breadth and prominence. The mouth was feminine, and took away from the strength of his [*the*] countenance; but the whole effect was spiritual. He might have been the embodiment of *one of* his airiest fancies, in no wise the lost soul one sees in some *of the* artistic creations of him of today. His voice was pleasant. There was nothing dramatic about his recitation. *One who loved him not called him a 'jingle man' and* like most poets he was sensitive to the music of his own verse*s*; and that was the element he emphasized in his delivery.

1. In the course of writing her compendious *Edgar Allan Poe, The Man*, 2 vols. (Chicago: John C. Winston, 1926), Phillips solicited reminiscences from those who might have memories of personal contact with the poet. Gildersleeve replied with a letter, abstracted on pp. 1442-43 of her book. He later sent an extract of the letter to James Howard Whitty (1859-1937), the editor of *The Complete Poems of Edgar Allan Poe* (Boston: Houghton Mifflin, 1911) and two other editions, and a great collector of Poeana, who was first president of the Poe Shrine in Richmond. That letter, dated 14 November 1921, exists in the Poe Museum, Richmond; the letter to Phillips is lost. Deletions made by Phillips are indicated in boldface. Whitty added footnotes to his copy as noted below.

2. "Swann Hotel, Broad, Northside, near Ninth Street" (Whitty).

3. "Southern Literary Messenger Office, then located Franklin near Governor St."(Whitty) "on Capitol Square and Franklin Street" (Phillips).

4. See No. 129, n. 12.

5. "Poe on his last trip to Richmond in 1849 had two suits of clothing; a black suit in which Dr. Gildersleeve recalls seeing him dressed and he also appeared on the streets in a loose fitting linen suit with a black velvet vest" (Whitty).

6. Whitty's copy reads "the fashion of his whole bearing," an obvious line-skip by the typist.

### 168 To: CHARLES FORSTER SMITH
*Smith*

[October 25, 1915]

Dear Charles Forster Smith: Your letters always set me thinking profoundly.[1] They are always full of praise, full of love. The love I accept freely and return as freely. But the praise leads to soul-searchings, and heart-searchings take the form of συντήρησις [preservation], which is the Greek aesthetic equivalent of remorse. I am an honest nature—so far as it is given any one to be honest—and I feel that I have not deserved a tithe of all the handsome things that have been said about me as the anniversaries come round and remind some people that I still make a fair show of being alive. Certain qualifications for higher work I recognize in myself—quickness of wit, a keen sense of duty, love of my subject—but unless 'love is the fulfilling of the law,'[2] I can't get the result out of the items—and if I have done all the good that has been attributed to me, if unwittingly I have served as a leader to those who are in the same line of work—I can only say with a reverence alien to my expression, not alien to my bringing up—it is a gift of

God, or, to quote a favorite line of mine from Goethe, *'Alles ist als wie geschenkt.'*[3] But a truce to analysis, which is fatal to that peace of mind I am cultivating in my old age. I rejoice in your good opinion of me and my work. I love to think of our first meeting,[4] of the tide of goodwill that has come from you to me and of its refluence.—You will be glad to know that I am in good health and in good spirits—barring this terrible war. I have organized my life so as not to miss my class work. I imagine that every day is a Saturday, a day on which I don't lecture. The mornings I spend in my study at home—chiefly in writing up things that I have had on my mind for a long time. The afternoons are taken up with work of the *Journal*, setting my house in order for the final break-up—*semper agens aliquid*[5]—one is tempted to call it pottering—but it is something more. I have in hand a compendium of my syntactical views. I intend to resume work on Plato's *Symposium*.[6] I expect to make a double extract of my olympiad of lectures—and so on. . . .[7] Continue to have me in loving remembrance and I shall not quarrel further with your over-estimate of yours faithfully and affectionately,

B. L. G.

1. Smith had sent greetings on Gildersleeve's eighty-fourth birthday.
2. 1 Cor. 13:10.
3. Goethe, *Zahme Xenien* 2; see No. 160 and n. 2.
4. At the APA meetings at Cornell, 13–15 July 1886.
5. Cic. *Fam.* 4.13.3: *Natus enim ad agendum semper aliquid dignum viro, nunc non modo agendi rationem nullam habeo, sed ne cogitandi quidem* (For though it is my nature to always be involved in something important and worthy of a man, I now not only have no plan of action, but not even a plan of thought). See also Cic. *De fin.* 5.20.55.
6. Cf. No. 128, n. 11.
7. Smith's ellipsis.

169 To: BENJAMIN IDE WHEELER<br>California

November 23, 1915

Dear President Wheeler:

I am highly honoured by your invitation to undertake the work of a Lecturer on the Sather Foundation.[1] The proposal of a sojourn in California is alluring, and my first impulse was that of acceptance without further ado. The climate, the surroundings, the companionship promised so much. I am entirely free from obligations to the Johns Hopkins, and I can provide for the Journal in my absence. Indeed, I have 'original articles' enough on hand to carry me through three numbers of the new volume. But I need more details as to the character of the work expected. Seminary work is excluded because my resignation[2] was based on the increasing difficulty of hearing. It is not a very serious difficulty, but it suffices. It was time for me to go before I could recognize any abatement in my resources as a teacher. My last session seemed to me one of my very best, but old men deceive themselves in such things.[3]

My general health is very good, although walking is no longer a pastime, and I am not the man physically that I was when we made the giro of the Peloponnesus together.[4] As to the mental activity, I expose myself to criticism every quarter, so that you can judge of that yourself. At all events, I am full of schemes, among them a review of my work as the Director of a Greek Seminary from the literary side of that work; and it has occurred to me that a series of familiar talks on what I should call 'Workaday aspects of Greek Literature' might be acceptable. Of course, these would have to be prepared on the spot from the material I should bring with me. I have a few epideictic lectures that might serve for larger audiences, and I might read Plato's Symposium with a class.[5] Pindar I leave out, because you have a Pindarist of renown in your faculty;[6] but for that matter I should have to subject myself to professorial criticism at any rate. How many hours would you expect a week?

I shall have to encounter some opposition on the part of my family, who think that I am happy enough as I am. Ordinarily the incarnegified man has to scramble in order to make up the difference between salary and pension, but I have retired on full pay, and as my children are independent, I am not troubled about money matters. As an old friend, you will be glad that my last years are not haunted by all manner of sordid considerations. At the same time I recognize the liberality of your offer,[7] which relieves me of my concern as to the expense of the trip, which was one of the considerations that prevented me from accepting previous invitations,[8] which I remember gratefully. You see I am not allowed to travel alone.

After receiving your answer, I will telegraph my decision as soon as possible.

I need not say that one great inducement will be the opportunity of renewing the memory of the days when we were so near to one another in Greece and in Germany.

With kindest regards to Mrs. Wheeler,

I am,

Yours faithfully
B. L. Gildersleeve

Professor Benjamin Ide Wheeler,
University of California,
Berkeley, California

1. The Sather Lectureship, "the most honorific of all annual Classical professorships anywhere in the world" (S. Dow, *Fifty Years of Sathers* [Berkeley and Los Angeles: University of California Press, 1965], 1), was begun in 1900 with an endowment of $75,000 by the great benefactor of the University of California, Berkeley, Jane K. Sather (1824-1911), to honor her husband, the wealthy banker Peder Sather (1810-86). Wheeler, who had been called from Cornell to the presidency of the University of California the year before, was instrumental in arranging the endowment and, undoubtedly, in having the lectureship be classical. At her death in 1911, her bequests of land and money to the university provided for a second lectureship (in history), in addition to a bell tower. Wheeler chose the professors for the duration of his presidency (1899-1919). The first Sather professor (1913-14) was Sir John Linton Myres (1871-1952), the ancient historian from New College, Oxford; the second, John Swinnerton Phillimore (1873-1926), Latinist of Glasgow, was prevented by the war from lecturing in 1914-15. Henry Washington Prescott (1874-1943) lectured in 1915. For the fourth course, Wheeler first contacted Edward Capps (1866-1950) of Princeton, then Gildersleeve, whom he had invited to California as early as 1904 (No. 128). See, further, Dow. Of the first eleven Sather professors, five had been Gildersleeve's students: G. J. Laing (No. 113, n. 1), F. G. Allinson (No. 142, n. 2), J. A. Scott, G. L. Hendrickson, and H. W. Smyth (for the last three, see "Correspondents").

2. See No. 166.

3. Gildersleeve had taught the tragic poets in addition to his regular "Practical Exercises" (No. 166, n. 3). There were only six graduate Greek students in 1914-15, none of whom achieved prominence.

4. No. 90, n. 4.

5. No. 168.

6. Edward Bull Clapp (1856-1919), author of *Hiatus in Greek Melic Poetry* (Berkeley: University of California, 1904) and *Homer's Iliad, Books XIX-XXIV* (Boston: Ginn, 1899). He provided reports on *Neue Jahrbücher* to *AJP* and wrote "Pindar's Accusative Constructions," *TAPA* 32 (1901): 16-42.

7. The honorarium was $3,000 for one semester (Wheeler to BLG, 15 November 1915 [California]), with the probable addition of $500 for travel, the amount offered Shorey the next year (Dow, 42).

8. See n. 1 above.


## 170 To: BENJAMIN IDE WHEELER
### *California*

December 9, 1915

President Benjamin I. Wheeler,
University of California,
Berkeley, California.
Dear President Wheeler:

The decision which I reached, reluctantly reached, after long and careful consideration of the problem was telegraphed to you yesterday.[1] If I were ten years younger, or had been invited six months earlier, the answer might have been different. Bu[t] the plan that I proposed, the only plan consistent with the scheme of work, that I had laid out for my few remaining years, turned out to be impracticable. So far from retiring after sixty years of teaching to a 'well earned rest'—as the phrase is, I have entered into a covenant with myself to gather up the fruits of the labor of my many years, and part of my programme was something that answered to what I called in my letter 'Work-a-day aspects of Greek literature.' Another was the completion of my projected edition of the Symposium. Neither of these is possible in the time allotted. And I am not willing to appear before your students with the imperfect preparation necessary under the conditions. Of course I am thinking only of lectures to special students. Nothing would induce me to give a long course of 36[2] lectures to a larger audience—lectures based on a hasty revision of discourses that have had their day. I am not suited for the function of a popular lecturer. I have, as you know, a poor voice,[3] and am besides subject to bronchial troubles,[4] which seem to have a pestilent way of attacking me, when I have a public function to discharge. Despite all drawbacks, however, the University of Texas has invited me for a short course in the month of April[5]—and New Orleans which lies on the way is tempting.

I must console myself as best I may for a grievous disappointment, but that is better than a dismal failure following hard upon an honorable retirement. Now that Europe is shut out, my thoughts have been turning to California for a holiday sojourn, and I may be privileged to visit your glorious state before I die.[6] But even if the way had been clear to accept your invitation, I should have seen nothing of the country except Berkeley and San Francisco, either, it is true, well worth the trip. Still one would like to see more and I should have been obliged to hurry back in order to set my house in order. I shall have to vacate my rooms at the Johns Hopkins in June, weed out and rearrange my library, and sort my multitudinous papers at a time when I should have been fagged out by the great strain. And after all I am in my eighty-fifth year,[7] and more of a cripple than I like to confess even to myself.

Pardon this long letter, which has its excuse in our old friendship. It would have been delightful to talk over the times we have had together, and to rejoice over all that you have accomplished at Berkeley.

With best regards to Mrs. Wheeler, I am

Yours faithfully,<br>B. L. Gildersleeve

1. See preceding letter.

2. The numeral is hand-written in this typed letter. Myres (No. 169, n. 1) had given no public lectures, but Prescott had given 20. From 1920 to 1955 the number was eight, and after that, six (Dow [No. 169, n. 1], 50–51).

3. Cf. *Culbreth*, 298, describing Gildersleeve: "voice of the upper gamut—clear, distinct and penetrating; delivery thoughtful, rather slow but not tedious." According to his grand-

daughter (No. 116, n. 7), he had no trace of a Southern accent, but Paul Shorey (see "Corres-pondents") said: "In some of our later conversations I noticed, or fancied that I noticed, what I had never observed before—an occasional recurrence or recrudescence of a recognizable Southern accent. Perhaps it was the call of the motherland as he drew nearer home" ("Gildersleeve the American Scholar and Gentleman," *Johns Hopkins Alumni Magazine* 13 [January 1925]: 140).

4. The official cause of his death was acute bronchitis. *NYTimes*, 10 January 1924: 21.

5. Probably invited by his pupil E. W. Fay (No. 95, n. 6) who was professor of Greek and Sanskrit at Texas (1899–1920).

6. Gildersleeve never visited California.

7. The oldest of the first fifty Sather lecturers was Paul Shorey in his third incumbency, at seventy-one; Myres and Prescott (No. 169, n. 1) were forty-three and forty-one respectively during their incumbencies (Dow, 48–49).

### 171 To: Charles William Emil Miller
### *JHU-BLG*

Febr. 7, 1916

Dear Miller:

The accounts of Vol. XXXVI of the Journal are closed. The net profits of the last six months during which you have acted as Assistant Editor[1] amount to $61—One third of this sum I have assigned to the Assistant Editor the remainder goes to a fund I am accumulating for tiding the Journal over hard times. Work for the Journal is practically a labor of love for us both—and you have declined to receive anything from me personally as a small evidence of my feeling of indebtedness but now that you are associ-ated with the fortunes of the Journal I hope you will consent to the dividing of the meagre 'spoils'—

Yours faithfully
B. L. Gildersleeve

1. Miller was named assistant editor in 1915, the year of Gildersleeve's retirement from Hopkins; he became joint editor in 1917, and editor in 1919.

### 172 To: Charles William Emil Miller
### *JHU-BLG*

March 1, 1916

Dear Miller:

Yesterday came very near being my final Brief Mention of all.[1] On the edge of Kokytos[2] I was tortured by something I would have had otherwise. The last revise of B.M. will not be needed perhaps. Please do the best you can with my scratches. The doctors think I shall pull through this time and last a little while longer.

Yours faithfully

B. L. Gildersleeve

I was not precipitate in furnishing myself with a sturdy ἔφεδρος [successor].

1. Gildersleeve suffered a heart attack on 29 February and, after his release from the Johns Hopkins Hospital, was for seven months "treated like a valetudinarian" (BLG to R. E. Harrison, 25 October 1916 [UVa]). See following letter.

2. The "river of wailing" in Hades.

173 To: WILLIAM MYNN THORNTON
*UVa-Thornton*

January 7, 1917

Dear Thornton:

Many thanks for your beautiful tribute to Abbot.[1] Quite apart from my personal interest in your biographical sketches[2] I delight in your delicate and sure literary touch, which distinguishes you from the herd and which is as characteristic of you as the wonderful handwriting which I have admired more than forty years, needless to say, without emulating.[3]

Abbot was the best man of my first Senior Greek (1856–1857), but we never became friends, perhaps because there was scant opportunity of closer intercourse, though I am free to say that we were naturally antipathetic. He seemed to me to take himself too seriously. That, as you know, is not my sort. Your memory has done much, if not everything, to give Abbot his dues [sic], in my mind—and I am glad to have it /so/, for with all my shortcomings I am a 'righteous beast', to use a schoolboy phrase—suggested by the story of a schoolmaster.[4]

Since my attack last spring[5] I have been under close guard and I have learned to renounce everything that can be called physical exercise. I do not suffer and keep up my reading and writing—though there is an end of serious research, as I am cut off from my library, which has been deported to the new site of the Johns Hopkins University, miles away.[6] It is a rehearsal of the conditions of a future life, as commonly imagined.

I have lived much longer than I had any right to expect. My eyesight is good. My hearing is somewhat impaired[7]—but that does not matter so much as I have little commerce with the outside world. My intellectual curiosity seems to know no abatement; and it is not likely that any one will call my attention directly to my intellectual decline.

My wife desires me to join in loving messages to you and to your wife,[8] who thank God still abides among the diminished ranks of our oldest and truest friends.

Yours faithfully
B. L. Gildersleeve

1. "A Virginian Schoolmaster," *UVa Alumni Bulletin*, 3d ser., 10, no. 1 (January 1917): 60–76. William Richardson Abbot (1839–1916), the son of a schoolmaster, attended the University of Virginia for only two years (1855–57), but received degrees at eighteen from all its academic schools except chemistry. After teaching in schools in Alexandria (1857–58), Albemarle Co., Va. (1858–60), and Louisiana (1860–61), he joined the Treasury Department of the Confederacy (1861–63) before his army service (1863–65). Following the war, he taught at the Charlottesville Institute (1865–70) before moving to the rich and exclusive Bellevue School in Bedford Co., Va., where he served first as associate principal (1870–73), then as one of the leading teachers and headmasters in the state (1873–1909), and where for one year (1873–74) he employed Thornton.
2. See No. 177, 181.
3. See No. 181.
4. Gildersleeve possibly refers to the well-known story of Frederick Temple (1821–1902), headmaster of Rugby (1858–69) and archbishop of Canterbury (1897–1902), who once, when a student athlete had neglected his work, "accidentally" sent for him just as an important match in which the student was to take a key role was about to begin. Temple dismissed the anxious boy only when the match was over, punishing him no further. Another boy told the student, "Of course, Temple's a beast, but he's a just beast" (J. B. Hope Simpson, *Rugby Since Arnold* [London: Macmillan, 1967], 52).
5. See preceding letter.
6. Despite the addition of McCoy Hall to the Howard Street site (No. 73, n. 7), Johns Hopkins rapidly outgrew its campus. In 1894, Gilman began the complicated negotiations that led to the acquisition, in January 1901, of a 120-acre estate, Homewood, two miles north of downtown Baltimore on the west side of Charles Street, as the new site of the university. In 1906 President Remsen appointed a committee to manage the planning of the campus and arrangement of buildings. See *French*, 119–30, 159–66. The Engineering and Academic buildings of the Homewood Campus (including Gilman Hall, where the new library was located) were dedicated 21 May 1915. See *Baltimore Sun*, 22 May 1915: sec. 14, 3 and the special issue, "The University in Its New Home," *JHU Circulars* 290 (December 1916).
7. See No. 169.
8. See No. 141, n. 10.

## 174 To: HAMLIN GARLAND
*Houghton*

Baltimore March 12, 1917

Dear Mr. Garland:[1]

Mr. Howells'[2] achievements are beyond my praise but every body takes credit for early discernment and before the judgment of the world had settled into a formula I looked upon Mr. Howells as the great literary exemplar of Americanism, as it is understood in the new era of the republic; and I remember sending to a foreign friend, curious in such matters, the Rise of Silas Lapham, when it first appeared, now an American classic, as a faithful mirror of the true American of the period.[3] Since then I have had abundant occasion to admire not only what Mr. Howells has done in the field of fiction but the masterly grace and skill and insight with which he has dominated from his throne—an Easy Chair to no one else[4]—the whole range of life and letters. Though not privileged to enjoy his personal friendship, I have felt the charm of his genial nature and regret that my great age—for I am older than Mr. Howells—and my somewhat precarious health prevent me from joining the Committee of Literary Arts in giving him by my presence as well as by my words my heartfelt congratulations my best wishes and the assurances of my highest esteem—

Yours sincerely<br>
B. L. Gildersleeve

1. Garland had solicited testimonials for a celebration of William Dean Howells' (1837–1920) eightieth birthday at the National Arts Club, but Howells, in Florida, could not attend (see *NYTimes*, 25 March 1917: sec. 1: 9; *Current Opinion* 62 [May 1917]: 357; and *Life in Letters of William Dean Howells*, ed. Mildred Howells [Garden City, N.Y.: Doubleday, Doran, 1928], 2: 368–70).

2. Howells' literary reputation began to grow after the Civil War. *The Rise of Silas Lapham* (Boston: Houghton Mifflin, 1884), a study of a self-made man in conflict with Boston society, was his most successful novel. An editor of *Harper's Monthly* and considered by many the leading man of letters in America, he was elected first president of the American Academy of Arts and Letters. On the suggestion of Richard Watson Gilder, Gilman had tried early to get Howells as professor of English, but he was unsuccessful (see *Hawkins*, 163–64). See, further, *Life in Letters* (cited n. 1 above), and *DAB* 9: 306–11.

3. Gildersleeve regularly sent Hübner American novels at Christmas (No. 68) and on 1 January 1886 had written his friend, "The present drift of American literature does not find a very enthusiastic admirer in me. I suppose I am getting too old for the analytical novels of Howells and James. While their heroes are taking a cup of tea an old fashioned novelist would have his man commit all the seven deadly sins.—Still they have a certain refinement of style in the non-dramatic part and in the present poverty of genius in England, the American story tellers are all the rage. I send you Howells' last—which some consider his best—I am afraid it will hardly interest you. The vulgar Yankee who is the hero of the book is as strange a creature to my social experience as he can be to yours. America holds many types—"

4. Howells wrote "The Easy Chair," a regular feature of *Harper's*, from December 1900 to April 1920.

175 To: WALLACE MARTIN LINDSAY<br>
St. Andrews

March 21, 1917

Professor Wallace M. Lindsay,
University of St. Andrews,
St. Andrews, Scotland.
Dear Professor Lindsay:

Your article on the St. Gall Glossary[1] is safe in my hands. I wish I could give you some assurance as to the time of publication. The pressure of the times, scarcity of paper, loss of foreign subscribers—all these things are so many troubles, and to this is added a great oversupply of material just at the time when prudence bids me reduce the bulk of the Journal. I will hold counsel with my Associate Editor, who is now practically the Managing Editor.[2] For the last year, I have been much limited in my physical activity by reason of a weakness of the heart which threatened to put an end to all my performances in this realm of Zeus.[3] Free access to libraries is an impossibility, and I must often trust to others for verification of my statements. There is an end of research for me. But I am in my eighty-sixth year and have no reason to complain. As a native expressed it, 'I have no kick coming'.

As I may not have another opportunity of writing to you, I must express my surprise at your statement that you do not approve my 'laxity about quantities'.[4] What laxity? I have simply emphasized the absurdity of making such an ado about an elementary virtue. Correct quantity is no more to be bragged about than cleanliness about which also English people talk too much. False quantity is an abomination to me as it ought to be to everyone who has any pretensions to being a scholar. I have prodded the Germans over and over again about their carelessness in that regard. They have winced at my footnote A.J.P. xxiii, 4 and would have winced at that other footnote A.J.P. xxxvii, 497, if the British patrol had not cut off all communication between America and Germany—a footnote inspired by an eminent British scholar not unknown to you. My sins are many but that is not one of them, and τό ὄν[5] is my standard as you say, and say truly, verum is yours.

Your ms. will be seen through the press when the time comes by Professor Miller, one of the most accurate scholars I know.

Yours faithfully,<br>[unsigned TL]

1. "The St. Gall Glossary," *AJP* 38 (1917): 349-69.

2. For Miller's *AJP* career, see No. 171, n. 1. For Gildersleeve's retirement from the journal, see *AJP* 40 (1919): 451.

3. See No. 171

4. At *AJP* 37 (1916): 497, Gildersleeve quotes from his 1854 essay, "The Necessity of the Classics," and n. 1 refers to the metrical error described at No. 132, n. 8. The "eminent British scholar" is not identified by Gildersleeve.

5. Originally used by Parmenides (fr. 8) for "being" (as opposed to non-being) the term is discussed in Plato *Ti.* 52a-c and *Sph.* 254b-d; it was taken by Aristotle (*Metaph.* 1003a) to mean "reality" ("what is"), the subject of metaphysics, while individual beings (τὰ ὄντα) are the subjects of other sciences. See *AJP* 38 (1917): 224: "My only standard is TO ON, not Teuton, not Briton. 'Nothing so brutal as a fact' said Ste.-Beuve, and I hate brutality; but τό ὄν is τό ὄν. In matters of philological accuracy, I am strictly impartial—as impartial as Dido. To me as to every scholar, as to everyone who has pretensions to scholarship, false quantities are an abomination and I should have been shocked, if I had not outlived of late the possibility of being shocked, when an eminent British scholar wrote, 'I cannot approve your laxity about quantities'. I could only parody my favourite poet John Bunyan, 'I such dirt heap never

was, since Ritschl discipled me'. What have I done to deserve such a rebuke? Where shown laxity? Have not the Germans winced at my footnote A.J.P. XXIII 4? The fact is, I am paying the penalty for the reproduction of my youthful essay in which I ridiculed English scholars for making such a parade of their correctness in the matter of quantity." In one of his memorial notices of Gildersleeve ([cited No. 170, n. 3], 139), Shorey spoke of this quality: "He was too true a Platonist, too genuine a Socratic, too conscientious a scholar, to desire any praise but the truth."

176 To: CHARLES WILLIAM EMIL MILLER
*JHU-BLG*

June 24, 1917

Dear Miller:

I appreciate your desire to spare me but I have abundance of time for such Journal work as I can do in the absence of references, which you are always able to supply and though reading proofs after you may well seem to be a working supererogation—'fissipant'[1] and Ribezzo's Greek[2] would not have been allowed to pass if I had had an opportunity to challenge these disfigurements of the Journal—I am still true to my boyhood's motto τρεῖν μ' οὐκ ἐᾷ Παλλὰς 'Αθήνη[3] and I am not afraid of offending my contributors on matters of that kind. I quite agree with you as to the stage of proofs to be submitted to me—In my own case I always ask for second galley proofs—and the Lord Baltimore Press[4] has never raised any objection. A second galley proof reduces the page proof to a minimum of trouble—You will have anticipated all the details and I can bring in such things as I deem advisable in the shape of footnotes such as I should have supplied to the Κυρήνη business[5]—

Of course, if extensive corrections not of the usual proof reading character are to be made, the expenses will be considerable, and, if it seems advisable, I am willing to go over MS in advance of committing it to the printer.—I am turning out a good deal of stuff—and I am still getting requests for articles and lectures so that the outside world has not discovered the 'wane of mind' of which Jefferson writes as inseparable from the twilight of years[6]—But for all that I invite your criticism—and expect to profit by it in the brief future as I have done in the long past of our association.

We have made our final arrangements and expect to leave Baltimore the night of July 3—After that date my address will be c/o Mrs. G. M. Lane Manchester Mass

Yours faithfully
B. L. Gildersleeve

1. At *AJP* 38 (1917): 228–29, E. W. Fay (No. 95, n. 6) had written this impenetrable sentence: "Given a wide literary documentation for the OEng. adjectives in -*bære*, no doubt as fissipant nuances might, with some finesse, be translated into them."

2. According to K. F. Smith's report (*AJP* 38 [1917]: 219), Francesco Ribezzo in *RivFil* 44 wrote γενετός for γενητός and used it with the dative rather than a genitive of source.

3. *Il.* 5.256: "Pallas Athena does not permit me to be frightened."

4. Possibly his mention of Apollo and Kyrene at *AJP* 37 (1916): 234 ( = *SBM*, 352).

5. With anti-German feelings high, the Friedenwald Press, which had published *AJP* from its inception, changed its name to the Lord Baltimore Press.

6. "Age, and the wane of mind consequent on it, have disqualified me from investigations so severe [into the conduct of the Supreme Court] and researches so laborious" (Jefferson to Judge William Johnson, 12 June 1823, in *The Writings of Thomas Jefferson*, ed. Andrew A. Lipscomb [Washington, D.C.: Thomas Jefferson Memorial Association, 1904], 15: 444; see also to Hugh P. Taylor, 4 October 1823, ibid., 473, and *AJP* 38 [1917]: 226).

### 177 To: William Mynn Thornton
#### UVa-Thornton

{ The Chimneys
Manchester, Massachusetts. }
July 27, 1917

My dear Thornton:

To-day's mail brought another specimen of the art in which you are past master, another addition to the portrait gallery all the numbers of which I could praise both as to the vividness and fidelity /and praise without reserve/[1] if it were not for a certain sketch in which the subject's ideal seems to have been taken for performance.[2] So you see I am still a devotee of truth. But what a man wills is after all the great thing. McGuffey you have hit off to the life.[3] In the introduction to my Hellas and Hesperia I have made a reference to McGuffey's end which you have treated so delicately.[4] It was a warning by which I have sought to profit in my old age. The strain of attempting to systematize a mass of doctrine characterized by a lack of system was fatal to brain and life. I was admitted to the secrets of the workshop he set up. It was something pitiful. And so in my retirement I keep to the lines I have followed so many years—and attempt nothing great. Noli altum sapere—sed time[5] is a motto I have had before me since 1855—and at last I have learned to apply it—The 29th of February 1916 revealed a weakness of the heart,[6] which perhaps I should not have heeded, if I had not been guarded by the loving care of wife and daughter. I am not allowed to indulge in any physical exertion deserving the name of exertion. I play with a few books and my pen, read and write even more than I did in my stalwart days. The war gets on my nerves and depresses my spirits. And then the bottom seems to have fallen out of /the/ jug in which I stored the wine of life[7] and a bottomless jug does not make a very good megaphone through which to shout the praises of classical study. We are spending July and August with our daughter at the beautiful place on the North Shore[8]— Every comfort—every attention. If my old age is not serene—it is no one's fault but my own.

Give my love to Rosalie[9] and Betty's love also—who bids me sign for her as for myself.

Your faithful and affectionate friend
B. L. Gildersleeve

1. See No. 172.
2. He means Thornton's sketch of him in *LSL* (see No. 141, n. 1).
3. W. M. Thornton, "The Life and Services of William Holmes McGuffey: Philosopher, Teacher, Preacher," *UVa Alumni Bulletin*, 3d ser., 10 (July 1917): 237-57. McGuffey (1800–1873) was educated at Washington College (now Washington and Jefferson) (A.B. 1826) and was appointed professor of ancient languages at Miami University, Oxford, Ohio, where he wrote the series of six readers by which his influence on American education was felt for over seventy-five years. In 1845 he was appointed professor of moral philosophy at Virginia, a position he held until his death. In a memorial minute of the faculty, Gildersleeve wrote: "Original in his methods, he surprised his pupils into knowledge. . . . To him the teacher's desk was no less sacred than the pulpit. His pupils were a charge to him from God" (Thornton, 253).
4. "As I take up the burden of this initial course of lectures on the Barbour-Page Foundation, I am sadly reminded of an old friend of mine who, towards the close of a useful career, attempted to gather up what he had learned and taught for so many years into a compact body of doctrine. He was younger than I am to-day, but the effort shattered him" (*H&H*, 10). "As the years drew on Dr. McGuffey's friends urged upon him more and more the duty of writing out his lectures on Moral Philosophy. The old professor would have been happy to achieve the task, and actually attempted it, piling sheet after sheet of manuscript upon his desk. It was too late; the habits of a life-time are not so easily broken. He had trained himself by years of assiduous practice to use the tongue and in his old age the pen no longer answered his command" (Thornton, 252).
5. *Rom.* 11:20: *Tu autem fide stas: noli altum sapere sed time* (But you stand fast only through faith: So do not become proud, but stand in awe). The motto of Robert Stephanus (No. 71, n. 12), quoted by Gildersleeve in "Henry Stephens," *Quarterly Review of the Methodist Episcopal Church, South*, n.s., 9 (January 1855): 2. See also *AJP* 35 (1914): 461; 38 (1917): 114.
6. See No. 171.
7. *Macbeth* 2.3.96: "The wine of life is drawn, and the mere lees / Is left this vault to brag of."
8. See No. 128, n. 1.
9. See No. 141, n. 10.


178 To: Leigh Robinson
*UVa-Robinson*

1002 N. Calvert St.
Baltimore
Nov. 14, 1917

Dear Robinson:

A Greek epigrammatist calls grammarians 'corner hummers'[1] and it is gratifying to an old corner hummer to find himself preserved in the amber of your great Gettysburg oration.[2] Corner hummer? Yes! But the sentence to which you refer was not confined in its utterance to the corner of my lecture room. You will find it published in my Hellas and Hesperia p. 14 where I am magnifying my office as a grammarian "It was a point of grammatical concord" said I and "that was at the bottom of the Civil War— 'United States are,' said one, 'United States is,' said another."[3] According to a marginal note of mine, John W. Foster wrote for the N.Y. Times a long article about "U.S. are" and "U.S. is".[4] It appears somewhere about 1909. I am glad that you remembered me when you were sending out presentation copies of your memorable speech at Gettysburg. All your deliverances are carefully preserved[5] and I am much heartened when I find my amateurish notions confirmed by your eloquent words[6]—To all appearances I am in fine health but every now and then I am admonished by a weakness of the heart that declared itself with Spring of 1916[7] that I am a very old man and that any little push will send me overboard. My wife thinks highly of her cousin Leigh[8] and so does her husband and we often refer to your flying visit, always with delight.

Yours faithfully<br>B. L. Gildersleeve

1. See No. 74, n. 4.

2. When Virginia erected a monument to those who fought at Gettysburg, Robinson gave the principal speech at the unveiling on 8 June 1917, privately printed as "Address" in *Ceremonies Attending the Dedication of the Virginia Memorial on the Battlefield of Gettysburg* (Richmond: Colonial Press, Everett Waddey Co., 1917), 17–47. The reference to Gildersleeve is on p. 22. It was also published in *So. Hist. Soc. Papers*, n.s., 4 (October 1917): 97–134 (Gildersleeve citation on pp. 102–3), and excerpted as "The Virginian Memorial at Gettysburg," *Confederate Veteran* 26, no. 4 (April 1918): 143–46 (Gildersleeve citation on p. 145) and summarized in the *Richmond News Leader*, 8 June 1917: 14. Robinson described the basis of the Southern cause and gave an account of R. E. Lee, "the warrior of the Cause of which he was the likeness." The account does not mention a reference to Gildersleeve.

3. Actually *H&H*, 16. See Charles McDonald Puckette, "Most Modern of the Grecians: Basil Lanneau Gildersleeve," *[New York] Evening Post Saturday Magazine*, 17 May 1913: 4, and "St. Basil of Baltimore," *NYTimes* 21 October 1923: sec. 2, 6.

4. John Watson Foster (1836–1917), former secretary of state, had been criticized for using a singular rather than a plural verb with "United States" throughout his *A Century of American Diplomacy* (Boston: Houghton Mifflin, 1900). He defended himself in remarks quoted in the *NYTimes* 7 May 190*1*: 8.

5. Particularly *A Souvenir of the Unveiling of the Richmond Howitzer Monument at Richmond, Virginia* (Richmond: J. L. Hill Printing Co., 1893) and *Address Delivered before the R. E. Lee Camp . . . in the Acceptance of the Portrait of General William H. Payne* (Richmond: W. E. Jones, 1909), which contains a respected description of Lee's tactics.

6. Robinson (p. 22 = *So. Hist. Soc. Papers* [cited n. 1 above]: 103 n. 2 = *Confederate Veteran* [cited n. 1 above], 146) cited the U.S. Constitution, Article 3.3, and a letter of George Washington's dated 1 December 1789 to the emperor of Morocco, both using a plural verb with "United States."

7. See No. 172.

8. Both Betty Gildersleeve and Robinson were of the Marshall family, whose noblest member was John Marshall, first chief justice of the United States Supreme Court. In addition, Robinson was married to a distant cousin, Alice Morson. See W. M. Paxton, *The Marshall Family* (Cincinnati: Robert Clarke, 1885), 334.

## 179 To: Angela Charlotte Darkow
### Dickinson College Library

1002 N. Calvert Street
Feb. 18, 1918

Dear D[r]. Darkow: (It is safer for me to think of you as D[r]. than as Miss D.) I do not deserve your thanks for my notice of your dissertation.[1] Your divining rod struck a spot which yielded a gush of autobiographical memory such as old men are sadly apt to indulge in.[2] I am only too glad that you have forgiven my frivolous summary. If I do not deserve thanks for what I have written about your Lysianic treatise, I hope I shall not encounter your displeasure for declining to discuss your paper on the Troades.[3] To be sure, you have furnished me with the apparatus—and that was well meant of you for I have nothing but the text.—and yet I cannot bring myself to revive the sad memories of my work as a teacher.[4] My only business is to amuse myself with my own fancies. A difficult passage, truly and I can't undertake to darken counsel.[5] Still I am willing to give evidence that I have read your paper with interest if not with insight. First and foremost—How did the Deïphobus interpolation get into the text?—Hecuba's βίᾳ [998] refers to Helen's βίᾳ (bis) [959-62] but Hecuba's βίᾳ means Paris— Deïphobus was Hecuba's son as well as Paris was and if we are dealing with Browning[6] and not with Euripides we might assume a half-hearing, a mixing up of the children.—As for the Epic tradition the dramatic poets take the wildest freedoms with characters—and one is rather surprised when Sophocles sticks to Homer's number—Hecuba's description of Helen's behaviour after Paris is [killed] may be considered a manner of reply to Helen's βίᾳ δ' ὁ καινός [959] and the ἀκόντων φρυγῶν [960; cf. 994]—Your understanding of ἐδούλευσα [964] as applying to Helen's forlorn condition as a captive has much in its favor—but I think you overdo the passionateness of the closing passage.— —The little article is not to be thrown rudely aside—but the Journal has no room for it—and when you are next in trouble, please remember that your leader, Professor Sanders[7] is a closer student of the tragic poets than I have ever been and that you yourself know more about the woman's soul than I can divine or have ever divined.

Yours sincerely
B. L. Gildersleeve

1. *AJP* 39 (1918): 455-57. Darkow's dissertation was "The Spurious Speeches of the Lysianic Corpus" (Bryn Mawr, 1917).

2. *AJP* 39 (1918): 457-459.

3. She had submitted to *AJP* "Note on *Troades* 959-964," which argues that 959-60 are an interpolation; she says, "Emotion, whether feigned or real, in her appeal to pity, the rhetorical ἔλεος of the day, and the climax of her speech, accounts for the incoherence and for the repetition . . . and for the juxtaposition . . . at which many scholars have taken offense."

4. Gildersleeve regularly taught the tragic poets at Virginia and at Hopkins. See Seth Schein, "Gildersleeve and the Study of Attic Tragedy," *Briggs-Benario*, 50-55.

5. Job 38.2: "Who is this that darkens counsel by words without knowledge?"

6. On Browning's carelessness and pedantry, see *AJP* 32 (1911): 483-485 ( = *SBM*, 238-40); *AJP* 33 (1912): 491 ( = *SBM*, 271-72), and *AJP* 34 (1913): 242 ( = *SBM*, 286).

7. Henry Nevill Sanders (1869-1943) studied at his native Edinburgh (1887-88), Göttingen (1894-95), and Trinity College, Toronto (A.B. 1894; A.M. 1897). He began work at Hopkins in 1895, was fellow in Greek (1897-98), and received his Ph.D. in 1903 with his dissertation, *The Cynegeticus* (Baltimore: Friedenwald, 1913). He was lecturer in Greek, Latin, and Sanskrit at McGill (1898-1902) before coming to Bryn Mawr (1902-35). He contributed one article and two notes to *AJP* during Gildersleeve's editorship, and also contributed to *Studies*. *NYTimes* 23 May 1943: 42; *WhAm* 5: 632.


### 180 To: CHARLES FORSTER SMITH
*Smith*

[October, 1918]

Your congratulations on my anniversary and especially your felicitations on my health of mind and body show how little one's best friends—who live at a distance—know of the real state of things. The ancients were wise. The powers gave a brace of sorrows for one blessing, and in the last seven months of suffering which have left me cast down but not destroyed, I have often and earnestly prayed for my release from this too-solid flesh[1] that would not let me go. From the eighteenth of March to the present day my life has been one of suffering and inexpressible weariness.[2] My birthday was celebrated by a departure for the hospital, and I am gradually mending and hope now in a few weeks to gather up my shattered faculties—moral, physical, mental. Your letter cheers me on the way. Yours faithfully and affectionately,

B. L. Gildersleeve.

1. *Hamlet* 1.2.129.

2. "This was the year [1918] in which Grandpa [Gildersleeve] became seriously ill and underwent an operation that at his age might have been fatal. He spent seven months in the hospital and on recovery was aware that his sight was failing" (K. L. Weems, *Odds Were against Me* [New York: Vantage Press, 1985], 31).

181 To: WILLIAM MYNN THORNTON
*UVa-Thornton*

1002 N. Calvert St.
Baltimore
Feb.ʸ 17, 1919

My dear Thornton:

Your sketch of Kent[1] with the accompanying letters from his friends I have read with great interest and I must thank you for the special copy you have sent me with a kind message in that wonderful handwriting of yours which has not varied in its perfection during all the years I have known you. Whenever I see it, I feel a pang of regret that my own chirography is so uncertain that I am often at a loss to make out my own marginalia. A past master at handwriting, you are also past master in the art biographical, and as I have profited by it in your account of me,[2] I ought not to venture upon any criticism. You seem to be inclined 'to turn the fair side outward' whereas I am only too prone to reveal the coarse lining of the robes of state. Some years ago I was requested to give some account of the faculty of the University of Virginia as it was in my day and I could not think of anything except what the English call 'funniments' and I declined the task. Since then I have read your tribute to Dr. McGuffey[3] and I felt a little or rather not a little ashamed of myself. All your biographies are incentives to better and higher work. Vollkommen ist die Norm des Himmels, Vollkommen wollen die Norm des Menschen?[4]—a sentence I have long cherished and alas! applied too feebly. If I am not mistaken Samuel Butler has expanded it without making it more forcible.[5] Kent came after my time—and I am not in a position to form a judgement of the man or the scholar—but I can readily understand that he was a power for good and everyone who reads what you and others have written about him must covet such a record.—I have been reading the remarkable book The Education of Henry Adams[6] and the chapter on Acceleration called up an absent figure out of my Un. of Va. days—The man lived in Charlottesville and wrote verses. One of his poems was addressed to one of the Mount girls[7] supposed to be heiresses and I remember one distich:

> Give me thy heart, give me thy hand
> And though I scorn it, give me thy land.

But I am not thinking of the poet but rather of the philosopher. His philosophic treatise was published by subscription and I recall the commendatory letter from Dr. McGuffey which he prints in the book. 'If you are determined to publish' wrote the Dr., 'I will take one copy' Dr. Davis[8] was fond of repeating one sentence of the seer's oracular deliverances. His thesis was the world was advancing from better to better—'going, glowing, growing', or something of the sort. His doctrine was absurdly like Henry Adams' and I would give more for a copy of the book than the fifty cents D$^r$ McG paid. I cannot recall the man's name. Perhaps the librarian may help you—if indeed you have forgotten. As you see, I am not quite dead yet. I have suffered much, been through several circles of the Inferno but I have gathered up what is left of my mind and managed to write a letter now and then—My wife is a ministering angel, not at all like the 'ministering minxes' of the hospital service. I have a trained attendant,[9] unusually intelligent and skilful and I am making some show of intellectual activity. Give my love to Rosalie.[10] My wife joins me in best regards to you both.

Yours faithfully and affectionately

B. L. Gildersleeve

1. *UVa Alumni Bulletin*, 3d ser., 12 (January 1919): 3–45; Thornton's memoir is on pp. 3–10. Kent (see "Correspondents") was Thornton's brother-in-law (No. 140, n. 9) and, as first editor of the *Bulletin*, employed Thornton to write sketches of illustrious faculty (Nos. 173, 177; see also No. 141, n. 1).

2. No. 173, n. 3.

3. No. 140, n. 6.

4. Goethe, *Maximen und Reflexionen*, 828: "Vollkommenheit ist die Norm des Himmels, Vollkommenes wollen die Norm des Menschen" (Perfection is the rule only in heaven, yet mankind wishes for something already perfected).

5. Gildersleeve may be referring to the "counsels of imperfection" in Butler's *Note-Books* ([1912; reprint, New York: AMS, 1968], 17–18), written to undercut absolutism. But perhaps he refers to the chapter entitled "The World of the Unborn" in *Erewhon* (1872).

6. On *The Education of Henry Adams* (Boston: Houghton Mifflin, 1918), see *AJP* 40 (1919): 335–37 ( = *SBM*, 391–93).

7. I.e., girls of the Taliaferro family who lived at their seventeenth-century ancestral home, The Mount Howse, on the Rappahannock River in Caroline Co., Va.

8. Noah Knowles Davis (1830–1910), professor of moral philosophy at the University of Virginia (1873–1906).

9. See No. 182, n. 3.

10. No. 141, n. 10.


182 To: CHARLES WILLIAM EMIL MILLER

*JHU-BLG*

Manchester, Mass.

July 14, 1919

Dear Miller:

The new A.J.P. came to hand last Saturday—a matter of keen interest to me, as always. Your careful management need not fear the closest scrutiny that interest would prompt—a scrutiny that the sad slits of my eyes make impossible.[1] I wish with all my heart that your conscientious exactness might have a more substantial acknowledgment from those who have the administration in their hands.

As you see, I am still able to write but it is only with difficulty that I can read what I have written and as my curator is in the same case, I shall have to resort more and more to dictation.—a process to which I am unaccustomed and seriously disinclined. Indeed I do not see how the best composition can be achieved in that way.

So much depends upon the revision by the oculi fideles,[2] so much at least in my case ~~by~~ /upon/ the subtle suggestion of the pen—The tool itself becomes animate. But as the trouble with my eyes cannot be stationary, although it may not culminate in my life time, I must brace myself for the inevitable and I have made some experiments, a specimen of which I am sending you under this cover. My aforesaid curator Neal[3] takes down my words faithfully—He is not a scholar but any difficulty to be encountered by the use of Greek words can be obviated by transliteration—and he writes an excellent hand and can use a type writer, if need be. Of course, the weakness of my eyes debars anything like research but Brief Mention of which alone I am capable has a wide scope and you are at liberty to discard anything you may consider too trivial even for that /fluffy/ department of the Journal and the accompanying paper—the first of a series of sketches of scholars whom I have known may belong to that class[4]—

Apart from my limitations in the matter of reading, I am having a happy summer in this beautiful country place of my daughter[5]—My general health is better than it has been for some years—I am tended with loving care—I have a faithful and skilful attendant who ministers to all my wants—A cheery companion who keeps me in touch with the human nature of a different class ~~than~~ /from/ mine—A good thing, as I learned from my experience in the army half a century ago—I take automobile rides through the lovely country—enjoy the riot of bloom and fragrance the wonderful gardens offer.—There is a slight haze over everything—but what can one expect of eighty-seven+?

Yours sincerely
B. L. Gildersleeve

1. Gildersleeve's cataracts had deteriorated.

2. Hor. *Ars* 181: *segnius irritant animos demissa per aurem / quam quae sunt oculis subiecta fidelibus et quae / ipse sibi tradit spectator* (Things coming through the ears arouse the mind more sluggishly than things which are delivered by the faithful eyes and which the spectator sees for himself).

3. E. Neal, about whom very little is known, was Gildersleeve's reader and amanuensis in his later years. He took dictation and typed Gildersleeve's letters, and though he did not know Greek, could recognize and type the letters, but see No. 186 and n. 6.

4. Sketches of G. G. Ramsay (No. 43, n. 3) and J. P. Mahaffy (No. 42, n. 2) at *AJP* 40 (1919): 446–48.

5. No. 128, n. 1.

183 To: Paul Shorey
*Chicago*

1002 N. Calvert Street
Baltimore, Md. April 28, 1920[1]

Dear Shorey:-

You promised to write to me, but you are a busy man, and move from West to East and East to West like a weaver's shuttle,[2] so that I cannot look forward to an early fulfilling of your promise. Meantime I, who continue to write, as that poor Frenchman said, incapable of doing anything else, have written a number of letters to you, which I have consigned to the waste-basket, as soon as completed. Many of them were letters of thanks, a most difficult branch of composition. Goethe maintains that gratitude is a feeling that ought not to be entertained by a high and mighty mind, that a lofty soul resents obligations,[3] but I am rather of Cicero's opinion which I incorporated half a century ago in my Latin Grammar, where one reads "Est animi ingenui cui multum debeas eidem plurimum velle debere"[4] and I am ready to accept any addition you may make to the kindness you shewed me during your stay in Baltimore.[5] Ordinarily, I fancy that my visitors get some return from their interviews with my derelict self, but I felt that I could not hold my own, indeed, did not wish to hold my own when you were willing to give me, and I was eager to receive, your views on matters in which you were a master. I was especially grateful for your consideration.

I am old enough to be your father,[6] and though as we go on in life even great differences in age always disappear, still there was [something] almost filial in your bearing and no one responds more readily than I do to affection. I wish that there had been time for you to read me some of your papers on Plato, just as you read your unforgettable lectures on Euripides.[7] I am looking forward with great interest to your review of Wilamowitz.[8] Of course, our talk turned every now and then on the philosopher whom you know more intimately than any one I have ever met, and more than once I have referred to our first interview, which made a deep impression on me, and is not unconcerned with your Platonic studies. I cannot recall the year. I telescope my years. I was proud of my young countryman, who was not afraid to face the great panjandrums of Germany,[9] and somewhere, in the mazes of my Mss. will be found an abstract of your doctoral dissertation,[10] which shewed a familiarity with Plato that I have not attained, and indeed, have never attained.

It was to that general period that some of my studies in the Symposium belong, and I am sending an old paper[11] which you have doubtless never seen. Put it among your Platonica, and continue to think kindly of the author, who was then only a boy of fifty-five.

In one of my sonnets,[12] I have explained the origin of a bad habit that I have acquired in the last twelve months or so. I grant this sonnet writing is my vanity, 'Tis an art, 'Tis nothing but a knack, with which I while away the darksome hours.[13] Most of these sonnets are mere embroideries,[14] of more or less familiar texts, they make no claim to poetry, at best they are bits of versified rhetoric.

The other day I undertook to turn Horace's "Ad Leuconoen"[15] into a sonnet, but after the first quatrain, a mischievous spirit entered into me, and the close illustrates the "Urceus exit"[16] motto of my old age.

Mrs. Shorey[17] thought one of my sonnets weepy, but many of them are shockingly frivolous and here is one that I dedicate to the charming proof-reader of your Horace.[18]

Yours faithfully and gratefully,
Basil L. Gildersleeve

Dic. E.N.

## AD LEUCONOEN.

**********************

Pry not into God's secrets, fair Lenore
Nor ask what end He hath decreed for us
Try not the fortune teller's abacus
But bear whate'er the future hath in store.

This is the substance of Horatian lore,
O'er which the world has made a needless fuss.
For this self-styled vates[19] Horatius
But curled the tails his fellow-porkers bore.

His motto was: I do not care a Damn.
His business was to pilfer from the Greek;
Most of his thefts have 'scaped the eye of day.

But all his loves are a transparent sham.
Mark you, against the bard I have no peak
I've just set down what Tyrrell has to say.

1. "April" is typed as rest of letter; "28, 1920" added by hand and as another copy of the same letter does not have that date, it must be considered uncertain.

2. Shorey gave his second Sather lectures in the spring of 1919, having given his first in the fall of 1916 (No. 169, n. 7), then conducted the Greek seminary at Johns Hopkins during the second trimester of 1919-20. See *JHU Circulars*, no. 327 (November 1920): 50.

3. *Dichtung und Wahrheit* 2.10.

4. Cic. *Fam.* 2.6.2; see *LG* para. 366, r. 1 (p. 234), where Gildersleeve translates, "It shows the feeling of a gentleman to be willing to owe very much to him to whom you already owe much."

5. See n. 2 above.

6. Gildersleeve was eighty-eight; Shorey was sixty-two.

7. Gildersleeve must refer to "Euripides and the Radicals," which he gave at Hopkins on 20 February 1920 (see *JHU Circulars*, no. 325 [July 1920]: 43–44); perhaps to "The Case of Euripides," which he gave at Oberlin in January 1912 and as one of the Lane Lectures at Harvard in March 1912; and possibly to "Athens: Fin de Siècle," given at Hopkins in March 1911 and elsewhere. It is not surprising that Shorey read his lectures to his virtually blind master.

8. Shorey may have contemplated reviewing Wilamowitz's *Platon* (see No. 188, n. 9), but never did so, perhaps for the reason stated in his "Classical Studies in America," *TAPA* 50 (1919): 50: "Who but the present writer, in whom it will be imputed to malice, will ever point out the long list of demonstrable errors, not in obiter dicta but affecting the argument, in Wilamowitz' *Plato?*" The next book of Wilamowitz's he would review was *Griechische Verskunst* at *CP* 17 (1922): 150–53.

9. Gildersleeve may mean Shorey's German education at Leipzig, Bonn, and Munich from 1881 to 1884, but more likely he refers to his appointment as Theodore Roosevelt exchange professor at the University of Berlin for 1913 and his direct conflict with Wilamowitz. See E. Christian Kopff, "Wilamowitz and Classical Philology in the United States of America: An Interpretation," in *Wilamowitz nach 50 Jahren*, ed. W. M. Calder III et al. (Darmstadt: Wissenschaftliche Buchgesellschaft, 1984); 569–76. Shorey had become the leading polemicist against the common view of the superiority of German over American scholarship in his papers "The Case for the Classics," *School Review* 18 (1910): 585–617, reprinted in *University Bulletin*, n.s., 11 (1910): 38–70; *Latin and Greek in American Education*, ed. Francis W. Kelsey (New York: Macmillan, 1911), 303–43; *Selected Articles on the Study of Latin and Greek*, ed. Lamar T. Beman (New York: H. W. Wilson, 1921), 125–52; "American Scholarship," *Nation* 92 (1911): 466–69, 553, reprinted *CW* 4 (1911): 226–30 and *Ed. Rev.* 42 (1911): 234–44; "The Assault on Humanism," *Atlantic* 119 (June 1917): 793–801, and 120 (July 1917): 94–105, (reprinted in book form, Boston: Atlantic Publishing Co., 1917); "What to Do for Greek," *CJ* 15 (1919): 8–19; and "Fifty Years of Classical Studies in America," *TAPA* 50 (1919): 33–61.

10. "The beginnings of my own work will always be associated in my mind with the promptness, the courtesy and intelligent appreciation of his reply to the letter which I sent him with a copy of my doctor's dissertation" (Paul Shorey, "Basil L. Gildersleeve, 1831–1924," *NYTimes*, 27 January 1924: sec. 4, 3). The dissertation is *De Platonis idearum doctrina atque mentis humanae notionibus commentatio* (Munich: T. Ackerman, 1884), reprinted in *Paul Shorey: Selected Papers*, ed. Leonardo Tarán, 2 vols. (New York: Garland, 1980), 1: 255–313, and by R. S. W. Hawtrey, *A Dissertation in Plato's Theory of Forms and on the Concepts of the Human Mind*, pref. by Rosamond Kent Sprague, *Ancient Philosophy* 2, no. 1 (Spring 1982).

11. "Studies in the Symposium of Plato," *JHU Circulars*, no. 55 (January 1887): 49–50.

12. Gildersleeve quotes from a sonnet he had sent Shorey entitled "Cup and Ball": I know this sonnet writing is inanity. / It is not art. 'Tis nothing but a knack / With which I while away the darksome hours." The poem is printed in "The Solace of Sonnetry," *Johns Hopkins Alum. Mag.* 9, no. 3 (March 1921): 179, and *NYTimes*, 11 January 1924: 16.

13. Carlyle's translation of Goethe's *Wilhelm Meisters Lehrjahre* 2.13: "Who never ate his bread in sorrow, / Who never spent the darksome hours / Weeping and watching for the morrow / He knows ye not, ye heavenly powers."

14. Greek ποικιλία, "embroidery," and, in literary style, "intricacy," "variety."

15. Hor. *C.* 1.11.

16. Hor. *Ars* 21–23: *Amphora coepit / institui: currente rota cur urceus exit? / denique sit quod vis, simplex dumtaxat et unum* (This began as an amphora, but, as I spin my potter's wheel, why is it coming out a pitcher? In short, do what you wish, only make it simple and uniform). Gildersleeve's innate modesty led him to inscribe copies of *H&H* alternately with

"Urceus exit" or the famous line, Soph. *OC* 273, "Albeit unwittingly I have come where I have come"; see No. 154. See BLG to O. P. Baldwin, 30 October 1915 [Va. Hist. Soc.].

17. Emma Large Gilbert (1868–1947) of Bucks Co., Pa., an honors graduate of Vassar (1890), was a graduate fellow in Latin at the University of Chicago (1893–95) when she married Shorey in June 1895.

18. *Horace: Odes and Epodes* (Boston: B. H. Sanborn, 1898; rev. ed. [with G. J. Laing], 1910).

19. Horace's word, originally "prophet," "seer," for poet; see *C.* 1.1.35, etc., and J. K. Newman, *The Concept of Vates in Augustan Poetry*, Collection Latomus, no. 89 (Brussels: Latomus, 1967).

### 184 To: PAUL SHOREY
*Chicago*

1002 N. Calvert St.
Baltimore, May 5, 1920

My dear Shorey:

I have formed the bad habit of ascribing all my qualities and their corresponding defects to my modicum of French blood. One of these defects is my propensity to indulge in the 'rime riche' so dear to French poets, so sedulously avoided by the English. Hence in revising my sonnets I am now and then forced to change a jingle which to the English ear is no jingle at all. In the Cantharides[1] sonnet[2] (sonnet)[3] which I sent you yesterday, I was so anxious to be discreet that I overlooked the sad fact that, according to English standards 'Phalarides' and 'Larides' do not rhyme at all and so I have substituted for the last line of the close these words:

Give me from all the heavy load I've carried ease.

I am sending you under the same cover ~~the~~ a reprint of what may prove to be my penultimate contribution to Brief Mention.[4] There is stuff enough left in Miller's pack for another number but without the help of my eyes I cannot look up those nugae[5] to my satisfaction.

My homage to Mrs. Shorey

Yours faithfully
B. L. G.

1. The plural of the Latin word for "blister beetle" or "Spanish Fly." The dried beetles were crushed into a preparation used externally as a vesicant in pleurisy, neuritis, and particularly for acute rheumatism, from which Gildersleeve suffered. It was used internally as either a poison or an aphrodisiac, depending, of course, on the dosage.

2.                                    Cantharides
The gentleman on the other side has made a vast display of classic learning. He has sock'd with Socrates, ripp'd with Euripides, and canted with Cantharides' old speech

\*\*\*\*\*\*\*\*\*\*\*\*\*\*\*\*\*

Sister of Lynceus' victim, brave Pyndarides,
Thou bidst me praise thy capillary tonic
'Tis proved naught in battle Laestrygonic
How could I dare to grapple with Cantharides.

Had Agrigentum's lord a son Phalarides
I'd call on him, in my distress mnemonic
Help, all ye gods, Olympian both and Chthonic
Help, all ye nymphs of Como's lake, ye Larides.

Of all these trumped-up rhymes, you've felt the rub
My ancient Muse, I will no further hurt you
Nor ask the tonic's merits to proclaim.

The Spanish daughters of Beelzebub
Rose Aylmer-like are dowered with every virtue
If virtue and efficiency are one.

B. L. G.

3. Written in Gildersleeve's hand thus.
4. Gildersleeve's last Brief Mention was *AJP* 41 (1920): 400–404.
5. "Trivialities"; Catullus's word for his poems (see Cat. 1.4).

## 185 To: Benjamin Ide Wheeler
*California*

The Chimneys
Manchester, Mass.
Aug. 20th. /20

Dear Professor Wheeler:-

The kind words of your letter were read to me as I was holding my quarterly debate with myself, whether I should withdraw from the B.M. game I have played so long.[1]

The failure of my eyes makes it impossible for me to read anything except the head lines of newspapers or the title pages of books. I lack the incitement of current philological literature, I have no access to the mass of MSS. from which I might draw something for the amusement or edification of my little public. I dare not trust the combination of a capricious memory.

I have emerged from months of suffering and disgust into a fair condition of health for a man of my great age and if my mind is not as active, it is as restless as ever, and I manage to while away the hours by verse composition and other devices and the besetting sin of my youth has become the stay of my old age, but I do not intend to flood the few pages I have reserved for myself in the A.J.P. with sonnets on classical themes.[2] I have hunted up my notes for another Mention, subject of course, to the censorship of the Editor, who is not over sympathetic with my prestidigitations.

This is not the first time that you have come to my help at a time of doubt and depression, and I shall always bear in grateful remembrance your invitation to join your staff in California, in the days when I was ruefully contemplating the close of my sixty years activity as a teacher.[3] But this manifestation of good will was not needed to quicken my concern at the report that after an administration of signal achievement, you had retired from the post which you had filled with so much distinction.[4] The cause was not known to me until your letter reached me[5] and you have my deepest sympathy in this temporary disability, due doubtless, to the strain of work from which a quiet student like myself is exempt. Among my multitudinous acquaintances you have a record that I am turning over in my mind as I write. You flashed across my path of life at Newport, Baltimore, Chicago, and New York.[6] I shall never forget the charming hospitality of your Ithacan home,[7] dare I call it the ξ of my Odyssey Χρυσοβραχίονος καὶ Τρόχιλου 'Ομιλία.[8] You shared with me the glorious vision of Greece,[9] and though the plans we worked over at Heidelberg came to nought,[10] there abides the memory of the days when I was admitted to your family circle, and made friends with Mrs. Wheeler and Poulaki. Present my homage to your wife, who holds a place of her own in my gallery of charming women.

I am spending the midsummer months with my daughter at her beautiful home on the North Shore,[11] and if it were not for the failure of my vision, I might be reconciled to the prolongation of my life, not only beyond the bourne of Mimnermus, but beyond that of his critic Solon,[12]

Yours faithfully<br>
B. L. Gildersleeve

Dic. E. N.

1. See No. 184, n. 4.
2. See *AJP* 40 (1919): 223, 451; 41 (1920): 201-2, and his final Brief Mention, 404.
3. Wheeler's invitation to the Sather professorship, see No. 169.
4. Wheeler retired from the presidency of Berkeley in 1919 with the title professor of comparative philology and president emeritus. For a year or so he offered courses in general linguistics and remained an adviser.
5. Wheeler's letter is lost.
6. The locations of APA meetings of 1875, 1877, 1893, and 1899.
7. Wheeler had invited Gildersleeve to lecture at Cornell on Friday, 1 February 1889; his topic was "The American Element in Greek Studies" (BLG to Wheeler, 26 January 1889 [California]).
8. "The communion of Gildersleeve and Wheeler." *Odyssey* 14 is largely devoted to a conversation between Odysseus disguised as a beggar and the swineherd Eumaeus. For "Chrysobrachion," see No. 3, n. 6, and for his nicknames for the Wheelers, No. 95, n. 2.

9. See No. 90, n. 4.

10. Plans for the Gildersleeve-Wheeler Series in 1896; see Nos. 103, 98, 98, 101, and 114.

11. See No. 128, n. 1.

12. Mimnermus (c. 670–c. 600 B.C.) wrote a couplet, "Oh that death, without disease and painful worries, might take me at sixty" (6 West). Solon (638–558 B.C.) replied: "Sing the line thus: 'Oh that death might take me in my eightieth year' " (20 West).

## 186 To: LANE COOPER
*Cornell*

1002 N. Calvert Street
Baltimore, Md
Oct. 4th/20

Dear Professor Cooper:—

Many thanks for the reprint of your article on Greek culture in the Encyclopedia Americana.[1] As you are doubtless aware, the failure of my vision debars me from reading, but I have had it read to me and after all nothing can take the place of the 'oculi fideles'.[2] Still it is only the ear that can catch the rhythm of artistic prose + my reader[3] proved sympathetic.

Jebb once told me that the hardest task he ever set himself was his primer of Greek literature,[4] and I can understand the difficulty you have had in bringing within so small a compass so vast a theme as Greek Culture—a task that you have dissolved as it seems to me—with rare grace + grasp.

I have more than once expressed to you the high esteem I have set upon your services to the good cause—the common cause—The praise of Hellenism comes with a more popular appeal when it comes from those who are not in the professional corps. When a Grecian pleads for Greek, his deliverance is usually set down to professional bias,[5] whereas /~~than~~/ when an English scholar champions the value of Hellenic study for his own work, he is sure of a hearing.

I have never rebelled against being considered, in the first line, a grammarian in the modern sense of the word but at heart I am a "γραμματικώσ" [sic][6] in the antique sense, and I am grateful to you as well as to the others who recognize me as a man of letters who has made his grammatical work ancillary to appreciation of literary art.[7]

Yours faithfully
Basil L. Gildersleeve

Per E. N.

1. *Encyclopedia Americana* (New York: Encyclopedia Americana Corp., 1918–20), 13: 385–87.

2. See No. 182, n. 2.

3. See ibid., n. 3.

4. *Greek Literature*, Literature Primers Series, ed. J. R. Green, (London: Macmillan, 1877; New York: D. Appleton, 1878).

5. See No. 125 and n. 2.

6. "Grammarian, teacher, critic." See *AJP* 33 (1912): 360 ( = *SBM*, 257). Gildersleeve's amanuensis Neal (No. 182, n. 3) has written an omega for an omicron and the wrong letter for a final sigma.

7. See *AJP* 25 (1904): 354–56 ( = *SBM*, 112–15).

187 To: JOHN CALVIN METCALF
*UVa-"Enchanted Years"*

March 3, 1921
1002 N. Calvert Street
Baltimore, Md.

Dear Mr. Metcalf:[1]—

The sonnet that I sent you some time ago was not meant as a contribution to the chorus of praise that will greet the centennial of the University, but merely as an expression of my regret that I could not respond to your invitation to join the concert. If however the verse should be thought worthy of publication among the poetical tributes to your great school, please change the wording of the second line from "bears an empty nest" to ["]holds an empty nest.["] You see, like most verse-wrights I am full of repentances.

Yours sincerely
Basil L. Gildersleeve

## TO THE UNIVERSITY OF VIRGINIA
\*\*\*\*\*\*\*\*\*\*\*\*\*\*\*\*\*\*\*\*\*\*\*\*\*\*\*\*\*\*\*\*\*\*

No summer rose my life-'Tis like a tree
An ancient tree which ~~bears~~ /holds/ an empty nest
Apples a few on topmost boughs,[2] the rest
Sun-dried, or strawn neglected on the lea.
\*\*\*\*\*\*\*\*\*\*\*\*\*\*\*\*\*\*\*\*\*\*\*\*\*\*\*\*\*\*\*\*\*\*\*\*\*\*

What fitting tribute can I pay thee?
How much I love thee, let those years attest
Those twenty years I served thee with my best
Poor best, perhaps, but all that lay in me.
\*\*\*\*\*\*\*\*\*\*\*\*\*\*\*\*\*\*\*\*\*\*\*\*\*\*\*\*\*\*\*\*\*\*

Twice twenty years I tilled another field—
Another? Nay. To me the two were one;
Love would not see the distance on the map
And bade me count whate'er I reaped thy yield;
And now that all my work in life is done,
Dear Mother, let me sleep upon thy lap.[3]

[signed]
Basil L. Gildersleeve

1. Metcalf, who succeeded C. W. Kent (see "Correspondents") as Linden Kent memorial professor of English literature at the University of Virginia, had solicited from Gildersleeve a contribution to *The Enchanted Years* (New York: Harcourt, Brace, 1921), a volume of verse he was editing with his colleague James Southall Wilson. Poets of England and America, including D. H. Lawrence, Vachel Lindsay, Amy Lowell, H. D., E. A. Robinson, Thomas Hardy, and Arthur Symons, dedicated poems to the University of Virginia on the centennial of its founding (No. 6, n. 5). Gildersleeve's sonnet appears on p. 106.

2. Sappho 105a (L-P): "As the sweet apple reddens on the top of the bough, on the top of the topmost bough: the apple-pickers forgot it—no, they did not forget it, they could not reach that high."

3. Gildersleeve was buried in Plot 58 of University Cemetery, Charlottesville, next to his two sons who had died in infancy (No. 12, n. 10; No. 13, n. 1). The apocryphal story of his desire to be buried in Charlottesville after death since he had been "buried" there for two decades of his life has been the most durable of the many anecdotes about him. Although not printed until twenty-five years after his death, the story obviously survived by the oral tradition, as witness the following, each version varying from the others: Paul B. Barringer, *The Natural Bent* (Chapel Hill: University of North Carolina Press, 1949), 206; Kathryn A. Jacob, "The Hopkins Four," *Johns Hopkins Magazine* 25 (July 1974): 24; Diana Lynn Walzel, "Basil Lanneau Gildersleeve: Classical Scholar," *Virginia Cavalcade* 25, no. 3 (Winter 1976): 116; George A. Kennedy, "Gildersleeve, the *Journal*, and Philology in America," *AJP* 101 (1980): 4–5 ( = *Briggs-Benario*, 44); Katharine Lane Weems (No. 116, n. 7), *Odds Were against Me* (New York: Vantage Press, 1985), 49.

188 To: EDWARD FITCH[1]
*Hamilton College Library*

The Chimneys[2]
Manchester, Mass,
[Aug. 22, 1921]

Dear Professor Fitch:-

I was glad to get your good letter of the 13th. The failure of my vision gives me more space for reminiscences than it has ever held in my daily life, so that I am able to dwell with pleasure on our association from the time of our first meeting on the deck of a German liner down to our last brief interview at Robinson's reception.[3]

So you have returned to Apollonius[4] from Thucydides and Plato, to whom you had recourse during the Great War more, I imagine for instruction than for repose. Certainly the actuality of Thucydides is not restful.

From your letter I gathered that your attitude toward Germany is much the same as mine. I have not allowed the turmoil of the terrible conflict to drown the voices that come to me from my years of study in the fatherland, and I have not suffered the lurid light of the great conflagration to distort the kindly features of my German masters and friends, as I remember them.[5]

The message you have brought me from Wilamowitz has touched me nearly. In the last forty years there has arisen no scholar to whom I owe so much for illumination and suggestion,[6] and I have delighted to give public expression to my admiration of his genius.[7] If I have not followed all his publications closely, it has been because to do so would have made it impossible for me to do anything else. I regret deeply that owing to my limitations, I have not been able to make the nearer acquaintance of his Homer[8] and Plato,[9] of which I have received glowing reports. I shall never forget his more than friendly reception of me in Berlin[10] and how he did honour to me then and has done since, by reason doubtless, of my long and loving service to our common cause,

Yours faithfully,
B. L. Gildersleeve

Dic. E. N.

1. This letter has been published by William M. Calder III, "B. L. Gildersleeve and Ulrich von Wilamowitz-Moellendorff: New Documents," *AJP* 99 (1978): 6–7 ( = *Selected Correspondence*, 146–47).

2. See No. 128, n. 1. For a description of Gildersleeve at The Chimneys in the following year, see Katharine L. Weems, *Odds Were against Me* (New York: Vantage Press, 1985), 43–44.

3. D. M. Robinson (No. 150, n. 7) may have held a reception at the APA meeting in Baltimore, 28–30 December 1920. Fitch described the meeting with Gildersleeve in a letter to Wilamowitz of 1 July 1921: "Etwa wie Teiresias er geht herum mit einem Studenten, der ihm Pindar und die Odyssee vorliest" (He goes around somewhat like Tiresias with a student [probably Neal; see No. 182, n. 3], who reads Pindar and the *Odyssey* aloud to him). W. M. Calder III, "The Correspondence of Wilamowitz-Moellendorff with Edward Fitch," *HSCP* 83 (1979): 88 ( = *Selected Correspondence*, 84).

4. See No. 136, n. 8. Fitch's 1896 dissertation was entitled *De Argonautarum reditu quaestiones selectae*. After this letter, his next publication on Apollonius was a review of Wilamowitz's *Hellenistische Dichtung in der Zeit des Kallimachos*, 2 vols. (Berlin: Weidmann, 1924), at *AJP* 47 (1926): 383–86. He never published on Thucydides or Plato.

5. Gildersleeve told a reporter for the *Columbia* [S.C.] *State*, 30 November 1919, "I am steadfastly opposed to all this crusade against German science, literature, and language. I owe all my professional success to German training and I have drawn much intellectual and spiritual nourishment from the great German poets and thinkers. I have scant sympathy with the Germany of the present, but I cannot and would not rid myself of the memories of the

past." See *AJP* 38 (1917): 233–34. He had no sympathy with those who associated "Prussian Junkerdom" with the Southern cause (*AJP* 38 [1917]: 339).

6. He used the words "illumination" and "suggestion" in the same context in 1907; see No. 136.

7. See No. 136, n. 3.

8. *Die Ilias und Homer* (Berlin: Weidmann, 1916).

9. *Platon I: Leben und Werke*; *II: Beilagen und Textkritik* (Berlin: Weidmann, 1919–20).

10. Gildersleeve visited Wilamowitz in May–June of 1907 and was graciously received. See Wilamowitz to Fitch, 12 June 1907, in Calder (cited n. 3 above), 379–80 ( = *Selected Correspondence*, 75–76) and Wilamowitz, *Erinnerungen, 1848–1914*, 2d ed. (Leipzig: K. F. Koehler, 1929), 312.


189 To: EDWIN ANDERSON ALDERMAN
*"Dr. Gildersleeve's Birthday," Alumni Bulletin,*
*University of Virginia, 3d ser., 17, no. 1 (January 1924): 200*

1002 N. Calvert Street,
Baltimore, Md.,
Oct. 24, 1923.

To President Alderman,
University of Virginia,
Dear President Alderman:—

The three-fold of love's labour and sorrow, of which I spoke when I left the service of the University of Virginia is still unbroken.[1] There has been no break in the unity of spirit, for the motto of the Johns Hopkins, Veritas Vos Liberavit, has been adopted by the elder sister,[2] and among the many expressions of interest in my 90th anniversary, none has given me more pleasure than your testimony to the honour paid me in my old academic home.[3]

With assurances of the highest esteem, I am

Yours faithfully,
Basil Lanneau Gildersleeve

1. *Culbreth*, 401, quotes Gildersleeve's impromptu farewell at the University of Virginia commencement of 1876: "I had not thought of saying farewell to you till I should bid the world good-night. Here to me love, labor and sorrow have found their keenest expression." See, further, introduction to chapter 3.

2. The University of Virginia has never adopted an official motto. Following the great fire that destroyed the Rotunda on 27 October 1895, the architect Stanford White (1853–1906) was engaged through the efforts of Thornton (see "Correspondents") to help restore what was lost and build much-needed new structures. Part of White's plan involved closing off the lower end of the Lawn with three buildings, one of which, Cabell Hall, directly faced the Rotunda. On the frieze of Cabell Hall, dedicated on 14 June 1898, is the Greek of John 8:32: καὶ γνώσεσθε τὴν ἀλήθειαν, καὶ ἡ ἀλήθεια ἐλευθερώσει ὑμᾶς ([Ye shall know the truth

and] the truth will make you free). At the dedication, A. C. Gordon (see "Correspondents") read his poem "The Fostering Mother," whose epigraph is this verse (*For Truth and Freedom* [Staunton, Va.: A. Schultz, 1898], see esp. 49–50). The biblical verse is called "the pregnant motto of the University" in *Jefferson's University*, ed. John Shelton Patton et al. (Charlottesville: Michie, 1915), 35.

3. Alderman had written Gildersleeve on 24 October 1923: "No where in the world is your great name and fame as a teacher and a scholar more genuinely cherished than at the University of Virginia. I send you the love and good will of the University and my own hearty wishes for your health and prosperity."

190 To: JAMES HENRY RICE, JR.
*Duke*

1002 N. Calvert Street, Baltimore, Md.,
November 15, 1923.

Dear Mr. Rice:-

In the last few weeks many tokens of friendly interest in my 91st[1] Anniversary have come to cheer me in my old age which, however lovingly intended, must necessarily for a man of my make up mean resignation.

Your good letter is the only one that has carried me back to the first quarter of my long life. As your congratulation was read to me I seemed to breathe again the atmosphere of my father's house,[2] to sit once more in the family circle at morning and evening prayer, and listen to the Scriptural phrases whose music has never ceased to haunt me, whose lessons have ever been before me, though sometimes only to rebuke.

And then the wonderful description of the present autumn in your own land, a description impossible for any one who has not, like you, made himself free of the great works of nature.

I have had that part of the letter read to me over and over again, then, thinking it churlish keeping it all to myself, as only a native could understand the intimate charm of your coast land, I have sent it to a friend, who knows and loves that stretch of South Carolina.

With best thanks for [your] delightful letter, and sincere regards, I am

Yours faithfully
Basil L. Gildersleeve

Mr. James Henry Rice, jr.,
Brick House Plantation,
Chee-Ha River, Wiggins, S.C.

1. He means ninety-*second*.
2. 5 Pitt Street, Charleston.

191 To: CARROLL SPRIGG
*"Dr. Gildersleeve at Ninety-Two," Alumni Bulletin,*
*University of Virginia, 3d ser., 17, no. 1 (January 1924): 132–33*

1002 Calvert Street,
Baltimore, Md.,
Nov. 20th, 1923.

Dear Carroll Sprigg:

The 23rd of October brought many friendly tokens of interest in my 92nd anniversary, none that I can recall from the palæozoic period that you represent; such a letter as yours[1] could not be fittingly answered in a few conventional phrases, and so I laid it aside for a season of greater leisure.

Correspondence is for me slow work, I cannot read anything but the largest type, I can write but I cannot revise what I have written, and at any rate my chirography is a hopeless puzzle to most persons,[2] but I manage somehow. Dictation is a process that does not suit my restless mind, but I must do my best.

Well, not to dwell on my infirmities, you may be interested to learn that out of the host of students of the late 60's, your face comes up to my mental vision with perfect distinctness, the laughing eyes, the fresh complexion. My wife does not help me and declines to confirm my impressions as to your presence on an occasion which has found a lodgement in my memory. I was married in '66, a portrait of my wife taken at that time was hanging on the wall of the reception room. It was not a good likeness, and one of the initiated explained the situation to a wondering freshman by telling him that the picture was a portrait of Mr. Gildersleeve's first wife.[3]

You have idealized the "Old Gil"[4] of your youth, a title I did not resent though my wife disliked—very much her scriptural name of Gilgal.[5] You have made me out a bright and shining light, and have not taken into account the charred wicks and the sputtering oil. In like manner you have idealized the "Old Gil" of to-day and accept the current story of my serene and happy old age. I will not enumerate the drawbacks to that estimate. I ought rather to count my blessings. I do not suffer. I am tended with loving care, every real want is met or even anticipated. My wife, whom you met in the flush of her youth, has set no bounds to her devotions. I have a faithful and intelligent attendant of whom I have made a friend.[6] My poor vision is supplemented by a succession of readers. I am only able to take a little bodily exercise. I while away the dark hours before dawn repeating Greek poetry or else fabricating rhymes that are not poetry at all but answer the purpose of intellectual dumb-bells,[7] and then I have messages from old friends and former students to cheer me on my way onward, the end of which I look forward to undismayed.

With thanks for the renewal of old associations, I am

Yours faithfully
Basil L. Gildersleeve

1. Sprigg had written Gildersleeve on 22 October 1923 (in part): "As a former Confederate soldier, a type of Southerner of the last century, a professor and tutor who deserved and won the admiration and affection of his students (but they were sometimes terrified at his wit), I am congratulating you upon your arrival at an age, that proves you have wronged no man, have looked upon the bright side of life, have generally eat and drunk without the aid of experts and legislatures, and have frequently been amused at seeing so many humans finding fault with their lot. That your remaining days may continue to bring you good health and spirits, freedom from all pain and trouble, is the sincere wish of one who in the 'Sixties' ventured, along with others, when you were not within hearing distance to call you 'Old Gil.' "

2. See No. 7.

3. *Culbreth*, 399: "During these [social] visits the Professor [Gildersleeve] would usually show himself in the parlor [of Pavilion I] for a few minutes, and those not under him, therefore unacquainted with his ready wit and repartee, often recounted their discomfort, not to say embarrassment, at something bright gotten off at their or another's expense, while those familiar with his characteristic gifts and inclination in never losing a good opportunity for witticism, accepted the situation with greater resignation."

4. "Old" may have been meant affectionately, but it may also have had a literal application. Culbreth, 397: "He was just forty-three years of age, but seemed to us youthful fellows at least fifty—due possibly to his sober reflective manner, general bearing, favorable reputation, and what he had accomplished already in the world of letters."

5. Gilgal ("circle of stones") is the name of several towns in the Old Testament, all probably having circles of sacred stones, or cromlechs. See Josh. 4; 1 Sam. 11:15; 2 Sam. 9:15, 40.

6. Neal, see No. 182, n. 3.

7. See *AJP* 40 (1919): 450: while "trying to work in the dark," he produced a version of Platen's sonnet, "The Death of Pindar."

# CORRESPONDENTS

**Edwin Anderson Alderman** (1861–1931), first president of the University of Virginia, was educated at the University of North Carolina, where he received a Ph.D. with honors in English and Latin (1882). The early years of his career were devoted to secondary education in his home state of North Carolina; he was superintendent of schools, conducted institutes for teachers across the state, and was instrumental in the founding of the State Normal and Industrial School (now the University of North Carolina at Greensboro) in 1891. Elected professor of the history and philosophy of education at Chapel Hill in 1893 and president in 1896, he inaugurated departments of pharmacy and education as well as an extension school and began to show his interest in Southern literature and history. He was president of Tulane from 1900 until 1904, when he went to Charlottesville. At the University of Virginia, Alderman helped unify the state's public education system and raise the academic standing of the university. Under his presidency, Gildersleeve was invited to give the inaugural Barbour-Page Lectures (No. 143), printed as *H&H*, and he declared Gildersleeve an official alumnus for his 1912 reunion of Confederate alumni (No. 153, n. 5). He was co-editor-in-chief (with Joel Chandler Harris) of *The Library of Southern Literature* (New Orleans: Martin and Hoyt, 1907) and co-author (with A. C. Gordon) of *J. L. M. Curry: A Biography* (New York: Macmillan, 1911). See D. Malone, *Edwin A. Alderman: A Biography* (New York: Doubleday, 1940). **Nos. 124, 143, 189.**

**Charles Wesley Bain** (1864–1915) attended the University of Virginia and received an M.A. from Sewanee (1895). He was first classical master at McCabe's School (No. 102, n. 2) and taught at the Sewanee Grammar School (1895–97), and was then professor of Greek at South Carolina College (now the University of South Carolina) (1898–1910) and at the University of North Carolina from 1910 until his death. His *First Latin Book* was one of the initial offerings of the Gildersleeve-Lodge Series (New York: University Publishing Co., 1898; rev. ed., 1914). He also edited *The Seventh Book of Homer's Odyssey* (Boston: Ginn, 1899) and *The Poems of*

359

*Ovid: Selections* (New York: Macmillan, 1902). He contributed a note to *AJP* 10 (1889): 84-85, and articles to the *Sewanee Review*. *WhAm* 1:45. **No. 104.**

**Benjamin Johnson Barbour** (1821-95), rector of the University of Virginia from 1866 to 1872, and the son of the famous Virginia governor and statesman James Barbour (1775-1842), graduated from the University of Virginia in 1839. A prominent Unionist, he was rector during the difficult period of Reconstruction, when students of Whig and Unionist sympathies were in greater numbers than before the war. Barbour recognized the need for increased technical education (applied mathematics, civil engineering, and applied chemistry were begun in his administration) and the need for postgraduate programs to train school teachers, an idea resisted by many faculty members, but embraced by Gildersleeve, who began the first such American programs in Greek (1859) and Latin (1866) (M. B. Pierson, *Graduate Work in the South* [Chapel Hill: University of North Carolina Press, 1947], 35, 57-59; R. J. Storr, *The Beginnings of Graduate Education in America* [Chicago: University of Chicago Press, 1953], 157, n. 45). On Barbour, see J. P. Maddex, Jr., *The Virginia Conservatives, 1867-1879* (Chapel Hill: University of North Carolina Press, 1970), 216. Barbour also served one term in the Virginia Legislature as representative of the Orange district. **Nos. 10, 75.**

**Friedrich Karl Brugmann** (1849-1919), one of the leading comparative grammarians of his day, trained at Leipzig, taught briefly at Freiburg, and returned to Leipzig in 1877 as professor of comparative philology. Following the departure of Herman Brandt (No. 47, n. 11), Gildersleeve wanted him to become professor of German and comparative grammar and head of the Romance languages department, but Brugmann declined, and Henry Wood, who also had a Leipzig Ph.D., was made associate professor of German in 1885. See further *Hawkins*, 162. Brugmann published *Ein Problem der homerischen Textkritik und der vergleichenden Sprachwissenschaft* (Leipzig: S. Hirzel, 1876) and "Griechische Grammatik" in Iwan Müller's *Handbuch der klassischen Altertums-wissenschaft* (Nordlingen: C. H. Beck, 1885-1923), 2: 1-126 (expanded in later eds.), but his great work was *Grundriss der vergleichenden Grammatik der Indogermanischen Sprachen*, 5 vols. (Strassburg: K. J. Trübner, 1886-93) ( = *A Comparative Grammar of the Indo-Germanic Languages*, trans. R. S. Conway and W. H. D. Rouse [New York: B. Westermann, 1895]). See *AJP* 37 (1916): 375 ( = *SBM*, 358). *NDB* 2: 667. **No. 64.**

**Ingram Bywater** (1840-1914), fellow and tutor of Exeter College, and Regius professor of Greek at Oxford, 1893-1908, edited Aristotle's *Nicho-*

*machaean Ethics* and *Poetics* (Oxford: Clarendon Press, 1890 and 1898 respectively), the latter reviewed by Gildersleeve in *AJP* 19 (1898): 233 ("The stamp of the master is on this work as on all that Bywater does"). Gildersleeve first met him in 1880 (No. 45). See also *AJP* 36 (1915): 476–77. W. W. Jackson's *Ingram Bywater: The Memoir of an Oxford Scholar, 1840–1914* (Oxford: Clarendon Press, 1917) concludes (p. 195) with Gildersleeve's obituary of Bywater from *AJP* and was warmly reviewed by Gildersleeve at *AJP* 38 (1917): 392–410; see, further, R. W. Chapman, *The Portrait of a Scholar* (Oxford: Clarendon Press, 1920), 9–23. **No. 142.**

**John Hampden Chamberlayne** (1838–82), Virginia journalist, was a native of Richmond, where he attended Socrates Maupin's school (probably after Gildersleeve taught there in 1849–50) and in 1858 received his M.A. from the University of Virginia. He was admitted to the bar in 1860, but when the war came, he volunteered as a private and rose to be captain of artillery in the Confederate Army. From July to November 1861 he was in the Cheat Mountain Campaign in Western Virginia, with Col. William Gilham's Regiment, Co. F, which Gildersleeve joined as a voluntary aide (No. 141, n. 21). He struggled greatly after the war before becoming editor of the *Norfolk Virginian* (1873–76). In March 1876 he founded the *Richmond State*, which inherited the "Bourbon" clientele of the *Richmond Enquirer* when it expired in 1877. Under his proprietorship, the *State* became the leading independent newspaper of the city, frequently siding with the (Conservative) Democrats, particularly on the question of funding rather than readjusting the debt (No. 32, n. 4). Chamberlayne also represented Richmond in the Virginia House of Delegates in 1879 and 1880. See further *Ham Chamberlayne—Virginian: Letters and Papers of an Artillery Officer in the War for Southern Independence, 1861–1865*, ed. C. G. Chamberlayne (Richmond: Press of Dietz Printing Co., 1932). **Nos. 13, 19.**

**Elizabeth Ellery Sedgewick Child** (b. 1824) was the wife of Francis J. Child (No. 21, n. 1). **No. 97.**

**Albert Stanburrough Cook** (1853–1927), professor of English at Berkeley (1882–89) and Yale (1889–1921), was an associate in English at Hopkins (1879–81) and is credited with organizing the department when, upon his return from Göttingen, a promised chair at Rutgers was not offered. He studied with Sweet (No. 44, n. 7) in London (1881–82) and was dismissed by Gilman in hopes that Sweet would come to Hopkins and received his Ph.D. from Jena in 1882, the year he took his post at Berkeley. He published over three hundred items, including his edition of *Judith* (Boston: D. C. Heath, 1888), *A First Book in Old English* (Boston, Ginn,

1894; 3d ed., 1903), *Select Translations from Old English Poetry* (Boston: Ginn, 1902), and his translation of Eduard Sievers, *An Old English Grammar*, 3d ed. (Boston: Ginn, 1903). In 1898 he was president of the Modern Language Association. His review of Skeat's *Etymological Dictionary of the English Language* is in *AJP* 1 (1880): 203-6. *DAB* 4: 370-71. **No. 105.**

**Lane Cooper** (1875-1959), one of America's first specialists in comparative literature, studied at Rutgers (A.B. 1896) and Leipzig (Ph.D. 1901), and in 1902 was appointed instructor in English at Cornell, rising to professor in 1915. He is best remembered for his *The Greek Genius and its Influence* (New Haven: Yale University Press, 1917), his translations *Aristotle on the Art of Poetry* (New York: D. Appleton, 1913; 2d ed., 1947) and *Aristotle's Rhetoric* (New York: D. Appleton, 1932) and his concordances to Boethius (Cambridge, Mass.: Mediaeval Academy of America, 1928), the Latin, Greek, and Italian poems of John Milton (Halle: Niemeyer, 1923), Wordsworth (London: Smith, Elder, 1911), and Horace (Washington: Carnegie Institute of Washington, 1916). He also wrote *Two Views of Education* (New Haven: Yale University Press, 1922). *NatCAB* 47: 380-81. **No. 186.**

**David Marvel Reynolds Culbreth** (1855-1943), member of a prominent Maryland family, was one of the last of Gildersleeve's University of Virginia students (A.B. 1877), and later attended the Maryland College of Pharmacy (Ph.G. 1879) and the College of Physicians and Surgeons, Baltimore (M.D. 1883). At Hopkins he studied vegetable histology with H. N. Martin (No. 44, n. 8). For thirteen years (1880-92) he operated his own drugstore in Baltimore, and in 1885 he was named professor of botany, materia medica, and pharmacology at the Maryland College of Pharmacy, in which position he served for thirty-five years. From 1897 to 1906 he held a similar position at the University of Maryland. His major works are *A Class Compendium of Pharmaceutical Botany* (Baltimore: Deutsch, 1893) and *A Manual of Materia Medica and Pharmacology* (Philadelphia: Lea Brothers, 1896). His *The University of Virginia: Memories of her Student-Life and Professors* (New York: Neale, 1908), 397-403, gives a detailed description of Gildersleeve in his latter years at the University of Virginia. **No. 119.**

**Angela Charlotte Darkow** (1889-1943), schoolteacher, was born in Vienna, Austria, was educated at Bryn Mawr (A.B. 1911, M.A. 1912, Ph.D. 1917), and spent her subsequent life there. Gildersleeve favorably reviewed her dissertation, "The Spurious Speeches of the Lysianic Corpus" (Bryn Mawr, 1917), at *AJP* 36 (1917): 455-57. From 1914 to 1917 she worked as a private tutor and taught at Miss Wright's School in Bryn Mawr, and in 1916 she became academic principal of the Harcum School there. **No. 179.**

**Joseph Villiers Denney** (1862–1935), dean of the College of Arts, Philosophy and Science at Ohio State, was a graduate of the University of Michigan (B.A. 1885), and rose from associate professor of rhetoric (1891) to head of the English department (1904–33) at Ohio State. From 1901 to 1921 he was dean, in which capacity Gildersleeve wrote him in 1914. He wrote numerous textbooks, as well as *The Value of Classics to Students of English* (Chicago: Scott, Foresman, 1913). *NatCAB* 44: 285–86. **No. 162.**

**John Dewey** (1859–1952) graduated from the University of Vermont (B.A. 1879) and Hopkins (Ph.D. 1884). Having taught at the universities of Michigan (1889–94) and Chicago (1894–1904), he brought his "new pedagogy" to Columbia in 1904 as professor of philosophy and won his first national fame arguing against the classical approach and aristocratic traditions that American education had inherited from Europe. See *My Pedagogic Creed* (New York: E. L. Kellogg, 1897), *The School and Society* and *The Educational Situation* (both Chicago: University of Chicago Press, 1899 and 1902 respectively). Among his other works are *The Significance of the Problem of Knowledge*, *Studies in Logical Theory* (Chicago: University of Chicago Press, 1897 and 1903 respectively), and *Human Nature and Conduct* (New York: Carlton House, 1922). For his life, see George Dykhuizen, *The Life and Mind of John Dewey* (Carbondale, Ill.: Southern Illinois University Press, 1973). **No. 165.**

**Richard Theodore Ely** (1854–1943), political economist, studied at Columbia (B.A. 1876), under Johannes Conrad at Halle, and under Karl Knies at Heidelberg (Ph.D. 1879). In 1881 he was appointed lecturer in political economy at Hopkins and in 1887 associate professor. While there he formulated his anti-classical, anti-Spencerian economic theory of selective intervention by the state for economic regulation and promulgated it through his writings, notably *The Labor Movement in America* (New York: T. Y. Crowell, 1886), through the American Economic Association, which he helped found in 1885 and of which he was president (1900–1901), and through his students, especially John R. Commons, Edward A. Ross, and Woodrow Wilson. Like Gildersleeve, Ely came from a deeply religious Presbyterian family, and the tenets of his Christianity informed all of his work, especially *The Social Aspects of Christianity* (Boston: W. L. Greene, 1888). Both men were contributors to the *Nation*. In 1892 Ely moved to the University of Wisconsin, where he endured a public hearing in 1894 on the charge that he was a socialist. He was cleared on the basis of academic freedom of speech, although he claimed to be an "aristocrat rather than a democrat." See his memoir, *Ground under Our Feet* (New York: Macmillan, 1938), dedicated to Gilman, and Benjamin G. Rader, *The Academic Mind and Reform: The Influence of Richard T. Ely in American Life* (Lexington, Ky.: University of Kentucky Press, 1966). **No. 159.**

**Henry Rushton Fairclough** (1862–1938), Stanford classicist and translator, was educated at the University of Toronto (B.A. 1883, M.A. 1886, Litt.D. 1922), where he was lecturer in Greek and ancient history from 1887 to 1893. He spent the year 1886–87 at Hopkins and was awarded a fellowship for the following year, but in April 1887 Canada federalized her universities, creating an immediate need for instructors, and Fairclough resumed his post. He taught at Stanford from 1893, with interruptions, until his death, and was president of the APA in 1926. Fairclough was considered the leading American Virgilian of his time, and translated Virgil's works for the Loeb series in two volumes, as well as Horace's *Satires, Epistles, and Ars Poetica* (both London: Heinemann; New York: Putnam, 1916–18 and 1926 respectively). He edited Terence's *Andria* (Boston: Allyn and Bacon, 1901) and Plautus's *Trinummus* (New York: Macmillan, 1909). His dissertation, *The Attitude of the Greek Tragedians toward Nature* was published in Toronto by Rowsell and Hutchison in 1897, and he returned to the theme later with *Love of Nature among the Greeks and Romans* (New York: Longmans, Green, 1927). He contributed one article to Gildersleeve's *AJP*, "Horace's View of the Relations between Satire and Comedy," 34 (1913): 183–93. See his autobiography *Warming Both Hands* (Stanford: Stanford University Press, 1941), esp. 75–85, 147–54. **Nos. 89, 100, 127.**

**Edward Fitch** (1864–1946), the only American to receive a doctorate under Wilamowitz, was educated at Hamilton College (B.A. 1886, M.A. 1889, LL.D [hon.] 1934) and, after three years of teaching at Park College, Parksville, Mo. (1886–89), went to Göttingen, where he studied for five semesters under Wilamowitz (see below) and received his Ph.D. in 1896. He returned to Hamilton, where he rose to become Edward North professor of Greek (1904–34) and dean (1926–32). He was also annual professor at the American School of Classical Studies at Athens (1932–33). He published six reviews and four articles in *AJP* during Gildersleeve's editorship, but though he produced many other articles, he published nothing of book length. See W. M. Calder III, "The Correspondence of Ulrich von Wilamowitz-Moellendorff with Edward Fitch," *HSCP* 83 (1979): 369–96, and esp. 370–72 ( = *Selected Correspondence*, 65–92; 66–69). **Nos. 136, 188.**

**Thomas Frank Gailor** (1856-1935), bishop of Tennessee, graduated from Racine College (A.B. 1876) and the General Theological Seminary, New York (S.T.B. 1879). He served Sewanee for over fifty-three years as professor of ecclesiastical history (1882-91), vice-chancellor (1891-93), chaplain (1893-1908), and chancellor (1908-35). On the death of Bishop Quintard (No. 71, n. 2), he became bishop of Tennessee. He was chairman of the Episcopal House of Bishops (1916) and presiding bishop of the council (1919-25), and was given an honorary D.D. by Oxford. Among his many publications are *A Manual of Devotion* (New York: J. Pott, 1897), *The Christian Church and Education: The Bedell Lectures of 1909* (New York: T. Whittaker, 1910), *The Episcopal Church, Its History, Its Prayer Book, Its Ministry* (Milwaukee: Young Churchman, 1914), and his autobiography *Some Memories* (Kingsport, Tenn.: Southern Publishers, 1937) (on Gildersleeve, see 91, 97-99). See *DAB Suppl. 1*, 329. **No. 84.**

**Hannibal Hamlin Garland** (1860-1940), novelist of the Prairie, was born in Wisconsin, the son of a farmer whom hard times forced to move about the Middle Border region of the United States, from Wisconsin to the Dakota territory. His early sketches detailing the hardships of life on the Middle Border were first published in *Harper's Weekly* and collected as *Main-Travelled Roads* (Boston: Arena, 1891), which was not a popular success, despite a review by William Dean Howells that praised his realism. In 1892 Arena of Boston published three novels by Garland that were frankly propagandistic: *A Member of the Third House, Jason Edwards: An Average Man*, and *A Spoil of Office*, all of which put forward his views on agrarian reform. In *Crumbling Idols* (Chicago: Stone and Kimball, 1894), he propounds his theory of "veritism" in novel writing. *The Captain of the Gray-Horse Troop* (New York: Harper and Bros., 1901), a story of injustice done to Indians by whites, was the best novel of his next period. By 1913 his best fiction had been written, and he wrote his autobiography, *A Son of the Middle Border* (New York: Macmillan, 1917), followed by the Pulitzer Prize-winning *A Daughter of the Middle Border* (New York: Macmillan, 1921). *DAB Suppl. 2*, 218-20. **No. 174.**

**Daniel Coit Gilman** (1831-1908), first president of Hopkins, after graduating from Yale in 1852, studied at Berlin under Karl Ritter, the Aristotelian F. A. Trendelenburg, and the Egyptologist Karl Richard Lepsius during 1854-55 before returning to Yale as assistant librarian and professor of physical and political geography in the Sheffield Scientific School (1855-72). More important, his position as secretary of the governing body of Yale helped prepare him for his role as president of the University of California (1872-75) and Hopkins (1875-1901), where he remained through financial vicissitudes (No. 92, n. 3), declining other offers (Nos. 92–93). Gildersleeve and Gilman first met in Charlottesville in the spring of 1875 when Gilman was touring the country in search of faculty. The two met again in Washington on 8 December 1875, talking long into the night about "the University that was to be" (No. 16, n. 1). Gilman had entered Gildersleeve's life at a crucial time: after nineteen years of collegiate teaching, with its drudgery of papers and its provincialism (No. 19, n. 1; No. 22), he was eager for a position whose lowest level would be the highest he had taught at the University of Virginia (No. 18) and in which he could organize and publish his accumulated work. He was forty-four, had published relatively little on classical subjects, even for that time, and clearly felt he was squandering his talents and education. Moreover, his beloved father had died on 20 June 1875, and the resulting change altered Gildersleeve's perspective on life and gave him the freedom to move (No. 62). From this time, Gilman would become as close to him as a member of his family (Nos. 46, 90), asking his counsel and sharing his confidences (No. 19), proselytizing for Hopkins (No. 28), and making appointments, particularly for the Latin chair (Nos. 18, 22, 24–25), but also for the chairs in English (Nos. 56, 73) and German (Nos. 27, 60). Gildersleeve was sent to Europe by Gilman in 1880 to advertise the university, make contacts for *AJP*, and find a Latinist, linguists (Nos. 41–50), and students (No. 44). Gildersleeve actually felt that his sense of "happiness and usefulness" (No. 93), if not his whole career (No. 131), was due to Gilman, and Gilman's resignation (Nos. 112, 118) caused Gildersleeve real anguish. See Gildersleeve's memorial address, *Daniel Coit Gilman: First President of the Johns Hopkins University, 1876–1901* (Baltimore: Johns Hopkins Press, 1908), 32–37, esp. 32:

> "It was the glory of the Johns Hopkins University that its President was foremost in every good word and work. It was no fountain sealed—it was a source of life and light. Such was the central sphere, such the ever enlarging cycles of his philanthropic endeavor; and so effective was his work that he seemed to be the one great champion of each cause he espoused. Wherever he appeared there came light and hope and confidence. His wide vision was matched by the discernment of spirits which is the secret of power, his marvellous resourcefulness by his wonderful sense of order."

From 1901 to 1904 Gilman was president of the Carnegie Foundation. His most notable papers are collected in *University Problems in the United States* (New York: Century, 1898). He wrote the biographies *James Monroe* (Boston: Houghton Mifflin, 1883) and *The Life of James Dwight Dana* (New York: Harper and Bros., 1899). His own account of the early years of Johns Hopkins is *The Launching of a University* (New York: Dodd, Mead,

1906). See further *Franklin* and *DAB*, 4: 299–303. **Nos. 15–18, 20, 22–25, 31–32, 30, 39–50, 55–56, 59–60, 63, 67, 73, 90–94, 96, 112, 118, 120, 131.**

**Thomas Dwight Goodell** (1854–1920), Yale classicist, received his B.A. (1877) and Ph.D. (1884) from Yale, where he was a student of Seymour's (see below). In 1888 he became assistant professor of Greek there, rising to full professor in 1893. A popular teacher at Yale, he was also annual professor at the American School of Classical Studies at Athens (1894–95), a member of its managing committee (1908–20), and president of the APA for 1911–12 (No. 155). He and Gildersleeve may have crossed the Atlantic together in 1907 or 1905 (No. 148, n. 5). In Goodell's obituary notice in *AJP* 41 (1920): 406, his colleague C. W. Mendell said the "three scholarly achievements . . . [that] will always overtop the rest, assuring him the lasting respect of the world of scholars" were his *Chapters on Greek Metric* (New York: Scribner, 1901); "*Hymnos Andron*: Greek Festival Hymn for Yale University . . .*" Yale Alumni Weekly* 11 (1902): 169–70; and *Athenian Tragedy: A Study in Popular Art* (New Haven: Yale University Press, 1920). He contributed one article to *AJP* (No. 155, n. 5), wrote over thirty articles, and, like Gildersleeve, composed sonnets. *NatCAB* 19: 146–47. **Nos. 76, 148, 155–56.**

**Armistead Churchill Gordon** (1855–1931), a prominent attorney from Staunton, Va., and a poet and biographer of some local fame (*Jefferson Davis* [New York: Scribner, 1918]), attended the University of Virginia from 1873 to 1875 and was a member of the board of visitors (1894–98; 1906–18). As rector (1897–98; 1906–18), he was one of the original proponents for change from faculty self-governance with oversight by a board of visitors to the appointment of a president. *WhAm* 1: 470 and *NatCAB* 8: 137. **No. 102.**

**James Francis Harrison** (1851–96) received his M.D. from the University of Virginia in 1874, where he became professor of medical jurisprudence, obstetrics, and the practice of medicine, and was secretary of the faculty from 1873 to 1886. **No. 31.**

**Joseph Edward Harry** (1863–1949), called by Gildersleeve "the most fecund conjectural critic in America" (BLG to Harry, 6 January 1915), was a Quaker who received both A.B. (1886) and Ph.D. (1889) from Hopkins, where he was a "jibbing pupil" of Gildersleeve's (No. 123). He taught at Georgetown College, Ky. (1889–1900), and the University of Cincinnati (1900–1916), where he founded the Classics Department and was also dean of the college of liberal arts (1904–6), acting president (1904), and dean of the graduate school (1906–16). He resigned to perform war service as a foreign-language censor for the Post Office, following which he lectured at the Sorbonne from 1919 to 1922. After a period of traveling and lecturing at various institutions, he was given a post at St. Stephens' (now Bard) College of Columbia University (1926–28) and was named Hoffman professor of Greek language there (1928–39). Principal among his many publications are *The Hippolytus of Euripides* (Boston: Ginn, 1899); *The Prometheus Bound of Aeschylus* (New York: American Book Co., 1905), which he dedicated to Gildersleeve (No. 123); *The Greek Tragic Poets* (Cincinnati: University of Cincinnati Press, 1914); and his translations, *Greek Tragedy* (New York: Columbia University Press, 1933). See *Bibliographical Record of Joseph Edward Harry, Ph.D.* (New York: American Book Co., 1938); *WhoAm* 2: 238; *NYTimes*, 13 August 1949: 11. **Nos. 110, 123.**

**James Morgan Hart** (1839–1916) graduated from the College of New Jersey (now Rutgers) in 1860 and took a J.U.D. *vera cum laude* from Göttingen in 1864. He abandoned the practice of law in 1868 and served for four years as assistant professor of modern languages at Cornell. Two years (1872–74) in Leipzig, Marburg, and Berlin focused his interest on English and Germanic philology, and he returned in 1876 to take the chair of modern languages and English literature at the University of Cincinnati, a post he held until 1890, when he returned to Cornell as professor of rhetoric and English philology. An early supporter of *AJP* (No. 38), he contributed two articles and three reviews while Gildersleeve was editor and also translated A. Laugel's *Angleterre, politique et sociale* as *England, Political and Social* (New York: Putnam, 1874), edited a number of school texts, wrote *German Universities: A Narrative of Personal Experience* (New York: Putnam, 1874), *A Syllabus of Anglo-Saxon Literature* (Cincinnati: R. Clarke, 1881), and *A Handbook of English Composition* (Philadelphia: Elldredge and Bro., 1895). He was president of the Modern Language Association in 1895 and, like Gildersleeve, he contributed numerous reviews to the *Nation*. *DAB* 8: 357–58. **Nos. 38, 54.**

**Sophia Lanneau Hart** (1862–1952), granddaughter of Charles Henry Lanneau (1808–75), brother of Gildersleeve's mother, Emma Louisa Lanneau (1805–59), lived a spinster with her married sister, Louise Stephens Hart Norwood (1865–1934; No. 144, n. 11) (S. R. Mowbray and C. S. Norwood, *Bazile Lanneau of Charleston, 1746–1833* [Goldsboro, N.C.: Hillburn Printing Corp., 1985], 139–44). **No. 144.**

**Paul Hamilton Hayne** (1830–86) was a schoolmate of the poet Henry Timrod's (No. 12, n. 1), but not of Gildersleeve's. He was at the College of

Charleston from 1847 to 1850, after Gildersleeve had moved to Richmond. An early member of the loosely knit literary circle that formed around the Charleston novelist and critic William Gilmore Simms (1806-70), he edited a number of short-lived Southern literary magazines, including the *Southern Literary Gazette* (1852-56), *Russell's Magazine* (1856-60), and *Southern Opinion* (1867-69). He was too sickly for extended war service and his lavish home and extensive library were destroyed during the Federal bombardment of Charleston. In 1865 he moved to "Copse Hill," near Augusta, Ga., and endured great financial hardship. His breakthrough year was 1872, when he published *Legends and Lyrics* (Philadelphia: Lippincott, 1872). For Hayne on Gildersleeve, Ramsay, and Lord, see "Ante-Bellum Charleston," *Southern Bivouac* 4 (n.s. 1) (November 1885), 329-30. Hayne there calls Gildersleeve "almost an 'admirable Crichton' even at his early age in the versatility of his classical attainments." On Hayne's life, see R. S. Moore, *Paul Hamilton Hayne* (Twayne: New York, 1972); *DAB* 8: 455-56; and *Charleston Sunday News*, 20 September 1903: 20. **Nos. 12, 14.**

**George Lincoln Hendrickson** (1865-1963) graduated from Hopkins in 1887, after attending Beloit College in his native Wisconsin (1883-85). He spent a year at Bonn and Berlin before taking positions at Colorado College (1889-91) and the Universities of Wisconsin (1891-96) and Chicago (1897-1907). He was professor of Greek and Latin at Yale (1907-9), then Lampson professor of Latin and Greek, a position he held until his retirement in 1933. He chaired the Yale classics department (1929-33), was both acting director (1913-14) and director (1919-20) of the American School of Classical Studies at Rome, Sather professor at Berkeley (1921-22), president of the APA (1936), and a member of the American Academy of Arts and Letters. For thirty years (1933-63) he was resident fellow of Branford College, of which he was one of the original five fellows. He wrote over seventy-five articles, translated Cicero's *Brutus* for the Loeb Series (Cambridge, Mass.: Harvard University Press; London: Heinemann, 1942), and revised (with Katharine Allen) F. De F. Allen's *The Life of Agricola and the Germania* (Boston: Ginn, 1913). *NatCAB* 47: 578-79. **No. 121.**

**Hamilton Bowen Holt** (1872-1951), editor, social activist, and college president, graduated from Yale (A.B. 1894) and went to work for his maternal grandfather's (Henry Chandler Bowen) *Independent*, a national liberal weekly of religious origin (see F. L. Mott, *A History of American Magazines, 1850-1865* [Cambridge, Mass.: Harvard University Press, Belknap Press, 1957], 367-79). He became managing editor (1897), owner (1912), and editor (1913), before selling the magazine in 1921. With the help of his magazine, he campaigned vigorously for the Eighteenth Amendment, helped found the National Association for the Advancement of Colored People, and lectured extensively on his view that world peace could be attained by a league of nations, helping to establish the League to Enforce Peace in 1915. In 1925 he was named president of Rollins College in Winter Park, Fla., where he began a number of experimental programs that involved the elimination of the traditional classroom lecture, required courses, and grades. See further W. F. Kuehl, *Hamilton Holt: Journalist, Internationalist, Educator* (Gainesville, Fla.: University of Florida Press, 1960). **No. 125.**

**Ernst Willibald Emil Hübner** (1834–1901) was the son of a prominent Dresden artist of the Düsseldorf school, Julius Hübner (1806–82), whom Gildersleeve visited twice (No. 62). A classmate of Gildersleeve's at Berlin, where he was a protégé of Theodor Mommsen's (No. 61, n. 4), and at Bonn (Ph.D. 1854), where he studied under Ritschl, he introduced Gildersleeve to Platen's poetry (*E&S*, 404–5 and n., and No. 11) and helped celebrate his twenty-first birthday (No. 4). Hübner early acquired an interest in epigraphy and, after obtaining his degree, went to Italy (No. 5) for some years. He returned to take a post as extraordinarius (1863–70), then ordinarius (1870–1901) at Berlin. Through Mommsen he became the first editor of *Hermes* (1866–81; see No. 61, n. 3) and *Archäologische Zeitung* (1868–72). His English was excellent and he delighted in receiving American novels of regional interest as Christmas gifts from Gildersleeve (No. 68). When Hopkins needed a Latinist, Hübner interceded with Wilhelm Wagner on Gildersleeve's behalf (No. 20, n. 1) and he taught one of Gildersleeve's first fellows, E. G. Sihler (No. 23). For an account of Hübner's at-home seminars, see Sihler, *From Maumee to Thames and Tiber* (New York: New York University Press, 1930), 62 - 63. When the illness of Minton Warren deprived Hopkins of a Latin professor in 1888–89, Hübner served as examiner in Latin, and the Latin doctoral candidates received reading-lists and examinations from Hübner by mail, the former published as "The Epistles of Cicero: Bibliography and Hints for Study" (*JHU Circulars*, no. 72 [April 1889]: 66–68; separately printed, Baltimore: Johns Hopkins Press, 1888). In the next year, when Gildersleeve's son Raleigh was studying architecture at Charlottenburg, Hübner was very helpful to Betty and Emma Gildersleeve, who knew little or no German and were living in Berlin. Their relations remained warm to the end (No. 117), despite the fact that Hübner's trouble with Mommsen (No. 61, n. 3) made him an outcast from the German philological establishment, and Gildersleeve's reputation in Germany suffered from the friendship in spite of (or perhaps because of) Hübner's regular mentions of his work in German journals (No. 117). Wilamowitz was led to believe that Gildersleeve hated him because Hübner and Wilamowitz's father-in-law (Mommsen) had quarreled, and relations between Gildersleeve and Wilamowitz were only repaired after the deaths of both Mommsen and Hübner (No. 150, n. 2). Gildersleeve faithfully continued to consider him his "nearest friend" in Germany (*AJP* 22 [1901]: 229 [ = *SBM*, 66]. In addition to a series of *Grundrisse* (No. 61, n. 2) and regular reviews in *Deutsche Rundschau* and *Deutsche Literaturzeitung*, Hübner was a renowned figure in Latin epigraphy, having edited *CIL II, Inscriptiones Hispaniae Latinae*; its *Supplementum*; *Inscriptiones Hispaniae Christianae*; *CIL VII, Inscriptiones Britanniae Latinae*; and *Auctarium: Exempla scripturae epigraphicae Latinae a Caesaris dictatoris morte ad aetatem Iustiniani* (Berlin: G. Reimer, 1869, 1892, 1871, 1873, and 1885 respectively). Nevertheless, his death was not noticed in the major classical journals of Germany (except *AA* 16 [1901]: 1), and the warmest notice came from his American friend of half a century, who regarded him "as the comrade of my youth, as the link that bound me to the period of revelation and aspiration, as the constant, generous friend of riper years" (*JHU Circulars*, No. 151 [April 1901]: 60 [ = *AJP* 22 (1901): 113]). **Nos. 2–7, 11, 51, 57, 61–62, 68–69, 72, 117.**

**Robert Underwood Johnson** (1853–1937), secretary of the American Academy of Arts and Letters, graduated at eighteen from Earlham College (Indiana) in 1871 and two years later joined Charles Scribner's Sons as an editorial clerk, remaining with the firm for over forty years and rising to associate editor (1881) and editor (1909) of the *Century* (formerly *Scribner's) Magazine*. A great literary and aesthetic conservative, he developed the "Century War Series" of Civil War memoirs that were eventually collected as *Battles and Leaders of the Civil War*, 4 vols. (New York: Century, 1887). Yosemite National Park was created in 1890 and the law of international copyright was passed in 1891 partially as a result of articles commissioned by Johnson. He was also ambassador to Italy (1920–21), director of the Hall of Fame at New York University (1919–37), and a founder of the American Academy of Arts and Letters, which he served as secretary (1904–37). He published poetry most of his life and collected much of his work in *Poems of Fifty Years* (New York: the author, 1931). See further his autobiography, *Remembered Yesterdays* (Boston: Little, Brown, 1923) and *DAB Suppl. 2*, 348–49. **Nos. 145, 152.**

**Charles William Kent** (1860–1917), editor of Poe and *The Library of Southern Literature*, a graduate of the University of Virginia (M.A. 1862) and Leipzig (Ph.D. 1887), was professor of English literature and modern languages at Tennessee (1888–93) and Linden Kent professor of English literature at the University of Virginia (1893–1917), where he inaugurated courses in biblical studies and journalism and was the first editor of the *UVa Alumni Bulletin* (1894–98). He was the author of numerous books, including *Cynewulf: Elene* (Boston: Ginn, 1889); *A Shakespeare Note-Book* (Boston: Ginn, 1897); and *Poems by Edgar Allan Poe* (New York: Macmillan, 1903), but his chief work was *The Library of Southern Literature* (New Orleans: Martin and Hoyt, 1908–13), of which he was literary editor (Edwin A. Alderman and Joel Chandler Harris were editors-in-chief). For tributes by Thornton and others, see *UVA Alumni Bulletin*, 3d ser., 12 (January 1919): 3–45. *Barringer*, 14–15. **No. 140**

**Gardiner Martin Lane** (1859–1914), prominent Boston financier, the son of Gildersleeve's Bonn and Göttingen classmate, George Martin Lane (No. 22, n. 1), and Frances Eliza Gardiner Lane, graduated from Harvard *summa cum laude* in 1881. After a three-year apprenticeship with the bankers Lee, Higginson and Co., he became assistant to Charles Francis Adams, president of the Union Pacific Railway. Helping Adams reorganize the railway led to his elevation to vice-president while still under the age of thirty. In 1892 his old firm, Lee, Higginson, made him a partner. Under his guidance, the firm helped finance the construction of the Interborough Subway system and the Hudson Tunnel in New York. He was president of the Boston Museum of Fine Arts for seven years (1907–13) and treasurer of the board of trustees and the managing committee of the American School of Classical Studies at Athens. On 8 June 1898 he married Gildersleeve's daughter, Emma (Nos. 107–8), and built her a magnificent summer house, The Chimneys, in Manchester, Mass. See K. L. Weems, *Odds Were against Me* (New York: Vantage Press, 1985), 1–3 (with portrait); *WhAm* 1: 702. **No. 150.**

**Jonas Marsh Libbey** (1857–1922), editor, graduated from Princeton in 1877, and did postgraduate work at Berlin (1878) and Leipzig (1879) after becoming editor of the *Princeton Review* (1877–85). He then attended Oxford (1885), during which time he made a survey of British industry and industrial depressions. *WhoAm* 1: 728. **No. 34.**

**Wallace Martin Lindsay** (1858–1937), one of Scotland's greatest Latinists, was educated at Glasgow and Balliol. As professor of humanity at St. Andrews (1899–1937), he was heavily influenced by the German scientific tradition. His first book, *The Latin Language* (Oxford: Clarendon Press, 1894), was singular for demonstrating Latin forms through Celtic. Among his many other publications are the Oxford Classical Texts *M. Valerii Martialis epigrammata*; *T. Macci Plauti comoediae*; and *P. Terenti Afri comoediae* (with R. Kauer) (Oxford: Clarendon Press, 1902, 1904–5, and 1926 respectively); *A Handbook of Latin Inscriptions* (Boston: Allyn and

Bacon, 1897); *The Captivi of Plautus* (London: Methuen, 1900); *Nonii Marcelli de compendiosa doctrina libros XX* (Leipzig: B. G. Teubner, 1903); *Syntax of Plautus* (Oxford: J. Parker, 1907; reprint, 1936); *Notae Latinae: An Account of Abbreviation in Latin MSS of the Early Minuscule Period (c. 700–850)* (Cambridge: Cambridge University Press, 1915); and *Early Latin Verse* (Oxford: Clarendon Press, 1922). He contributed six articles to *AJP* and visited Baltimore (staying with Minton Warren) while he was in America to lecture at Harvard. See, further, H. J. Rose, "Wallace Martin Lindsay, 1858–1937" *PBA* 23 (1937): 487–512 (with bibliography); *DNB (1931–1940)*, 537–38. **Nos. 132, 175.**

**Gonzalez Lodge** (1863–1942), Gildersleeve's student and collaborator, was a student of Chapman Maupin's (No. 11, n. 5) at Baltimore City College and graduated from Hopkins (A.B. 1883, Ph.D. 1886), where he was a fellow in Greek (1885–86). He taught for two years at Davidson (1886–88), spent six months in Germany and Greece (1888–89), and then rose from associate to professor of Greek at Bryn Mawr (1889–1900). In 1900 he was appointed professor of Latin and Greek at Teachers College, Columbia University, where he is credited with introducing the oral method of Latin instruction (see his "The Oral Method of Teaching Latin," *Nat Educ Assn Proc* [1910]: 493–97) and where he remained until his retirement in 1929. He compiled the *Lexicon Plautinum* in 2 vols. (Leipzig: B. G. Teubner, 1901–33); substantially revised Gildersleeve's *Latin Grammar*, the school edition of same, and *Latin Composition* (all New York: University Publishing Co., 1894, 1898, and 1899 respectively); edited Plato's *Gorgias* (Boston: Ginn, 1891); wrote *The Vocabulary of High-School Latin* (New York: Teachers College, Columbia University, 1907; reprinted through 1928); and was managing editor of the Gildersleeve-Lodge Series (16 vols., 1894–1908). He also edited *Classical Weekly* from 1907 to 1913. He wrote a memorial notice of Gildersleeve at *CW* 17 (1924): 113–14. *Nat-CAB* 31: 59; *NYTimes*, 25 December 1942: 17; *WhAm* 4: 582. **Nos. 113, 115, 126.**

**Socrates Maupin** (1809–71), a friend of the Gildersleeve family's, was chairman of the department of ancient languages, Hampden-Sydney College, taught at Richmond Academy, then founded his own school in Richmond, where he employed Gildersleeve for the school year between his graduation from Princeton and his departure for Germany (1849–50). Maupin became chairman of the chemistry department at the University of Virginia in 1853, and, as chairman of the faculty, at that time chief administrator of the university, from 1854–70, he was instrumental in hiring Gildersleeve as professor of Greek in 1856. *Barringer*, 1: 359. **No. 9.**

**Charlotte Lanneau Mead** (b. 1879), was descended from Pierre Lanneau IV (No. 144, n. 8), brother of Gildersleeve's grandfather, Bazile Lanneau (No. 144, n. 3). **No. 161.**

**John Calvin Metcalf** (1865-1949), professor and dean at the University of Virginia, was educated at Georgetown (Ky.) (M.A. 1888), Chicago, and Harvard (A.M. 1905). He taught English at Georgetown (Ky.) (1895-1904), Richmond (1905-17), and the University of Virginia, where he was Linden Kent memorial professor of English literature (1917-40) and dean of the Graduate School (1923-37). He was literary editor of the *Library of Southern Literature* (see Kent, above) and wrote *English Literature, American Literature* (both Richmond: B. F. Johnson Publishing Co., 1912, 1914 respectively), *The Stream of English Biography* (New York: Century, 1930), *De Quincey: A Portrait* (Cambridge, Mass.: Harvard University Press, 1940), and an edition of Coleridge's *Biographia Litteraria* (New York: Macmillan, 1926), in addition to *The Enchanted Years* (No. 187). *NatCAB* 36: 449. **No. 187.**

**Charles William Emil Miller** (1863-1934), Gildersleeve's first assistant and successor on *AJP*, graduated from Baltimore City College in 1880 and received his A.B. (1882) and Ph.D. (1886) from Hopkins. During 1890-91 he was professor of Latin and English at Walther College in St. Louis. At Hopkins, he rose from special assistant (1891-92) to associate in Greek (1892-97), to associate professor (1897-1915), and was Gildersleeve's successor as Francis White professor of Greek from 1915 to his retirement in 1933. He was assistant editor (1916-18), managing editor (1918-20), and editor (1920-34) of *AJP*, co-authored *Syntax*, edited *SBM*, and wrote obituaries of Gildersleeve for *AJP* 45 (1924): 97-100 and *PAPA* 56 (1925): xix-xxii, xxviii-xxxii. *WhoAM* 1: 839-40. For his role in the *Syntax*, see No. 155. **Nos. 171-72, 176, 182.**

**Edwin Mims** (1872-1959), historian of Southern literature, was educated at Vanderbilt (B.A. 1892, M.A. 1893) and Cornell (Ph.D. 1900) and was professor of English literature at Trinity College (now Duke University) (1894-1909), the University of North Carolina (1909-12), and Vanderbilt (1912-42), where from 1928 to 1942 he was also chairman of the division of humanities. In addition to his *Sidney Lanier* (Boston, Houghton Mifflin, 1905) (see No. 129), he edited Thomas Carlyle's *Essay on Burns* (New York: American Book Co., 1903), *Southern Prose and Poetry for Schools*; *Past and Present*; (both New York: Scribner, 1910 and 1918 respectively); and the "Southern Fiction" volume in *The South in the Building of the Nation*, of which he was an editor (Richmond: Southern Historical Publications Society, 1909-13), and wrote *The Advancing*

*South* (Garden City, N.Y.: Doubleday, Page, 1927), *The History of Vanderbilt University* (Nashville: Vanderbilt University Press, 1946), *Great Writers as Interpreters of Religion*, and *Christ of the Poets* (both New York: Abingdon-Cokesbury, 1945, 1948 respectively), in addition to numerous articles for the *Encyclopedia Britannica*, *DAB*, *Atlantic*, and others. *NatCAB* 49: 570-71. **Nos. 129, 133, 138-39.**

**John Barbee Minor** (1813-95) graduated from the University of Virginia with a B.L. in 1834. After six years of practice in Buchanan, Va., he returned to Charlottesville, and in 1845 he was elected to the chair of law there, which he held for fifty years. Perhaps because Betty Gildersleeve was related to Minor by marriage, Gildersleeve rented a house, "Oakhurst," near the campus from Minor, as a family house in addition to his formal address at Pavilion I. Minor's scholarly monument is his four-volume *Institutes of Common and Statute Law* (Richmond: the author, 1875-95). He also published *The Virginia Reports, 1799-1800* and *Exposition of the Law of Crimes and Punishments* (both Richmond: the author, 1850, 1894 respectively). *DAB* 7: 26-27. **Nos. 32, 35.**

**Charles Eliot Norton** (1827-1908) graduated from Harvard in the same class with George M. Lane (No. 22, n. 1), Francis J. Child (No. 14, n. 1), and Charles Short (1821-86), president of Kenyon College and Latinist at Columbia. As professor of fine art at Harvard (1873-97), Norton was one of its most influential figures and forms an interesting contrast with Gildersleeve: he had no Ph.D., was a dilettantish critic rather than a scientific scholar, and was decidedly anti-German (and pro-Italian) in his sympathies. A founder of the *Nation* (1865) and co-editor of the *North American Review* (1864-68), he also wrote extensively for the *Atlantic*. His best-known works are his prose translation of *The Divine Comedy*, 3 vols. (Boston: Houghton Mifflin, 1891-92); *The Poems of John Donne*, 2 vols. (New York: Grolier Club, 1895); and *The Early Letters of Thomas Carlyle*, 2 vols. (London: Macmillan, 1886). Gildersleeve may have known Norton first through the Huntingtons of Charleston, who were close friends of the Nortons in the 1850s. Norton and Gildersleeve may have discussed Pindar (No. 109) over dinner in Cambridge on 12 April 1898. Norton lectured at the Peabody in Baltimore in 1877 (see *Franklin*, 236). See *Letters of Charles Eliot Norton with a Biographical Comment by His Daughter Sara Norton and M. A. DeWolfe Howe* (Boston: Houghton Mifflin, 1913) and K. Vanderbilt, *Charles Eliot Norton: Apostle of Culture in a Democracy* (Cambridge, Mass.: Harvard University Press, 1959). **No. 109.**

**Walter Hines Page** (1855-1918), editor and diplomat, was born near present-day Cary, N.C., and entered Trinity College (now Duke University) in 1871, but transferred to Randolph-Macon in 1873, where he fell under the influence of Thomas Randolph Price (No. 19, n. 4; No. 70, n. 3). Page was hired as assistant in Greek upon his graduation in 1875 and, with Price recommending him to Gilman and Gildersleeve, was encouraged to apply for a Hopkins fellowship. He stayed at Hopkins for two years, but had to withdraw pleading ill health (No. 33). Following his years as a journalist in St. Joseph, Mo., New York, and Raleigh, he made his name as a magazine editor first with the *Forum* (1891–95) and later with the *Atlantic* as associate editor and editor (1895–99), in which capacity he solicited *60 Days* from Gildersleeve. Page also edited *The World's Work* (1900-1913). In 1899 he helped found the Doubleday, Page publishing firm. An early supporter of Woodrow Wilson's, he was named ambassador to the Court of St. James (1913-18). He fell out with the president as a neutralist at the beginning of World War I, but ultimately supported American involvement, and so overstrained himself in his duties that he was forced to resign his post, and died shortly afterwards. John Milton Cooper, *Walter Hines Page: The Southerner as American, 1855-1918* (Chapel Hill: University of North Carolina Press, 1977); B. J. Hendrick, *The Life and Letters of Walter H. Page*, 3 vols. (Garden City, N.Y.: Doubleday, Page, 1922-25); and *DAB* 7: 142. **Nos. 26, 33.**

**Mary Elizabeth Phillips** (1857-1950), biographer of Poe, was born in Chicago, educated at a convent in Ohio, and lived most of her adult life in Boston, where she wrote *A Handbook of German Literature* (London: G. Bell and Sons, 1895), *Laurel Leaves for Little Folk* (Boston: Lee and Shepard, 1903), *James Fenimore Cooper* (New York: John Lane, 1913), and the compendious *Edgar Allan Poe, the Man*, 2 vols. (Chicago: John C. Winston, 1926). **No. 167.**

**Emily McKim Reed** (1840-1924) was a Baltimore socialite, the granddaughter of one of the founders of the Baltimore and Ohio Railroad and president of the Merchants National Bank in Baltimore. During the Civil War she bravely demonstrated her sympathies for the South by smuggling supplies of food, medicine, and clothing across Union lines to Confederate soldiers. After the war, she headed the Southern Relief Association in Baltimore, and during the Spanish-American War and World War I, she organized benefits and rallied volunteers to work in service centers in Baltimore. In 1878 she founded the Decorative Art Society of Baltimore, of which she was president until her death, and in 1891 she founded the Maryland Society of the Colonial Dames of America, of which she was president (1909-20); she was also secretary of the national society for eight years and vice-president for two. A member of the Daughters of the American Revolution, she was honorary president of the National Society United

States Daughters of 1812, and founder of the Maryland Society of the Daughters of the Confederacy. See *Tercentenary History of Maryland*, ed. H. F. Powell (Baltimore: S. J. Clarke, 1925), 4: 98–101. **No. 163.**

**Lulu Gildersleeve Reed** (b. 1876) was the daughter of Hannah Leland (1837–1916) and Rev. William Gildersleeve (No. 122, n. 7) and wife of Samuel Norris Reed, Jr. W. H. Gildersleeve, *Gildersleeve Pioneers* (Rutland Vt.: Tuttle, 1914), 250, 320. **No. 122.**

**James Henry Rice, Jr.** (1868–1935), a South Carolina naturalist, conservationist, and local historian, graduated from South Carolina College (now the University of South Carolina) in 1886 and taught for a while in the local public schools. He wrote editorials for the *Columbia* [SC] *State* (1896–98) and was chief game warden of South Carolina (1911–13). In 1922–24, he wrote a series of sketches for the *State* called "Paladins of South Carolina," one of which treated Gildersleeve (27 January 1924: sec. 1: 15). He wrote two books, *Glories of the Carolina Coast* (Columbia, S.C.: R. L. Bryan, 1925) and *Aftermath of Glory* (Charleston, S.C.: Walker, Evans and Cogswell, 1934). *Who's Who in South Carolina, (1934–35)*, 396. **No. 190.**

**Leigh Robinson** (1840–1922), attorney and orator, was a native of Richmond and a student of Gildersleeve's at the University of Virginia (1858–61). When war was declared, he joined the Richmond Howitzers and fought in over twenty engagements, facetiously calling himself the "only private in the Confederate army." After the war, in which his two brothers were killed, he joined his father's law practice in Washington and achieved such prominence that he was named to defend Charles Guiteau, the assassin of President Garfield (No. 57, n. 8), a commission he declined. He became commander of the Confederate Veterans' Camp 171 in Washington and was a sought-after speaker for dedications of Confederate monuments. He published *The South before and after the Battle of the Wilderness* (Richmond: J. E. Goode, 1878), *Joseph E. Johnston* (Washington, D.C.: Government Printing Office, 1891), and *A Souvenir of the Unveiling of the Richmond Howitzer Monument at Richmond, Virginia* (Richmond: J. L. Hill, 1893). **No. 178.**

**Alexander Duncan Savage** (1848–1935), one of the first Greek fellows at Hopkins, was born the son of an Episcopal missionary in Sumterville, Ala. After taking a B.Litt. from the University of Virginia in 1870, he studied Hebrew, Sanskrit, Latin, and Greek at Bonn and Leipzig from 1871 to

1873 and began teaching in a school in Kingston, N.Y., in 1873. He received an honorary A.M. from Yale in 1876, and, probably in part because as a University of Virginia student he had checked references for Gildersleeve's *Latin Reader*, entered Gildersleeve's first class at Hopkins (1876-79), serving as acting librarian in 1879, and providing reports for vols. 1-2 of *AJP*. His varied later career never found him associated with a university. He was assistant curator of antiquities at New York's Metropolitan Museum (1879-81) under the notorious Luigi Palma di Cesnola, but he resigned in protest of Cesnola's fraudulent "restorations" of his findings in Curium and elsewhere. See J. Royce, *The Philosophy of Loyalty* (New York: Macmillan, 1908), and E. McFadden, *The Glitter and the Gold* (New York: Dial, 1971), 193, 196, 212, 221. After leaving the Metropolitan, Savage organized a school for girls, was reference librarian at Princeton (1906-7), assistant curator of fine arts at the Brooklyn Museum (1907-12), librarian of the American Numismatic Society (1912-15), and a transcriber and editor for the Hispanic Society of America (1915-29). **No. 29.**

**Johann Hermann Heinrich Schmidt** (1830-1913), whose metrical theories (later known as the "Old Metric") greatly influenced Gildersleeve and a generation of German-trained American classicists and their pupils, was *Oberlehrer* in the gymnasium at Wismar, Mecklenburg. He developed his views on metrical theory and practice largely by examining the choral and lyric poetry itself rather than the prosodic theories of the ancients. His *Leitfaden in der Rhythmik und Metrik der Classischen Sprachen* (Leipzig: F. C. W. Vogel, 1868) was translated by J. W. White (No. 50, n. 9) as *An Introduction to the Rhythmic and Metric of the Classical Languages* (Boston: Ginn, 1878). *Die Eurythmie in dem Chorgesängen der Griechen*, *Die Antike Compositionslehre*, *Die Monodien und Wechselgesänge der Attische Tragödie*, and *Griechische Metrik*, were collected as *Die Kunstformen der Griechischen Poesie und ihre Bedeutung* (all Leipzig: F. C. W. Vogel, 1868, 1869, 1871, 1872, and 1872 respectively). He also did noted work on synonyms, *Handbuch der Lateinischen und Griechischen Synonymik* (Leipzig: B. G. Teubner, 1889) and *Synonymik der Griechischen Sprache*, 4 vols. (Leipzig: B. G. Teubner, 1876-86) (see *AJP* 7 [1886]: 406-7). *Sandys*, 158-59. **No. 158.**

**Max Paul Ernst Schneidewin** (1843-1931), son of Friedrich Wilhelm Schneidewin (1810-56), under whom Gildersleeve studied Latin syntax (summer semester 1851) and Greek syntax and elegiac poetry (winter semester 1851-52). Max, trained at Göttingen and Berlin, was professor at Hameln from 1887, and wrote *Drei populär-philosophische essays* (Hameln: T. Fuendeling, 1883), *Die juedische Frage im Deutschen Reich* (Hameln: T. Fuendeling, 1894), and *Die antike Humanität* (Berlin: Weidmann, 1897). *Wer ist's, 1928* 9: 1389. **No. 157.**

**John Adams Scott** (1867–1947), one of America's leading Homerists, was educated at Northwestern (A.B. 1891), was Greek fellow at Hopkins (1895–96), and received his Ph.D. the following year with his dissertation, *A Comparative Study of Hesiod and Pindar* (Chicago: University of Chicago Press, 1898). He also returned to his alma mater where, in his forty-year career, he rose from instructor to professor (1901) and ultimately John C. Schaffer professor of Greek (1923). He gave the Sather lectures in 1920–21, published as *The Unity of Homer* (Berkeley: University of California Press, 1921), and one of the first Martin Lectures, "The Poetic Structure of the *Odyssey*." He was president of the APA (1919–20) and the Classical Association of the Middle West and South (1916–17) and was associate editor of *Classical Journal*. He wrote *Homer and His Influence* in the "Our Debt to Greece and Rome" Series (Boston: Marshall Jones, 1925), as well as *Socrates and Christ*, and *Luke, the Greek Physician* (both Evanston, Ill.: Northwestern University Press, 1929 and 1930 respectively), and *We Would Know Jesus* (New York: Abingdon Press, 1936). He contributed eight articles and one review to *AJP*. *NatCAB* 35: 221. On his trip with Gildersleeve (Scott left him on 17 May), see *PAPA* 56 (1925): xxvii–xxviii. He was probably instrumental in bringing Gildersleeve to Northwestern to lecture (No. 101) and wrote memorial notices at *CJ* 19 (1923–24): 306–8 and *CP* 19 (1923–24): 66. On Scott's anti-Germanism, see E. C. Kopff, "Wilamowitz and Classical Philology in the United States of America: An Interpretation," in *Wilamowitz Nach 50 Jahren*, ed. W. M. Calder III et al. (Darmstadt: Wissenschaftliche Buchgesellschaft, 1985), 576–77. **No. 166.**

**Horace Elisha Scudder** (1838–1902), best known as the writer and editor of books for children, such as *Dream Children* (1864), *The Dwellers in Five-Sisters Court* (1876), and *Childhood in Literature and Art* (1894), edited the *Atlantic* from 1890 to 1898, in which capacity he encouraged Gildersleeve to write *Creed*. *DAB* 8: 522–23. **No. 77.**

**Thomas Day Seymour** (1848–1907), whom Gildersleeve called "America's leading Homerist" (*AJP* 29 [1908]: 118 [ = *SBM*, 159], also 123–25), graduated from Western Reserve, and returned there after two years of study at Leipzig and Berlin as professor of Greek (1872–80). He was professor of Greek at Yale from 1880 until his death. Gildersleeve's initially negative opinion of him (No. 50) changed greatly, for by the time of his death, Seymour had written commentaries on *Iliad* 1-3 and 4-6, *Introduction to the Language of Homer* (Boston: Ginn, 1885), and his masterpiece, *Life in the Homeric Age* (New York: Macmillan, 1907). He was president of the APA (1888-89), associate fellow of the American Academy of Arts and Sciences (1900), and president of the AIA (1903-7). See, further, J. W. White, *Thomas Day Seymour, 1848-1907* (New Haven: Classical Club of Yale, 1908); *DAB* 17: 10-11. **Nos. 128, 130, 135.**

**Henry Elliott Shepherd** (1844-1929), educator and college president, was Gildersleeve's student for one year (1860) before he joined the Confederate Army. Wounded and captured at Gettysburg, he was released from prison (see his *Narrative of Prison Life at Baltimore and Johnson's Island, Ohio* [Baltimore: Commercial Printing and Stationery Co., 1917]) at the war's end. He became professor of history and English at City College, Baltimore (1868-75), and, like Sidney Lanier, was one of many Baltimoreans who coveted a post at the new university. He had hoped to further his chances with his *History of the English Language* (New York: E. J. Hale and Son, 1874), but when he failed to get the post, he became superintendent of Baltimore's public schools and from 1882 to 1897 was president of the College of Charleston. He then returned to Baltimore, where he lived near Gildersleeve (1707 N. Calvert St.). He lectured and wrote widely and popularly until his death. *NatCAB* 33: 442-43. For Shepherd on Gildersleeve, see his *Representative Authors of Maryland* (New York: Whitehall Publishing, 1911), 154-56. **No. 21.**

**Paul Shorey** (1857-1934), second only to Gildersleeve among American classicists, was educated at Harvard (A.B. 1878). After being admitted to the Chicago Bar in 1879 and practicing for a few years, he went to Europe to pursue his interest in classics. He attended Leipzig (1881-82), Bonn (1882), and the American School of Classical Studies at Athens (1882-83), whose annual associate director he was in 1901-2. He received his Ph.D. from Munich in 1884 under Wilhelm Christ and was professor of Latin and philosophy at Bryn Mawr from 1885 to 1892 (he taught Greek from 1886 on) before being called by President William Rainey Harper to the new University of Chicago in 1892. There, like Gildersleeve, he began a major graduate program in classics, which he headed (1896-1927), and helped found a journal, *Classical Philology*, which he edited (1908-34). The bulk of his work was on Plato, beginning with his dissertation, *De Platonis idearum doctrina atque mentis humanae notionibus commentatio* (Munich: T. Ackermann, 1884), and continuing with "The Idea of Good in Plato's Republic," *Chicago Studies in Classical Philology* 1 (1895): 188-239 ( = *University of Chicago Decennial Publications* 1, no. 6 [1904]: 127-214); *The Unity of Plato's Thought* (Chicago: University of Chicago Press,

1903); the Loeb *Republic* (London: Heinemann; New York: Putnam, 1930-35), and *What Plato Said* (Chicago: University of Chicago Press, 1933). His *Horace: Odes and Epodes* (Boston: B. H. Sanborn, 1898; rev. ed. [with G. J. Laing, 1910]) is still in print. He gave the Turnbull Lectures at Hopkins in 1912, the Martin Lectures at Oberlin (*Sophocles* [Cambridge, Mass.: Harvard University Press, 1931], 57-95), and was three times Sather lecturer at Berkeley (1916: "The Broader Aspects of Platonism in European Literature"; 1919: "Aristotle and Aristotelianism"; and 1928: *Platonism Ancient and Modern*, Sather Lectures, vol. 14 [Berkeley: University of California Press, 1938]). He held lectureships at Harvard and Northwestern, was president of the APA in 1910, and, on Gildersleeve's nomination (No. 145), was elected to the American Academy of Arts and Letters in 1918. He wrote obituaries of Gildersleeve for the *NYTimes*, 27 January 1924: sec. 4: 3 and 14, and *Commemorative Tributes of the American Academy of Arts and Letters, 1905-1941* (New York: American Academy of Arts and Letters, 1942), 148-60, and gave a memorial address at Hopkins (*Johns Hopkins Alumni Magazine* 13 [January 1925]: 136-48). See *Paul Shorey: Collected Papers*, ed. L. Tarán, 2 vols. (New York: Garland, 1980). *DAB* 17: 125-26. **Nos. 151, 183-84.**

**Charles Forster Smith** (1852-1931) was a native of South Carolina, graduated from Wofford College in 1872, and did postgraduate work at Harvard (1874) and Leipzig (Ph.D. 1881). After teaching for a year at Williams (1881-82), he became professor of Greek at Vanderbilt (1882-93) and, following the death of his wife, chairman of the department of Greek and classical philology at Wisconsin (1894-1917). He was associate editor of *Classical Philology* and in 1902-3 president of the APA. His books include *Thucydides VI* (Boston: Ginn, 1886); *Ancient Greece* by G. F. Hertzberg, trans. Smith (Philadelphia: Lea Bros., 1902); *Xenophon's Anabasis: The First Four Books* (New York: D. Appleton, 1905); *Greek Literature* (New York: Columbia University Press, 1912); and the Loeb *Thucydides*, 4 vols. (London, Heinemann; New York: Putnam, 1919-23). He first met Gildersleeve at the Sewanee summer session of 1887 and became a close friend. He contributed one apticle, two notes, four reports (on *Philologus*), and two reviews to *AJP* and wrote a warm memorial, "Basil Lanneau Gildersleeve: An Intimate View," *Sewanee Review* 32 (April 1924): 162-75. See his autobiograpical *Reminiscences and Sketches* (Nashville: Methodist Episcopal Church, South, 1908) and *DAB* 17: 247-48. **Nos. 154, 160, 164, 168, 180.**

**Kirby Flower Smith** (1862-1918), was educated at the University of Vermont (A.B. 1884, LL.D. 1910) and Hopkins (Ph.D., 1889). He rose from instructor to professor of Latin at Hopkins (1889-1918) and in 1900 was associate professor while H. L. Wilson (No. 113, n. 12) was associate. Smith is best known for his *Elegies of Albius Tibullus* (New York: American Book Co., 1913; reprint, Darmstadt: Wissenschaftliche Buchgesellschaft, 1964). His collected essays were published posthumously as *Martial the Epigrammatist and Other Essays* (Baltimore: Johns Hopkins Press, 1920), and he contributed six articles and twenty-seven reviews to *AJP*. He was also acting director of the American School of Classical Studies in Rome in 1914-15. See Gildersleeve's obituary notice, *AJP* 40 (1919): 110-11, and "IN MEMORIAM K.F.S." (a sonnet), *Johns Hopkins Alumni Magazine* 7 (March 1919): 131 ( = *Johns Hopkins News-Letter*, 1 April 1919) *WhAm* 1: 1146. **No. 147.**

**William Robertson Smith** (1846-94) was assistant professor of natural philosophy at Edinburgh (1868-70), professor of oriental languages and exegesis of the Old Testament at Aberdeen (1870-81), and a member of the Old Testament Revision Committee (1875). Following his conviction of heresy for his questioning of the traditional date of Deuteronomy, he became a fellow of Trinity College, Cambridge, where he had his greatest influence. He was also an editor of the *Encyclopedia Britannica*. His great work was *Lectures on the Religion of the Semites* (Edinburgh: A. and C. Black, 1889), written during the trial. On the trial, see Nos. 43, 48, n. 5, and 53, and, in general, J. S. Black and G. Chrystal, *The Life of William Robertson Smith* (London: A. and C. Black, 1912), 235-451. **No. 53.**

**Herbert Weir Smyth** (1857-1937) was perhaps Gildersleeve's successor as the premier American Greek grammarian. He studied at Swarthmore and Harvard (A.B. 1878), Leipzig (1878-80), and Göttingen (1880-82; Ph.D. 1884), where he was a student of August Fick's (No. 66 and n. 2). After two years teaching German and Sanskrit at Williams (1883-85), he was lecturer and reader in Greek at Hopkins (1885-88) and taught a course in Greek lyric poetry. One of his students was Fairclough (see above). He gave four lectures on the same topic at Hopkins Hall, 12-22 March 1888. Moving on to Bryn Mawr (1888-1901) and finally to Harvard (1901-25) as professor of Greek, he had initially become known for *Der diphthong EI im Griechischen unter Berücksichtigung seiner Entsprechungen in verwandten Sprachen* (Göttingen: Dieterischen University, 1884; reprint, Göttingen: Vandenhoeck and Rupprecht, 1885), but he is best remembered for his major works, *The Sounds and Inflections of the Greek Dialects: Ionic* (Oxford: Clarendon Press, 1894) (No. 87); *Greek Melic Poets* (New York: Macmillan, 1900) (No. 114); *A Greek Grammar for Schools and Colleges* (New York: American Book Co., 1916) (No. 114, n. 6); the Loeb *Aeschylus*, 2 vols. (Cambridge, Mass.: Harvard University Press, 1922-26); his Sather Lectures, *Aeschylean Tragedy* (Berkeley: University of California Press, 1924); and the successful "Smyth Series" ("Greek Series for Colleges and Schools") that ran to over twenty volumes. He was secretary (1889-1904) and president of the APA (1904-5) and visiting professor at the American School of Classical Studies at Athens (1899-1900). *DAB Supp. 2*, 620-21, and C. N. Jackson, "Herbert Weir Smyth," *HSCP* 49 (1938): 1-21. **Nos. 81, 87, 111, 114.**

**Carroll Sprigg** (1849-1928), a native of Cumberland, Md., attended the University of Virginia from 1867 to 1869, where he was a student of Gildersleeve's. He became a successful businessman in New York. **No. 191.**

**Edmund Clarence Stedman** (1833-1908), poet and stockbroker, was originally from Hartford, Conn. His best-known poem is probably "Pan in Wall Street," from his collection *The Blameless Prince and Other Poems* (Boston: Fields, Osgood, 1869). He was an esteemed poet only in his time, but his *Poets of America*, 2 vols. (Boston: Houghton Mifflin, 1885); *A Library of American Literature* (with Ellen Mackay Hutchinson), 11 vols. (New York: C. L. Webster, 1888-90); his edition of Poe (with George E. Woodberry), 10 vols. (Chicago: Stone and Kimball, 1894-95), and *An American Anthology, 1787-1900* (Boston: Houghton Mifflin, 1900) helped extend the appreciation of American literature at the turn of the century. Stedman was chosen to inaugurate the Turnbull lectureship in poetry at Hopkins in 1889, and having postponed his appointment for a year because of the demands of the *Library* and his health, he delivered eight lectures on "The Nature and Elements of Poetry" in the spring of 1891, which he repeated at Columbia and the University of Pennsylvania in 1892, published serially in the *Century*, and then collected (Boston: Houghton Mifflin, 1892), a copy of which he sent to Gildersleeve, occasioning No. 83. On Stedman see Laura Stedman and George M. Gould, *The Life and Letters of Edmund Clarence Stedman*, 2 vols. (New York: Moffat, Yard, 1910), and, on the lectures, R. J. Scholnick, *Edmund Clarence Stedman* (Boston: Twayne, 1977), esp. pp. 107-16. **No. 83.**

**Martha Carey Thomas** (1857-1935), president of Bryn Mawr, was the daughter of one of the original trustees of Johns Hopkins, James Carey Thomas (No. 106, n. 1). After graduation from Cornell (the only university in the East that enrolled women as regular students) in 1877, she applied for admission to Gildersleeve's seminary. The board of trustees decided that she was "to have the direction of studies by University Professors, and the final examination for degrees without class attendance in the University." So great was this handicap and so heavy was the imposition on Gildersleeve that, although she passed her first year with commendation, she withdrew from the university on 8 October 1878. She went on to study in Leipzig (No. 49, n. 15), which would not grant women degrees, was denied admission to Göttingen, and finally took a Ph.D. in philology *summa cum laude* from Zürich in November 1882. She became dean (the first time the title was used in America) and professor of English literature at the new Bryn Mawr College and was its second president (1894-1922). Drawing on the Hopkins model and her European experiences, she organized the first "group system" for undergraduate instruction and the first graduate school connected with a women's college. See *Hawkins*, 260-62; E. Finch, *Carey Thomas of Bryn Mawr* (New York: Harper and Bros., 1947), 69-83; and *Martha Carey Thomas: The Making of a Feminist; Her Early Journals and Letters*, ed. M. H. Dobkin (Kent, Ohio: Kent State, 1979). **Nos. 66, 106.**

**William Mynn Thornton** (1851-1935), dean at the University of Virginia, was educated at Hampden-Sydney (A.B. 1868), attended the University of Virginia for two years, and graduated in Greek (see his "Memorial Address," No. 140, n. 6), mixed mathematics, and six other schools of the university. After teaching at McCabe's School (No. 102, n. 2) during 1870-71 and Abbot's Bellevue School (No. 173, n. 1), he was professor of Greek at Davidson (1874-75) before being called back to the University of Virginia as adjunct professor of mathematics, rising to professor of applied mathematics and civil engineering (1883-1931). He was chairman of the faculty (1888-96) and dean of engineering (1904-25) and retired after fifty-six years of continuous teaching at the University of Virginia. When fire destroyed many buildings in 1895, Thornton arranged for Stanford White to oversee their rebuilding. *NatCAB* 30: 444-45. **Nos. 141, 153, 173, 177, 181.**

**John Randolph Tucker** (1823-97), Virginia congressman, received his law degree from the University of Virginia in 1843, was attorney general of Virginia (1857-65), and for the rest of his life taught law at Washington and Lee University (1870-74; 1888-97). The son and father of U.S. representatives from Virginia, he served as a Democrat in Congress (1875-87), was a leading Democratic champion of states' rights, and was particularly interested in tariff reform, serving on the Tariff Bill conference in the second session of the 47th Congress (1882). After refusing to be renominated, he returned to Washington and Lee as professor of constitutional law, was president of the American Bar Association (1892-93), and finished his great work, *The Constitution of the United States*, ed. H. St. George Tucker, 2 vols. (Chicago: Callaghan, 1899). *DNB* 20: 34-35. **No. 58.**

**Hermann Karl Usener** (1834-1905), called by Gildersleeve "my friend" (*AJP* 37 [1916]: 499), was educated at Heidelberg, Munich, Göttingen, and Bonn, where he was professor of Greek (1866–1905) and numbered Wilamowitz among his students (*Usener und Wilamowitz: Ein Briefwechsel, 1870–1905*, ed. Hermann Dieterich and Friedrich von Hiller [Leipzig: B. G. Teubner, 1934]). In 1866 he married Lily Dilthey (1846–1920), sister of the philosopher Wilhelm Dilthey (1833–1911). Gildersleeve met him in 1880 and their friendship remained warm (*AJP* 27 [1906]: 102–3). Usener wrote on a vast range of subjects, but is particularly known for his work on ancient philosophy and religion, such as *Epicurea* (Leipzig: B. G. Teubner, 1887), *Götternamen* (Leipzig: B. G. Teubner, 1896; 2d ed., 1929), and *Die Sintfluthsagen Untersucht* (Bonn: F. Cohen, 1899), all three reviewed by Gildersleeve at *AJP* 9 (1888): 229; 17 (1896): 356–66; and 20 (1899): 210–15 respectively. He also published *Scholia in Lucani bellum civile* (Bonn: F. Cohen, 1869), *Altgriechische Versbau* (Bonn: M. Cohen und Sohn, 1887), and, posthumously, *Kleine Schriften* (Leipzig: B. G. Teubner, 1912). See *Sandys*, 184–85. For Gildersleeve's correspondence with Usener, see R. L. Fowler, "The Gildersleeve Archive," *Briggs-Benario*, 82–85; biographical sources in n. 119. See also *Aspetti di Hermann Usener filologo della religione*, ed. G. Arrighetti et al. (Pisa: Giardini, 1982). **Nos. 52, 116.**

**Benjamin Ide Wheeler** (1854–1927), president of the University of California, Berkeley, graduated from Brown (B.A. 1875) and Heidelberg (Ph.D. 1885) and was instructor in Greek and Latin at Brown (1879–81). After a year at Harvard following his German tour, he taught comparative philology, Latin, and Greek at Cornell, before being named professor of Greek and comparative philology in 1888. One of Gildersleeve's closest friends, he agreed to edit a Gildersleeve-Wheeler textbook series, which was never realized (Nos. 88, 103, 114). Following his stint as professor of Greek literature at the American School of Classical Studies at Athens in 1895–96, he and Gildersleeve toured the Peloponnesus (No. 169). He also sought Gildersleeve's students for positions at Cornell whenever vacancies occurred (Nos. 74, 85–86). In 1899 he became president of the University of California and presided over its expansion for the next twenty years, playing an instrumental role in establishing the Sather lectureship, to which he invited Gildersleeve (No. 177). He was Theodore Roosevelt professor at Berlin in 1909–10, from which came his lectures *Unterricht und Demokratie in Amerika* (Strassburg: K. J. Trübner, 1910). Known as a highly effective teacher, he also published his dissertation, *Der Griechische Nominalaccent* (Strassburg: K. J. Trübner, 1885); *Analogy and the Scope of its Application in Language* (Ithaca, N.Y.: Cornell University Press, 1887); *Introduction to the Study of the History of Language*, with H. A. Strong and W. S. Logeman (London: Longmans, Green, 1891), *Dionysus and Immortality* (Boston: Houghton Mifflin, 1899), and *Alexander the Great: The Merging of East and West in Universal History* (New York:

Putnam, 1900). *DAB* 21: 44–46. **Nos. 74, 85–86, 88, 95, 98–99, 101, 103, 108, 169–70, 185.**

**William Dwight Whitney** (1827–94), America's great Sanskritist, began to study medicine after his graduation at the top of his class at Williams (1845), but contracted measles in October of that year. While ill, he read Franz Bopp's (1791–1867) *Comparative Grammar* (1833) and became in time, in Gildersleeve's words, "the most earnest of American philologians," a man "who vindicated the right of Americans to share in the processes of the philological thought of the world, and showed in all that he wrought the unmistakable stamp of the American genius" (*AJP* 15 [1894], 258–59). In 1850 Whitney went to Berlin to study under Bopp himself, Albrecht Weber, and Karl Richard Lepsius, with an additional year at Tübingen under Rudolph Roth. He returned to America in 1853 and was named professor of Sanskrit at Yale, where he remained for forty years. His greatest work was his *Sanskrit Grammar* (Leipzig: Breitkopf and Härtel, 1879), a descriptive rather than comparative survey. By 1858 Whitney had already published the first edition of the *Atharva Veda Samhita*, edited with Roth (Berlin: F. Dümmler, 1856) and "Alphabetisches Verzeichniss der Versanfänge der Atharva-Samhita," *Indische Studien* 4 (1864): 9–64. His later publications covered a broad range: *Language and the Study of Language* (New York: Scribner, 1867; 6th ed., 1901), *A Compendious German Grammar* (New York: Leypoldt and Holt; Boston: S. R. Urbino, 1870; 6th ed., 1888), *The Life and Growth of Language* (New York: D. Appleton, 1875), *Goethe's Faust* (New York: H. Holt, Boston: Schönhof and Möller, 1878), *Indische Grammatik* (Leipzig: Breitkopf & Härtel, 1879), and *A Practical French Grammar* (New York: Holt, 1886). As evidence of his professional stature and of Gildersleeve's affection, the lead article of the October issue of *AJP* (15 [1894]: 271–98) was an appreciation of Whitney by his colleague Thomas Day Seymour. See, further, "Classics and Colleges," 80 ( = *E&S*, 62), and *DAB* 20: 166–69. **Nos. 8, 36.**

**Benjamin Lawton Wiggins** (1861–1909), Sewanee classicist and close friend of Gildersleeve's, was a native of Sand Ridge, S.C., graduated from Sewanee (B.A. 1880, M.A. 1882) and was fellow by courtesy at Hopkins (1882–84). He began his teaching career at Sewanee in 1881 as professor of ancient languages, and in 1893 he was made vice-chancellor of the university. Gildersleeve was a guest in his home during the summer session of 1887. He published nothing of note, but as Gildersleeve says in an unpublished testimonial in the Hopkins Archive, "his extraordinary ability as a man of affairs was happily paired with a deep and fervid love of letters." **Nos. 65, 71, 78, 80, 82, 107, 137.**

**Ulrich von Wilamowitz-Moellendorff** (1848–1931), the preeminent German classicist of his day, succeeded Ernst Curtius as professor of rhetoric at Berlin in 1897, wrote major works on nearly every phase of Greek literature and life, and was especially renowned not only as editor and commentator on Aeschylus (*Aischylos: Interpretationen* [Berlin: Weidmann, 1914]) and Euripides (*Euripides' Herakles* [Berlin: Weidmann, 1889]), but also as a translator of Greek verse. On the relationship of Gildersleeve and Wilamowitz, see W. M. Calder III, "B. L. Gildersleeve and Ulrich von Wilamowitz-Moellendorff: New Documents," *AJP* 99 (1978): 1–11, and idem, "The Correspondence of Ulrich von Wilamowitz-Moellendorff with Edward Fitch," *HSCP* 83 (1979): 369–96. For most of their careers, Gildersleeve and Wilamowitz developed neither a personal nor professional relationship, largely because of ill will between Hübner and Theodor Mommsen (1817–1903), Wilamowitz's father-in-law. See Wilamowitz, *Erinnerungen, 1848–1914*, 2d ed. (Leipzig: K. F. Koehler, 1929), 130, 175, 189. The misunderstanding was repaired through the agency of Wilamowitz's only American doctoral student, Edward Fitch. **No. 146.**

**Mary Gildersleeve Wylie** (1903–), born in Lancaster, S.C., is the sixth child of Louise Gildersleeve (1866–1958), the daughter of Gildersleeve's sister Johannah Frances (1836–1904) and Henry B. Pratt (1832–1912). She is now resident in Spartanburg, S.C. **No. 149.**

# ❦ INDEX ❧

NOTE: **Boldface** references indicate the principal biographical notes on correspondents and certain significant family members, students, and classicists who occur more than once. Illustrations are indicated by *italic* numbers.

*The Letters of Basil Lanneau Gildersleeve*

*Designed by Ann Walston.*

*Composed by Action Comp Co., Inc.
in English 49.*

*Printed by Thomson-Shore, Inc.
on 60-lb. S. D. Warren's Olde Style
and bound by John H. Dekker & Sons, Inc.
in Holliston Roxite A.*